Proclaim Christ Until He Comes

Proclaim Christ Until He Comes

Calling the Whole Church to Take the Whole Gospel to the Whole World

J. D. Douglas, Editor

Lausanne II in Manila
International Congress on World Evangelization, 1989

World Wide Publications
Minneapolis, Minnesota

Proclaim Christ Until He Comes

Library of Congress Catalog Card Number: 89-051973

ISBN: 0-89066-190-1

Printed in the United States of America

Contents

84171

II. A. The Whole Gospel

II. B. The Whole Gospel: Bible Studies

Lausanne Occasional Papers

Further presentations relating to Lausanne II, as well as more in-depth versions of many of the presentations in this volume, will be subsequently published in the *Lausanne Occasional Papers*, available from the Lausanne Committee, 2531 Nina St., Pasadena, CA 91107, USA.

Editor's Preface

Lausanne II has been described as the most representative gathering in the history of the church. From nearly every nation came believers to worship and pray, to share and encourage, and under God to plan a strategy toward world evangelization.

This volume includes plenary talks, track reports, the scripts of those videos which are meaningful apart from their visual components, and miscellaneous items, notably the Manila Manifesto. A considerable amount of editing was necessary, partly because of limitations imposed by space and the need to avoid overlapping. No attempt has been made to stifle the unique flavor of some of the pieces, however, and we trust that none will feel themselves misrepresented.

Separate from the presentations, the sturdy independence shown in that uniqueness reminds us that evangelicals are not carbon copies. Thus, there is a healthy liberty of expression which might not necessarily reflect the position of the Lausanne Committee.

Because of the uncertainties that dogged us all (not least those that came from trying to decipher handwritten reports), a greater load than usual fell on DeWayne Herbrandson, Bill Deckard, and their colleagues at World Wide Publications, including Helen Hanson, Mary Petrie-Terry, and Nedine Kolmodin. We are grateful to them. We are also indebted to Program Director Edward Dayton, and to Helen Mooradkanian who had to cope initially with a daunting mass and variety of revised and unrevised manuscripts. When we fell victim to vagaries of machines, human and mechanical, largely outside our control, their unfailing good humor was a tonic to us all.

A Spanish saying asserts that words fly, writing remains. We pray this written record of thoughts shared on a historic occasion will prove to be a blessing, an encouragement, and a reminder to those who seek to "Proclaim Christ Until He Comes," and who labor among those who die so fast.

—J. D. Douglas

Foreword

Since 1974 "Lausanne" has become the name for more than a city or for the International Congress on World Evangelization held in that city. Lausanne has become known around the world as a movement which stands for completing the task of world evangelization, for cooperation in that cause and for networking between evangelical leaders in that task. Lausanne II in Manila has played a significant role in that movement.

It was significant in its *purpose:* to focus the whole church of Jesus Christ in a fresh way on the task of taking the whole gospel to the whole world.

It was significant in its *representation:* 4,300 in attendance from 173 countries, including the Soviet Union and Eastern Europe, and with a larger proportion of women, lay persons and younger leaders than at previous conferences.

It was significant in its *timeliness:* building on the foundation of Lausanne '74, on the work which has taken place since then, and leading into the final decade of this century.

It was significant in its *breadth:* consideration was given to scores of important topics, ranging from the A.D. 2000 movement, to the work of the Holy Spirit, to liberating lay people, to the heart-cry of the poor of our world—and all related to Christ's global cause.

Ultimately, however, the significance of Lausanne will be judged not by the event, but by significant advances in world evangelization which will follow in the decade ahead. This compendium is a digest or summary of Lausanne II and can be both an important record and a valuable resource in the years ahead for all concerned with world evangelization. The pages of this book contain much of the important material from Lausanne II, but still only a small proportion of all that happened.

It is also fitting to express thanks to Thomas Wang, the Congress Director, and the key members of his Congress staff: Paul McKaughan, Ed Dayton, Brad Smith, Jim Newton, Joe Sindorf, Ric Jumawan, and many others who made Lausanne II possible. I particularly want to single out our good friend Jim Douglas, who once again has masterfully edited a vast amount of material into this readable book.

On behalf of the Lausanne Committee for World Evangelization, I commend this work with the prayer that all who read may find their hearts kindled again with the "spirit" of Lausanne, and may be moved with fresh urgency, sacrifice, and cooperation to proclaim Christ until he comes.

—Leighton Ford

Introduction

Lausanne II in Manila was the second International Congress on World Evangelization. The Congress drew its name from the first International Congress which was held fifteen years ago in Lausanne, Switzerland.[1] The years between these two Congresses were a dynamic time in the spread of the gospel around the world. In 1974 we were alarmed to hear that there were over two billion people who had never heard the gospel. In 1989 we were still challenged by two billion people who had yet to hear, but we were also encouraged by the large number of people groups within which there was now an evangelizing church. We were encouraged by the fact that a much greater percentage of the world had had an *opportunity* to hear the gospel. We are amazed by the fact that, in order for Christianity to stay equal with the population growth during this period, it was necessary to have a thousand new churches every day of every year!

Lausanne I and II

Lausanne I focused very much on the major issues that faced Christians in the task of world evangelization. The papers prepared for Lausanne I were distributed a year in advance of the Congress so that each participant had the potential opportunity to interact with the writer. The plenary presentations at Lausanne I utilized *responses* to the papers and the authors' responses to the comments as the basis for presentation. This produced a wealth of well-thought-out material.

The philosophy behind the design of Lausanne II was different. Although the Planning Committee worked diligently to identify the major issues that were facing the church in its evangelistic intent, the plenary presentations were designed to be as much motivational and inspirational as informational. The music of Lausanne II was drawn from over twenty different languages.[2] The musicians came from many different countries and many different cultural backgrounds. The intention was to expose one

---

[1] The papers of Lausanne I are published in *Let the Earth Hear His Voice*, ed. J. D. Douglas (Minneapolis: World Wide Publications, 1975).
[2] See *Alleluia: The Music of Lausanne II*, available from Corean Bakke, 5255 North Paulina, Chicago, Ill. 60640

another to all of the richness of the church in its varied forms of worship and celebration (see the following article).

The "grass roots" people of the church were brought into the Plenary Hall through the medium of eighteen different video presentations. (As you read the plenary papers in chapters that follow, you will find the text for these video presentations intertwined with them.) These video presentations, combined with the multicultural music and worship brought a new dimension to our understanding of what God is doing and saying throughout the world.

The participation process for Lausanne II was one of encouraging local Participant Selection Committees to recommend a broad representation from the church within each country. The qualification for being recommended as a participant was that the participant "agree with the biblical teaching on the gospel and evangelization as presented in the Lausanne Covenant," that the participant agree to be involved in work leading up to the Congress, and to return to his or her country to share the results with others. Participants were also chosen on the basis of the type of ministry they were carrying out and the people they were trying to reach. Fifty percent of the participants were under the age of forty-five. Twenty-two percent were women.

The results of the participant selection process were that large numbers of people discovered one another. Delegations from a particular country were made up of many people who had never met each other, and the opportunity to meet and share formed vital new links for future communication and cooperation. An interesting example was the sixty-seven members of the Russian delegation. These people were drawn from all over that huge country. Because of some visa problems, they spent two days together in Moscow before leaving for Manila and had a marvelous time of meeting one another.

Forty-five different networks (referred to as "tracks" at the Congress and in this volume) of people were identified before the Congress. Such networks as those interested in reaching Muslims, those interested in promoting tentmaker missionaries, those interested in women's issues, those interested in ministering in urban areas were noted and key individuals in these networks were invited to recommend participants who were involved in such areas of interest.

Representatives from 173 countries attended the Congress.[3] Each participant had an opportunity to attend nine workshops that were specifically designed for a particular track, or to move between the various tracks to get a broader overview. The material that was prepared for the 425 workshops provided an amazing amount of resources for future efforts of evangelization. The amount of these resources was far greater than could be included in one volume. Rather, summaries of the work of each track are given, starting on page 383.

The ultimate result of the planning of the Congress and the type of participants who were there was a marvelous "town meeting" of people from all over the world who could find new networks, new relationships, new challenges, and thus move toward the goal of the Lausanne movement: to "build bridges of cooperation and understanding between Christian leaders interested in world evangelization."

---

[3] Because of security considerations, the presence of some countries was not made public knowledge. Many of these countries had not been represented at Lausanne I. The Congress was held at the beginning of the *Glasnost* era in Eastern Europe. Lasting impressions were made on many participants who had never been able to attend such a conference before.

Congress Structure

An outline of the ten day Congress program is shown on page 461. The three streams of content for the plenary sessions were drawn from the Congress subtheme: "Calling the Whole Church to Take the Whole Gospel to the Whole World." Each day had three parts, each aimed at focusing first on the whole gospel, second on the whole world, and third on the whole church.

Each day was begun by an exposition from the book of Romans led by Rev. John R. W. Stott, Rev. Ajith Fernando and the late Archbishop David Penman.[4]

There were three opportunities during the ten days for national groups to meet together, in addition to the nine opportunities for workshops.

The Future of the Lausanne Movement

A meeting of the Lausanne Executive Committee and representatives of the four Lausanne Working Groups and the track leaders from the Congress was held on January 21–25, 1990, at Arrowhead Springs, California. In preparation for this meeting, all of the various reports and papers that are included in this volume were analyzed, along with future plans from each of the participating countries. A meeting of the full (seventy-five-member) Lausanne Committee is planned for the summer of 1990.

Lausanne II in Manila needs to be understood as part of a process, rather than an event. Ideally, it was an accelerator of things that were already happening. The country reports that have subsequently come from all over the world indicate a great moving of the Spirit, a deepening of commitment to world evangelization, and a new sense of partnership in the task that lies ahead.

In addition to this volume, a wealth of material in the form of audiotapes, videotapes, Congress reports and other books is now appearing.

—Edward R. Dayton

---

[4] Archbishop David Penman was unwell at the Congress in Manila. On his return to Melbourne, he suffered a major heart attack and for some weeks hovered between life and death. On October 1 he died at the age of fifty-four years. From a human point of view, his death is a very great loss.

He was a New Zealander by birth and he and his wife, Jean, had served as C. M. S. missionaries in Pakistan and Lebanon. He founded the IFES work in Pakistan. He gained a Ph.D. in Islamic studies from Karachi University. His election as Archbishop of Melbourne was unexpected. However, he set a cracking pace. He was committed to evangelism. In the midst of his many duties, he headed a team of people who visited parishes for evangelistic meetings. He took his team to South Africa recently at the invitation of Archbishop Desmond Tutu. He established a Department of Evangelism in his Diocese.

In Australia his interest was the relation of the gospel to society. He became a spokesman for multiculturalism, was a critic of government policy, and won the respect of civic leaders for his wide interests and his commitment to justice issues. Overseas he had many contacts, particularly in the Middle East, and from time-to-time had been involved in government and church conversations.

Movements like Lausanne were close to his heart because it brought the gospel and people of different backgrounds and cultures together.

He is greatly missed and widely mourned. His three Bible studies from Lausanne have been published by the Diocese of Melbourne as a memorial to his last act in a distinguished ministry.

Edward R. Dayton is Vice President-at-Large for World Vision International and founder of Missions Advance Research and Communications Center (MARC). He was also Program Director for the Lausanne II Congress, and is Chairman of the Strategy Working Group and a citizen of the United States.

The Music of Lausanne II

Corean Bakke, Worship Coordinator for the Lausanne II Congress in Manila, first conceived the idea behind the worship at the Congress from a Japanese ethnomusicologist—a specialist in the study of music which emerges from the cultural roots of ethnic peoples.

She learned that the specialist divided the world into seven musical regions: Asia, Northern Africa/Middle East, the rest of Africa, North America, South America, Western Europe and Oceania. As she spoke with him, Corean's dream of seeing true multi-cultural worship at international meetings suddenly became tangible for the first time.

"I had travelled in India as a pianist until I realized that that was the worst thing I could be," she said. "The piano is not used there at all." Corean decided that the piano and the organ cannot be defined as truly international instruments because it is difficult and expensive to make them. She found three instruments complying with her stipulation of accessibility to anyone in any church: the guitar, because almost all cultures have stringed instruments; the flute, which can be made easily from bamboo; and the drum.

Corean found the guitarist and flautist for the team easily. Ren Merry from Nagaland, India, guitarist, and Pedro Eustache from Venezuela, flautist, were studying music in different parts of the United States. Corean heard their music and immediately invited them to come to Lausanne II. The male vocalist for the team, Najeeb Labeeb, a specialist in indigenous Egyptian music and the a'youd (an Arabic lute) agreed to come as well.

Finding a drummer was a bit more challenging. One week before the Congress, Corean had not spoken directly with Steven Agyaku from Ghana. This would be the first time Agyaku played before this size of crowd. "I have been overwhelmed by how people receive my music. I did not know God could use me this way. I have also learned that I am precious in his sight . . . I wept all one afternoon; the thought just overwhelmed me. You see, I was on the verge of leaving the group I used to play with. In fact, I was going to stop going to church altogether. And now this . . . God loves me so . . . oh . . ." his voice trailed off.

With the team taking shape, Corean began seeking someone who could lead them. Her prerequisite for this task: no limitations on style and respect for all types of music. "I asked myself who fits this description and thought immediately of Ken Medema." Medema, a resident of California agreed to work with the team.

Corean was still searching for a female vocalist ten days before the Congress. She heard about Deyanira Torufio of Nicaragua, who was in the United States seeking political asylum. However, her application for asylum was not scheduled to be processed for four months. Until then Torufio would be required by law to remain in the country. The process of securing an exception to this rule is lengthy.

Corean said a prayer, picked up the phone and within twenty-four hours secured permission for Torufio's trip to Manila with the help of Christians throughout the United States in bureaucratic positions.

The team met for the first time on the first day of the Congress and practiced together briefly before leading worship at the opening ceremony. Corean also invited Kerygma, a five-man ensemble from Peru, and the Thai Drama Troupe to participate in worship at the Congress.[*]

---

[*] Reprinted by permission from Alan Nichols, ed., *The Whole Gospel for the Whole World* (Ventura, Calif.: Regal Books, 1989), 39.

The Lausanne Covenant

Let the earth hear his voice.

Introduction

We, members of the church of Jesus Christ, from more than 150 nations, participants in the International Congress on World Evangelization at Lausanne, praise God for his great salvation and rejoice in the fellowship he has given us with himself and with each other. We are deeply stirred by what God is doing in our day, moved to penitence by our failures and challenged by the unfinished task of evangelization. We believe the gospel is God's Good News for the whole world, and we are determined by his grace to obey Christ's commission to proclaim it to every person and to make disciples of every nation. We desire, therefore, to affirm our faith and our resolve, and to make public our covenant.

1. The Purpose of God

We affirm our belief in the one eternal God, Creator and Lord of the world, Father, Son, and Holy Spirit, who governs all things according to the purpose of his will. He has been calling out from the world a people for himself, and sending his people back into the world to be his servants and his witnesses, for the extension of his kingdom, the building up of Christ's body, and the glory of his name. We confess with shame that we have often denied our calling and failed in our mission, by becoming conformed to the world or by withdrawing from it. Yet, we rejoice that even when borne by earthen vessels the gospel is still a precious treasure. To the task of making that treasure known in the power of the Holy Spirit we desire to dedicate ourselves anew.

Isa. 40:28
Mt. 28:19
Eph 1:11
Ac. 15:14
Jn. 17:6, 18
Eph. 4:12

Ro. 12:2
I Co. 5:12
2 Co. 4:7

2. The Authority and Power of the Bible

We affirm the divine inspiration, truthfulness and authority of both Old and New Testament Scriptures in their entirety as the only written Word of God, without error in all that it affirms, and the only infallible rule of faith and practice. We also affirm the power of God's Word to accomplish his purpose of salvation. The message of the Bible is addressed to all men and women. For God's revelation in Christ and in Scripture is unchangeable. Through it the Holy Spirit still speaks today. He illumines the minds of God's people in every culture to perceive its

2 T. 3:16;
2 Pe. 1:21

Isa. 55:11;
Ro. 1:16;
I Co. 1:21

Jn. 10:35;
Mt. 5:17, 18;
Jude 3

Eph. 1:17-18 truth freshly through their own eyes and thus discloses to the whole church ever more of the many-colored wisdom of God.

3. The Uniqueness and Universality of Christ

We affirm that there is only one Savior and only one gospel, although there is a wide diversity of evangelistic approaches. We recognize that everyone has some knowledge of God through his general revelation in nature. But we deny that this can save, for people suppress the truth by their unrighteousness. We also reject as derogatory to Christ and the gospel every kind of syncretism and dialogue which implies that Christ speaks equally through all religions and ideologies. Jesus Christ, being himself the only God-man, who gave himself as the only ransom for sinners, is the only mediator between God and people. There is no other name by which we must be saved. All men and women are perishing because of sin, but God loves everyone, not wishing that any should perish but that all should repent. Yet those who reject Christ repudiate the joy of salvation and condemn themselves to eternal separation from God. To proclaim Jesus as "the Savior of the world" is not to affirm that all people are either automatically or ultimately saved, still less to affirm that all religions offer salvation in Christ. Rather it is to proclaim God's love for a world of sinners and to invite everyone to respond to him as Savior and Lord in the whole-hearted personal commitment of repentance and faith. Jesus Christ has been exalted above every other name; we long for the day when every knee shall bow to him and every tongue shall confess him Lord.

Gal. 1:6-9

Ro. 1:18-32

I Ti. 2:5-6

Ac. 4:12
Jn. 3:16-19

2 Pe. 3:9
2 Th. 1:7-9
Jn. 4:42

Mt. 11:28

Eph. 1:20-21
Php. 2:9-11

4. The Nature of Evangelism

To evangelize is to spread the Good News that Jesus Christ died for our sins and was raised from the dead according to the Scriptures, and that as the reigning Lord he now offers the forgiveness of sins and the liberating gift of the Spirit to all who repent and believe. Our Christian presence in the world is indispensable to evangelism, and so is that kind of dialogue whose purpose is to listen sensitively in order to understand. But evangelism itself is the proclamation of the historical, biblical Christ as Savior and Lord, with a view to persuading people to come to him personally and so be reconciled to God. In issuing the gospel invitation we have no liberty to conceal the cost of discipleship. Jesus still calls all who would follow him to deny themselves, take up their cross, and identify themselves with his new community. The results of evangelism include obedience to Christ, incorporation into his church and responsible service in the world.

1 Co. 15:3-4

Ac. 2:32-39
Jn. 20:21

1 Co. 1:23;
2 Co. 4:5

2 Co. 5:11,20
Lk. 14:25-33
Mk. 8:34
Ac. 2:40,47
Mk. 10:43-45

5. Christian Social Responsibility

We affirm that God is both the Creator and the Judge of all. We, therefore, should share his concern for justice and reconciliation throughout human society and for the liberation of men and women from every kind of oppression. Because men and women are made in the image of God, every person, regardless of race, religion, color, culture, class, sex, or age, has an intrinsic dignity because of which he or she should be

Ac. 17:26,31
Ge. 18:25
Ps. 45:7;
Isa. 1:17
Ge. 1:26-27

respected and served, not exploited. Here, too, we express penitence both for our neglect and for having sometimes regarded evangelism and social concern as mutually exclusive. Although reconciliation with other people is not reconciliation with God, nor is social action evangelism, nor is political liberation salvation, nevertheless we affirm that evangelism and socio-political involvement are both part of our Christian duty. For both are necessary expressions of our doctrines of God and man, our love for our neighbor and our obedience to Jesus Christ. The message of salvation implies also a message of judgment upon every form of alienation, oppression, and discrimination, and we should not be afraid to denounce evil and injustice wherever they exist. When people receive Christ they are born again into his kingdom and must seek not only to exhibit but also to spread its righteousness in the midst of an unrighteous world. The salvation we claim should be transforming us in the totality of our personal and social responsibilities. Faith without works is dead.

Lev. 19:18;
Lk. 6:27,35

Jas. 3:9

Jn. 3:3,5
Mt.5:20;
Mt. 6:33
2 Co.3:18
Jas. 2:14-26

6. The Church and Evangelism

We affirm that Christ sends his redeemed people into the world as the Father sent him, and that this calls for a similar deep and costly penetration of the world. We need to break out of our ecclesiastical ghettos and permeate non-Christian society. In the church's mission of sacrificial service evangelism is primary. World evangelization requires the whole church to take the whole gospel to the whole world. The church is at the very center of God's cosmic purpose and is his appointed means of spreading the gospel. But a church which preaches the cross must itself be marked by the cross. It becomes a stumbling block to evangelism when it betrays the gospel or lacks a living faith in God, a genuine love for people, or scrupulous honesty in all things including promotion and finance. The church is the community of God's people rather than an institution, and must not be identified with any particular culture, social, or political system, or human ideology.

Jn. 17:18; 20:21
Mt. 28:19-20

Ac. 1:8; 20:27

Eph. 1:9-10; 3:9-11
Gal. 6:14, 17
2 Co. 6:3-4
2 Ti. 2:19-21

Php. 1:27

7. Cooperation in Evangelism

We affirm that the church's visible unity in truth is God's purpose. Evangelism also summons us to unity, because our oneness strengthens our witness, just as our disunity undermines our gospel of reconciliation. We recognize, however, that organizational unity may take many forms and does not necessarily forward evangelism. Yet, we who share the same biblical faith should be closely united in fellowship, work, and witness. We confess that our testimony has sometimes been marred by sinful individualism and needless duplication. We pledge ourselves to seek a deeper unity in truth, worship, holiness, and mission. We urge the development of regional and functional cooperation for furtherance of the church's mission, for strategic planning, for mutual encouragement, and for the sharing of resources and experience.

Eph. 4:3, 4
Jn. 17:21, 23
Jn. 13:35

Php. 1:27

8. Churches in Evangelistic Partnership

We rejoice that a new missionary era has dawned. The dominant role of western missions is fast disappearing. God is raising up from the younger churches a great new resource for world evangelization, and is, thus, demonstrating that the responsibility to evangelize belongs to the whole body of Christ. All churches should, therefore, be asking God and themselves what they should be doing both to reach their own area and to send missionaries to other parts of the world. A reevaluation of our missionary responsibility and role should be continuous. Thus, a growing partnership of churches will develop and the universal character of Christ's church will be more clearly exhibited. We also thank God for agencies which labor in Bible translation, theological education, the mass media, Christian literature, evangelism, missions, church renewal and other specialist fields. They, too, should engage in constant self-examination to evaluate their effectiveness as part of the church's mission.

Ro. 1:8;
Php. 1:5; 4:15;
Ac. 13:1-3;
1 Th. 1:6-8

9. The Urgency of the Evangelistic Task

More than 2,700 million people, which is more than two-thirds of all humanity, have yet to be evangelized. We are ashamed that so many have been neglected; it is a standing rebuke to us and to the whole church. There is now, however, in many parts of the world an unprecedented receptivity to the Lord Jesus Christ. We are convinced that this is the time for churches and para-church agencies to pray earnestly for the salvation of the unreached and to launch new efforts to achieve world evangelization. A reduction of foreign missionaries and money in an evangelized country may sometimes be necessary to facilitate the national church's growth in self-reliance and to release resources for unevangelized areas. Missionaries should flow ever more freely from and to all six continents in a spirit of humble service. The goal should be, by all available means and at the earliest possible time, that every person will have the opportunity to hear, understand, and receive the Good News. We cannot hope to attain this goal without sacrifice. All of us are shocked by the poverty of millions and disturbed by the injustices which cause it. Those of us who live in affluent circumstances accept our duty to develop a simple lifestyle in order to contribute more generously to both relief and evangelism.

Mk. 16:15

Jn. 9:4

Mt. 9:35-38

Isa. 58:6-7;
Jas. 2:1-9
1 Co. 9:19-23;
Jas. 1:27;
Mt. 25:31-46;
Ac. 2:44-45; 4:34-35

10. Evangelism and Culture

The development of strategies for world evangelization calls for imaginative pioneering methods. Under God, the result will be the rise of churches deeply rooted in Christ and closely related to their culture. Culture must always be tested and judged by Scripture. Because men and women are God's creatures, some of their culture is rich in beauty and goodness. Because they are fallen, all of it is tainted with sin and some of it is demonic. The gospel does not presuppose the superiority of any culture to another, but evaluates all cultures according to its own criteria of truth and righteousness, and insists on moral absolutes in every culture. Missions have all too frequently exported with the gospel an alien culture and churches have sometimes been in bondage to culture rather than to Scripture. Christ's evangelists must humbly seek to empty themselves of all but their personal authenticity in order to become the

Mk. 7:8-9, 13
Ge. 4:21-22

1 Co. 9:19-23

Php. 2:5-7
2 Co. 4:5

servants of others, and churches must seek to transform and enrich culture, all for the glory of God.

11. Education and Leadership

We confess that we have sometimes pursued church growth at the expense of church depth, and divorced evangelism from Christian nurture. We also acknowledge that some of our missions have been too slow to equip and encourage national leaders to assume their rightful responsibilities. Yet, we are committed to indigenous principles, and long that every church will have national leaders who manifest a Christian style of leadership in terms not of domination but of service. We recognize that there is a great need to improve theological education, especially for church leaders. In every nation and culture there should be an effective training program for pastors and laity in doctrine, discipleship, evangelism, nurture, and service. Such training programs should not rely on any stereotyped methodology but should be developed by creative local initiatives according to biblical standards.

Col. 1:27-28;
Ac. 14:23

Tit. 1:5,9

Mk. 10:42-45

Eph. 4:11-12

12. Spiritual Conflict

We believe that we are engaged in constant spiritual warfare with the principalities and powers of evil, who are seeking to overthrow the church and frustrate its task of world evangelization. We know our need to equip ourselves with God's armor and to fight this battle with the spiritual weapons of truth and prayer. For we detect the activity of our enemy, not only in false ideologies outside the church, but also inside it in false gospels which twist Scripture and put people in the place of God. We need both watchfulness and discernment to safeguard the biblical gospel. We acknowledge that we ourselves are not immune to worldliness of thought and action, that is, to a surrender to secularism. For example, although careful studies of church growth, both numerical and spiritual, are right and valuable, we have sometimes neglected them. At other times, desirous to ensure a response to the gospel, we have compromised our message, manipulated our hearers through pressure techniques, and become unduly preoccupied with statistics or even dishonest in our use of them. All this is worldly. The church must be in the world; the world must not be in the church.

Eph. 6:12
2 Co. 4:3-4
Eph. 6:11, 13-18
2 Co. 10:3-5
1 Jn. 2:18-26; 4:1-3;
Gal. 1:6-9;
2 Co. 2:17; 4:2

Jn. 17:15

13. Freedom and Persecution

It is the God-appointed duty of every government to secure conditions of peace, justice, and liberty in which the church may obey God, serve the Lord Christ, and preach the gospel without interference. We, therefore, pray for the leaders of the nations and call upon them to guarantee freedom of thought and conscience, and freedom to practice and propagate religion in accordance with the will of God and as set forth in "The Universal Declaration of Human Rights." We also express our deep concern for all who have been unjustly imprisoned, and especially for those who are suffering for their testimony to the Lord Jesus. We promise to pray and work for their freedom. At the same time we refuse to be intimidated by their fate. God helping us, we, too, will seek to stand

1 Ti. 2:1-4

Col. 3:24
Ac. 4:19; 5:29

Heb. 13:1-3
Lk. 4:18
Gal. 5:11; 6:12

Mt. 5:10-12;
Jn. 15:18-21

against injustice and to remain faithful to the gospel, whatever the cost. We do not forget the warnings of Jesus that persecution is inevitable.

Ac. 1:8;
1 Co. 2:4
Jn. 15:26-27
Jn. 16:8-11;
1 Co. 12:3;
Jn. 3:6-8;
2 Co. 3:18
Jn. 7:37-39;
1 Th. 5:19
Ps. 85:4-7
Ga. 5:22-23
Ro. 12:3-8;
1 Co. 12:4-31
Ps. 67:1-3

14. The Power of the Holy Spirit

We believe in the power of the Holy Spirit. The Father sent his Spirit to bear witness to his Son; without his witness ours is futile. Conviction of sin, faith in Christ, new birth, and Christian growth are all his work. Further, the Holy Spirit is a missionary spirit; thus, evangelism should arise spontaneously from a Spirit-filled church. A church that is not a missionary church is contradicting itself and quenching the Spirit. Worldwide evangelization will become a realistic possibility only when the Spirit renews the church in truth and wisdom, faith, holiness, love, and power. We, therefore, call upon all Christians to pray for such a visitation of the sovereign Spirit of God that all his fruit may appear in all his people and that all his gifts may enrich the body of Christ. Only then will the whole church become a fit instrument in his hands, that the whole earth may hear his voice.

15. The Return of Christ

Mk. 14:62
Heb. 9:28
Mk. 13:10
Mt. 28:20;
Ac. 1:8-11
Mk. 13:21-23;
1 Jn. 2:18; 4:1-3
Lk. 12:32
Rev. 21:1-5;
2 Pe 3:13
Mt. 28:18

We believe that Jesus Christ will return personally and visibly, in power and glory, to consummate his salvation and his judgment. This promise of his coming is a further spur to our evangelism, for we remember his words that the gospel must first be preached to all nations. We believe that the interim period between Christ's ascension and return is to be filled with the mission of the people of God, who have no liberty to stop before the end. We also remember his warning that false Christs and false prophets will arise as precursors of the final Antichrist. We, therefore, reject as a proud, self-confident dream the notion that people can ever build a utopia on earth. Our Christian confidence is that God will perfect his kingdom, and we look forward with eager anticipation to that day, and to the new heaven and earth in which righteousness will dwell and God will reign forever. Meanwhile, we rededicate ourselves to the service of Christ and of people in joyful submission to his authority over the whole of our lives.

Conclusion

Therefore, in the light of this our faith and our resolve, we enter into a solemn covenant with God and with each other, to pray, to plan, and to work together for the evangelization of the whole world. We call upon others to join us. May God help us by his grace and for his glory to be faithful to this our covenant! Amen, Alleluia!

International Congress on World Evangelization,
Lausanne, Switzerland, July 1974

The Manila Manifesto

Calling the whole church to take the whole gospel to the whole world

In July 1974 the International Congress on World Evangelization was held in Lausanne, Switzerland, and issued the Lausanne Covenant. Now in July 1989 over three thousand of us from about 170 countries have met in Manila for the same purpose, and have issued the Manila Manifesto. We are grateful for the welcome we have received from our Filipino brothers and sisters.

During the fifteen years which have elapsed between the two Congresses some smaller consultations have been held on topics like Gospel and Culture, Evangelism and Social Responsibility, Simple Lifestyle, the Holy Spirit, and Conversion. These meetings and their reports have helped to develop the thinking of the Lausanne movement.

A *manifesto* is defined as a "public declaration of convictions, intentions, and motives." The Manila Manifesto takes up the two Congress themes, "Proclaim Christ Until He Comes" and "Calling the Whole Church to Take the Whole Gospel to the Whole World." Its first part is a series of twenty-one succinct affirmations. Its second part elaborates these in twelve sections, which are commended to churches, alongside the Lausanne Covenant for study and action.

Twenty-one Affirmations

1. We affirm our continuing commitment to the Lausanne Covenant as the basis of our cooperation in the Lausanne movement.

2. We affirm that in the Scriptures of the Old and New Testaments God has given us an authoritative disclosure of his character and will, his redemptive acts and their meaning, and his mandate for mission.

3. We affirm that the biblical gospel is God's enduring message to our world, and we determine to defend, proclaim, and embody it.

4. We affirm that human beings, though created in the image of God, are sinful and guilty, and lost without Christ, and that this truth is a necessary preliminary to the gospel.

5. We affirm that the Jesus of history and the Christ of glory are the same person, and that this Jesus Christ is absolutely unique, for he alone is God incarnate, our sin-bearer, the conqueror of death and the coming judge.

6. We affirm that on the cross Jesus Christ took our place, bore our sins, and died our death; and that for this reason alone God freely forgives those who are brought to repentance and faith.

7. We affirm that other religions and ideologies are not alternative paths to God, and that human spirituality, if unredeemed by Christ, leads not to God but to judgment, for Christ is the only way.

8. We affirm that we must demonstrate God's love visibly by caring for those who are deprived of justice, dignity, food, and shelter.

9. We affirm that the proclamation of God's kingdom of justice and peace demands the denunciation of all injustice and oppression, both personal and structural; we will not shrink from this prophetic witness.

10. We affirm that the Holy Spirit's witness to Christ is indispensable to evangelism, and that without his supernatural work neither new birth nor new life is possible.

11. We affirm that spiritual warfare demands spiritual weapons, and that we must both preach the Word in the power of the Spirit, and pray constantly that we may enter into Christ's victory over the principalities and powers of evil.

12. We affirm that God has committed to the whole church and every member of it the task of making Christ known throughout the world; we long to see all lay and ordained persons mobilized and trained for this task.

13. We affirm that we who claim to be members of the body of Christ must transcend within our fellowship the barriers of race, gender, and class.

14. We affirm that the gifts of the Spirit are distributed to all God's people, women and men, and that their partnership in evangelization must be welcomed for the common good.

15. We affirm that we who proclaim the gospel must exemplify it in a life of holiness and love; otherwise our testimony loses its credibility.

16. We affirm that every Christian congregation must turn itself outward to its local community in evangelistic witness and compassionate service.

17. We affirm the urgent need for churches, mission agencies, and other Christian organizations to cooperate in evangelism and social action, repudiating competition and avoiding duplication.

18. We affirm our duty to study the society in which we live, in order to understand its structures, values, and needs, and so develop an appropriate strategy of mission.

19. We affirm that world evangelization is urgent and that the reaching of unreached peoples is possible. So we resolve during the last decade of the twentieth century to give ourselves to these tasks with fresh determination.

20. We affirm our solidarity with those who suffer for the gospel, and will seek to prepare ourselves for the same possibility. We will also work for religious and political freedom everywhere.

21. We affirm that God is calling the whole church to take the whole gospel to the whole world. So we determine to proclaim it faithfully, urgently, and sacrificially until he comes.

A. The Whole Gospel

The gospel is the Good News of God's salvation from the powers of evil, the establishment of his eternal kingdom, and his final victory over everything which defies his purpose. In his love God purposed to do this before the world began and effected his liberating plan over sin, death, and judgment through the death of our Lord Jesus Christ. It is Christ who makes us free and unites us in his redeemed fellowship.

Col. 2:15
1 Co. 15:24-28
Eph. 1:4;
Col. 1:19
Tit. 2:14

1. Our Human Predicament

We are committed to preaching the whole gospel. That is, the biblical gospel in its fullness. In order to do so, we have to understand why human beings need it.

Ac. 20:27

Ge. 1:26-27

Men and women have an intrinsic dignity and worth, because they were created in God's likeness to know, love, and serve him. But now through sin every part of their humanness has been distorted. Human beings have become self-centered, self-serving rebels who do not love God or their neighbor as they should. In consequence, they are alienated both from their Creator and from the rest of his creation, which is the basic cause of the pain, disorientation and loneliness which so many people suffer today. Sin also frequently erupts in antisocial behavior, in

Ro. 3:9-18
2 Ti. 3:2-4

Ge. 3:17-24

Ro. 1:29-31

Ge. 1:26, 28; 2:15
Ro. 1:20; 2:1; 3:19
Mt. 7:13

violent exploitation of others, and in a depletion of the earth's resources of which God has made men and women his stewards. Humanity is guilty, without excuse, and on the broad road which leads to destruction.

Mt. 5:46; 7:11
1 Ti. 6:16
Ac. 17:22-31

Although God's image in human beings has been corrupted, they are still capable of loving relationships, noble deeds, and beautiful art. Yet, even the finest human achievement is fatally flawed and cannot possibly fit anybody to enter God's presence. Men and women are also spiritual beings, but spiritual practices and self-help techniques can, at the most, alleviate felt needs; they cannot address the solemn realities of sin, guilt, and judgment. Neither human religion, nor human righteousness, nor socio-political programs can save people. Self-salvation of every kind is impossible. Left to themselves, human beings are lost forever.

Ro. 3:20
Eph. 2:1-3
Gal. 1:6-9;
2 Co. 11:2-4

1 Jn. 2:22-23; 4:1-3
1 Co. 15:3-4
Jer. 6:14; 8:11

So we repudiate false gospels which deny human sin, divine judgment, the deity, and incarnation of Jesus Christ, and the necessity of the Cross and the resurrection. We also reject half-gospels, which minimize sin and confuse God's grace with human self-effort. We confess that we ourselves have sometimes trivialized the gospel. But we determine in our evangelism to remember God's radical diagnosis and his equally radical remedy.

2. Good News for Today

Eph. 2:4
Lk. 15: 19:10
Ac. 8:35
Mk. 1:14-15
2 Co. 5:21;
Gal. 3:13
Ac. 2:23-24
2 Cor. 5:17
Ac. 2:38-39
Eph. 2:11-19
Rev. 21:1-5; 22:1-5

We rejoice that the living God did not abandon us to our lostness and despair. In his love he came after us in Jesus Christ to rescue and remake us. So the Good News focuses on the historic person of Jesus, who came proclaiming the kingdom of God and living a life of humble service, who died for us, becoming sin and a curse in our place, and whom God vindicated by raising him from the dead. To those who repent and believe in Christ God grants a share in the new creation. He gives us new life, which includes the forgiveness of our sins and the indwelling, transforming power of his Spirit. He welcomes us into his new community, which consists of people of all races, nations, and cultures. And he promises that one day we will enter his new world, in which evil will be abolished, nature will be redeemed, and God will reign forever.

Eph. 6:19-20;
2 Ti. 4:2
Ro. 1:14-16
Jer. 23:28

This Good News must be boldly proclaimed, wherever possible, in church and public hall, on radio and television, and in the open air, because it is God's power for salvation and we are under obligation to make it known. In our preaching we must faithfully declare the truth which God has revealed in the Bible and relate it to our own context.

Php. 1:7
Ac. 18:4; 19:8-9
2 Co. 5:11
1 Pe. 3:15

We also affirm that apologetics, namely "the defense and confirmation of the gospel," is integral to the biblical understanding of mission and essential for effective witness in the modern world. Paul "reasoned" with people out of the Scriptures, with a view to "persuading" them of the truth of the gospel. So must we. In fact, all Christians should be ready to give a reason for the hope that is in them.

Lk. 4:18; 6:20; 7:22
Dt. 15:7-11

We have again been confronted with Luke's emphasis that the gospel is Good News for the poor and have asked ourselves what this means to the majority of the world's population who are destitute, suffering, or oppressed. We have been reminded that the law, the prophets, and the wisdom books, and the teaching and ministry of Jesus, all stress God's concern for the materially poor and our consequent duty to defend and care for them. Scripture also refers to the spiritually poor who look to God alone for mercy. The gospel comes as Good News to both. The spiritually poor, who, whatever their economic circumstances, humble themselves before God, receive by faith the free gift of salvation. There is no other way for anybody to enter the kingdom of God. The materially poor and powerless find in addition a new dignity as God's children, and the love of brothers and sisters who will struggle with them for their liberation from everything which demeans or oppresses them.

Am. 2:6-7; Zec. 7:8-10

Pr. 21:13

Zep. 3:12

Mt. 5:3

Mk. 10:15

1 Jn. 3:1

Ac. 2:44-45; 4:32-35

We repent of any neglect of God's truth in Scripture and determine both to proclaim and to defend it. We also repent where we have been indifferent to the plight of the poor, and where we have shown preference for the rich, and we determine to follow Jesus in preaching Good News to all people by both word and deed.

3. The Uniqueness of Jesus Christ

We are called to proclaim Christ in an increasingly pluralistic world. There is a resurgence of old faiths and a rise of new ones. In the first century too there were "many gods and many lords." Yet, the apostles boldly affirmed the uniqueness, indispensability, and centrality of Christ. We must do the same.

1 Co. 8:5

Because men and women are made in God's image and see in the creation traces of its creator, the religions which have arisen do sometimes contain elements of truth and beauty. They are not, however, alternative gospels. Because human beings are sinful, and because "the whole world is under the control of the evil one," even religious people are in need of Christ's redemption. We, therefore, have no warrant for saying that salvation can be found outside Christ or apart from an explicit acceptance of his work through faith.

Ps. 19:1-6; Ro. 1:19-20

Ac. 17:28

1 Jn. 5:19; Ac. 10:1-2; 11:14, 18; 15:8-9

Jn. 14:6

It is sometimes held that in virtue of God's covenant with Abraham, Jewish people do not need to acknowledge Jesus as their Messiah. We affirm that they need him as much as anyone else, that it would be a form of anti-Semitism, as well as being disloyal to Christ, to depart from the New Testament pattern of taking the gospel to "the Jew first." We, therefore, reject the thesis that Jews have their own covenant which renders faith in Jesus unnecessary.

Ge. 12:1-3; 17:1-2

Ro. 3:9; 10:12

Ac. 13:46; Ro. 1:16; 2:9-10

What unites us is our common convictions about Jesus Christ. We confess him as the eternal Son of God who became fully human while remaining fully divine, who was our substitute on the cross, bearing our sins, and dying our death, exchanging his righteousness for our unrighteousness, who rose victorious in a transformed body, and who will return in glory to judge the world. He alone is the incarnate Son, the Savior, the Lord and the Judge, and he alone, with the Father and the Spirit, is worthy of the worship, faith, and obedience of all people. There is only one gospel because there is only one Christ, who because of his death and resurrection is himself the only way of salvation. We, therefore, reject both the relativism which regards all religions and spiritualities as equally valid approaches to God, and the syncretism which tries to mix faith in Christ with other faiths.

Jn. 1:1; 14:18; Ro. 1:3-4

1 Pe. 2:24; 1 Co. 15:3 2 Co. 5:21

1 Co. 15:1-11

Mt. 25:31-32; Ac. 17:30-31

Rev. 5:11-14

Ac. 4:12

Php. 2:9-11
2 Co. 5:14
Mt. 28:19-20

Jn. 10:11-16
2 Co. 11:2-3

1 Ti. 2:5-7

Moreover, since God has exalted Jesus to the highest place, in order that everybody should acknowledge him, this also is our desire. Compelled by Christ's love, we must obey Christ's Great Commission and love his lost sheep, but we are especially motivated by "jealousy" for his holy name, and we long to see him receive the honor and glory which are due to him.

In the past we have sometimes been guilty of adopting towards adherents of other faiths attitudes of ignorance, arrogance, disrespect, and even hostility. We repent of this. We, nevertheless, are determined to bear a positive and uncompromising witness to the uniqueness of our Lord, in his life, death and resurrection, in all aspects of our evangelistic work including interfaith dialogue.

4. The Gospel and Social Responsibility

1 Th. 1:6-10
1 Jn. 3:17
Ro. 14:17

Ro. 10:14

Mt. 12:28
1 Jn. 3:18
Mt. 25:34-46

Ac. 6:1-4;
Ro. 12:4-8
Mt. 5:16
Jer.22:1-5, 11-17; 23:5-6

Am. 1:1-2, 8

Is. 59

Lev. 25
Job 24:1-12

The authentic gospel must become visible in the transformed lives of men and women. As we proclaim the love of God we must be involved in loving service, and as we preach the kingdom of God we must be committed to its demands of justice and peace.

Evangelism is primary because our chief concern is with the gospel, that all people may have the opportunity to accept Jesus Christ as Lord and Savior. Yet, Jesus not only proclaimed the kingdom of God, he also demonstrated its arrival by works of mercy and power. We are called today to a similar integration of words and deeds. In a spirit of humility we are to preach and teach, minister to the sick, feed the hungry, care for prisoners, help the disadvantaged and handicapped, and deliver the oppressed. While we acknowledge the diversity of spiritual gifts, callings, and contexts, we also affirm that Good News and good works are inseparable.

The proclamation of God's kingdom necessarily demands the prophetic denunciation of all that is incompatible with it. Among the evils we deplore are violence, including institutionalized violence, political corruption, all forms of exploitation of people and of the earth, the undermining of the family, abortion on demand, the drug traffic, and the abuse of human rights. In our concern for the poor, we are distressed by the burden of debt in the Two-Thirds World. We are also outraged by the inhuman conditions in which millions live, who bear God's image as we do.

Eph. 2:8-10
Jn. 17:18; 20:21

Php. 2:5-8

Ac. 10:36

Mt. 6:33

Our continuing commitment to social action is not a confusion of the kingdom of God with a Christianized society. It is, rather, a recognition that the biblical gospel has inescapable social implications. True mission should always be incarnational. It necessitates entering humbly into other people's worlds, identifying with their social reality, their sorrow and suffering, and their struggles for justice against oppressive powers. This cannot be done without personal sacrifices.

We repent that the narrowness of our concerns and vision has often kept us from proclaiming the lordship of Jesus Christ over all of life, private and public, local and global. We determine to obey his command to "seek first the kingdom of God and his righteousness."

B. The Whole Church

The whole gospel has to be proclaimed by the whole church. All the people of God are called to share in the evangelistic task. Yet without the Holy Spirit of God all their endeavors will be fruitless.

5. God the Evangelist

The Scriptures declare that God himself is the chief evangelist. For the Spirit of God is the Spirit of truth, love, holiness, and power, and evangelism is impossible without him. It is he who anoints the messenger, confirms the Word, prepares the hearer, convicts the sinful, enlightens the blind, gives life to the dead, enables us to repent and believe, unites us to the body of Christ, assures us that we are God's children, leads us into Christlike character and service, and sends us out in our turn to be Christ's witnesses. In all this the Holy Spirit's main preoccupation is to glorify Jesus Christ by showing him to us and forming him in us. *(2 Co. 5:20 / Jn. 15:26-27 / Lk. 4:18 / 1 Co. 2:4; Jn. 16:8-11 / 1 Co. 12:3; Eph. 2:5 / 1 Co. 12:13; Ro. 8:16 / Gal. 5:22-23; Ac. 1:8 / Jn.16:14; Ga. 4:19)*

All evangelism involves spiritual warfare with the principalities and powers of evil, in which only spiritual weapons can prevail, especially the Word and the Spirit, with prayer. We, therefore, call on all Christian people to be diligent in their prayers both for the renewal of the church and for the evangelization of the world. *(Eph. 6:10-12 / 2 Co. 10:3-5 / Eph. 6:17 / Eph. 6:18-20; 2 Th. 3:1)*

Every true conversion involves a power encounter, in which the superior authority of Jesus Christ is demonstrated. There is no greater miracle than this, in which the believer is set free from the bondage of Satan and sin, fear and futility, darkness and death. *(Ac. 26:17, 18 / 1 Th. 1:9-10 / Col. 1:13-14)*

Although the miracles of Jesus were special, being signs of his Messiahship and anticipations of his perfect kingdom when all nature will be subject to him, we have no liberty to place limits on the power of the living Creator today. We reject both the skepticism which denies miracles and the presumption which demands them, both the timidity which shrinks from the fullness of the Spirit and the triumphalism which shrinks from the weakness in which Christ's power is made perfect. *(Jn. 2:11; 20:30-31 / Jn. 11:25; 1 Co. 15:20-28 / Jer. 32:17 / 2 Ti. 1:7 / 2 Co. 12:9-10)*

We repent of all self-confident attempts either to evangelize in our own strength or to dictate to the Holy Spirit. We determine in future not to "grieve" or "quench" the Spirit, but rather to seek to spread the Good News "with power, with the Holy Spirit and with deep conviction." *(Jer. 17:5 / Eph. 4:30; 1 Th. 5:19 / 1 Th. 1:5)*

6. The Human Witness

God the evangelist gives his people the privilege of being his "fellow-workers." For, although we cannot witness without him, he normally chooses to witness through us. He calls only some to be evangelists, missionaries or pastors, but he calls his whole church and every member of it to be his witnesses. *(2 Co. 6:1 / Ac. 8:26-39; 14:27 / Eph. 4:11; Ac. 13:1-3 / Ac. 1:8; 8:1, 4 / Co.1:28)*

The privileged task of pastors and teachers is to lead God's people (*laos*) into maturity and to equip them for ministry. Pastors are not to monopolize ministries, but rather to multiply them, by encouraging others to use their gifts and by training disciples to make disciples. The domination of the laity by the clergy has been a great evil in the history of the church. It robs both laity and clergy of their God-intended roles, causes clergy breakdowns, weakens the church, and hinders the spread *(Eph. 4:11-12 / Mt. 28:19; 2 Ti. 2:2 / 1 Th. 5:12-15)* of the gospel. More than that, it is fundamentally unbiblical. We, therefore, who have for centuries insisted on "the priesthood of all believers" now also insist on the ministry of all believers.

We gratefully recognize that children and young people enrich the church's worship and outreach by their enthusiasm and faith. We need to train them in discipleship and evangelism so that they may reach their own generation for Christ.

God created men and women as equal bearers of his image, accepts them equally in Christ, and poured out his Spirit on all flesh, sons and daughters alike. In addition, because the Holy Spirit distributes his gifts to women as well as to men, they must be given opportunities to exercise their gifts. We celebrate their distinguished record in the history of missions and are convinced that God calls women to similar roles today. Even though we are not fully agreed what forms their leadership should take, we do agree about the partnership in world evangelization which God intends men and women to enjoy. Suitable training must, therefore, be made available to both.

Lay witness takes place, by women and men, not only through the local church (see section 8), but through friendships in the home and at work. Even those who are homeless or unemployed share in the calling to be witnesses.

Our first responsibility is to witness to those who are already our friends, relatives, neighbors, and colleagues. Home evangelism is also natural, both for married and for single people. Not only should a Christian home commend God's standards of marriage, sex, family, and provide a haven of love and peace to people who are hurting, but neighbors who would not enter a church usually feel comfortable in a home, even when the gospel is discussed.

Another context for lay witness is the workplace, for it is here that most Christians spend half their waking hours, and work is a divine calling. Christians can commend Christ by word of mouth, by their consistent industry, honesty and thoughtfulness, by their concern for justice in the workplace, and especially if others can see from the quality of their daily work that it is done to the glory of God.

We repent of our share in discouraging the ministry of the laity, especially of women and young people. We determine in the future to encourage all Christ's followers to take their place, rightfully and naturally, as his witnesses. For true evangelism comes from the overflow of a heart in love with Christ. That is why it belongs to all his people without exception.

7. The Integrity of the Witnesses

Nothing commends the gospel more eloquently than a transformed life, and nothing brings it into disrepute so much as personal inconsistency. We are charged to behave in a manner that is worthy of the gospel of Christ, and even to "adorn" it, enhancing its beauty by holy lives. For the watching world rightly seeks evidence to substantiate the claims which Christ's disciples make for him. A strong evidence is our integrity.

Our proclamation that Christ died to bring us to God appeals to

---

Margin references:

1 Co. 12:4-7;
Eph. 4:7

Mt. 21:15-16
1 Ti. 4:12

Ge. 1:26-27
Gal. 3:28
Ac. 2:17-18
1 Pe. 4:10

Ro. 16:1-6, 12
Php. 4:2-3

Mk. 5:18-20;
Lk. 5:27-32

Ac. 28:30-31

Ac. 10:24, 33;
18:7-8, 24-26

1 Co. 7:17-24
Tit. 2:9, 10
Col. 4:1
Col. 3:17, 23-24

Ac. 4:20

2 Co. 6: 3-4

Php. 1:27
Tit. 2:10
Col. 4:5-6
Pr. 11:3
1 Pe. 3:18

people who are spiritually thirsty, but they will not believe us if we give
no evidence of knowing the living God ourselves, or if our public worship
lacks reality and relevance.

1 Jn. 1:5-6
1 Co. 14:25-26

Our message that Christ reconciles alienated people to each other
rings true only if we are seen to love and forgive one another, to serve
others in humility, and to reach out beyond our own community in
compassionate, costly ministry to the needy.

Eph. 2:14-18
Eph. 4:31-5:2
Gal. 5:13
Lk. 10:29-37

Our challenge to others to deny themselves, take up their cross and
follow Christ will be plausible only if we ourselves have evidently died
to selfish ambition, dishonesty and covetousness, and are living a life of
simplicity, contentment and generosity.

Mk. 8:34

Mt. 6:19-21, 31-33
1 Ti. 6:6-10, 17-18

We deplore the failures in Christian consistency which we see in
both Christians and churches: material greed, professional pride and
rivalry, competition in Christian service, jealousy of younger leaders,
missionary paternalism, the lack of mutual accountability, the loss of
Christian standards of sexuality, and racial, social, and sexual discrimination. All this is worldliness, allowing the prevailing culture to subvert
the church instead of the church challenging and changing the culture.
We are deeply ashamed of the times when, both as individuals and in our
Christian communities, we have affirmed Christ in word and denied him
in deed. Our inconsistency deprives our witness of credibility. We acknowledge our continuing struggles and failures. But we also determine
by God's grace to develop integrity in ourselves and in the church.

Ac. 5:1-11
Php. 1:15-17
1 Co. 5:1-13
Jas. 2:1-4
1 Jn. 2:15-17

Mt. 5:13
Mt. 7:21-23
1 Jn. 2:4

Eph. 4:1

8. The Local Church

Every Christian congregation is a local expression of the body of
Christ and has the same responsibilities. It is both "a holy priesthood" to
offer God the spiritual sacrifices of worship and "a holy nation" to spread
abroad his excellences in witness. The church is thus both a worshipping
and a witnessing community, gathered and scattered, called and sent.
Worship and witness are inseparable.

1 Co. 12:27

1 Pe. 2:5, 9
Jn. 17:6, 9, 11, 18

We believe that the local church bears a primary responsibility for
the spread of the gospel. Scripture suggest this in the progression that
"our gospel came to you" and then "rang out from you." In this way, the
gospel creates the church which spreads the gospel which creates more
churches in a continuous chain-reaction. Moreover, what Scripture
teaches, strategy confirms. Each local church must evangelize the
district in which it is situated, and has the resources to do so.

Php. 2:14-16

1 Th. 1:5, 8

Ac. 19:9-10

We recommend every congregation to carry out regular studies not
only of its own membership and program but of its local community in
all its particularity, in order to develop appropriate strategies for mission.
Its members might decide to organize a visitation of their whole area, to
penetrate for Christ a particular place where people assemble, to arrange
a series of evangelistic meetings, lectures or concerts, to work with the
poor to transform a local slum, or to plant a new church in a neighboring
district or village. At the same time, they must not forget the church's
global task. A church which sends out missionaries must not neglect its
own locality, and a church which evangelizes its neighborhood must not
ignore the rest of the world.

Col. 1:3-8

Ac. 13:1-3; 14:26-28

Php. 1:27

In all this each congregation and denomination should, where possible, work with others, seeking to turn any spirit of competition into one of cooperation. Churches should also work with para-church organizations, especially in evangelism, discipleship, and community service, for such agencies are part of the body of Christ, and have valuable, specialist expertise from which the church can greatly benefit.

Lk. 12:32

Ro. 14:17

1 Th. 1: 8-10
1 Jn. 4:12;
Jn. 13:34, 35; 17:21, 23
Gal. 3:28; Col. 3:11

The church is intended by God to be a sign of his kingdom, that is, an indication of what human community looks like when it comes under his rule of righteousness and peace. As with individuals, so with churches, the gospel has to be embodied if it is to be communicated effectively. It is through our love for one another that the invisible God reveals himself today, especially when our fellowship is expressed in small groups, and when it transcends the barriers of race, rank, sex, and age which divide other communities.

Ac. 2:47

We deeply regret that many of our congregations are inward-looking, organized for maintenance rather than mission, or preoccupied with church-based activities at the expense of witness. We determine to turn our churches inside out, so that they may engage in continuous outreach, until the Lord adds to them daily those who are being saved.

9. Cooperation in Evangelism

Jn. 17:20-21
Php. 1:27
Php. 1:15, 17; 2:3-4
Ro. 14:1-15:2

Php. 1:3-5

Eph. 2:14-16; 4:1-6

Evangelism and unity are closely related in the New Testament. Jesus prayed that his people's oneness might reflect his own oneness with the Father, in order that the world might believe in him, and Paul exhorted the Philippians to "contend as one person for the faith of the gospel." In contrast to this biblical vision, we are ashamed of the suspicions and rivalries, the dogmatism over non-essentials, the power-struggles and empire-building which spoil our evangelistic witness. We affirm that cooperation in evangelism is indispensable, first because it is the will of God, but also because the gospel of reconciliation is discredited by our disunity, and because, if the task of world evangelization is ever to be accomplished, we must engage in it together.

Eph. 4:3-7

"Cooperation" means finding unity in diversity. It involves people of different temperaments, gifts, callings and cultures, national churches and mission agencies, all ages and both sexes working together.

Ac. 20:4

We are determined to put behind us once and for all, as a hangover from the colonial past, the simplistic distinction between First World sending and Two-Thirds World receiving countries. For the great new fact of our era is the internationalization of missions. Not only is a large majority of evangelical Christians now non-western, but the number of Two-Thirds World missionaries will soon exceed those from the West. We believe mission teams, which are diverse in composition but united in heart and mind, constitute a dramatic witness to the grace of God.

Our reference to "the whole church" is not a presumptuous claim that the universal church and the evangelical community are synonymous. For we recognize that there are many churches which are not part of the evangelical movement. Evangelical attitudes to the Roman Catholic and Orthodox Churches differ widely. Some evangelicals are praying, talking, studying Scripture and working with these churches.

Others are strongly opposed to any form of dialogue or cooperation with them. All evangelicals are aware that serious theological differences between us remain. Where appropriate, and so long as biblical truth is not compromised, cooperation may be possible in such areas as Bible translation, the study of contemporary theological and ethical issues, social work, and political action. We wish to make it clear, however, that common evangelism demands a common commitment to the gospel.

Some of us are members of churches which belong to the World Council of Churches and believe that a positive yet critical participation in its work is our Christian duty. Others among us have no link with the World Council. All of us urge the World Council of Churches to adopt a consistent biblical understanding of evangelism.

We confess our own share of responsibility for the brokenness of the body of Christ, which is a major stumbling-block to world evangelization. We determine to go on seeking that unity in truth for which Christ prayed. We are persuaded that the right way forward towards closer cooperation is frank and patient dialogue on the basis of the Bible, with all who share our concerns. To this we gladly commit ourselves.

Jn. 17:11, 20-23

C. The Whole World

The whole gospel has been entrusted to the whole church, in order that it may be made known to the whole world. It is necessary, therefore, for us to understand the world into which we are sent.

Mk. 16:15

10. The Modern World

Evangelism takes place in a context, not in a vacuum. The balance between gospel and context must be carefully maintained. We must understand the context in order to address it, but the context must not be allowed to distort the gospel.

Ac. 13:14-41; 14:14-17; 17:22-31

In this connection we have become concerned about the impact of "modernity," which is an emerging world culture produced by industrialization with its technology and urbanization with its economic order. These factors combine to create an environment, which shapes the way we see our world. In addition, secularism has devastated faith by making God and the supernatural meaningless; urbanization has dehumanized life for many; and the mass media have contributed to the devaluation of truth and authority, by replacing word with image. In combination, these consequences of modernity pervert the message which many preach and undermine their motivation for mission.

In A.D. 1900 only 9 percent of the world's population lived in cities; in A.D. 2000 it is thought that more than 50 percent will do so. This worldwide move into the cities has been called "the greatest migration in human history"; it constitutes a major challenge to Christian mission. On the one hand, city populations are extremely cosmopolitan, so that the nations come to our doorstep in the city. Can we develop global churches in which the gospel abolishes the barriers of ethnicity? On the other hand, many city dwellers are migrant poor who are also receptive to the gospel. Can the people of God be persuaded to relocate into such urban poor communities, in order to serve the people and share in the transformation of the city?

Modernization brings blessings as well as dangers. By creating links of communication and commerce around the globe, it makes unprecedented openings for the gospel, crossing old frontiers and penetrating closed societies, whether traditional or totalitarian. The Christian media have a powerful influence both in sowing the seed of the gospel and in preparing the soil. The major missionary broadcasters are committed to a gospel witness by radio in every major language by the year A.D. 2000.

Ro. 12:1-2

We confess that we have not struggled as we should to understand modernization. We have used its methods and techniques uncritically and so exposed ourselves to worldliness. But we determine in the future to take these challenges and opportunities seriously, to resist the secular pressures of modernity, to relate the lordship of Christ to the whole of modern culture, and thus to engage in mission in the modern world without worldliness in modern mission.

11. The Challenge of A.D. 2000 and Beyond

The world population today is approaching six billion. One third of them nominally confess Christ. Of the remaining four billion half have heard of him and the other half have not. In the light of these figures, we evaluate our evangelistic task by considering four categories of people.

First, there is the potential missionary work force, the committed. In this century this category of Christian believers has grown from about forty million in 1900 to about five hundred million today, and at this moment is growing over twice as fast as any other major religious group.

Second, there are the uncommitted. They make a Christian profession (they have been baptized, attend church occasionally and even call themselves Christians), but the notion of a personal commitment to Christ is foreign to them. They are found in all churches throughout the world. They urgently need to be re-evangelized.

Third, there are the unevangelized. These are people who have a minimal knowledge of the gospel, but have had no valid opportunity to respond to it. They are probably within reach of Christian people if only these will go to the next street, road, village, or town to find them.

Fourth, there are the unreached. These are the two billion who may never have heard of Jesus as Savior and are not within reach of Christians of their own people. There are, in fact, some two thousand peoples or nationalities in which there is not yet a vital, indigenous church movement. We find it helpful to think of them as belonging to smaller "people groups" which perceive themselves as having an affinity with each other (e.g., a common culture, language, home, or occupation). The most effective messengers to reach them will be those believers who already belong to their culture and know their language. Otherwise, cross-cultural messengers of the gospel will need to go, leaving behind their own culture and sacrificially identifying with the people they long to reach for Christ.

There are now about twelve thousand such unreached people groups within the two thousand larger peoples, so that the task is not impossible. Yet, at present, only 7 percent of all missionaries are engaged in this kind of outreach, while the remaining 93 percent are working in the already evangelized half of the world. If this imbalance is to be redressed, a strategic redeployment of personnel will be necessary.

A distressing factor that affects each of the above categories is that of inaccessibility. Many countries do not grant visas to self-styled missionaries, who have no other qualification or contribution to offer. Such areas are not absolutely inaccessible, however. For our prayers can pass through every curtain, door, and barrier. And Christian radio and television, audio and video cassettes, films and literature can also reach the otherwise unreachable. So can so-called "tentmakers" who like Paul earn their own living. They travel in the course of their profession (e.g., business people, university lecturers, technical specialists, and language teachers), and use every opportunity to speak of Jesus Christ. They do not enter a country under false pretenses, for their work genuinely takes them there; it is simply that witness is an essential component of their Christian lifestyle, wherever they may happen to be.

Ac. 18:1-4; 20:34

We are deeply ashamed that nearly two millennia have passed since the death and resurrection of Jesus, and still two-thirds of the world's population have not yet acknowledged him. On the other hand, we are amazed at the mounting evidence of God's power even in the most unlikely places of the globe.

Now the year 2000 has become for many a challenging milestone. Can we commit ourselves to evangelize the world during the last decade of this millennium? There is nothing magical about the date, yet should we not do our best to reach this goal? Christ commands us to take the gospel to all peoples. The task is urgent. We are determined to obey him with joy and hope.

Lk. 24:45-47

12. Difficult Situations

Jesus plainly told his followers to expect opposition. "If they persecuted me," he said, "they will persecute you also." He even told them to rejoice over persecution, and reminded them that the condition of fruitfulness was death.

Jn. 15:20
Mt. 5:12
Jn. 12:24

These predictions, that Christian suffering is inevitable and productive, have come true in every age, including our own. There have been many thousands of martyrs. Today the situation is much the same. We earnestly hope that *glasnost* and *perestroika* will lead to complete religious freedom in the Soviet Union and other Eastern bloc nations, and that Islamic and Hindu countries will become more open to the gospel. We deplore the recent brutal suppression of China's democratic movement, and we pray that it will not bring further suffering to the Christians. On the whole, however, it seems that ancient religions are becoming less tolerant, expatriates less welcome, and the world less friendly to the gospel.

In this situation we wish to make three statements to governments which are reconsidering their attitude to Christian believers.

First, Christians are loyal citizens who seek the welfare of their nation. They pray for its leaders and pay their taxes. Of course, those who have confessed Jesus as Lord cannot also call other authorities Lord, and

Jer. 29:7
1 Ti. 2:1-2;
Ro. 13:6-7

Ac. 4:19; 5:29   if commanded to do so, or to do anything which God forbids, must disobey. But they are conscientious citizens. They also contribute to their country's well-being by the stability of their marriages and homes, their honesty in business, their hard work, and their voluntary activity in the service of the physically impaired and needy. Just governments have nothing to fear from Christians.

Second, Christians renounce unworthy methods of evangelism. Though the nature of our faith requires us to share the gospel with others,

2 Co. 4:1-2   our practice is to make an open and honest statement of it, which leaves the hearers entirely free to make up their own minds about it. We wish to be sensitive to those of other faiths, and we reject any approach that seeks to force conversion on them.

Third, Christians earnestly desire freedom of religion for all people, not just freedom for Christianity. In predominantly Christian countries, Christians are at the forefront of those who demand freedom for religious minorities. In predominantly non-Christian countries, therefore, Christians are asking for themselves no more than they demand for others in similar circumstances. The freedom to "profess, practice, and propagate" religion, as defined in the Universal Declaration of Human Rights, could and should surely be a reciprocally granted right.

2 Co. 6:3   We greatly regret any unworthy witness of which followers of Jesus
1 Co. 1:18, 23; 2:2   may have been guilty. We determine to give no unnecessary offense in
Php. 1:29   anything, lest the name of Christ be dishonored. However, the offense
Rev. 2:13; 6:9-11; 20:4   of the cross we cannot avoid. For the sake of Christ crucified we pray that we may be ready, by his grace, to suffer and even to die. Martyrdom is a form of witness which Christ has promised especially to honor.

Conclusion: Proclaim Christ Until He Comes

"Proclaim Christ Until He Comes." That has been the theme of
Lk. 2:1-7   Lausanne II. Of course, we believe that Christ has come; he came when Augustus was Emperor of Rome. But one day, as we know from his
Mk. 13:26-27   promises, he will come again in unimaginable splendor to perfect his
Mk. 13:32-37   kingdom. We are commanded to watch and be ready. Meanwhile, the gap between his two comings is to be filled with the Christian missionary
Ac. 1:8   enterprise. We have been told to go to the ends of the earth with the
Mt. 24:14   gospel, and we have been promised that the end of the age will come only when we have done so. The two ends (of earth space and time) will
Mt. 28:20   coincide. Until then he has pledged to be with us.

So the Christian mission is an urgent task. We do not know how long we have. We certainly have no time to waste. And in order to get on urgently with our responsibility, other qualities will be necessary, especially unity (we must evangelize together) and sacrifice (we must count and accept the cost). Our covenant at Lausanne was "to pray, to plan, and to work together for the evangelization of the whole world." Our manifesto at Manila is that the whole church is called to take the whole gospel to the whole world, proclaiming Christ until he comes, with all necessary urgency, unity, and sacrifice.

Opening Addresses

Setting the Stage

Producer: Jodi Berndt

Narrator: Beatenberg, Switzerland, 1948. Billy Graham was but one of 150 young Christian leaders who gathered to pray, study, and plan for sharing the gospel with a divided, post-war world. Encouraged by that historic meeting, Dr. Graham launched a ministry that would draw hundreds of thousands to Christ. But even as he preached, the great evangelist knew there had to be more. He envisioned a day when Christians would come together—a day when resources, strategies, and prayer for global evangelization could be shared around the world. Fifteen years ago, in Lausanne, Switzerland, that dream became a reality.

As 2,700 committed believers from over 150 countries converged on Lausanne, many recognized the vibrant heritage which had helped shape that Congress. Eight years earlier, in 1966, the World Congress on Evangelism in Berlin had laid a strong biblical foundation for taking the gospel to the ends of the earth. In the years which followed, the Berlin Congress gave rise to regional conferences on evangelism: in Singapore, Minneapolis, Bogota, and Amsterdam. Within this historic framework, the 1974 Congress was attended by Christians who were united in mind and purpose, ready to discover the vision and strategy they needed to reach the world.

Billy Graham (1974): I have come to Lausanne with great hope and great expectation and great spiritual need, asking God to enlarge my vision, as I'm sure you have.

Narrator: Spurred on by Dr. Graham, and challenged by speakers like the late Bishop Festo Kivengere of Uganda and the late Francis Schaeffer, the Lausanne participants grappled with a number of strategic factors as they looked to increase the tempo of world evangelization—factors like the need for cooperation among believers, the difficulty of restricted access countries, and the awesome challenge of unreached people groups. Participants like Leon Ferraez remember feeling somewhat overwhelmed.

Leon Ferraez: When we learned there were three billion people who had never heard about Christ, it was a frightening experience. I realized how little I had done, how little we had done as an organization, and even how little Christians had done to evangelize the world.

Chua Wee Hian: At the '74 Congress, I had the privilege of moderating and chairing a session entitled "The Hard-to-Reach Places of the Earth." At that gathering we spoke of countries where it was extremely difficult to present the gospel. One of the men taking part in that session was Archbishop Luwum of Uganda. A few months later, he was killed by Idi Amin.

Narrator: World evangelism was indeed a formidable mission, but even in the face of these hurdles, the '74 Congress was marked by an unquenchable optimism. In the Two-Thirds World, an unparalleled surge of evangelistic effort was taking place—a fire which fueled the hopes of Christians around the world. At Lausanne, speakers like Malcolm Muggeridge focused on the urgency of evangelism, stressing the need for unity among believers, and, in an unprecedented spirit of cooperation, Christians from each of the 150 countries represented at Lausanne began to pray, plan, and work together on evangelistic strategy.

Chua Wee Hian: Through Lausanne, people were able to function together, not as structures or rigid bureaucratic organizations, but as task forces, with the desired aim of spreading the gospel, particularly to unreached segments of the population.

Dr. Howard Jones: The thing that blessed my heart was the fact that we came together not to exalt any denomination, not to exalt any particular religious persuasion. The Holy Spirit drew us together and we felt a closeness, that oneness in Christ.

Narrator: One immediate result of this newfound unity was the signing of the Lausanne Covenant, a landmark document drafted by a committee chaired by British theologian John Stott.

John Stott: I suppose every conference has a report of some kind, and this was the report which was to conclude the Lausanne Congress. But in God's goodness and providence it proved to be more influential than any of us had expected, partly because of the definiteness of its commitment: to Scripture, to the uniqueness of Jesus Christ, to evangelism, to social responsibility, and to the role of culture. And it seemed to clarify a number of these areas which people from different backgrounds and denominations were able to accept.

Gottfried Osei-Mensah: The Covenant defines our cooperation in a positive way. We are not saying, "If you belong there, you cannot belong here." We are saying, "This is what we believe. This is where we stand, and this is our purpose: To take the gospel of the Lord Jesus Christ so those who can agree on this basis, and who share our purpose, can feel that they can be a part of the Lausanne movement.

Narrator: The Covenant provided a rallying point for Christians of all denominations, and in this spirit a new banner was raised.

Billy Graham: The whole church must be mobilized to bring the whole gospel to the whole world! This is our calling. These are our orders!

Narrator: Armed with this vision, the Lausanne participants went out, renewed in their desire to see the Great Commission fulfilled. The Congress was over, but a *movement* had begun!

Thomas Wang: We feel the Congress in 1974 was as if God threw a big rock into the still water. The church scene at that time was like a still water: without stirring, without spiritual renewal and revival. God threw a rock into the water and the spiritual ripple has been ever-widening until today it touches all the shores of the world.

Don Stephens: I live on a ship—I have for the past ten years, one of YWAM's mercy ships—and at Lausanne, what I think I saw was a course change, like a captain on the bridge saying, "We're going to go fifteen degrees in a direction we haven't been going." And it gave us a focus. It's like you could watch the water part on both sides of the bow. I began to believe it *is* possible; completion of the Great Commission is possible!

Narrator: To continue the important work started at Lausanne, a committee on world evangelism was formed; and as the movement gained momentum, the years following 1974 were marked by scores of national and international conferences, strategy planning meetings, and concerted prayer for global evangelization. New inroads for the gospel were made all over the world by groups like Dr. James Kennedy's Evangelism Explosion, the Chinese Coordination Center of World Evangelization (CCCOWE) movement, and Bishop David Gitari's work with the unreached people of Kenya.

David Gitari: We identified twenty-six tribes in Kenya who fell into the definition of "unreached people" according to the Lausanne movement, and we have made churches aware of those groups of people. The church in Kenya is growing and some of the tribes that had not heard the gospel have now heard and have responded, and the church continues to grow from day to day.

Narrator: It has been fifteen years since the first Lausanne Congress, and now, in 1989, we gather in Manila. Today there are new barriers to be crossed, as Islam vies for a place as the dominant world religion and Hinduism becomes militant. New religious movements penetrate the secular societies in the West, and all around the globe more and more countries turn their backs on traditional missionary efforts. At the same time, though, there are fresh opportunities, as revival sweeps across South America, Africa, and Asia.

Chua Wee Hian: In 1974, we had very little news about the church in China. But in 1978 or 1979, after the cultural revolution, with the new era, we observed that the church in China had grown by leaps and bounds. Today it is estimated there are between forty to fifty million Chinese who are believers, who profess the name of Jesus.

Narrator: As the church continues to grow, Christians all over the world are sensing an urgency about fulfilling the Great Commission. Literally hundreds of different plans have been made for world evangelization by the year 2000, and in the days ahead we will unite our efforts, gaining the strategy and momentum that's needed as we move toward the twenty-first century.

Gottfried Osei-Mensah: I think what I'm expecting from Manila is that there are credible networks being put in place to reach out to the unreached peoples. We've talked about them, we've defined them—many of us know where they are. And now we need to bring the forces together to reach them.

Joni Eareckson Tada: It's not like we don't know our message. It's not like we have to rehearse it, or memorize it, or think of different ways to share it. We just have to get out there and do it!

Thomas Wang: World evangelization is possible by the end of this century. I can't think of anything else that should excite a real Christian more than this.

Narrator: Today, there are still two billion—or two thousand million—people who remain unreached by the gospel. We are the ones who must evangelize our own generation, and we must pray, plan, and work together. The time is now!

Message to the Congress

Corazon Aquino
President of the Philippines

On behalf of the Filipino people, I extend a warm welcome and our world-renowned tradition of friendship and hospitality to the Lausanne II delegates. I wish to express my appreciation to the leaders and organizers of this conference for choosing Manila as the venue for this gathering of more than four thousand delegates from all over the world. I understand this conference is being held for the second time, since the 1974 meeting at Lausanne, Switzerland.

As President of the Philippines, I urge the delegates to include in their discussions pressing problems besetting Third World nations today. The discussion of spiritual topics in this conference is well appreciated, but I take cognizance of the fact that in some Asian countries there are other imperatives which will have to be resolved, particularly those that involve the physical being such as hunger and poverty. My wish is that this gathering of spiritual leaders will be able to offer alternatives to modern day problems that beset cities around the world.

In a world ravaged by war, pain, hunger, and disease, accompanied by a definite trend in the breakdown of moral strength, Christian conferences which encompass all faiths are a welcome respite. I send my best wishes for the success of Lausanne II in Manila.

(Mrs. Aquino's message was read, in her absence, by her special assistant Ruth Romero.)

Welcoming Remarks

Jovito R. Salonga
President of the Philippines Senate

On behalf of the evangelical community in the Philippines, and on my own behalf, I am honored to greet and welcome the delegates to the Lausanne II International Congress on World Evangelization.

I understand there are more than four thousand people from 173 countries attending this ten-day gathering in this historic city. To each and everyone of you I say in Filipino, our national language: *"Maligayang pagdating. Tinatanggap namin kayo ng buong lugod at kaslyahan."* ("A happy welcome. We receive you with great joy and pleasure.")

It is our earnest prayer that the God of all nations, the Lord of all history, will bless your deliberations so from here we may go forth into all the corners of the world with a new spirit and a new resolve—namely, to proclaim the Good News not only from the church pulpit but in public and private offices; in the factories and the farms; in the classrooms or in dark prison cells; in the refugee camps of the hungry and the homeless; in all places where fear, anxiety, suffering, and despair plague humanity; and there, point to our Lord and Master, Jesus Christ, and say, "There is the Light of the World."

The Philippines is a country where your prayers and discussions will sound familiar. As far back as I can remember, our people have been described as "the only Christian nation in Asia." We say that with pride since 90 percent of our people, mostly Catholics, profess the Christian faith. But sometimes I wonder whether that is a compliment or a cause for continuing reproach.

During the twenty-year rule which ended in February 1988, we were also described as the most corrupt nation in Asia. Corruption and Christianity are simply incompatible.

Even now graft and corruption seem to dominate the news reports in this city of twenty-five competing daily newspapers—a record seldom equalled in any place in the world. (New York has only three or four dailies, and all of Sweden has only two morning and two evening newspapers.) But let me add that our people are not easily fooled. During the days of dictatorship, we believed only three things printed in the newspapers: the classified ads, the death notices, and the comics!

The gospel teaches us to accord great respect to the sacredness of human life. But unfortunately, this is a country torn by insurgency. Assassinations, ambushes, and massacres are daily occurrences. It is tragic that church pastors and workers are not spared by the extreme right or the extreme left. On May 1, 1989, paramilitary forces identified with the government reportedly killed a woman pastor and her husband. And on June 25, 1989, an entire congregation of almost forty members, including the lay pastor and his children, were brutally massacred during Sunday school by Communist-led rebels in Davao del Sur. These two tragedies occurring in the southern island of Mindanao show what it means to live the gospel in a Christian country rent asunder by insurgency.

The roots of that insurgency may be traced in part to our massive, grinding poverty and the host of injustices poverty breeds. We have a population of almost sixty million in a country blessed with abundant natural resources. There is the heart of paradox. Italy was once described by a U.S. ambassador as "a poor country full of rich people." The Philippines, by way of contrast, is a rich country full of poor people. Around 60 to 70 percent of our people live below the poverty level. Eighty-five percent of our school children suffer from malnutrition, and according to the research of one Jesuit priest, only eighty-one families—apart from the big corporations—control the wealth of this nation. We are burdened by a huge foreign debt of almost thirty billion dollars. Servicing our total debt consumes more than 40 percent of our national budget. This is the context in which the Good News is being preached today in the Philippines. In metro Manila alone, where this Congress is being held, roughly 30 percent of the inhabitants are slum dwellers; that is to say, squatters in their own country, without any home they can call their own.

That is why Jesus Christ's inaugural sermon in a synagogue in Nazareth, quoting from the prophet Isaiah, contains a wealth of meaning:

The Spirit of the Lord is on me, because he has anointed me to preach good news to the poor. He has sent me to proclaim freedom for the prisoners and recovery of sight for the blind, to release the oppressed, to proclaim the year of the Lord's favor (Luke 4:18).

I understand this Congress will deal with the problems of working among the urban poor. That is good news to us. One of the things we learned during our years of struggle is that we achieve spirituality not only when we are in the privacy of our individual worship, but also when we are out in the busy streets or in the crowded marketplace among the oppressed and the poor, identifying ourselves with the lowliest of them and struggling with them for a free, open society where—we pray and hope—the weak shall be strong and the strong shall be just.

I believe the time is past when we could build our own separate, individual stairway to heaven, away from the sufferings of our people. In the tragedy of our Philippine condition, God's kingdom may also be found where we struggle together with those who yearn to work for truth, justice, freedom, and a better life for all.

Welcome again, and may your ten-day gathering exert a profound influence in the lives of people all over the world. Best wishes and, as we say here, *"Mabuhay! Salamat po."*

VIDEO PRESENTATION

A Message to the Congress

Billy Graham

Greetings in the name of our Lord Jesus Christ. I'm speaking to you from a Methodist church here in London, just around the corner from where John Wesley lived. And so this is a very historic place for us to be when we talk about evangelism. I suppose that it's almost as hot here in London as it is in Manila. But I want to take this opportunity to thank Dr. Leighton Ford and all of those, such as Thomas Wang and Ed Dayton, who have worked long and hard to make this Manila conference possible.

I regret that three things have kept me from being there. First, physical depletion. After the six weeks of our mission here in England, I am physically exhausted. Second, the overwhelming blessings of the Lord on these British meetings that went so far beyond anything we could have ever dreamed. Not only the evening meetings where thousands of people made their commitments to Christ, but also the scores of additional meetings. Third, the challenge of Hungary, where in just a few days we will be having a week of meetings ending in their great People Stadium seating seventy-five thousand. And we need your prayers for that.

This Manila conference is a far-reaching and historic gathering for which we have been praying for many months. I'm praying that God is going to use this Manila meeting to touch the church throughout the whole world, and that all denominations and other related organizations will sense the presence and power of this conference because it's needed in our world.

And certainly this conference is needed if we are to evangelize the world in the next few years. It can be done. The technology is there. People are hungry for the gospel. I heard about a man in China the other day: There were people passing by who were Christians, and as they were passing by one of them said, "I'm going to stop and talk to that poor old man about Jesus." They were on the way down the mountain, going for a little holiday; they stopped, and they looked at him and talked to him. And he cried.

He said, "You know, I prayed to him all my life, but I didn't know his name." And I think there are millions of people like that, people throughout the world whose hearts God has prepared. And I believe that this Manila Congress can be a tremendous inspiration, encouragement and blessing to the whole world church.

I wish with all my heart that I was with you, because I would like to sit in those workshops. And I would like to hear those great messages that are going to be brought in the plenary sessions. May God bless you all.

Thank you very much for giving me this opportunity of saying a few words to you.

Billy Graham is the Honorary Chairman of Lausanne II.

OPENING ADDRESS

"Proclaim Christ"

Leighton Ford

Fifteen years ago this week, the First International Congress on World Evangelization convened in Lausanne, Switzerland, on the shores of Lake Geneva.

Now we are gathered in sight of Manila Bay for Lausanne II in Manila. "Why Lausanne II?" some have asked. "Why not call it the Manila Congress?"

Our son, Kevin, who is here as a participant, was born twenty-four years ago this September. There have been many exciting moments in his life since, but we have never forgotten that birthday. In a very real sense, Lausanne 1974 was a birthday—the birthday of a movement, and we never really forget birthdays.

The "spirit of Lausanne" emerged in July of 1974—the spirit of a new vision and cooperation in world evangelization. There we signed the Lausanne Covenant: to pray, to plan, and to work together to evangelize the world.

Out of that Congress grew the Lausanne movement—a fellowship of leaders from all parts of the world committed to further biblical evangelization. Out of the spirit of Lausanne, literally hundreds of evangelistic movements and organizations have been born. The movement has given birth to many other movements and this is why we still call it "Lausanne." Our prayer is that July 1989 will also become one of God's *kairos* moments and many other births will be traced back to "Manila 1989."

Much is still the same in 1989 as it was in 1974—the need of a lost, broken, lonely world; the mandate of Christ; and the message of salvation. But much has also changed: Then, in 1974 we were looking back on twenty-five tremendous years of church growth worldwide. Now, in 1989 we look forward to the incredible evangelistic opportunities of the last decade of this millennium.

Then, the world had just emerged from the traumas of the sixties. Now, we wait expectantly to see what the new openness and longing for freedom in our world—as shown in the spirit of *glasnost* and the events in China—will mean for the future of the gospel.

Then, a bloody conflict in Indochina had just ended. Now, we have pastors from Vietnam among us in Manila.

Then, youthful protestors raised their voices against injustice around the world. Now, some of those same protestors are here among us as followers of Christ seeking his kingdom of righteousness.

Then, we became aware that God was raising up a group of outstanding leaders in

Leighton Ford is President of Leighton Ford Ministries, and Chairman of the Lausanne Committee for World Evangelization. He is a citizen of Canada.

the Third World such as Gottfried Osei-Mensah, Lausanne's first executive secretary. Now, we see God raising up younger men and women who are moving into positions of leadership. Half of those are under forty-five. Some of you here are even too young to remember Lausanne 1974!

Then, there was only one participant from one Eastern European nation. Now, in the age of *glasnost* we are deeply moved to welcome scores of fellow believers from the Soviet Union, Poland, Czechoslovakia, Hungary, East Germany, Romania, Cuba, Mozambique, and other socialist countries.

Then, the status of the church in China was shrouded in mystery. Now, we know the growth of the church there is one of the great miracles of our time. Until several weeks ago, we had hoped to have several hundred Chinese leaders among us. But the tragedy of Tiananmen Square has closed that door. The empty seat in this room is a silent reminder for us during these days to pray for them and a handful of believers of other nations who are not represented.

Then, in 1974 a layman said, in frustration, that he felt many church leaders expected laypeople to do no more than support the programs, pay the bills, and try not to change anything. Now, we are newly conscious that laity are on the cutting edge of world evangelism, that we are going through a second reformation in which God is putting his work into the hands of ordinary lay-Christians just as in the first reformation he put his Word into their hands.

Then, few women came as participants. Now, we are thankful for the many gifted women among us (and we wish there were more) who have come, not so much in the cause of feminism as for the cause of evangelism, ready to play their full role in Christ's global cause.

Then, the fledgling Third World mission agencies were sending out some three thousand or more missionaries. Now, the Third World churches are sending out twenty thousand cross-cultural missionaries.

Then, many denominational groups were calling for a moratorium on missions. Now, we do not hear the word *moratorium;* many of these same historic churches are rethinking the need for aggressive missionary outreach, and some have called for the nineties to be a decade of evangelism.

Then, there was, sad to say, some mutual suspicion between charismatic and non-charismatic believers. Now, there is a new sense of respect and a desire for partnership in world evangelization.

Then, the concept of two and one-half billion unreached people was new to many of us. Now, that idea has gripped missions around the world, and churches have been planted among hundreds of unreached people groups in the last fifteen years.

Then, social responsibility was clearly recognized as an integral part of the church's mission, remembering that evangelism is primary. Now, in thousands of exciting instances, evangelistic and social ministries have become creative partners—albeit the injustices of our world still stir our consciences.

Then, there was no Lausanne Committee. The 1974 Congress was envisioned, organized, and financed largely by Billy Graham and his organization. I firmly believe that Congress and its results will be one of Dr. Graham's great historic legacies. Now, Lausanne II is sponsored by the Lausanne Committee. And, Lausanne II in Manila has come together, not because of one large organization, but because literally hundreds of churches, scores of organizations, and hundreds of individuals on every continent have sacrificially provided the prayer, the staff, the funds, and the time to make this Congress possible.

Then, there was no Lausanne movement. Now, there exists the worldwide Lausanne movement, not a structured hierarchy, but a network of leaders linked together in a common commitment under the Lausanne Covenant to work with others in their areas of ministry to advance the gospel.

Then, the World Evangelical Fellowship was a historic long-standing, but struggling group. Now, our sister international movement, the WEF, has a clearly established identity, a growing role, and many effective national affiliates. We are grateful for the many cooperative conferences LCWE and WEF have held together.

But with all the cause for thanks, there are reasons to be sober.

Then, we did not have to live with the worldwide scandal of certain Christian leaders whose conduct has obscured the gospel. Now, we do.

Then, we were not so aware of the rise of aggressive missionary efforts by the non-Christian religions worldwide. Now, we are.

Then, we had not seen fully the devastating results of secularization on church, workplace, and family, or on morals and the meaning of life. Now, we are seeing that.

Then, our world was not quite so clearly aware of the "troubles" in Northern Ireland or of apartheid in South Africa where the gospel has been wrapped in the sectarian robes of race and power. Now, we are aware and we stand with our brothers and sisters in those areas where they seek to live and speak faithfully for Christ.

Then, we were not so caught up, especially in the developed world, with comfortable lifestyles, and lavish buildings which have sometimes cut deeply into sacrificial support for evangelism, relief, and development. Now, we do face these issues—and many other challenges.

Then, we met with the theme: Let the Earth Hear His Voice. Now, we meet with the theme: Proclaim Christ Until He Comes, a biblical theme which calls us forward to the year 2000 and beyond, to the completion of the task, and to the return of the Lord.

Within that theme, I suggest three hopes and prayers for the next ten days.

First, in the theological dimension, I hope and pray that we will come to a convincing reaffirmation of the uniqueness, adequacy, and attractiveness of the Christ we proclaim as the only hope of our world and of eternal salvation.

Second, in missiological terms, I hope and pray that we may receive fresh, sensitive, and compelling insights into the ways in which Christ is and must be made known in the various situations of our world in which people seek life abundant and eternal.

Third, in spiritual terms, I hope and pray that God would give us a renewed outpouring of his Holy Spirit which will enable all God's people—especially laymen and laywomen, and the emerging younger leaders—to proclaim Christ with creativity and authority, with integrity and unity in the decades ahead.

Our sub-theme is: Calling the Whole Church to Take the Whole Gospel into the Whole World. And who calls? Not us, but Christ.

I wish that in these days we could relive that captivating scene where the risen Christ appeared to his first followers on the evening of the first day of the week. They had gathered in a house with doors locked, with fear of what was on the outside and with a sense of failure on the inside. Then Jesus walked through those walls, stood among them, and gave them three keys that opened the doors and sent them out to proclaim him.

He gave them the key of new peace: the call to proclaim Christ as he did.
Who is this Christ we are called to proclaim? He is the:

- Word to be spoken
- Truth to be told
- Way to be walked
- Light to be shown
- Life to be lived
- Joy to be shared

But here he shows himself as the peace to be given.

"Shalom," he said, as the Jews did; or as an Arab would say, "Salaam." It was a common everyday greeting. But it was an uncommon gift that he was giving. It was a deep peace he was bringing, peace with his Father, peace with themselves, and peace with the world. His peace was not the absence of problems, but the presence of himself.

It was a peace that was costly. He showed them his hands and side as if to say, "Recognize me, and recognize at what cost this peace is given."

"Christ," says the Scriptures, "is our peace." We proclaim not Christianity, but Christ—not ideology, but Christ; not our experience, but Christ; not even our faith, but Christ.

What will it mean to proclaim Christ's peace to young men in Lagos and Soweto, who can find no work to support their families?

What will it mean to proclaim Christ's peace to the harried businessman in Tokyo who knows *karoshii*—sudden death from overwork—is growing at an alarming rate?

What will it mean to proclaim Christ's peace to the mother in Mozambique whose starving child is dying in her arms?

What will it mean to proclaim Christ's peace to the youth of New Zealand with the highest suicide rate in the world?

What will it mean to proclaim Christ's peace to parents in America, whether in affluent suburbs or the inner city, who hear that their child has died of an overdose of drugs?

What will it mean to declare Christ's peace to our world, and what will it cost?

God will help us to learn from his Word and each other what this means. Jesus is like a beautiful diamond, cut with many facets. As the diamond turns in the light, different gleams of beauty shine forth. There is more to Christ's beauty and power than any one of us can describe. Indians see Christ's peace in a way that Englishmen don't. Brazilians see it in a way that Nigerians don't. Pacific Islanders see it in a way that Germans don't. But as we focus on these next ten days on Christ, we may learn to proclaim his peace as he did.

He also gave them the key of new purpose: the call to proclaim Christ in his way.

"As the Father sent me, so I send you," he said to those first followers. Here is the call to proclaim Christ, not only as he did it, but in his way.

He was saying to them as he is saying to us, "I want you to be a little 'me' in this world." He proclaimed at his Father's command as One who was sent. Do we evangelize in that way? We are not the self-appointed saviors of the world. We are sinners sent by our Sovereign Lord.

He proclaimed to glorify the Father. Do we proclaim to glorify ourselves?

He did it with caring personal love. Even on the way to the Cross he had time to stop for one blind beggar.

He proclaimed not just with words, but with a life that attracted. We have many powerful means of communication at our disposal today, but we should remember that Paul could write to powerless slaves that they could "make the gospel attractive" by their lives.

And Jesus did it, not from a distance, but by drawing close. Is there any such thing, really, as long-distance evangelism? Evangelism in Jesus' way meant touching people—life rubbing life. He didn't tell us to do witnessing, but to be witnesses.

During these days we can learn from Joni Eareckson Tada how Christ touches the physically impaired, and from Caesar Molebatsi how Christ touches the youth of Soweto, and from Lucien Accad how Jesus touches the refugees of Lebanon.

Gottfried Osei-Mensah was the first Executive Secretary of Lausanne. As a boy in Africa, he attended a school with an English headmaster. He was quite amazed that the headmaster knew and called him by his name. He was even more amazed when the headmaster invited him to the Bible class at his house. When Gottfried arrived, he saw there were no chairs left, and being shy, he began to leave. The headmaster called, "Here, Gottfried, I have a seat for you." Then the headmaster put him in his own chair and sat on the floor while he taught. Gottfried was mortified and hardly remembered what was said. But that unconscious Christlike act of sitting on the floor touched him. Years later Gottfried reminded the headmaster about that moment and he didn't even remember, but he proclaimed Christ in such a way that a life was forever changed.

The third key he gave them was new power: we are called to proclaim Christ not only as he did and in his way, but by his Spirit.

He "breathed" on them and said, "Receive the Holy Spirit."

Can you imagine that little band of brothers and sisters, of men and women, when Jesus said, "As my Father sent me, I send you. You are going to be a little 'me'" Can you imagine them looking around at each other and saying, "Who? Us?"

James and John had been arguing not long before about which one was important enough to sit by Jesus' side. Thomas wouldn't even believe in the Resurrection. Peter denied him three times. The women were looked upon as nothing in that day. How could they be "little Christs"?

So when he breathed on them, he was acting out a parable of the Pentecost that was to come. When he breathed, his breath was the wind, the Spirit of God. He was breathing himself to them.

Just as the Father showed himself in the Son, so the Son was reproducing himself in his followers.

This is the secret of world evangelism:

Christ in us, the hope of glory.
Christ in us, the peace of the world.
Christ in us, the bread of life.
Christ in us, the light of the world.

Of course, those first evangelists were failures. And so are all of us. We have all failed. As the great inventor, Charles Kettering, once said, "The only time you don't fail is the last time you try something and it works."

So during these days, we who have failed many times will listen to the call of Christ and pray for the breath of Christ. "Breathe on us, breath of God." We will be fanning into flame the gift of God which is in us, knowing that he has not given us "a spirit of fear, but of power, love, and a sound mind."

Is world evangelization possible by the year 2000? I want to believe it is. I am tempted to believe it is not. Is it possible for people like you and me to do it? I would like to think it is. But deep within, I fear it is not. But is it possible for Christ in us to do this through his Holy Spirit? I am sure that it is!

It is even possible that Jesus Christ may do this greatest work through some people who aren't at this Congress and might never be invited. And it might be possible that he will work through some at this Congress that you and I don't agree with.

In the next ten days we will hear many ideas. We will agree with some and we will disagree with some. But we are here to hear Christ's call and to learn from one another.

And as we focus on proclaiming Christ—as he did, in his way, and in his Spirit— may we find renewed among us that unifying passion which is "the spirit of Lausanne" and which is at the heart of all true world evangelization.

Several years ago one of the world's leading newspapers was shut down because of labor/management strife. Finally an agreement was reached and a new publisher was appointed. The first day he went to work and found the front doors were chained, as they had been for months because of the violence. So he went in the back door and gathered the staff around him in the newsroom. No one had told him what to say or do. So on the spur of the moment he climbed on the desk and said, "Let's open up those front doors!" There was silence. Then the whole crowd cheered. Grown men and women stood with tears flowing down their faces. It was a moment of new beginning.

May this be the prayer of each of us: that Lausanne II in Manila will be a new beginning; that Jesus, the crucified, risen Christ, will walk within this Philippine International Convention Center, show us his hands and side, give us the keys of new peace, new purpose, new power, and say to us, "Let's open up those front doors!"

And so, may we proclaim Christ as he did, in his way, and by his Spirit until he comes.

The Challenge Before Us

Producer: Jim Keen
Writers: Phil McHugh, Greg Nelson

Jesus said:

> Go and make disciples of all nations, baptizing them in the name of the Father and of the Son and of the Holy Spirit, and teaching them to obey everything I have commanded you. And surely I am with you always, to the very end of the age (Matthew 28:19–20).

Where the gospel has gone, people's lives are changed and churches are being established. But there are many groups of people who have not yet had an opportunity to hear that God loves them.

That is the challenge before us. The word Jesus used as *nation* in the Great Commission does not refer to just a political boundary. It refers to ethnic groups or unique communities of people. Our challenge is to provide every people and population on earth with a valid opportunity to hear the gospel in a language they can understand, establishing a mission-minded church planting movement within every unreached people group, so the gospel is accessible to all people.

In 1974, it was estimated there were approximately seventeen thousand unreached people groups, as defined by subculture and dialect. Since then, missions researchers estimate churches have been planted among five thousand of those unreached groups.

But the world's population continues to grow, and there are still twelve thousand groups containing vast multitudes of people that have not yet had an opportunity to hear about Jesus—let alone belong to a caring church. The challenges facing the church are greater than ever before.

Every day the world is becoming much more complex and urbanized. Nearly everywhere, people are moving from the countryside and villages to the cities. Mexico City, for example, has a population of 17.3 million. That is larger than the individual populations of 134 countries. Many of these migrants to the cities are illiterate and poor. At the present rate, one-fourth of the world's population will be urban-poor by the year 2000. These people are poor economically and they are poor spiritually. Many even live off the garbage thrown away by others. How can we win them for the Lord and disciple them if we don't minister to them physically as well?

In contrast, consider the material wealth of Tokyo. And think of the vast multitudes living there who are heading into a Christ-less eternity because no one has told them of the love of God. But a person living in Tokyo has far more opportunities to hear the gospel than people living in cities like Teheran, Pyongyang, Ankara, Tianjin, or Dacca. Many major cities of the world like these have few, if any, churches.

There are now 317 cities of over one million people. Jesus said, "The harvest is plentiful but the workers are few. Ask the Lord of the harvest, therefore, to send out workers into his harvest field" (Matthew 9:37–38). In addition to the large number of cities that need to be impacted for Christ, there are twenty-five entire countries where there are only a few Christians. We need to make a greater commitment to take the gospel to countries like Turkey, Mongolia, North Korea, Afghanistan, and Morocco.

In some parts of the world, there are still many rural people who have not had an opportunity to hear about God's love. It is not so much that there are barriers of distance or geography to the gospel, but it is linguistic barriers that need to be overcome. Many people do not yet have the Bible in their native languages.

> How then shall they call on Him in whom they have not believed? And how shall they believe in Him of whom they have not heard? And how shall they hear without a preacher? And how shall they preach unless they are sent? (Romans 10:14–15, NKJV)

Today, 93 percent of the world's missionary force works among half of the world's population and only 7 percent works among the other half. This neglected half is made up mostly of Hindus, Buddhists, and Muslims.

There are almost seven hundred million Hindus. Millions are willing to acknowledge Christ as one of their many gods, but they see no need to turn from their ancient beliefs to the one true and living God.

Nineteen countries claim Islam as their state religion. Mohammed is their prophet, and the Koran is their scripture. They need to see people living in their countries whose lives demonstrate hope and joy—lives that make it possible to believe the truth of the gospel. Buddhists as well as traditional religionists turn from the gospel. They make attempts to fill the God-shaped void that is part of every person's life—a void which can only be filled by God's Spirit.

If we want to be faithful to our Lord's command to take the gospel to the whole world, the whole church must cooperate to correct this imbalance. New ways must be found to penetrate unreached areas. Churches and mission boards must commit more people to cross-cultural ministry in this other half of the world. Reassignment of some missionaries must be considered. Laymen need to become more involved in sharing their faith. If the world is to be evangelized, the vast majority of the work will be done by laypeople. Tentmakers and nonresidential missionaries need to be employed in areas where traditional missionaries can't go. It is estimated that during the next decade four out of every five countries will officially not welcome those who bring glad tidings.

Creative Christian partnerships need to be established to share moral, spiritual, and financial support, especially in poorer and limited-access countries and where the Christian population is small. Churches in the West and in the rapidly expanding economies in the Pacific-rim countries can greatly enhance the work of the Lord by generously sharing their resources. Cooperation and partnership are absolute necessities if the Great Commission is to be fulfilled.

One of the things we are witnessing today is the amazing growth of the church outside of the Western world. In 1900, only 5 percent of all evangelical Christians lived outside the West. By 1980, half of all the evangelical Christians lived outside the Western world. It is estimated that by 1990, three-fourths of all evangelical Christians will be non-Western. Most of these people are poor in material wealth, but rich in the things of God.

The mobilization of cross-cultural missionaries from this new Christian majority is crucial to accomplishing the task of planting a church among every group of people in the world. The world needs more women like Ninette and Julita. They are from El Salvador, but they are working with Ixil-speaking Indians in Guatemala. They lead Bible studies, work with children, and teach simple health and hygiene. The Indians love them and have responded readily to the gospel. The world needs more people like Brother Weedodo in Indonesia. A requirement for graduation from the evangelical seminary in Indonesia is that you must start at least one church of thirty members before graduation. Brother Weedodo started nine such churches before graduation and saw four thousand people accept the Lord in these churches.

Every day the signs of our Lord's return are increasing. We live in a world of war and injustice—a world full of hurting people. One-third of humankind has some form of physical or mental impairment. If all the blind and deaf people lived in one country, the population of that country would make it the seventh-largest country in the world. Jesus loves them. Do we?

Among the part of the world considered "reached" are many millions of nominal Christians—those who are Christians in name only. Life in the body of Christ has never become real for them because they have not experienced the new birth. There are also many who consider themselves to be Christian solely by virtue of their culture. They have never accepted Christ, so they might be called "notional" Christians. There are churches in their language and culture, so they are not unreached; but they have yet to be effectively evangelized.

With the turn of the century just a few years away, Christian leaders of each country, region, and network need to set goals focused on the year 2000. God's people everywhere need to mobilize into action for a major harvest as we approach the year 2000.

James 1:22 (NASB) says, "But prove yourselves doers of the word, and not merely hearers who delude themselves." As we develop strategies for the challenges before us, as leaders, we need to put this verse into practice, lest we appear to be like young people relaxing in a park, listening to their music. They are so captured by the music that it appears they are asleep. In the hour or so that they are lying there, thousands of people pass by, and they do not even notice them. Let's be careful that spiritually we are not so involved in our own little worlds that we are not aware of the millions of people passing right by us into eternity without Christ.

The Challenge Before Us

Luis Bush

How can we describe the challenge before us at the Lausanne II Congress in Manila? Perhaps it can be described by something we have experienced. This was true for me one day right here in Manila, when I met Andrew. For two years, he had been proclaiming Christ in a community of some seven thousand people who made their living off the garbage dump of Manila.

We put on boots, and as we walked to the dumps, I saw a group of people swimming in the river that flows out to the Manila Bay and to the Pacific. As in other cities around the world, the water is completely polluted. The houses are one-room shacks where entire families live.

While we were in the area, a woman approached us. She was crying. In her hand, she carried a bag which contained the remains of her infant baby who had died only a short while before. She did not have the money needed to give the baby a decent burial, and had approached Andrew for help.

Trucks daily unload the garbage onto a smoldering heap of refuse. At the top of the dump, which smokes six months out of the year, it was a shock to see young and old scavenging—picking up broken bottles and old tin cans to sell to recyclers.

As I looked over the smoking dump on the one side and the community of people on the other with the river in the distance leading out to the Manila Bay, I thought, *What a graphic picture of the world in which we live. What a graphic picture of the challenge before us.*

The challenge before us is to work together with understanding, in a rapidly growing urban world which is increasingly unfriendly. We need to work together in an attitude of dependence on the Lord Jesus Christ and the Holy Spirit, to mobilize all the forces within the body of Christ in every country of the world to fulfill the Great Commission. We must strive to proclaim the gospel to every people group, and to obey the Great Commandment by demonstrating love for the whole person as we approach the year 2000 and until he comes.

"To Work Together With Understanding"

During my time at the dump community in Manila, I was moved by what I saw. There was a team of about twenty people working together in harmony. They proclaimed the gospel and sacrificially served the community. Among them were young

Luis Bush is International President of Partners International. He is a citizen of Argentina.

and old, men and women, charismatics and non-charismatics. Over half of the workers were national Christians from the Philippines. There were people from six different countries and from a number of different Christian organizations working together to share Christ's love. This is the kind of cooperation needed.

The challenge before us is to build new bridges of understanding. We must build a strong bridge of understanding between the younger, rapidly growing churches in the Two-Thirds World countries and the matured and financially blessed churches in the West.

We need to build a bridge which brings together the younger generation and the older generation of Christian leaders. While younger leaders are looking for ways to have meaningful involvement in Christian work by horizontal networking, older leaders, used to working with "top-down" authority lines, need to look for creative ways to support the developing gifts of younger leaders. This requires new and creative styles of leadership.

We must build a bridge to unite the rapidly growing charismatic movement with the more traditional forms of Christianity. The one emphasizes the supernatural power of God operating in spiritual gifts and signs and wonders, while the other underscores the Word of God. We need *both* the power of God and the Word of God.

The fourth bridge would bring together with understanding the call of God for both evangelism and social responsibility, sacrificial service in the world and preaching the gospel of Christ to the world, of both word and deed, proclamation and presence.

Our goal is to build bridges of understanding during the next ten days in our national delegation meetings, in the different tracks, over meals, and when we all meet together. The spirit of cooperation we experience in the next ten days could well be a foretaste of the kind of cooperation we will enjoy over the next ten years.

"In a Rapidly Growing Urbanizing World"

The world is moving to the cities. In 1900, a little more than one out of ten people were urban dwellers. One hundred years later, in the year 2000, almost eight out of ten will be urban dwellers, according to United Nations statistics. The world is becoming one gigantic city.

Moody said, "If we reach the cities we reach the nation. But if we fail in the cities, they will become a cesspool that will infect the entire country."

For all the "human family," this is an increasingly unfriendly world. Major threats to the earth's environment drive one hundred species of plants and animals to extinction every day because of the gases from automobiles, factories and power plants, toxic and household waste, and overpopulation. One out of every five people in the world go to bed hungry every night.

It is also an increasingly unfriendly world for Christians. In the year 1900, virtually every country was open to expatriate missionaries of one tradition or another. This is no longer true. Major changes are taking place in the ability of expatriate missionaries, particularly from the West, to move into unreached areas. By the year 2000, at present trends, over eight out of ten people of the world will be living in countries with restricted access to traditional missionaries.

"In an Attitude of Dependence"

It is Jesus who is Lord. It was Jesus who said: "All authority in heaven and on earth has been given to me. Therefore go. And surely I am with you always, to the very end of the age" (Matthew 28:18–20). "The horse is made ready for the day of battle, but victory rests with the Lord" (Proverbs 21:31).

It is the Holy Spirit who empowers the church. We have experienced three mighty waves of worldwide Pentecostal/charismatic renewal in this century. There is a fourth wave of those of us who desire to hear what the Spirit is saying to the churches through these other waves and join them in the task of spreading the kingdom of God throughout the earth to the year 2000 and until he comes.

"To Mobilize the Body of Christ"

There is a shift in the center of gravity in Christianity from the West to the East and from the North to the South. This growing, global church is becoming mobilized for world evangelization. As John Stott wrote in his commentary on the Lausanne Covenant, "Unless the whole church is mobilized, the whole world is not likely to be reached."

In the Lausanne Covenant, embedded within fourteen other affirmations, one stands out like a precious jewel because it is the only article which speaks of rejoicing. It is article 8, titled "Churches in Evangelistic Partnership," which begins: "We rejoice that a new missionary era has dawned."

The dawn of partnership with missions movements around the world has become at least mid-morning of a new day in Christianity—a day in which the responsibility for world evangelization is being taken up by the "whole body of Christ." More Christians from more countries are seeking to fulfill the Great Commission than at any time in history. The internationalization of missions is the great new fact of our time. Our challenge is to encourage the new world-evangelization initiatives from Africa, Asia, and Latin America, which at the present rate will place more than one hundred thousand missionaries in the field by the year 2000.

But not only that, we are challenged by the need to unleash all the forces within the church in this mobilization. Particularly, we need to see women, young people, and laypeople within our churches renewed, moved into action, and growing as they discover and fulfill their role in world evangelization.

Andrew described to me the tremendous ministry a single laywoman had at the Manila dump over the years. I was also impressed that a man as young as Andrew had such compassion and vision. When we got to the top of the dump and saw those children bent over, picking up garbage, he said two things that I will never forget, "These are beautiful people." And then he added, "It is a privilege to work here."

How much he was like Andrew, the brother of Peter, who kept on bringing people to Jesus. And this Andrew was only twenty-one years old. We need to give the youth of our generation room to grow, and even allow them to make mistakes, and release them in ministry along with other people. All these vital forces need to be released in order to achieve our goal.

"To Fulfill the Great Commission"

This means going beyond "near neighbor" evangelism. This means we need to take the gospel cross-culturally to those groups of unreached people who have never had an adequate internal witness. Cross-cultural evangelism to the unreached is our highest priority. These people groups have never had an indigenous church movement in their midst.

This point was highlighted at Lausanne I. Fifteen years ago there were an estimated seventeen thousand unreached people groups, defined by dialect and sub-culture which needed to be reached. Today, that number has been reduced to some twelve thousand.

Most of these people groups live in a belt that extends from West Africa across Asia, between ten degrees north of the equator to forty degrees north of the equator. This includes the great Muslim block, the Hindu block, and the Buddhist block. And today, only seven of every one hundred missionaries are working among these peoples.

We must refocus our efforts in evangelization. We must redeploy our missionaries. We must think of new creative ways of partnership. And we must not forget the need for the re-evangelization of Europe.

"To Obey the Great Commandment"

A recent study indicated that a great deal of the lost are poor and a great deal of the poor are lost. It also became evident that those in greatest need are living in the midst of Muslim contexts in the Third World.

By the year 2000, one out of every four people will be urban poor. Our challenge is incarnational missions—to respond to the needs of the whole person as we proclaim new life in Christ.

Andrew and his team have learned to minister to the whole person. There is a food program for the children under five living in the community. Many of the workers are trained in primary health care and lovingly minister to the sick and suffering. While I was there they were preparing a room that was to be used as a Christian preschool.

"Until He Comes"

As Christians approach the end of this century, many groups within the worldwide body of Christ are setting the year 2000 as a symbolic milestone for humankind. This milestone year serves both as a focal point for evangelization plans and as a transition time into a new century of world evangelization.

Several countries, including the Philippines, already have a "2000 Plan" and national A.D. 2000 task forces. Others, like Costa Rica in Central America, have already planned their meetings. They are expecting over one thousand Christian leaders in San Jose, Costa Rica in August for what they have called *Alcance 2000,* "reaching out to the year 2000."

Other remarkable national initiatives are taking place. There will be time during this Congress for delegations to come together and discuss what can be done in their country as we approach the year 2000 and beyond.

Preliminary rough-draft plans setting goals by the year 2000 are being laid out and considered by leaders in the continents of Southeast Asia, South Asia, Africa, Latin America, the Middle East, and North America.

The challenge at this Congress is to see those plans mature and expand so every country and continent will have aggressive faith goals for the last ten years of this century and millennium.

As you gather in your national meetings, begin to think of the mandate of Scripture, the context and the issues facing the church in your country, the unreached people groups, the great cities, and the twenty-five most unevangelized countries that your national church can reach. And seek to answer the question: *What can be done by the year 2000?* Set a date for yourself—December 31, 1999. Prepare to involve the wider Christian constituency from your country. Over the next three years, we would like to see 150 countries have national consultations to set faith goals and discover national strategies.

There are also local and global plans focused on the year 2000 by Christian organizations, local churches, denominations, Christian movements, and affinity groups.

The challenge before us is to set significant goals. Ten year goals can become steps of faith that take us from present limitations to future possibilities—goals that are specific, measurable, and achievable. Let us trust God together to do great things.

At the Manila dump community, I also observed signs of joy and peace in the midst of all the agony. Children could be seen playing soccer on the dirt streets and were laughing. An older woman with a big smile came up and gave Andrew a loving embrace.

I also learned something as I heard from others outside of the team. The community had gone through a transformation over the previous two years. Signs of the presence of God among his people were everywhere: in the fourteen home Bible studies, in the church filled with children at mid-morning, and throughout the community as Christians became salt and light.

Brothers and sisters in Christ, if it can be done in a dump community, then why can we not strive to proclaim the whole gospel to the whole world with the whole church by the year 2000 and until he comes?

Looking Ahead

Floyd McClung

I was asked to comment on looking forward—in light of the next ten days, but also in light of the next ten years. Senator Salonga helped us to put the seriousness of talking about world evangelization into perspective.

We have ten days together—ten very important days. We've all come with expectations. We bring our weaknesses, our disappointments, our personal histories, and we even carry some failures with us. We also come as leaders. God has used us in spite of our weaknesses; he has called us and he has blessed us.

Some of us also come from suffering situations. Last night I sat in the balcony, behind me were brothers from Mozambique and in front of me were brothers from Laos. I was deeply moved by realizing they come from intense situations where suffering is all too real.

Some of us come to this conference with certain misgivings about other people who are here. We carry with us our disagreements, our tensions, our questions. Part of the challenge before us is to receive what God has for us personally. And to be able to receive from the Lord what he has for us in the conference, we must have humility in our hearts and we must have faith. We must be willing to lay aside our fears of one another. We must be willing to lay aside our own weaknesses. And, indeed, we must look to the Lord. We can go through these ten days and approach it from a human perspective: evaluate it with human standards and judge it from what we think about it. And we can miss what God has for us.

I would like to challenge you to ask God to speak to you in these days. I would like to ask you to open your heart to the Lord and receive what he has for you personally. If this Congress is going to make a difference in your life, and in my life, then we must hear from God. We can listen to men and women all week long and miss hearing God unless our hearts are open.

Let's open our hearts in a spirit of humility and teachableness. We need to come as receivers. Perhaps one of the greatest criticisms of Christians in our world is that we often carry with us the sense of triumphalism—a kind of cultural imperialism. It is insensitive to impose the gospel upon people. Perhaps as we look forward, one of the things the Lord wants us to do is to humble ourselves and to adopt a spirit of servanthood toward one another.

If we're going to look forward in the proper spirit then there must also be a spirit of

---

Floyd McClung is International Executive Director of Youth With a Mission.

faith and expectation. I talked to a brother from Africa last night and asked him, "What are you expecting in this conference?"

He said, "I have come with a sense of destiny. I am looking to God to give me direction for my life." What a wonderful attitude to have!

If we're going to look forward, we must look forward together. I was thrilled to hear about missionaries going from a non-Western nation to a Western nation. God wants to do something new for us, a paradigm shift in attitude and in constituency. It is a new world in which we're serving. We're to look at the needs of our world, and the vast numbers of people who have not been reached, with a new attitude and a new kind of partnership to work together in missions.

As we consider the challenge that is before us, three brothers who have looked at the challenge and have accepted it are going to share what God is saying to them. First, we're going to hear from Edison Queiroz. Edison is from Brazil and he is the South American Director for COMIBAM.

"CHALLENGE" TESTIMONY I

Edison Queiroz

Brothers and sisters, God is doing tremendous things in Latin America! In November of 1987, we had a Congress in San Paulo, Brazil, called COMIBAM. In that Congress, God pushed his church and told us clearly that we *must* reach the unreached people with the gospel of Jesus Christ. The Congress focused on the local church as the instrument of God to go and to reach the world for Christ. And now in Brazil and Latin America we have a strong awakening of the church and are training pastors to go into missions. It's amazing what God is doing!

In May of 1989, I was in El Salvador, Central America. I was to preach there, but five minutes before I arrived, two bombs exploded at the door of the church. When I got there I said, "What happened here?"

"This is the welcome for you!" I replied, "What a crazy kind of welcome!"

Yet, in the middle of that situation, even though there was shouting and helicopters flying around, the people were singing and saying to one another, "Let's go into missions."

At the end of that conference, one local church raised a faith promise of $55,000. El Salvador is a small country with a bad economy. Many poor people are living in an environment of war, yet one church can raise $55,000 in a faith promise. This is a miracle! God is pushing his church and doing something to reach the world for Christ.

This church in El Salvador asked to support a missionary couple in the Middle East and another couple in Spain. That is beautiful: A small country, a poor country sending their own missionaries. God is doing a tremendous thing. When you leave this Congress, I want to challenge you to go to your churches and push the people, challenge them, encourage them to go into missions.

Latin America is sponsoring several original efforts to reach the world for Christ. We're helping Costa Rica with a strong congress to help reach all of Central America with missions. We have another congress on the south coast.

I am so glad to share this with you. Pray for Latin America as well as the work in your own country .

"CHALLENGE" TESTIMONY II

Chris Marantika

It is an exciting privilege to be a child of God during this period of the history of the church of our Lord Jesus Christ. In spite of the difficulties the church is facing throughout the world today, exciting things are happening. The church of our Lord is growing. In Indonesia, there is a great movement toward the evangelization of the nation.

There are sixty-seven thousand villages in Indonesia—fifty thousand of them are unreached. But the churches of Indonesia are committed to evangelizing the entire nation. They have initiated a program called "Indonesia One, One, One." We are praying and working toward the year 2000, as *one* generation to plant *one* church in every*one's* village.

Many of the churches have set goals. The Free Evangelical Church of Indonesia, headed by Dr. Sutjiono, has plans to plant four hundred churches every four years. They call this plan Four-by-Four. The Bethel Church of Indonesia is focused on planting ten thousand churches by the year 2000. The Indonesian Union of Indonesian Baptist Churches set a goal to plant five hundred churches every five years. And also, the Indonesian Baptist Convention plans to plant two hundred churches by the year 2000.

The churches in Indonesia are working diligently to fulfill their dream to plant one church in every village.

Evangelization in Indonesia is not easy because 80 percent of the population is Muslim. It is the fifth largest nation in the world, yet it's still an underdeveloped country. But the Scripture says that nothing is too hard for God.

The evangelization of the whole world in this generation is not an impossible task. We challenge you to work and pray to reach every community in your country in your lifetime.

Last year we held Tacata '88. Four thousand church leaders, pastors, and evangelists from twenty-seven provinces, from different tribes and denominations came together to plan how to reach Indonesia with the gospel. A challenge was given to the pastors and leaders to pray and dream to have one hundred-thousand Christian workers, evangelists, and pastors by the year 2000. That would make fifty thousand villages seem like a small challenge. We want to reach it, and we need your prayers.

You may forget the things I have said, but try to remember us with this simple prayer, "Lord Jesus, bless Indonesia One, One, One."

"CHALLENGE" TESTIMONY III

Gus Marweigh

Never in the history of Liberia has the nation's only television station, which is owned by the government, pre-empted its major news time to permit a preacher of the gospel of the Lord Jesus Christ to deliver a message. But on June 29–July 1, 1989, a miraculous broadcasting event occurred. The government television station set aside its news time to give Billy Graham an opportunity to preach during prime time as the whole nation listened. Liberia is blessed with the privilege of having only one television station, so when you're on television, everybody listens to you.

The entire nation listened as Billy Graham spoke directly from London by satellite. Later, the Speaker of the House of Representatives, the Honorable Samuel Hill, was interviewed by a television crew that went to Liberia. He said that as people sat before their television sets during those three nights, when Billy Graham give an invitation, people knelt down in front of their televisions to receive the Lord Jesus Christ as their personal Savior.

God is doing something spectacular in Liberia. In addition to what is happening in the cities, God has given strategies to put evangelists and holistic evangelistic strategy teams in various villages. These teams consist of an agriculturist, a building technician, a church planter, a church trainer, and a public health worker. We place a team in a village and operate from there as a public elementary school and teach the children the various trades. We then organize these children into teams. They become teachers who plant churches in various villages.

The first two teams we developed have planted nineteen churches. We feel this is a very effective method to reach the nation with the gospel. We began by recruiting students as teachers, and today we have twenty-nine missionaries in different parts of Liberia.

Please pray God will raise more workers. The harvest is ripe, and the people are ready! God is ready to equip the people. Are the Christians ready to share their resources so the task may be accomplished by the year 2000?

I. The Whole Church

Primacy of the Local Church in World Evangelization

Jong-Yun Lee

When we examine Paul's epistle to the Ephesians, we find some of the clearest statements on the nature of the church. We find:

1. *The primacy of the Lord Jesus Christ.* Jesus is the head, the cornerstone of the church (Ephesians 1:22–23).
2. *The primacy of the Scriptures.* The apostles and prophets are the foundation of the church (Ephesians 2:20), but the Scriptures are still the only rule for our faith and practice (2 Timothy 3:15–17).
3. *The primacy of connectional unity.* The church is a single body of living members, a single temple of living stones (Ephesians 2:21; 4:13,16).
4. *The primacy of the local church.* There are many references throughout the New Testament to locality, including that of the saints in Ephesus, which indicate the significance of locality for identifying the church. Each local church visibly represents the whole church. When we call for "The Whole Church to Take the Whole Gospel to the Whole World," we are calling for each and every local church to take the whole gospel to the whole world.

The churches at Jerusalem and Antioch provide a biblical model as we face the challenge of the primacy of the local church in world evangelization. Four distinct lessons may be learned from the Jerusalem church model: gathering, anointing, teaching, and witnessing.

The Challenge of Gathering

Ekklesia, the New Testament word for *church,* means "assembly," with the action of gathering being primary. The *ekklesia* at Jerusalem gathered often (Acts 1:4,8,12–13; 2:1,44,46). The church gathered for worship as a large group (Acts 3:11; 5:12) and in small groups from house to house (Acts 2:46; 5:42). Togetherness as expressed in regular gatherings for worship, was and is a power source for world evangelization.

The whole church today faces a crisis of individualism which threatens to splinter the church, and thereby reduce our effectiveness in evangelization. Gathering for worship as local churches is one key remedy. Gathering provides an atmosphere for spiritual anointing, a crucible for sound teaching, and a platform for bold witnessing.

Jong-Yun Lee is the Senior Pastor of Choony Hyun Presbyterian Church in Seoul, Korea. A former professor of theological studies and President of Jeon Ju University, he is a citizen of Korea.

The Challenge of Anointing

As Jesus had promised (Luke 24:49; Acts 1:8), the church received the anointing of the Holy Spirit for world evangelization (Acts 2:1–4; 4:24–31). The anointing of the Holy Spirit was evident in their devotion to fellowship (Acts 2:42,44–45; 4:32–35) and in their devotion to prayer (Acts 2:42; 4:23–31). The power of the Holy Spirit is evident in Korea in the prayer life of the Korean churches. Each morning we gather in local churches for pre-dawn prayer meetings (*sae byuk kido*). These include singing, preaching, and extensive prayer. One of the most powerful features of our prayer life is our intense, simultaneous prayer (*tong song kido*). We intercede as one great voice, asking for God's power to be poured out upon us.

The whole church today faces a crisis of misplaced emphasis. With modernization comes materialism, which causes our emphasis to be placed on visible material blessing, rather than on the invisible spiritual blessing of the Holy Spirit. We can learn a great deal from our brothers and sisters in Christ who are suffering under the hand of persecution. Patient endurance and evangelization in the face of persecution is an indication of the power of the Holy Spirit at work in the church.

The Challenge of Teaching

The anointing of the Holy Spirit upon the Jerusalem church was also evident in their devotion to the apostles' teaching (Acts 2:42). Sound teaching is based on the infallible and inerrant Word of God. Even as inspired men of God, the apostles based their entire ministry on the Word of God (Acts 2:16–21,25–28,34–35; 4:25–26; 6:4).

Apostolic teaching set the standard for sound doctrine (Acts 4:25; 5:3,9; 4:2; 5:25,42; 6:2; 8:25). Early response to the gospel, at times numbering into the thousands, resulted from authoritative preaching and teaching of the Word of God (Acts 2:41,47; 4:4; 6:7; 8:4,12; 12:24). Sound teaching kept the gospel and the church pure as the Jerusalem church grew.

The whole church today faces a crisis of authority. We are in danger of losing our identity if we compromise on the infallibility and inerrancy of the Scriptures. We will no longer be the pillar and foundation of the truth (1 Timothy 3:15) if we fail to meet this challenge. Unwavering reliance upon the Scriptures within each and every local church is the key. As pastors stress the authority of God's Word in the local church, the direct result will be a movement of evangelization. Sound teaching is the basis for bold witnessing.

The Challenge of Witnessing

In the same way that the Scriptures are for the whole church, so also the Great Commission is for the whole church, for each local church, and each member of the church.

Witnessing in Jerusalem was based upon the Word of God, supported in prayer, accompanied by wonders (Acts 2:43; 5:12), and expanded geographically and cross-culturally (Acts 1:8; 8:1; 11:19). This witnessing resulted in increasing numbers of converts to faith in the Lord Jesus Christ, sometimes by the thousands, sometimes by daily increases, but always by the power of the Holy Spirit which filled their evangelism.

The whole church today faces a crisis of priorities. Witnessing the gospel must be maintained as our top priority, with ministries of education and compassion working in support of our witnessing efforts. Local churches play the key role, especially each local pastor and the trained laity. We owe a debt of gratitude to Dr. Thomas Wang for his unending emphasis upon the role of the local church in world evangelization. If this one man can accomplish so much, how much more could be done if we all would carry the burden of world evangelization to each local church represented here.

Church extension is often the result of spontaneous evangelism. Such was the case in the development of the church in Antioch. God had prepared the church at Jerusalem to act as a "mother church" to the church at Antioch. Spontaneous preaching to the Gentiles in Antioch led to a great number of converts (Acts 11:19–21). Barnabas was then sent from the church at Jerusalem as an organizing pastor in Antioch (11:22). Four additional lessons may be learned from the Antioch church model: training, praying, calling, and sending.

The Challenge of Training

The church at Antioch developed from a daughter church into a sister church under the ministry of trained leaders. Five ministers are listed in the Antioch church (Acts 13:1). These men are gifted—prophets and teachers. They are tested—leading worship on a regular basis (13:2). It was from among these trained ministers in this local church at Antioch that the Lord chose two, Barnabas and Saul, to go on the first missionary journey.

The whole church today faces a shortage of trained leaders. This decreases our ability to train local laity, as well as to send trained laborers into the worldwide harvest field. Tested service and ministry within the local church are still the best methods for recognizing those whom God has gifted and chosen as whole church leaders.

The Challenge of Prayer

We must continue to pray the Lord of the harvest to raise up workers for his harvest. The leaders in the early church were selfless, sacrificial, cooperative, forgiving, loving, morally noble, and they possessed international vision. This is the type of leader which is still needed today.

If prayer is neglected, then fasting is even more neglected. The ministers of the Antioch church prayed and fasted on a regular basis (Acts 13:2; 14:23). Fasting prayer increases sensitivity to the Word of God and to the leading of the Holy Spirit, and is a great resource for power in evangelism. The Antioch church matured through prayer and fasting.

The whole church today faces a crisis of commitment which threatens to dilute our evangelism. Our commitment must include obedience before activity, quality before quantity, power before effort, the eternal before the temporal, and the historical facts of the gospel before theories. Prayer and fasting within the context of the local church will bring about spiritual renewal. Local pastors are the key in calling for such a renewal.

The Challenge of Calling

In one sense, every Christian is called to evangelize. However, the Holy Spirit still leads local church leaders to recognize God's call on the lives of those whom he wishes to send as evangelists. Within the Antioch church the call came for Barnabas and Paul.

Barnabas and Paul were called to plant churches (Acts 14:23). The local church is primary both in terms of the call and the task of workers in the harvest field. The call is issued from within the local church and the task is to plant more local churches.

The whole church today faces a crisis of consecration. Regionalism, racism, and even denominationalism, threaten to reduce our efforts for world evangelization. Motivation for world evangelization should come from no other source than the powerful conviction of God in our hearts— by the power of the Holy Spirit working through the Word of God. Let us issue a call for repentance to pastors, seminarians, and laity— a call which challenges them to fasting and prayer, evaluation, confession of sin, repentance, and renewal. In this atmosphere we will be able to recognize those who have been truly called as evangelists, to lead the way in taking the gospel to the remainder of the world. The purpose of our training, praying, and calling is that we might be involved in sending.

The Challenge of Sending
Those duly sent by a local church have been sent by the Holy Spirit himself (Acts 13:3–4), such is the primacy of the local church in world evangelization.

Barnabas and Paul preached the gospel and planted churches until their work was completed. Upon returning they gave a full report to the sending church (14:26–28). Our missionaries today should do the same.

The whole church today faces the challenge of sacrificial sending. It is much easier to sing, "We will give, we will pray, we will witness every day," than it is to actually accomplish these tasks. This is why we need to re-emphasize the power of the Word of God, the power of the Holy Spirit, the power of prayer, and the power of evangelizing. World evangelization calls for sacrificial giving, sacrificial praying, and sacrificial witnessing. May each and every local church rise to the occasion, based on the authority of God's Word, and fulfill the responsibility to pray for, to send, and to support laborers in the worldwide harvest field.

Let us pray and set goals under the direction of the Word of God and the leading of the Holy Spirit. And let us expect the Lord to do more than we could ask or imagine! May God be glorified in the church, in each local church, and in Christ Jesus throughout all generations.

The Importance of the Local Church to World Evangelization

Eduardo M. Maling

I represent thousands of pastors from small local churches scattered in different parts of the world. I used to think small local churches were insignificant because large churches have all the attention and we were seldom noticed. But this is not true today. Large and small local churches are equally significant and important to world evangelization. As a matter of fact, it is the *key* to world evangelization.

According to David B. Barrett, the total world population in 1989 is 5,200,782,100. By the year 2000, the total will be 6,259,642,000. Today the total number of Christians is only 1,721,655,700. And the total number of practicing Christians is even lower at 1,193,073,400. It has been claimed that 2.5 billion souls have never heard the gospel of salvation. Who will reach them for Christ?

People are important to God. He is a people-seeking God. The Bible says God is "not wanting anyone to perish, but everyone to come to repentance" (2 Peter 3:9). God loves people.

For God so loved the world that he gave his one and only Son, that whoever believes in him shall not perish but have eternal life. For God did not send his Son into the world to condemn the world, but to save the world through him (John 3:16–17).

This is the gospel of the kingdom: In Christ alone, there is hope and salvation. "Salvation is found in no one else, for there is no other name under heaven given to men by which we must be saved" (Acts 4:12).

The entire world must hear the Good News of God. The gospel of the kingdom is "the power of God for the salvation of everyone who believes" (Romans 1:16). But,

How, then, can they call on the one they have not believed in? And how can they believe in the one of whom they have not heard? And how can they hear without someone preaching to them? (Romans 10:14).

God is calling the whole church to take the whole gospel to the whole world—proclaiming Christ faithfully until he comes.

The church is the key to world evangelization. The church is a gathered and scattered community of God's people throughout the world in different situations and

---

Eduardo M. Maling is Senior Pastor of the Tanauan Bible Church, Tanauan, Philippines and is a senior leader of his denomination in that country.

contexts. The church is a called-out people placed in the world and being sent into the world to evangelize and do good to all people. The apostle Peter said,

> But you are a chosen people, a royal priesthood, a holy nation, a people belonging to God, that you may declare the praises of him who called you out of darkness into his wonderful light" (1 Peter 2:9).

The church has been chosen to demonstrate and declare the Good News of salvation to the whole world. It is God's will that the entire world be evangelized before he comes.

God will not do it alone. He can, but decided not to. He chose a human instrument to do his will in his own way. God chose Israel to be his instrument. To bless them, to be blessings to the nations, and to be his servants and light to all the world, but they failed. Christ came through the faithful remnant and said, "I will build my church and the gates of hell will not prevail against it." Christ, the Good Shepherd, died for church growth and world evangelization. He commissioned and commanded his church to do the same. "As the Father has sent me, I am sending you" (John 20:21). God will not do it alone. He has chosen and is calling his church, the local churches gathered and scattered around the world, to carry on his work of proclaiming him until he comes.

God has given the local church all the resources to do the needed task entrusted to her:

1. *We have the Word of God* in our hands. Says the Lausanne Covenant:

> We affirm the divine inspiration, truthfulness and authority of both Old and New Testament Scriptures in their entirety as the only written Word of God, without error in all that it affirms, and the only infallible rule of faith and practice. We also affirm the power of God's Word to accomplish his purpose of salvation. The message of the Bible is addressed to all men and women. For God's revelation in Christ and in Scripture is unchangeable. Through it the Holy Spirit still speaks today. He illumines the minds of God's people in every culture to perceive its truth freshly through their own eyes and thus discloses to the whole church ever more of the many-colored wisdom of God.

2. *We have God himself* in the person and power of the Holy Spirit to bear witness to the Son. The Holy Spirit is to enable and empower his people to do the work that Christ began. As Christ said, "I tell you the truth, anyone who has faith in me will do what I have been doing. He will do even greater things than these, because I am going to the Father" (John 14:12). The Holy Spirit came to teach, guide, and empower the church. World evangelization will become a reality only when the Holy Spirit renews and revives the local churches in truth, wisdom, faith, holiness, love, and power.

3. *We have other members* of the body of Christ. We may vary greatly, but we are all part of one body. Local churches have a variety of settings and approaches to world evangelization. As the apostle Paul said, "From him the whole body, joined and held together by every supporting ligament, grows and builds itself up in love, as each part does its work" (Ephesians 4:16). In all our doings, we should make every effort to keep the unity of the Spirit in peace to accomplish together our evangelistic and cultural mandate.

4. *We have spiritual gifts* to prepare and equip God's people to do the ministry. Spiritual gifts are a special attribute given by the Holy Spirit to each member of the body of Christ, according to God's grace, for use within the context of the body. The body is an organism with Jesus Christ as the head and each one of us are members functioning with one or more gifts. It is our responsibility as pastors and Christian leaders of local churches to assist our members to discover, develop, and use their spiritual gift(s) respectively. If our spiritual gifts are being discovered, developed, and used, we will know our "spiritual job description." Our attitudes will be changed, the body of Christ will grow and multiply, the world will be evangelized, and God will be glorified.

God has given us all the resources we need in our local churches to be active participants in world evangelization. The church has never stopped growing since the Day of Pentecost. The church is God's instrument, chosen to demonstrate and declare to the whole world Jesus Christ, the Savior and Lord. God will hold us responsible and accountable to him.

The urgency of the task is before us. God has not changed his plan. The local church plays an important role in world evangelization. But the problem is the church is not growing fast enough. Total commitment, unity, and sacrifice to world evangelization is greatly needed.

As a young pastor in 1968, I looked after a small congregation—the Tanauan Bible Church. It was located in the municipality of Tanauan, in the province of Batangas, Philippines—about thirty-five to forty miles south of Manila. For seven to ten years, I had struggled and was ready to quit the ministry because I could not see growth in the church. But God reminded me of his Word saying, "I will build my church and the gates of hell will not prevail against it." *I will build my church.* . . . As I pondered those words, the Lord brought me to my knees in prayer—searching, fasting, and waiting upon him for guidance and clear direction.

The field director of the mission working with us came to visit. He asked, "What can we do as a mission to help the Tanauan Bible Church grow, mature, and reach out for others?"

In humility and honesty, I responded, "You can help the church grow, mature, and reach out to others by leaving us alone and by you moving to the next city to begin a new work."

They did. What was the result? Growth!

In our case as a congregation, this was a real challenge. God gave us courage to welcome the difficulty as a challenge to prove the sufficiency of God's grace. I began sharing my burden and vision to the people through prayer, training, modeling, teaching, and preaching the Word of God by the help of the Holy Spirit. My goal was clear: To see Tanauan Bible Church mature in spiritual qualities, leadership ability, financial stability, and in effective ministry—that is, an extension, expansion, and cross-cultural ministry. The people began to see and understand the scope of God's redemption and the seriousness of their role, as the people of God. I often told them:

We are not here for ourselves only, but we are here for God and for others. God has given us all the resources we need to bear witness. We have the Word of God in our hands. We have the Holy Spirit in our hearts to dwell in and empower us. The Holy Spirit has given us a variety of spiritual gifts for the building up of the body and to do the work of

Christ in today's world. We are to discover, develop, and use those gifts in serving God, because God will hold us responsible and accountable to him.

The congregation was moved mightily by the Holy Spirit. Their lives were renewed and revitalized. Faith and vision were enlarged. Burden for lost souls was evident. Consequently, they renewed their commitment to God in Christ. They renewed their commitment to the local congregation and to loving and serving one another. The community was amazed by the lifestyle God's people displayed; they gained much respect and credibility. And they renewed their commitment to the work of Christ in the world.

We are all ministers of God—servants to serve, not to be served. We are to give our lives for the salvation of many and for world evangelization. We are to act local, but our thinking and vision are global.

We need unity and cooperation in local churches, missions, and para-church organizations. But we already have unity in Christ. Our responsibility is to keep, preserve, and work within that unity to be more effective witnesses in our community, in our country, and in the world.

I took the initiative to call and invite all the local pastors and Christian leaders to have a fellowship and sharing time as appointed leaders in our municipality. Our main purpose was for fellowship, to know each other better, and to give the ministry focus and direction. We have also elicited respect and cooperation from each other as brothers and sisters in the Lord, both co-laborers of God in his vineyard. Consequently, we have resolved to keep and preserve our unity in Christ. Our responsibility is to manifest and demonstrate that spirit of unity and mutual understanding in the ministry locally. This spirit prevailed, and we want this to be evident in our district and in the entire nation. As a nation, we are committed to plant fifty thousand local churches by the year 2000. On a global scale, as in the case of Lausanne, we want to evangelize the world by the year 2000. We need to work together in unity and mutual cooperation to fulfill the Great Commission and the Great Commandment.

The Tanauan Bible Church, which struggled with non-growth for at least a decade, found its way through the Word and Holy Spirit. The church is now experiencing tremendous growth and maturity, and has an effective ministry planting daughter churches in satellite towns and has active participation in cross-cultural ministry. The Tanauan Bible Church became a model to others in our district, regional, and national organization. It has been noticed by the nation and by the world. There is no doubt in my mind that the local church is central to world evangelization.

Because the local church is important to world evangelization, there is need for simple planning for future growth and multiplication of responsible and reproducing local churches.

As a local church, we need to set goals for future growth and multiplication. We are convinced that goal setting is biblical, natural, and practical. We have adopted a twofold evangelistic goal: to make responsible and reproducing disciples; and to plant responsible and reproducing local churches. These goals should be relevant, measurable, significant, manageable, and personal.

We need to formulate a simple strategy to guide us. We can start by finding contacts from relatives, friends, interested people, and people groups. Then, we can conduct an evangelistic Bible study for those interested. Through the Word, the Holy Spirit, and the faithfulness of God's people to share the gospel, the Holy Spirit converts people to Christ. New converts need to grow and have fellowship, so we form a congregation or join an existing congregation, as the case may be. A church is then established and organized to have regular worship, instruction of the Word, fellowship, and expression of the members' faith.

Consequently, a new church is born. As this church grows and matures, they will communicate the gospel to others—to the community they are in and to other communities. Then, the cycle repeats: contacts, conduct, converts, congregation, church, and communication.

Our approach needs to be flexible. Sensitivity to the real context is important. In much of the Philippines, we cannot preach the gospel outside the context of poverty. We must be sensitive to the real needs of the people. For the Tanauan Bible Church, we use a holistic ministry approach. It is an integration of the two mandates—evangelistic and cultural: fulfilling the Great Commission and fulfilling the Great Commandment.

No matter how small your local church, God can make it grow and multiply. It can make an impact on your community, district, region, country, to the nations, and to the entire world. The local church is central to world evangelization. World evangelization will be fulfilled if we work together locally *and* globally in unity and sacrifice.

Together let us aspire to be great for God, as Christ was. He came not to be served, but to serve and give his life as ransom for evangelization. May we, the church—the local churches of the Servant, do the same. May we serve as faithful servants and willingly give our lives to world evangelization.

Primacy of the Local Church

Producers: Ty Bragg, Tawnia Wilson

I looked and there before me was a great multitude that no one could count, from every nation, tribe, people and language, standing before the throne and in front of the Lamb (Revelation 7:9).

God has a plan for the nations, and that is to restore men and women to a right and vital relationship with himself. To accomplish this task, God has chosen his body, the church—the local church. And it can be found all over the world. It can be found wherever a group of believers come together to pray, worship, and witness to God's power.

The local church today comes in different shapes and sizes. Some churches use beautiful liturgies, and others prefer to worship in more simple ways. Some churches meet in cathedrals, while others congregate in the most humble of settings. Some churches are visible, yet some are underground because of repressive governments.

Despite the variety of doctrines which shape the various churches and expressions of faith as well as their forms of worship, at the heart of every church is the Evangel, the Good News that Christ died for our sins and rose again; that through his death and resurrection all men and women, everyone, might be reconciled to God and become part of a new community. It is that new community which has been asked to share the Good News with the whole world.

Go in the midst of their doctrinal distinctions. There is a common core to what the local church is and does.

Before our Lord left this earth, he commissioned his church to go and make disciples of all nations. That Great Commission was not given selectively, but to *all* churches. It is just as binding for the largest as for the smallest, from the most wealthy to the poorest of congregations. Indeed, to accomplish this great task of reaching every nation for Christ, congregations from every denomination must discover their special place in sharing the Good News in the world. The church must become mission-minded. But how?

Mobilizing churches for missions, Reverend Thomas Telford believes, is not another elective church program, but is required by our Lord, who is the head of the church:

I think first of all, you accept Jesus Christ as Lord of your life; then you accept his people, the church; and third, you accept the Great Commission and your marching orders. That does not necessarily mean you are going to be a missionary, but it means you are going to be a missions-person—or, to use today's terminology, a "world-Christian."

Missions leader and Partners International president, Luis Bush, agrees. He says the pattern for missions was established by the church at Antioch nearly two thousand years ago:

> As those Christians met, they prayed and fasted. As the Spirit of God spoke to them, they began to send out missionaries. And I think that is the biblical base. But also, when you see what God is doing around the world today—especially in Latin America, Asia, and Africa—it is the local church that is having a key role in the effort of missions launching out from these different continents.

Many of the church leaders in the Two-Thirds world see true revival sweeping their countries. Even in revival, the General Secretary for the Evangelical Churches of West Africa (ECWA), Panya Baba, says the churches must have unity to keep up with the challenges facing them:

> The time for cooperation is critical because the remaining unfinished task is too great for one single church or mission to complete it. And with the church maturity in Africa today, I think this is the best time for us to cooperate more and become partners in the Lord's work.

Current methods of outreach are inadequate for completing the Great Commission. With the current world population explosion, it is estimated that a thousand churches must be established each and every day just to maintain the percentage of Christians we have in the world today.

In 1900, the world population was estimated at 1.6 billion people. About one-third of the world's population were called Christians. At that time, about half of the world population had been evangelized, while the other half had never heard the gospel message. Today, the world population has increased 600 percent to nearly six billion, but only about one-third of the world population calls itself Christian. Another third of the world population has been evangelized, and the remaining third (two billion souls) have never heard the Christian message of salvation. They will only hear if the church goes to them. How will that happen?

The biblical pattern is for the pastor to care for, serve, and train the people of God to become ministers of God. According to Reverend Telford:

> The pastor is to be the trainer—the trainer of people to minister. The pastor is only successful when he can train other people to do what he does, and they become his arms and his legs. And I think our Lord did that, the model, with his disciples. The laity is probably the most important part. That is where we are going to get our missionaries.

A prime example of the laity expanding the church occurred when the Communists took governmental control of China in 1948, and forced all foreign Christian missionaries out of the country. It was estimated there were about one million Christians in China at that time, and many Christian groups believed that the church would not survive. Today we hear reports that the church has grown to at least fifty million believers and, according to the Lausanne International Director Thomas Wang, that estimate is low. He has stated, "Fifty million is a conservative estimation. Actually, the figure goes as high as seventy million."

Reverend Wang says that nothing paralleling the Chinese revival has ever happened before in history:

> After forty-eight years of oppression and suffering, the number of Christians grew like wildfire at the grass roots level. There are many of what we would call "barefoot evangelists" in China today. They pedal a bicycle, they visit from village to village, and they preach a basic, pure, simple gospel.

It is estimated that by the year 2000, 83 percent of the people of the world will live in countries which have limited access to traditional missionaries. Yet, the local church can play an enormous role even when invisible.

Noman is a former Muslim and is a leader in the invisible church in the Middle East. His conversion came only two years ago. Through his efforts and that of a handful of others, their extended church has grown to over five hundred believers.

Noman says the church is strong and the fields are ripe in the Moslem world, but there are not enough laborers:

> I heard it a lot of times when I was Muslim, from many American preachers on TV: They used to say we never can reach Muslims, we never can reach Arabs. Why? They *can* reach us. We are sons of God, too. We are seeds of Abraham. We have the same color blood. Our blood is red, the same as yours. So there is nothing impossible for God. There is nothing impossible for God.

God's church, the church triumphant and universal, marches on. It retains the potential for tremendous works yet to be imagined by man. God has provided it with all the gifts, all the resources it needs.

When each Christian is active, using their gifts in the local church, when each local church sees itself as having within itself all the resources of God and appointed for a unique part of this great task, then the world will be evangelized.

The Laity

Pete Hammond

Hundreds of thousands of laity are represented at this Congress by their pastors or para-church staff. What will be the impact on the laity through them? How will God's church be affected as a result of our labors here?

Today's church is too dependent on hired staff in the roles of pastors, nuns, evangelists, and missionaries. The latest Roman Catholic book on the laity aptly describes us as it says, "The church bureaucracy has successfully convinced its pew-sitters that their role in the kingdom is to *pray*, *pay* and *obey*—mostly pay."

This immobilization of 99 percent of God's people is both unbiblical and discriminating, while making our task of world evangelization impossible. It is our struggling pew-sitters who are:

1. in contact with the non-believer daily at work;
2. fluent in their language of heart and mind;
3. unintimidating as friends at work together; and
4. the best evidence that the Good News works for average people.

For instance, in Ephesus it was through merchants, chariot drivers, and relatives that allowed Luke to report, "All of Asia heard the Word of the Lord, both Jews and Greeks ... and the Word of God spread widely and grew in power as Paul argued the gospel daily in the Ephesian Hall of Tyrannus." What must we learn for that to happen again in the barrios and cities, industries and farms, alleys and airways, institutions and families of our troubled and unreached billions today? It will require a renewed understanding of where the church is Monday through Saturday.

For too long, we have viewed the church as a building similar to the diagram on the following page:

John "Pete" Hammond is director of Intervarsity's Marketplace and has been on the staff of IVCF since 1966. He is a citizen of the United States.

I. THE CHURCH - UPSIDE DOWN

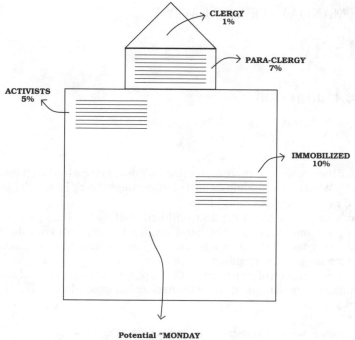

At the top are the "ordained." Especially favored are the "paraclergy." These people volunteer for all the programs within the building or within congregational life. As church staff conceive of things, these members are ready to serve. This gives them elevated status in the eyes of the staff and their level of Christian commitment is clear to all.

Next are the "activists." They focus on issues of controversy within or outside of church life ranging from remodeling the church, to abortion, to pacifism. They often make the whole congregation sweat as they stir up controversy, but their zeal is never in doubt.

Finally, there are the "immobilized." These people are in the midst of crisis. Death, divorce, or unemployment are dominating their lives. Their dilemma arouses our compassion and we seek to care for them.

These four groups cover 23 percent of the congregation. The remaining members live under a cloud of suspicion. Their lack of involvement inside the life of the church is confusing and leads to questions about their level of dedication to the Lord.

The majority of faithful worshipers available for ministry (77 percent) remain uninvolved. They are usually ill-thought-of by church leaders. They are often seen as uninvolved and spiritually questionable. We see them as passive, instead of ready to serve. Shouldn't they be the primary members who need to be affirmed, equipped, and supported?

Correctly portrayed, this would be the "upside down church" as seen in the following diagram:

II. THE CHURCH - RIGHT SIDE UP

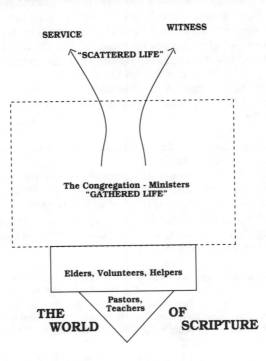

In this portrayal, we see the people of God acting as agents of the kingdom of God in the world. The church is pictured as a "leaky bucket building" inverted. The pastors, teachers, and paraclergy are rooted in the disciplines of mining the Scriptures. They face inward as "internists" in the body of Christ. They are to "equip all the people for ministry" by making Scripture come to life in their minds and wills.

The larger congregation (the 77 percent in the previous diagram) face outward in ministry as the "church scattered." They spend the bulk of their lives representing the kingdom "in the world." The "gathered" and "scattered" life of the church are interdependent.

In contrast, we have developed another unfortunate set of images that betray our non-biblical understanding of the church on earth. We may cringe at these, but it is what the watching world sees as we carry out our sub-biblical agenda. Some of these images are:

- Pirates or looters scavenging the ruins of earth for personal gain and enhancing the furnishing of heaven for their enjoyment
- Empire builders trying to establish a safe and distant environment as they wait out their time on earth safely protected from everyone else's pain
- Little rabbits fearfully running from safe hole to control group totally incapable of doing battle with the roaring lion, Enemy of God in the world
- Addicted junkies spending their energies on personally gratifying experiences instead of being waiters or hosts inviting the hungry to a banquet

We must resist building protective enclaves or hiding places to escape the world. In stark contrast, the New Testament speaks of everyone being central to ministry. A good illustration of this is in Peter's letter to the "scattered ones." The word *called,* in 1 Peter 2:9–10, is *kleros* from which is derived the word *clergy.* Therefore, all the people are clergy. We are all priests with various ministries—some are practiced internally, most function externally for the benefit of the fallen world.

This view of the church's call to live in the world is emphasized with biblical images and metaphors describing involvement with "outsiders" in an environment hostile to kingdom values. We see this as:

- Soldiers and their armor as they wrestle against principalities and powers (Ephesians 6:10–18; 2 Timothy 2:3–4).
- Wheat among the tares in harvest (Matthew 13). We are mixed in with the lost and God will do the sorting in his time.
- Salt bringing restraint and purification to decay (Matthew 5:13). The removal of the salt of the church from society has a devastating effect on the world and the church. As pointed out by Stephen Neiland Hans Rudi-Weber in *The Layman in Christian History*:

    Kingdom salt was never meant to be kept bottled up in a salt shaker. Now the various activities of man's mind and hands seem to have fallen apart. Religion has become interested in religion, and has in consequence become anemic. Culture has declared its emancipation from its religious past, and has therefore become demonic ([Westminster, 1963], 21).

- Leaven that enriches the whole loaf (Matthew 13:33; Luke 13:20–21)
- Light that reveals, penetrates, and heals in darkness (Matthew 5:14–16)
- Seeds that are sown freely and mixed with stifling, hostile environments (Matthew 13:1–23,31–43)
- Living stones for a new reality in a broken creation (1 Peter 2:4–8) and as a holy temple for the Lord, God's dwelling place on earth (Ephesians 2:19–22)

These images speak of sacrificial involvement in a world gone astray. We must re-establish a positive, biblical answer to the question, "Where is the church on Monday?" Instead of the church *scattered*, meaning "disconnected, adrift, confused, unproductive, and weak"; we must redefine it with meanings like "involved, fruitful, called, strategic, and powerful." Then world evangelization will be possible, because it is the task of *all of us* wherever we are.

VIDEO PRESENTATION

Clergy Affirmations; Lay People Minister

Producer: Cheryl Settoon

Narrator: As light reveals and penetrates the darkness, as seeds of life are sown freely in every place, so shall the scattered church be in a hurting world. What Christ has set before us is such a lofty goal, the only way it can be reached is by clergy and laypeople working hand-in-hand for the sake of the gospel.

Edwin Catucutan is one layman who got excited about sharing his faith. After a near fatal blow to his practice, he dared to believe that God would use him in his profession. Edwin gave his heart, mind, and career to Jesus Christ, and soon found he could offer more than just wise counsel.

Edwin Catucutan: After I work on their case, while the papers are being typed by the secretary, I share the gospel. In my office, the Lord allowed me to be a willing vessel. I think about six or seven people were born again.

Narrator: Edwin reaches out with the blessing of his pastor.

Pastor Ed Fernandez: Brother Edwin is mightily used by the Lord. Wherever he goes, he testifies. He presents the Lord to the people and not only that, he brings many people to the Lord.

Narrator: Pastor Fernandez and Edwin are a success story, but too often we see a different picture. The clergy, who make up less than 1 percent of Christendom, are shouldering too much responsibility and are breaking under the burden. The majority of Christians, the laypeople, have not come to the understanding that the task of world evangelism belongs to them. Yet, some laypeople *have* caught the vision!

Marilyn Martinez, an entertainer from Manila, desires to reach out to the world with the love of Christ.

Marilyn Martinez: I've prayed to the Lord about this. The Lord told us to extend our hands to other people. We cannot stay among our own kind, nothing will happen. We need to go out there and help those who do not understand.

Narrator: Marilyn understands a biblical truth. When pastors train and ignite the fire under the laity, it starts a chain reaction. The hurt find healing. The laypeople discover their identity in Christ. And there's an added blessing: churches that serve the laity experience growth. But when the laypeople see the church as only the four walls of a building, the congregation stagnates. Laymembers suffer defeat, feeling like second-class citizens. Dr. Wathanga from Nairobi, Kenya, sees the scriptural path.

Dr. Wathanga: We don't want them just to draw converts to Christ. We want people to be transformed to the likeness of Christ. We want them to be mature Christians.

Narrator: He advises thousands of young people, most of whom will not enter paid Christian service, to surrender their life, time, money, family work, talents, and leisure to Jesus Christ.

Dr. Wathanga: Then as they go out, they ask themselves such questions as, "Where is God sending me?" And wherever they go to work, they are not just professionals who happen to be Christians, but are Christians who happen to be professionals—first and foremost, ambassadors to the Lord Jesus Christ.

Miltinne Yih

Q. Miltinne, I understand you became a Christian through some school teachers in Germany during a period of marital stress. What happened?

A. I had never felt the need for anyone, outside of myself, until I had been married for one year. It was the first time I felt I couldn't cope with everything happening in my life. Then God brought a Christian couple into our lives that exhibited something I knew I needed. I had only known them for about two weeks and I couldn't stand it, I finally asked them, "What is it about you two that makes you so different?" I still remember their answer. They said, "We have a personal relationship with Jesus Christ." I was flabbergasted. I said, "What else."

Q. Thank God for school teachers who know Jesus. You and your husband Lee have an autistic child, what does that mean?

A. Autism is a severe form of mental retardation. Our son was born several years after my husband and I became Christians. Many people asked us why would God allow something like that to happen. And I myself asked, "Why would God do something like this? Why to me? Why to my family? Why to my little son?" But as I asked why, I realized I was asking the question. The question is not *why*, it's *who?* Who is in charge? And as I began to understand *God* was in charge, I no longer had to know *why*. God has used this little boy in my life, in my husband's life, and in the lives of many people.

Q. How are you involved with seekers and non-believers in Hong Kong?

A. I used to think if I got involved with non-Christians they would weaken my faith. But I realized if I was willing, God would use me. And the way he uses me is through natural contacts I have through common interests. For instance, my life at home with my husband and my children provide natural bridges to people.

Q. I understand you get acquainted with many parents by helping them with their troubled children. You even did that in Beijing recently. Tell us about that.

A. Because of my son, I'm involved in the Hong Kong Association for the Mentally Handicapped. Last summer there was a special education conference in Beijing, and I was invited to attend as one of their members. I wanted to attend because the keynote speaker was Dung Pu Pang, who is Chairman Dung Chao Pang's son. During the Cultural Revolution, he was thrown from a balcony. He became paralyzed and is in a wheelchair. Because his father is Chairman, he was placed in charge of all the handicapped services.

I began to pray that perhaps God would in some way use an article I had written about our son and how God has used him in our lives. At the conference, as I sat in the Great Hall of the People listening to Dung Pu Pang speak, I felt strongly that I should go up and try to give him a copy of the article.

In the moments before I approached him, I flashed back to ten years earlier when I first heard that my son was handicapped. I remembered asking why this was happening. I could have never imagined that ten years later I would be sitting in Beijing poised to give the son of the chairman an article about Jesus Christ.

God allowed me to give him the article. Later I found out that he lives with his father and his entire family, and they share and talk about everything. I don't know if anything happened, we just do what we can, and God does the rest.

Q. A final question: Do you believe that you're where God wants you though you're not a professional Christian worker or, as some say, you haven't been called to full-time Christian ministry?

A. Every Christian is in full-time Christian work. Actually, I know many people who avoid vocational Christian workers because they're afraid of being proselytized. Because I am the wife of a stock broker, they do not feel they are in danger when they talk to me or get close to me. With the layman, they can let their guard down. I may not look like it, but I assure you I am "dangerous."

Working—
Past, Present, and as Worship

Producer: Cheryl Settoon

Each day, all over the globe, modern Jobs, Lydias, and Josephs are busy at work. They are current reminders that 75 percent of the better-known men and women of the Bible held full-time secular jobs, yet were called and used by God. They are the laity, as important in today's world as in biblical times, since each one of us has a special calling on our lives. Stuart Chen is one such layman who is eager to fulfill his mission. As a businessman from Taipei, he sees the financial growth of his country as an open door for sharing the gospel. He uses business to share his faith in Christ with other countrymen, often from Buddhist backgrounds.

Stuart Chen: Taiwan is growing at a tremendous speed economically and materially, so people feel more and more hungry in their spirit. They are searching for something that satisfies the heart.

Narrator: In Lima, Peru, Elena and Cesar Pando provide another example of effective laity. Both have their own business. Elena offers spiritual as well as physical food at her restaurant. Her husband, Cesar, gives Bibles to his employees at the fish cannery, and supports a Bible study there. His decision to follow Christ affects even the way he conducts business.

Cesar Pando: In business there are always opportunities to cheat, bribe, and swindle, but I learned you don't have to stoop to those activities to conduct business successfully. You can conduct business in a wholesome manner and be satisfied.

Narrator: In a remote area of the Philippines, Dr. Sarmiento uses his medical skills to bring light to his part of the world. The doctor treats physical and spiritual needs. While some might be put off by this rugged terrain, Dr. Sarmiento finds great satisfaction working in these mountains.

Dr. Sarmiento: After all, the secret of the joy of life is to live for the Lord and to live for other people.

Narrator: Concern for their classmates who might never hear of Jesus spurs these Thai students to action. If all Christians reached out to people they come into contact with in their neighborhoods or on the job, half of the world's population would hear the gospel! But that will never happen until the clergy realize that their work is God's plan for them and world evangelism—not just a mundane chore to fill their days.

Pete Hammond: In answer to the questions, *Is work God's dirty trick? Is it the long dark tunnel between Sundays?* The answer is an absolute *no.* It is not the first picture God gave of himself for a work week. He went to work for six straight days and we've forgotten that redeemed view of work.

Narrator: If clergy help the laity to recapture the view that work is part of our worship to God, and work can open doors to spread the gospel, then lay people will find more spiritual, mental, and physical fulfillment on the job. This newfound joy will be like water to a dry seed. It will transform the body of Christ from a fruitless to a fruitful state, one which produces light in the darkness and life in every nation.

A Theology of the Laity

Lee Yih

Proverbs 30:24–28 (NASB) says there are four things that are small on earth, but they are exceedingly wise:

> The ants are not a strong folk, but they prepare their food in the summer; the badgers are not mighty folk, yet they make their houses in the rocks; the locusts have no king, yet all of them go out in ranks; the lizard you may grasp with the hands, yet it is in kings' palaces.

These four small but exceedingly wise things on earth perhaps also describe the Christian layperson, with his weaknesses and strengths.

The layperson by himself may seem insignificant, not able to accomplish much, but like the ant, he can steadily do his part and in the end a great task is accomplished.

The lay person may not be mighty or strong, but like the badger, he lives and moves about in a dangerous place—the world—which is enemy territory.

The layperson has no recognized leader or organization, but like the locust, he knows the goal and serves the plan of God.

The layperson is individually vulnerable, but like the lizard, there is no place where he is not found.

Given the enormity of the task, the dangers of the environment, the difficulties of staying with the task, and the logistical problems of evangelizing the world today, we need to look to something small like the ant, the badger, the locust, and the lizard. The thesis of William Garrison's paper is that the layperson, small but wise, is God's chosen instrument for the task of world evangelization in the next decade.

Although conventional wisdom says the layperson is insignificant and small, God's wisdom has always been to mystify the world in his choice of instruments. This is illustrated well in 1 Corinthians 1:27–29 (NASB):

> But God has chosen the foolish things of the world to shame the wise, and God has chosen the weak things of the world to shame the things which are strong, and the base things of the world and the despised, God has chosen, the things that are not, that He might nullify the things that are, that no man should boast before God.

Lee Yih is a businessman and works with the Morgan Stanley Company in Hong Kong. Mr. Yih's message is based upon a paper by William Garrison, titled "A Theology of the Laity." Mr. Garrison is a businessman in Fort Worth, Texas.

When we examine church history, three major paradigms or stages are evident They are the result of the churches' response to the cultural, sociological, and political milieu of its day. These three paradigms involve the ancient church, the state church, and the liberated church.

The Apostolic or Ancient Church

The first paradigm we observe is the apostolic, or ancient, church. The early church experienced heavy persecution, which only served to scatter the church. Thus, the gospel was spread to more than two hundred communities by the end of the third century.

It is not known who started the churches at Phoenicia, Cyprus, and Antioch. Secular history did not record any well-known figures, leaders, or visionaries behind their incredible growth. One strong possibility is that it had something to do with the endless travel of people along the Roman network of roads.

However, those who understand the working of God, and how the church was truly inauspicious and ubiquitous, would say it had something to do with ordinary lay people carrying out the command of Paul to Timothy when he said,

> The things which you have heard from me in the presence of many witnesses, these entrust to faithful men, who will be able to teach others also (2 Timothy 2:2, NASB).

This period is known as the Golden Age of the church, a time when the gospel spread dramatically like a prairie fire throughout the Roman empire in spite of heavy Jewish, as well as Roman, persecution.

This paradigm ends with the reign of Constantine, the first Emperor of Rome to become a Christian.

The Imperial or State Church

The conversion of Constantine, and the subsequent Edict of Milan in A.D. 313, dramatically changed the operating environment of the church. It changed from a group constantly facing the threat of martyrdom, into a self-confident institution ready to confront the world on its own terms. One hundred years later, Augustine's view of the Millennium as the time in which the church would conquer the world, provided the theological basis for the rise of the Imperial Catholic Church and the Holy Roman Empire.

During this period, the inauspicious church began to be auspicious and the ubiquitous church became defined, precise, and identifiable. The prominence and authority the church experienced caused it to change its mission away from evangelism and toward one of dominating and absorbing an entire empire. And the church began to look like the secular institutions of the day.

Even the Reformation in the sixteenth century did not much affect this self-view of the church. And it was not long before Protestants started looking like the Catholic Church they were trying to reform. To quote Howard Snyder: "The fact is that Protestantism has never developed a fully biblical doctrine of the church."

As the Protestant church grew strong enough so their survival was assured, the drift to the Augustinian model of the church became irresistible and the state church was created.

The Wesleyan Model of the Liberated Church

The revivals of John Wesley during the Industrial Revolution in mid-eighteenth century England signaled a shift to a third paradigm for the church. Wesley was denied access to the pulpits of the English churches, so he got on his horse, went to the fields of Bristol, and did open-air preaching. He developed special societies and when people were converted, they were placed into groups which employed methodical follow-up systems, thus, gaining the name of Methodist for his followers. It is said the revivals of Wesley had the greatest impact on society of any revivals in history.

Wesley went about the ministry without worrying about the institutional church. That is, he did not allow the goals of the institutional church to stop him from preaching the gospel. He was liberated from the persistent notion that the grace of God could only be channeled and controlled through institutions and their liturgies. He was actually a part of the church, but did not have a need to reform it. Instead, he channeled his efforts into creative and resourceful ways of participating in the Great Commission. Wesley was the forerunner of a church that would see leaders serve Christ and his body in nonsectarian ways never before seen in history.

Observations on the State of the Church of the Third Paradigm

The church of the third paradigm is creative, resourceful, pragmatic, and even liberated in its desire to fulfill the Great Commission in the face of a fast-paced and ever-changing society.

There are a great number of examples of this shift. We see it in the nineteenth century with the formation of organizations like the Clepham Sect, and in lay leaders like Wilberforce, Raikes, and Booth. We see it in the model for nonsectarian missions set up by a shoe cobbler named William Carey, a missionary to India. In the twentieth century, we have witnessed the proliferation of parachurch organizations. Howard Snyder acknowledged the church's new self-understanding when he told us fifteen years ago in Lausanne, "No one single expression of the church could ever be thought of as anything more than a 'parachurch.'" We even see it in the incredible rise of the charismatic movement during the last twenty years, a movement which has infused new application into the concept of the priesthood of the believer.

Ford Madison's committee has discovered more than one hundred lay affinity groups across the United States serving everything from doctors and lawyers to hard hats and truckers, as they organize for the purpose of promoting Christ within their professions. At a meeting of about thirty of these groups in Denver in 1985, I was impressed by the creative expressions of the laity as they sought to bring Christ to the marketplace.

These groups have mobilized the laity to witness for Christ to a degree never before realized. Thus, a strong point can be made that this third and most recent paradigm of the church relies heavily on the creative energies of an inauspicious laity. Although stated in a different context, the principle of James Engel and Wilbert Norton in their book, *What's Gone Wrong With the Harvest?* rings true:

> The gospel communicator has the obligation to focus theological truth in such a way that it brings light upon each person's unique situation. This of course cannot be done only by pontificating in the pulpit or by occupying the pew. Witnessing for Christ requires contact with people.

There seems to be strong evidence that God is behind this paradigm shift, which, according to J. Christy Wilson, is essentially returning us to the lay evangelism methods which prevailed during the apostolic era. For example, missionary researchers like David Barrett and others affiliated with the LCWE, say that by the year 2000, fully 83 percent of the world's non-Christian population will reside in 120 nations closed to traditional missionary methods. Since the Bible states that no national government can come into existence unless established by God, then it must be God who is orchestrating a major departure from traditional methods of evangelism. Thus, it seems that God is behind a shift that will of necessity feature a strong lay or tentmaker participation in these latter days.

A critical case in point today is mainland China. In the late 1940s, an estimated five million believers suddenly lost all of their vocational Christian workers as the Communist government expelled all foreign missionaries and imprisoned church pastors and leaders. The church in China became the object of an intense intentional effort to destroy it. Today, some well-respected estimates number the church in excess of fifty million, a tenfold increase. What happened? It had to have grown through the efforts of the ordinary layperson left behind, who was prepared to share the hope within him to comrades hungry for hope.

God is raising up a laity that refuses to be limited to the confines of an institutional church and whose ministry refuses to be counted, created, or controlled. The prominence of the laity is clearly the distinguishing mark of the third paradigm. With so many new groups on the scene and here to stay, the church must redefine its identity or enter into a crisis.

However, it is sad to say that the institutional church does not always respond well to this new and growing role for the layperson. To quote Dr. William Lawrence of Dallas Theological Seminary:

> There is this very subtle mentality that exists everywhere, that for ministry to be legitimate you need to get it down to the church house. It's better there because that's where it belongs.

This thinking is an anachronism, because in this developing third paradigm for the church, ministry belongs in the marketplace.

There are now instances of parachurches growing prominent enough to also want to control the ministry. The institutional church, and institutional Christianity for that matter, can respond in one of three ways to the role of the laity in this new paradigm. They can either fight it, deny it, or help it.

If they choose to fight it, they risk opposing God himself, as Gamaliel warns in Acts chapter 5.

If they choose to deny it, they will worsen what is already called a worldwide "effectiveness crisis" in the church. In these cases, congregations sometimes plunge into theological squabbles or rally around some effort to Christianize society instead of fulfilling the Great Commission. Bear in mind that this paradigm is already two hundred years old.

If they choose to help, the institutional church must take on a new self view and mission. They need to become a *servant church*—to serve the people, and to equip and encourage them to do the work of the ministry that God is leading them into, rather than use the people to do the work of the programs the institution wants achieved. Thus, the only corporate mission of the church is to build itself up spiritually. Any organizational form it adopts is to facilitate that process.

Frogs Versus Lizards

Have you ever noticed how differently frogs and lizards acquire their food? The frog just sits and waits, and lets the food come to him. As soon as an insect gets close enough, all the frog has to do is stick out his tongue and get it.

On the other hand, if the lizard did what the frog does, it would soon starve. It cannot afford to sit and wait, but must go out into his world, know where his food can be found, and hunt.

The vocational Christian worker is like the frog. He goes off to seminary, gets a degree, goes on staff somewhere, and somehow people know he is in the business of meeting spiritual needs. Ministry comes to him and before long, he has his hands full. Many evangelists today are frogs in that when they come to town, with no effort on their part, an audience always assembles to hear them speak.

The layperson on the other hand, is a lizard. In order for him to have a ministry, he has to learn to hunt. If he were to put out a notice saying that he was coming to town, no one would care. Ministry does not come seeking him out. Instead, like the lizard, he must move around in the environment he lives in, assess his sphere of influence, sow broadly, build bridges, establish friendships, and then, when he has earned the right to be heard, be ready to give an account for the hope that is in him, with gentleness and reverence.

The ministry of the laity is as different from the vocational Christian worker's ministry as the lizard's food gathering techniques are different from the frog's. Frogs usually cannot teach the lizard ministry. They can get the lizard to act like a frog, however, and get him to teach Sunday school or even give a thirty-minute talk during an evangelistic outreach lunch. Unfortunately there are many sad lizards out there who think that to have a ministry, they must act like frogs. What a limited view of the ministry. The lizard needs to know how God can use him as the lizard!

In Amsterdam '86, Stephen Olford declared that the days of mass evangelism were over. Perhaps he meant the job of world evangelization is a lizard's job. He represents the church's contact point with the world as he lives and works in it. He understands it and is familiar with its ways. When he is differentiated by his faith, the world takes note. As Howard Hendricks says, "The world is not looking for perfection, just reality. When the vocational Christian worker is good it is because he is paid to be good, the layperson on the other hand, is good for nothing."

The lizard must be given a sense of ministry, and must be equipped and encouraged by the frog. One layman recently said to me, "I must work out the tension between raising my family, holding down a job, and participating in the Great Commission. Men and women like me must learn how to make it because there will never be enough vocational Christian workers to get the job done."

At first, I thought we needed to present these ideas about the importance of the laity in world evangelization in the form of a plea, the way that Ford Madison has been doing since Lausanne I in 1974. After seeing William Garrison's paradigm shifts and observing firsthand the layman in action both in the United States and Hong Kong, I realized what is needed here at Lausanne II is not so much a plea as a proclamation.

We are here to proclaim that we are in the midst of a paradigm shift that is featuring the priesthood of the ordinary believer in God's "end game strategy" to reach the world. Will you be a player or a spectator?

VIDEO PRESENTATION

Tentmakers

Producer: Cheryl Settoon

Narrator: Now that we've discussed the value of the laity mobilized and ministering in their own cultures, let's look at the church as it is scattered cross-culturally.

By the year 2000, it's estimated that 83 percent of the world's unreached population will live in countries with restricted access to career missionaries. Millions will be trapped behind bankrupt ideologies and false religions. How will they hear of the love of Jesus Christ? Many church leaders are looking to tentmakers to help meet this challenge.

Dr. J. Christy Wilson: Tentmaker has come to describe a person who is a missionary, but self-supporting like the apostle Paul.

Dr. Ted Yamamora: They are people who are biblically informed, missionary-committed, and professionally trained.

Narrator: Tentmakers will not replace the missionaries who have successfully spread the gospel for centuries.

Dr. Wilson: But along with missionaries we need tentmakers, or self-supporting witnesses, in order to evangelize the whole world.

Dr. Yamamora: Given the context of the increasing inaccessibility of the gospel, we can't afford not to consider the method of tentmaking if we believe in the Great Commission.

Dr. Ken Touryan: Tentmakers are there, right in the pews looking for ways they can serve the Lord.

Narrator: Dr. Touryan speaks from experience. Trained extensively in aerospace science and technology, he's been invited to a number of countries to give lectures. The scientist says these trips open doors outside of the classroom.

Dr. Ken Touryan: I started using vacation time—two weeks, three weeks, up to five weeks at a time—to go to Lebanon, the Soviet Union, and other places to give lectures in science and technology and then use that to minister or share the gospel.

Narrator: In these foreign countries, the local church serves as a springboard for ministry.

Dr. Touryan: I contacted the local churches and then helped in the ministry of starting new churches and Bible groups.

Narrator: But what about countries which have no local church to draw on? Dr. Wilson found tentmaking provided the answer in places like Afghanistan.

Dr. Wilson: My parents were missionaries in Iran. As a child, I heard Afghanistan was closed, that it didn't have any Christians or any churches, and I felt God calling me to go there. I had to go in as an English teacher, so that's the way I got involved in tentmaking.

Dr. Touryan: This is not just American tentmakers going into the world, but all nations to all nations. In fact, the Koreans and Brazilians can gain easier access to countries that are closed or restricted than the Americans, so tentmaking needs to become a worldwide network.

Narrator: When you consider the millions who travel as part of their job description—military, shipping, airline workers—it's clear the potential for tentmaking hasn't yet been tapped. Tentmakers do not have to come from a certain socio-economic group: from laborers to university students, each can have an impact on foreign soil. Muslims have put this into action for years.

Dr. Wilson: Consider the religion of Islam. It has spread mainly through tentmakers: not by those who are fully supported but by students, diplomats, and business people. They are the ones spreading the Muslim religion today.

Narrator: Perhaps those who believe in tentmaking the most are those who have been won to Christ through a tentmaker's message.

Afghan Surveyor: A few years ago, a man came to my country from America to teach us civil engineering. A few years later, while helping to build a hospital in a remote area, he was accidentally killed. One of my co-workers who was transporting the body said, "I know this man. He was my teacher at the university." Some one asked him, "What did he teach?" He replied, "He taught me to survey the wondrous Cross." My friend and I may never have heard about Jesus if not for this man.

Luis Palau: My father wouldn't be in heaven today if it wasn't for a tentmaker who came to Argentina and South America and brought the gospel of Jesus Christ. The man's name was Charles Rogers. He was an executive with the Shell Oil Company, and he came to South America with the specific purpose of winning men and women to Jesus Christ—and he did! My father, my mother, my whole family came to Christ.

Narrator: There are many people out there like Luis Palau and his family longing for a tentmaker's message of love. Let's not keep them waiting!

Mandate of the Laity

Ford Madison

Ordinary People

While traveling to several parts of the world for the Lausanne movement, I conducted a survey to see who God was using in different countries. I wonder what this same survey might reveal at this Congress.

How did you come to Jesus Christ? Sometimes God uses famous celebrities on TV or radio to bring people to Christ. He also uses mass evangelism as a method of conversion.

Many people meet Jesus through an ordinary person: their mother, father, brother or sister, or maybe some other relative or friend. Perhaps the lay person was a teacher, co-worker, neighbor, or Sunday-school teacher.

Through this survey, we've discovered that just as in the Bible times and every year since Pentecost most often God uses common people.

But this truth raises some important questions. First, what about the everyday, ordinary women and men in our own churches? Do we believe Christ really lives in them? Do we see each one of them as a minister of Jesus Christ? It's hard to believe, especially if the church has members like Bob Griffin.

Bob Griffin is a small man, and he is handicapped. It's impossible for him to speak clearly. I first met Bob after a seminar which challenged us to get a vision that God could use lay people. At the end of the meeting, a woman and I were Bob's prayer partners. We were to tell each other what we'd learned, and then pray for one another.

Bob spoke first. In broken English he said, "I'b guttun uh visun that God cun ooze evn me."

My heart sunk into my shoes because I could not imagine *how* God could use him. But, by God's grace, I said, "Oh good! How did you get this vision and what is it?"

In broken words, he explained his hearing and speaking impairments, and that he worked in a department for the government for handicapped people where he had developed special communication skills. Bob's local church had asked him to consider teaching a Bible study for their handicapped members. Bob met Christ at a university where he learned to study the Bible through InterVarsity. We affirmed his vision and prayed for him. We told him "Go for it!"

Months later, the woman from our prayer group sent a newspaper with several

---

Ford Madison is a businessman in the United States. He has been active in lay movements throughout the world.

photographs of Bob Griffin using an overhead projector to teach a Bible study to more people each week than had attended that whole seminar.

"Ooze evn me." God will—with "faith-vision"! But that kind of "faith-vision" is hard to develop, especially if we haven't thought it through.

For example, we heard of a pastor with two Ph.D.s and a Th.D. from a world-renowned seminary, telling how wonderful the people in his church were to give money and to help *him* in *his* ministry. When asked, "What are you doing to help these ordinary members in *their* ministry," this theologically degreed man said, "It's never occurred to me!"

If you believe everyone in Christ is in the ministry, then the second big question is: *What can you do to help mobilize them?*

Leighton Ford said, "If our goal is penetration of the whole world, we must aim at nothing less than the mobilization of the whole church." This takes leadership. It requires the kind of servant leadership that not only trusts, but also equips others.

A great example of a servant leader is Frank Butler, the head of a manufacturing division of the Kodak company, who said of his employees, "I don't fill the boxes we sell, but I'm here to serve those who do by providing them with whatever it takes for them to get the job done!"

Whatever it takes! We need a servant attitude that helps provide whatever it takes for us to get the job done.

An Appeal to Work Together

Let me appeal to you as an ordinary lay person on behalf of millions of lay people—that big 90 percent—many of whom are potential laborers. We don't want your job, nor your pulpit! But neither do we want to be stuck on the sidelines, limited to cheering from the spiritual grandstand. We want to be full partners with you on Christ's team: everyday women and men working wholeheartedly for Christ in the world. That's full-time Christian service and we are all called to it!

But to accomplish this we need you, the church leaders. We need your encouragement to use our God-given ministries out in the world, not just in church buildings, budgets, and meetings. The battleground between Sundays is with people, lost people, out in the real world.

If you support this and will commit to it, then as leaders you need to help provide whatever it takes to support your people out in their world as they serve Christ.

Wouldn't it be wonderful if out of Lausanne II grew a new challenge of serving one another instead of looking after our own self-interests? We'd be full partners—no clergy/laity barriers—who are one in the Spirit of Jesus Christ, with the oneness Jesus prayed for to let the world know that the Father sent him and loves them—even as God loved Jesus. Together, let's love and serve our Lord Jesus Christ.

The old adage says, "The journey of one thousand miles begins with the first step." For any group, this needs the first step of a leader. Will you, as leaders, step out for your lay people? Maybe God wants you to change your vision of where the battleground is for lost people; or your perception and attitude toward the laity and their ministries. Perhaps he wants you to trust the Holy Spirit to use them, or maybe you need to make a commitment to do whatever it takes to equip them. Whatever you need, may God help us to cooperate with each other so the whole church can reach the whole world.

The Work of the Holy Spirit in Conviction and Conversion

J. I. Packer

I live in Vancouver, Canada, where the wind rarely rises beyond a gentle breeze. But in Britain, where I lived before, gales would strip branches from trees, roofs from sheds, and make it hard to stand. The power of a hurricane or tropical typhoon is awesome. Yet, the wind is God's picture of the activity of the person whom Charles Williams rightly and reverently called "our Lord the Holy Spirit."

The biblical words for *Spirit* (*ruach* in Hebrew, *pneuma* in Greek) signify breath breathed or exhaled hard such as when you blow up balloons, blow out candles, or breathe hard as you run. The words also signify the blowing of the wind, which is sometimes barely perceptible, but at other times becomes a roaring, shattering thing— an overwhelming display of power. The Spirit's action takes both forms, and many in between. The Spirit is God's power in human lives.

Eighty years ago, a breath of revival struck the church in Manchuria. Missionaries wrote home these words: "One clause in the Creed that lives before us now in all its inevitable, awful solemnity is, 'I believe in the Holy Ghost.'" I dare to hope and pray that we shall be impacted by that same "inevitable, awful solemnity" at this Congress. Should a "Holy Ghost hurricane" hit us, there will be some disruption—I promise you that—but we, and our ministries, will be blessedly marked for life; not by chaos and darkness such as natural hurricanes bring but by light, order, and Christlikeness.

The man with whom I began as a pastor and a another close friend in the ministry for over twenty-five years are both now in glory. They were revival converts. I have never known men of deeper humility and honesty, of greater sensitivity to sin, of a stronger sense of God's holiness, or of shrewder discernment of the human heart. As one who has long coveted these qualities for himself, so I covet them now for us all.

Much is said nowadays about the need for worldwide revival and the renewing ministry of the Holy Spirit. That is good, but care is needed lest this new emphasis goes astray, and its correcting of one error produces a greater error. In my youth, all the talk was about Jesus and far too little was said about the Spirit. It became vogue to call the Spirit "the displaced person of the Godhead" and "the Cinderella of theology." Today, people are being promised an experience of the Spirit in situations where far too little is being said concerning Christ. That can be disastrous. Knowledge of Christ and fellowship with him is what the Holy Spirit's ministry since Pentecost is all about.

James I. Packer is Professor of Theology at Regent College in Canada, and a citizen of that country.

The Spirit focuses attention, not on himself, but on the Savior. He has a ministry of illumination through the Word that convinces us of the reality of Christ; a ministry that leads us to see our need of Christ so that we embrace him in faith and love; a ministry that keeps us prayerfully in touch with Christ and assured of salvation by Christ; and a ministry of oneness which connects us to Christ in such a way that his risen life flows into us and he ministers to others through us. The Reformers, Puritans, Pietists, and older evangelicals in the West understood this. They insisted that the only proof of religious experiences came from the Spirit of God. Through those experiences the men, women, and children concerned were being prepared for, and then pointed and led to, fellowship by faith with Christ as their Savior and Lord.

But today any experience of quietness replacing mental distress, hopefulness replacing depression, or behavioral order replacing behavioral chaos tends to be treated as a work of the Holy Spirit, even when no reference to Jesus Christ enters into it. On that basis, one would have to treat the experiences of Jewish, Hindu, Buddhist, Islamic mystics, and the "altered states" of consciousness promised by North America's New Age movement and sought by many through drugs as saving manifestations of the Holy Spirit. Some people actually do, but biblically this is incorrect. Religious experiences which keep people from seeking and finding Christ are sponsored by a spirit quite different from the Holy Spirit of God.

My focus is the work of the Holy Spirit in the experienced event of personal conviction and conversion. Conversion is a vital necessity. Without conversion, no one beyond the state of infancy who has ordinary mental powers can be saved.

Conversion is a much misunderstood subject. Some think it must be an intense experience, a rush of feeling associated with revivalist campaigns and choirs singing, "Just as I Am," or accompanied by the experience some refer to as being "slain in the Spirit." But some conversions are entirely unemotional.

Conversion involves much more than new feelings, and clarity about conversion is important. There are three issues regarding conversion that I will attempt to clarify: (*a*) the Spirit as the author of conversion; (*b*) the work accomplished by the Spirit in conversion; and (*c*) the means used by the Spirit in conversion.

The Holy Spirit as the Author of Conversion

The word *conversion* means "turning from one thing to another." The concept of Christian conversion, according to the New Testament, is of turning from idolatry and sin to God through Jesus Christ. This turning is analyzed as repentance towards God— which means first a change of thoughts, then a change of ways. It is also analyzed as faith in Jesus Christ—which means a trustful commitment. This repentance and faith is the response that the gospel requires.

But fallen human hearts are gripped by sin. None of us have it in us by nature to take the gospel seriously and turn to God in complete trust. It often looks as though evangelism will always be an impossible task; that no one will ever respond to the Good News. But, thank God, that is not so! Many, in fact, do turn to God and are committed to him. How is this possible?

The New Testament explains it in terms of sinners being *called*. That is, not just told the truth about salvation, but led by God to embrace it as the truth, and to repent and receive Christ; after which they are "kept by the power of God." Christian conversion, which is an act of man, is thus revealed as being also a work of God.

Conversion is an exercise of divine sovereignty. Psychologically, the discernment and the decisions are ours, yet God turns us to himself by his own initiative and power.

When we look back on our conversion, both Scripture and our own hearts tell us that we turned because we were turned. We came to trust the Lord because we were turned. We came to trust the Lord because God himself drew us to him. This explains why English-speaking Christians for more than four centuries have talked about "being converted," as the King James Version also does, even though the Greek word for convert, *epistrepho,* is always used in the New Testament in the active voice. In this act of almighty grace, the Holy Spirit is the direct agent. He illuminates, convinces, quickens, induces new birth, imparts repentance, and prompts the converted soul's confession, "Jesus is Lord."

Psychologically, conversions take countless forms. Some are quiet, some tumultuous. Some are quick and clear, occurring the moment the gospel is understood, others take years before faith in Christ is confidently professed. Some occur so early in life that there is no conscious memory of them; some are deathbed occurrences.

In ministering conversion to us, however, the Spirit makes our ways converge. Wherever we start, and whatever differences we begin with—racial, social, sexual, cultural, or religious—we all end up in the same place. We enter into the same relationship of faith and love with the Lord Jesus Christ, our Savior and Master. The Spirit's uniform success in bringing us all to this same joyous and peaceful state of mind and heart shows that the title, "Lord of grace," which an English hymn gives him, is well deserved.

The Work Accomplished by the Holy Spirit in Conversion

The New Testament interprets conversion Christologically and pneumatologically—that is, in terms of starting life afresh with Christ through the Spirit. It exhibits conversion as an entirely new beginning, miraculous in the sense that you cannot account for it in terms of anything that preceded it. New Testament concepts used to delineate conversion include new birth; new creation; the quickening of the dead; sharing in Christ's death and resurrection; and putting off the old self and putting on the new. These are startling images and are powerful in their meaning.

1. *New birth* (John 3:3–8) means a change in our way of existing so radical and far-reaching that the only adequate comparison is our emergence from the womb into a world unknown.
2. *New creation* (2 Corinthians 5:17) means a change of outlook and attitudes that is inexplicable in terms of what we used to be.
3. *Quickening the dead* (Ephesians 2:1–5) means the end of corpse-like unresponsiveness to God and the start of a relationship with God that is true human life.
4. *Sharing* (literally, being "grafted into") *Christ's death and resurrection* (Romans 6:3–11), that is, being crucified, buried, and raised with him (Galatians 2:20; Colossians 2:11–13,20; 3:1), means a miraculous motivational change at the core of our being, which Scripture calls our *heart.* The essence of the change is that the character qualities that marked the perfect humanity of the Lord Jesus are now implanted in us. Our strongest inner drives are opposing, if not always fully overcoming, the sinful habits that previously mastered us. Our moral nature is made new and we find ourselves desiring to know, love, trust, obey, honor, and please our Savior-God more than we desire anything in the world. Every lapse into sin makes us deeply miserable in a way that was never true before.

5. *Putting on the new self in place of the old* (Ephesians 4:22–24; Colossians 3:9–10) means embracing this new life of Christlikeness that God both prescribes and bestows.

All of this becomes reality "in Christ." Union with him, across all boundaries of time and space, is the objective fact that produces these immense changes in what we are. When we speak of conversion, therefore, both the objective fact and the subjective results should be in our minds, for both are aspects of the one reality.

Conversion, thus appears as the most significant thing that ever happens to any human being. It makes God our focus, Christ our glory, the Spirit our life, and heaven our home forever. And it is the Holy Spirit himself who effects this union, who sustains it by his indwelling presence, who makes it fruitful in Christlike living, and who will one day finish his transformation by giving us new bodies to match our renewed hearts. The Puritan, Thomas Goodwin, said that it is the Holy Spirit who "takes all the pains with us." This, and nothing less, is his work in conversion. It is for us who believe to wonder, to adore, and to know ourselves as new creatures in Christ. We need to make it our daily goal to live out, with the Spirit's help, what has been wrought in us by the Spirit's power. True conversion is known by the new quality of life that it produces.

The Means Used by the Spirit in Conversion

The Holy Spirit is truly God the evangelist: He brings sinners to conversion. He does this through a variety of means. The Western habit of theological abstraction might lead us to believe (as evangelical theologians have said for four centuries) that the means in question are: (*a*) the preaching and teaching of the gospel, along with its visible embodiment in the two sacraments, and also with signs and wonders; (*b*) the demonstration of the gospel in the worship, fellowship, holiness, love, and good deeds of the church and Christian individuals; and (*c*) backing all of this—prayer.

Such a statement would not be false—it is, indeed, profoundly true—but it could blur our awareness of the reality behind it that sinners saved by grace are called to become the means of evangelism as we preach, teach, witness, serve, and pray. In this sense, we are all fellow workers with God. God lays upon us the awesome privilege and responsibility of being used evangelistically because in evangelization the Holy Spirit respects human nature as God made it. The Spirit employs a mode of communicating the gospel that is truly convincing simply because it is authentically incarnational.

The fullest and most potent revelation of God's graciousness was given by our Lord Jesus Christ himself. He was in person (and in heaven still is) God incarnate. To most fully show us God's grace, the Word became flesh. As the Gospels show, his personal impact was uniquely arresting and powerful; no one spoke like him, or behaved like him, and no one could ignore him. And other things being equal, the fullest and most potent proof that the gospel of salvation through Christ is true will be given by persons who are most clearly seen to be living in its power, and whose lives are most decisively different from the lives of those around them.

The Spirit works in us through our minds. Any genuine decision to receive the new life will be the result of conscious conviction, and conscious conviction can only be expected when the new life is visible in its exponents. Otherwise, in whatever reasons for faith we might give, credibility will be lacking, just as it would be if a bald man attempted to sell you hair restorer, or if one who had just crashed his car offered to teach you to drive. The world has a right to ask that the gospel be not only shared with them, but shown to them in the lives of the gospel's spokesmen. We have a duty to serve the world in both these ways.

The New Testament norm for evangelization is and always will be communication through persons. In regular pulpit preaching and in the most informal sharing of the gospel, and in all evangelistic activity in between, personal sanctity needs to be visible in the communicator. The messenger of this life-transforming gospel is at least half of the message. The most compelling communicator in the Spirit's hand will ordinarily be the person who most honestly speaks out of personal realization of spiritual need and personal experience of the new life that remedies it. Their personal desire is to share the riches of that life with others.

The worship and service of a Christian congregation which expresses the reality of the new life can be a potent evangelistic force. Spirit-filled worship and service can convince and convert through the Spirit's power in an amazingly effective way.

We also need to recognize the intrinsic superiority of nationals evangelizing within their own or similar cultures. This is more effective than having others bear the brunt of evangelizing cross-culturally where the receiving culture differs from their own in a radical way.

National evangelism is superior to cross-cultural evangelism because: (a) nationals have freedom of movement, whereas by A.D. 2000, 83 percent of the world's population are expected to be living in lands to which church-planting Western missionaries will not be admitted; (b) throughout Asia, and in other parts of the Two-Thirds World, anti-Western prejudice is strong; (c) in Asia and Africa, missionary money from the West goes much further when supporting nationals rather than Westerners; (d) pioneering by Western missionaries perpetuates the myth that Christianity is the religion of the West as Hinduism, Buddhism, and Islam are religions of the East, in other words, that Christianity is an ethnic rather than a universal religion; and (e) the efforts of Western missionaries in the East so easily look and feel like neo-colonialism and denominational imperialism. But the deepest reason is that appreciating the full humanity of a person who culturally is not felt to be "one of us" is harder than when a person is felt to be a part of that culture. This makes it more difficult for cross-cultural communication to be perceived as incarnational and, therefore, as convincingly true. It is as simple, and as far-reaching, as that. In lands where there are no churches, cross-cultural missionary work remains the only way to begin.

In those parts of Asia, Africa, India, China, and Latin America where the church now exists, it seems the Holy Spirit is drastically shifting the center of gravity in evangelism and church-planting from Western cross-cultural pioneering and modeling to more indigenous national movements. This is a tremendous move forward in God's global strategy. His pattern of action is, and always was, that once cross-cultural evangelism has planted a church, national evangelists, who can achieve incarnational identification with their hearers more profoundly and effectively because of the common culture, should sustain and extend the outreach.

We need to honor our Lord the Holy Spirit. Honor him by letting him remold the raw clay of our lives into a Christlike model of holy love, purity, and passion for both sanctity and souls. Honor the Spirit by confessing that in evangelism everything depends on him, and by committing ourselves to labor in evangelism as if everything depends on us. Honor the Spirit by giving ourselves afresh to Jesus Christ, whom the Spirit honors, to be his means of evangelism wherever he leads.

Ministry of the Spirit

Producers: Mike Quintana, Stuart Bennett

Narrators: "You will receive power when the Holy Spirit comes on you; and you will be my witnesses" (Acts 1:8). To be his witnesses is the call of the church: to be his witnesses to the uttermost ends of the earth. And so his witnesses have gone—to Ecuador, Mexico, Nigeria, and Korea.

Just as on the day of Pentecost when the Holy Spirit imbued power and boldness to the disciples, present-day apostles are being filled so they can take the gospel of Jesus to the world with a power and boldness that can only be described as supernatural.

Yet, for many, the supernatural represents a spirit-world filled with strange, frightening creatures. The idea of the spirit-world is nothing new in many places of the globe including, South America—Quito, Ecuador to be exact. There, the Holy Spirit touched the lives of Mario and Janette Torres.

Out of work and in debt, Mario and his wife had exhausted every physical means of solving their problems.

Mario: The truth is, it was an insurmountable situation: bitterness, arguments, lack of things in the house. In fact, we even went to see a witch doctor to see what she could do for us.

Narrator: When the spiritual answer never came, Mario and his wife turned to some people who claimed they could actually speak to God. That same day, they attended a church and were so moved by the Holy Spirit that they accepted Christ and were filled with his power.

Mario: I was afraid of it because we were all standing and praying and I felt as if my tongue was all tied up, as if it wasn't me talking.

Narrator: Loaded with questions, Mario tried to sleep that night, but he was awakened every fifteen minutes with a new word from God that comforted, assured, and affirmed his salvation and new power in the Lord.

Mario: I finally said to the Lord, "Thank you for what you have done for me. Thank you for the answers you have given me."

Narrator: Soon after that, Mario began to witness and the Lord began to work.

Mario: I saw how the blind were healed, how the lame walked, and people were healed of cancer, of heart problems. I saw these things and knew that only God could do it. Only God could manifest his power this way.

Narrator: Today Mario is a full-time evangelist. He preaches in his home church and helps out in tent meetings. Both he and his wife recognize it is only through the power of the Holy Spirit that they are able to minister to others and draw them to Christ. As Mario's wife, Janette, explains, it is something deeply personal that happens when the Spirit touches you.

Janette: I was baptized in the Holy Spirit. It was a marvelous experience. You don't know what to expect beforehand: you think it is unreal—that it is impossible. But the moment you trust God, it's something only you yourself can understand—the marvel of what God can do inside.

Narrator: Reverend William Kumuyi is another person who has been changed from the inside out by the Holy Spirit. A pastor in the city of Lagos, Nigeria, Reverend Kumuyi had a desire to see the Lord move in a supernatural way.

Reverend Kumuyi: First I had a desire. I had read in the Word about Moses, Elijah, Elisha, Daniel, Shadrach, Meshach, Abednego, Jesus Christ, Paul, and Peter. They moved in the supernatural. And I thought these men didn't just rely on the Bible or theology alone, they went to the miraculous. Every person that Jesus chose, he anointed to move in the miraculous.

Narrator: As Nigeria bustled around him, Reverend Kumuyi spent hours in prayer and reading the Bible. He started a Bible study with fifteen people. Soon it grew to one thousand, then to six thousand as he continued to seek God. The Holy Spirit fell on him and filled him with Christ's power.

Reverend Kumuyi: On Sunday, February 6, 1963, I found myself saying something I had no knowledge of, except by the Spirit of God. I then ministered to someone who had been demon possessed for eighteen years and the Lord gave us a breakthrough. People were healed, eyes were opened, people were drawn to the study, and we went from six thousand to forty-five thousand. And this was just the beginning.

I read that in the Lord all things were possible, that greater works would we do, and that Jesus is the same yesterday, today, and forever. So what he did in Matthew, Mark, Luke, and John, he is able to do today, and he must need someone to use. I said to myself, *If it is possible with anyone on the face of the earth, it should be possible with me, also.*

Narrator: From Nigeria we look east to Korea—to another man who has opened his life to the evangelizing power of the Holy Spirit. Few will argue that Dr. Paul Yonggi Cho is on the forefront of Korea's Christian movement. His church has seen unprecedented growth, and according to him it has been only by the power of the Holy Spirit that these works were possible.

Dr. Paul Yonggi Cho: I usually pray three to five hours a day. Without prayer, you don't have the spiritual resources you need to build this kind of church. But along with prayer, you need to work with the Holy Spirit. Before I go to preach, I say, "Dear Holy Spirit, let's go. We are all going to do this together." When I finish, I say, "Holy Spirit, I thank you. You did a marvelous job," because he is the one who is working with us, who is helping us.

Narrator: Whether it is in the awe-inspiring movment of thousands, as in Dr. Cho's church, or in the simple reverence of a child's prayer, the Holy Spirit moves in his own way. Filled with his power, we can surge forward into the thirsting hearts of people and quench them with the living water of the Lord.

If we will open ourselves to the power of his Spirit, then supernatural works like those in Africa, or Korea, or Colombia will abound. And if reaching the 5.2 billion people on earth is our goal, then it is going to take supernatural power to do it.

A Passion for Fullness

Jack W. Hayford

"But I know that when I come to you, I shall come in the fullness of the blessing of the gospel of Christ" (Romans 15:29, NKJV).

That He would grant you, according to the riches of His glory, to be strengthened with might through His Spirit in the inner man. . . . To know the love of Christ which passes knowledge; that you may be filled with all the fullness of God (Ephesians 3:16,19, NKJV).

In discussing the power of the Holy Spirit in evangelism, we are at the cutting edge of the miraculous. God's works are all wondrous, but five definite points mark the Spirit's miracle workings in the spread of the gospel:

1. The immersion of power by which the Spirit calls, equips, and anoints the messenger to bear witness to the gospel
2. The quickening of the Word proclaimed, as the Holy Spirit causes it to become prophetic and powerful—penetrating and convicting the hearer
3. The confirmation of the Word with signs and wonders, by which the Holy Spirit verifies the living presence of Christ Jesus and demonstrates his superiority over all human and satanic power
4. The regenerating power, by which the Holy Spirit transforms souls from spiritual death to eternal life and brings abiding peace, hope, and joy
5. The reproductivity of this grace, by which each disciple may also be empowered by the Holy Spirit as the cycle of witness renews itself

The process of evangelism is wholly miraculous. The essence of the word *witness* is "to bear testimony," "to give evidence for the case." Evangelism is not merely conveying a message, but the delivery of power. It is the proof that Jesus is still alive; still working as miraculously as he is saving and forgiving. Without *all* his fullness we have no adequate resource to make global impact. Thus, the passion for fullness rises among all who want to see sin conquered and human need met.

In John 9, Jesus healed a man who had been born blind. When questioned about

Jack W. Hayford is pastor of the Church on the Way in Van Nuys, California and is a citizen of the United States.

Jesus and the miracle, the man began to describe his experience by saying: "One thing I know: . . . now I see" (John 9:25, NKJV).

He claimed no great wisdom or accomplishment; what he knew was the result of Jesus' miracle. We can all appreciate how that blind-now-healed man felt. He was a classic Bible example of McCandlish Phillip's comment, "A man with an experience is never at the mercy of a man with an argument." We all have an *experience* of salvation, not just a theology. Our testimonies, therefore, include the experiences of the Holy Spirit's miraculous power.

As an infant I was healed of a life-threatening affliction through the prayers of a congregation in Long Beach, California. Our family physician told my parents that my healing was unexplainable apart from God. The Holy Spirit had gained my parents' attention and as a result, they were later converted at the church which had prayed for their baby.

A few years later, I contracted polio. I was completely healed through the laying on of hands and anointing with oil by the church elders. By God's grace through the Holy Spirit's miraculous power, my parents were born again and I can walk and stand before you today.

As a teenager, I answered God's call to a ministry committed to allow and expect Christ's miracles, signs, and wonders because my life was a result of them. Though I have often been frustrated by witnessing excesses, fanaticism, and foolishness among some who exercise such gifts, I have held constant in this community because I have found that for every case of lamentable excess there are a hundred examples of depth, reality, and divine power.

For the past twenty years, I have ministered God's Word simply and without sensation in one pastorate: The Church on the Way, in Van Nuys, California. In that time I have watched the church grow from less than thirty believers to more than ten thousand. Thirty thousand decisions for Christ have been registered, dozens of churches have been planted, and scores of workers have been commissioned to minister the gospel across the nation and around the world. Only God deserves the praise for these miraculous results. I exclaim with the blind man, "This is all I know—I couldn't have accomplished this; Jesus did it!" Such results have become common worldwide, replicated in scores of nations and vastly exceeded in hundreds of cities—especially in the last fifteen years.

The Lausanne Covenant

This is the fifteenth year of the Lausanne movement. Together, we have witnessed and continue to see a phenomenal proliferation of the Holy Spirit's works of power throughout the church. Church growth and ministry are increasing and abounding at an exponential rate, as at no other time in history. Often, it is a direct by-product of God's Word being confirmed by signs, wonders, and the manifestation of the Holy Spirit's gifts. Though an enormous unfinished task is still before us, faith for its completion is rising as a renewed passion. The fullness of the Holy Spirit's power is resulting in Christ being glorified in *all* his works as he confirms *all* his Word.

In 1974, the first Lausanne Congress made a bold, welcoming declaration concerning the ministry of the Holy Spirit. In speaking for such a broad representation of evangelicals, it was unlike any such statement before:

> We believe in the power of the Holy Spirit. . . . Worldwide evangelism will become a realistic possibility only when the Spirit renews the church in truth and wisdom, faith, holiness, love, and power. We therefore call upon all Christians to pray for such a visitation of the sovereign Spirit of God that all his fruit may appear in all his people and

that all his gifts may enrich the body of Christ. Only then will the whole church become a fit instrument in his hands, that the whole earth may hear his voice (Lausanne Covenant, article 14).

In view of what has happened the past fifteen years, who can estimate the degree to which the Lausanne Covenant has been key in welcoming a release of the Holy Spirit's power across the earth? The words of that covenant have opened doors for multitudes of leaders:

- A doorway to investigating the Word of God and its present promise of power, with signs and wonders;
- A doorway to broadening fellowship, overcoming fears, and dissolving stereotypes which hinder boldness in faith and divide brethren; and
- A doorway to God Almighty, giving his Spirit license to move freely in our midst, unshackled by the restraints of our doubt and unbelief.

A new passion for the fullness of the Spirit's power has released a new presence of the fullness of Christ's works. Something has undoubtedly begun and is moving forward. But what is this "something," and how can we respond most fully?

Affirming the Biblical Base

This "something" is, as Peter said of the miracles at Pentecost: "That which was spoken of by the prophet." He noted the biblical basis of the phenomena at hand, and thus, revealed how this ministry of the Holy Spirit's power is rooted in the Scriptures.

Christ's Continuing Ministry

The book of Acts opens by asserting that what follows—the church at work—was, and is, a direct continuation of Christ's ministry: "The former account I have written, O Theophilus, of all that Jesus began both to do and teach" (Acts 1:1, NKJV). The text declares that the *actions* (what Jesus began to do) are as essential to this mission as the *proclamation* (what Jesus began to teach).

Jesus' ministry was *both* a teaching/preaching ministry and a miracle/healing ministry. For example:

So they were all amazed . . . saying, "What a word this is! For with authority and power He commands the unclean spirits, and they come out" (Luke 4:36, NKJV).

Now Jesus went about all Galilee, teaching in their synagogues, preaching the gospel of the kingdom, and healing all kinds of sickness. . . And they brought to him all sick people who were afflicted with various diseases and torments, and those who were demon-possessed, epileptics, and paralytics; and He healed them. And great multitudes followed Him" (Matthew 4:23–25, NKJV).

Acts begins by presuming the church's intended dimensions of ministry are defined in the Gospels, as Jesus said: "The works that I do, he [you] will do" (John 14:12, NKJV). Acts shows how the Holy Spirit has come to help us continue all Jesus began, both to teach and to do—to help us proclaim the Word and expect the wondrous.

The Bible itself removes any excuse for reticence to expecting the supernatural signs of Jesus at work in a ministry. Candor with the text makes us accountable today to allow Jesus to do through our ministries the kinds of things he did in his. In whatever part of his church he places us, we need to encourage and sustain this balance: *to declare* the Word Christ proclaimed, *to show* the love the Father revealed in him, and *to expect* miracles as the Holy Spirit works.

Today's "world need" calls for no less power than he displayed in the first century. Only as God's eternal Word is confirmed by the Holy Spirit's mighty works, can New Age error be exposed at its deceptive roots, Muslim nations be penetrated by God's love, urban centers be visited by divine grace, and campus intellectualism be shown inadequate. Only God's miracle grace can overthrow satanic strongholds and break demonic bondage.

And Jesus wants to touch today's lepers—all who suffer amid the welter of pain and disease. He wants to heal today just as surely as his love touched the sick long ago. Beyond whatever superficiality we may deem present in some who practice healing ministries, we need a personal passion for fullness to answer the human passion for wholeness.

A balanced ministry is possible. More and more in the church hunger and thirst for Christ's fullest works in every dimension: his truth, love, and character, *with* his healing, authority over demons, and resurrection power displayed.

Christ's Continuing Power

The biblical call for Jesus' complete ministry includes a promise by which Jesus' power may be received. Jesus said, "You shall be baptized with the Holy Spirit . . . You shall receive power" (Acts 1:5,8, NKJV). Whatever "the baptism with the Spirit" may mean to us, whenever we may feel it is experienced, or however it may be evidenced, this much is sure: Jesus said it is to provide us a resource for fullness; with power to minister everything Jesus has and is to the world he loves, died to redeem, and wants to touch with his forgiveness, healing, and wholeness.

Explosive and expanding results are present today where Christ's disciples seek and welcome a distinct experience of the Holy Spirit's infilling. It is often inappropriate and unnecessary to debate differing theological viewpoints. They are essentially immaterial in the light of the larger question, "Is the power of God's Spirit as evident in our works as the truth of God's Spirit is in my words?

In his book, *Joy Unspeakable,* Martyn Lloyd-Jones acknowledges the need for each believer being baptized in the Holy Spirit as a distinct experience, but concludes in saying:

> May God give us all grace in this matter. It is not a matter for controversy, nor for proving who is right and who is wrong. The issue before us is the state of the Christian church, her weakness, her lethargy, with a world on fire, a world going to hell. We are the body of Christ but what do we need? The power! The Pentecostal power! Shall we not with one accord, mind, and spirit, during these coming days, wait upon him and pray that again he may open the windows of heaven and shower down upon us the Holy Spirit in mighty reviving power? . . . The need today is for an authentication of God, of the supernatural, of the spiritual, of the eternal, and this can only be answered by God graciously hearing our cry and shedding forth again his Spirit upon us and filling us as he kept filling the early church ([Wheaton, Ill.: Harold Shaw, 1985], 265, 278).

It is clear the first church had no restricting notions about when or where they had been filled with the Spirit. The issue for them was *being* filled—for this moment—for God's present purposes to be served by the Spirit's present surge of supernatural power.

When Paul confronts the satanically inspired Elymas, whose demonic control over the regional governor parallels barricades to evangelism we face today, Acts 13:9 (NKJV) says he was "filled with the Holy Spirit." In the fresh anointing of that moment, Paul moves to confound the works of hell and advance the purposes of God. This passion for the Spirit's present fullness explains Paul's words to the Romans (15:29, NKJV). He declares his expectation of coming to them, "in the fullness of the blessing of the gospel of Christ." The same passion marks his prayer for the Ephesians (3:14–21, NKJV), that they may be "filled with all the fullness of God."

Whatever our various traditions may hold regarding Jesus' words, "You shall be baptized with the Holy Spirit . . . You shall receive power," we should not be satisfied with only a theological position. Doctrinal precision is no substitute for the Holy Spirit's demonstration. Paul said,

> And my speech and my preaching were not with persuasive words of human wisdom, but in demonstration of the Spirit and of power, that your faith should not be in the wisdom of men but in the power of God (1 Corinthians 2:4–5, NKJV).

Re-studying the biblical call to Holy Spirit-filled ministry is not to question doctrinal positions, but to re-stir our passion for fullness, that we "stir up the gift of God which is in [us] . . . For God has not given us a spirit of fear, but of power and of love and of a sound mind" (2 Timothy 1:6–7, NKJV). In the light of God's Word, hosts of leaders and laity are responding. Recent research indicates explosive evangelism and church growth where the spirit of fear is overcome and the Holy Spirit is revealing the fullness of Christ through the church.

Confirming the Evidence Today

David Barrett's monumental work as the editor of the *World Christian Encyclopedia* (Oxford: Oxford U. Press, 1982) has provided a wider perspective on the church's world witness. Objective analysis of its report shows the widest growth in most areas regularly correlates with one given feature of Christ's ministry: the ministry of the supernatural—of the Spirit's gifts, with signs and wonders.

Miracles and Miraculous Growth

Barrett's study records good growth where evangelistic vigor is alive, Christ is exalted, and the Word of God is preached. But it also notes "many situations of explosive, uncontrollable growth," where the Holy Spirit's gifts are active and where signs and wonders confirm the Word (see D. B. Barrett, "The Twentieth Century Pentecostal/Charismatic Renewal," in Burgess, McGee and Alexander, eds., *Dictionary of Pentecostal and Charismatic Movements* [Grand Rapids, Mich.: Zondervan, 1988], 811).

Statistics reveal this segment of the global Christian community, which in 1900 represented only 7 percent of all Christians, now involves almost one of every four believers (*Dictionary*, 812). Another researcher notes that while a general awareness of this phenomenal growth still exists, some prominent evangelical journals seem to ignore it. This reticence is provoked by prevailing and perfectly understandable fears.

Fears of the Miraculous

Two kinds of fear seem to relate to the Holy Spirit's supernatural workings. Some leaders are often bewildered or frustrated—especially in the realm of miracles, signs, wonders, and manifestations of the gifts of the Spirit. Fear blocks freedom in ministry, and those fears *can* be overcome.

The first is *fear of the unfamiliar*. I remember, as a boy, the first time I ever swam in a river. Until then, I had only been in public swimming pools. I found myself caught up in a slow but mighty stream, which relentlessly carried me beyond my entry point in the water. It was a new sensation, and a memorably frightening one. Much in the same way, first contacts with the dynamics of the Holy Spirit can be very disconcerting; where the miraculous occurs, where demons are confronted, and where spiritual gifts that before were only verbal ideas are being manifest as vital realities.

Compounding the fear of the unfamiliar, is an even more troublesome fear: *the fear of fanaticism*. It is justifiable that people fear the risk of fanaticism when the Spirit's mighty works are present. Sensationalism and exploitation have always been a problem. Peter faced that long ago, and in rebuking Simon the Sorcerer he provided us with a challenging model (Acts 8:18–23). Could the Holy Spirit be calling *all* of us, to exercise today the choice Peter did then?

As a Christian leader, it is worth my determination to gain an acquaintance with the supernatural operations and manifestations of the Holy Spirit. I can't let him have full control and not risk losing control of some situations. But I can learn to trust him, and learn how to move with his power in a way that restrains foolishness and releases fullness. We need to be open to the moving of the Holy Spirit. He's clearly ready to bring broader breakthroughs in evangelizing every nation. If we as leaders, are open to him, two tragedies can be avoided: (1) Ministry in the gifts of the Spirit with signs and wonders will be shaped by leaders who prioritize biblical values, rather than be forfeited to the few who may seem indifferent to those priorities; and, (2) We shall all be equipped throughout all the church to reach to all the world with all the resources Jesus promised; rather than attempting to pursue all the task without all the power he commanded us all to receive.

We all feel a passion for fullness. We all hunger for the Spirit's works of power. With the Word of God unfolding before us and the Holy Spirit poured out upon us, let us reach out to the world with power. The world needs Jesus—in all his *saving* power, in all his *healing* power, in all his *delivering* power.

Reaffirming Our United Quest

A dear friend of mine, who pastors one of America's most respected traditional evangelical churches, said:

> Jack, I want to find a word that describes us both. Because my heart is as yours and I know yours is as mine, we want all the power, gifts, and miracles the Holy Spirit has to give, and I don't want people putting us in separate pockets because you're Pentecostal and I'm not.

He has addressed a point critical to the subject of the Holy Spirit's power in evangelism. As long as we either hedge on the Spirit's call to us, or build hedges against our unity in answering that call, something of pure power will be sacrificed. Christ's prayer for our unity, "that the world may know," is not his mandate to our total doctrinal agreement or our uniformity in church policy. But he *is* calling us all to acknowledge his fullness—to be people with a passion for "all the fullness of God"; people who all are candidates to minister in the power, gifts, and grace of the Holy Spirit.

A Spirit-filled ministry is characterized by all that Jesus is, all that Jesus does, and all that Jesus wants. Spirit-filled ministry is Christ-filled ministry; when Christ, the Anointed King, is manifest in and through us by the anointing of the Holy Spirit. His anointing enables, ensures, and enlarges.

The Spirit enables the believer for service and witness, giving gifts which focus on answering human need, not personal, selfish, or private interests; gifts that bear witness to the faithful Word, exalting Christ and the triumph of his Cross as signs and wonders confirming his resurrection rule.

The Spirit ensures the uniqueness of each personality. He doesn't violate the Father's handiwork by forcing any of us into a robot-like mold. He'll use each of us in different ways—even in the same gifts.

The Spirit will enlarge our heart and vision. He will make us more like Jesus and help us love all who are his. He will deal a deathblow to sectarian smallness, and help us understand the vastness and variety of the members who form his body.

Lausanne II and "All the Fullness"

In Paul's prayer "that you may be filled with all the fullness of God," *pleroma* is the word translated "fullness." This grand New Testament word is most often used to describe the "full content, entirely, and whole sum" of the person of Christ (Gerhard Friedrich, ed., *Theological Dictionary of the New Testament*, vol. 6, trans. and ed. Geoffrey W. Bromiley [Grand Rapids, Mich.: Eerdmans, 1968], 298). Perhaps *pleroma* is the word for a new millennium. As we stand on the threshold of the twenty-first century, could it be that this is the word—the ministry—he would give us; a ministry which breaks through in all Christ's fullness and power as we are filled and energized by the Holy Spirit?

The result would be a fullness in evangelism; our ability to say with Paul, "And when I come to you, I shall come in *pleroma*—the fullness of the blessing of the gospel of Christ."

That fullness brings breakthrough because it declares the Word of the Cross and the glory of Christ. That fullness brings breakthrough because it confronts demonic powers in the power of the blood of the Lamb and the spirit of prayer. That fullness brings breakthrough because it is attended by signs and wonders as the Lord works with us, confirming his Word with signs following.

That's the ministry of the people of the *pleroma,* the fullness of Christ. Their ministry is filled with the Holy Spirit and his power. They preach the Word, but they're more than biblical. They baptize their converts, but they're more than Baptist. They govern their congregations in orderly ways, but they're more than Free Church, Presbyterian, Episcopalian, or Congregational. They may speak with tongues, but they're more than Pentecostal. They move in the resources of the Spirit's gifts, but they're more than charismatic. They flow in the river of the Spirit's power, but they're more than Third Wave.

What shall we call these people who want the full power of the Holy Spirit? Since they're people of the *pleroma*, the fullness, we might call them pleromatics; that is, people committed to witness God's Word in all the Spirit's workings until all the world is reached with all Christ's fullness! Or, we might call them believers, saints, or disciples. But perhaps, we may best return to the label the world hung on us long ago, when Holy Spirit-filled people first shook a pagan city through God's miracle grace and power: "And the disciples were first called Christians at Antioch" (Acts 11:26, NKJV).

Christ is Jesus' title as the Anointed One. *Christian* is the name given people who continue in that anointing.

We need to give full acknowledgment to the biblical basis for our call to continue Jesus' ministry, both in the Word of truth and in the Spirit of power. We should accept and rejoice in the evidence that such fullness of ministry is available and abounding today. And, with one heart together, we need to affirm our passion for that fullness; answering anew the call of the Lausanne Covenant, to "pray for such a visitation of the sovereign Spirit of God that all his fruit may appear in all his people and that all his gifts may enrich the body of Christ"; and then "the whole church become a fit instrument in his hands, that the whole earth may hear his voice."

Living Holy

Carmelo B. Terranova

The first Lord's Supper developed in an environment laden with fear, treason, and uncertainty. However, the whole environment was immersed by the holiness of the blessed person of the Lord Jesus Christ.

Time has passed, but the stage hasn't changed much. On occasion, the truth of the revelation has been betrayed; at other times, fear has invaded large areas of the church, and uncertainty has multiplied in the ministry and faith of the mission fields. But always, in the hopeless crises as well as in the uncertain decisions, the radiant figure of the Lord's holiness has covered the church and its ministers with glory. It is as true now as it was before that: He lives and is the Lord of the church.

We are a step away from the twenty-first century. Looking back with gratitude and ahead with hopeful perplexity, we find that the greatest need for the church and for the world is that of producing men and women who know, live, and communicate holiness. This is not a simple statement; it is an urgent demand—not only from God, but from a mankind paralyzed in amazement by so many moral crises and so many spiritual disappointments.

What Is the Model of Holiness?

There have been—and still are—good models of holiness. God has placed men and women in each era who reflect his holiness. They are attractive and convincing, but the true model is Jesus Christ. An imitation of Christ is a poor copy of a model that cannot be imitated. Authentic holiness exposes and displays itself from the inside out. We have imitated the exterior of Jesus' life, and that replica consists of reproducing his miracles, teachings, promises, and even his charisma. The results have not been very convincing. We get the mistaken impression that the one who makes miracles, or astonishes with his biblical discoveries or his charismatic gifts, is a saint. We can be wrong when we use this reference as a standard.

Holiness, as well as the total Christian life, should be a reproduction of Jesus' inward life—not his exterior life—of the pure and transparent character of Jesus Christ. The holy person does not imitate Jesus, he just looks like Jesus. The world is continually searching for people who look like Jesus. We have had a sufficient number of gifted

---

Carmelo B. Terranova *is pastor of the Christian and Missionary Alliance in Puerto Rico. He is a citizen of Argentina.*

people and eloquent speakers. We desperately need saints with the fragrance of Jesus Christ and the aroma from heaven.

The Price of Holiness

When we speak of *price* we think of the cost we have to pay or we think of sacrifice, renouncement, self-denial, or of taking up the cross. We are mistaken if we begin from this viewpoint, as if the core of holiness has to do with us. This could explain our natural unconscious rejection of holiness.

When we truly speak of holiness, we speak of renouncing, of crucifying, of dying. This is true and it is painful. But the pain is a profitable exchange. We renounce even that which is good, to obtain that which is better. To renounce is not always to lose; it is to yield to God all things—even the most beloved—so that he will return them beautified and enriched with the touch of his approval. It is an exchange. Paul expresses it with these words:

> I am crucified with Christ: nevertheless I live; yet not I, but Christ liveth in me: and the life which I now live in the flesh I live by the faith of the Son of God, who loved me, and gave himself for me (Galatians 2:20, KJV).

We look at the marks of the Cross. Paul spoke of the marks of Christ in his life. This is the difference between religion and holiness.

Holiness reflects itself in the suffering of humble pastors in poor villages of the Third World, but it also should reflect itself among computers and high-tech equipment. The price of holiness is the renouncement of all so God can beautify everything that touches our lives.

Holiness is the presence of God in our lives. Not only do you have to desire it, you have to claim it. Moses was boldly clear; "If thy presence go not with me, carry us not up hence" (Exodus 33:15, KJV). And God heard him. Jacob wrestled with the angel of the Lord. He knew his precise need and said, "I will not let thee go, except thou bless me" (Genesis 32:26, KJV). And God responded: "For as a prince hast thou power with God and with men, and hast prevailed" (v. 28, KJV). This is holiness—to claim the presence of God. This is our struggle with God. This is the cost; we must say, "If thou go not with me, I go nowhere; and if thou dost not bless, I will not let thee go." If we cannot say this, we will know a great deal of the theory of holiness but very little of the reality.

The true price of holiness is what it is worth, what it signifies, what it represents, and what it produces in our lives in relation to the model which is Jesus Christ. The cost of holiness is insignificant, overwhelmingly insignificant compared to the price we pay for it and what we receive. Holiness is attractive, optimistic, contagious, and exuberant.

The Urgency of Holiness

Everyone demands urgency for their priorities. There is an urgency to evangelize. There is an urgency to pray. There is an urgency for missionaries. There is an urgency for the return of Jesus Christ. But all these urgencies are under the urgency of holy lives.

When we look at the model of holiness, which is Christ in us, we discover the true price of holiness. As we examine our motives, our ethics, our finances, our relation toward others, and the secret world of the heart that only God knows, then we perceive not only the importance of, but also the urgency for, men and women who are holy before God and have the approval of men.

Yet, I ask myself some questions:

We have many specialists that are a great help to the church, but where are the special men who look like Christ?

Every day there are more and more doctorates in our modern churches and the fashion continues to be in obtaining the greatest amount of credits to gain the greatest amount of approval, but where are the saints who look like Christ?

Our colleges and seminaries are being directed by excellent and experienced professionals, but where are the prophets of God who can say with the overwhelming authority of a saint: "Thus saith the Lord," and at the same time have a resemblance to Jesus?

A holy life, a holy church will evangelize, pray, and open new mission fields with greater efficiency and better results than any other priority out of the context of a holy life. Holiness is not a magic touch or an instantaneous prescription, but it involves an instantaneous decision and a process that embraces the whole life. Lausanne I produced one of the best statements of faith in history. Lausanne II should produce the best people of faith in history. Men of God, holy men; women of God, holy women—that is our greatest need and our greatest goal.

Christian Community and World Evangelization

Roberta Hestenes

"My command is this: Love each other as I have loved you" (John 15:12).

Be kind to one another, tenderhearted, forgiving one another, as God in Christ forgave you (Ephesians 4:32, RSV).

We put no stumbling block in anyone's path, so that our ministry will not be discredited. Rather, as servants of God we commend ourselves in every way: in great endurance; in troubles, hardships and distresses; in beatings, imprisonments and riots; in hard work, sleepless nights and hunger; in purity, understanding, patience and kindness; in the Holy Spirit and in sincere love; in truthful speech and in the power of God; with weapons of righteousness in the right hand and in the left (2 Corinthians 6:3–7, NIV).

So much of our thought and energy is devoted to the visions, methodologies, and strategies for worldwide evangelization that we need the help which Scripture provides to sort our priorities. To what will we give our major attention? Of all the things which should or could be done, which ones will capture our energy and our commitment?

We are finite human beings with limited time and energy. While we can accomplish great things by the grace and power of God, no one of us can do everything which needs to be done. We are not the saviors of the world; we are ambassadors for Christ who alone is the Savior. We must make choices. The need of the world does not determine our particular and specific callings. Only through prayer, worship, and attentive study of Scripture can we determine what God is calling us to and what our priorities should be.

Priorities not only relate to which work we do but also to the ways in which we accomplish our work. Jesus and the apostles in the New Testament said little about specific methodologies and strategies; however, they said a great deal about the character and relationships of those who are sent by God into the world to proclaim the gospel and make disciples.

Large sections of the Epistles are devoted to the themes of Christian character and Christian community. A foundational assumption of biblical Christianity is the membership of each Christian believer in the body of Christ—the church. The Great Commission is given to the church, the whole community of believers. The empower-

Roberta Hestenes is President of Eastern College in Pennsylvania, United States. An ordained minister, and former Associate Professor at Fuller Theological Seminary, she is a citizen of the United States.

ment of the Holy Spirit is poured out on the gathered community, not simply on isolated individuals (Matthew 28:18–20; Acts 1:1–4; 2:1–4; 1 Corinthians 12; Galatians 6:10).

Just as the first disciples discovered when they responded to the invitation to follow Jesus, contemporary Christians discover that Christ's call to faith and obedience is also a call to community. Just as the Twelve did not choose each other, so we find ourselves alongside those of different backgrounds and nationalities, preferences, and temperaments in this marvelous, complex, perplexing, exciting, and disturbing set of relationships which is called the church. Our unity and life together in the church is to be a witness to the world of Jesus as the beloved Son of the Father who gave his life for the redemption of the world. Our unity is centered in our common confession of Jesus Christ as Savior and Lord, and is demonstrated by the love which we express to one another.

The New Testament is full of instructions and examples of how Christians are to relate to one another. The quality of our life together should be a powerful demonstration of the reality and power of God to transform every form of isolation, sin, and brokenness. The Good News we preach is made credible by our acts of love and service within the church as well as outside the church. Every one of the numerous biblical texts on unity and relationships within the Christian community can be seen as an explication of Jesus' "new" commandment that Christians are to love one another as Christ loves them.

This is not merely a sentimental regard for each other. This love which Christ commands is more than a tolerant forbearance of different traditions, denominations, or agencies. It is not a capitulation to relativism which is to characterize every Christian person and group of persons. It is an intentional commitment to costly, sacrificial, compassionate, caring, and self-denying service to the Christian community. We are called by Jesus Christ to be committed to each other as we walk together as disciples, ambassadors, and agents of reconciliation in all the world (John 15:9–17; 2 Corinthians 4:5; 5:16–21; 6:3–10).

A Barrier to Worldwide Evangelization

One of the great barriers to effectiveness in worldwide evangelization is the way Christians treat each other. All too often what the world says when it sees the church up close is *not,* "See how they love one another," but "See how they attack and hurt each other." In spite of the prayer of Jesus for complete unity among his followers, it is shocking to see alongside wonderful manifestations and expressions of spiritual unity an almost casual acceptance of competitive rivalry, disunity, and hostility. This can be seen in all levels of life in the church from the individual to the congregation, to the national and international reality of a divided church. Over the many decades of the missionary movement, literally thousands of missionaries and church workers have given up their posts and returned home in discouragement and despair long before work was done or the mission assignment accomplished. Many reasons are often given including physical disability, spiritual burnout, or circumstances within the family. There are often other reasons, less respectable to mention and more painful to acknowledge, which hinder the ability of many people to sustain their commitment to Christian ministry.

Symptoms of Brokenness

One of the most significant discouragements for many young idealistic Christians who move into full-time Christian service is their persistent experience of conflict, rivalry, and uncaring behavior among those who are supposed to work together in love and harmony. They join, hoping for a fellowship of common love and common purpose, but their experience may fall far short of their expectations. Often, their expectations were unrealistic. More often, in all their preparation and training for service, little was said about the basic reality of most ministry assignments.

Ministry is carried out through a group of persons who may not know or understand how to build positive relationships, how to handle conflict, or how to work together in caring ways to accomplish the common ministry. The issue of how to develop and maintain community and unity among Christians is crucial to sustained and effective service.

There are other problems which can contribute to a lack of a spirit of unity and caring in a particular group of Christians. Sometimes cohesion and commitment within one group is sought by joining in a common attack on some other group of Christians outside the circle of acceptance. Joining together as "insiders" against "outsiders" does build a sense of group loyalty. When Christians do this, however, our witness to the watching world is damaged.

Another issue is envy or jealousy. These feelings are seldom acknowledged or addressed as temptations and problems even though they are almost always present in any large group with levels of leadership.

At times, problems may center on leaders; at other times, on issues of loyalty and trust among participants. Strong leaders of Christian organizations are occasionally seen as those who have great visions, yet may be prone to use people to accomplish those visions without adequately caring for them. One common temptation is to judge other people's motives and ministries as inadequate or misguided while hoping we will be judged more positively ourselves.

Another sign of a lack of compassion may come when people sin and fall. Instead of the gentleness leading toward restoration spoken of in Galatians 6:1, some organizations may solve a problem by discarding or setting aside even the repentant wounded or fallen worker. This is in contrast to Jesus who tenderly restored Peter after his bitter failure with his threefold denial (John 21:15–19). The terrible joke is too often repeated, and believed, that "the Christian church is the only army that shoots its wounded."

We seem to struggle between two extremes: one, of denying the importance of purity, holiness, and appropriate accountability and discipline within the Christian community; and the other, of harsh judgment and a critical spirit which can damage the faith and hope of those who fail to measure up or meet expectations. In all the complexities of our relationships, when we work together as Christians, our ministry priorities can become distorted if the drive for success in our programs crowds out the biblical requirement of active love.

During my twelve years as a professor of Christian formation and discipleship at an evangelical seminary, I worked with young students and older career Christian workers from over eighty countries and at least as many different denominations, mission organizations, and theological traditions. I have often heard thrilling stories of the power of God in transforming people, bringing new life and spiritual vitality into some of the most difficult situations imaginable. And all too often, I have also heard heartbreaking stories of painful, broken relationships which led to divisions and strife, suffering and sorrow. Many times this resulted in separation among Christians and difficulties in ministry.

Biblical faith takes seriously the pervasive effects of sin and spiritual warfare. And though a loving and sovereign God can bring good out of every evil, much of this suffering is an additional burden which should not be accepted as inevitable or impossible to change.

Our Need for Love and Community

Too many Christians are suffering from a lack of love which leaves them feeling isolated and lonely, uncared for and discouraged. They feel used instead of loved, criticized rather than affirmed. This can affect our marriages and families, as well as our daily work in the tasks of worldwide evangelization. This is not a lack in God's love, which overflows constantly towards us, but a lack of love in the Christian community. When we have a great task to accomplish, we sometimes forget that the people who are called to accomplish that extraordinary task are ordinary people who need to receive and give love.

The triune God, who lives eternally in relationship, created us for relationships. We were made for fellowship with God and with each other. We truly need each other to be fully human, fully Christian, and fully effective. We need each other for comfort in times of suffering. We need each other to rejoice when we rejoice and weep when we weep. No matter how strong we are, we need to bear one another's burdens and receive help with our own burdens. We need each other's gifts. We need to hear truth spoken in love. We need relationships which help us and nourish us as we seek to give ourselves to others. We need people to whom we can confess our sins, with whom we can pray for healing and wholeness. We need conversations which build us up and affirm our gifts and abilities (Genesis 1–2; Romans 3:9–20; 2 Corinthians 1:3–7; Ephesians 4:14–16; James 5:13–16).

Along with our planning and programs, we need spiritual direction and discernment of the will of God. We need strength and support for the spiritual battle. These needs can never be adequately met in impersonal, task-oriented structures. They can only be met in significant relationships which encourage and empower us for service.

The great model of this is the committed relationships of Jesus and the Twelve. We see this pattern continued in Acts 2:42–47, where large meetings of new Christians were interspersed with the smaller groups of home fellowships, or house churches, which became the primary form of gatherings for the early centuries of the Christian movement. It was in a small group of Christians described in Acts 13 that the missionary movement was born. It was to these relatively small fellowships of Christians that most of the New Testament letters were written with their instructions for appropriate conduct in their relationships with one another.

Down through the centuries, we have continually rediscovered that meaningful relationships of integrity and caring are nourished in communities who take seriously the command of Jesus to practice love within the fellowship while doing the work to which we have been called.

Temptations That Hinder Growth in a Caring Community

A possible cause of an uncaring community is an unrecognized yet common acceptance of the secularized Western values of competitive individualism and success. Instead, we need a practical involvement in the biblical visions of a covenant community of caring and outreach. The Western, and particularly the North American world, tends to focus on pragmatic goals and innovative entrepreneurship as a preferred style of organization-building and success.

There are significant strengths in some aspects of these values but there are dangerous weaknesses as well. There is a danger that we will conceive our work in terms of competition with other Christian groups rather than in terms of our faithfulness and courage in doing the work that God has given us to do.

A second contributor is the assumption that the best leader is the "task-oriented" leader. This type of leader can fall into the trap of being so consumed with work that there is little time for nurturing relationships either with God or with other people. One young missionary leader shared his astonishing discovery after becoming ill and unable to work, that he had always believed that the Westminster Catechism taught: "What is the chief end of man? The chief end of man is to glorify God and *work for him* forever!"

We will never be the kind of leaders who truly bring glory to God unless we develop and nurture a deep relationship with God and deep relationships with other Christians. Relationships take time; they take attention; they take intentional effort. Jesus led the disciples by modeling a life of prayer, a life of service, and a life lived in community. We are called to no less.

A third contributor to the lack of caring community is the common dichotomy in the Protestant missionary movement separating the congregation from the larger church with an accompanying split between responsibility for discipleship and missions. Congregations are sometimes presumed to own the responsibility of spiritual growth and care for personal needs, while Christian organizations and institutions are to accomplish tasks in the larger world. This assumption can contribute both to weak churches with an inadequate involvement in ministry, and larger organizations who feel little or no responsibility for the spiritual development, nurture, and care of their people.

Congregations support ministry while denominational and mission agencies accomplish the work. Pastoral care and its related ministries are usually seen as the responsibility of the congregation, while evangelism, church growth, education, relief, and development ministries are seen as the primary responsibility of separate organizations. Workers are supposed to arrive at their positions fully developed spiritually with all the resources necessary to sustain themselves through the years of service with minimal time and effort from the ministry organization.

This runs contrary to the increasing reality that some of those who offer themselves for service are long on enthusiasm and willingness, and short on adequate biblical and theological foundations, spiritual depth, and discipline necessary to sustain quality ministry. And many of the Protestant mission-oriented groups fail to make adequate provision for the spiritual and emotional nurturing of their people. The assumption that congregations in expatriate contexts provide depth, understanding, and personal care for employees of Christian organizations is often unrealistic. Generalized exhortations do not substitute for the personalized attention which matters of the spiritual life and Christian service require.

Annual retreats or weekly chapels in our offices, although worthwhile, simply do not provide the quality of love and care which is needed to sustain ministry day after day, year after year. We need to be able to pray together and talk with each other, not only about our work, but also about our lives. The provision of spiritual directors and the encouragement of Christian small groups are only two of the possibilities which could be used to enrich the life of ministry communities.

Two questions which every Christian leader should ask regularly are: *What are we doing to help nourish and express Christian faith and love for each other?* and, *What am I doing to encourage and practice spiritual accountability and growth in my own life and the lives of those around me?*

A fourth factor which may inhibit development of a caring community is an organizational culture which inhibits expressions of struggle, suffering, brokenness, confession, and repentance. This occurs through failure to provide an environment that facilitates careful listening, gentleness, tenderness, forgiveness, and a constant goal of encouragement and restoration. Sometimes we miss the biblical teaching that the need for firmness in conviction is to be accompanied by patience and tenderness. Strength may be expressed in honest openness and vulnerability as well as in other ways. Paul often shared his struggles and burdens as he sought to care for the young churches. Jesus was the great author and perfecter of our faith, yet he was not afraid to show his need or to weep at the grave of a friend.

Biblical Requirements for Building Christian Community

Ephesians 4:32 gives three instructions to Christians: be kind; be tenderhearted; and be forgiving as God in Christ has forgiven you. These instructions are so simple they are often overlooked in the larger, more grand challenges. Yet, they reveal God's will for our priorities as people working in the tasks of ministry.

We are to be kind. The dictionaries define *kindness* as "well-meaning, helpful, charitable, sympathetic, pleasant towards other people." This is the opposite of acting or speaking in rough, brutal, or harsh ways. We are to treat people in such a way that we build them up, not tear them down; that we affirm, rather than attack; that we hope for the best, rather than assume the worst; that we rejoice in the good and keep no list of evil.

This does not mean that we will never disagree with people or need to find ways to handle significant differences. Conflict and disagreements have always been present in the church from the first century until today. Yet in the midst of differences, we are to treat each other with kindness. Without gentleness and kindness toward others, we become unable to acknowledge our own limitations, weakness, and vulnerability and then we may fall ourselves. When we draw up our lists of qualities of leadership, kindness is seldom mentioned, yet it is to shape our behavior toward each other.

The second part of the instruction is that we are to be tenderhearted. The obvious opposite is to be hardhearted, cold, or indifferent. Tenderheartedness is defined as being "humane, sensitive, compassionate, open to the needs and desires of the other person." To be kindhearted does not mean that we are "soft-headed" or thoughtless in our actions. We are to be warmly affectionate to one another rather than manipulative, calculating, cautious, or withholding of warmth and concern.

Without tenderness, our fellowships can become dishonest because of fear. We may hide our weeping if we think people will criticize, ignore, or be made anxious by our tears. Expressions of honest perplexity or struggle can be disdained as signs of weakness or incompetence. It sometimes seems as if no new questions are to be allowed, even though the world around is rapidly changing. When tough realities force new questions or doubts, a harsh community which insists on only repeating the same formulaic answers can crush a struggling spirit.

To confess our sins or to acknowledge our weakness does not automatically disqualify us from all future leadership. The lives of David and Peter illustrate the awfulness of sin and the restoring mercy of God. Paul often shared his struggles. When allowed to guide our behavior, tenderheartedness and kindness encourage unity and reduce conflict.

The third part of the instruction is that we are to forgive each other as God in Christ has forgiven us. Forgiveness is necessary in our relationships because we do hurt each other and we need to confess our sins in the appropriate way. To practice forgiveness is not a compromise with sin; it is a biblical requirement. True forgiveness is not an easy toleration of evil but acknowledges that there has been a wrong committed or a right left undone which must be dealt with.

We are to seek purity, holiness, and righteousness, but we must also acknowledge the reality of sin and failure as we are continual receivers of the grace and mercy of God.

As God has forgiven us in Christ, so we are to forgive one another. This is not an easy discipline, yet it is a critical one.

A lack of forgiveness in the life of a fellowship can leave an organization vulnerable to deceit and pretense because the truth will not be handled sensitively and will be forced into hiding. Forgiveness opens the door to restoration and renewed service. It proclaims our belief in our own identity as forgiven people who have wonderful news to share with the world about the love of God in Christ.

As we come to the Communion table of our Lord in the midst of a broken world, we find the center of our unity and a rebuke to all forms of our conflict. It is a powerful reminder of the Upper Room where Jesus commanded us to love and prayed that we might live in unity. We are reminded of the great price paid for our redemption so that we could be adopted into the family of God. However great our sin, greater is the mercy and forgiveness of God. As we have freely received the kindness, tenderheartedness, and forgiveness of God in Christ Jesus, so may our communities of worship and service be true fellowships of love. The world will then truly see and receive our witness because they see how we love each other.

The Church in Challenging Situations

Lucien Accad

We want to remind you, brothers and sisters, of the trouble we had in Beirut, Lebanon. The burdens laid upon us were so great and so heavy that we gave up all hope of staying alive. We felt that the death sentence had been passed on us. But this happened so that we should rely, not on ourselves, but only on God, who raises the dead. From such terrible dangers of death he saved us, and will save us; and we have placed our hope in him that he will save us again, as you help us by means of your prayers for us (2 Corinthians 1:8–10, TEV—author's paraphrase).

Saturday, 5 February 1983, 2:00 P.M. A terrible explosion shook us as we were eating our lunch. I ran out of the house to see what had happened. People were going in the direction of the street where the Bible Society shops and offices are located. A car loaded with 240 kilograms of dynamite had exploded right in front of the Bible Society building. A few minutes later ambulances rushed to the building and rescue teams helped the wounded. Many were taken to the hospital.

The screams of women and children were heartbreaking. A mother and father were trying to find their eight-year-old son. The small bicycle he was riding at the time of the explosion was there, all twisted and torn, covered with rubble and blood. The little boy was never found. Fire and smoke erupted and teams of young people from several churches in the neighborhood arrived to help us save as many precious books as possible from the fire and from the water used to extinguish the fire. At the end of that terrible day, nineteen people were dead and 136 were wounded.

We knew we were not the target of this tragedy; above our shop was a research center for the Palestinians and opposite us a Libyan office. We were thankful to the Lord because no one on our staff was injured—the office had closed twenty minutes before the explosion.

It was not the first time, or the last that some of us would go through a similar experience. A few months later, the house of George, a member of the Bible Society staff, was destroyed in a similar explosion. His younger sister was killed as the balcony she was standing on collapsed. Today this young man is married and their first child was named after that sister. They repaired their home with the help of their many Christian friends. This experience of solidarity touched the rest of every member of George's family who had not previously expressed any interest in spiritual matters.

What should be our reaction in such a situation? Since the mid-1970s when civil

---

Lucien F. Accad is General Secretary of the Bible Society in Lebanon and a citizen of that country.

war broke out in Lebanon, life and work inside the country have been extremely difficult. Many have left the country, including pastors and church leaders. They felt it was no longer possible to live in a situation where the future of their lives and that of their families was threatened. Foreign missions decided to close down and evacuate their members. The last group of Baptist missionaries from the United States left in 1987 because of the new policy of their government and the feelings of their constituencies back home. All these people left the country at a critical time, seemingly abandoning us to our fate, and at the same time fulfilling the wishes of extremists who were kidnapping foreigners. Those who remained asked themselves: "Should we stay on? Should we leave? How can we have any future for ourselves and our families? Is it fair for our children to be raised in such an atmosphere?"

Others, for different reasons, can't leave Lebanon and feel very frustrated. They have been displaced from their hometowns or villages during fighting. Many have lost everything they owned. Those who have also lost loved ones are in despair. If they don't have relatives abroad who can assist them with money or tickets to leave Lebanon, they feel completely abandoned.

My personal experience has been to depend entirely upon the Lord for guidance, knowing that if he wants me in Lebanon, he can also protect me. This has been the conviction of many others, and we have encouraged each other in this decision which we made at the beginning of the war. What were the results of such a decision on our lives?

We went through many hardships, losing houses, furniture, and other personal belongings, and sometimes losing loved ones as well. At the same time, our miraculous escapes from death are a real and continuous story of divine protection for which all glory should be attributed to God.

One of the great dangers is kidnapping. The international media speak about it often because of the many westerners kept as hostages, some of them for years. But Lebanese people face the same danger. Thousands have been kidnapped. Many of us went through miraculous interventions from God who kept us or delivered us from this traumatic experience.

I was living in West Beirut, but had to cross to the other side every day because our offices are located on the East side. One afternoon, as I was preparing to go home someone told me, "Be careful, there is a group of young men who are kidnapping people trying to cross from our side."

I said, "Well, what can I do? This is the only crossing point and I'm doing this every day. We'll see what happens." When I reached the crossing point, the last Lebanese army check point, they told me, "Stop, you can't cross now." "What's going on?" I asked. "There is a sniper; someone was injured while trying to cross to the other side."

"Should I turn back? When are you going to reopen the passage?" "No, wait a little bit," they answered. "This will not take very long." After fifteen minutes they said to me, "Now you can go."

"How do you know it's safe?" I asked.

The guard shrugged and said, "Well, someone has to try."

You really get a terrible feeling when you are caught in such a situation. That is when you need special encouragement from the Lord.

But that was not the end of my experience that day. I started my car and drove toward West Beirut. There they were, these young men, a few hundred meters from the army checkpoint. They stopped me and asked me to pull over to the side of the road. I didn't like that very much because that is sometimes the first step towards disappearing completely. I drove ahead two meters, a little bit to the right, and stopped again. A young militiaman came over to the car and said, "Show me your papers. Who are you?"

I thought to myself, *What should I show them? They seem to be the young fanatic Muslims that I have been warned about. If I show my usual identity card, they may not like it that I'm a Christian coming from a Christian area. I have another card which indicates that I am an evangelical pastor. Which one is the best?* I thought, *If I have to be kidnapped let it be as a pastor on duty!* So I showed my card as a Christian worker. The young man had problems reading it. He probably had not received much education, yet, he was a fifteen-year-old boy with a machine gun! He said, "What is the meaning of *pastor?* Does this mean that you are a man of religion? Sorry, sir, we don't want you to have any inconvenience or problem. What are you doing?" I explained that we print Bibles. Then he asked, "Can we have some copies? We need the Bible here because we have only received some calendars with Scripture verses that you distribute at the beginning of the year. We have been waiting for a long time to find a copy of the whole Bible. Can we get one?"

What an experience! When I left the young men, I was shaking from tension and fear. But I was glad to discover that the Lord has a message for all and that in all situations he wants to have witnesses of his love.

Both experiences of suffering and deliverance have been beneficial, bringing us closer to the Lord. They also demonstrate to the non-Christian that evil and good are realities even in the lives of believers, but that our Lord is alive and intervening directly in the affairs of his children today.

How can witness and evangelism take place without the presence of people who live out their Christianity? I think that God wants some of us to be present, to live in this situation with the rest of the people of the country, sharing the daily experiences of people at all times.

Another incident took place in 1985. It was past midnight and two of our children woke us up saying, "Don't you hear the heavy bombardments? We can't sleep. Can we come to your bed? If we have to die, let's die together." The shelling was very hard. We decided to pray together, then after some singing the children quieted down and slept. I was not able to sleep so I got up and started to think about the many times the Lord had protected us. But this time I wondered if it was not wiser to go to the nearby shelter. I went out on the balcony of our house and looked in the direction of the shelter, not very far from us. The shelling had hit a car in front of the shelter, and the car was burning. Close to the place where our own car was parked, other cars were burning and the heavy black smoke was going in the direction of the shelter where people were caught. From the floors above the shelter people were trying to help by throwing buckets of waters on the burning cars, but it didn't help much. In my heart I thanked God for his shelter which is stronger than human-built shelters.

While I was still meditating, our non-Christian neighbors from the floors above us knocked at our door. The electricity was off because the shelling had hit wires and poles. I opened our door and asked if there was something I could do for them. "May we come and stay in your home?" they asked. "Your home is a safer place than the shelter because it is also a place of prayer and reading of the Bible."

The war situation has opened many hearts to the gospel. In spite of fanaticism which stirs up many incidents there is a real receptivity to the message of the Good News. The pressure of the events and the suffering force many to ask questions they have never asked before. When they don't find answers in human resources, they try to see if answers can be found somewhere else.

Our family has just lived through one of the worst periods of this war. Bombing and shelling around our home and office make it very unnerving. The past month has been very difficult as we could not sleep very well. For the first time we have decided to stay in the basement of our new home during the bombardments. One of our friends with whom we spent last Christmas died in his home recently because of shrapnel. Heavy artillery is used between armies and militias fighting in the middle of neighborhoods of innocent civilians who are paying a very heavy price in lives and properties. We have already lost some windows but no one has been injured. This is the sixth home in which we have lived since the beginning of the war. We have lost the previous houses so we know that we should not worry about material possessions.

Sunday, 16 April 1989. We have been unable to reach the church to worship. The services have taken place in our homes instead for the past few weeks. The noise of the bombardments gets on our nerves, but we try to use this time to make new friends. Some of our neighbors were unknown to us, after moving to this part of Beirut, but the bombing has brought us together and provided many opportunities to share the gospel. During the evenings in the shelter we also had new opportunities of witnessing to neighbors.

In talking with some of those who left Lebanon, I have discovered that those who left without clear direction from the Lord seem to be feeling more unsettled than those who have stayed. People who were sure of God's will in their remaining in the country and have stayed are content. Along with their families, they have the Lord's peace and his blessings. Those blessings do not always manifest themselves in material possessions. The severe economic chaos into which Lebanon has plunged since 1986 is forcing more people to leave the country. Those of us who have resisted all kinds of pressure before find that it is more difficult to persevere in God's guidance when our income is reduced to 10 percent of our previous income. This is one of the new challenges for Christians in our churches today.

What is our hope for the future in such a country? Will we be allowed to survive as a nation or will we become part of another country? Will we keep our freedom? The main question for the committed Christian should be, what does God want me to do *now?* What should *I* do? The destiny of the entire nation may rest on the decisions of these Christians.

Although during the hardest times of fighting the priority is for survival, Christians need to be present as a witness of God's grace to people living around them. They have to be the "salt of the earth" both to give flavor to life and to prevent the decay of the society in which they live. They have to "stand before God for their country" in prayer and fasting. In the presence of God the course of history can be changed and nations can turn back to the Lord in repentance and new life.

Areas of the world living in war, violence, and other disturbances are on the increase. This is another challenge for the church of Jesus Christ today. Are we to go on the offensive, or will we restrict ourselves to affluent nations where people are hardening their hearts to the gospel? Evangelization there is becoming difficult also in the midst of materialism and indifference.

For Paul the questions of life and death had a clear answer. He wanted to please God, his Master, and do his will. He said to the Philippians:

My deep desire and hope is that I shall never fail in my duty, but that at all times, and especially right now, I shall be full of courage, so that with my whole being I shall bring honor to Christ, whether I live or die. For what is life? To me, it is Christ (Philippians 1:20–21, TEV).

Paul also knew that his presence with the believers was important so he added in verse 24, "for your sake it is much more important that I remain alive."

Christianity and Christian ministry is not mainly a set of activities or a successful program. It is a maturing relationship of the individual with the Lord, based on faith. Out of this relationship comes a sense of community with fellow believers—a feeling of responsibility in helping each other, sharing what we have, and encouraging each other.

A Paradox Regarding the Church

Because our church building was hit twice last week, we are not able to meet in that building for the time being. The damage caused by the explosion of the bombs gives a sense of loss to our community. It is not the first time our members have lost property. Most of us are refugees from other parts of the country. But this physical rallying point has been a symbol for us in recent months and in many ways a unifying factor. Several other churches have gone through the same experience. Yet, the struggle reminds us that the real church is its people, the community of believers. In fact, the services are often held in the shelters during the bombardments.

It is easy to get lost in the day-to-day struggle of politics and survival and to be swayed by the ups and downs of public moods. We get caught up in trying to "solve the country's problems." To a certain extent we should become involved, but we should not put our trust in certain leaders, plans, or power. Our only real trust is in our Lord, who can change the hearts of people and start a new community. With his help we can rise above the situation and lead people to Christ.

It is also easy to get attached to material things—home, money, furniture, cars. We are learning that relationships with people are more important than things. We need to put into practice our theories to *love people more than things*. This should apply to people who are causing us harm as well as those who are close to us.

At times I feel I'm carrying a burden too heavy to bear for a man. I'm living in a country torn apart by a war that has claimed tens of thousands of victims throughout the last fourteen years. With my own eyes I've seen the devastation, and at times I've "touched evil" as people attack others made of the same flesh and blood and created in the likeness of God.

My home is in a country which, strategically speaking, hundreds of people like you and me have considered "ripe" for reaching out to all parts of the Middle East. In Lebanon, about one hundred missionary agencies issued papers, did research, printed books, and told everybody how to evangelize, yet, did very little in practice. In Lebanon, all the different religious communities were living side-by-side without too many obvious tensions. More than ten different Christian communities exist in Lebanon—of which six are Catholic. The others are Orthodox groups, and the Protestants (evangelicals) are only a very small minority (around 1.6 percent of the population). While we were researching and writing our papers most of our communities were left without the proper leaders, and we are reaping what we've sown. We certainly never carried out Jesus' call to present the gospel to all Lebanese.

The cause for such a variety of communities in Lebanon is the geography of the country. Formed of three main mountain ridges, it has been a safe place in the Middle East for persecuted groups. Christians that suffered persecutions through several centuries, found refuge in those hills. Later the country developed politically into the only democratic state of the region. Christian communities and churches lived side-by-side with Muslim communities, exchanging cultures and resources. Christian communities have always had an element of *entente,* and this coexistence was unique in the

Middle East. In this context, new channels of collaboration have also started to develop in recent years between the different Christian groups.

Evangelical church members represent a small minority that is being decimated year by year. We often lose members as our leaders are offered lucrative positions in the West, while the local churches cannot produce good leadership at the pace needed. Today there are more Armenian and Arab pastors in America than in Lebanon, and those who are still here are also being lured to leave their flocks for security.

We need committed Christians willing to stay in Lebanon and other troubled areas of the world to share the gospel. At times we watch the news and are relieved that the violence and suffering in the world is far away from our own quiet little corner. We need to react adamantly when we hear of twenty-six hundred Chinese slaughtered as the madness of militarism takes its toll. We must respond with compassion when thousands of people in Sudan die from starvation or a quarter of a million people lose their homes. If we get together and enjoy the luxury of a holiday in Manila and then decide that our budget can't pay for Scriptures or any other evangelistic effort in Sudan or China, then we need to get back to the Cross of Jesus—with the compassion of Jesus.

The Church That Loves

Brother Andrew

"We are ragged and we are poor, but we will conquer the world, we will change the world."

Eight abreast they marched, faces beautiful, because they were dedicated to a cause, a cause they believed in, and were therefore willing to die for.

Warsaw, 1955. I stood there all alone and watched the "evangelists" of the twentieth century, the vanguard of the unstoppable revolution. Proudly holding their red banners, the young communist pioneers marched through the center of Warsaw. In astonishment and confusion I clutched my little Bible and pressed it to my heart. What could I say? What could I do?

Casually I turned over the pages and then God spoke. In an almost audible voice he said: "Every knee shall bow . . . and every tongue shall confess that Jesus Christ is Lord" (Philippians 2:10–11, TLB).

Again I looked at the seemingly endless stream of young people. They were still marching, still chanting; but now a deep love and compassion filled my heart. They were not a threat, they were an opportunity!

That same week I visited a local church, where they allowed me to say a few words. At the end of my little talk the pastor said something I'll never forget as long as I live: "Andrew, I want to thank you for being here, it means more to us than ten of the best sermons."

Later when I was alone, as I thought about the words of this pastor, God spoke again—this time from Revelation 3:2 (RSV): "Awake, and strengthen what remains and is on the point of death." These two basic truths from the Bible have become the foundation of innumerable last-days ministries into the restricted-access world.

First, the ultimate goal: Every knee will bow and every tongue will confess Jesus Christ as Lord. Second, the ultimate care: Awake! A remnant of my children will die, unless *you* strengthen them.

The miracles that followed in the years since my first encounter with the Marxist revolution proved that God's calling was not my own invention. The fact that today more and more attention is given to missions into the restricted-access world makes me happy and thankful. But now we have to analyze our behavior and of that of our opponents in order to be more effective than in the past.

Brother Andrew is Founder/President of Open Doors International and is a citizen of the Netherlands.

How did the Marxist ideology so easily get a grip on masses of young people? They offered a program for the here and now and for the future. And the church failed to offer such a challenging program. Instead, the church compromised with the ruling powers of their time and did not set the example of the love of Jesus Christ for a lost world.

If Christians had remained real disciples of Jesus Christ and had never accepted compromise within the body, semi-religions like atheism would not have arisen. There might have been only a straightforward persecution of Christians as in the days of Nero.

In those early days of the church, persecution was limited to smaller areas, cities, or provinces. Later, the persecution became more organized when the established church persecuted spiritual movements within the church—often coinciding with the persecution of Jews. But since the atheistic revolution, the fundamental pattern of persecution has changed from a local threat to a global ideology with the shameless claim: There is no God!

And, as if inspired by the revolutionary movements of this age, the Islamic giant woke up and began its own revolution with the even more penetrating question: Who is God?

Muslims estimate their number around 1.1 billion. But the people living under Islamic governments, and thus living in restricted-access countries, number a little more than 20 percent of the world population.

The communist dominated area is much larger. By forcing whole nations to become atheistic, the communist revolution grew by territory but not by ideology. Today a third of the entire world is governed by communist regimes.

During the last decade, however, communism has lost millions of supporters in many countries—certainly in Poland, Hungary, the Soviet Union, and in China. But not only there; in which country are the masses still voluntarily and wholeheartedly chanting communist phrases and waving red banners?

In most countries where communism is settled, the church now attracts millions. In the midst of persecution people flock to the remaining churches or meet in the open. In Romania, one of the most oppressed countries in Eastern Europe, we find the largest evangelical gatherings in Europe.

We welcome such political changes especially when they are positive for the church. Our praises belong to the Father who answers prayers. The changes that are taking place prove that the Marxist revolution is reversible—but only by the prayers of God's people and by *obeying* the call to go into the *whole* world with the *whole* gospel and to strengthen what remains, regardless of the man-made barriers and restrictions.

But the opposite is also possible: recent events in China have shown that democratic developments are equally reversible. I have no guarantee that the same cannot happen to *perestroika*.

In spite of all the changes, laws are not adjusted properly to protect individual Christians and churches that take the Great Commission seriously. The ultimate goal has *not* been reached, either in the Soviet Union or in the other communist countries, like Albania, Mongolia, and North Korea. I believe that God is eager to penetrate these three hostile fortresses of the Enemy. He awaits servants who are indeed willing to give their lives for this cause.

More is happening in the world than a simple change from one political system to another or changing attitudes of worldly rulers. More is happening than communism, even more than the larger Muslim threat. A spiritual reality lies behind all this. A war is raging. The only people on this earth that are aware of this war are God's praying servants. Although they may seem insignificant they are the only force that will overcome "by the blood of the Lamb, and by the word of their testimony; and they loved not their lives unto the death" (Revelation 12:11, KJV).

There is a tremendous need for scientific research and faithful reporting in order to mobilize God's army for prayer. Who would have thought that while at the beginning of this century some 30 percent of Iraq was Christian, today there is a scant 3 percent? In the whole country there is not a single national evangelical pastor! At the beginning of this century Syria was 40 percent Christian. And now, what is left of them? And what about Iran or Afghanistan?

History repeats itself. Recently a pastor in Beirut said to me, "Andrew, your being here means more than all the preaching you can do—because everybody runs away and *you* come!"

I have heard that before—in Warsaw, in Moscow, in Kampala. But, are we learning the lessons of history? Are we ready this time?

There is one hopeful sign that did not exist the first time when I heard the words, "the enemy image." Held for many years and finally falling away is the preconception that all Russians are communists and all Arabs are terrorists. Instead of viewing them as threatening, we begin to see them as people for whom Jesus died. This development is absolutely unparalleled in history, both ancient and modern. We now see that loving our enemies changes them into friends, and that we can win them for Christ. We can now listen to their hearts as they open up.

I recently met the spiritual head of the most fanatical Muslim sect, the Hezbollah, in his headquarters in Beirut. He said, "Andrew, if only the Christians would live according to their Book, and the Muslims would live according to their Book, we would not have all these problems."

The cry I hear in all this is, "Can we go back to our roots—to our source?" We must return to him who said, "Fear not—I am always with you. Go into all the world—I am the Way, the Truth, the Life!"

All of our statements and actions have to be based on the infallible Word of God and are, therefore, prophetic. "Every knee shall bow and every tongue confess that Jesus Christ is Lord" is a prophecy and will be fulfilled—even in the Muslim world.

Then, we will anticipate change because God's people pray, and because they will be ready to move in with all the help that is needed: personnel, Bibles, literature, and Christian education.

By doing that we will help stop the current retreat of the church in the Middle East. By "being there" we bring them the encouragement they need to accept the challenge and to endure suffering. Because "all that will live godly in Christ Jesus shall suffer persecution" (2 Timothy 3:12, KJV).

We can enter the battle prepared, because we know the spiritual warfare behind all cruelties, bloodshed, and persecution. We know and will not be astonished as John was, when he saw for the first time the revelation of the woman, "drunk with the blood of the saints, the blood of those who bore testimony to Jesus" (Revelation 17:6).

"Why are you astonished?" the angel asked John. God asks the same question of us today: "Why are you amazed? Did you not understand that you should expect persecution?" All the anti-God forces in the world will join together in one last desperate war on the Lamb. Remember, the sole object of the persecution has been and will be the life of the Son of God in us.

I firmly believe that the end of the life of the church here on earth will be similar to the end of Jesus' life on earth—on a cross, in seeming defeat. But *that* will be our greatest victory!

Whenever the message of the gospel is preached, it clashes with the religions and philosophies of the time. It inevitably results in persecution, because Jesus said, "If they persecuted me, they will persecute you also" (John 15:20). If we seriously prepare to reach the world by the year 2000, we must go beyond mere slogan shouting.

1. We need to make a concentrated attack on the last remaining bastion of the countries hardly, if ever, penetrated by the gospel. Only 2 percent of the missionary force, including the tentmakers, is concentrating on the Muslim world!
2. There will be a terrific resistance. The opposition is often translated into political pressure on the sending countries, and there definitely will be a greatly accelerated pace of persecution.

Are we ready? That is the big question. In the short time remaining for us to finish the task, we will see persecution on a global scale as we have never seen before.

But this is not the end. They make war on the Lamb, but the Lamb conquers them! Jesus wins, and *we* are with him (Revelation 17:14). That is our joyful message. We have nothing to be afraid of, nothing of which to be ashamed. Everyone who is persecuted can hold his head up high and face the future, knowing that "if God is for me, who shall be against me?" And if we obey God's calling to go into the whole world and to strengthen what remains, he will be with us until his victorious coming.

The final frontier is *not* a physical border or a forbidding cultural, political, or religious "line." It is instead our lack of obedience to him who saved us and our lack of passion for souls! The greatest heresy is a church that does not *love!*

CHALLENGING SETTINGS TESTIMONY I

M. Y. Chan

I was imprisoned in a labor camp. The authorities thought the best way to "reform" me, to torture me, was to appoint me to empty the cesspool of human waste. All the human waste collected from the entire camp stagnated in a cesspool until it was ripe, then it was dug out and sent to the fields to be used as fertilizer.

The cesspool was very large—more than two meters in depth. It was so deep that I could not empty it on the surface of the ground, so I had to walk into the disease-ridden mass to empty it. And all the time, I had to inhale that horrible stench. My captors thought it was the best place for a Christian leader: working in the human waste pit with a shovel in my hands. But I enjoyed working in the cesspool, because I liked the solitude.

In the labor camp, all prisoners were under constant surveillance—none of us could be alone. Only when I worked in the cesspool on Saturdays, could I be alone. Then I could pray to our Lord as loudly as I wanted. I could recite the Scriptures and psalms of the Bible that I still remembered. No one would come close enough to protest!

That's why I loved to work in the human waste cesspools. I could pray loudly and recite Scriptures. I also sang hymns as loudly as I could.

In those years, one of my favorite hymns when I worked in the pit was "In the Garden." And when I sang this hymn in the cesspool, I understood the meaning of *garden* and I knew where God was. I met my Lord in the garden of the cesspool.

CHALLENGING SETTINGS TESTIMONY II

Ali Sougou

Brothers and sisters, I greet you in the name of our Lord Jesus Christ. I come from a Muslim country with three governments. The first government is for the older people of the villages; the second one is the Muslim association which has its members in every village or every town; and the third is the official government. All of these governments are anti-Christian. Before 1973, there were no converted Christians in my country. I was the first to convert to Christianity. I was witnessed to by a missionary who was just passing through in 1970. But it took me two years to decide to become a Christian.

In 1976, on my way back home from Bible school, I was arrested. Sent directly to prison, I was thrown into a very small cell. It was so small that I was unable to even kneel—I had to lean on a wall for three months. They fed me nothing except rice full of salt and just once a day. The first day in that room, when the food was sent to me, I stood like this and tried to put it into my mouth but it was too salty. Then I held it in my hands and prayed, "Lord Jesus Christ, please provide me with nice food." The answer came to eat the very food I had in my hand. So, I obeyed and that food miraculously tasted very delicious. I never slept lying down, because the space was too small. But the Lord was good to me because I felt as if I was sleeping on a double bed.

After three months, I was taken before a special court arranged by Muslim leaders, army people, and elders of the villages. When I appeared in front of the gathering, the head of the Muslims stood and said, "Do you know what you have done? We don't want you to explain yourself, and we don't want you to ask questions. We have three punishments selected for you to choose between." I started trembling a bit. One choice was to be imprisoned forever; the second was to be shot to death; and the third was to be deported from the country. As a family man with eight children and two grandchildren, it was very hard for me to choose. I had nothing to say, but I felt somebody come from behind me, put hands on my shoulders, and pull me down. I went down, closed my eyes and prayed loudly in the language that everybody there understood. I said, "Lord, Jesus Christ, here I am. I need your answer for these people, and I ask this in your precious name. Amen." The whole gathering stood and started shouting, "You people, this man is foolish; let him go away." So, they released me, and that is why I'm here today.

When I was released, I started walking among my people. The first person that I led to Christ was a police inspector. He was the one who was sent to watch me. This man came to know the Lord, after I gave him a New Testament to read.

On Sunday he came to me and said, "Brother, I want to ask you a very, very important question."

I said, "What do you want?"

He said, "I want to know God the Father, God the Son, and God the Holy Spirit. Do you believe in three gods?"

I said, "No just one God." Then I asked him, "Brother, tell me, what is your work?" He said, "I'm a police officer."

"Are you married?"

"Oh, yes, I'm married."

"Have you got children?"

"Oh, yes, I have two children."

I said, "In the morning when you are in your office, do they call you inspector? Does your wife call you husband? And do your children call you Daddy? But, you are only one person. You are a police officer, a husband, and a father."

He then asked me if he could become a Christian. I asked him if he really *wanted* to become a Christian. He said, "Yes." So we went down to our knees and prayed together. Right then and there he received the Lord and now he's working with me.

In my village there are now 107 Muslims who are born-again Christians. I praise the Lord who allowed me to come to this gathering. Please pray for us. God bless you.

CHALLENGING SETTINGS TESTIMONY III

Mikhail Savin

Peace be to you, dear children of God. I'm very glad that today I could greet you with the words of Paul the Apostle. They're recorded in 2 Corinthians 2:14: "But thanks be to God, who always leads us in triumphal procession in Christ and through us spreads everywhere the fragrance of the knowledge of him."

Just a few words about how we are spreading the Good News in our own region. Last year was very special for our country—we celebrated a thousand years of Christianity in Russia. The good Lord has given us opportunities to conduct many evangelistic services in palaces, sports arenas, and open-air assemblies. It was so moving it brought tears to our eyes. A hundred hands were eagerly outstretched to receive one simple gospel track. When people received copies of the New Testament, some of them would press those New Testaments against their hearts as a sign of gratitude towards God. They even kissed copies of the New Testament.

In Krasnodar, where I live, the young people go into the center of the city. Right there in the middle of the street, they put out tables filled with New Testaments and other Christian pamphlets, books, and magazines. They sing and preach about the good Lord and the people listen. Praise the Lord.

One day at such an event, all the literature was handed out. There was only one magazine left and there were so many people who wanted that one magazine that they tore it up page-by-page and parceled it out to everyone. And that magazine was spread among all those who wanted it.

One of the methods our young people use to spread the gospel is to go door-to-door. They go into the streets of the village where they talk to the people, inviting them to come to evangelistic meetings. Very often these services are so enthusiastically attended that they continue on even past midnight. Praise the Lord.

My prayer is, "Lord, please teach us how to pray for those who are lost. Oh, teach us to take the gospel to those who are perishing. Help us to be faithful. The Soviet Union is the largest country in the world. There are approximately 138 different nationalities. Dear God, please open the door even wider so that we can take the gospel to the people of our country. Amen.

The Challenge of the Restricted-Access World

George Otis Jr.

When Marcus Dods was an old man, he said, "I do not envy those who have to fight the battle of Christianity in the twentieth century." Then, after a moment, he added, "Yes, perhaps I do, but it will be a stiff fight."

It is doubtful, however, that Dr. Dods could have known just *how* stiff the battle would be. Who could have predicted, for example, that an elderly Shiite cleric would leave the French hamlet of Neauphle-le-Chateau, in 1979, to launch a worldwide Islamic revolution that would profoundly challenge the strategic interests of both superpowers—not to mention the church of Jesus Christ? At the end of the 1980s, who was prepared for the fact that two-thirds of the world's population would live beyond the reach of conventional missions programs? And who has yet fully realized the implications of such diverse, present-day phenomena as hyperinflation, *perestroika,* or the fact that, since 1975, the Mormon Church has more than tripled in size?

Despite the contention of the great Roman leader Marcus Arelius that, "He who has seen present things has seen all," contemporary history is proving to be extraordinarily fluid. While historical precedent may have provided a useful tool for decision-making in the past, the current flow of human activity and achievement is such that precedent is no longer a reliable methodology. As the British futurist Arthur C. Clarke quipped during the 1960s, "The future just isn't what it used to be."

Crucial Questions

The church today is in the midst of what scientists call a "paradigm shift." The business world refers to it as a "discontinuity." Put simply, we are in a process of transition away from ministry perspectives and tactics that are nearing the limits of their performance capabilities, to emerging ideas and methods with the potential to raise or extend current performance limits. Many of our standard modes of picturing and responding to the task of world evangelization no longer mesh with the current contextual realities of life, therefore, any future success on the evangelistic battlefield will require us to relinquish many of our cherished, but vintage, wineskins.

The issue before us is not one of efficiency, but of effectiveness. The need is not simply for a few minor adjustments in our "evangelistic engine," but for a revolutionary new design.

George Otis Jr. is founder of Issachar Frontier Mission Strategies and is a citizen of the United States.

Three areas in particular need immediate attention: our mission, our market, and our methods.

Is the primary mission of the church today to reinforce the faith of the believer, or to evangelize the unbeliever? Given David Barrett's recent observation that, "Ninety-nine percent of all global Christian resources are consumed by Christians themselves for their own purposes," our *de facto* answer to this question would seem obvious. A few years ago, the "Voice of Calvary's" John Perkins startled his church audiences by declaring, "Let's be honest, we tithe to ourselves." But when existing Christians are the prime beneficiaries even of the church's foreign mission money—86 percent of it to be exact—can anyone argue with his conclusion?

The second area in which radical change needs to occur is our ministry marketplace. Whom, exactly, are we trying to reach with the gospel? Most Christian mission agencies and workers today will respond that their desire and intent is to evangelize unreached peoples, but with few exceptions, their resources are targeted on the Christian world. Out of a global foreign mission force of some 262,000 workers, only 21,000—or 8 percent—of its foreign missionaries and 14 percent of its missions budget reach the nearly 3.5 billion people living outside the Christian world. If the world is to be evangelized anytime soon, a major redeployment of our resources is clearly in order. We must leave the one that is found and go to the ninety-nine that are lost.

Finally, we must look at our current methodologies. Will the deployment of conventional, resident missionaries remain a viable and effective ministry approach in the years ahead? If the majority of the world's unreached people live in nations whose governments prohibit or severely limit traditional Christian missionary presence and/or activity, how will we reach them?

Preparing for the Battle

If we are to successfully evangelize the world in light of these and other important questions, we must first gain a thorough understanding of: (1) the times, (2) the battlefield, and (3) our identity.

To understand the times, the church needs prescient Christians—those who see the future and responsibly prepare to live and minister in it. A quick glance through Scripture reveals many such men and women. Noah, for instance, saw a coming flood and prepared an ark. Rahab perceived the Israeli conquest of Jericho and hid the spies. Joseph predicted an impending famine and instructed Pharaoh to take action. Mary sensed the imminence of her son's public ministry and commanded Cana's servants to obey him. Peter recognized God's desire to release the gospel to the Gentiles and traveled to the home of Cornelius.

In 1 Chronicles 12:32 (KJV), the sons of Issachar are described as being men that "had understanding of the times, to know what Israel ought to do." God, in similar fashion today, is prepared to give his people insight into events and circumstances that have "ripened" (*kairos*), along with the corresponding wisdom to take appropriate action. Vivid present-day examples of *kairos* include the Iranian revolution and resurgent Islam; the new opening of China; and *perestroika* in the Soviet Union.

While the future is largely determined by God, preparation for it is man's responsibility. Seeing the future, in other words, means nothing if no appropriate action is taken today. Conversely, those with no detailed expectations for the future have nothing to drive their present actions and decisions.

In addition to understanding the times, however, we must also become intimately familiar with today's spiritual battlefield. To do this, we must learn to identify two important areas of concern: (1) prevailing strongholds (superintended by powerful demonic powers and principalities), and (2) active or emerging spiritual convergence zones (areas where onrushing deceptive forces attempt to fill spiritual vacuums created by retreating or spent ideologies). Contemporary examples of the latter would include Afghanistan, Cambodia, the People's Republic of China, Mozambique, and the Soviet Union. If understanding the times provides us with insight into what is happening and when, familiarity with the spiritual battlefield gives us answers to the question of *where*.

Last, but not least, successful evangelization in the 1990s and beyond will require that we clearly understand who we are and how we fit into this grand process. In the days of the early church, this issue of identity was first broached when the pagan communities of the eastern Mediterranean referred to local Christians as the "third race." Not fitting the mold of traditional Jews, and plainly not espousing a polytheistic worldview, they were a curious anomaly.

Whether we call it strategic non-assimilation, or something else, Herbert Schlossberg is right in saying in his *Idols for Destruction,* "The repeated New Testament call for separation demands that we refuse to think and act like those around us."

Knowing that the kingdoms of this world are destined to become the kingdom of Christ, and that, as Schlossberg observes, "those who seek their ultimate value in the next world are the only ones able to do much good in this one," we must nevertheless take care that our message remains pro-Christ and not anti- any particular political or economic system. Paul's experience in Ephesus is a good example of this. Although the apostles were brought before a restless mob intent on doing them harm, the town clerk in Acts 19:37 (RSV) declares: "You have brought these men here who are neither sacrilegious nor blasphemers of our goddess." In the two years Paul spent in Ephesus, he took a stand for Christ, not against the existing system. He remained focused, remembering that his task was to win a bride for God's Son.

Essential Elements of Victory

As the church approaches the year 2000, the battle to access and win the hearts of lost peoples will intensify—particularly in areas dominated by rival belief systems. In these frontline mission fields, evangelistic progress will require that our understanding of strategic timing, placement, and calling be followed up with a strong commitment to the other essential elements of victory: collaboration, innovation, and activism.

Collaboration

If the rallying cry of the Lausanne Covenant, "That the whole church might take the whole gospel to the whole world" is to be realized, we must first command a whole church. Regrettably, despite the absence of any scriptural justification for a segmented body, many of us continue to view the subjugation and isolation of certain of our brethren by various man-made barriers and human edicts as simply an unfortunate fact of life. What we do not see, but must begin to perceive, is the fact that these segregative devices contain nothing more than a potential to divide; they are empowered only through our passive acquiescence of their intent.

By referring to the body of Christ alternately as the "persecuted church" and the "free church," we tend to perpetuate a harmful and unbiblical "us/them" mentality. Fortunately, this can be replaced with a healthier "we, together" perspective simply by re-labeling these same references (i.e., the "Forward-Positioned" church and the "Partner-Provider" church) in such a way so as to suggest their unified relationship.

International partnership has much to commend it. A good way to illustrate this is to examine the respective asset and liability sheets of the Forward-Positioned and Partner-Provider units of Christ's church. When this is done, it readily becomes apparent that the strengths of one are the precise remedy for the weaknesses of the other. The Partner-Provider's problems with access, language, culture, and general proximity to the field, for instance, are dealt with through relational linkage with his Forward-Positioned brother. In similar fashion the Forward-Positioned church's lack of adequate manpower, training materials, finances, and political freedoms are needs which can be positively addressed by its Partner-Provider. Partnership, in other words, is the only means by which the whole church will be able to take the gospel to the whole world.

However, contemporary attitudes are working against this as seen in paternalism and exclusivism. Advocates of paternalism tend to view the Forward-Positioned church not as partners to work with, but as victims to be comforted. Given their circumstances, these frontline believers are considered generally incapable of either discerning or implementing a ministry plan for their homelands without external guidance. Unfortunately, some Western-based ministries have found it profitable to perpetuate this notion; and, as a consequence, efforts to dispel it often meet with considerable resistance.

Champions of exclusivism, meanwhile, argue that national churches should be solely responsible for the evangelization of their countrymen. This is energetically touted as God's ordained plan, and "outsiders" are encouraged not to interfere with the process.

This position, however, not only negates the concept of cross-cultural work, but it also serves to isolate believers living in politically restrictive societies from the rest of the body of Christ. It suggests that it is necessary for one part of the body to live and function independent of its other members.

But what if these believers, like Apollos in Acts 18, are fervent in spirit but are teaching only that portion of the gospel they have been exposed to? Where, apart from an integrated relationship with the wider body of Christ, will they encounter the Priscillas and Aquilas who will be able to "explain the way of God more accurately"? What if they do not have, and cannot officially secure, copies of God's Word? Apart from access to the Bible, how can believers in closed societies build their faith so as to withstand severe temptations and persecutions?

Innovation

With many traditional mission programs currently operating under increased governmental scrutiny, and others struggling for measurable results, there is a growing sense among those working in frontier areas that conventional tactics are probably more important for what they have contributed in the past than for what they are going to contribute in the future. The times, in other words, appear ripe for some interesting detours.

Departing from the status quo, however, can be a difficult business. People whose identities are tied to traditional structures and methodologies are often deeply threatened by change. A typical feature of their defense mechanism is to throw up a critical attitude toward almost any new proposal. In response to this, one of the co-founders of artificial intelligence, Massachusetts Institute of Technology professor Marvin Minsky, offers the following warning: "There is always something wrong with a new idea. But you have to be careful of people who say there are no new ideas because they are likely to fool you into never getting any."

History is not prescriptive; and as one astute writer has pointed out, "Neither heroism nor invention emerged from doing things as one did them in the past." If progress is to be achieved in the spiritual or any other arena of life, prevailing assumptions about what is necessary and possible must be periodically challenged. This is not out of a juvenile desire to be deliberately provocative, but rather comes of the understanding that times change, and that many widely held assumptions in the past have proven to be faulty and inaccurate.

In the scientific realm, for instance, men used to hold fast to the belief that the world was flat, and that the sun revolved around the earth. The year before the Wright brothers' successful first flight at Kitty Hawk, astronomer Simon Newcomb proclaimed: "Flight by machines heavier than air is unpractical and insignificant, if not utterly impossible." In 1923, Nobel Prize-winning physicist Dr. Robert Millikan demonstrated a similar pessimism when he prematurely declared: "There is no likelihood that man can ever tap the power of the atom."

On the spiritual plane as well, evangelistic progress has been, and continues to be, hampered by many such negative and false assumptions. Perhaps the biggest of these—that evangelism cannot be conducted in so-called "closed" societies—is in fact no more sound than the prevailing notion in earlier ages that the world was flat.

In truth, many of us stand in need of a fresh revelation from God as to what is possible and what is not. A good starting point might be admitting that we have confused government opposition to Christianity with rejection of the gospel by the resident people groups; and that we have judged these mission fields to not be "white unto harvest" without having first attempted to seriously evangelize there. (Or, in other cases, failing to recognize it may not be the gospel that is being resisted but rather our methods of presenting it!) By acknowledging that our notions are untested, and that we have made our determinations on the basis of assumption rather than experience, we clear the way for God's purposes to be revealed.

If the prerequisite to innovation is the discarding of dated assumptions, then innovation itself begins with the formation of new ones. In this regard, deliberate, firsthand exposure to current challenges is critical. Not only does this provide useful protection against the malignancy of apathy, but it also affords God the opportunity to birth creative vision in our hearts. When this happens, however, we must dream largely; because as Malcolm Muggeridge wrote in the early 1970s, "Experience shows that those who ask little tend to be accorded nothing."

The encouraging news is that the last few years have evidenced a significant upsurge in large-scale dreaming relative to evangelism in politically changing settings. Even the descriptive label "restricted-access nations," itself a replacement for the theologically troublesome term "closed countries," is in the process of evolving. As previously daunting restrictions are transformed into surmountable challenges, the new, more appropriate, emphasis is on "creative-access nations."

Several promising methodologies are also emerging. Some of these are new, while others have been remodeled to meet the requirements of today's spiritual battlefield. All represent viable alternatives to conventional approaches which are fast reaching the limits of their effectual life spans in the world's growing community of creative-access nations.

In addition to the multiple entry evangelism of nonresident missions and the persistence of gospel broadcasting, the rapidly growing potential of indigenous missions and tentmaking gives the church a formidable arsenal with which to approach the ministry-access challenges of tomorrow.

National missions are now virtually unstoppable. In addition to holding their own strategy consultations, such as the recent Third World Missions Advance at Portland's Western Conservative Baptist Seminary, they are developing extraordinarily creative, diverse, and bold ministry initiatives. Examples from within the creative-access world include the David Evangelistic Outreach in Nepal; two highly effective indigenous ministries operating within the Arab world—the Lord's Army in Romania and the Society for Propagation of Christian Ethics; and the Light and Life Movement in Poland.

By taking advantage of opportunities uniquely open to them, many non-Western Christians are moving into positions and places of strategic influence. An Indian ministry is recruiting believers from the subcontinent to take employment openings in the Arabian Gulf. African exchange students in the Soviet Union have been used by God to evangelize and disciple unreached young people there. Koreans, Filipinos, and Nigerians have been effective witnesses in some of the most tightly controlled nations of the Middle East and North Africa. Eastern Europeans have been instrumental in presenting the gospel to Mongolia. Five new Latin missions are presently focusing their attention on North Africa. And the list goes on.

Tentmaking's growing appeal is due to its ability to simultaneously provide access to unreached peoples, involve the laity in missions, and keep costs in check. While tentmaking is hardly a new idea, and in fact can be traced back to Paul (Acts 18:3), it has never fit the prevailing mission context as snugly as it does today. The role of modern communications in diminishing isolation, growing economic interdependence, burgeoning tourism, and increasing technical and educational exchanges brought on by the advent of the information age all pave the way for, and indeed beckon, tentmaker missionaries to come to the forefront of world evangelization.

While tentmaking may appear one-dimensional to some observers, this is not the case. For in addition to standard international employment opportunities, there is today virtually unlimited potential for entrepreneurship. If we can stem the "brain drain" in the church by helping our more talented and enterprising lay people to decompartmentalize their vocational and spiritual callings, "missionary corporations" and "companies for Christ" will abound on their own accord.

Finally, though hardly an innovation, we must not overlook the role and gifts of the Holy Spirit in areas where spiritual breakthroughs are needed. In many lands today, including—and perhaps especially—within the Muslim world, we cannot afford to come in with our doctrine but not with power. People will often have been prepared by the Holy Spirit for our arrival; and they expect an encounter with the supernatural.

Activism

Having joined ranks with our fellow believers and examined fresh approaches to the task, it remains for us to act. For as Peter Wagner puts it: "God brings the harvest to ripeness, but he does not harvest it."

Activism—a term not to be confused with busyness—is the inevitable result of a soul that moves into close proximity to the heart and purposes of God. It is the natural response to the realization that the will of God is the highest and most profound cause which may be served.

Jeremiah cried under the weight of prophetic anointing: "His word was in my heart like a burning fire shut up in my bones; I was weary of holding it back, and I could not" (Jeremiah 20:9, NKJV).

Peter and John argued before the Sanhedrin: "For we cannot but speak the things which we have seen and heard."

The apostle Paul reasoned with the Corinthians: "For if I preach the gospel, I have nothing to boast of, for necessity is laid upon me; yes, woe is me if I do not preach the gospel!" (1 Corinthians 9:16, NKJV)

Jesus declared to his disciples: "I must work the works of Him who sent Me while it is day; the night is coming when no one can work" (John 9:4, NKJV).

In Paul's epistle to the Romans, he exhorts them to be "not lagging in diligence, fervent in spirit, serving the Lord" (Romans 12:11, NKJV). Proverbs declares: "If you faint in the day of adversity, Your strength is small." An even stronger admonition is found in Jesus' parable of the talents where indolent servants are called "lazy" and "unprofitable" and given their dread release.

The strong intimation in this latter parable is that God will judge us not on the basis of what we have done, but rather on the basis of what we could have done and chose to neglect. The central question at all times involves what we are doing with what we have been given. To ensure we are able to provide a satisfactory answer to this question, it is crucial that we maintain a conscious inventory of the resources God has entrusted to our stewardship.

The Partner-Provider church, in particular, must also remember that God's definition of stewardship requires investment; although not, it should be added, in comfortable zones of control where those who pay homage to the Christian message can congregate in peace.

After a recent lengthy tour of American Christian churches and media ministries, a Polish pastor was asked to summarize his impressions. His reply was piercing:

> The American church is captive to freedom. . . . To American Christians the most important thing about freedom is that they have it. To those of us in Eastern Europe, however, the most important thing about freedom is what one does with it.

As the church proceeds toward the year 2000, there is perhaps no other warning more appropriate to the occasion. Multitudes still wait in the valley of decision, but the question remains as to who will reach them first. Never before has the competition for souls been as fierce. Never before has the church had to contend with such a diverse assortment of rivals so utterly committed to the principles of activism.

All of this raises significant questions when it comes to sharing our faith with others—particularly when in so doing we can be relatively certain that it will stir up fierce opposition. If, for example, we know there will be persecution, should we attempt to gauge its probable severity before we extend a witness? If our calculations indicate that the reaction will be severe, even life-threatening, can we biblically justify a conscious decision to avoid the confrontation?

Should the church in politically or socially hostile circumstances remain covert to avoid potential eradication by forces hostile to Christianity? Or would a more open confrontation with prevailing spiritual ignorance and deprivation—even if it produced Christian martyrs—be more likely to lead to evangelistic breakthroughs?

Islamic fundamentalists claim that their spiritual revolution is fueled by the blood of martyrs. Is it conceivable that Christianity's failure to thrive in the Muslim world is due to the notable absence of Christian martyrs? Can the Muslim community take seriously the claims of a church in hiding?

Advocates for a more covert approach argue that it is essential for young national churches to be allowed to mature undisturbed until they reach a point of "assured viability." Once the church grows beyond this critical threshold, it can, and inevitably will, become public knowledge. Even if stiff persecution follows, proponents of this position claim that the church's roots at this stage will be deep and wide enough to sustain it.

The question remains, however, as to whether it is possible to bring a covert church to a point of assured viability. Can enough converts be won and effectively discipled in the absence of fearless role models, or living examples of God's ability to deliver and sustain his people in the teeth of adversity?

There is surely biblical precedent for strategic seclusion. David hid out from the relentless anger of Saul, Rahab hid the Jewish spies in Jericho, and Joseph and Mary took the infant Jesus into Egypt in order to escape Herod's massacre of the innocents. The question, then, is not one of whether it is at times wise to keep worship and witness discreet, but rather how long this may continue before it becomes a matter of "hiding our light under a bushel."

Admittedly, these are issues which most Western Christians can only deal with vicariously. There is unquestionably a danger in allowing those of us who live in the hills of freedom to thrust our sometimes all-too-rational perspectives on those who live in the valley of the shadow of death. Still, God has called us in the spirit of unity to "remember those that are in bonds as bound with them." He further reminds us in his Word that "all that live godly in Christ Jesus shall suffer persecution." If this blessed privilege has not yet touched our lives, perhaps it is time for us to ask why not.

At the same time, those who pray for the spiritual awakening of unreached peoples in restricted lands, but cannot at the same time abide the thought of a church in confrontation, might wish to reconsider the likely implications of answered prayer.

The first book of the prophet Samuel records a truly dramatic encounter between God's people and the spirit of fear and intimidation. The account involves the armies of Israel and Philistia who had set themselves for battle in the Valley of Elah. As they faced each other atop parallel ridges, a monstrous Philistine warrior broke ranks with his fellows to defy Saul's troops. For forty days, this giant presented himself, morning and evening, before the armies of God. As he bellowed his hostility across the valley, we are told that "all the men of Israel, when they saw the man, fled from him and were dreadfully afraid."

In these modern times, our fears over what might happen have resulted in an increasing incidence of missionary detours and evangelistic paralysis. All too often the primary question to be answered today is not: "Is the field ripe," but, "Is it safe?" If relative freedom and safety cannot be satisfactorily affirmed, the only prudent option is to step back and wait for God to "open doors."

But what is meant by the phrase *open doors*? If one surveys its popular definition, the concept clearly involves more than mere assurances of personal safety. Opportunity and feasibility are cast as equally important components, demanding, in the first case, some kind of legitimizing invitation or welcome to minister, and in the second, a resources-to-challenge ratio that is realistic. Should any of these factors be absent, the assumption is made that the doors to effective ministry are, for the time being at least, "closed."

Despite the prevalence of such notions, a careful re-examination of the New Testament places them in clear conflict with the views and practices of the early church. The idea, for instance that God's servants must or will be welcomed in their ambassadorial roles is nowhere encountered. From Jerusalem and Damascus to Ephesus and Rome, the record shows that the apostles were beaten, stoned, conspired against, and imprisoned for their witness. Invitations were rare, and never the basis for their missions.

In fact, it is a crucial point of spiritual engagement that God almost never calls his people to a fair fight. The recurring theme of Scripture is one of giants and multitudes. Time and again, Christian warriors were asked to face foes whose natural resources exceeded their own.

The script is the same for us today. As we face the emerging challenges of urbanization, massive refugee populations, militant Islams, and growing numbers of totalitarian governments opposed to the spread of the gospel, there are no fair fights.

Spiritual inroads into enemy territory are nearly always the result of godly initiatives rather than heathen invitations. God's strategy in reclaiming his fallen creation is decidedly aggressive; rather than waiting for captive souls to petition for liberation, he instead dispatches his servants on extensive search and rescue missions. It is a slippery and deadly serious business, for outside the perimeter of the kingdom of God, divine emissaries are immediately confronted with the gates of hell. Fearful in their imagery, these malevolent structures have persuaded more than one expedition to turn back for safer havens.

Those who proceed, however, do so in the double confidence that Christ has promised to go with them, and that he has passed through these portals before. Additional encouragement, if any is needed, is afforded in Jesus' declaration of Matthew 16:18 (KJV) that "the gates of hell shall not prevail" against either the church or her truths. In glorious strokes, the dynamic characteristics of the Lord's army are highlighted against the static and essentially defensive structures of the enemy. As for the myriad of supposed "closed doors" facing Christian believers today, the reality is that very few are the work of God. Most are deceptive barriers that have been erected to ward off divine arrows of truth, and are, therefore, legitimate targets for spiritual conquest. All represent golden opportunities to prove his resources and promises afresh.

Today, Goliaths stand all about us—in our society and throughout the earth. The Mongolias, Libyas, and Albanias of the world mock us, because for decades we have displayed neither the courage nor faith to penetrate their ramparts with the gospel. Do we hear them? Are we, like David, shocked at their defiance of the armies of God? If so, the time has come for us to fulfill our duty. And as an old Talmudic proverb observes: "These things are good in little measure and evil in large: yeast, salt, and hesitation."

II. A. The Whole Gospel

Good News for the Poor

Edna Lee de Gutierrez

I grew up in Mexico City. Although my family was financially sound when I was born, sickness, injustice, and other factors contributed to leaving us in poverty. However, my childhood was very happy and I have sweet memories of life at home with my family.

My parents were committed Christians and I was raised in an atmosphere of understanding. They taught me that we were rich because we had God's abundant wealth in Jesus Christ. There were days when we didn't have much to eat, but love, care, encouragement, faith, and hope were always plentiful. The experience of the psalmist became existentially ours: "I have been young, and now am old; yet I have not seen the righteous forsaken or his children begging bread" (Psalm 37:25, RSV). We used to repeat every day, "Bless the Lord, O my soul; and all that is within me, bless his holy name! Bless the Lord, O my soul, and forget not all his benefits" (Psalm 103:1–2, RSV). The Reina Valera Spanish version reads, "and forget not any of his benefits."

The Good News in Jesus Christ is ours. The Good News can make the whole and decisive difference in the life of any person. Once we belong to the kingdom of God, we have a new attitude towards life and find renewed strength to face our problems and adversities.

The Poor

The poor have common problems whether they live in rural, semi-urban, or urban communities. They barely have the means to meet their primary needs of food, housing, health, and education. Malnutrition, unsanitary living conditions, and sickness, abound among the poor. There is a saying that "poverty is a bad counselor" and at the same time, it is a good soil for promiscuity, delinquency, and ignorance.

The social, moral, emotional, psychological, and spiritual problems of the poor are complex. The poor face poverty with different attitudes. Some react with resentment, animosity, and hatred; others have a self-destructive attitude of passivity, low self-esteem, and impotence; still others have a favorable, healthy reaction of earnest desire to overcome their problems and attain success in life.

Women and children are particularly affected by poverty. Most of the women stay at home with the responsibility of caring for a large family under tremendous stress and anguish. At times they suffer their husbands' abuse and mistreatment as the men try to "forget" their problems with alcohol and drugs. Many of the women are illiterate.

Edna Lee de Gutierrez is President of the Women's Department of the Baptist World Alliance; she is a citizen of Mexico.

Children suffer abandonment and quite often develop bitterness and resentment. Their mothers are busy with housework and doing what they can to earn a little money, and children have to look after their younger brothers and sisters. They attend school sporadically or not at all. If they do attend school, their school performance is handicapped by malnutrition and weakness.

Good News for the Poor

"Good News for the poor" is a tremendous challenge for Christians. We must be aware of the causes and effects of poverty and recognize the problems we face in this particular ministry. We must learn to make the best use of any and all resources to achieve our goal.

We frequently hear comments like, "There are so many wonderful projects we would like to carry out but we have no money." And so, we turn our heads and stretch out our hands to the wealthy.

Partnership is important in the task of taking the Good News to the unreached—most of whom are poor. But we should not wait for help from the wealthy to do our work. We have spiritual, human, and material resources at hand and must learn to be good stewards of them. We are Christ's servants who have been put in charge of God's secret truths. And the one thing required of servants is that they be faithful to the Master (1 Corinthians 4:1–2).

Today, many countries are closed, or are in the process of being closed, to foreign missionaries and evangelists. China teaches us a good lesson for evangelization. During the years of the cultural revolution, Christians around the world wondered about the future of the gospel in China: no missionaries, no church buildings, no Bibles, no religious freedom. But Chinese Christians kept faith alive by nurturing their faith in their families, gathering to worship in their homes, and by evangelizing through the testimony of their lives. They took the responsibility of evangelization and the Lord is blessing China with a wonderful harvest of people accepting Jesus Christ as their Savior.

The economies of many countries today are becoming poorer. We are reaching the point where the poor are evangelizing the poor. Evangelization is coming not only from the wealthy to the poor, but from the poor to the poor.

Church Interaction With the Poor

In January 1968, my husband accepted the pastorate of Horeb Baptist Church, a small congregation of not more than thirty people. His ministry began with the particular goal of ministering to the young and has expanded over time. Today, we minister in a variety of areas. We work with victims of illiteracy, drug addiction, and prostitution. We also have a prison fellowship and work with socially underprivileged people. Horeb is a church of prayer with a wide concept of what ministry means and a strong desire to execute God's will and to meet our neighbors' needs.

Ten years ago, a member of our church whose heart is in missions and evangelism invited a woman she had met in her evangelistic work to attend a service. After the service, the church had a fellowship gathering.

The visitor had a background of poverty and unfortunate consequences. She became angry when the ladies at church invited her to the kitchen to help with the dishes. Later on, she confessed she had made a vow never to go back to the church where she had been insulted by being asked to help with the dishes.

But she went back.

Eventually, she and her sister began a congregation in a community called San

Francisco Culhuacan, with the orientation and support of our church, which became the Mount of Olives Baptist Church. Although the members are economically poor, they are self-supporting.

Many opportunities to minister the Good News came after the tragedy of the earthquakes in September of 1985. Our sister's house, and many others in the community where she lives, were severely damaged. Many families were forced to evacuate their houses and the city government granted permission to use a parking lot as a shelter for forty-five families.

Our sister saw this opportunity to minister among the families living together in the shelter. Our church supported her initiative. World Vision Mexico joined hands with us in meeting the immediate needs: tents, kitchen utensils, blankets, food, and water. Retired teachers volunteered to teach the children whose school buildings had been destroyed. Later, the tents were exchanged for prefabricated one-room houses through the help of a Canadian agency.

This community was known in Mexico City as "the cradle of thieves" and right in the middle of it the gospel was preached in words and deeds. The first converts were baptized in our church. The families living in the parking lot were eventually relocated in different neighborhoods and some of the people have joined different churches.

The people in this shelter experienced a variety of incidents that sometimes caused those involved to feel a sense of failure and frustration and the consequent temptation to give up. But there were also rewarding experiences which made us remember that God is in control of everything.

This is only one example of a project carried on through the initiative of one poor woman with the support of her church and the cooperation of a parachurch organization.

Our sister is an effective evangelist among the poor. They cannot say "She doesn't know what it is like." She *does* know and understand. Her burden for women and children compels her to minister to prostitutes, women in prison, and abandoned children.

What happened to her poverty when she became a Christian? Her economic poverty was not "magically" transformed into economical wealth, but her vision of life and her life *were* transformed. She was aware that her children were not condemned to live as she lived before; she became strong in the Lord and helped them to trust him through her own example. She encouraged them to study and the two youngest have obtained scholarships for further studies. She has not been as successful with all of her children, but she keeps on praying for them.

She progressed only as far as the third grade in elementary school but she has taken the courses offered at the Bible institute at church and was one of our first graduates.

"When anyone is joined to Christ he is a new being: the old is gone, the new has come" (2 Corinthians 5:17, TEV). Her new being is committed to serving the Lord.

Something to Pray for and to Think About

Because the doors of our Christian churches are open to everybody without barriers with regard to nationality or race, economic or social status, or any other consideration, the church's ministry is broadened to reach out to diverse groups. We have "evangelists" from different contexts.

In ministering to the economically poor, we must not make them dependent on our giving but rather help them to be self-sufficient.

The church is a channel of love, understanding, and encouragement, as well as a source of diverse opportunities to learn and work and experience new avenues of service and cooperation.

There is a blessing in the partnership in the ministry but let us not forget that we have our own resources. Freely we have received, let us freely give what we have. We may be economically limited, but we can take the message to the "lame men" of the world:

"We have no money at all, but we give you what we have: in the name of Jesus Christ of Nazareth . . ."

As Christians, poverty is not a handicap to serving the Lord. He uses our experience to minister to the poor and all men as well.

Good News for the Poor

Tom Houston

There is something almost absurd about my discussing "Good News for the Poor." I come from a wealthy country. I am one of the affluent. I have no grounds to speak, yet I must.

For years I have had two burdens about the evangelization of the world. One, is the vast populations in resistant countries with no knowledge of the Father's love, the Savior's cross, or the Spirit's power to bring them out of darkness into light. These countries form a great swath on the map of the world starting with Japan, moving on to China, the Soviet Republics in Asia, Thailand, Indochina, the Indian subcontinent, Indonesia, West Asia, the Middle East, Turkey, North Africa, and Muslim West Africa.

My second burden is the great landslide away from the Christian faith in the West, in Eastern Europe, and in the countries of the British Commonwealth. They are abandoning the Father's love, despising the Savior's cross, and adopting an attitude of self-sufficiency with no need of the Spirit's power (see Table 1).

If we are serious about world evangelization, then we need to find answers to both of these challenges.

It is interesting to note that the resistant countries have never been evangelized in modern times and, with the exception of Japan and some oil producing countries, they are poor. On the other hand, the countries of the West that are becoming secular *have* been evangelized in the past and are now relatively rich.

This broad contrast is intriguing. Are the two challenges and their answers related? Is there one answer that would address both problems?

The Gospel of Luke contains material not included in the other Gospels—about 40 percent. A significant part is focused on the rich and the poor, and there are ways in which they are directly linked to each other. It suggests that what the gospel says about the poor is connected to what it says about the rich.

Good News for the Poor

Luke uses the expression *preaching*, or *bringing* (TEV) *Good News to the poor* twice in his Gospel. Luke indicates that Jesus saw bringing, or preaching, Good News to the poor as central to his mission. The questions that arise are:

Thomas Houston is the International Director of the Lausanne movement, was formerly a missionary to Kenya, head of the British and Foreign Bible Society, and for five years President of World Vision International. He is a citizen of Scotland.

- Who are the poor—then and now?
- What is the Good News?
- How significant to the task of evangelization are they meant to be?
- What are the implications for the rich and for those who feel the call to evangelize?

VIDEO PRESENTATION

Is There Good News for the Poor?

Producer: Eric Miller
Writers: Tom Houston, Eric Miller

Tom Houston: In the Gospel of Luke, Jesus visits the synagogue in Nazareth immediately after he had resisted the temptations to use popularity, publicity, or power to accomplish his mission.

Standing, Jesus read from Isaiah 61:

> The Spirit of the Lord is upon me. He has anointed me to preach the Good News to the poor, he has sent me to proclaim liberty to the captives, and recovery of sight to the blind, to set free the oppressed, to announce the year when the Lord will save his people (Luke 4:18–19, TEV).

Later, when John the Baptist sent his disciples to ask about his credentials as the Messiah, Jesus healed many people of their sickness, diseases, evil spirits, and gave sight to many blind people. He answered John's messengers,

> Go back and tell John what you have seen and heard: the blind can see, the lame can walk, the lepers are made clean, the deaf can hear, the dead are raised to life, and the Good News is preached to the poor (Luke 7:22, TEV).

For Luke, bringing or preaching Good News to the poor is clearly central to Jesus' understanding of his mission. The poor are to be special beneficiaries of his Good News.

As I studied Luke's Gospel, I was puzzled because Luke sees the poor as central to the mission of Jesus and then seems to say little about the poor as such. I felt I was missing something that was there.

As I looked closer, I noticed something similar in both places where Luke talks about Good News for the poor. In Jesus' announcement of his mission in Luke 4:18–19 (TEV), he proclaimed,

> The Spirit of the Lord is upon me. He has anointed me to preach the Good News to the poor, he has sent me to proclaim liberty to the captives, and recovery of sight to the blind, to set free the oppressed, and to announce the year when the Lord will save his people.

Could it be that Jesus was including the captives, the blind, and the oppressed among those whom he calls poor?

Then I looked at Luke 7:22 (TEV), at the evidence Jesus gives that he is the Messiah,

Go back and tell John what you have seen and heard: the blind can see, the lame can walk, the lepers are made clean, the deaf can hear, the dead are raised to life.

In other words, the Good News is preached to the poor. Perhaps the blind, the prisoners, the oppressed, the lame, the lepers, and the deaf are examples of the poor that Jesus is speaking of. Blind and lame people in the Gospels were often beggars. Prisoners were often in jail for debt or theft and did not come out until they had paid the last penny. Lepers were outcasts from society and were cut off from all means of making a living. If "the year when the Lord will save his people" was a reference to the Year of Jubilee, that year was intended to benefit debtors, slaves, and those dispossessed of their land.

The two words used for "the poor" in the New Testament are *penes* and *ptochos*. *Penes* refers to the person who is oppressed, underpaid, and the working poor. *Ptochos* refers to the person who has no work to do and has to beg. It is sometimes translated "poor" and sometimes "beggar." The basic idea is dependence on others for the essentials of life: food, clothes, shelter, and health.

With that in mind, when we read Luke and Acts with this linguistic clue, we discover many references to the poor:

1. The hungry and their children, that Mary says will be filled with good things (Luke 1:53);
2. The people, and their children, who are oppressed by tax collectors who take more than their due, and by soldiers and policemen who take their money or bring false charges against them (Luke 3:12–14);
3. The disabled blind, deaf, lame, paralyzed, lepers, and demon possessed, and their children, who cannot work for a living and are cut off from society (Luke 3–7);
4. The widows, like the one in Nain, whose only son died, leaving her with no breadwinner in her home (Luke 7:11–17);
5. The widows who cannot get justice from judges (Luke 18:2–5), whose houses are expropriated by hypocritical religious leaders (Luke 20:47);
6. The women with medical problems who have spent all their money on doctors (Luke 8:43);
7. The victims of famine in Judea, and their children, who were helped by the Christians in Antioch (Acts 11:27–30).

It is evident in Luke and Acts that the poor to whom Jesus and the early church brought Good News included the naked, the hungry, the disabled, the oppressed, the imprisoned, the sick, the bereaved widows, and orphans. But the question remains, *What kind of Good News was needed by all these people?*

What Was the Good News?

It was the kind of Good News that brought a prostitute to wash Jesus' feet with her tears and wipe them with her hair, and then hear Jesus say, "Your sins are forgiven" (Luke 7:36–50, TEV).

It was the kind of Good News that brought the leper to kneel and say, "If you want to, you can make me clean," and feel Jesus' touch and hear him say, "I do want to. . . . Be clean!" (Luke 5:12–15, TEV)

It was the kind of Good News that prompted a disabled man's friends to bring him to Jesus and have their faith rewarded by hearing Jesus say, "Your sins are forgiven you, my friend. . . . Get up, pick up your bed, and go home" (Luke 5:17–24, TEV).

It was the kind of Good News that challenged a prominent religious leader to think about inviting the poor, the crippled, the lame, and the blind, who could not repay him, to a banquet as the true way to blessing (Luke 14:1–14).

The Good News of the kingdom of God is that sin, disease, and oppression are never the last word. Where Jesus is King, he brings forgiveness, healing, and liberation.

Jesus expected—and it should be expected today—the preaching of the Good News to bring help and hope to the sinner, help and hope to the poor. Because evangelism and social concern were inseparable in the mind of Jesus, they must be inseparable in our minds and ministry.

As representatives of Jesus, we must ask, *Who are the poor today who are desperately calling for Good News?*

Who Are the Poor—Today?

Young voices: We are the blind.

Narrator: Two hundred fifty thousand children will become permanently blinded this year for lack of a ten-cent vitamin A capsule or a daily handful of green vegetables (*The State of the World's Children 1989* [London: Oxford University Press], 40.) And that is only one instance where people become blind because they are poor.

Young voices: We are the lame.

Narrator: Each year two hundred thirty thousand children are struck by polio because they do not receive the immunization which has virtually eliminated polio in the West.

Female voices: We are the mothers who lose our children before they are five years old.

Narrator: Fourteen million children will die this year from common illnesses and malnutrition. Most could be saved by relatively simple, low-cost methods. Two and a half million of them die from dehydration due to diarrhea, yet a solution of eight parts sugar and one part salt in clean water could save their lives.

Male and young voices: We are the husbands who lose their wives, and the children who lose their mothers and become orphans from preventable deaths in childbirth.

Narrator: In the next twenty-four hours more than a thousand young women will die because of something going wrong at childbirth. As long as the nutrition of girls is placed second to that of boys, as long as women eat last and least and work hardest and longest, as long as half of the babies in the developing world are delivered with no trained person in attendance, child bearing will remain one hundred fifty times as dangerous as in the West.

Mixed voices: We are the people who cannot read.

Narrator: Many are poor because no one has taught them to read. They are cut off from much that could enrich their lives.

Young voices: We are the children who cannot go to school.

Narrator: In the last few years, governments of the thirty-seven poorest nations have cut spending on health by 50 percent and on education by 25 percent, in order to pay the West the interest that they owe on their huge debts.

Mixed voices: We are the refugees who have lost our homes.

Narrator: Today fourteen million displaced people have lost citizenship, homeland, relationships, and the opportunity to work, and much that gives life meaning.

Young voices: We are the orphans.

Narrator: Thousands of children are orphaned by war, civil strife, revolution, and terrorism. Millions more are being abandoned by their parents. There are three million of these in Brazil alone.

Women's voices: We are the prostitutes.

Narrator: To provide for their children, many women are forced to turn to prostitution. Many children in cities like Bangkok are sold by desperate parents as slave labor or for sexual exploitation.

Young voices: We are the children of the streets.

Narrator: One hundred million children living in the streets of our great cities are drawn inevitably into a life of crime and corruption.

Young voices: We are teenagers, losing our future.

Narrator: The future of many teenage boys and girls in our cities has been taken captive by drug pushers, violence, and promiscuity; they end up as unmarried mothers, victims of drug violence, or wasting away from AIDS.

Mixed voices: We are the prisoners.

Mixed voices: The world's prisons are overcrowded. Some are in prison for crimes, some for conscience, others are the victims of unjust legal systems. All their families suffer.

Mixed voices: We are the destitute.

Narrator: There are nearly one billion people who are defined as "the absolute poor," whose existence is characterized by malnutrition, illiteracy, and disease, and is beneath any reasonable definition of human decency.

Tom Houston: Yes, that is who the poor are, but if we are to bring them Good News, then we must also know where they are today.

Where Are the Poor Today?

Tom Houston: The five countries with the largest number of absolute poor are China, India, Bangladesh, Indonesia, and Pakistan (see Table 2).

The five countries with the highest percentage of absolute poor are Bangladesh, Burkina Faso, Burundi, Haiti, and Papua New Guinea (see Table 3). The five countries with a GNP per capita less that $150 per year are Chad, Ethiopia, Nepal, Burkina Faso, and Bhutan (see Table 4).

Six countries where 20 percent of the population gets less than 2 percent of the income are Botswana, Brazil, Iraq, the Philippines, Jamaica, and Peru (see Table 5).

The five countries with the highest "under five" infant mortality rate are Afghanistan, Mali, Mozambique, Angola, and Sierra Leone (see Table 6).

More than half the world's population live in these twenty-four poor nations. Yet the poor of the world, the hungry, the disabled, the oppressed, the sick, and the marginalized are found in every country and Jesus says we must bring Good News to them.

How Significant Are They to the Task of Evangelization?

Nearly half the world's population is poor and the world will not be evangelized until the Good News is brought to them.

Today, eight of the ten countries with the largest number of non-Christians have serious problems with poverty. The ten are China, India, the Soviet Union, Indonesia, Japan, Bangladesh, Pakistan, Vietnam, Nigeria, and Thailand (see Table 7). They need to be given priority and there is no exaggerating the magnitude of the task of bringing the Good News to the poor in these countries.

Yet, when all is said and done, the church must bring Good News to the poor for more than strategic reasons. The Lord Jesus so identified with the poor that unless we serve the poor, we do not serve him.

(END VIDEO SCRIPT, RESUME ADDRESS FROM PAGE 154)

After the video we are left with the question, *What are the implications for the rich?*

We need to go back to Luke. Jesus asked some of those who wanted to follow him to sell all their belongings and give the money to the poor (Luke 12:33). Luke alone records that the four fishermen and Matthew actually did that when they followed him (Luke 5:4–11,28).

It is important to notice that by doing so, they put themselves into the same category of dependence on others that defines the poor. Jesus became poor when he left the carpenter's shop. His disciples became poor when they left their homes and their means of earning a living. Luke then tells three stories that are built around the same challenge.

The first is the story of the rich young ruler who wanted to know how he might inherit eternal life. He was told that he should sell all that he had, give the money to the poor, and follow Jesus; then he would have riches in heaven or eternal life he was looking for. He refused to do this and walked away with the sad verdict implied by Jesus to his disciples that he had missed the kingdom of God (Luke 18:18–30).

The second is the story of Zacchaeus, the tax collector who, without being specifically challenged, gave half of his goods to the poor and set out to restore fourfold any taxes he had taken beyond what was due. Jesus responded by saying that he had been lost but was now found and saved, and he was shown to be a true son of Abraham (Luke 19:1–10).

The third story is about the rich man who went about enjoying life and failed to do what Jewish law required for the beggar Lazarus, who was laid daily at the gate of his compound. Jesus indicated that he thought he was a son of Abraham but did not reach Abraham's bosom. Instead, he ended up condemned (Luke 16:19–31).

When we consider these stories in the context of Jesus' declared mission to bring Good News to the poor, we come to this conclusion: Jesus intended to have Good News brought to the poor by his followers identifying with the poor, as well as telling them about him and urging them to turn from their sins.

One part of compassion is economic. We may not be required to give up our jobs or sell our property, but we must give up something significant if the compassion of Jesus for the poor is to be seen in us.

Another part of compassion has to do with meeting the other needs of the poor. When Jesus "saw the crowds, he had compassion on them, because they were harassed and helpless, like sheep without a shepherd" (Matthew 9:36). Jesus was quoting from Ezekiel. The shepherds or rulers of Israel had not taken care of the weak ones, healed those that were sick, bandaged those that were hurt, or looked for those that were lost, so the people of Israel were like sheep without a shepherd (Ezekiel 34:4–5).

Jesus urged his disciples to pray that the Lord would send out workers into his harvest, shepherds who would have compassion and truly care for the weak, the sick, the hurt, the wandering, and the lost among the sheep.

It would appear that the rich man in Lazarus's story had no compassion. The dogs who licked his sores did more for Lazarus than the rich man, who lost heaven by his neglect. We run the same risk. If economic and human compassion is not seen in the lives of those who follow Jesus, an enormous number of the poor will never have convincing evidence to believe the Good News of the kingdom.

The tragedy is that many of our churches contribute to this credibility gap. For example, the affluent and nominally Christian countries of Europe, North America, and the Commonwealth are becoming wealthier. The GNP of the top ten countries is 123 times greater than the GNP of the bottom ten. Yet with the growth in material prosperity, there is a great exodus from the churches and it seems likely to continue. Wealth leads to forgetting God, which is the essence of secularization. The message of Jesus becomes less palatable to people in the West as their prosperity increases. While nearly one billion people live in absolute poverty, in their desire to have more, the followers of Jesus are not easily distinguishable from others.

If Luke were paraphrased today, it might sound like this:

The prosperous are still living in luxury and paying little attention to the poor outside their door or half a world away. The rich fools are still going for the bigger and better and losing their souls in the process. The unjust businessmen are still obsessed by their margins of profit and will end up without friends in eternity. Wealthy, upright leaders still want to believe they can have eternal life without any significant parting with their goods for the benefit of the poor. Religious leaders still pass by those on the other side who have been robbed on the highways of life and economics.

Today, many who were in the church are moving away from trust and belief in God;

they believe in mammon. Some nominal Christians who still try to serve God and mammon, do not believe Jesus when he says it is impossible. Even some evangelical Christians have a long way to go before they are distinguishable from the mammon worshippers.

According to David Barrett, 52 percent of all Christians live in affluence. Thirty-five percent are comparatively well off. Only 13 percent live in absolute poverty. The influential worldwide community of evangelicals alone have personal income totalling just under $1 trillion a year. He maintains that the global sharing by Christians of money, wealth, property, and goods could solve most of the world's problems including those of famine, poverty, disease, unemployment, unsafe water supplies, and so on (*International Bulletin of Missionary Research*, [October, 1983], 147).

What an impact it would have on the poor's perception of the Good News of Jesus Christ if his followers were seen sharing in that way. A major way in which we can make the Good News of Jesus convincing in a hostile or reluctant world is to show by our compassion its relevance to the poor and their needs. We will also be able to combat secularism in the West if we restore this kind of authenticity to the Good News of Jesus Christ.

What Are the Implications?

We all must go back to our countries, open our eyes to the needs of the poor, and become poor in spirit. That is, identify with them and share the Good News of Jesus Christ. There is no general blessing on the poor apart from their response to him. The blessings of the kingdom for them are forgiveness for the repentant and acceptance for the excluded. They need to hear that in a credible way.

It will mean challenging the rich inside and outside of our churches to remember the poor. We all need to preach Luke's stories until their impact is felt deeply and controls the way we follow the Master.

Second, we must focus on massive prayer, generosity, and evangelism in the neediest countries of the world. China, India, Bangladesh, Pakistan, Indonesia, and Indochina need to be given priority.

One hundred ninety-five million of our Christian brothers and sisters live in absolute poverty. David Barrett says, "This Church of the Poor is the only part of global Christianity whose lifestyle is similar to that of Jesus on earth" (Barrett, *Missionary Research*, 8, 151). They are the key to the evangelization of the world. They are the ones we need to learn from. They are the ones we need to support in the task. If, together, we have the determination, we will find ways of bringing Good News to the poor.

Perhaps it is time for the churches to begin to surpass our governments in both the giving and receiving of aid. Perhaps it is time for the Christian citizen to change the attitudes of our governments, business, and banking communities to do something about Third World debt.

In 1979, a net $40 billion flowed from North to South. Today, the South, while still poorer, is transferring a net $20 billion to the North. If we add the reduction of commodity prices in the same period, the annual flow from the poor South to the rich North might be as much as $60 billion (*World's Children 1989*, 15).

Without a massive increase in practical compassion for the poor, there will be little increase in world evangelization. We need to proclaim the Good News fully by word, deed, and sign (Romans 15:18–19). Only as we do so, will we have the power of the Spirit with which to face the task (Luke 4:18–19).

In the last forty years there have been two great trends in world evangelization. One has been the growth of organizations such as CAFOD, Caritas, Church World Service, Compassion International, Inter-Church Aid, Lutheran World Federation, Mennonite Central Committee, Tear Fund, World Concern, World Relief, World Vision, and others who have witnessed to the truth of the Good News of Jesus by deeds of mercy and compassion. Christian relief and development agencies have mushroomed and have begun to make their mark on the world. Proclaiming by deed is taking place and it must continue and intensify.

In the same period, there has been the remarkable growth of the Pentecostal and charismatic movement. David Barrett and C. Peter Wagner have shown us that the Pentecostals and charismatics are one-fifth of the Christian population, one-fourth of the workers, and are responsible for half of the growth in the worldwide church—and their force is by no means spent (*International Bulletin of Missionary Research* [July, 1988], 119). They have gone to the poor and, as with Jesus, they have been anointed by the Spirit to heal the sick and cast out demons. Proclamation by signs is also happening, and it must continue and intensify.

We need both of these thrusts. For not all the sick and disabled are going to be healed by miraculous signs today any more than in Jesus' day. In the Old Testament, when God proclaimed, "I am the Lord, who heals you" (Exodus 15:26), it was in the context of his people obeying his laws, many of which were about health and cleanliness. We need to proclaim both the Good News that Jesus can heal the sick, and the Good News that there are better ways to live together to please God so that people do not become sick, or can be cured by skills that can be learned.

But we must not disregard the need for the Good News to be proclaimed by *word*. A second look at the Pentecostal growth and impact on both urban and rural poor shows that they communicate the word of salvation more effectively than traditional churches. They emphasize the spoken word more than the written Word, as does the New Testament. They are an audio church, which is necessary for illiterate people. They have effective music. They continually preach and teach with great joy and perseverance, the Good News that Christ died for our sins. This is the only way to communicate in poor societies where the homes are hovels and people cannot read or have nothing to read.

While "It is written" is the essence of revelation, it will be a continuing limitation in bringing Good News to the poor if the churches do not learn about identification with the poor and master skills of communication to non-reading cultures.

The use of the movie *Jesus* is a powerful illustration. Half a million people a day are viewing that film in 130 languages with remarkable response in some of the most unlikely places. Many of those responding could not read a Gospel of Luke if they had one. But seeing the Gospel of Luke acted out as well as spoken in film or video, they can *see* Jesus as the compassionate Savior we have been talking about, delivering the captives, healing the blind, the lame, the deaf, and the brokenhearted.

In my Father's house are many mansions, and Jesus speaks about feasts and banquets in these mansions. He says that some who were invited to the feast will not be there because they were preoccupied with lands and cattle and family. But others who will be there are from the poor, the sick, the lame, and the blind. And they will respond more readily than the sophisticated people who are better off (Luke 14:15–24).

Our Father wants his house to be full. Will we go out into the highways and byways to help him fill it?

TABLE 1
Landslide from the Churches 1900-1985

Source: *World Christian Encyclopedia* country tables, adding the Non Religious and Atheist categories both in percentage and numbers. In descending order of 1985 percentages of "non religious" plus "atheist". This takes no account of nominal Christians.

	1900		1985	
	ATHEIST OR NONRELIGIOUS			
	%	(in millions)	%	(in millions)
First World Countries				
Sweden	1.1	0.06	28.7	2.5
Italy	0.2	0.06	16.2	0.1
France	0.3	0.12	15.6	8.6
Australia	1.0	0.04	14.9	2.2
Netherlands	1.5	0.08	12.1	1.7
UK	1.9	0.7	9.5	5.4
New Zealand	0.6	0.005	8.0	0.26
Belgium	0.8	0.06	7.5	0.8
USA	1.3	1.5	6.9	15.3
Canada	0.2	0.01	6.3	1.5
Finland	0.0	0.0	5.5	0.2
Luxembourg	0.0	0.0	4.9	0.017
Portugal	0.0	0.0	4.6	0.4
Germany, West	0.3	0.009	4.6	2.9
Denmark	0.2	0.006	3.6	0.18
Spain	0.0	0.0	2.9	0.88
Austria	0.1	0.01	2.7	0.2
Iceland	0.1	0.0	2.1	0.04
Switzerland	0.2	0.1	1.9	0.12
Norway	0.6	0.01	1.7	0.07
Malta	0.0	0.0	1.0	0.03
Ireland	0.0	0.0	0.4	0.01
Greece	0.0	0.0	0.3	0.03
Total		**2.68**		**43.44**
Eastern Europe and USSR				
Albania	0.1	0.001	74.1	2.1
USSR	0.2	0.25	51.2	158.3
Germany, East	0.3	0.03	25.3	4.4
Bulgaria	0.1	0.004	24.8	2.2
Czechoslovakia	0.4	0.04	20.3	3.1
Yugoslavia	0.1	0.008	16.7	3.7
Hungary	0.5	0.03	15.9	1.7
Romania	0.3	0.03	15.9	3.5
Poland	0.1	0.025	9.5	3.4
Total		**0.42**		**182.40**
Total of Both		**3.1**		**225.84**

TABLE 2
10 Countries with largest number of Absolute Poor

	Millions		Millions
China	?	Mexico	35.90
India	380.50	Nigeria	31.60
Banladesh	89.50	Brazil	28.70
Indonesia	67.40	Ethiopia	28.20
Pakistan	65.20	Philippines	21.90

TABLE 3
11 Countries with the highest percentages of Absolute Poor

	Percentage
Bangladesh	86
Burkina Faso	75
Burundi	75
Haiti	72
Papua New Guinea	67
Sudan	65
Benin	65
Pakistan	64
Uganda	64
Ethiopia	63
Afghanistan	63

TABLE 4
6 Countries with a GNP per Capita $150 or less

GNP $pc	Country
80	Chad
80	Laos
120	Ethiopia
150	Nepal
150	Burkina Faso
150	Bhutan

TABLE 5
9 Countries where 20% of Population get less than 2.5% of the income

(%of income received by lowest 20%)	
Botswana	1.6
Brazil	2.0
Iraq	2.0
Philippines	2.0
Jamaica	2.0
Peru	2.0
Panama	2.1
Kenya	2.3
Tanzania	2.3

TABLE 6
Countries with the highest Under 5 Mortality rate

1. Afghanistan
2. Mali
3. Mozambique
4. Angola
5. Sierra Leone
6. Malawi
7. Ethiopia

Figures taken from The State of World's Children 1989, *supplemented by* The 1988 World Population Data Sheet.

TABLE 7
The 10 most populous and least Christian nations

Country	Total Population	Non Christian Population	Percentage
	(in millions)		
China	1087.0	1032	95
India	816.8	792	97
USSR	286.0	191	67
Indonesia	177.4	157	89
Japan	122.7	120	98
Bangladesh	109.5	109	99.6
Pakistan	107.5	105	98.4
Vietnam	65.2	60	92.5
Nigeria	111.9	57	51
Thailand	54.7	54	99

Numbers taken from Operation World *by subtracting the percentage Christian from 100%*

VIDEO PRESENTATION

Sin and Lostness

Producer: Rick Quintana

Narrator: During the reign of King Ahab and his wicked queen, Jezebel, God appointed his prophet Elijah to preach against the sin and lostness of his people, Israel. Today, the same seed which sprouted into sin and lostness for Israel is being sown across the world by the master grower of alienation, discord, and guilt—Satan. The nations are his planting ground and not one is safe from the cold, sharp blade of his plowshare— temptation.

Despite the scientific advancements of our age, the technological developments, the sociological changes in almost every segment of our societies, there is still one common problem for all mankind—sin. The great problems which plague humanity: wars, starvation, crime, disease, social inequities, and poverty have sin as their root cause.

In the West, sin has been redefined as a benign character weakness which can be corrected through behavior modification, social adjustments, or even economic reposi- tioning. The reality that sin separates man from God and leaves him eternally lost until he is reconciled to the Father is largely scoffed at, even by many church leaders. In the East, sin is defined in relative terms. It is treated as lesser degrees of goodness.

Culture now decides what is sin. Politicians declare that the good of the state is the only good which matters. God and his laws of right and wrong are relegated to myth and useless fiction. Lostness steals across countries, covering entire continents with a satanic delusion, robbing millions of souls of eternal life.

Pablo: Satan has deceived man about the reality of sin and its absolutely unavoidable consequence without Christ. Multitudes are doomed to be lost and separated from the loving Savior who sacrificed himself for them. By God's grace and mercy, we have seen our sinfulness and lost state. We have sought and received his forgiveness and reconciliation.

It is our utter and absolute duty and privilege to go into the highways and byways and compel unbelievers to forsake sin and accept the Son of Righteousness—to leave their lostness and find the true Way.

Sin and Lostness

Stephen Tong

The unconsciousness of danger is a greater threat than the danger itself. In the same way, indifference to and misinterpretation of sin are greater dangers than the sin itself.

God does not divide mankind into two categories when he says, "I come not to call the righteous, but the sinners to repentance." It is an irony of sinners that they are not conscious of their own status. The Bible teaches that sin is a fact—a fact revealed by a righteous God to sinful men. The difficulty lies in the question, *How can sinners properly understand?* Sin has deprived them of the aspect of godly understanding. The Bible, therefore, continues to teach that the only way to become conscious of human sin is through the illumination of the Holy Spirit.

Throughout history, we have always tried to ignore the fact of sin—to believe we were free from any bondage of evil power. Yet, that effect has proven to be self-deceptive, which is shown clearly in the existence of strife—both cultural and personal.

Since the days of the Renaissance, the anthropocentric worldview of natural man has tried to interpret *God* and *soul* through the sinful *self* of man. This worldview sees man as the central point of the universe, who lifts up reason as the absolute tool for discovering truth and considers nature as the final aim of achievements in science, economics, politics, education, psychology, philosophy, and even religion.

There is a common and consistent cause of imbalance and problems. Our societies are full of empty souls, in spite of material abundance; full of the anxiety of war, in spite of unceasing peace talks; and full of insecurity, in spite of the most powerful weapons ever produced. The rate of suicides increases in spite of better living standards; and more families are broken in spite of more freedom practiced in sex and love.

From the Renaissance to the twentieth century, we have been dreaming of human autonomy from the interference of God. Since the nineteenth century, many ideologies have risen to create a modern naive optimism, including liberal theology, evolutionism, and communism. The result has been terrifying wars in the twentieth century. Then followed international revolutions of communism, nationalism, and existentialism—all of which have tried to solve human problems, yet we are still living in a chaotic situation without knowing where the future is heading. To date, the search for man's identity remains a key issue.

Doesn't this tell us that sin and lostness is an undeniable fact? It is no wonder that Karl Barth fought against his two liberal professors, Adolf von Harnack and William

Stephen Tong *is an evangelist-at-large to over twenty countries. Born in China, he is a citizen of Indonesia.*

Hermann, who taught the "brotherhood of mankind" on the one hand and agreed with the Nazi invasion on the other. It is no wonder that the liberal leader, Harry Emerson Fosdick, had to acknowledge the liberals had neglected the teaching of sin and that conservatives understand it better. It is no wonder that Niebuhr had to insist on the biblical teaching for the understanding of sin as inspired by the World War, in his book *The Nature and Destiny of Man*. It is the same reason Paul Tillich wrote in his diary during World War I, "I see not the ruins of the buildings before me, but the ruin of the culture."

Our cultures seem dead. Even in Russia and China after their victory over the old political systems and after practicing communism for decades, their leaders feel the urgency of renewal. They have many problems yet within themselves.

What Sin Is Not

Though man has tried to escape the fact of sin to dilute and reinterpret it—man can never escape God's references to it in the Bible. The Bible clearly teaches that sin began with the historical fall of Adam, the first and the representative of mankind. Before discussing what sin is, let us first consider what sin is not.

The Bible leaves no room for the concept of the eternal pre-existence of sin. Sin is not an entity of self-eternal existence. Sin and evil are not self-dependent realities, neither are the Devil and the demonic powers. Nothing and no one but God himself is the only self-existent and eternal reality. Only God is without beginning and ending. The Bible rejects ontological dualism in religion.

The Bible leaves no room for the concept that sin was created by God or caused by him. God is neither the cause nor the source of evil. The word *evil* in Isaiah 45:7 (KJV), refers to the punishment of God in history as the manifestation of his righteousness and sovereignty to this sinful world, but not ontological or moral evil.

The Bible leaves no possibility for God to be held responsible for sin. The only reference is the mysterious permission of God for the occurrence of evil, which was the result of the misuse of the freedom created within spiritual beings.

Sin emerged from the creatures themselves. It was the creation of created ones against their Creator. About this, Jesus said, "When he [the Devil] speaketh a lie, he speaketh of his own: for he is a liar, and the father of it" (John 8:44, KJV).

What Sin Is

The Bible teaches that sin is more than ethical failure. To merely equate sin with misconduct is too simplistic.

Philosophically, *sin* means "missing the target." The New Testament uses the Greek word *hamartia* to indicate that man is created with a standard, or target, as the purpose of life and conduct. This means we are responsible to God. When sin occurs, we fail to achieve God's standard. After the Fall, man's view of the target became blurred, and the standards of conduct were missing. God sent his Son to delineate the standard again and made him our righteousness and holiness. The rediscovery of the aim of human life can only be found through the perfect example of the incarnated Christ.

Positionally, sin is the removal of the original state. Man was created distinctively, in a unique position, in order to be a witness of God. We were created in between God and the Devil, good and evil, after the fall of Satan. Man was created in a neutral state of goodness, yet to be confirmed through the way of obedience; created a little bit lower than God, yet in dominion over nature; and created after God's image and likeness. The true submission of man before God's sovereignty is the secret of governing nature, and to achieve the true aim of glorifying nature's Creator in man's life. Temptations come in the sense of trying to draw man away from his original God-planned position. Then comes misconduct. The same happened with even the archangels. The Bible says, "They kept not their first state," to describe their fall.

Sin is also the misuse of freedom. The greatest honor and privilege God gave man was the gift of freedom. Freedom has an undiminishable factor as the foundation of moral values. Moral achievements can only be rooted in willingness, they cannot be forced. Spiritual freedom offers two choices: God-centered life or man-centered life. When man submits in his freedom to God, it is a return of that freedom to its original master. Man chooses to seek the joy of freedom within the limits of God's truth and righteousness. God is the reality of righteousness, and any departure from him will cause unrighteousness. The self-centered life is the cause of sin, and self-centered intention is the beginning of unrighteousness. Freedom without the limits of the righteousness of God becomes false freedom. It is not the freedom Jesus spoke of when he said, "No one can follow me without denying himself."

Sin is a destroying power. Sin is not merely a failure in conduct, rather, it is a consistent, binding power which indwells sinners. Paul uses both the singular form and the plural form of *sin* in the book of Romans. The plural form of *sin* indicates wrongdoings, but the singular form means the power that drives sinful conduct. Sin has deprived life to such a degree that there is not one single aspect of life which has not been distorted or polluted. The Reformers insisted on and persisted in fighting against the incomplete understanding of the power of sin in medieval scholasticism. Sin not only pollutes the sphere of the will, it penetrates emotion and reason as well. The ultimate result of this destroying power is to cause man to be self-abusing and self-killing. As Kierkegaard said, men are born in sin. The only power we possess is the power to kill ourselves.

Sin is the rejection of God's eternal will. The ultimate result of sin is not only to harm man, but to oppose the eternal will of God through man. Calvin said, "Nothing is greater than the will of God except God himself." The creation of the universe, the salvation of mankind, and eternal glory all exist by the will of God. Sin is the rejection of the will of God, so Christians need to be conscious of the importance of faithful obedience. As Christ taught his disciples to pray, "Let thy will be done, on earth as in heaven." The Bible also teaches us, in 1 John 2:17 (NKJV), that "the world is passing away, and the lust of it; but he who does the will of God abides forever."

Sin and Cosmic Relations

The event of sin did not stop, it is an ongoing evil within the sinner and a disturbance to cosmic order. Sin destroys relationships, both personally and cosmically, including the relationships between man and nature, and man and men. Sin also destroys the relationship between man and himself. Therefore, sin makes harmonious life impossible. Yet, deepest of all is the destruction of the relationship between man and God.

From the original privilege, we are created higher than nature, and nature is created for man. Man is to appreciate, enjoy, govern, preserve, and interpret nature as man's prophetic function. But sin turned man into the abuser, the enemy, and even the destroyer of nature. Searching nature and discovering the truths of God revealed in it, is the foundation of science. Yet, since the appearance of sin, science has failed to function as a tool to glorify God and has been used as a demonic instrument to destroy nature and man.

As the result of broken relationships between man and men, man has lost the potential to reflect the love of the triune God, which is the model of human community. It makes mutual respect, trust, edification, and mutual accomplishment in our society impossible. Instead, we see the absoluteness of the individual "self" to reject others with the self-centered life that causes tension and unceasing hatred. Man has become his own enemy. He has lost all spiritual peace, eternal security, and confidence of life's meaning. Therefore, the existence of man has become an isolated island in the universe. Others' existence has become a hell which threatens us. These are all reflected in modern atheistic existentialism.

The most serious broken relationship is between man and God, which is the cause of the brokenness of other relationships. When man is separated from God, no other relationship is able to be restored. It blocks all possibilities of personal peace in our spirits and universal peace on earth. The twentieth century was the practical field of nineteenth-century ideologies, yet we see no true hope for our future, even now in the final decade of this century. More than at any other time, we need to seriously rethink and reevaluate the shortcomings of the ideologies derived from anthropocentric humanism.

The Bible says, God is Love, God is Life, God is Light. He is also the God of truth, righteousness, and holiness. What kinds of societies will exist if we depart from such a God as is revealed in Christ? The only possibilities left will be hatred, death, darkness, deception, injustice, and corruption. This is precisely what we see in our world today.

Sin and Lostness

Separation from God leads sinners into a state of lostness—lostness from the countenance and presence of God. Sin causes man to fall short of God's glory. The Augustinian concept of sin as the lacking of good needs to be understood as a result of sin in man, rather than as the interpretation of sin itself. When sin occurs, the glory of God is immediately removed. The privilege of man as the representative of God and the reflector of his glory ends. The removal of the glory of God from man leaves him in a pitiful state. Man will live without honor and greatness, education will be devoid of truth, human rights will contain no righteousness, knowledge without wisdom, lust without love, science without conscience, and freedom without control. As reflected in the book of Ezekiel, the glory of God removes gradually and departs from the temple of God. It means the judgment of God is near, the doom for the world is at hand.

The effects of the state of lostness are seen in many areas:

1. *Universal identity.* Separation from God makes man a universal prodigal, determined to be tired of his ungrounded existence and uncontrolled freedom.
2. *Spiritual dignity.* Man was crowned with glory. Sin destroys the unity between man and God, and dignity becomes an idea without reality.
3. *Inner security.* Men are created for God and can only obtain peace and security in God himself. When the separation occurs, our peace is ended.
4. *Eternal direction.* God is our origin and our conclusion. Potentially, the image of God indicates that man is created to be like God. Theologically, man is to live for him as life's final goal. When sin occurs, eternity loses direction.

Not only this, lostness affects sinners themselves. Men are lost from the presence of God forever. Man is lost from the source of truth, righteousness, love, and eternal blessings. The result of sin is more than terrifying. The judgment of God will be upon sinners; then will follow the second death, which the Bible calls hell where the love and truth, and the presence and holiness of God are eternally withdrawn.

Believers and evangelicals all over the world need to reaffirm the seriousness of the fact and the effect of sin, as it is taught in the Bible. This affirmation is crucial in this post-liberal and post-modern era, both theologically and socio-politically. We also need deep conviction for the need of sinners for salvation, and fervent affection to love sinners. Let us faithfully proclaim the gospel to the sinful world.

"Repent ye, for the kingdom of God is at hand." "Behold the Lamb of God, who takes away the sin of the world." These great forewords of the gospel remain valid until the end of the world. Let us shout, "Repent, ye people, rend your hearts but not your garments!" to the leaders and the people of the world. Let's lift the Cross of Christ high, which is the only hope of mankind, so the Holy Spirit will illuminate our generation to accept Christ. Let us humbly confess our sins before God, to reopen the door of heaven and regain the mercy and forgiveness of him.

Worthy is the Lamb that was slain! Glory be to him forever and ever more.

Cross-Cultural Evangelism

Panya Baba

And the gospel of the kingdom shall be preached in all the world for a witness unto all nations and then the end will come (Matthew 24:14).

About a year ago, one of the village heads posed this challenging question to a cross-cultural missionary: "Do you really believe what you are preaching to us?"

"Yes," replied the missionary with conviction.

"How long ago did your people get this news?" he asked.

"About sixty years ago," replied the missionary.

The leader paused and asked, "Why didn't you come to tell us before my father and other relatives died? If God will judge those who do not believe, what will God do to those who receive the message and do not quickly tell others?"

The unfinished task of world evangelization in our generation is still too enormous to be left to a *few* active Christian workers and missionaries. The task calls for the involvement of the universal church of Christ in evangelism regardless of geographical boundaries. Existing local churches, denominational and non-denominational agencies, parachurch agencies, lay people, and individual believers of Christ are to proclaim Christ cross-culturally until he comes.

Cross-cultural evangelism means evangelizing and planting new churches among people groups culturally different from the evangelizing Christians.

The Unfinished Task

It is shocking to see that more than two billion people, or 40 percent of the world's population, have yet to hear the gospel of Christ. According to the record of provisional data from Lausanne II:

There are about two thousand ethno-linguistic groups of people among whom there is no indigenous community of Christians with adequate members and resources to evangelize their groups. There are also about one thousand unevangelized cities and thirty unevangelized countries.

We have heard by the speakers at this Congress that most of the unreached groups live in countries where normal missionary work is restricted and where there is no

---

Panya Baba is President of the Evangelical Churches of West Africa (ECWA). He has served as missionary, pastor, and director of the Evangelical Missionary Society in his country of Nigeria.

existing church to witness to them, such as in socialist countries or in countries where other world religions dominate. Here we must include those unreached religious groups living even in the so-called Christian countries like the thousands of Muslims who live in Western countries today.

In Nigeria alone, there are still over one hundred unreached people groups. The Butawa people received their first missionary couple just three years ago. The three largest unreached tribes in Nigeria are Muslim groups. Research reveals that there are fifteen thousand towns and villages in the whole country of Ghana without Protestant churches. There are two million unreached people in Southern Ghana and three million unreached people in Northern Ghana.

There are many other countries that have people yet to be reached with the gospel. These are the lost sheep that must be brought into the fold (John 10:16). The key is for cross-cultural missionaries to go there first to witness and evangelize.

Trends in Our World

As the result of God's punishment for the pride of mankind at Babel, the world is filled with an incredible patchwork of cultures. This multi-cultural setting makes the task of reaching the world a difficult one. However, this also makes the need for cross-cultural evangelism an imperative. Some of these people groups are being absorbed by others within the country, but most have retained their cultural uniqueness. Each culture has its own language and social structure and would need a viable strategy for their evangelization.

Traditional homelands are gradually being deserted and large-scale migration to urban centers is increasing. The question arises as to how the giant cities with different immigrants having different cultures will be evangelized. Christians are seen in the large cities setting up churches of their own tribes or groups. The implication of this is that they can still be identified in the urban areas.

The fulcrum of missions is rapidly moving from the West to the Two-Thirds World. As we have heard, there are over twenty thousand cross-cultural missionary workers from the Two-Thirds World alone. The church in this part of the world is facing the task with great courage. And it is hoped that by the year 2000 there will be 160 thousand cross-cultural missionaries from the Two-Thirds World alone.

Let us also not forget that recent statistics show that 93 percent of all cross-cultural missionaries are working in churches or church-related projects and only 7 percent are working among unreached people. This is an unbalanced missionary focus.

The growing evangelical movement in the Two-Thirds World is offsetting the loss experienced in Europe. For example, it took less than ten years for the Nigerian student movement to become one of the world's largest evangelical student movements.

The Possibility of the Great Commission

Despite the trends in our world, reaching the unreached people groups is not impossible. We are commanded to preach the gospel to every creature (Mark 16:15), and we are to make disciples of all nations (Matthew 28:19–20).

During the Global Consultation on World Evangelization by A.D. 2000, an encouraging statement was made. "We believe that we can bring the gospel to all the people by the year 2000." This can be accomplished with sufficient dedication, unity, and mobilization of available resources, powered and directed by God.

As we seek to finish the task, we can see that there is no alternative to cross-cultural evangelism. Saved Christians must go to proclaim the gospel to unreached people wherever they are. "How shall they hear without a preacher? And how shall they preach except they are sent?" (Romans 10:14–15). The Turkana tribe in Kenya was counted as an unreached group until missionaries went to settle among them ten years ago. Now the tribe is being touched with the message of salvation. Five of the unreached people groups in Nigeria, namely the Gwandara, Koma, Koko, Dirim, and Kambari are also being reached. More than three hundred new churches have been planted among these tribes during the past seven years because cross-cultural missionaries were sent to them. They would still have remained unreached today if no one had been sent.

The Emerging Harvest Force

We live in an exciting missionary era. The Lord of the harvest is doing a new thing as we work on the final harvest for world evangelization:

1. *The rise of the new missionary force from the Two-Thirds World.* Some receiving countries are now beginning to send missionaries.
2. *The growth in Christian workers.* It is encouraging to notice that in 1989, the total number of Christian workers has risen to 3.8 million while the number of Protestant and Roman Catholic missionaries alone is about .27 million or 270,000.

There is no doubt that there has been appreciable growth of the missionary work force. However, even with this number of workers, we still need more workers to cope with the unfinished task. We need to mobilize Christian professionals, "tentmakers," students, lay people, and women for cross-cultural evangelism and church planting.

Obstacles or Hindrances

1. *Lack of Vision.* "Where there is no vision, the people perish" (Proverbs 28:18). There are many local churches that are yet to catch the cross-cultural missionary vision. We need to pray fervently for the renewal of the vision of cross-cultural evangelism in our local churches. Some local churches are evangelizing successfully in Jerusalem and Judea, but have yet to enter Samaria and the uttermost parts of the world. If each local church would make it a goal to send or add just one new couple or two couples of cross-cultural missionaries from now until 2000, we would see a great increase. My denomination alone could come out with three thousand missionary couples by 2000.
2. *Denominational Differences Resulting in Strife.* This hinders the coopera-tion vital for cross-cultural evangelism. We should work together instead of separating from one another. This togetherness does not demand an organic organizational structure. Each church can have autonomy, but we must remember that there is no church, mission, or organization that can finish the task alone.
3. *Economic Constraints.* Many Two-Thirds World mission agencies who serve countries across their national borders cannot support their mission-aries because of foreign-exchange restrictions. The principle of partnership should be applied as the Holy Spirit guides. A two- or three-party partnership could be considered.
4. *Lack of Burden, Compassion, and Genuine Love for the Lost.* Romans 9:22–23, Matthew 9:36, and 2 Corinthians 5:14 give the motivation for

mobilizing more Christians for cross-cultural witnessing.

5. *Entry Restrictions.* Some countries close doors to cross-cultural missionaries. Various categories of missionaries should be utilized to overcome these barriers.

6. *People Missionary Movement.* Most of the major religions spread through the process of immigration and trade. In the early church, God used the persecution of the church for a "People Missionary Movement" (Acts 8:1–4). Members of our local church today should be taught how to be a part of a People Missionary Movement during persecution or in time of relative peace. We are all witnesses for Christ wherever we go.

7. *Inadequate Training.* The principles of cross-cultural evangelism and discipleship must be taught to the workers to equip them for the most effective service.

Proposed Strategies

1. *Prayer Cells.* Each local church should organize prayer for cross-cultural evangelism programs. Jesus told his disciples, "Pray ye the Lord of the harvest, that he will send forth laborers into his harvest" (Matthew 9:38). In the Bible, when the Antioch church devoted itself to prayer, the Holy Spirit ordered the separation of Paul and Barnabas for cross-cultural evangelism (Acts 13:2–3).

   A good example of this kind of praying is found in the Korean church, when its members devote themselves to prayer on the mountains. As a result, members and churches multiply. Prayer is like the electrical switch to the power of the Holy Spirit. We do nothing apart from the power of the Holy Spirit. It is not by might, nor by power, but by God's Spirit (Zechariah 4:6). The power of the Holy Spirit is not limited. The Bible is still the same. The Spirit is far ahead of us—preparing people to receive the Word. But we are reluctant to go and share.

2. *Provide Adequate Cross-cultural Training for the Workers.* Adequate training is imperative. The training need not be identical everywhere. We should not transfer patterns wholesale without considering the cultural relevance of such patterns to the receiving countries. We must study their beliefs and their social and traditional practices. The World Evangelical Fellowship (WEF) missions commission spent several days discussing this issue. We agreed to print, at some time in the future, a pamphlet on effective training procedures.

   Areas that we need to look at with greater flexibility than we have done in the past are: (*a*) verbal communication, (*b*) non-verbal communication, (*c*) individual personal approach, (*d*) family or relative approach

3. *Emphasize the People Concept.* Each mission agency, local church, and parachurch group should adopt the unreached people concept as we seek to finish the task. As we do this, let us begin as Paul did by reaching out to places where Christ had not been made known (Romans 15:20–21). I like the goal of, "A church in every unreached people group by the year 2000."

4. *Mobilizing the Local Church.* Pastors and mission leaders should get together and organize more Mission Awareness programs, conferences, and seminars. The church needs to release many types of missionaries— tentmaking missionaries, professionals, short- and long-term missionar-

ies—all are needed to fill vacancies on the fields.

5. *Cooperation or Partnership.* It is not possible for one single organization to finish the task of world evangelization. It is, therefore, necessary for us to keep providing a forum for cooperation or partnership between emerging and established missions, parachurch, and denominational missions so that we can avoid competition and duplication. Examples are:

- The Southern Baptist Foreign Mission Board in cooperation with others. "More than a dozen sister denominations overseas are coordinating their mission efforts in this worldwide movement called Bold Mission Thrust."
- During the past three years, the Sudan Interior Mission (SIM) Board in the United States has entered into cooperative agreement with several other mission agencies in Asian and Latin American countries in order to give the final thrust for cross-cultural evangelism.
- The Cooperation of three major Christian radio ministries (HCJB, FEBA, and TWR) with a common goal of reaching the entire world by the year 2000 is a very challenging development. They are presently proclaiming the gospel in more than one hundred languages. According to information given Dr. Ron Cline, more than 90 percent of the world's population can now hear the Good News in a language they can understand.
- The Indonesian Missionary Fellowship provides opportunity for both western and non-western missionaries to work together towards a common goal in cross-cultural missions.

6. *Redeployment of Some Missionaries.* Our missionaries should be redeployed to work in unreached areas. We need to balance the distribution of the force we have.

7. *Planting Mission-Minded Churches.* Many church members are not interested in cross-cultural evangelism. The whole idea is foreign to their thinking. We need an effective missionary endeavor based on the local church in order to produce workers and support for cross-cultural evangelism. The mission of the church is not only local, but global. Pastors are the key for training laity in discipleship and mission awareness.

8. *Applying the Right Cross-Cultural Approach or Method to the Unreached People.* The right strategy speeds up understanding of the gospel and hastens the work of cross-cultural church planting. Some unreached people have very strong family ties, and decisions have to be made by the head of the family or religion or village. We need to be sensitive. Both people movements and the individual approach should be utilized where appropriate (Acts 8:26–39, John 4:10–42, Acts 16:32–34).

- Verbal and non-verbal communication of the gospel in cross-cultural evangelism should be considered.
- Sacrifice is needed in order to identify with people from other cultures. We need to learn from the Master himself who emptied himself and "made himself of no reputation, and took upon him the form of a servant, and was made in the likeness of men" (Philippians

2:7, KJV). We are to learn from Paul who said, "To the weak I became weak, to win the weak" (1 Corinthians 9:22).

A case in point is the Dirim people, who live high in the mountains of Nigeria near the boundary of Nigeria and Cameroon. For several years, the first three Evangelical Missionary Society (EMS) couples sent to the Dirim had trouble in evangelizing the people. They had isolated themselves from other tribes due to long years of tribal warfare. They rejected any attempt by the government to develop their areas and ran away from any visitor or stranger who attempted to get near them. They regarded any person apart from their tribe as an enemy, therefore, an enemy could bring them no "Good News."

When the EMS discovered this secret they began the non-verbal approach to building bridges of friendship and reducing their fears. They did this by spending days helping them in farming, free of charge. The missionaries' wives also fetched drinking water from the streams and would carry it to their wives' small thatched kitchens, without mentioning anything about the gospel.

After several weeks some of them began to come nearer and question the missionaries. "Tell us who you are? Why are you different from other tribes people who fight against us? Why are you so kind and helpful to us?"

When the missionaries responded to their questions and shared the love of God with them, the Dirim village leaders summoned a meeting of the village heads and discussed the uniqueness of the missionaries and their message and then passed the information to all the family heads and relatives. They said, "We recognize these preachers as people of a different God from our gods. They are so kind with love to us. We also agree that their message is true and for our welfare. Therefore, anyone interested can accept them and their message because they came and are here for our good." Within a short time there was a breakthrough. Fifteen of them accepted the Lord Jesus. Now, new churches are being planted among the Dirim tribe. Let us remember that Jesus didn't say let your light be shown only, but rather, "Let your light so shine before men, that they may see your good works, and glorify your Father which is in heaven" (Matthew 5:16, KJV). In the Gospel of John, Jesus said, "By this shall all men know that ye are my disciples, if ye have love one to another" (John 13:35, KJV).

Conclusion

The challenge must go beyond this Congress. We should be good stewards who carry the cross-cultural missionary vision to the grass roots of our local churches. Each local church's vision for cross-cultural evangelism must not stop in its Jerusalem and Judea, but go beyond that to Samaria and the uttermost parts of the world. We are called to repentance from our past failure to accomplish the task of world evangelization. According to the *Global Consultation of World Evangelization A.D. 2000 Manifesto*:

> We humbly confess our pride, prejudice, competition, and disobedience that have hindered our evangelization. These sins have impeded God's desire to spread abroad his gracious provision of eternal salvation through the precious blood of his Son Jesus Christ. The revelation of God in Christ is plain. The commission to his church is clear. The unfinished task is apparent. The opportunity to work together is ours.

We are called to rededicate ourselves to a deeper commitment to the unfinished task of cross-cultural evangelism, so that our work force will be increased as we seek to complete the task by A.D. 2000 and beyond. We need to produce more audiovisual materials that are applicable to the people we reach. In this way, more cross-cultural missionaries will he recruited. May the vision of Lausanne II teach us to see we have been too long reluctant to accomplish the task of cross-cultural evangelism. It is our responsibility to proclaim the gospel to all peoples, tribes, and tongues of the world so that they will stand before the Lamb clothed with white robes and with palms in their hands, worshiping with a loud voice, saying, "Salvation to our God which sitteth upon the throne, and unto the Lamb" (Revelation 7:9–10).

VIDEO PRESENTATION

The Challenge of Other Religions

Producer: Richard Klein

From earliest times, man has sought to know the unknowable, touch the untouchable, and to find peace for his troubled soul. His search for God has followed many paths, from paganism to the occult. Man has worshipped his deities in the smallest of objects and the largest of celestial bodies.

But while man's individual creeds are innumerable, there are only a few religions of significant historical, cultural, and apostolic importance. And only one is the truth.

Perhaps the oldest and the most complex challenge to Christianity is Hinduism. Based in India, and tracing its origins to the third millennium B.C., Hinduism has no central, discernable founder. The word *Hindu* refers to an array of beliefs, encompassing nearly every form or style of religion that has been conceived or practiced, not all of which are consistent with one another.

Hinduism has regularly absorbed internal and external challenges throughout history. It is seen as the most tolerant of the world's great religions. Permeating the Hindu faith is a pervasive sense of reality in the unseen or spiritual. The Christian concept of forgiveness is alien to the devout Hindu. In its place is the doctrine of *karma,* or "retribution." Today, as it has in the past, modern Hinduism has sought to incorporate the ideals and ethics of other major religions, such as Christianity, while simultaneously adapting itself to human secularism and the science of evolution.

Presently, there are 690 million adherents of Hinduism, representing 13.3 percent of the total world population. Hindus are predominantly born into their faith, rather than converted, and are, therefore, found mainly in India. However, Hinduism can be found in those areas of the globe where large numbers of Indians have migrated, including Malaysia, Java, Borneo, Fiji, and East Africa.

Buddhism, an outgrowth of Hinduism, was founded by Siddhartha, a prince of sixth century B.C. India. The word *Buddha* was, in fact, a somewhat generic title, meaning "the enlightened one."

Defied by his followers in the centuries after his death, Buddha never intended to found a new religion, or even to reform Hinduism. His original teachings dealt more with ethics and self-awareness than anything resembling doctrine or dogma. However, in a movement resembling the geographical expansion of Christianity under Constantine, Buddhism developed a distinctly non-Hindu missionary imperative during the third century B.C. The new faith swept through Asia, replacing or absorbing existing religious systems, while at the same time losing its foothold in India.

Within this century, Buddhism has begun a fresh revival. Spurred in part by Western interest in the exotic religion, Buddhism gained new popularity following the post-World War II collapse of colonialism. The rise of Asian nationalism created a new sense of ethnic and religious pride, while to many, the preternatural Buddhist concept of tolerance seemed more in keeping with mankind's needs in the advent of the nuclear age.

In 1989, Buddhists number 320 million, or 6.2 percent of the world's people. Buddhism is still the predominant belief of much of the Far East, from Manchuria to Java, Central Asia to the islands of Japan.

Matching, and perhaps surpassing, the recent resurgence of traditional Eastern religious belief is the modern mutation known as the New Age movement. A spiritual hybrid, New Age incorporates the essence of Eastern mysticism with diverse occult practices, from clairvoyance to channeling, astral projection to astrology. The New Age movement does, however, reflect a definitive Western orientation, replacing the asceticism of mainstream Eastern ideology with twentieth-century hedonism. For the New Age adherent, worldly success is not incompatible with enlightenment.

Transformation of society is the open goal of the New Age movement, though propagation sometimes employs bizzare techniques. The recent "harmonic convergence" saw participants gathered across the planet in key locations, such as the great pyramids in Egypt. At an agreed moment, a global "hum" arose, in a consciousness-raising attempt to speed the dawn of the New Age.

The New Age movement sees every man as a god. But the world's fastest growing religion, and the one which poses the most serious challenge to Christianity, is noted for its strict monotheism—Islam. It has been argued that the seventh century A.D. Arabian prophet Muhammad's vision was to give his people a contextualized version of the monotheism which he saw among the Christians and Jews living in and around Arabia. But while Christians can say, "The word became flesh," Muslims say in effect "the word became book," that is, in the *Quran*. The word *Islam* means "submission," submission to the will of God.

Islam is the only faith besides Christianity which claims to be a universal religion, and in fact, the one and only true religion. Incorporated in the Islamic belief system is a fervent missionary zeal, which has spread the faith to over nine hundred million followers. The world is 17.5 percent Muslim, with the largest numbers concentrated in countries ranging from Morocco to Indonesia.

Hinduism, Buddhism, Islam, and the New Age movement are not the only religious challenges to Christianity at the end of the twentieth century. Another 9.6 percent of the world's population is involved in a variety of other faiths, from various ancient and new Asian religions, to Judaism, Sikhism, and African tribal religions. What is the challenge of these faiths to the third of the world that considers itself Christian?

Before any person can be brought to a saving knowledge of Jesus Christ, there must be a penetration beyond religious and cultural barriers. Instead of passing judgment from the outside, Christians need to look beneath the surface and understand other ways of life from within. Beneath the layers of culture, tradition, and dogma, there remains in each person the fundamental desire to know the truth. And across the globe, God's truth is penetrating to the hearts of the people all around us.

The Challenge of Other Religions

Colin Chapman

When we speak about "other religions," we are speaking about people who make up two-thirds of the human race. Since a large proportion of them are poor and hungry, it's hardly an exaggeration to say that two of the most important issues we have to tackle at this Congress are poverty and other religions. In our concern for the two billion who haven't heard the gospel, we have to reckon not only with the situations in which they live, but also with the religions to which they already belong.

But why do we consider other religions a "challenge"? Part of the reason is because they have worldviews which conflict at many points with our own, but also because instead of disappearing or disintegrating, as some of our forefathers thought they would, almost all of them have grown in numbers, and at least one of them has its own vision of winning the world.

How do we attempt to discuss the challenge of other religions? It's not enough to simply work out strategies for reaching people of other faiths. While we set about that huge task, or perhaps even before we do so, we need to do some hard thinking about other religions in general. Their very existence, their numbers, their vitality, and their resistance to the Christian message should force us to wrestle with the difficult theological questions which the church as a whole in the twentieth century has been slow to face. We need cool heads as well as warm hearts!

Where do we begin? Because the subject is so vast and complex, I have prepared some discussion materials to go with this address which suggest ways of mapping out the ground and isolating the crucial questions. It includes case studies from different parts of the world, illustrating some of the dilemmas which Christians face today in relating to their neighbors of other faiths ("Feeling the Dilemmas"). It then addresses how we should interpret the statistics ("Interpreting the Statistics"). The next section deals with deciding what's different and special about the context in which we approach the subject today ("Understanding Our Context"). Finally, we outline a whole range of questions which need to be faced ("Asking the Right Questions").

Let's take four of these major questions and explore briefly how we can use the Scriptures to help us to find relevant and appropriate answers.

What Is Our Theology of Other Religions?

Evangelical Christians tend to emphasize passages in Scripture which present other

Colin Chapman *is Lecturer in Mission and Religion at Trinity College, Bristol, England. He is a citizen of Great Britain.*

religions in a negative light. In the Exodus, for example, God brings judgment on the gods of Egypt (Numbers 33:4). At Sinai he declares, I am the Lord your God, . . . You shall have no other gods before me" (Exodus 20:2–3). The people are not to copy the religious practices of the Canaanites "because in worshiping their gods, they do all kinds of detestable things the Lord hates" (Deuteronomy 12:31). And the psalmist knows that "all the gods of the nations are idols, but the Lord made the heavens" (Psalm 96:5).

Is the total picture throughout Scripture as clear-cut as this? Genesis 1–11 teaches a theology of the nations, in which Yahweh is no mere tribal God, but is concerned with all seventy nations. Melchizedek is described as a "priest of God Most High" (el elyon), and Abraham seems to identify Melchizedek's God with Yahweh when he speaks of "God Most High, Creator of heaven and earth" (Genesis 14:18–22). This same God of Abraham communicates with an outsider like Abimelech in a dream. And Job, who lives in the land of Uz, perhaps during the time of the patriarchs, has no contact with them, and yet has personal dealings with Yahweh (Job 38:1; 40:1; 42:1). Several of the prophets have to challenge the attitudes of arrogance, superiority, and complacency which often go with convictions about uniqueness. Amos, for example, says that while the Exodus was a unique event, it doesn't mean that God has only been at work in the history of Israel, and not in the history of other peoples (Amos 9:7). Jonah is a reluctant missionary, who finds to his surprise that people of another faith are more responsive to God than his own people (Jonah 3–4). And Malachi shocks his listeners when he suggests the sacrifices offered by their pagan neighbors may be more acceptable to God than their own careless worship (Malachi 1).

Similarly, the disciples of Jesus find their attitudes toward people of other races and faiths need to be changed. As a result of what happens to Cornelius, Peter says, "I now realize how true it is that God does not show favoritism" (NIV), "but in every nation any one who fears him and does what is right is acceptable to him (RSV)" (Acts 10:34–35). Cornelius needs to respond to the gospel before he can experience salvation. The word acceptable (dektos) doesn't mean "justified" or "saved." But it says something significant about the status of individual people of other faiths who have the fear of God in their hearts.

What then is our theology of religions? We can hardly say that other religions are simply "satanic delusions," or simply "human attempts to find the truth," or simply "preparations for the gospel." If we are to relate all we know about other religions today to all we find in Scripture, our theology of other religions will have to be flexible enough to include elements of all three of these explanations.

What About People Who Have Never Heard the Gospel?

This difficult question is raised partly because there is some uneasiness with the answers that have been given in the past, and partly because many liberals suspect that we've never really faced the dilemma or tested the logic of our answers.

In its simplest terms, the question is this: Is salvation only for those who consciously and openly profess faith in Jesus Christ? Are people of other faiths, before and after the time of Christ, who haven't heard the message, excluded from the possibility of salvation?

Putting the question in these terms helps us understand why the current debate is much more complicated than it used to be. In the past, it seemed as if we had a simple choice between the traditional Christian answers and the universalism which says that everyone will be saved. But now the number of options has increased:

1. *The exclusivist* believes Christ is the only path to salvation.

2. *The inclusivist* believes that while Christ is the final and definitive revelation of God, his presence and saving activity are also found in non-Christian religions. The salvation offered by Christ can, therefore, be mediated in and through faiths other than Christianity.

3. *The Pluralist* believes that all religions provide ways of salvation which are equally valid, and that Christianity cannot claim to be either the only path (exclusivism) or the fulfillment of other paths (inclusivism).

All of us who subscribe to the Lausanne Covenant affirm that salvation comes only through Christ, and, therefore, probably place ourselves firmly within the exclusivist position. But we don't all agree when we come to work out its implications for those who don't have the opportunity to hear the gospel. We all agree that salvation is an undeserved gift of God's grace which is received through repentance and articulated in response to the proclamation of the gospel. Others, however, without wanting to go the whole way with the inclusivists, have at least some sympathy with their concerns, and believe that God must have his own way into the human heart and know where there is evidence of genuine repentance of faith, even when they are not expressed in words. I hope we are willing to allow differences of this kind within our shared conviction that salvation is found in no other name (Acts 4:12).

Where do we go in the Scriptures when we feel perplexed about these difficult questions? Among other places, we go back to the promise of God to Abraham, that his descendants would be as numerous as the dust of the earth, the stars in the sky, and the grains of sand on the seashore (Genesis 13:16; 15:5; 22:17). Remember also how Jesus answers the question, "Lord, are only a few people going to be saved?" He refuses to reply in terms of numbers, and instead challenges us to make every effort to enter through the narrow door, and beware of an unhealthy concern about numbers. People from every corner of the earth will be at the feast, and there are going to be some surprises in heaven (Luke 13:22–30)!

To Dialogue or Not to Dialogue?

Part of the problem is that the word *dialogue* means different things to different people. For some it simply means a conversation between two or more people, while for others it implies a particular open-ended attitude to other faiths. To open up the question, we will begin at an unexpected place—with Luke's description of Jesus in the temple at the age of the twelve (Luke 2:46–47). Jesus is with some of the religious leaders, sitting among them, listening to what they're saying, and asking questions. His audience is amazed at his understanding and his answers.

The value of this picture is that it shows what's involved in *any* genuine meeting of minds in dialogue. "Sitting among them" means working through our fears and trying to relax in the company of people of other faiths. "Listening to them" involves hearing their testimony, reading what they write, and watching what they present on television. We ask questions because we want to understand their worldview, and appreciate their hopes and fears. We need to pray constantly for the special discernment which enables us to see where we have common ground and where we differ, so when we have opportunities to speak of Jesus, our testimony is related to *their* questions and not only to ours.

What happens later when Jesus enters into dialogue with the religious leaders during his public ministry? The Synoptic Gospels reveal the main issues over which he is challenged, and many of these are still relevant to our discussions with people of other faiths. The Gospel of John, however, recounts dialogues of a slightly different kind which focus on the one fundamental objection to the claims of Jesus, "You, a mere man, claim to be God" (John 10:33). In this way, the fourth Gospel makes it clear that for Jesus dialogue is much more than "mutual sharing," because ultimately it leads him to the cross.

If we need an example of Paul practicing dialogue, we can't find a better one than the way he explores common ground with his audience in Athens. Although he's deeply distressed by the idolatry that he sees all around him (Acts 17:16), he doesn't begin his address on a negative note. He isn't mocking their beliefs or pouring scorn on their practices when he describes the Athenians as being "very religious." Throughout the address, he chooses his words carefully, deliberately engaging with each of the different groups in his audience. He certainly challenges some of their ideas when he says, "We should not think that the divine being is like gold or silver or stone" (v. 29), and proclaims without apology that God "commands all people everywhere to repent" (v. 30). But Paul recognizes what is genuine in their worship and searching and begins his proclamation there, "Now what you worship as something unknown I am going to proclaim to you" (v. 23) or "What you worship but do not know—this is what I now proclaim" (NEB).

These models of Jesus and Paul in dialogue convince us that it's nonsense to try to separate proclamation and dialogue. Does our dialogue with people of other faiths ever lead in the same direction as the dialogues of Jesus and of Paul? With these examples before us, is there any reason to be afraid of the word *dialogue* or to be reluctant to practice it?

How Should We Pray About Our Witness?

Paul's prayer at the end of Ephesians has special relevance for the way we pray about the challenge of other religions. When he speaks of "the mystery of the gospel," he uses the world *musterion*, which comes straight out of the mystery religions of his day. But for Paul the Good News about Jesus is not a mystery to be shared only with the initiated; it's an open secret to be shared with the world.

Paul then uses the word *parrhesia*, which comes out of Athens with its tradition of free speech. And he asks others to pray that he will have the courage to speak fearlessly and have the wisdom to find the right words to communicate the Good News to each different audience (Ephesians 6:19–20).

There's another context in which a whole group of Christians pray for this same gift of *parrhesia*—when Peter and John lead the Jerusalem church in prayer. They ask God to release them from their fears and loosen their tongues, "Enable your servants to speak your word with great boldness" (Acts 4:29). At the same time, they realize that their words are limited and ask God to act in his sovereign way to reveal his power, "Stretch out your hand to heal and perform miraculous signs and wonders through the name of your holy servant Jesus" (4:30).

Whatever we think about the so-called "charismatic question," I trust that we all recognize the special relevance of the Apostles' Prayer to our prayer for people of other faiths. It's often a special demonstration of the power of God mediated through Jesus that has brought Muslims, Hindus, Buddhists, and people from traditional religions to trust Jesus as Lord. And if all our churches were praying regularly in these terms, we might perhaps develop a greater sense of expectancy, and begin to look for those ways in which the Holy Spirit is working among people of other faiths and pointing them to the person of Jesus.

I want to close with a short and simple prayer, based on this and other passages of Scripture, which sums up how we can respond in prayer to the challenge of other faiths. Our thinking about the challenge of other religions should lead into prayer, and the way we pray will affect the way we act on our theology. And perhaps at the end of the day, our prayer will be the truest test of our theology.

O God, Creator, Savior, and Guide, we thank you that you have created all people in your image to seek after you and find you, and have sent your Son Jesus that we may know you as the only true God.

Look upon the people of our world in all their need, and forgive us for our failure to show your love and proclaim your truth.

Enable us, your servants, to speak your Word with all boldness, while you stretch out your hand to show your power, through the name of Jesus Christ, our Lord and Savior. Amen.

The Challenge of Other Religions

Martin Alphonse

Today, as we face the challenge of other faiths to evangelism two questions must be raised: *Why are they challenging us?* and *How are they challenging us?*

The Reasons for the Challenge

Historically, the challenge emerged from three factors deeply rooted in the socio-political missionary context of the colonial and post-colonial eras: (*a*) in reaction to the colonial rule, which was mistakenly identified with Western Christianity; (*b*) in defense of the vigorous evangelistic activities of Christian missionaries; and (*c*) in response to ethical questions and criticisms raised by national Christians, as well as by devotees of other faiths who had been enlightened by Christianity.

Combined, these three factors posed a threat to the survival of other faiths in several nations. Many had anticipated the end of the colonial era would result in suspension of the evangelistic missions of the church. On the contrary, most of the national churches revived traditional evangelistic work, and some have become more vigorous than ever before. The number of converts to Christianity has continued to increase in several nations in the post-colonial era and in an unprecedented number in some cases. The escalation and influence of national missionary movements in recent decades is a power to reckon with. Some religious leaders see the Christian evangelistic endeavor as a threat to the survival of their faiths. As a result, in a counterattack, people of other faiths have thrown us some strong challenges.

The Ways of the Challenge

J. T. Seamands identifies two kinds of challenges of other faiths to Christianity today: *intrinsic* and *interactional*.

Intrinsic challenges merge from within the religions, relating to beliefs, systems, and structures and have resulted in the resurgence of non-Christian religions. This resurgence is expressed in four distinct forms:

1. *Revival of the religious spirit.* In reaction to colonial rule and continued Christian missionary enterprise, some religions, such as Hinduism, have

---

Martin Alphonse is a pastor in the Methodist Church of Madras, India. An evangelist, church planter, and lecturer, he is a citizen of India.

founded counter-missionary movements. Others have taken political coverage. For instance, Islam has been established as the state religion in Pakistan and Malaysia, two former British colonies.

2. *Reformation of religious practices.* Reform is carried out by means of "acceptance and incorporation of new ideas and practices." Organized reform movements have been effective in winning back converts from Christianity and in preventing potential aspirants from converting to Christianity.

3. *Reinterpretation of religious doctrines.* In defense against accelerated evangelistic activities of Christianity, some religions have been pressured into making radical reinterpretations of some important doctrines. In the process, the old faith acquires a new meaning, new resilience, and new vitality. In Hinduism, idol worship, myths, and caste systems are now explained in new and relevant ways. In Islam, *Jihad,* the "Holy War," is now redefined as a spiritual warfare between the faithful and the infidels. In Buddhism, *Nirvana*—whose original meaning of "blow out" or "extinguish"— is now reinterpreted as "a state of perfect bliss and contentment."

4. *Relevancy of one's own faith.* If religion is primarily a means of meeting basic, human spiritual need, especially in relation to destiny and salvation, then most people are content with what their religion offers. Hence, there is an absence of a "felt need" for replacement of their faith by Christianity. To many, religion is synonymous with the culture to which they are inseparably attached. Religion is a way of life which is biologically inherited; you are born with it, therefore, you are bound by it. For example, many educated Hindus will respond, "A Hindu is born, not born again." Christians are seen as culturally distant and alien.

There are also interactional challenges. The resurgence of these faiths has yielded desired results. Evidently, people of these faiths are confident not only about their survival, but also about their competency in being easy and effective rivals to the unique claims of Christ and Christianity. The spirit of rivalry is evident in the following criticism.

1. *They criticize our failure.*

- They cannot distinguish between true Christians and nominal ones. They point out increases in the rate of divorce, crime, and licentiousness among Christians, especially in the so-called "Christian" West.
- They are confused by the multiplicity of denominations and their competition in a small area. They are confused by our diversity.
- They accuse us of being unpatriotic. To them, Christians are too "other-worldly," too spiritual, and have no concern for people's immediate needs. Conversion is seen as an expression of arrogance. They feel it symbolizes a superiority complex and a disrespect for other religions.
- They say our lifestyle is incompatible with the gospel we preach. As E. Stanley Jones used to say when missionaries first preached the gospel to India, the Hindu intelligentsia responded saying, "What you say is not *true*." When the missionaries proved it to be true, they

took a second defense and said, "Well, it is not *new!*" When the missionaries proved it also to be new, they are making a final defense saying, "The gospel is not in *you!*"

Brethren, let us examine our hearts. The gospel has no credibility to people of other faiths unless and until they see the gospel lived out by us visibly.

2. *They challenge our claims.*

- They say that Jesus is only one way. There are many other ways, too.
- They insist that every religion is unique and complete in itself.
- They argue that traditional religions, older than Christianity, must not be dispensed with.

3. *They claim universality of all religions.*

- To them all religions share the same content, though they may differ in form. They argue that "all roads lead to Rome."
- They emphasize that service to humans is indeed service to God which is "true religion." Hence, missionary service is no longer the monopoly of Christians.

4. *They invite us to compromise and cooperate.*

- They suggest, "Let us work together to fulfill a common task—build a global society, fight paganism and secularism, and strive for peaceful coexistence."
- They proclaim "God is our Father. We are all his children. Come join the universal brotherhood."

The intensity of the challenge before us makes the task of evangelizing peoples of other faiths impossible. Yet, the commission of Jesus Christ to his church is clear: "Go and make disciples of all peoples." He meant business. He would not have told them to do something that was humanly impossible. Therefore, there must be a sure way to penetrate the impenetrable, reach the unreachable, and gain access to the inaccessible.

The Great Commission is clear. It commands us to "make disciples of all peoples," not all religions. Colin Chapman reminded us that "What we're talking, thinking, and praying about here is not other religions but other people—people of other faiths or of no faith." We are dealing with people in need—in all kinds of need. The three great elemental needs are said to be an adequate goal for character, a free and full life, and a God. Religion is believed to meet these needs squarely. To most humans, religion is inevitable. Our call is to "evangelize the inevitable."

In facing these challenges, it is not Islam, Hinduism, or Buddhism that we will confront with the gospel, but people who cling to these religions for meeting their essential needs.

As E. Stanley Jones suggests,

We need not mention the non-Christian religion but speak to persons in spiritual need. Jesus Christ has met (our) needs, and he would meet theirs. It would be a head-on presentation of Christ.

How, then, do we proclaim Christ relevantly to people of other faiths who totally reject his unique claims as *the* Lord, *the* Savior of the world? How do we convince the Hindu who considers Jesus as only one of the 330 million *avatars* or "incarnations" of God? Or reach the Muslim who acknowledges Jesus only as a prophet and says it is blasphemous to call him the Son of God? How do we persuade a Buddhist, Jain, or Sikh who respects Jesus as nothing but a supreme guru or teacher?

Where there has been a ready and phenomenal response to Christ and his gospel, there is cause for celebration. There have been mass movements in South India in the early century, and ongoing people movements in South Korea, Indonesia, and in several nations south of the Sahara in Africa. But where there is reluctance, resistance, or rejection we need to prayerfully explore new ways and means of evangelization.

The answer is found in developing a need-oriented Christology, placing the right emphasis on the right point in the right context.

Developing a Contextual Christology

Evangelistic proclamation should begin at a point of relevancy. As they say, the first impression is the best impression. To make our entry into the hearts of people of other faiths easy and natural, we must first decide where our emphasis should fall. The need for an appropriate entrypoint leads to the formulation of what may be called *situational accentuation.*

The Theory of Situational Accentuation

This theory is based on certain assumptions:

1. *The gospel is multi-dimensional and wholistic in nature.* It meets not only the spiritual needs of humans, but their total needs such as emotional, moral, social, and physical.
2. *Humans differ in their basic needs.* Although every human need is wholistic, the intensity of a particular need in a given moment varies from person to person. But the gospel is able to meet the need of any human— anytime, anywhere.

The "Nazareth Manifesto" in Luke 4:19 affirms this. Christ is saying the Good News is good news to the spiritually, economically, physically, and socially disenfranchised humanity. This is a gospel which meets the total needs of the total human. Charles Taber speaks of Jesus who in a "sensitive and careful way ... offered each person a gospel tailored to his or her own context." Thus, depending on the situation, the particular dimension of the gospel which meets that situation should be accentuated.

The theory of situational accentuation has an entrypoint and a finish line. The entrypoint is the particular felt need which Christ can meet adequately. It is the person's first encounter with Jesus Christ. At this point, Christ may be seen as a supreme deity, an affectionate mother, a cordial friend, or a venerable guru. This first encounter with Christ by an adherent of another faith must be further developed. As they get closer to Christ, they develop a deeper relationship with him, eventually leading to the finish line as they realize Christ is more than a teacher or friend. But the final realization of the fullness of Christ cannot happen except for their first encounter or experience with the Living Christ.

My father—a staunch, orthodox Hindu—was converted to Christ as a result of a miraculous healing. He had prayed to Jesus when the physicians had given up all hope.

The entrypoint of conversion was an immediate *physical need* met by Jesus.

I was a Roman Catholic, a former Jesuit novice, and a Marxist sympathizer. I was converted to Christ when Jesus liberated me from a severe inferiority complex. The entrypoint of my conversion was an immediate *psychological need* met by Jesus.

There is a Brahmin family—father, mother, and three beautiful daughters—who are members of our church. The entire family was converted to Christ when they realized Jesus alone could grant the *shanti* or the "inner peace" they had been long searching for. The entrypoint of conversion was an immediate *emotional and spiritual need* met by Jesus.

Two days prior to leaving Madras for Lausanne II in Manila, I had the thrill of baptizing eleven Hindu converts to Christ. They live in one of the pitiable slums in Madras. They were converted to Christ when they discovered that Jesus alone could give them a true sense of identity and restore their dignity, which was being destroyed by the discriminatory caste structure of Hindu society. The entrypoint of their conversion was the immediate individual and collective *social need* met by Jesus.

Jesus Christ did not die on the cross to heal my father of an incurable sickness, or to emancipate me from an inferiority complex, or to give inner peace to a few Hindu seekers, or to liberate the socially oppressed people of India. He died on the cross to take away our sins.

Yet, the fact that he does meet physical, emotional, psychological, spiritual, and social needs cannot be ignored or denied. Therefore, in situations of evangelistic impenetrability, the entrypoint is essential for conversion.

Evangelists have often erred by beginning their communication at the wrong point. Eddy Asirvatham suggests:

> Perhaps the wise thing to do is to invite the non-Christian to accept Jesus Christ as a perfect man, a perfect teacher, and a perfect revealer of God, and to hope that as he personally comes in contact with the spirit of the living Christ, he will be led to further truth and to the acknowledgment of Jesus as his Lord and Savior. To demand that this final stage be made the initial one is to put the cart before the horse.

The theory of situational accentuation has a classic example in the ministry of Jesus in his encounter with the Samaritan woman at the well (John 4:7–42). He began with an accentuation of the human need for water. The woman's first encounter with Jesus was at the level of an ordinary Jew. From that starting point, she gradually began to see him as a teacher, a prophet, the Messiah, and, finally, the whole community acknowledged him as the Savior of the world. The emphasis on the incarnate, immanent God in Christ who meets a particular need of a particular person in a particular moment seems to be the best entrypoint in communicating the gospel.

The task of evangelizing the people of other faiths still seems breathtakingly impossible when we think of it in statistical terms—900 million Muslims, 690 million Hindus, 320 million Buddhists, and so on. Yet, we are not going to meet millions of them at a time or in one large geographical location. We need to think in terms of organized world evangelization by local ministries, reaching a few here and a few there, eventually making the gospel spread everywhere.

This concern demands the discovery of an effective method of evangelism which will not be seen as a threat or an open onslaught on other faiths. Yet, by playing it low-key, the gospel can permeate the various spheres of other faiths in a quiet but firm way.

Determining an Effective Method

In situations of evangelistic impenetrability, the most effective means for opening channels of communication seems to be in dialogue. Colin Chapman has argued forcefully in favor of dialogue as the most effective method of evangelism in this context. He has laid theological and biblical foundations, citing the excellent examples of dialogue our Lord Jesus Christ and the apostle Paul held with their contemporaries. By and large, evangelicals have remained ambivalent toward the use of dialogue in evangelism. Some fear it might become a mere academic discussion rather than a persuasive proclamation of the gospel. Also, the fact that dialogue as an evangelistic method originally emerged from the conciliar circles aroused evangelical suspicions about dialogue as merely intended to foster syncretistic tendencies in religiously pluralistic societies.

Such fears are unwarranted. By dialogue, we are referring to Christocentric discussions between evangelists and non-Christians on the relevance of Christ in their lives. It is strictly an evangelistic methodology, a type of "conversational evangelism." The goal of an evangelistic dialogue is to persuade the non-Christian participants to accept Christ as Lord and Savior. Interfaith dialogue presented in creative and dynamic ways has produced amazing results.

The Round Table Conference of E. Stanley Jones

This method involved bringing together a group of about twenty Christians and non-Christians seated in a circle. They would share what their respective religions meant to them in personal life experience. No one would be allowed to argue, lecture, or criticize other religions—not even to compare one's faith with others. Each person would simply state what his religion meant to him in real life. The evangelist would speak last, not preaching Christ as at other times, but, like everyone else, sharing what Christ meant to him in his personal daily life experience.

Jones saw two main functions of dialogue as an evangelistic method:

1. *Evangelism through personal experience.* The main challenge of dialogue was to put each faith represented to the "acid test" of authenticity, verifiable by experience in down-to-earth, day-to-day life context. Each participant was to speak for their own faith, not based on traditions and doctrines, but from first-hand life experience. This provided a unique opportunity for the evangelist to share Christ and the gospel straight from the heart. It was a spirit witnessing to another spirit—deep calling to deep. It was evangelism done at the deepest level of human personality.
2. *Establishment of the moral supremacy and spiritual uniqueness of Jesus.* The participants who had come expecting some sort of a discussion on comparative religion were much surprised and challenged. The supremacy and uniqueness of Jesus was established on the basis of his being the embodiment of true religion. When true Christianity was defined in terms of the person of Christ and what he stood for, there was little room for criticism or complaint, dispute or debate. As a result, the participants were challenged to consider the content and concern of religion in the light of Christ who stood out as morally supreme and spiritually unique. No religion had the capacity to match his personality.

This new realization of Christ introduced the participants to the inescapable influence of Christ in a short span of time. Jones recalls that there was not a single situation where "before the close of the Round Table Conference Christ was not in moral and spiritual command of the situation. . . . At the close everything had been pushed to the edges and Christ controlled the situation."

Jones presents a vast amount of documented evidence to prove that the evangelistic use of dialogue was extremely successful at those Round Table Conferences. Such a proven method can work in similar situations of evangelistic impenetrability anywhere.

There is a story about a young man who was jogging along a seashore. One morning, he noticed an older person involved in a sort of childlike play. The old man was rhythmically bending over, picking up a handful of objects, and flinging them into the ocean. Driven by curiosity, the young man stopped jogging and asked the old man what he was doing. The old man replied, "You see, these little creatures belong to the waters. They have been washed ashore by the rough tides of the night. If we let them lie on the sand, they all will die. By throwing them back into the sea, I am giving them life!"

The young man smiled rather sarcastically and said, "But, you see, this seashore stretches hundreds of miles. If you walk down, you will find thousands of these creatures washed ashore all along. So, by throwing a few of them back into the sea, what difference does it make to the rest of them?"

The old man looked intently into the eyes of the young man and said firmly, "What difference it makes to the rest of them, my son, I do not know. But as far as these few are concerned, it does make a difference." Then he bent over again, picked up a handful more, and flung them into the sea.

As we reach out to a few Hindus here, and a few Muslims and Buddhists there, we may never know what difference it will make to the rest of the millions who follow these faiths. But as far as the few Hindus, Muslims, Buddhists, Sikhs, Jains, Shintoists, Taoists, Confucianists, and Baha'i are concerned, the gospel we share does and will make a difference. And as long as there are people in need—in need of an adequate goal for character, a full and free self, and a God—and as long as they are searching in their respective religions to meet these elemental needs, our job will not be over. As long as even a handful of people of other faiths are eagerly searching for the truth, we must not tire of reaching out to them. He who said "Behold I am with you to the ends of the world" is still with us. In this confidence and trust, we face the challenges of other religions with the gospel of Jesus Christ and his uniqueness of being the one and the only Lord and Savior of the world!

The Gospel and Salvation

Tokunboh Adeyemo

John Newton was a notorious slave master. During the inhuman and cruel period of slave trade, he was the captain of one of the ships that transported Africans from West Africa to work in the sugarcane plantations of North America. Newton was a product of his day—brutalizing and exploiting those he regarded as nonbeings. How natural it is to be greedy, self-centered, hateful, and indifferent!

But something happened to Newton. He was confronted with the gospel and the claims of Jesus Christ. Convicted of his wickedness in the light of God's righteousness and judgment, Newton, in repentance, submitted his life to Jesus Christ as Savior and Lord. What a transformation! Not only did Newton renounce his involvement in slave trade, but he spent the rest of his life fighting against it and defending the rights of slaves. He was no longer of the world once he met Jesus. Out of this experience of new life in Christ, he wrote one of the church's favorite hymns:

> Amazing grace, how sweet the sound
> That saved a wretch like me!
> I once was lost, but now am found,
> Was blind, but now I see.

Newton's testimony of a life that honored God confirms the words of 2 Corinthians 5:17, "If anyone is in Christ, he is a new creation; the old has gone, the new has come!"

These words were born out of the experience of the writer, Saul of Tarsus, who was to become Paul, the apostle to the Gentiles. A religious fanatic, arrogant, boastful, proud, and a killer of the people of the Way, this former Pharisee met Jesus Christ on the Damascus Road and was completely transformed. His life was never the same. He was translated from darkness to light, from wickedness to righteousness, from following the god of this world to following the Lord Jesus Christ. No longer of this world, he wrote, "Our citizenship is in heaven" (Philippians 3:20). From the point of his conversion Paul lived for Christ. He could write: "For to me, to live is Christ and to die is gain" (Philippians 1:21).

It does not matter that Newton was a Gentile or that Paul was a Jew; whether ancient

Tokunboh Adeyemo is General Secretary of the Association of Evangelicals of Africa and Madagascar, and a citizen of Nigeria.

or contemporary; neither do the genders nor socioeconomic classes make any difference: the eternal gospel is the power of God for the salvation of everyone (Revelation 14:6) who believes (Romans 1:16). For purposes of clarification, we ask: *What is the gospel?* and *What is salvation?*

A Definition of the Gospel and Salvation

Occurring over seventy-five times in the New Testament, *evangelion* simply means "good news," or "joyful tidings." Originally, it denoted a reward for good tidings. Later, the idea of reward was dropped and the word stood for the Good News itself. Theologically, the Good News is that God is in Christ reconciling the world to himself, not counting our sins against us (2 Corinthians 5:19). While this was crystallized in the New Testament, especially in the Christ-event (i.e., the incarnation, crucifixion, and resurrection of Christ), the concept has its root in the Old Testament. In the Greek translation of the Old Testament Hebrew, the verb *euangelizomai,* "bring good news" is used of the declaration of Jerusalem's deliverance from bondage (Isaiah 40:9; 52:7) and also of a wider announcement of liberation for the oppressed (Isaiah 61:1–2).

We are not surprised, therefore, to note that Christ's inaugural address and the manifesto of his ministry (Luke 4:18–19) was taken from this Isaiah passage: For the Messiah is the Good News!

We err if we confine the gospel to the New Testament alone. The central theme of the whole Bible is nothing but Good News through and through! If I were asked to define the central concepts of the gospel, I would put it this way: It is the triumph of good over evil; of light over darkness; of life over death; of sight over blindness; of order over anarchy; of righteousness over wickedness; of purity over profanity; of justice over corruption; of Christ over Antichrist; of God over god substitutes; and of the kingdom of God over the kingdoms of this world. The gospel announces:

- Good news to the poor
- Freedom for the prisoners
- Recovery of sight for the blind
- Release for the oppressed, and
- The year of God's favor for all humanity

God grants *soteria* which denotes "deliverance," "preservation," and "salvation"— to those who accept his conditions of repentance and faith in the Lord Jesus, in whom alone it is to be obtained (Acts 4:12), and upon confession of him as Lord (Romans 10:10). For this purpose the gospel is the saving instrument (Romans 1:16; Ephesians 1:13). Salvation is both instantaneous and continuous. These two aspects are expressed by the terms "justification" and "sanctification."

To preach the gospel, therefore, is to lift up Jesus Christ as Savior and Lord (Romans 10:9–10); to invite sinners to the Cross where God's free offer of new life in Christ can be obtained.

Justification	Sanctification
God's external work outside us and for us, like clothing	God's internal work inside
God reckoning sinners to be right	God working within sinners to make them holy in heart and behavior
The declaration of the Father	The internal working of the Spirit
Concerns guilt	Concerns pollution
Righteousness imputed	Righteousness imparted
Complete and perfect	Never complete or perfect in this life
A gift which entitles us to heaven	A work which prepares us for heaven
Relates to our standing	Relates to our condition

In Nigeria lived a professor of medicine at the University of Ibadan—a Rhodes scholar, brilliant, proud, and reckless. He lived a loose and wayward life until he met Jesus. By the power of the gospel a revolution took place in his life. He was delivered from a life of sin. Today, he humbly serves the Lord as a parish pastor at Kano in northern Nigeria, turning others to true life in Jesus.

As a politician depends upon public opinion and a military general upon soldiers in warfare, the church depends upon the Holy Spirit and the Word (the gospel) in matters of world evangelization and salvation of the lost. "Faith comes from hearing, and hearing by the Word of God" (Romans 10:17, NASB). God has ordained that by the preaching of the gospel—simple and ridiculous as it may sound—men and women who believe shall be brought into the kingdom of God. The apostle Paul condemns anyone who preaches another gospel (Galatians 1:6–9).

Demands of the Gospel

Throughout Bible history, the gospel made demands on whoever embraced the good tidings. The first of these is separation. To embrace the gospel is to follow Jesus Christ; and to follow Jesus demands a radical break with the former ways of life. Christ does not call us to a set of *do*s and *don't*s but to himself. "Follow me," "Learn of me," "Come to me," are some of the expressions of his invitation. Jesus calls us away from corruption, wickedness, injustice, and violence and unto himself—his peace, forgiveness, joy, and righteousness. At conversion every believing sinner is ushered by the power of God into a new life—a life in Christ—diametrically opposed to the former life. God's Holy Spirit is deposited within us in order to produce God's holy nature in us. The implication of this is threefold: (*a*) we are obliged to be pure and live a holy life as God who called us is holy (1 Peter 1:15–16)—Christian integrity rests on this fact; (*b*) we are not to be conformed to this world but rather to be transformed by the renewing of our minds (Romans 12:2)—the Christian principle of nonconformity rests on this fact; and (*c*) we are Christ's ambassadors sent to this world as its only salt and light with the message of reconciliation (2 Corinthians 5:19–20)—Christian stewardship rests on this fact.

The gospel demands separation: contact without contamination. As Paul aptly states: "No one serving as a soldier gets involved in civilian affairs—he wants to please his commanding officer" (2 Timothy 2:4).

Second, the gospel demands self-denial and cross-bearing (Luke 14:27). Self-denial is willingly saying *No* to one's fleshly desires and *Yes* to the things of Christ. It is living a life of obedience to the commands of God, which often involves suffering. In fact, the Bible says: "All that will live godly in Christ Jesus shall suffer persecution" (2 Timothy 3:12, KJV). Those who became Christians in the New Testament and the first three centuries of the Christian era became "marked people." They automatically became targets of persecution and attack. Christians' refusal to worship Caesar caused them to be considered enemies of the state; their intolerance and nonviolent disobedience of unjust laws made them rebels; their indiscriminate love and acceptance of one another—Jews and Gentiles—was more than the Pharisees could take; and their loyalty and total allegiance to Jesus as Lord was unpopular. But this is part of what cross-bearing meant to them. It cannot mean any less for us today. The gospel demands from every believer the testimony: "Not my will but yours, O Lord."

Third, the gospel demands perseverance. To persevere is to continue steadfastly, to bear up courageously, to endure patiently. The gospel is not a drug for occasional relief; neither is salvation in Christ a fad. Rather, the new life in Christ is equipped by the Word of God and the power of the Holy Spirit to weather all storms. Those who once kept company with Paul but later fell away—such as Hymenaeus, Alexander, and Philetus—were treated as nonbelievers (1 Timothy 1:20; 2 Timothy 2:16–19). In Colossians 1:22–23 (NASB), Paul minces no words concerning the necessity to persevere. He writes:

> He has now reconciled you in his fleshly body through death, in order to present you before him holy and blameless and beyond reproach—if indeed you continue in the faith firmly established and steadfast, and not moved away from the hope of the gospel that you have heard, which was proclaimed in all creation under heaven, and of which I, Paul, was made a minister.

This remark does not limit God's ability to keep whom he saves, rather, it addresses personal responsibility and warns against false pretenses.

Salvation in Christ is a small gate and a narrow road. It is free for anyone but it costs everything. The gospel that offers us salvation when we believe also makes demands on us. We cannot be godly and worldly at the same time.

Demonstration of the Gospel

Almost invariably in the ministry of Jesus Christ as recorded in the synoptic Gospels, preaching, and healing go hand-in-hand. Matthew records the triple formulae of teaching, preaching, and healing while Mark and Luke simply speak of preaching and healing (Matthew 4:23; 9:35; Mark 1:34,38; Luke 4:40, 43–44). One word that stands out in Christ's healing ministry is *compassion,* which, I believe, is a demonstration of the gospel. In its original root, *compassion* is "love in action." When translating the Greek word into English in the New Testament, it is usually accompanied by action verbs such as *moved* or *filled* to convey the real meaning of the concept.

Compassion wells up from within—down deep at the gut level—and propels one into action. Compassion made Jesus heal every sickness and disease (Matthew 14:14); cleanse the lepers (Mark 1:41); give sight to the blind (Matthew 20:34); raise the dead

(Luke 7:15); and feed the hungry multitude (Matthew 15:32). Jesus was moved to compassion by the world's pain and sorrow, especially of those who were gripped by demonic affliction (Mark 9:20–27; Luke 8:27–38). The sight of a leper, banished from society, living a life of loneliness and abandonment drew sympathy and love from Christ. He also saw the world as a confused mob without a sense of direction and had compassion for it. It is only logical that part of Christ's gospel message is healing (Luke 4:18) and that when he sent out the Twelve and the seventy he gave them power to heal.

Another word which aptly describes Christlike compassion is *altruism,* which has been defined as "regard for and devotion to the interest of others." No other story has vividly drawn out the demonstration of love as the parable of the good Samaritan (Luke 10:30–37). Triggered by a lawyer's question, *And who is my neighbor?* Jesus, by this parable, draws our attention to the master plan for world evangelization. Love sees beyond the accidents of race, tribe, color, nationality, and religions, to people made in the image and likeness of God. Neighborly concern ceases to be drawn along tribal, class, national, or racial lines. People are seen no longer as objects to be exploited but in their true humanness as God's image for whom Christ died. The good Samaritan saw not a Jew (though he was), but a man in need. One's personal security is not what matters, but others' redemption. In the words of Dietrich Bonhoeffer: "The church is the church only when it exists for others." One can say that the ultimate measure of a church is not where it stands in moments of comfort and convenience, but where it stands at times of challenge and crisis as in nations like Ethiopia, Namibia, South Africa, El Salvador, Nicaragua, Northern Ireland, the Middle East, Vietnam, and Armenia.

Furthermore, Christlike healing ministry demands involvement. With his own hands the good Samaritan bound the wounds of the man, set him on his own beast, and paid the hospital cost from his own pocket. This is much more than the wounded might deserve. Compassion is empathy for the person in need. It is bearing others' pain, agony, and burdens by which, Paul says, the law of Christ is fulfilled (Galatians 6:2). This principle can make us love our enemies, bless those who curse us, do good to those who hate us, and pray for those who despitefully use and persecute us (Matthew 5:44).

St. Basil, styled as "the Great," a hermit theologian and one of the Cappadocian Fathers, founded a complex of charitable institutions during the fourth century. Around the church building and the monastery, there arose a whole new city consisting of hotels, almshouses, and hospitals for infectious diseases. The bishop himself took up residence there. The establishment was regarded as a threat to the state. At the risk of his life Basil resisted the objection. During the great famine of the year A.D. 368 he organized free meals for the people as well as the immigrants, foreigners, pagans, and even the infidel children of Israel. Charity to Basil, as well as to other church Fathers, is giving what we have and not what we have left over (Mark 12:44).

The gospel in demonstration takes the church out of its comfortable environment, places it in the marketplace, in ghettos, in prison cells, in refugee camps, in rural as well as urban centers—wherever people are, people wounded and bruised by the scourge of sins and violent brutality of man against man. It disallows evangelism at arm's length and speaks of "release" rather than "relief." The ministry of Mother Teresa, for example, is internationally recognized as a ministry of healing, a significant link in the chain of peace. The church of Jesus Christ all over the world is under obligation to respond to human need with Christlike compassion. How better can the gospel be demonstrated than by acts of love?

William Wilberforce fought relentlessly against all odds for the abolition of slave trade in the nineteenth century. Martin Luther King, Jr. was assassinated in the struggle against racial segregation. Lord Shaftesbury dared to stand for justice for the poor in the midst of the Industrial Revolution of the early nineteenth century. All these men shared in God's desire for justice based on love. Speaking of their heroic example, the late Francis Schaeffer said: "These men did not do these things incidentally, but because they saw it as a part of the Christian Good News" (*A Christian Manifesto* [Westchester, Ill.: Crossway Books, 1981], 65).

The gospel is not only a creed to believe, but a life to live! With untold billions still unevangelized; with escalation of violence and unrest all over the world; with the economic hope of the world waning as nations from the Third World sink deeper and deeper into debt; what better gift can come from Manila than to call on the church of Jesus Christ "to take the whole gospel to the whole world!" The need is more desperate than ever; the call is more urgent today! Like the apostle Paul, may the Lord lay the burden upon us so that we may say: "Woe is me if I do not preach the gospel" (1 Corinthians 9:16).

How to Teach the Truth of the Gospel

Peter Kuzmic

The saying "It's the gospel truth" is frequently used by people who insist on the total reliability of their statements. However, in our age of relativity, agnosticism, and denial of absolutes, the very truth of any truth is questioned and the validity of the gospel truth denied. Carl Henry rightly asserts that at the heart of the "modern eclipse of God" is the crisis of truth:

> Such double loss of the gospel's truth and of all truth—as an objective and transcendent claim upon the human mind—is an unmistakable facet of the civilizational crisis that has engulfed modern Western culture.

Belief in God is considered to be part of an obscurantist, outdated, and pre-scientific way of thinking. Not only in the communist dominated areas and under the influence of Marxism, but also in the so-called Christian West. Henry continues:

> God's very existence, and with this the objectivity of truth, have been submerged in tidal waves of modern doubt. The spiritual crisis of mankind is also intellectual crisis, in as much as the modern temper is now disposed to consider God unthinkable, unchanging truth an illusion, and gospel truth a fiction.

The result of the denial of divine revelation is stated by the apostle Paul, "They exchanged the truth of God for a lie, and worshipped and served created things rather than the Creator (Romans 1:25). Similarly, people today have become victims of modern idolatries and secular substitute religions. Modern man seems to be caught between the materialistic individualism of the West and the ideological totalitarianism of the East. Individualistic consumerism and collectivistic communism are both inherently idolatrous and are dangerously enslaving in their fanatic forms. Carl Henry again has said:

> Multitudes of people are gripped by totalitarian lies, snared by commercial slogans and popular cliches, entranced by vogue ideas and warped words. It is fashionable to be committed to scientific revisability, resigned to the historical character of all men's knowledge, fascinated with evolutionary development, reliant upon historical method,

Peter Kuzmic is Director of Biblijsko-Teoloski Institut, an evangelist, teacher, member of the Theology Working Group and citizen of Yugoslavia.

devoted to dialectical paradox, preoccupied with existential decision, and derisive of God talk.

In this context, and in the context of "relativity of all religions," we must insist on the factual Christ-event and the historical reliability of the gospel story. According to David Read, the "first question about religion is not whether or not it is useful but whether or not it is true." Truth is foundational for trust. Stephen Neill in his *Call to Mission* says "The only reason for being a Christian is the overpowering conviction that the Christian faith is true."

Jesus is the heart of the gospel; he is the truth of God incarnate, the truth that liberates (saves) men (John 8:32,36; 14:6). By his claim, "For this reason I was born, and for this reason I came into the world, to testify to the truth," he provoked Pilate into asking the resounding question of all ages: "What is truth?" (John 18:37–38)

The apostle Paul considered himself to be a herald and defender of "the truth of the gospel" (Galatians 2:5). He was convinced that faith, love, and hope are fruit of the hearing of "the word of truth, the gospel" (Colossians 1:5). "And you also were included in Christ when you heard the word of truth, the gospel of your salvation" (Ephesians 1:13).

Due to the truth-character, historical accuracy and doctrinal content of the gospel, a preacher is inevitably also a teacher. "We proclaim him [Christ] . . . teaching everyone with all wisdom" (Colossians 1:28). In one of his succinct summaries of the grace and power of the gospel, Paul brings the divine revelation and the human apostolic task together,

> It has now been revealed through the appearing of our Savior, Christ Jesus, who has destroyed death and has brought life and immortality to light through the gospel. And of this gospel I was appointed a herald and an apostle and a teacher (2 Timothy 1:10–11).

Paul saw himself as a trustee of "the sound doctrine that conforms to the glorious gospel of the blessed God" (1 Timothy 1:10–11). We are called to the same sacred task and trust.

Proclamation of the gospel is communication of knowledge: exposition and explanation of the glorious facts of incarnation of the eternal *Logos;* of the life, teachings, and deeds of the Lord Jesus Christ; of the meaning of his atoning death; of the significance of his resurrection; of the convicting and equipping power of the Holy Spirit; and of Christ's offer of forgiveness and a new life to all who would put their trust in him.

> By this gospel you are saved . . . That Christ died for our sins according to the Scriptures, that he was buried, that he was raised on the third day according to the Scriptures, and that he appeared (1 Corinthians 15:2–5).

Wherever the gospel is preached, these foundational facts of the universally valid truth must be taught. William Temple said, "The gospel is true always and everywhere, or it is not a gospel at all, or true at all."

Though not always equally emphasized, *kerygma* and *didache* are actually insepa-rable. Evangelism does not bypass the God-given intellect of the hearer by appealing to his more responsive emotions. In the Parable of the Sower, Jesus explains why such an approach remains without fruit. "When anyone hears the message about the kingdom and does not understand it, the evil one comes and snatches away what was sown in his heart" (Matthew 13:19). Theology and evangelism should not be viewed as separate fields of activity.

In the chapel of Trinity College in Glasgow, there was a stained-glass window in memory of James Denney, with the inscription: "Supreme alike as scholar, teacher, administrator, and man of God, to whom many owed their souls." It was Denney's view we would be closer to an ideal church if "evangelists were our theologians or theologians our evangelists." His major theological preoccupation was the analysis of the atoning work of Christ. His conclusion: "The simplest truth of the gospel and the profoundest truth of theology must be put in the same words—he bore our sins."

We are not faithful to the gospel, nor will our work of evangelism be effective, unless we are gripped by the soteriological significance of the Cross-event, the death of Jesus, and the importance of his resurrection apart from which "our preaching is useless" (1 Corinthians 15:14).

May it be said of us, as it was of James Denney by one of his successors as principal of Trinity College:

> As theologian and as man, there is no one like him. I have known many theologians both scholarly and devout, but I have never known his equal for making the New Testament intelligible as the record and deposit of an overwhelming experience of redemption and for generating in those who listened to him the conviction that the gospel incarnate in Jesus is the only thing that matters.

Renew the Credibility of the Christian Witness

The answer to the question of world evangelization, *How shall they hear?* is inextricably linked to and conditioned by the answer to the related question, *What shall they see?* It is not primarily a question of methodology but rather of authenticity. Our message has no credibility apart from its visibility as expressed in the quality of new life, new sets of relationships in the believing community, and a loving concern and sacrificial service on behalf of the needy.

The evangelist is not only a proclaimer and teacher of the gospel, he is an inseparable part of the message he communicates. So is the Christian community. The problem today is not that we lack a credible message—for indeed the gospel of Christ is the most glorious and powerful Good News for the world—but, rather, that we so often lack credible messengers, those whose lives are irrefutably in harmony with the gospel, and are thus able to carry it with authenticity and power.

Christian religion has a long and heavy historical ballast that presents a serious hindrance to world evangelization. In Eastern Europe we have learned that Marxist criticism of religion is not all wrong and have come to acknowledge that the rise and spread of both Western and Marxist atheism is proportionally related to the shrinking credibility of the Christian church. Much of communist atheism is at least partially a reaction against a backslidden Christianity and may even be interpreted as God's judgment on the historical unfaithfulness of the church.

When going out to evangelize in Yugoslavia, I tell our seminary students that our main task may be to "wash the face of Jesus," for it has been dirtied and distorted by both the compromises of the Christian church through the centuries and the propaganda of atheistic communism in recent decades.

Viewing it from the biblical perspective, no one can justify the "unholy alliance of throne and altar" and its many negative consequences since the Constantinian era up to the present. We must humbly acknowledge that frequently religion was used as a manipulative tool of the powerful and mighty, and has often served as an ideological screen justifying the actions of the oppressors and deceptively comforting the oppressed and exploited. Whitewashing unjust wars, justifying economic injustices, and smokescreening racial discrimination are only some of the obvious evils the Christian church has practiced for ages and, in some of its segments, participates in even today. In the perception of many, especially the youth and the intelligentsia, the church is not a credible institution. That is why, when challenged with the claims of the gospel, many today will respond with the slogan: "Jesus—yes! Church—no!"

Evangelism is a life before it is a task; it is a question of being before it becomes an agenda of doing. The believing community will either evangelize by its attractive quality of new life or it will create barriers to the gospel by its old way of life. It will by its integrity enhance the gospel or it will discredit and hinder it by lack of it.

This is illustrated by recent scandalous behavior and related worldwide negative publicity of prominent American television evangelists and other evangelical leaders. These TV scandals show unmistakably what the "cheap gospel," based on financial gain rather than rooted in the Cross of Christ, does and how it links with the sinful human nature. Asked to comment on this by a provocative communist journalist, I blurted out: "Charisma without character is catastrophe!" I was forced to categorically deny that their "gospel" and the gospel of Jesus Christ are the same.

How unfortunately prophetic appears the statement of Charles P. Templeton in his *Evangelism for Tomorrow* of more than thirty years ago. He said:

> The church stands in danger that the time will come when (to paraphrase G. K. Chesterton) it can pick up a microphone and address the entire world—only to find out it has nothing to say.

The world is watching carefully to see whether the Christian people really believe what they proclaim and live up to the demands of the holy gospel.

The eloquence of the preacher, the size of the annual budget, the rise of modern technology, and the employment of social sciences, effective strategies, top management, and impressive missionary agencies will not do it. It will take genuine repentance, divine cleansing, holy living, and a new empowerment by the Holy Spirit if the world is to be evangelized in the last decade of our millennium.

Much Western "evangelical religiosity" is shallow and selfish. It promises so much and demands so little. It offers success, personal happiness, peace of mind, material prosperity, security, and a moral fiber for the nation; but it hardly speaks of repentance, sacrifice, self-denial, holy lifestyle, and willingness to die for Christ. It tends to forget that Jesus Christ is not only a Savior to be trusted, but also the Lord to be obeyed.

Our modern preoccupation with money, buildings, and programs, however validly we try to justify it, is still foreign to the New Testament and may be the most serious sign that Christianity has been captivated by a secular, materialistic "cash-register" culture.

Evangelical leaders and evangelists must be aware of the potential sin of professionalism. Perfected techniques and visible results can easily make evangelism degenerate into "patterns without power." We need to remember that people are not digits to be totaled on an adding machine.

Recover the Whole Gospel

Our Congress is "A Call to the Whole Church to Take the Whole Gospel to the Whole World." We need to recover the whole gospel and renounce all "half-gospels" that have invalidated much of the Christian mission around the world. According to P. T. Forsyth, "Half-gospels have no dignity and no future. Like the famous mule, they have neither pride of ancestry nor hope of posterity." Carl Henry agrees: "Half-gospels deceive and defraud, demote and degrade, and dead-end in disillusion and dishonor."

The whole gospel means total commitment to all the demands of Jesus Christ, including the whole spectrum of ethical requirements that are inherent in the gospel message. It means for us to live "worthy of the gospel of Christ" (Philippians 1:27). The whole gospel implies joyful celebration of God's gift of salvation and continuous openness to the Holy Spirit to confirm the Word by signs and wonders. The whole gospel covers proclamation of truth and exhibition of love, manifestation of power and integrity of life. In the task of world evangelization, it will also require less competition and more cooperation, less self-sufficiency and more self-denial, less ambition to lead and more willingness to serve, less of the drive to dominate and more of the desire to develop.

We need to continue asking ourselves the painful question: *How can a sinful and divided church announce to the world the gospel of salvation and reconciliation?* Our distinction between the visible and invisible church is not biblical and is totally meaningless and hypocritical to the watching world. The whole gospel reminds us that although salvation is primarily a spiritual and personal experience, it has much wider cultural, social, and political implications. The Lausanne Covenant (article 5) states:

> The message of salvation implies also a message of judgment upon every form of alienation, oppression, and discrimination, and we should not be afraid to denounce evil and injustice wherever they exist. When people receive Christ they are born again into his kingdom and must seek not only to exhibit but also to spread its righteousness in the midst of an unrighteous world. The salvation we claim should be transforming us in the totality of our personal and social responsibilities. Faith without works is dead.

The New Testament does not drive a wedge between a "personal gospel" and a "social gospel." There is only one gospel of Jesus Christ which is both personal and social because it has two focal points: the individual person and the kingdom of God. This is clearly taught and consistently practiced in the ministry of Jesus.

We want to bring the whole gospel to the whole world, but we must never allow it to become captive to the spirit of the world. The church is a fellowship of pilgrims, never completely at home, nor comfortable in any culture of socio-political order. We are a *communio viatorum,* still on the way to the eternal city. The scenery around us is constantly changing but our mandate remains the same: to authentically represent Christ and faithfully proclaim the gospel to our lost contemporaries so they may join us in the way of salvation.

Translate the Gospel

The evangelical reading of the New Testament leads to the inevitable conclusion that there is only one gospel. It is the gospel of God (Romans 1:1,9,15–16), because it came from God; and "the gospel of Christ" (Romans 15:19; 1 Corinthians 9:12; 2 Corinthians 9:13), because he and his redemptive work are its content. The New Testament never uses the word *gospel* in plural. It "is not something that man made up" for it was received "by revelation from Jesus Christ" (Galatians 1:11–12). That is why, in expounding and defending it, the apostle Paul speaks of eternal condemnation for those who would dare to preach a "different gospel" (Galatians 1:6,9). However, Jesus and other New Testament evangelists portray considerable flexibility and creative freedom in adapting and variously communicating the gospel in different settings.

While the basic content is always recognizable and unchanging, the presentations are never the same. There are no "pre-packaged, universally applicable" formulations. The *Willowbank Report on Gospel and Culture* summarized it well:

> The Bible proclaims the gospel story in many different forms. The gospel is like a multifaceted diamond, with different aspects that appeal to different people in different cultures. It has depths we have not fathomed. It defies every attempt to reduce it to a neat formulation.

Messengers of the gospel are called to be bridge-builders spanning the wide gap between the ancient world of the biblical story and the modern technological age and culture. We are to bring the answer of Christ in a relevant and meaningful encounter with the spiritual needs of our contemporaries. The late Helmut Thielicke reminds us:

> The gospel must be preached afresh and told in new ways to every generation, since every generation has its own unique questions. This is why the gospel must constantly be forwarded to a new address, because the recipient is repeatedly changing his place of residence.

We must be firmly rooted in the Word of God, while at the same time lovingly concerned and knowledgeably involved in the world of men. There is no effective evangelism without transposition and translation of the biblical *kerygma* into the lifestyle, culture, and thought forms of our audience.

For missionaries, this requires a thorough knowledge of the history, language, and customs, accompanied by constant cross-cultural sensitivity and respect for the people to whom God has sent them. For all who are involved in evangelism, this means that while faithfully expounding the divinely revealed truth, our preaching must also be people-, situation-, and issue-oriented.

Along with renewing the credibility of the Christian witness, we must also renew the intelligibility of the Christian message. In some parts of the world, the radical, ideologically inspired secularization and other developments in the society have either totally distorted or completely abolished the basic facts of the Christian faith. Most of the young people in Eastern Europe are biblically illiterate to the extent that they don't understand much of the famous historical art and literature in which biblical personalities and motifs are used. The message of the Cross and salvation can have little meaning for those who grew up in a system which claimed monopoly on truth, thought that historically Jesus never existed, and scientifically argued that any belief in God is superstition. Soviet government, for example, claims that one of the successes of its educational system is evident in the fact that around 90 percent of their young people, ages sixteen to nineteen, adhere to atheism as their worldview.

All of these and billions of other people need to hear and read the gospel translated into their thought categories in order to understand its significance for their own salvation. If we love them with the love of Christ, we will grapple with their prejudices and study their beliefs in order to understand them better and to be able to respond by articulating the gospel with intelligence, clarity, and relevance. The Holy Spirit will help us to be courageous and creative, and the love of Christ in us will cross all barriers in order to find, understand, and redeem.

Attempts to interpret the gospel in order to make it relevant are not without dangers. Some Western Protestant "apostles of modernity" have amputated the biblical message and rendered it powerless. In their almost neurotic anxiety about the relevance of

Christianity in an age of prevailing secularity, they have emptied their faith of its biblical contents. While seeking to incarnate the gospel, they have instead buried it in the process.

We must avoid total rigidity and pious "other-worldliness" in the name of faithfulness and also avoid "this-worldliness" in the name of relevance and modernity. Both betray the gospel of Jesus Christ, for the first renders it meaningless and the other leaves it powerless. We have no freedom to restructure, reduce, or in any other way compromise the message in order to make it more attractive and palatable to secularized minds or adherents of other religions. We must firmly refuse to participate in any syncretistic processes, remembering always that "salvation is found in no one else, for there is no other name under heaven given to men by which we must be saved" (Acts 4:12).

Our theology must not be reduced to ethics or our agenda set by the world rather than by our Lord. Dialogue with the world is a constant necessity. Its purpose in the evangelistic arena is not content transformation, but, rather, the contextual translation of our message. If the message is transformed in the process of communication, it will lose its own transforming power and cease to be the gospel of Jesus Christ. If it is faithfully preserved while meaningfully translated in order to be understood, it will retain and effectually manifest its evangelical power to transform human lives. This, and nothing less, is the task and purpose of the Great Commission.

While identifying in redemptive love with the lost humanity, we must watch to preserve our own spiritual identity and power, for in it lies the secret of our spiritual authority in this world. The incarnation of Jesus is the supreme example of identification without the loss of identity. John Stott reminded us that in this complex, and yet joyous task of world evangelization, the incarnational model of Jesus is not only instructive but also normative. For as John stated in his version of the Great Commission: "As the Father has sent me, I am sending you" (John 20:21).

Cooperation in Evangelism

Bill O'Brien

God revealed himself as one in community: the Trinity. God created humankind in his image: in community. We were assigned as stewards of all the components of the household. In Genesis 12, God established his covenant with Abram through whom all peoples would be blessed. In the new covenant the disciples were an instrument through which all peoples would be served and blessed. In 1 Corinthians 3, Paul indicates we are all God's fellow workers. We are laborers together with God in a common cause for God's own mission.

Peter reminds us we are the people of God, a royal priesthood.

Cooperation

From the Edenic Fall to the present time, human nature has worked against cooperation. Left to ourselves, we isolate, insulate, exclude, and put "self" in first place. From the Lausanne Congress in 1974 have come many efforts in cooperation, and many good models exist. One contribution made subsequent to the Congress was the little book, *Cooperating in World Evangelization: A Handbook on Church/Parachurch Relations*. It outlines obstacles, or barriers, to cooperation. It is helpful to identify things which work against such efforts and become traps. In the Bible, there are clear principles which enable us to deal with those barriers under the lordship of Christ. That lordship provides the guidelines for cooperation and its parameters.

Setting the Scene

An episode in the ministry of Jesus illustrates some needed lessons. One account of the story is in Luke 5. Inherent in the story is a consuming confidence in the person of Jesus—a confidence that evoked cooperation.

Beyond the facts of the story, it is likely that the four men who carried the paralytic to Jesus were not totally like-minded on other things. What if those other differences had taken precedence over their common cause—bringing the paralytic to Jesus—and their common hope in Jesus?

Let us suppose these men represented some very normal first-century attitudes:

William R. O'Brien *is Executive Vice President of the Foreign Mission Board of the Southern Baptist Convention. A former missionary to Indonesia, he is a citizen of the United States.*

Simon

The first attitude represented might have been in a man named Simon, a Zealot. Old Testament history provided strong models for Simon: Simeon, Levi, Phineas, and Elijah. He was an agent of God's wrath and judgment against all forms of apostasy. He took seriously what it meant to be a chosen people:

> We are a special people, a chosen race. If not, why would God have chosen us? At one time I was willing to kill Gentiles, even a fellow Jew, out of my zeal for the Law. But at some point, pride in my race and nation took precedence over my worship of the one true God. I felt superior, but I disguised that attitude with religious jargon. Racial and national pride kept me from seeing others the way the Nazarene Rabbi saw them.
>
> I still believe in *our people* and *our land*. But, something troubles me deeply about what it has done to me, especially when I am in his presence. But what is happening now is the most important thing for the moment. I've got to pick up my corner of the mat and help get this man to Jesus.

Zadok

And perhaps there was Zadok, a Sadducee. His tradition descended from Aaron, but took the form of a Sadduccean party after the Maccabean rebellion. His party felt they must hold the line against the more accommodating Pharisees:

> I've given my life to the service of the temple in the tradition of our fathers. Even my name calls up memories of Solomon's priest. These wretched Pharisees have been willing to include writings other than the Law. There is an insidious and undermining para-temple movement emerging. Should this continue, not only our rituals but our base of support will be seriously endangered.
>
> There was a day when my temple calling would have never allowed me to do what I'm doing today. I first heard this Galilean Rabbi in the temple—intriguing. But, he spoke in various synagogues and even in the households of publicans and sinners—troubling!
>
> My uncle raised me after my father died. One day, out by the well, he talked to me about the troubling things this Rabbi was saying and doing. Now, my uncle lies here helplessly paralyzed. What if Jesus really could do something about it? If he can, then maybe God will forgive me for associating with the Pharisee Lazarus in this "endeavor."

Lazarus

The third man was Lazarus, one of the Pharisees whom Zadok used to despise:

> I have been doubly cursed among my people. Earlier, as a scribe, I was the target of attack by the temple priests. When this man Jesus came into our family, life took another turn. Even my own Pharisee group turned on me. But through him my perspective of all creation gradually changed.
>
> My two sisters came alive as a result of him. Many of their friends experienced the same thing. I am accused of having gone soft, transgressing both the Law and tradition as it relates to our Hebrew women.
>
> I believe that Jesus is the Way and he is Life! He is also Truth—the kind of truth that set me and my sisters free. Yet, it still feels cold and lonely in my religious community which has not experienced that freedom.

John Mark

The fourth member of the team was a lad who had been coaxed into helping. He was only fourteen but was strong and athletic. He was obviously a child of privilege, from a family of wealth. He was on his way home from tutorials when he paused to see what the commotion was about. It centered around three men and a paralytic on a mat. Upon hearing of their proposed mission to get the man to Jesus, young John Mark's curiosity took over:

> From earliest memory I have instinctively known that to be rich is a sign of God's favor. The physical and intellectual advantages that money buys guarantee one's place in society. God can trust us to run things on his behalf! Obviously this poor man on the mat is not blessed; he is probably the victim of sin. I wouldn't even be seen with this group except I want to see Jesus up close. I have heard the stories about him; now is my chance. Uncle Barnabas is coming from Cyprus today. Wait till he hears about this!

Paralyzed. Who was paralyzed in the story? The man on the mat or the four others by their attitudes? What is the real miracle in the story—that the man was healed or that the four overcame their attitudes and cooperated to take him to Jesus?

The group picked up the man on the mat and carried him to the house where Jesus was. True to reality and the experience of every generation, the environment produced factors beyond their control. Seemingly, there was no way to get where they wanted to go. At best, this house was a limited-access situation—at worst, a "closed country." Whether their faith produced determination or their determination fueled their faith, we do not know. However, we do know their faith and determination would have been to no avail had the four not cooperated to reach their objective.

Modern Echoes

To be redeemed and a part of the body of Christ does not automatically deliver one from conflicting attitudes. In fact, the greatest barrier to the spread of the gospel today lies within the church. Apathy, competition, and outright sin and disobedience prevent a shared stewardship of the gospel that would reflect the unity Jesus prayed would characterize his body.

Racial and National Superiority

Our generation is one of rising nationalism coupled with strong ethnic consciousness. A healthy "selfhood" enriches the diversity God has created. Rightfully, churches reflect our ethnic and cultural diversity.

However, when prompted by haughtiness, signs of racial or national superiority will negatively affect the church. The potential for cooperation is jeopardized. Outside the church, many have never taken Christ seriously because of the way Christians view other Christians. Ralph Winter reminds us in his message, "The Future of the Church: The Essential Components of World Evangelization," that even after the Resurrection the agenda of the disciples was still different from that of Jesus:

> In Acts 1:6 (TLB), their own agenda surfaces, "Lord, are you going to free Israel [from Rome] now and restore us as an independent nation?" Jesus, in his reply in Acts 1:8, sidestepped their patriotic concern, their nationalism, their basically self-directed thinking by simply restating once more God's unchanging and decisively larger concern for all other human societies.

Winter reminds us that God's Spirit not only gives us a new and different power, but also a new and different perspective.

There are modern zealots exclaiming, "My people, my land." Even in this room, thousands gather under the lordship of Christ. We look different, we talk differently. And down deep, the tendency is to differentiate between us for many reasons, even as we wear the label "Christian."

"I beseech you therefore, brothers and sisters, by the mercies of God . . ."

Ecclesial Superiority

The names of the actors have changed, but the first-century drama is still playing. "Sadducees versus Pharisees" are present in interchurch, intrachurch, and parachurch rivalries. From bases of tradition, doctrine, or praxis, the competition has escalated until today there are more than twenty-two thousand denominations and twenty thousand parachurch entities in the world. The validity of one is questioned by the other, resulting in competition and conflict. Within many of these rage clergy-laity battles that drain spiritual energy. They fail to capitalize on the availability of gifts and commitment that could become the salt penetrating a lost world.

Modern Zadoks are exclaiming, "My church, my tradition, my movement." Even in this room, there may be the tendency to discriminate from a competitive or superior stance.

"I beseech you therefore, brothers and sisters, by the mercies of God . . ."

Gender Superiority

A confusing principle among believers today is the role of gender in the mission and purpose of our Lord. There is no consistent parallel from culture. Even within Scripture, there are examples and principles which mean different things to different people. How can we arrive at a common understanding of cooperation under the lordship of Christ as it relates to gender?

Jesus' own example is our surest foundation. Within a culture and tradition that segregated and differentiated on the basis of sex, Jesus dealt justly both in relationships and in ministry. When he ascended to the Father and the Spirit of truth came, the giving of spiritual gifts bore no gender distinction. The conflict comes in the interpretation of the application of those gifts. If the sovereign Spirit distributes those gifts according to the will of the Father, we must be careful as to how we differentiate to whom the gift is given and how it is applied. If the lost of the world are to hear the gospel in the next ten years, we must see greater male-female partnering in the shared task.

If the truth has set us free, why does it feel so cold and lonely in the church for so many? Even in this room, there may be the tendency for some to say, "My gender, my role."

"I beseech you therefore, brothers and sisters, by the mercies of God . . ."

Economic Superiority

Throughout the past twenty centuries, the corporate bodies of Christ have been rarely viewed apart from a national, geopolitical, and economic context. Often the churches began to look like the environment in which they existed. We live with a growing gap between the rich church and the poor church. The illusions of superiority are assumed by the ecclesial "haves," and because they have so much they begin to assume God is the one blessing them. The mixture of feelings evoked within those who "have not" range from envy, to hostility, to an inverted pride for not being like the "ecclesial colonialist."

Those who claim some relationship to Christianity worldwide receive 62 percent of the global income. But only about one-tenth of 1 percent goes to evangelize the unreached billions. If the world is ever going to take the church seriously, it must see the church act dramatically and drastically at the point of the distribution of its resources. We must find new common ground for the integration of our corporate giftedness and corporate calling.

"I beseech you therefore, brothers and sisters, by the mercies of God . . ."

Believers around the world today should join hands and hearts—without regard to race, gender, or economic status. Out of our love for Christ, we must pour out our resources—material, physical, and spiritual—to the end that all persons may hear of the Christ who brings us together and restores our relationship with the Father.

We are standing at the four corners of the "global mat." Who is the paralytic lying on the mat—the world, or the church? Perhaps time for confession and forgiveness is what we need most. Then *together* we can pick up our share of the load.

Lord, by our renewed faith may you touch and transform a paralyzed, lost, and dying world!

VIDEO PRESENTATION

Cooperation: No Time To Hold Back!

Producer: Christine Rylko
Writer: Phill Butler

Narrator: When the task is hardest, when the forces are most united against Christianity, when talking about Christ is illegal, when money is scarce, when time is short, *then* certain words are heard over and over: unity, cooperation, and collaboration.

Christian leaders, some working in places where it is illegal for Christians to witness, and who must keep their identity secret to protect their ministry, report from their personal experiences.

Tim Lewis: No organization, no matter how much power or money a particular denomination or church might have, has enough organizational clout, muscle, or resources to finish the job of world evangelization, or to penetrate the unreached people groups at any time in the near future by themselves.

Dave Adams: I would like to encourage the leadership of ministries to assess for themselves what they are wanting to do. What has God called them into existence to accomplish? What can they contribute to the partnership? And in that process of self-awareness, what role will they play in the cooperation?

Narrator: A few years ago, several Christian ministries in a closed country agreed to coordinate their outreach for a more strategic presentation of Christ. People who responded to radio broadcasts were followed up by another agency's Bible correspondence courses. A different agency provided personal follow-up. Another provided Christian literature. Christian nationals within the country visited them regularly. Each ministry contributed in its most effective way. The result: Souls were won to Christ!

Another dramatic partnership example started fifteen years ago. A group of Christian agencies, working separately in a closed country, were seeing about eight hundred to a thousand inquiries a year about Christ.

They decided to come together in a formal partnership. Within three years, the inquiries about Christ had gone up to seven to eight hundred thousand a year!

Some people aren't surprised by ministry partnership success.

Pablo Carillo: The concept of unity itself has some sort of power that is conveyed to the people they're trying to reach.

Phill Butler: At the highest level, partnership is doing God's work God's way. He suggests to us that his own message is more credible as his people dwell in unity.

Mark Holthaus: Partnerships are important to the future of worldwide evangelism because they make sense. It's not only practical, but it's also God's will.

Narrator: Cooperation's positive influence on the people Christians are trying to reach with the Good News is undeniable.

Keith Fraser Smith: It means they get a consistent presentation of the gospel. We've noticed that people will take courses and listen to programs from various centers and stations, and when they hear the same thing, they're more convinced of the truth of the gospel.

Ab: When they see we are working together, that we are one in Christ, and following the same God, they appreciate that and accept our message.

Farida: Often we ask a young brother or sister, "What is it that led you to be converted to Christ? What led you to approach him?" Often the answer is, "It was the love we saw in you."

Narrator: But the partnerships are sometimes difficult to form because they require Christian ministries to do something they're not used to doing.

Henri Auon: It has been difficult. Everyone thought they could do the job alone, and people had fear and a sense of competition.

Dave Adams: Each organization develops quite a different style of ministry, and when we come into cooperation together, we find that sometimes those styles come into conflict.

Narrator: Under any name, Christian disunity has proven to be a bad witness. After meeting two young believers in a closed country, this man felt he was in competition for converts.

Henri Auon: I discovered I had no right to bring him to my home because he was followed up by another organization and they wouldn't allow me to. I was discouraged. I hope it didn't discourage him as well.

Narrator: This woman found that a convert from her closed country was confused by the question: "Which church do you belong to?"

Farida: It was really quite shocking for her to see that, in fact, here people were unable to cooperate and that it was necessary for her to wear a "label" or pronounce a "doctrine" in order to be understood or to be fully integrated into the church.

Phill Butler: We have seen cases in the past, where many individual ministries have been trying to witness in a single area, and multiple ministries keep contacting the same person. The police are sitting across the street having coffee and three weeks later, that person is in jail.

Narrator: Christian men and women who have overcome organization obstacles to work in unity with other Christian agencies say they have experienced an unusual releasing of the Holy Spirit.

Tim Lewis: It's not an easy thing; it's a process that requires time and commitment. Once you make the commitment, there's a growing trust that you must take step by step.

Dave Adams: One of the most important benefits of cooperation is that it purifies our own understanding of the task. When you're face to face with different ministries, trying to do the job together, it forces you to evaluate yourself.

Phill Butler: I sat at a meeting a year and a half ago with sixteen men gathered around a table. In the beginning, they all wondered why they were even in the room. There was fear—people were concerned about the future. Three days later, I saw those same men embracing each other, tears running down their faces, passing communion elements to each other, and praying for each other's ministries.

Narrator: As we escalate towards the end of this century, many Christian leaders are seeing an increase in hostilities between the kingdom of Light and the kingdom of darkness.

From Christian men and women who are working every day to reach the remaining men and women who do not know Christ as their Savior, the message is clear: Go find people of like biblical conviction, and join hands with them to carry Christ's message of Good News. This is no time to hold back.

Dave Adams: The scale of our challenge is enormous. The vast range of people groups and the enormous spread of languages seems insurmountable.

Tim Lewis: I think every organization needs to take a look at what they consider the "non-negotiables" they must work with, and look for other organizations and movements with whom they can cooperate.

Ab: A work that has no collaboration, no help, cannot exist, and even the Lord Jesus has said, "A kingdom that's divided cannot stand."

Henri Aoun: I think we need to realize we're one body worldwide. We are the body of Christ, and each body has different members. God has ordained all these organizations to fulfill a certain part of world evangelization.

Phill Butler: If you want to be more effective, if you want to see Christ's desire for people coming into his kingdom fulfilled, then please consider joining hands with other people to maximize the amazing resources he's giving us these days, to carry out his ministry more effectively.

Tim Lewis: I'm not saying give up your integrity organizationally, or as a movement, or as an individual. But find other people who are like-minded, with a similar heart, who are doing the kinds of things that will be helpful. We will then see the cause of Christ move forward in a magnificent way in the time that remains.

Cooperation in Evangelism

Robyn Claydon

The fingers on the hand were having a rather heated discussion on who was the most important. When the discussion turned into an argument, the thumb decided to intervene. He suggested everyone sit down and each finger be given the opportunity to state why he thought he was the greatest. The thumb would be the judge.

The index finger was called on. He stood up and said, "I'm the most important because I'm the one that points the way. I'm also the most important because when people count they start with me."

The middle finger was called to stand but refused saying, "If all the fingers will stand with me you will see that I'm the most important." When they stood, the middle finger said, "It is clear that I am the greatest as I stand head and shoulders above the rest."

The next finger was called and he said, "I'm the most important because people load me with riches. I have gold, silver, and precious stones put on me. I am, therefore, the most important because people value me the most.

Lastly, the little finger stood, saying, "I'm the greatest because I'm the strongest. When anyone wants to make a point vehemently they bang their fist on the table and I take the full force of the attack. I'm the greatest because I am the strongest."

The thumb then took a tennis ball and said, "Each one of you come and pick this up." Each finger tried, but none succeeded.

Then he said, "Now work together and try to pick up the ball." They each held a different part of the ball and found they could lift it. It wasn't very easy, but they could at least do better then when they each tried to pick up the ball on their own.

The thumb then said, "Now try again and let me help you."

The whole hand, fingers and thumb, all worked together and lifted the ball easily.

There are some things we can do alone, and more we can do when we work together, and still more when we work together and with God.

When the term cooperation is used the emphasis is usually on "co"—together. There is action involved in cooperation, but it is an action undertaken in unity. It is not enough for us to nod assent at the notion of cooperation. What is required is a determination to take the initiatives needed to move ourselves, our congregations, our churches, our groups into cooperative endeavor.

Unity does not mean that we are all the same, as we saw in the example of the hand.

Robyn M. Claydon is Vice Principal of Abbotsleigh School, Sydney, Australia and a citizen of that country.

Rather, it means mutuality and interdependence. It means being united in purpose while giving each member freedom to exercise his or her own strengths.

If we look at Paul's letters we see that unity is characterized by the giving of mutual encouragement (Romans 1), by commending one person to another (Colossians 4:7–14), praying for one another (Philippians 1:4), exhorting one another (Philippians 2:14), and encouraging each other not to lose heart (Colossians 3). How well do we encourage each other, commend each other, pray for each other, and encourage each other to keep going?

In Philippians 2:2–4, Paul urges his readers to be "one in spirit and purpose," not to do anything out of "selfish ambition," and asks each to look "not only to your own interests, but also to the interests of others."

During this Congress we have been studying the book of Romans, and we are given a wonderful picture of cooperation in the early church. In Romans, we are invited to glimpse an international fellowship of believers who are working to spread the gospel. This fellowship is made up of women and men, of young and old, of experienced Christians and new Christians, of people representing different countries, different gifts, different opportunities, and different levels of society.

Paul commends these Christian workers to each other: Phoebe, a minister of another church at Cenchrea is to be received in a way that is worthy of the saints. Timothy, Gaius, Erastus, and others working for the gospel with Paul in Ephesus, send encouragement to those working at Rome.

Clearly, unity was not to be confused with uniformity. We hear too of Priscilla and Aquila, in whose home the church meets; Epenetus, the first convert to Christ from Asia; Andronicus and Junia, who had suffered in prison with Paul, and who, he said, were "outstanding among the apostles"; and others, some of whom were members of slave households and some of the imperial household.

What diversity in unity! All were "fellow workers" in the gospel, but their ethnic, educational, social, and religious backgrounds were very different, as were their responsibilities, opportunities, and experiences. Yet they all had a significant role in the spread of the gospel. The range of ministries created diversity, but the workers were bonded by a common purpose.

Paul could have listed many more names from other cities and from other places and ministries, but instead sums them up in the words, "All the churches of Christ send greetings." Is this true of us? Do we send greetings to one another? Does the church in Australia send greetings, encouragement, and support to the church in Zaire? Does the church in India send greetings, encouragement, and support to the church in Finland? Certainly this Congress gives an opportunity for this to be done.

The workers then were as international and, in other ways, as multifaceted as was the task they undertook, and the need for recognition of each other's work, the value of praying one for the other, and the encouraging of each other, was a vital aspect of cooperation in evangelism.

It was a cooperation which recognized different gifts and roles, that recognized the primacy of the task, accepted the inevitability of suffering, and warmly and generously gave encouragement. It was not a superficial cooperation which tolerated and even perpetuated divisions, or that encouraged individualism and needless duplication. Nor was it characterized by competitiveness. Recent research from the Cooperative Learning Center at the University of Minnesota has shown that too much competition is bad for our health and can bring out the "beast" in us. Cooperation is conducive to good health and brings out the "best" in us.

Cooperation means non-competitive partnership. It requires humility and the recognition of others, their gifts, and their ministry. Cooperation means genuine partnership between men and women, clergy and laity, young and old, First World and Third World, North and South, church and para-church.

We cannot be partners and co-workers until we recognize our oneness in the Spirit, and until we come in humility asking forgiveness for the divisions we have created, the polarity we have tolerated, the opportunities we have wasted through suspicion and territorialism, the hurts we have administered to one another, and the opportunities we have denied each other. And let us recognize that we have done all these. We allowed personal ambition, rivalry between ministries, dogmatism about nonessentials, denominational distinctiveness, continued paternalism, and corporate individualism to cloud our commission and contaminate our call. But it is not enough to acknowledge it; we must do something about it.

The fact that we are here at this Congress on World Evangelization shows that we share a common vision. We recognize the primacy and urgency of making known Christ's saving work to all people, and it is becoming an increasingly obvious fact that the whole gospel will not be taken to the whole world unless it is taken by the whole church.

No one of us can do it alone. No denomination can do it alone. No mission body can do it alone. No country can do it alone. No gender, age, or race can do it alone. It can, however, be done, if we work in cooperation with God and with each other.

In the nineteenth century, the scientists Marie and Pierre Curie had been experimenting with radioactivity. After years and years of work Pierre was one day discouraged and daunted by the magnitude of the task. Turning to his wife he said, "It can't be done. It can't be done. It will take one hundred years!" To which she replied, "It will be done. Even if it takes one hundred years! We can do no less than work for it while we have breath."

They kept working and they discovered radium.

Let's not be daunted by the magnitude of the task of world evangelization. It can be done no matter how long it takes! And it will be done faster and more efficiently if we, as individuals, local churches, and parachurch organizations, work together.

The October '88 issue of the *Prayer Countdown to Lausanne II in Manila* said,

A new spirit of cooperation pervades Christianity everywhere. International radio broadcasters have banded together to more effectively sound out the gospel message to the world; expatriate Chinese churches around the world have come together under the Christian coordination Center for World Evangelization, and different organizations are working together in a number of countries to bring the whole gospel to their entire nation.

Have you been receiving as I have, these prayer countdowns to Lausanne II saying "four months to go," "three months to go," "two months to go ... ?" Well, the countdown has ended. Lausanne II is here. We are Lausanne II. The countdown has stopped. Now is the time for the launch!

Today is the time for cooperative action. Cooperation, however, has a cost. It may mean that the church will need a greater openness to the work of parachurch and house churches. It may mean denominational sharing of tasks and personnel; it may mean conservatives and those not so conservative—and the charismatic among them both—listening to and learning from each other; it may mean men recognizing women's calling to ministry and mission; it may mean mission boards working more closely and more humbly with the national churches they have brought into being. It may mean cooperation between international and multinational organizations. It may mean this and more, and more!

We need to ask for forgiveness for our pride, our self-seeking, our denominational divisiveness, our exclusive structures, and our failure to put first God and his call to world evangelization. But let us remember that when we ask for that forgiveness, we stand forgiven. The past with all its failures is behind us and glorious opportunities lie ahead. We must not, like Marley's ghost in Charles Dickens's *A Christmas Carol*, drag the chain of the past with us wherever we go. We are the forgiven, cleansed, renewed people of God.

Today we can say, "Lord forgive us." We can also say, "Lord, help us to learn from our mistakes and from this day forward go forth together to take your Good News to the world."

The Lausanne Covenant, paragraphs 6 and 7 read:

> We affirm that Christ sends his redeemed people into the world. . . . We affirm that the church's visible unity in truth is God's purpose. Evangelism also summons us to unity, because our oneness strengthens our witness, just as our disunity undermines our gospel of reconciliation. . . . We who share the same biblical faith should be closely united in fellowship, work, and witness.

The task of taking the whole gospel to the whole world will only be effective if the whole church catches the vision of working with God and with each other, acknowledging each other and each other's ministries, encouraging each other, praying for each other, strengthening, and supporting each other, so that there will be an ever-growing, dynamic network of God's believing, praying, called, and commissioned witnesses covering the whole world.

It can be done, and we can do no less than work for it while we have breath!

II. B. The Whole Gospel: Bible Studies

Eagerness to Preach the Gospel

John Stott

Paul and the Gospel (Romans 1:1–5)

Paul's letter to the Romans is a type of Christian manifesto—a manifesto of freedom through Christ. Once we grasp the Good News which it contains, we are eager to share it with the world, and no one is able to silence us.

The book of Romans contains fundamental teachings about:

- Human beings—sinful, guilty, and without excuse
- God—revealing his wrath against evil and his mercy in the gospel
- Jesus—who died for our sins and rose again to prove it
- Salvation—justification by faith alone, life in the Spirit, and the glory yet to be revealed
- History—God's unfolding purpose for Jews and Gentiles
- Believers—their responsibilities to God, to the state, to other believers, and to the world

The truths God reveals in this book are enough to stretch our minds, liberate our consciences, set our hearts on fire, and open our mouths in praise and testimony. May God speak to us through his Word and give us grace to listen and respond!

Paul and the Gospel (vv. 1–5)

At this time, Paul has not yet visited Rome. The people he addressed his letter to were not known to him personally, nor was he known to them. He introduces himself as a servant (or slave) of Jesus Christ, which is a title of great humility, and as one called to be an apostle, which is a title of great authority.

On the Damascus road, Saul of Tarsus was not only converted, but he also was commissioned as an apostle, indeed, as an apostle to the Gentiles. He did not appoint himself to this task. He was called to it—called to be an apostle. He was set apart for the gospel of God, which he describes to the Romans in six aspects, which are as true for us as they were for him.

John R. W. Stott is President of Christian Impact, and Rector Emeritus of All Souls Church, London. He is a citizen of Great Britain.

1. *Its origin is God (v. 1).* The Christian Good News is the gospel of God. Paul and the other apostles did not invent it, it was revealed and entrusted to them by God. This is the first and most basic conviction which underlies evangelism. Specifically, what we have to share with others is not human speculation, not just one more religion to be added to the rest, not actually a religion at all but the gospel of God—God's Good News for a lost world. Without this conviction there can be no evangelism, no world mission.

2. *Its attestation is Scripture (v. 2).* The gospel of God is a message which he promised beforehand through his prophets in the Holy Scriptures. Although God revealed it to the apostles, it was no novelty, because he had already promised it through his prophets. As Paul wrote to the Corinthians, "Christ died for our sins according to the Scriptures, . . . was raised on the third day according to the Scriptures" (1 Corinthians 15:4). The gospel has a double attestation: by the prophets in the Old Testament and the apostles in the New. Both bear witness to Jesus Christ, which is what Paul discusses next.

3. *Its substance is Jesus Christ (vv. 3–4).* Paul states he was set apart for the gospel of God . . . regarding his Son. The gospel of God concerns the Son of God. The Good News is about Jesus, who, Paul says, "as to his human nature was a descendant of David, and who through the Spirit of holiness was declared with power to be the Son of God by his resurrection from the dead" (vv. 3–4). We could spend hours meditating on the profound implications of these two verses. There are references, direct and indirect, to the birth, death, resurrection, and reign of Jesus Christ. It is a statement of both his humiliation and his exaltation. These verses make the claim that he is both fully human and fully divine; his human descent is traced to David and his divine Sonship demonstrated by the Resurrection. Further claim is made that this historical person is our Lord, who owns and rules our lives.

4. *Its scope is the nations (v. 5).* Paul's grace and apostleship (the undeserved privilege of being an apostle) is "to call people from among all the Gentiles." Although Paul was a Jew—previously, a narrow-minded Pharisee—he had been gloriously liberated from his racial prejudice. He retained a patriotic love for his own people, and longed passionately for their salvation, but now he loved the Gentiles too and longed for their salvation as well. If we are to be committed to the Christian world-mission, we need to be delivered from all pride of race, nation, cast, tribe, and class, and to acknowledge that God's gospel is for everybody without exception.

5. *Its purpose is the obedience that comes from faith (v. 5).* The obedience of faith is Paul's definition of the response which the gospel demands. Its importance is emphasized by its mention at both the beginning and the end of Romans. In Romans, Paul outlines more clearly than anywhere else that justification is by grace alone—through faith alone. Yet, the response to the gospel is not just "faith" but the "obedience that comes from faith." Paul is not contradicting himself with that statement. The obedience the gospel requires is not the obedience of *law* but the obedience of *faith.* The proper response to the gospel is indeed faith alone, but a true and living faith in Jesus includes an element of submission and inevitably leads into a life of obedience.

6. *Its goal is the honor of Christ's name (v. 5).* As Christians, we desire to call the nations to the obedience of faith "for his name's sake" (v. 5). God has

exalted Jesus and given him the name that is above every name, that at the name of Jesus every knee should bow (Philippians 2:9–11). If God desires every knee to bow to Jesus, so should we. We should be jealous for the honor of Christ's name, troubled when it remains unknown, hurt when it is ignored, indignant when it is blasphemed, and all the time anxious that it should be given the honor and glory due it. Henry Martyn once said, "I could not endure existence if Jesus were not glorified." This is the highest of all missionary motives. It is not obedience to the Great Commission, nor love for sinners who are perishing, but zeal for the glory of Jesus Christ. Some evangelism is a thinly disguised form of imperialism—ambition for the honor of our own race, nation, church, or organization. Only one form of imperialism is Christian, and that is concerned for the empire, or kingdom, of Jesus Christ. "For his name's sake " expresses the supreme missionary goal, before which all unworthy motives wither away and die.

There are six fundamental truths about the gospel. Its origin is God the Father, and its substance Jesus Christ, his Son. Its attestation is the Scripture and its scope all the nations. Our immediate purpose in preaching it is to bring people to the obedience of faith, but our ultimate goal is the glory of the name of Jesus.

Or, to sum up these six truths by six prepositions: the Good News is the gospel of God, about Christ, according to Scripture, for the nations, unto the obedience of faith, for the sake of Christ's name.

Paul and the Romans (vv. 6–13)

Having described himself and his gospel, Paul now describes his readers—the Christians in Rome. According to Paul, they are "loved by God," "called to belong to Jesus Christ," and "called to be saints" (vv. 6–7).

Similarly, if we are Christians, we are also called and loved. Not because we decided for Christ, but because God first loved us and called us to himself. In consequence, we belong to him and Paul wishes for us a continuing enjoyment of "the grace and peace" which we have already begun to receive.

After this introduction, Paul tells the Romans of his feelings towards them:

1. *He thanks God for them (v. 8)* "because your faith is being reported all over the world." Paul was not responsible for bringing the gospel to them, yet this did not hinder him from giving thanks that Rome was evangelized.
2. *He prays for them (vv. 9–10).* He does not know them personally; yet he prays for them "constantly" (v. 9), and "at all times" (v. 10). He prays especially that "now at last by God's will the way may be opened" for him to come to them (v. 10). His prayer was answered, although neither at the time nor in the manner that he had envisaged. Paul reached Rome about three years later, not as a free man but as a prisoner, having appealed to the emperor. God sometimes has unexpected ways of answering our prayers.
3. *He longs to see them (vv. 11–12),* and tells them why. His motivation is partly to impart some spiritual gift, perhaps his teaching or exhortation, but also to receive something from them. He knows about the mutual encouragement of Christian fellowship. Although he's an apostle, he is not too proud to acknowledge his need for encouragement. Modern missionaries who go to another country or culture in the same spirit of humility and

receptivity, anxious to receive as well as to give, to learn as well as to teach, to be encouraged as well as to encourage, are likely to be fulfilled and content.

4. *He had often planned to visit them (v. 13),* not only to give or to receive, but to "reap some harvest" among them (RSV), as among other Gentiles, that is, to win some of them for Christ. It was appropriate that the apostle to the Gentiles should do some evangelistic reaping in the very heart of the Gentile world.

Paul and Evangelism (vv. 14–16)

Paul makes three strong personal statements about his anxiety to preach the gospel:

- I am under obligation (v. 14)
- I am eager (v. 15)
- I am not ashamed (v. 16)

These affirmations are striking because they are in direct contrast to the mood of many people in the contemporary church. Today people regard evangelism as an option and even a charity, but to Paul it was an obligation. The modern mood is one of reluctance, but Paul's was one of eagerness and enthusiasm. Many today are ashamed of the gospel, but Paul declared that he was not.

Paul had as many reasons to feel as reluctant or embarrassed as we have. Rome was the capital of the world—the symbol of imperial pride and power. People spoke of Rome with awe. Everybody hoped to visit Rome once in their lifetime, in order to look, to stare, and to wonder. Paul wanted to visit Rome, not as a tourist but as an evangelist He believed he had something to say, which Rome needed to hear. According to tradition, Paul was an unattractive man with bad eyesight and no great oratorical gifts. What could he hope to accomplish against the proud might of imperial Rome? Would he not be wiser to stay away? Or if he must visit Rome, would it not be prudent for him to keep silent? Paul did not think so. On the contrary, he was under obligation, eager and not ashamed to preach the gospel. What, then, were the origins of his evangelistic eagerness?

1. *The gospel is a debt to the world (v. 14).* The expression, "I am under obligation" (NIV) is correctly translated in the King James Version as "I am debtor" or in debt.

   There are two possible ways to get into debt. The first is to borrow money from someone, and the second is to be given money for someone by a third party. For example, if I borrowed $1000 from you, I would be in your debt until I had repaid it. Equally, if a friend of yours had given me $1000 to bring to you, I would be in your debt until I gave it to you. In the first case, I got myself into debt by borrowing, but in the second case, your friend put me in your debt by entrusting me with $1000 for you. It is in this second sense that Paul was in debt to the Romans. He had not borrowed anything from them, which he needed to repay. But Jesus Christ had entrusted him with the gospel for them. Several times in his letters Paul uses the expression, "I have been put in trust with the gospel." It was Jesus who had made him a debtor. And as the apostle to the Gentiles, he was specially in debt "to Greeks and non-Greeks, to the educated and the uneducated" (v. 14).

   Similarly, we are in debt to the world. If the gospel has come to us, we cannot keep it to ourselves. Nobody can claim a monopoly of the gospel. The Good News is for sharing. We have a universal obligation to make it known. Such was Paul's first incentive. He was eager to preach the gospel because he was in debt. It is universally regarded as a dishonorable thing to leave a debt unpaid. We should be as eager to discharge our debt as Paul was to discharge his.

2. *The gospel is God's power for salvation (v. 16).* "I am not ashamed of the gospel," Paul wrote, "because it is the power of God for the salvation of everyone who believes" (v. 16).

The apostle's almost fierce negative is surprising. The suggestion that Paul could have felt ashamed of the gospel sounds ludicrous, but it is not. I once heard Professor James Stewart of Edinburgh preach on this text. In the course of his sermon he said, "There is no sense in declaring that you are not ashamed of something unless you have been tempted to feel ashamed." And without doubt Paul had been tempted. He knew that the message of the Cross was a stumbling block to the proud. We sometimes experience the same temptation.

How did Paul overcome this temptation to feel ashamed? Only by remembering that the gospel, which some despise for its weakness, is God's power to save sinners. We know this because we have experienced it ourselves. The gospel has saved us, brought us into a new and right relationship with God, so that he is our Father and we are his children. How then could we be ashamed of a gospel which has transformed us?

Paul and Righteousness (v. 17)

The logic of verses 16 and 17 is clear: "I am not ashamed of the gospel, because it is the power of God for the salvation of everyone . . . For in the gospel a righteousness from God is revealed." The power of God is in the gospel because the righteousness of God is revealed in it. This expression is crucial for our understanding of Romans.

What did Paul mean by "the righteousness of God"? Is it a divine attribute? Our God is a righteous God. Is it a divine activity? God coming to rescue and vindicate us. Or is it a gift? God bestowing a righteous status on sinners.

All three positions are held by different commentators. The most satisfactory solution seems to be to combine them. In the letter to the Romans, "the righteousness of God" is God's righteous way of putting people right with himself by bestowing on them a righteousness which is not their own but his. "The righteousness of God" is God's way of justifying sinners, by which he both demonstrates his righteousness and gives righteousness to us. It is God's righteous way of declaring the unrighteous righteous. It is God's act of putting us right with himself, without thereby putting himself in the wrong.

He does it through Christ, the righteous one who died for the unrighteous, and he does it by faith, that is, when we put our trust in him or cry out to him for mercy. Indeed, what God does, he does "from faith to faith," (v. 17, KJV), or "by faith from first to last" (NIV). For God affirmed it centuries before through Habakkuk, "But the righteous will live by his faith" (2:4).

God's enlightenment of Martin Luther to grasp this truth sparked the Reformation. When he was preparing his lectures on the letter to the Romans in 1514, he wrote:

I greatly longed to understand Paul's epistle to the Romans, and nothing stood in the way but that one expression "the righteousness of God," because I took it to mean that righteousness whereby God is righteous and deals righteously in punishing the unrighteous. . . . Night and day I pondered until . . . I grasped the truth that the righteousness of God is that righteousness whereby, through grace and sheer mercy, he justifies us by faith. Thereupon, I felt myself to be reborn and to have gone through open doors into paradise. The whole of Scripture took on a new meaning, and whereas before "the righteousness of God" had filled me with hate, now it became to me inexpressibly sweet in greater love. This passage of Paul became to me a gateway to heaven.

Paul's eagerness to preach the gospel arose from his recognition that the gospel was (*a*) an unpaid debt, and (*b*) the saving power of God. The first gave him a sense of obligation because he had been put in trust with the gospel, and the second, a sense of conviction because the gospel had saved him and it could save others.

Today, the gospel is still both a debt to discharge and a power to experience. Only when we have grasped these truths shall we be able to say with Paul "I am not ashamed of the gospel. I am under obligation. I am eager to share the gospel with the world."

The World's Guilt

John Stott

Nothing keeps people away from Christ more than their inability to see their need of him, or their unwillingness to admit it. As Jesus said, "It is not the healthy who need a doctor, but the sick. I have not come to call the righteous, but sinners" (Mark 2:17). This does not mean that some people are righteous and do not need salvation, but that some people *think* they are. In that condition of self-righteousness, they will never come to Christ. Just as we go to the doctor only when we admit that we are ill and cannot heal ourselves, we go to Christ only when we admit that we are guilty sinners and cannot save ourselves.

This is the principle which lies behind the long passage before us. Paul's purpose is to "lay the charge that Jews and Gentiles alike are all under sin" (3:9) and that "there is no difference" between us (3:22). Paul does more than bring an accusation; he marshals the evidence against us, proves our guilt, and secures a conviction. All men and women, without exception, from both the Jewish and the Gentile worlds are sinful, guilty, and without excuse before God. Therefore, they are under his wrath. Already they stand condemned. It is a theme of great solemnity and an indispensable foundation for world evangelization.

Paul demonstrates the universality of sin and guilt by dividing the human race into several sections, and then arraigns them one by one. In each case his procedure is identical. He reminds each group of their knowledge of God and of goodness. He then confronts them with the uncomfortable fact that they have not lived up to their knowledge. Instead, they have suppressed it, and even contradicted it, by continuing to live in unrighteousness. And, therefore, they are guilty, inexcusably guilty, before God. No one can plead innocence, because no one can plead ignorance. This is the thrust of Paul's argument throughout.

He addresses four sections of people. He describes the depraved Gentile world in its idolatry, immorality, and anti-social behavior. He addresses critical moralists (both Gentiles and Jews), who profess high ethical standards and apply them to everybody except themselves. He turns to self-righteous Jews who boast of their knowledge of God's Law, but do not obey it. And then, he encompasses the whole human race and concludes that we are all guilty before God.

To each group his message is substantially the same:

> You know the righteous character and requirements of God. Yet you have persisted in your unrighteousness, so you are guilty. You have no excuse. You have no hope either—apart from the grace of God who justifies those who believe in Jesus.

The Depraved Gentile World (Romans 1:18–32)

In verses 16–20, the apostle develops an argument of relentless logic as he refers successively to the power of God, the righteousness of God, the wrath of God, and the glory of God in creation.

Our text begins with verse 18, "The wrath of God is being revealed from heaven." This reference to God's wrath raises three questions:

1. *What is the wrath of God?* It does not mean God loses his temper or is malicious or spiteful. God's wrath is his righteous hostility to evil, his refusal to condone it, and his just judgment upon it.
2. *Against what is God's wrath revealed?* Paul answers that it is revealed "against all the godlessness and wickedness of men who suppress the truth by their wickedness" (v. 18). In other words, all human beings know something of God from the creation. The creation is a visible disclosure of the invisible God. That is why godless people are without excuse. They deliberately suppress the truth about God which they know. It is against this willful rebellion that God's wrath is revealed.

   Idolators are also inexcusable, for "although they knew God, they neither glorified him as God" (v. 21). Instead, they exchanged the glory of God for images of human beings, birds, beasts, and reptiles (v. 23). "They exchanged the truth of God for a lie" (v. 25), indeed, the supreme lie of worshipping created things as if they were the Creator. This condemnation applies not only to primitive idolatry but equally to the more sophisticated idolatry of Western materialism. It is a deliberate denial of the transcendent reality of God.
3. *How is God's wrath revealed?* God's wrath will be revealed in the future, in the judgment of the Last Day, for there is such a thing as "the wrath to come." But meanwhile, there is a present disclosure of the wrath of God, which Paul describes in his terrible threefold refrain:

   - God gave them over to immorality (v. 24).
   - God gave them over to "shameful lusts" (v. 26). In particular to homosexual practices which are against nature and are a violation of God's created order.
   - God gave them over to "a depraved mind" (v. 28) which leads to antisocial behavior. Paul lists twenty-one examples such as greed, envy, slander, malice, and murder. He concludes that people practice these things and encourage others to do so, even though they know God's righteous decree is that those who practice them deserve death.

In summary, Paul describes the wrath of God as: (*a*) God's righteous hostility to evil, (*b*) directed against people who know something of God's truth and righteousness but deliberately suppress it, and (*c*) it is being revealed in the process of moral and social degeneration.

Critical Moralists (2:1–16)

Paul turns from a world characterized by shameless immorality to a world characterized by self-conscious moralism. Far from approving of lawless behavior (1:32), these people deplore and condemn it (2:1–3). Who are they? Twice in the Greek sentence (which is obscured by the NIV), Paul addresses them as,"O man" (vv. 1,3, KJV), indeed, "O [critical] man." He is referring to every human being, whether Jew or Gentile, male or female, who is a moralist and passes moral judgments on other people.

Paul's argument is basically the same with moralizers as with those who are openly immoral: both groups have a certain knowledge of righteousness; both contradict their knowledge by their behavior; and both are, therefore, without excuse (1:20; 2:1).

Paul draws attention to three things about the moralizers, which are surely true of us:

1. *Our hypocrisy (2:1–3)*. Paul uncovers a strange human foible. It is our tendency to be critical of everybody except ourselves. We are as harsh in our judgment of others as we are lenient towards ourselves. We work ourselves up into a state of self-righteous indignation over the disgraceful behavior of others, while somehow the very same behavior seems not nearly as serious when it is ours and not theirs. We even gain a vicarious satisfaction from condemning in others the very faults which we excuse in ourselves. Freud called this moral gymnastic "projection," but Paul described it centuries before Freud.

    This practice, Paul argues, leaves us without excuse. If our critical faculties are so well-developed that we become experts in the moral evaluation of others, we can hardly plead ignorance of moral issues in ourselves. On the contrary, in judging others (v. 1), we thereby condemn ourselves who do the very same things. This is the hypocrisy of the double standard—a high standard for others, but a conveniently low one for ourselves.

2. *Our impenitence (vv. 4–5)*. Sometimes, Paul says, we take refuge in the theological argument that in the "riches of his kindness, tolerance and patience" (v. 4) God will condone our sin. That is, he is too kind and loving to punish anybody. But such trust in God's patience is not faith; it is presumption. The kindness of God is intended to lead us to repentance, not to give us an excuse for sinning. If it does not lead us to repent, then because of our stubbornness and unrepentant hearts (v. 5), we are storing up wrath, God's holy wrath, against ourselves on the Day of Wrath when his righteous judgment will be revealed.

3. *Our works (vv. 6–11)*. Paul emphasizes the indispensable necessity of good works if we are to escape the judgment of God. In verse 6, he states the inflexible principle, laid down in the Old Testament (e.g., Psalm 62:12; Proverbs 24:12) and repeated by Jesus and his apostles, that God will give to "each person according to what he has done" or God will "requite a man according to his work" (RSV).

Some people are immediately indignant at this statement. "Have you taken leave of your senses, Paul?" they ask. "Do you begin by affirming salvation by faith alone, and then destroy your own gospel by saying that it is by good works after all?" Paul is not contradicting himself. He is describing God's universal principle of judgment that, although his justification is by faith alone, his judgment will be according to our works.

The reason for this is not hard to find. The Day of Judgment will be a public occasion. Its purpose will be less to determine God's judgment than to declare and vindicate it. The divine process of judgment, which is a process of separation, is secretly going on all the time; but on the Day of Judgment, its consequences will be made public. The day of God's wrath will be a "revelation" of the righteous judgment of God (v. 5).

Such a public occasion (on which a public verdict will be given and a public sentence passed) will require public appeals and verifiable evidence to support them. The only public evidence available will be our works—what we have done and have been seen to do. The presence or absence of saving faith in our hearts will be disclosed by the presence or absence of good works of love in our lives. Paul and James teach the same truth: saving faith issues in good works, and if it does not, it is bogus or dead. Verses 7–10 enlarge on this: our works will be the basis of God's judgment.

Paul applies this general principle of God's judgment according to works applies in particular to Jews and Gentiles (vv. 12–16). They differ from one another in that while Jews possess the Mosaic Law, the Gentiles do not. Yet, there is no distinction between them either in the sin they have committed, in the guilt they have incurred, or in the judgment they will receive, unless they cry to God for mercy. Gentiles, although they do not possess God's Law as an external revelation, sometimes "do by nature things required by the law" (v. 14). God has created them as self-conscious moral beings, on account of which they do not have the law in their hands (as the Jews do), but nevertheless, they show by their behavior that they have it in their hearts (v. 15). For God has written it there, not in the sense that he has regenerated them, but in the sense that he has created them with a moral instinct. Moreover, their conscience also bears its witness, their thoughts accuse them and sometimes even defend them.

This teaching is important. The same moral law which God has revealed in Scripture is also stamped on human nature. God has in fact written his law twice: once on stone tablets and once on human hearts. There is a fundamental correspondence between God's Law in the Bible and God's law in our hearts. Therefore, we are authentically human only when we obey the law of God. If we disobey it, we contradict not only what we know to be right, but our own human being. To do this is to be without sense as well as without excuse.

Let's remember in our evangelism that the other person's conscience is on our side!

Self-righteous Jews (2:17–3:8)

In 2:1, Paul addressed human beings, " O man." In 2:17, he addresses a Jew, "Now you, if you call yourself a Jew." He anticipates Jewish objections to what he has written:

> Surely, Paul, you cannot possibly treat us as if we were the same as those Gentile outsiders? Have you forgotten that we have both the Law (the revelation of God) and circumcision (the sign of the covenant of God)? Are you saying that we Jews are no better off than Gentiles?

Paul answers these objections by referring to the Law in verses 17–24 and to circumcision in verses 25–29. He insists that neither gives the Jews any immunity to the judgment of God.

1. *The Law (vv. 17–24).* Paul gives a full description of Jewish self-righteousness:

> You rely on the law and brag about your relationship to God. . . . you know his will. . . . you are convinced that you are a guide, "a light," an instructor of the foolish, . . .you, then, who teach others, do you not teach yourself? (vv. 17–21).

It is the same argument as at the beginning of the chapter: If we judge others, we should judge ourselves; if we teach others, we should teach ourselves. If we set ourselves up as either judge or teacher, we cannot possibly claim to be ignorant of morality. Instead, we invite God's condemnation of our hypocrisy.

2. *Circumcision (vv. 25–29).* Jewish knowledge of the Law did not exempt them from the judgment of God, neither did their circumcision. Circumcision was the God-given sign of his covenant, but it was not a magical ceremony and was no substitute for obedience. On the contrary, the true Jew is one inwardly, not outwardly, and the true circumcision is in the heart, not the body (v. 29). One could say the same of the true Christian and of the true baptism.

It is not difficult to imagine that Jewish people would listen to Paul's teaching with incredulity and indignation, so Paul responds to further questions about the character of God. Would God's judgment on Israel contradict his faithfulness and his justice? Paul emphatically denies it. God's faithfulness is not nullified by Israel's unfaithfulness (3:3–4) and God's justice is equally unstained (3:5–8). God is going to judge the world, how could he possibly be guilty of injustice? (v. 6).

The Whole Human Race (3:9–20)

Paul is approaching the conclusion of his argument. He has exposed in succession the blatant unrighteousness of much of the ancient Gentile world, the hypocritical righteousness of moralizers, and the legal self-righteousness of Jews who boast of God's Law. "We have already made the charge that Jews and Gentiles alike are all under sin," that is, "under the power of sin" (v. 9, RSV, NEB). Sin is personified as a tyrant who holds all human beings imprisoned in guilt and under judgment.

Paul goes on to support this fact of the universal bondage of guilt from Scripture. In verses 10–19, he gives a list of six Old Testament quotations, all of which bear witness in different ways to the universality of human sin and guilt. Two features of this biblical portrait stand out:

1. *It teaches the ungodliness of sin.* For example, there is "no one who seeks God" (v. 11) and "there is no fear of God before their eyes" (v. 18). Sin is fundamentally the revolt of the self against God, the dethronement of God and the enthronement of self. Sin is "getting rid of the Lord God" (Brunner), in order to proclaim our own sovereignty. Ultimately, sin is self-deification.
2. *It teaches the pervasiveness of sin.* Sin affects every part of our human constitution—every human faculty and function. In the Old Testament quotations there seems to be a deliberate listing of these: our "throats are open graves"; our tongues deceive; our lips spread poison; our "mouths are full of cursing and bitterness"; our "feet are swift to shed blood," scattering ruin and misery in our paths instead of walking in the path of peace; and, we do not keep God before our eyes or reverence him (vv. 13–18).

   All of these parts of our bodies—our throat, tongue, lips, mouth, feet, and eyes—were created and given to us to glorify God, and are in rebellion against him. This is the biblical doctrine of total depravity, which is rejected only by those who misunderstand it. It has never meant that all human beings are as depraved as they could possibly be. Such a notion is manifestly absurd and untrue, for we are not all drunkards, thieves, adulterers, and murderers. The "totality" of our corruption refers to its extent (affecting every part of us), not its degree (depraving every part of us absolutely). As Dr. J. I. Packer has said, total depravity means, "Not that at every point man is as bad as he could be, but that at no point is he as good as he should be."

These six texts certainly describe Gentile sinners but in verse 19, Paul argues that they apply to Jews also, "those who are under the law." In fact, they are God's portrait of all humankind. Their purpose is to stop every mouth, silence every excuse, and make the whole world "accountable to God" and liable to his just judgment. The words *that every mouth may be silenced* (v. 19), comments Professor Charles Cranfield:

> Evoke the picture of the defendant in court who, given the opportunity to speak in his own defense, is speechless because of the weight of the evidence which has been brought against him.

This is the point toward which Paul has been steadily moving: the idolatrous and immoral Gentiles are "without excuse" (1:20); all critical moralists, whether Jewish or Gentile, are also "without excuse" (2:1); in fact, "the whole world" and all its inhabitants, without any exception, are inexcusable (3:19).

And the reason? All have known God's law to some degree, and all have disregarded it. That is why "no one will be declared righteous in his sight by observing the law" (v. 20). Rather, what the law brings is the knowledge of sin, not the forgiveness of sin. Its function, as Luther said, is not to justify, but to terrify, and so to drive us into the arms of Christ.

How should we respond to this devastating exposure of universal human sin and guilt? We need to be as certain as we can that we have accepted the divine diagnosis as true, and that we have fled from the judgment of God to the only refuge there is—Jesus Christ. We have no merit to plead. We have no excuse to make. We stand before God condemned and speechless. But God in Christ on the cross has borne our condemnation. This is the only way that we can be justified, if we take refuge in Jesus.

And we simply cannot keep this Good News to ourselves. All around us are men and women who know enough about God's glory and holiness to make their rejection of him and his law inexcusable. They too stand condemned. Their only hope of justification is in Christ. How can we keep this Good News from them? Let us speak boldly to them of him! Their mouths are closed in guilt; let our mouths be opened in testimony!

Amazing Grace

John Stott

All human beings are sinful and guilty before God—the moral and the immoral, the educated and the uneducated, the religious and the irreligious. "There is no one righteous, not even one" (3:10). "All have turned away" (3:12). That was Paul's terrible theme. There was no ray of light, no flicker of hope, no prospect of salvation. There was nothing but darkness, nothing to do but to wait speechless for the final outpouring of the wrath of God.

"But now," Paul suddenly breaks in (v. 21), God himself has intervened. After the long and starless night, the sun has risen and a new day has dawned. For "now a righteousness from God, apart from law, has been made known" (v. 21). Over the unrighteousness and self-righteousness of human beings, Paul sets the righteousness of God. Over God's wrath revealed from heaven, he sets God's righteousness revealed in the gospel. Over against our pitiful works, he sets the atoning work of Jesus Christ, appropriated by faith. Over our guilt he sets God's grace—his free and unmerited favor towards sinners.

The Manifestation of God's Grace (Romans 3:21–26)

"The righteousness of God," which has been made known in the gospel, is God's righteous way of "making right" the unrighteous—his justifying grace which alone can overcome our guilt. Paul describes its source (where it comes from), its ground (on what it rests), and its means (how we receive it):

1. *The source of our justification is God and his grace.* Justification is God coming to the rescue—God coming in Christ to put the unrighteous right with himself.

   Fundamental to the gospel of salvation is the truth that the saving initiative, from beginning to end, belongs to God the Father. No formulation is biblical which takes the initiative away from him and attributes it to us, or even to Christ. It is certain that we did not take the initiative; for we were sinful, guilty and condemned, helpless and hopeless. Nor was the initiative Jesus Christ's, as if he did something which the Father was reluctant or unwilling to do. The initiative was God the Father's. If we are justified, then we are justified "freely by his grace" (v. 24). Grace is God loving, God stooping, God coming, and God giving.

2. *The ground of our justification is Christ and the Cross.* If God justifies sinners freely by his grace, then on what grounds does he do so? How can

the righteous God declare the unrighteous to be righteous without compromising his own righteousness?

No expression in Romans is more startling than in 4:5, "God who justifies the wicked." In the Old Testament, God repeatedly told the judges of Israel to "justify the righteous and condemn the wicked." He added that anyone who "justifies the wicked or condemns the righteous" is an abomination in his sight, and he declared of himself, "I will not justify the wicked." Then how can Paul affirm that God does what he forbids others to do, and does what he says he will never do? Justify the wicked? It is preposterous! It is unbelievable! Or rather it would be, were it not for the Cross of Christ.

Without the Cross, the justification of the unjust would be impossible. The only reason God can justify the ungodly (4:5) is because "Christ died for the ungodly" (5:6). He shed his blood (3:25) in a sacrificial death for sinners. Indeed, God presented him as a sacrifice of atonement, that is, as a propitiatory sacrifice, or means of propitiation.

Propitiation means placating the wrath of God. We need not be shy of using this word, as long as we remember that Christian propitiation is totally different from pagan notions of propitiation. In particular, that it was God himself who took the initiative, who in his great love propitiated his own wrath through his Son, Jesus Christ, who took our place, bore our sins, died our death, and so has provided a righteous basis on which the righteous God may forgive the unrighteous. Professor Cranfield has stated it tersely:

> God, because in his mercy he willed to forgive sinful men, and, being truly merciful, willed to forgive them righteously, that is, without in any way condoning their sin, purposed to direct against his own very self in the person of his Son the full weight of that righteous wrath which they deserved.

In the Cross, God has perfectly expressed both his love for sinners and his wrath against sin. In and through Jesus Christ, and him crucified, he has borne the fearful condemnation which our sins deserved. This is the very heart of the Christian Good News. It is enough to break the hardest heart.

Through the sin-bearing death of Jesus, God has propitiated his wrath, demonstrated his justice (3:25), and redeemed and justified those who put their trust in Jesus.

3. *The means of our justification is faith.* The apostle repeats this truth three times: "Through faith in Jesus Christ" (v. 22), "through faith in his blood" (v. 25), and God "justifies those who have faith in Jesus" (v. 26). Indeed, justification is by faith alone—*sola fide*. Although the word *alone* is not in Paul's text, it was a true instinct of Luther's to add it. Far from distorting Paul's meaning, the word clarifies and emphasizes it.

It is vital to understand there is nothing meritorious about faith. Salvation is not a cooperative enterprise between God and us, in which he contributes the Cross and we contribute faith. The value of faith lies entirely and exclusively in its object—Jesus Christ and him crucified. As Richard Hooker said in the sixteenth century, "God justifies the believer—not because of the worthiness of his belief, but because of his worthiness who is believed."

Justification by grace alone, in Christ alone, and by faith alone is unique to

Christianity. No other religion proclaims free forgiveness to those who have done nothing to deserve it. On the contrary, all other religions teach some form of self-salvation through good works of religion or righteousness. Christianity, by contrast, is not a religion at all. It is a gospel: the Good News that God has mercy on the undeserving, that God's grace has turned away his wrath, for God's Son has died our death and borne our judgment. There is, therefore, nothing left for us to do or even to contribute—only to receive what he offers.

The Implications of God's Grace (3:27–31)

Paul anticipates the questions which the gospel was bound to raise in Jewish minds.

1. Where then is boasting? (v. 27). The Jewish people were immensely proud of their privileges as the chosen people of God. But the gospel excludes all boasting, except boasting in Christ. Praising, not boasting, is the characteristic activity of justified believers.
2. Is God the God of the Jews only? (v. 29). Jewish people were extremely conscious of their special relationship to God, which the Gentiles did not share. But the gospel excludes discrimination as well as boasting. The one God has one way of salvation: he justifies both Jews and Gentiles in the same way—by faith.
3. Do we then nullify the Law? (v. 31). The Law was the Jews' most treasured possession and the gospel seemed to contradict it. But on the contrary, the gospel establishes the Law, since it justifies those whom the Law condemns.

These questions represent three implications of God's free, justifying grace: it humbles sinners and excludes boasting, it unites believers and excludes discrimination, and it establishes the Law and excludes contradiction.

An Illustration of God's Grace (4:1–25)

Paul chooses Abraham as his illustration of justification by faith because Abraham was the founding father of the Jewish people, and they regarded him as having been justified by works.

But in verse 3, Paul directs his readers' attention to Genesis 15:6, "Abraham believed God, and it was credited to him as righteousness." In other words, he was justified by faith. Paul then elaborates upon two particular features of Abraham's faith: its priority and its reasonableness.

1. *The priority of Abraham's faith (4:3–16).* Abraham's faith preceded anything else on account of which he might have been justified. Abraham was justified by faith before he did any good works, righteousness was credited to him not as a wage he had earned, but as a gift he received (vv. 3–4). He was justified by faith before he was circumcised (vv. 9–12). Abraham was justified in Genesis 15, and circumcised in Genesis 17. His circumcision was a sign, or seal, of the justification he had already received by faith while he was uncircumcised. Abraham was justified by faith before the Law was given (vv. 13–16). God gave Abraham a promise to be believed, not a law to be obeyed.

In summary, Abraham was not justified by works or by circumcision or by law. These all came later, his justification preceded them: it was by faith.

Abraham today, is the father not of those who trace their physical descent from him, but of those who belong to his spiritual lineage—the lineage of faith. The true children of Abraham are believers in Jesus, regardless of whether they are Jews or Gentiles.

2. *The reasonableness of Abraham's faith (vv. 17–25)*. Some people are surprised to hear faith described as "reasonable." They have always supposed that faith and reason exclude one another, and that *faith* is another word for "superstition or credulity." True faith always has a rational basis. Faith is believing somebody's word, and its reasonableness depends on the reliability of the person who spoke the word. It is always reasonable to trust the trustworthy. And there is no one more trustworthy than God.

As Abraham realized, the trustworthiness of God arises both from his power (he is able to keep his promises) and from his faithfulness (he can be relied on to keep his promises).

God's power is indicated at the end of verse 17, where he is described as the God "who gives life to the dead and calls into existence the things that do not exist" (RSV). He is the God of resurrection and the God of creation.

The creation of the universe and the resurrection of Jesus are the two major manifestations of the power of God. "Nothingness" and "death" utterly baffle us, but they are no problem to God. God creates even out of nothing, and God raises even out of death.

Both are seen in the birth of Isaac. According to the second part of verse 19, Abraham's body was as good as dead and Sarah's womb was also dead. Yet out of that double death, God brought a new life! It was at the same time an act of creation and of resurrection.

We are much more fortunate than Abraham, and have no excuse for our unbelief—we live after the resurrection of Jesus. We also have a completed Bible, in which both the creation of the universe and the resurrection of Jesus are recorded. It is even more reasonable for us to believe God than it was for Abraham.

And, there is the faithfulness of God—the fact that he keeps his promises. Abraham knew all about his senile body and Sarah's barren womb. He did not underestimate the problems. But he set the problems in the light of the promises of God. He was "fully persuaded that God had power to do what he had promised" (v. 21). All human faith reckons and rests on the divine faithfulness.

The People of God's Grace (5:1–11)

Immediately noteworthy at the beginning of Romans 5 is Paul's change of pronoun. He has been writing of believers in the third person plural. For example, "He is the father of all who believe" (v. 11). But suddenly in 4:16, he switches to the first person plural, "He is the father of us all." And Paul continues to write in the first person plural in chapter 5, with a series of six "we" sentences. They are bold affirmations in the name of all God's people who have been justified by faith.

1. *We have peace with God through our Lord Jesus Christ (v. 1)*. The pursuit of peace is a universal obsession, whether it be international peace, industrial peace, domestic peace, or personal peace. Yet more fundamental than all these, is peace with God—reconciliation to him through Jesus Christ.

"We have it," Paul writes, as a present possession. The prophets foretold it as the supreme blessing of the messianic age. It is the very essence of the *shalom* of the kingdom of God.

2. *We are now standing in grace (v. 2).* "Through whom we have gained access by faith into this grace in which we now stand." Grace is not so much a quality of God, as the state of favor into which he has brought us. We continue to stand in it continuously, firmly, and securely.

3. *We rejoice in the hope of God's glory (v. 2).* From the present (peace with God, standing in grace), Paul turns to our Christian hope for the future. It focuses on the glory of God, his radiant splendor, and the outward shining of inward being. One day it will be fully revealed, for Jesus Christ is coming again in the glory of his Father and then we will both see and share his glory. Even the groaning universe will be set free from its bondage to decay into the freedom of the glory of the children of God. The new heaven and the new earth will be suffused with the glory of their Creator.

4. *We also rejoice in our sufferings (v. 3).* Paul has written of peace, joy, grace, and glory, but that is only one side of the picture. The other side is suffering. Not sickness, pain, bereavement, and poverty, but rather *thlipsis*, which refers to the pressures and persecutions of the world, which Jesus and the apostles told us to expect.

We are to rejoice in them: partly because suffering is the necessary path to glory, partly because suffering is the means to Christian maturity (vv. 3–4), and partly because suffering is the context in which we become assured of the love of God. Twice in these verses, the apostle refers to God's love:

- "God has poured out his love into our hearts by the Holy Spirit"
- "God demonstrates his own love for us in this: While we were still sinners, Christ died for us" (v. 8).

This is a marvelous combination of history (the Cross) and experience (the Spirit), the objective and the subjective, the past and the present. First God proved his love for us by the death of his Son, and now he pours his love into us by the indwelling of his Spirit. From this perspective we can confront evil with defiance. We can even rejoice in our sufferings because we know God loves us.

5. *We shall be saved through Christ (vv. 9–10).* Verses 9 and 10 concern our future salvation. Both include the identical words "shall we be saved"— "from God's wrath" (v. 9) and "through his life" (v. 10). We may be sure of this future salvation. If we already have been justified and reconciled by God, then how much more will he complete the salvation which he has begun?

6. *We also rejoice in God through our Lord Jesus Christ (v. 11).* We not only rejoice in our sufferings and in our hope of glory, we also rejoice in God himself. It is a final, comprehensive Christian affirmation. Indeed, joy in God is a major characteristic of justified believers, that is why we should be the most positive people in the world. Whatever our circumstances, God is there in his grace and we can exult in him.

The Reign of God's Grace (5:12–21)

Paul has surveyed both the universal extent of human sin and guilt and the glorious adequacy of God's saving grace through Jesus Christ. He now gives his philosophy of history by comparing and contrasting Adam and Christ—Adam, the head of the old, fallen human race; Christ, the head of the new, redeemed human race.

The essential similarity between them lies in the contrast between the one and the many: Each was a single human being, yet what each one did affected many people.

But the dissimilarity between them is even more pronounced. "The gift is not like the trespass" (v. 15). Five times the contrast is drawn, although each time in different words and with a different emphasis. For example, the trespass resulted in death, the gift in life (v. 15); God's judgment brought condemnation, God's gift brings justification (v. 16); Adam's disobedience made many sinners, Christ's obedience will make many righteous (v. 19).

Even more striking is Paul's use of "kingdom language." He repeats the verb to "reign" or "rule" five times.

Before Christ, the throne was occupied by sin and death, and the world was strewn with corpses. Since Christ, the throne has been occupied by grace, and by those who have received God's grace—their reign being marked by life through Jesus Christ, for they have both received life themselves and are seeking to bring life to others.

Verse 21 sums up the argument. Just as during the centuries before Christ, sin reigned in death, so now grace reigns, bringing eternal life through Jesus Christ to all who repent and believe.

Is this our vision? In our view of reality, who or what is occupying the throne today? Are we still living in the Old Testament with the whole scene dominated by Adam, or is our vision filled with Christ? Do we think of guilt still reigning, or of grace—of death, or of life?

Our Christian conviction is that grace reigns—the grace which took Christ to the cross, the grace which has justified us freely through the redemption that is in Christ Jesus, the grace which sends us out in mission.

The Christian and Sin

Ajith Fernando

At the end of Romans 5, Paul completed his explanation of the heart of the gospel—justification by faith. But the Christian life does not climax with a mere change of legal status in our relationship with God. Justification is the beginning of a great pilgrimage. Chapter 6 begins the next section of Romans—the exposition of the way of holiness.

In typical Pauline style, the section on justification is made to flow logically into the section on sanctification. There is an inseparable connection between justification and sanctification. Paul begins by addressing those who object because they think there is no such connection in the gospel he proclaims.

Christians Cannot Go on Sinning (6:1–2)

Verse 1 presents the objection: "What shall we say, then? Shall we go on sinning so that grace may increase?" This is still one of the most important questions addressed in evangelism. The fact that we receive salvation from Christ because of what he has done and not because of any merits of our own is a revolutionary idea to most people.

When people hear this for the first time, their initial reaction is often a negative one. They think it is impossible for one to die for another; and if salvation is obtained in this way, then it is cheap and results in irresponsible behavior. They believe people will take morality lightly because they know that God's grace will forgive them anyhow.

Non-Christians often ask the same type of question that Paul is responding to. It is asked by secular people from Western backgrounds as well as by those following other religions. This, incidentally, was one of Mahatma Gandhi's strongest objections to the Christian doctrine of atonement.

We must preach Christ crucified. That is the heart of the Christian gospel. But we must be aware of the fact that most non-Christians may misunderstand it at first.

As the preachers of Acts did, we must reason with the non-Christians. We must seek to persuade them that the work of Christ can indeed save them, that grace is not cheap, and that it is the only legitimate way to salvation. This should be a key element of our preaching of the Cross to non-Christians.

Paul's first response to this question is his famous emphatic negation, "By no means!" (6:2). The Greek expression *me genoito* is the most emphatic means Paul uses to repudiate an idea.

Ajith R. Fernando is the National Director of Youth for Christ in Sri Lanka and a citizen of that country.

This is an age when the church seems to be focusing little on the seriousness of sin in the believer. When it is discussed, it is often excused as inevitable, given the weaknesses of Christians.

It is important to note how strongly Paul reacts to the idea that sin in the believer can be excused. This certainly will be necessary if we hope to make any impact on the non-Christian religions. They are now seeking to send missionaries to so-called Christian lands because the Christians are so lacking in moral self-control.

Union With Christ's Death and Resurrection (6:2–10)

Paul goes on to explain why it is unthinkable that Christians can go on sinning. "We died to sin; how can we live in it any longer?" (6:2). "We died" is in the aorist tense. It points to a definite act that took place in the past. This act was our conversion. When we first came to Christ for salvation, we made a decisive break with sin. We said sin would no longer be acceptable to us. We turned from our past ways to trust in Christ alone for salvation.

Trusting in Christ for salvation means that we no longer trust in sin to give us satisfaction or to be the answer to any given situation we face. We say with Paul, "How can we live in it [sin] any longer?"

Before we accepted Christ as Savior, when someone hurt us, we saw fulfillment in anger and revenge. Or when a document was being delayed in a government office, our solution was to pay a bribe so we could get on with our work. As Christians, we do not trust in such solutions to our problems. Our trust is in the way of Christ which is opposed to such actions.

Being born again includes repentance, which is a decision on our part to be done with sin. That decision is made from within the perspective of grace. We acknowledge that we cannot overcome sin of our own strength; we trust in Christ to give us the strength to do it. We say we are done with sin. A gospel without repentance is no gospel. It is like giving a sick person food to eat without treating the stomach infection that has caused the illness.

Paul emphasizes his point by reminding his readers about what happened at their baptism. He asks, "Or don't you know that all of us who were baptized into Christ Jesus were baptized into his death?" (6:3). Note that he makes his point in the form of a question. This is something they are supposed to know. The baptism was a sign of something that had happened in their lives.

Leon Morris reminds us that today the word *baptism* brings to mind a comforting ritual, to the first-century Christians there was an element of violence associated with this word. It was used of a deluge—a flood. Josephus used it when he talked about how the crowds flooded into Jerusalem and "wrecked the city." Christ used it to describe his death. Baptism meant death, a violent spiritual revolution that resulted in death to a whole way of life.

Verse 4 says, "We were therefore buried with him through baptism into death in order that, just as Christ was raised from the dead through the glory of the Father, we too may live a new life."

After death, we are raised into a new life. Paul is speaking from the perspective of one of his favorite themes—the believer's solidarity with Christ. What happened to Christ happens to the believer also. Just as he died, was buried, and was raised; we also die, are buried, and will be raised to live a new life.

Paul describes the solidarity with Christ in terms of union with Christ: "If we have been united with him like this in his death, we will certainly also be united with him in his resurrection" (6:5). To Paul, the figure of union with Christ is a key to understanding the nature of the Christian life. We enter the kingdom through faith, but faith is not merely an act of giving mental assent to some facts about Christ and his work; it is that and more. Salvation is not only a legal transaction resulting in a change of status; it is that and more.

The act of faith is an entrusting of ourselves to Christ. Salvation is entering into a union with Christ. And because Christ was raised, when we are united with Christ, we also enter into an experience of his resurrection. If this is so, we must live as resurrected people would live.

This process is described again in verse 6: "For we know that our old self was crucified with him." Paul said previously that we have died to sin. Now he says it again, it is our "old self" which has died; that is, our fallen human nature.

The word translated "old" often has the connotation of being antiquated and worn-out. When we come to Christ, we don't give up some valuable treasure so we are to be pitied because of the great sacrifice we have made. Everything we give up is like dung, as Paul said in Philippians 3:8 (KJV).

When someone told David Livingstone that he must have sacrificed much for the sake of the gospel, we are told that Livingstone got angry. "Sacrifice," he said, "the only sacrifice is to live outside the will of God!"

God is the creator of life. To come to him is to come to the source of life. We die to things that could never truly satisfy us. They will only destroy us in the end. But Satan, who blinds the eyes of unbelievers so that they do not see the truth, will try to deceive people into thinking that the cost of discipleship is too much to pay.

There is a price to pay, and it is a high price because we are so accustomed to the life of sin. Yet, what we give up is useless, and what we gain is a treasure of immeasurable worth.

Paul says, "Our old self was crucified with him." Paul is using the language of identification with Christ. The phrase *crucified with* is a single word in the Greek. This is the same word which appears in Galatians 2:20. It can be translated "co-crucified."

He is with us in the process of crucifying the flesh. He has gone before us and suffered a more serious crucifixion than we have. When we crucify our old self, he is beside us. That gives us courage.

Yet we must bear in mind as C. E. B. Cranfield said, "The reference to crucifixion is a stark reminder—the harsh word *cross* had not yet been rendered mellow by centuries of Christian piety." Just as *baptism* is a violent word, so is *crucifixion*. However painful it is to extricate ourselves from the sin which clings to us so closely, we *must* do it when we come to Christ.

This is the paradox of conversion. It is hard, and it is easy. It is hard because we say we are done with sin, which has been our close companion. It is done away with decisively, violently. But it is easy because Christ has gone before us and done all that is necessary for our salvation. All God needs is our willingness to accept Christ as Lord and Savior, which includes saying no to sin. That is what faith is.

Salvation, and its accompanying sanctification, is no great achievement on our part. It is a great achievement on Christ's part. No one is too weak to come to him. Anyone may come and be saved and sanctified.

Paul goes on to explain that freedom from sin takes place by the person dying to sin (6:6–7). But the process does not end with death to sin. Verse 8 says, "Now if we died with Christ, we believe that we will also live with him." One of the great implications of the fact that we have been raised with Christ is that we live with him. Now life means living with Christ.

In verse 4, Paul said that we are resurrected with Christ so that "we . . . might walk in newness of life" (RSV). The key feature of walking in newness of life is living with him. All responsible people and all religions agree there is an element in us which has to be put to death. The uniqueness of Christianity is that it presents a new life lived with a living Savior.

When a Muslim who came to Christ was asked why he became a Christian, he said:

It is like this; say you are walking along a road and you suddenly come to a fork, and you don't know which way to turn. At that fork there are two men—one dead and one alive. Which one do you think I would ask for directions as to where to go?

Christianity is a life lived with a living Savior. If we were asked to summarize the Christian life, we would not say it is the following of a set of principles. We would not say it is crucifying the old life. We would not say it is living a righteous life. It is all of this. But these do not come to the heart of describing the Christian experience. For that we need to say with Paul, "To me, to live is Christ" (Philippians 1:21). "Christianity is Christ," as the old saying goes.

Verses 9 and 10 show the logical impossibility of a Christian living in sin. "For we know that since Christ was raised from the dead, he cannot die again; death no longer has mastery over him. The death he died, he died to sin once for all; but the life he lives, he lives to God." The great theme of this section is that sanctification is not an option for a Christian. It is a normal experience. One of our problems has been that we have tried to separate the various stages of salvation in a way that Paul never did.

Perhaps the linear logical thinking which has provided a framework for theology for centuries has had an influence in the separation that is common when we think about salvation. Therefore, we have justification as a distinct experience, followed by sanctification, and culminating in glorification.

This made it possible for us to think of one stage independently of the other. Some who think this way are not scandalized as Paul would be if a person continues in sin after receiving salvation. They would say, "Well, at least this person has entered the eternal kingdom. And that's what is most important." Paul would react to such thinking with his outraged, "By no means!" We need the integrated view of salvation that is found in the Bible.

We cannot excuse sin in the life of the Christian. Christians may sin, but sin is never to be excused. Sin in a Christian is always a denial to the world of the reality of the atonement of Christ.

I think the bumper sticker that says, "Christians are not perfect, just forgiven" is repulsive. It tries to excuse sin in the believer, and does so before a watching world. This is a blatant affront to the honor of Christ who commanded us to be without sin. It is a symptom of the fact that the church has begun to pander so much to the self that no all-out war is being waged on sin and selfishness.

I don't think Jesus meant an absolute perfection when he asked us to be perfect. But he certainly meant that a Christian has the power to be totally given to God, to love the Lord with all his heart and soul and strength. Paul told the governor Felix, "I strive always to keep my conscience clear before God and man" (Acts 24:16). May we also strive to do the same.

What We Must Do (6:11–14)
Yet, because we die to sin at our conversion, it does not mean that we are immune to sin. Vestiges of the old nature still remain, so there is an active part that we play in sanctification.

The Way of Faith (6:11)
"In the same way, count yourselves dead to sin but alive to God in Christ Jesus" (6:11). What does this mean? Does it mean that we are to try to convince ourselves of something that is not real? That would be a case of self-deception—like telling a person who is dying, "You're going to be fine."

In chapter 4, the same word *count* or *reckon* was used of the way God regards us after we exercise saving faith. It was used to say that if God regards us as righteous, then we are indeed righteous. In the same way, we are asked to do this type of reckoning regarding our relationship with sin. God accepted our action of dying to sin when we were converted as being valid. If so, we too must accept it as valid. C. E. B. Cranfield translates this verse as, "Recognize the truth that you yourselves are dead to sin. . . ." We are simply accepting a fact about ourselves.

How can we accept such a fact? By faith. By faith we accept the fact that we have died to sin and have been made alive to God. If God regards us thus, then we should too. We believe that what God said he will do in us, he has indeed done. Faith is an important key both to justification and to sanctification.

The Way of Resistance (6:12)
Verse 12 gives the next requirement for being holy. Paul says, "Therefore do not let sin reign in your mortal body so that you obey its evil desires." We don't simply rest passively on the fact that we have died to sin. We get actively involved in this process by not letting sin reign in our mortal body.

Note that Paul begins this verse with *therefore*. The act of resisting sin arises directly out of our reckoning ourselves dead to sin and alive to God. Because we know that we are dead to sin, we have the confidence that the sin can be overcome, and so we act to overcome it.

Satan will try to make us think that we cannot overcome sin. Our sin nature, which has not been totally eradicated, will try to convince us that we are incurably sinful. If we believe these lies of Satan and of our sin nature, we will yield to the temptation. But they *are* lies.

The truth is that we are dead to sin. It is not necessary for us to commit any sin. Christ has won the victory over sin and made us participants in that victory. If we believe this, that is, if we reckon ourselves dead to sin and alive to God, we will have the confidence to resist our sinful nature and to resist the devil. And as James 4:7 says, when we resist the devil, he will flee from us.

Faith helps us overcome sin. It tells us that we are victors and gives us the courage to battle temptation without passively yielding to it. This is not a case of self-deception. It is a case of facing up to the truth of who we are, and through that, having the confidence to battle sin. It is believing that what God promised to do in us, he has indeed done.

Paul says, "Do not let sin reign in your mortal body." Siegfried Wibbing has said, "In Paul, [the word translated "body"] *soma* has a specialized meaning in the sense of person." *Bodies* here could be translated as "selves."

Paul describes these bodies as "mortal." The wages of sin have touched our whole being, so we cannot be overconfident. We must be aware that none of us are immune to sin. This is why, just before 1 Corinthians 10:13 which talks about there being no temptation that we cannot overcome, Paul says, "If you think you are standing firm, be careful that you don't fall!" (1 Corinthians 10:12).

Victory is available to all, but we must never forget that we are mortal and, therefore, not immune to sin.

The Way of Dedication (6:13–14)

In verse 13, Paul presents the way of dedication. He first says, "Do not offer the parts of your body to sin, as instruments of wickedness." The word translated "offer" is sometimes used of sacrifices. It has the idea of presenting something. Sin is personified and portrayed as the recipient of the part of the body that yields to temptation. Paul urges us not to let this happen.

Living in a land torn by racial strife, I have come to believe that racism is one of the last things that the process of sanctification touches in the life of a Christian. We often encounter people who are speaking in ways that do not promote harmony. People of both races can find much to say against the other race. When there is a racist conversation going on, Christians are often tempted to join in and add to the ill will generated through such conversations. After all, they also have feelings towards their race. But if a Christian joins in, he is offering his mouth to sin as an instrument of wickedness. Though he may wish to add some points which would increase the ill will, he must say no to the temptation. Paul is talking about an act of total commitment. He goes back to the parts again and says, "Offer the parts of your body to him as instruments of righteousness" (6:13).

There is an interesting change of tense here. When Paul said, "Do not offer the parts of your body to sin," he used the present tense. This is why some translations render this as, "Do not go on presenting the members of your body" (NASB). Paul is talking about the habit of sinning.

In the rest of the verse, he gives the solution to the problem of habitual sin in the believer. He uses the same word *offer*, but he shifts from the present tense to the aorist tense. The aorist tense is usually used to describe a definite act that took place in the past.

The shift is significant. He is not talking of a habitual offering, but of a definite act of commitment. Leon Morris shows the differences in the tenses with this rendering: "Do not keep on presenting your members to sin . . . but once and for all present yourselves to God."

Paul is speaking of that conscious act of total commitment when we say, "God will have all of me." He seems to be referring to an act that usually takes place after conversion.

This act of commitment often takes the form of a crisis. It could be after God has spoken to the Christian through a sermon, or it could be alone at home, or with a friend after God has spoken to the person quite clearly.

We may not even remember exactly when we made this commitment, but we know that at some crucial time in our spiritual pilgrimage we came to the point when we said to God, "I give you my all." We became totally dedicated to him. George Mueller expresses this crisis in a famous statement:

> There was a day when I died: Died to George Mueller; to his tastes, his opinions, his preferences and his will. Died to the world—its approval or censure—died to the approval or blame even of my brethren and friends. Since then I have studied only to show myself approved unto God.

Sometimes in a person's spiritual pilgrimage there may be more than one such crisis experience, when the Spirit of God convicts the person of the lack of total commitment and leads them to a fresh act of rededication. Many of us can testify to many such crises when we gave ourselves totally to God.

Both the crisis act of total commitment and the daily acts of dedication are important for the Christian. Our act of total commitment is put to the test in the daily challenges we face after making it.

It has been said that a crisis that is not followed by a process becomes an abscess. At each step, our total commitment is confirmed as we act in accord with that commitment in our day-to-day activities. We are all called upon daily to reaffirm the commitment of our whole lives to God which we made at some time in our spiritual pilgrimage.

Paul goes on to say, "For sin shall not be your master" (6:14). When we give our whole selves to God, sin is no longer going to be lord of our lives. A new Lord has taken over.

And why is this? "Because you are not under law, but under grace" (6:14). Paul is talking about our state in Christ—the positional blessings that are ours by virtue of our salvation. The knowledge of our position in Christ gives us the courage to be obedient to God.

Note that Paul is responding to the accusation that the emphasis on grace leads to more sinfulness in practice. He is stating the exact opposite: the fact that we are under grace causes us to overcome sin. When we are under law, we are under condemnation. The guilt only serves to bring us into slavery. Because we are unable to meet the demands of the law, in frustration we may end up deeper in despair and defeat.

When we are under grace, we are not under condemnation. Instead, we are freed to live the resurrection life in union with Christ. We believe victory is possible and, therefore, we strive towards it. The result is victory over sin and its accompanying condemnation.

The Slave Market Analogy (6:15–23)

In verses 15–20, Paul goes back to his original question about whether grace causes people to sin and he answers it using the slave market analogy. Once we were slaves of sin, but now we are slaves of righteousness. Therefore, we do not continue in sin.

Note that verse 20 says, "When you were slaves to sin, you were free from the control of righteousness." Some people today might claim that freedom from the control of righteousness is a happy position to be in. But we know better, for we know what sin produces.

Paul continues, "What benefit did you reap at that time from the things you are now ashamed of? Those things result in death!" (6:21). Sinners may claim to be alive or "living it up." But this leads to death; there is nothing to envy. The people who make use of the numerous temptations in life are not to be envied.

Satan may at times cause us to regret that we cannot participate in such things because of our commitment to Christ, but these things are a diabolical trap. Satan tries to make us think that they are enjoyable, but all they do is to give some fleeting pleasure for a moment. After that, it makes the sinner a slave to the misery of sin.

But that is not all. The righteous have some positive benefits too. Paul says in verse 22, "But now that you have been set free from sin and have become slaves to God, the benefit you reap leads to holiness, and the result is eternal life."

Paul mentions two great rewards of obedience. The first is holiness. Holiness describes in one word what is meant by the image of God; that is, the image according to which man was originally created. Without it, our souls are restless. We may strive to satisfy ourselves through other means. We may neglect the pursuit of holiness in our eagerness to succeed in our careers. We may be so busy writing a book or administering the expanding ministry which we are leading that we neglect our quiet time with God. The ministry may grow, but the sense of fulfillment that we seek through the success will elude us. Fulfillment comes only when we become like what we were created to be. We were created to be like God, and becoming like God is the only achievement that truly satisfies.

Why is it so satisfying? Because we are creatures of eternity. Ecclesiastes 3:11 explains, "He [God] has also set eternity in the hearts of men." We will never be fully satisfied with the temporal. We long for the eternal.

This is the second thing we reap when we live according to God's way: eternal life. It is eternal in quality in that it fulfills the restless longing for more than the temporal that is implanted in us. And it is eternal in duration in that it goes on forever.

In verse 23 Paul summarizes this matter of rewards, "For the wages of sin is death, but the gift of God is eternal life in Christ Jesus our Lord."

An Analogy With Marriage

Paul again answers the question of whether freedom from the law increases sinfulness in Romans 7:1–6, this time using an analogy from marriage. He describes those who are under the law as bound to it like a wife is bound to her husband.

Just as death breaks the marriage bond, when the believer dies with Christ he is freed from the law to be united with Christ. Before this freedom from the law, Christians found the law stimulated the very sins it prohibited. Now we live in the freedom of the Spirit.

The Relationship Between Law and Sin (7:7–13)

From what has been said, someone could infer that Paul viewed the law as being sinful. In verse 7, Paul responds to this emphatically saying, "Certainly not!" In verses 7–13, he substantiates this. He moves to the autobiographical first-person in this section, but he does so because what he has gone through is what all people experience.

There has been a lot of discussion and disagreement in the church on the question of what events Paul is talking about. Some even say that this is not autobiographical. This is not the forum for us to go into detailed discussions about these issues, but there are some general principles we can all agree on.

First, this passage affirms that the law is not sinful (v. 7). In fact, it says that the law is "holy, . . . righteous and good" (v. 12). But when this righteous law interacts with our sinful nature, the result could be disastrous. Sin, which lies dormant in our being, can be aroused simply by hearing a prohibition which is given in the law. For example, simply hearing the command, "Do not covet" may give opportunity for sin to produce in us "every kind of covetous desire" (v. 8).

Verse 10 says, "The very commandment that was intended to bring life actually brought death." Paul goes on to say this is because "sin, seizing the opportunity afforded by the commandment, deceived me, and through the commandment put me to death. . . . Through the commandment sin might become utterly sinful" (7:11–13).

The Struggle Between Unspiritual Man and the Spiritual Law (7:14–25)

Next comes Paul's famous passage which describes his inner struggle with sin. Two themes are clearly presented. In his inner self, Paul wants to do what is right, but the sin nature residing in him drives him in a different direction. This is said many times in different ways in these verses:

- "For what I want to do I do not do, but what I hate I do" (v. 15).
- "I do what I do not want to do" (v. 16).
- "For I have the desire to do what is good, but I cannot carry it out" (v. 18).
- "For what I do is not the good I want to do; no, the evil I do not want to do— this I keep on doing" (v. 19).
- "I do what I do not want to do" (v. 20).
- "So I find this law at work: When I want to do good, evil is right there with me" (v. 21).

This inability to do what he should do is a source of deep disappointment to Paul. He says in verse 24, "What a wretched man I am! Who will rescue me from this body of death?"

No one really enjoys sin. The great American preacher, Henry Clay Morrison, said: "God never fixed me up so that I could not enjoy sin; but he fixed me up so that I couldn't sin and enjoy it." The Christian particularly finds sin unenjoyable because he has tasted of the joy of righteousness.

Paul talks about this in verse 22, when he says that the life of holiness brings deep satisfaction to him. He says, "For in my inner being I delight in God's law." This is because his true nature is holiness. As one sanctified by Christ, all "un-Christlike" activity is out of character for him.

On the other hand, in his inner being he delights in God's law (v. 22). That word *delight* is a beautiful word. It is used many times of our attitude toward the law, especially in the Psalms. The law is not something we usually associate with joy.

We delight in God's law because it helps us to fulfill our total humanity; and also because we know that it is the will of the one we love so deeply. If the things that are supposed to be gloomy about Christianity are sources of joy, then is it any wonder that C. S. Lewis and others have claimed that joy is the hallmark of the Christian life?

As long as there is a thirst for holiness, there is hope for us—for holiness is a possibility. Christ has made ample provision for it in his scheme of salvation. Paul is speaking of the battle that commonly takes place in the lives of many Christians, as the sin nature wars against the nature of Christ implanted in them. For one who carries out the battle with sin in the way described in Romans 6, there is hope of victory. So Paul can conclude this chapter by saying, "Thanks be to God—through Jesus Christ our Lord!" (v. 25).

Was Paul speaking of his present state? The context of this passage, especially chapters 6 and 8, suggests this was not his present state. But it could be the state of many Christians.

Perhaps some of us at this Congress are going through a similar experience in our lives. We wish we would have more time to spend with God, but the urgent demands of ministry have so tyrannized us that we can't find the time. We wish we could take away the lustful thoughts from our minds, but they seem to be ever present when we are alone. We wish we would not be so impatient with our spouses, but when we are home we seem to act in ways that are out of character to our real selves.

To all such strugglers there is a word of hope: What you are going through is not unique. Even the great apostle Paul went through such experiences. There is hope of recovery. Christ has made provision for such situations. As Paul experienced victory, so can we. We can live as people who have been sanctified.

We must first reckon ourselves as people who are dead to sin and alive to God in Christ Jesus. That is our true nature. Sin is the exception, and not the norm. Such faith will give us the courage and confidence to yield ourselves completely to God.

When temptation comes, this faith tells us we are victors in Christ, and so we have the courage and confidence to yield to God the part of the body facing temptation. This is not done alone through some herculean effort on our part; we are in union with Christ. He has gone before us in crucifying himself. Now we are asked to be co-crucified with him. He is with us in the struggle.

Therefore, when we think of life we don't think of it as a great struggle. Rather, we say, "For to me, to live is Christ." May God grant such an experience to each of us!

The Spirit-Filled Life

Ajith Fernando

The eighth chapter of Romans describes the Spirit-filled life. It is a gold mine of spiritual truth and could cover a whole series of expositions. Instead, we will focus on the last major section which deals with suffering.

The Spirit-filled Life (8:1–17)

The first seventeen verses of chapter 8 describes what it means to be filled with the Holy Spirit. This fullness is God's answer to the problem of how we can be holy.

In this chapter, Paul affirms life through the Spirit. We have freedom from an accusing conscience because we have been freed from the control of sin (vv. 1–2). This victory over sin was secured for us through the work of Christ (v. 3). And the righteous requirements of the law can be fully met in us (v. 4). As F. F. Bruce says, "God's commands have now become God's enablings." We can live holy lives. This means our minds are controlled by the Spirit. And the result of this is life and peace (vv. 5–6).

In this way, Paul gives affirmation after affirmation of what the Spirit does in us.

Suffering and the Spirit-filled Life (8:17–39)

The Holy Spirit witnesses to us about the great heritage we have as children of God (vv. 14–16). Paul says that as children we are heirs to a heavenly inheritance. Immediately after mentioning the heavenly reward, Paul presents the fact that suffering is a prerequisite for inheriting this reward.

"Now if we are children, then we are heirs—heirs of God and coheirs with Christ, if indeed we share in his sufferings in order that we may also share in his glory" (v. 17). For the second time, Paul brings up the topic of suffering in this book. Both times we see a familiar pattern: a long process of argumentation, climaxing with a major theological affirmation, and then the inevitable question: *Why do Christians have to suffer?*

Paul argued for the affirmation that justification is by faith in chapters 1–4. Then in chapter 5, he tackled the question of suffering. He said that suffering is God's way of helping us along the path to glorification. In chapters 6 and 7, he grappled with the question of whether people can be holy. He came to the climax of his argument in chapter 8 with another great theological affirmation: The key to holiness is the Spirit-filled life. Then he returns to the question, *Why do people who are filled with the Spirit suffer?*

The victory we have in Christ is the great message we give to the world. Confidence in that victory gives us the courage to tackle the problem of suffering. We don't glibly preach power and prosperity in Christ and ignore all the suffering in the world. In fact, we affirm that we are called to participate in this suffering—to taste some of its bitter cup.

Paul gives a fivefold answer to the question as to how suffering can coexist with the Spirit-filled life.

Sharing in Christ's Suffering (8:17)

His first answer is given almost in passing in verse 17, when he says that when we suffer "we share in his [Christ's] sufferings." Because Christ is a suffering Savior, those who follow him must also suffer. Suffering is an essential ingredient of union with Christ. Paul expressed a desire to know "the fellowship of sharing in his [Christ's] sufferings" (Philippians 3:10). There is a depth of oneness that we share with Christ which can only be achieved when we are one with him in suffering.

Paul found out about this at the start of his Christian life on the road to Damascus when Christ asked him, "Why do you persecute me?" (Acts 9:4). Paul was attacking the church, but Christ was feeling the pain. Christ and the church had become one in suffering.

The fullness of the Spirit is not simply some ecstatic experience that we have only when things are going our way. Paul affirms that we can be filled with the Spirit amidst the darkness of suffering, too. The heart of the fullness of the Spirit is having an intimate relationship with Jesus, and for that, suffering is an essential ingredient.

Acts 7:54 says that Stephen's opponents "were furious and gnashed their teeth at him." The most creative theologian in the church was about to undergo a painful martyrdom. "But Stephen, full of the Holy Spirit, looked up to heaven and saw the glory of God" (v. 55). He was full of the Spirit as he was awaiting the painful blows of the stones. Stephen had entered into the fellowship of Christ's sufferings. This fellowship reached its peak when he was going through his darkest hour. He first had a vision of Christ (vv. 55–56). Then he began to say some of the same things that Jesus said when he was on the cross. He asked God not to hold this sin against his murderers (v. 60). And he asked God to receive his spirit (v. 59). He had become like Jesus when he suffered. And to become like Jesus is what it means to be filled with the Spirit.

When we suffer for Christ, Christ suffers with us. There is a depth of unity with Christ that can come only through suffering. There have been times when Christians, in their thirst for a deep unity with Christ, desire the fellowship of sharing in Christ's sufferings. This is the desire that Paul expressed in Philippians 3:10. A vivid instance of this is from the life of Ignatius, Bishop of Antioch in Syria, who lived at the end of the second century. He asked the church not to attempt to deprive him of the honor of martyrdom. He said, "Let fire and the cross, let the companies of wild beasts, let breaking of bones and tearing of limbs, let the grinding of the whole body, and all the malice of the devil, come upon me; if only I may gain Christ Jesus."

An implication of this passage is that suffering is not optional for a few Christians. It is an essential ingredient of following Christ. If this is so, suffering must come into our basic descriptions of the Christian life. When Christ called people to follow him, he asked them to take up the cross of suffering. Therefore, this ingredient must enter into our evangelistic proclamation also. Honesty requires us to inform people about the life they are to expect when they come to Christ.

Hoping for the Redemption of Creation (8:17–25)

Paul's next point in his discussion of suffering is that our suffering is born from the perspective of looking forward to the final redemption of creation.

Paul says, "We share in his sufferings in order that we may also share in his glory"

(v. 17). Note those words, *in order that.* F. F. Bruce points out that "there is an organic relation between suffering and future glory." If we hope to share in the future glory, we must be willing to share in present suffering.

In verse 18, Paul says, "I consider that our present sufferings are not worth comparing with the glory that will be revealed in us." Note that this glory is going to "be revealed," not created. This is not just some faint hope that we have. Christ has risen from the dead. And his resurrection is the firstfruits of our resurrection (1 Corinthians 15:20). He is now enthroned above; he has already been glorified. But this glory is still to be fully revealed. The kingdom has come, now we await its consummation. We have been "marked in him with a seal, the promised Holy Spirit, who is a deposit guaranteeing our inheritance until the redemption of those who are God's possession" (Ephesians 1:13–14).

The suffering that God calls many to today may include failure in society, because they refused to compromise their principles. This is hard to take, especially as we see others doing better than us financially, socially, or in terms of ecclesiastical status.

But there is a logic behind this suffering. This does not come from a masochistic desire to experience pain. We don't suffer only because it is a fulfilling of our duty as Christians. The choice of the cup of suffering is a carefully calculated choice of a wise person. There is wisdom here, and not folly, as is often supposed. The Christian has weighed the options, and has decided that suffering for Christ is the wisest course to take. It is the best investment to make; the investment is secure and the yield is good. These are the two factors a prudent market analyst would look for when recommending an investment—security and yield.

Recently, many people in Sri Lanka lost their savings because they invested their money in unstable establishments. These investments gave a very high interest for a time but they crashed and the high yield was temporary. Not so the investment made through costly discipleship. It will produce a huge yield in heaven, and there is no uncertainty to it. It lasts forever.

Verse 19 presents the coming Judgment in a positive light. "The creation waits in eager expectation for the sons of God to be revealed." "Eager expectation" is one word in the Greek. The basic idea of the word is "stretching the neck or craning forward." It refers to an anxious longing for the end.

Note that the longing is attributed to the creation. It seems most likely that what Paul meant here is the subhuman creation, what we would call *nature.* This is another of the many passages in the Bible which shows that nature is not exempt from God's plan of redemption. God has not abandoned this world as hopelessly irredeemable. On the contrary, he has a plan for its glorification.

What creation waits for eagerly is "for the sons of God to be revealed." The chief characters in the cosmic drama are the children of God. At the moment we may be insignificant, often despised, for our commitment to God. But the God we are committed to will be the final conqueror of the universe. At his conquest our status will be revealed.

It is significant that Paul uses the word *revealed.* It suggests what we know in our hearts to be true is going to be made public. We are princes and princesses in the kingdom of God and we will reign with him when he comes in glory.

This is a particularly significant feature for those who come from countries where Christianity is a minority religion. Our distinguished service for the kingdom wins no praise from the powers that rule. They may regard our work as being destructive to the national life of the people. We do not need public-relations agents to publicize what we are doing. Publicity may be harmful for us. At times it is better that this work be done quietly without attracting much attention. But one day this work is going to be revealed. Then recognition will be given—not the passing earthly accolades that sometimes don't even survive our lifetime, but a crown of glory that lasts forever. A great reward will be given in the final day to those who persevere.

Verse 20 describes what happened to creation: "For the creation was subjected to frustration, not by its own choice, but by the will of the one who subjected it, in hope . . ." In Genesis 3, we are told that even the ground was cursed because of the Fall. The whole of nature lost its equilibrium. There is still beauty there, but there are also destructive storms, terrible droughts, and a host of other natural disorders. Therefore, at the present time, as Ecclesiastes 1:2 and 12:8 says, everything under the sun is utterly meaningless. The Greek word translated as "frustration," is what is used often in Ecclesiastes in the Septuagint (Greek translation). It appears thirty-seven times in Ecclesiastes and is translated as "meaningless" in the NIV and "vanity" in the AV.

"The creation was subjected to frustration." "Was subjected" is in the aorist tense, suggesting that it was a distinct event. If so, this must refer to the Fall. Paul says the subjection was done "not by its own choice, but by the will of the one who subjected it." This refers to the curse when God decreed the world would suffer the effects of the Fall. But this decree was made "in hope" (v. 20). As Leon Morris puts it: "The cosmic fall is not the last word; the last word is with hope." The Creator is going to redeem his creation.

Verse 21 states what this hope is: "The creation itself will be liberated from its bondage to decay and brought into the glorious freedom of the children of God." Revelation 22:3 looks to the day when "no longer will there be any curse." This verse reflects the same hope, but verse 21 describes it as liberation from "bondage to decay." Death and decay are found all around us as one of the realities of the present age.

According to this verse, when the creation is changed to its glorious state, it is not going to be annihilated. Paul says "the creation itself will be liberated." It is going to be transformed rather than annihilated. In this transformation it will receive a glory that corresponds to the glory that we are going to receive.

Our eternal home will contain the good things about the present creation in a perfected state but without its decay. It is not going to be a strange place with an "otherworldliness" that some find unattractive to consider. It will be a place of beauty, of the type of beauty we have come to appreciate. But this beauty will be perfect. Because of our mortality, all pleasure on earth is temporary and incomplete. Not so heaven! Indeed, this is why there is such an eager longing in us as we look forward to it.

This longing is described as a groaning in verse 22: "We know that the whole creation has been groaning as in the pains of childbirth right up to the present time." Two vivid words are used here. The first *sustenazo* is translated "groaning" and has the idea of lamenting. The second word *sunodino* is used for the pains of childbirth. This brings in the idea of anticipation into the travail. This groaning and travailing is going on even now. Paul says it is taking place "right up to the present time." It is a day-to-day experience in this present age.

There is lament, but it is a lament of one who knows the pain is going to end. It is lament tinged with hope. It is like the lament of a person whose beloved has left the country for an extended period of time. The separation is hard to bear, but one day there is going to be a glorious reunion.

This groaning is experienced not only by the sub-human creation, it is a factor in the experience of the average Christian, too. "Not only so, but we ourselves, who have the firstfruits of the Spirit, groan inwardly as we wait eagerly for our adoption as sons, the redemption of our bodies" (v. 23). His language here is significant. We are people who "have the firstfruits of the Spirit." That is, we have tasted of the Spirit's fullness. What we have experienced is a foretaste of glory divine. It tells us of the glory of sonship—of having an intimate relationship with God.

What we have experienced of this relationship gives us a longing for the fullness. So, says Paul, "We groan inwardly as we wait eagerly for our adoption as sons."

On that day we will also experience "the redemption of our bodies." Today, our bodies give evidence of mortality. They are susceptible to illness and aging. Our resurrection bodies will not have these limitations of mortality.

There is a dual theological emphasis in this passage. On the one hand, there is a healthy view of creation that sees it as something that is going to be redeemed and not annihilated. This world is made of "stuff" that is not intrinsically bad. This gives us the courage to persevere in costly service on earth. We do not view the world as a place abandoned by God. Rather, it is the arena of God's activity now. Thus, it should be the arena of our service now.

Yet at the same time, the Christian is realistic about the limits of what can be achieved on earth. The world is suffering from the consequences of the Fall. We cannot expect a utopia here. This world is groaning, waiting for its redemption. We will serve faithfully and sacrificially, but we will not expect our final rewards and comforts here. On earth we are groaning, waiting eagerly for the return of our Lord. The idea of waiting eagerly for the consummation is a common theme in the New Testament. Our greatest ambitions in life are related to the next life. Here we labor and toil to bring eternal blessing to as many as we can. There we will rest from our labors.

Is this groaning reflected in our preaching today? Is the healthy disdain for earthly reward that Paul constantly reflects in his writings reflected in our thinking and our ministries? When Paul returned to the new churches he had helped to found, his message was: "We must go through many hardships to enter the kingdom of God" (Acts 14:22).

Preachers today may hesitate to preach on such themes because members of their congregations may feel uncomfortable with the message. This worldly preaching is attracting large crowds today. If we promise people groaning and travailing in this life they may go to another church. This would be considered a failure for the preacher who will go down the ecclesiastical "status ladder" as a result. That is a cost that some find too big to pay.

If contemporary Christians say they are groaning, waiting for the return of Christ, we would probably pronounce them as unsuitable for ministry because they have too negative an attitude to life. Jeremiah would fail most of our tests for ministry. But the fact is that our roots are in the next world. And this is what makes it possible for us to be willing to suffer loss in this world for the sake of our ministry.

It is people with this perspective who will be able to persevere in difficult settings. They won't give up and go elsewhere because their gifts are not being fully used. The topic of fulfillment is one of the latest fads in ministerial education. We are encouraged to go to places of ministry where we can be fulfilled. And fulfillment is understood as the use of our gifts to the fullest. There is some truth here. But with too much of this kind of emphasis we will have a generation of disillusioned Christian workers. They will expect the wrong rewards from ministry, rewards developed using this-worldly criteria.

Consider the example of the call to go to the unreached or to difficult places of ministry. One will not see much "earthly" fulfillment and success in that type of work, especially during the first few years. You may be a great preacher, but if you go to the unreached, at the start you would have a congregation of one person—yourself! Is that a price worth paying? History tells us that it was indeed worth it. Some of the men and women the world considered most brilliant and talented went to the unreached and worked amidst hardship and frustration. They saw little fruit during their lifetimes, but today there are churches all over the world as evidence of the fruit of their labors.

This does not imply that those who go to difficult areas are not fulfilled. There is a deep fulfillment that comes from doing the will of God. It is only when we do the will of God that we are fully human. And to be fully human is to be complete, to be fulfilled. There is the great peace and joy of moving along the stream of God's sovereignty, the stream which will culminate in the consummation of the eternal kingdom.

Many contemporary strategies to determine the will of God ignore the call to suffer. They have forgotten that our rewards are in heaven. Often people make a decision aimed at going up in this life. But in reality, that decision takes them down. They have gotten disoriented, their thinking is so far removed from God's ways of thinking that they don't realize they are going down. Often people who are doing God's will are disillusioned because they seem to be lacking in earthly success. They need to be reminded that the final reckoning about the significance of their work will be revealed not in this life but in the next.

We must not be surprised when we encounter suffering, for we are people who groan in this life. We have a whole eternity to enjoy rest from and rewards for our labors.

One of the key concepts in the heavenly perspective is that of hope. "For in this hope we were saved" (v. 24). This hope had a big part to play in our salvation. "We were saved" is in the aorist tense, indicating that it is an act that took place in the past. When we were saved we experienced some great blessings. But we knew these were only a foretaste of the heavenly blessing. Hope is one of the things that attracts us to Christianity.

There is an eschatological element to the basic evangelistic message. We invite people to come to Jesus and receive many blessings such as freedom from guilt, fulfillment in life, the presence of God with us, and the power of the Holy Spirit at work in us. But we also point them to eschatological blessings whose attractiveness far outweighs the attractiveness of the present blessings. We tell people that if they come to Christ, then they will avert the eternal punishment of hell and will inherit the eternal reward of heaven.

I have just completed writing a book on the doctrine of hell. A number of those whom I talked to about this book told me that the thing which ultimately resulted in their conversion was the prospect of going either to heaven or to hell. That is just one evidence that the hope of reward in the afterlife is still an important and relevant aspect of the Christian gospel. In verse 24, Paul says the prospect of avoiding hell and inheriting heaven was a significant feature of the gospel which the Roman Christians accepted.

Heaven and hell seem to have disappeared from modern preaching. That makes the evangelistic message incomplete. Missing a key aspect of the gospel impoverishes the church. This "worldly" preaching has produced a plague of selfishness and worldliness in today's church.

In the second part of verse 24, Paul states that Christian hope has to do with the future: "But hope that is seen is not hope at all. Who hopes for what he already has?" Hope in the Christian gospel indicates that we have not yet experienced the full blessings of salvation.

Verse 25 gives an implication of living in hope: "But if we hope for what we do not yet have, we wait for it patiently." We wait for what we hope patiently. The Greek word translated "patiently" is *hupomone*. It does not mean what usually comes to our mind when we think of patience. What usually comes to our mind is of people stoically enduring hardship with a passive acceptance of circumstances. Christian patience is positive endurance, rather than a quiet acceptance. Leon Morris says, "It is the attitude of the soldier who in the thick of the battle is not dismayed but fights on stoutly whatever the difficulties."

Recently, the Christian hope of heaven fell into disrepute because of what we may call the "pie-in-the-sky-in-the-world-by-and-by" religion. It was like an opiate which lulled people to acquiescence amidst hardship, to a fatalistic acceptance of injustice. They did not fight for legitimate rights because they were assured of a home in heaven for which they waited in eager anticipation. This is not Christian hope. Christian hope is the hope of a soldier enduring in the heat of battle.

We need to redeem the concept of future reward and give it its biblical thrust. Christian hope motivates us to service on earth. It gives us a sense of mission and of militancy. It convinces us that the price of trying to apply kingdom principles in this fallen world is worth paying. And so it helps us persevere in service amidst hardship.

Verses 17–25 gives an "eschatological perspective" on suffering. It reminds us that our sufferings are temporary. We now live in hope, persevering in obedience and spurred on by the prospect of a day of final redemption of ourselves and of the whole creation.

The Spirit Helps Us in Our Weakness (8:26–27)

But hope is not all we have to cheer us amidst hardship. Paul says that the Spirit is there to help us as we face the limitations of our weaknesses (vv. 26–27). This is Paul's second point in his answer to the paradox of suffering and the Spirit-filled life.

God Will Fulfill His Purpose for Us (8:28–30)

The fourth point in Paul's exposition on suffering and the Spirit-filled life is presented in verses 28–30. There may be problems, but through it all God is at work and will achieve good even through the problems.

Paul defines that good in verses 29 and 30. The final goal is glorification. When we are glorified, one of the most important things about us is that we will be like Jesus. As Paul puts it, we were "predestined to be conformed to the likeness of his Son." But this is not going to be a new nature that is suddenly invested on us. Daily, God is making us more and more Christlike. That is the goodness which God strives to achieve through all things. Even suffering is a means of doing that in us. Because God has implanted in us a thirst for holiness, the knowledge that the suffering is going to be a means of God achieving this ambition of ours help make the suffering bearable.

But there is an even more pleasant consideration for us to think about regarding our sufferings. Paul's fifth point on suffering and the Spirit-filled life is that amidst the suffering, God is for us.

God Is for Us (8:31–38)

Five great affirmations that are all related to the fact that God is for us are contained in verses 31–38. First, if God is for us, no one can be against us; that implies that no one can defeat us. Second, in view of the fact that God expressed his commitment to us in sacrificing his own Son, we can rest assured that he will give us all the things that we need. Third, the accusations that people may bring against us are of no consequence because we have been justified by virtue of the sufficient work of Christ, and we have this same Christ as our advocate in the only court that really matters—the heavenly court.

Fourth, nothing can separate us from the love of Christ. And fifth, in all these things we are more that conquerors through him who loved us.

Paul does not end this section with his fifth point. He goes back to his fourth point that nothing can separate us from the love of Christ, and he repeats it with even greater emphasis than before. He wants to end the section with this favorite theme of his, which is a key to the Christian's response to suffering: the love of God.

> For I am convinced that neither death nor life, neither angels nor demons, neither the present nor the future, nor any powers, neither height nor depth, nor anything else in all creation, will be able to separate us from the love of God that is in Christ Jesus our Lord" (vv. 38–39).

Suffering is not a pleasant word—but love is. If there is love in our hearts we can experience beauty amidst the ugliness of suffering. The beauty of the Spirit-filled life is that there is such love which helps us face suffering. In Romans 5:5 (TEB), Paul said that "God's love has flooded our inmost heart." When love floods our inmost heart, it washes away the bitterness that may have come into our lives because of suffering.

To be filled with the Spirit is to have a love relationship with God. Nothing brings true radiance to a person's life as much as love does. And we are people who have been loved. People may have been wicked to us, but God's love is greater than man's wickedness. The pain of that wickedness may remain, but love takes away the bitterness of it. Amidst the pain, we are radiant.

In the early centuries when Christians were severely persecuted, a martyr was smiling as he was being burned at the stake. His persecutor was annoyed by his smile and asked him what there was to be smiling about. He replied, "I saw the glory of God and was glad." The pain of the flames, the anger of the opponents of the gospel, had not separated him from the love of Christ.

Paul begins and ends this discussion of suffering by talking about the primacy of our relationship with Christ. In verse 17, he said we share in Christ's suffering, which is an affirmation of the fellowship of suffering. He ends by saying that nothing can separate us from our love relationship with Christ. This implies that when trials come our way, we should make it our first priority to cultivate our love relationship with God. We must look for a solution for the problem, but that is not what's most important. Our priority is to maintain our love relationship with God.

Psalm 42 begins with the words, "As the deer pants for streams of water, so my soul pants for you, O God." This is the heart cry of a person who is suffering. He has lost the sense of God's presence and now he prays to God to give him the joy that he once knew. It is a Psalm that shows the struggle of a sufferer who feels that God is far away. But it also shows the determination of the psalmist to get back to a warm relationship of love with God. In the same way, we, too, must seek first to deepen our relationship with God when we encounter difficulties.

Someone once asked Charles Spurgeon, "What persuasion are you of?" I suppose they expected a philosophical or intellectual answer. Today this would mean something like, "Are you a Calvinist or an Arminian—charismatic or a non-charismatic?" Spurgeon's response was: "I am persuaded that neither death, nor life, nor angels, nor principalities, nor powers, nor things present, nor things to come, nor height, nor depth, nor any creature, shall be able to separate us from the love of God, which is in Christ Jesus our Lord." That was the most important thing about Spurgeon. He was a person who was loved by God. And that is the most important thing about us too!

We may be called to suffer, but we are loved. And because we are loved, we are radiant.

How Can They Hear?

David Penman

How, and Through Whom, Will They Hear the Message? (Romans 10:14–17)

For eight full mind-stretching chapters, the apostle Paul outlined the plan God had established for the redemption and salvation of humanity. He repeatedly makes it clear: Those who put their faith in Jesus the Messiah will be justified before God and given the power of the Holy Spirit to enable them to live a good and holy life. His language is complex, and the ideas are difficult, but there is no doubting their intention. Those who are in Christ, who accept and follow him, are the true people of God. Those who don't, whether Jew or Gentile, are *not* the people of God. This is painful, but the message and emphasis of Scripture is unequivocal on this point.

This great theological argument comes to a triumphant conclusion in Romans 8:35–39:

> Who shall separate us from the love of Christ? Shall trouble or hardship or persecution or famine or nakedness or danger or sword? As it is written: "For your sake we face death all day long; we are considered as sheep to be slaughtered." No, in all these things we are more than conquerors through him who loved us. For I am convinced that neither death nor life, neither angels nor demons, neither the present nor the future, nor any powers, neither height nor depth, nor anything else in all creation, will be able to separate us from the love of God that is in Christ Jesus our Lord.

Following the dramatic and exultant expressions of his own previous words, it is almost as if Paul is suddenly reminded of what he has been repeating for eight chapters about the glory, the wonder, the indescribable joy of recognition, and the potential adoption of all humankind into God's special precious family. Suddenly, he comes back to earth!

Alexander Whyte once wrote in response to this passage: "What will it be to *be* there?" Then suddenly and solemnly, he added, "And what will it be *not* to be there?"

"What if you are not there?" or, in the context of the passage, "What of the Jews?" Paul had already begun to face the implications of this question earlier, especially in chapters 3 and 4, but now he must do so again and at length, so there is no misunderstanding.

---

*The late **David Penman**, Archbishop of Melbourne for the Anglican Church of Australia, died October 1, 1989. See page 15 for a fuller biographical statement.*

A shadow continues to emerge in this letter to the Romans. What about the Jews, to whom the indescribable gift was first offered? What of God's purpose and plan for them? In the light of all that has been said and written, where do they now fit into the kingdom? As one writer has said:

> They were Paul's own people, his own flesh and blood. More than that, they were God's own people. Everything that could have been done to prepare them for their supreme privilege, he had done for them. Out of Egypt, God had called his own (Hosea 11:1); his glory had gone before them in the pillars of cloud and fire (Exodus 13:21); he had made his covenants with them, and given them the Law, the temple worship, and the prophetic promises. He had raised up Christ himself as one of themselves (Romans 9:4–5); yet they had rejected him. He came to his own, and his own did not receive him (John 1:12). No wonder Paul was wracked with grief and ceaseless pain (9:2), willing to suffer a curse if his brethren might be saved (9:3). And if it was bad for Paul, what must it have been like for God, as the Gentile world accepted the gospel, and the Jews turned it down?

The story is now well known. In this Congress few, if any, would doubt or reject the clear teaching of the apostle of God, that the true children of God are those according to the Spirit and not the flesh (2:28–29). Abraham is our father, because we are children of that righteousness which comes through faith (4:13).

We, my dear friends, are the Israel of God. We are the fulfillment of the promises of God. We are those who, by faith, can move mountains! We stand justified, not by works, not by evangelical faith, not even by the Lausanne Covenant, but by the grace and mercy of our God—freely, generously, and lavishly poured upon us so we might be among the adopted children of God.

What then of the Jews? The text is stark in its clarity:

> It is not the natural children who are God's children, but it is the children of the promise who are regarded as Abraham's offspring (9:8). It does not, therefore, depend on man's desire or effort, but on God's mercy (v. 16). As he says in Hosea: "I will call them 'my people' who are not my people; and I will call her 'my beloved one' who is not my loved one" (v. 25). What then shall we say? That the Gentiles, who did not pursue righteousness, have obtained it, a righteousness that is by faith (v. 30).

It is abundantly clear that those who are in Christ are the Israel of God, whether they are of Jewish descent or not. Those who by faith have accepted the Messiah are members of the messianic community. They are the people of Jesus, the Israel of God, the true descendants of Abraham. We need to do everything in our power to lovingly and sensitively share this Jesus with all those who do not know him, whether Jew or Gentile.

These words imply a warning. It is the same warning given to his people long ago:

> You only have I chosen of all the families of the earth; therefore I will punish you for all your sins (Amos 3:2).

As the inheritors of the promises, as the recipients of the privileges, as those upon whom his abundant mercy has been lavished—great will be our judgment if we continue in our sin, fail to obey his commands, and ignore the injustices borne by the peoples of the world for whom Jesus died.

In this context, consider Romans 10:9–13:

If you confess with your mouth, "Jesus is Lord," and believe in your heart that God raised him from the dead, you will be saved. For it is with your heart that you believe and are justified, and it is with your mouth that you confess and are saved. As the Scripture says, "Anyone who trusts in him will never be put to shame." For there is no difference between Jew and Gentile—the same Lord is Lord of all and richly blesses all who call on him, for, "Everyone who calls on the name of the Lord will be saved."

I want to focus on three emphases in the questions asked in the verses which follow:

How then, can they call on the one they have not believed in? And how can they believe in the one of whom they have not heard? And how can they hear without someone preaching to them? And how can they preach unless they are sent? As it is written, "How beautiful are the feet of those who bring good news!" (Romans 10:14–15)

The Recurring Use of the Word *They*

The emphasis is overwhelming. In these two brief verses, "they" are mentioned at least seven times. It is an all-embracing term, from which there is no exclusion.

Who are these multitudes mentioned here? At the Congress on World Evangelism (COWE) in Thailand, in 1976, we identified them as the three billion people made up of over seventeen hundred separate people groups. On a global scale, they can be described as the world of Islam, the world of Hinduism, the world of Marxism, and so on. Locally, for many of us, they are the recently formed community groups of our complex multicultural societies.

During that conference in Pattaya, several of us traveled to the Thai/Kampuchean border to spend a weekend at the Kam Put refugee camp near Thap Sal. It was a moving time for me, not just because of the terrible suffering of those beautiful people, but also because of the physical, emotional, and spiritual progress they had made since their arrival in their temporary homes in Thailand. These are part of the "they" of the passage.

I will never forget my first visit to Dacca in Bangladesh. There seemed to be people everywhere. "Wall to wall people," someone once said to me, reflecting every dimension of human hope, endurance and despair. These too are the "they" mentioned in Romans 10.

Some years ago, my daughter, Christine, and I traveled from Addis Ababa to the Tigray provincial town of Mekelle in Ethiopia. More than a hundred thousand refugees encircled the town in three vast feeding centers. On the day we arrived, 146 people had died from hunger, cold and disease. It was a terrible experience, which defies meaningful description. In one small medical tent we discovered several rows of critically ill people. Christine and I stood awkwardly in the midst of that dramatic little group, not knowing what to do or what to say. In fact, on reflection, words would have been an intrusion. Our attention was drawn to a couple lying in the corner, on either side of their desperately ill baby. We felt so helpless, and as we turned to go, the woman looked up from where she was lying, and with a tremendous effort raised her hand from across her body and indicated she knew we were there. It was almost as if she understood how we felt, and wanted to tell us that she was pleased that we had come. The Lord Jesus died not only for us, but also for such people in every corner of our needy world.

The decade my family spent working among Muslim peoples in West Asia and the Middle East continues to affect and influence my ministry profoundly. The whole area touches my heart and brings tears to my eyes every day. Not just because of a spiritual lostness, real though it is, but because of their overwhelming social and emotional needs as well.

I have made a point in recent years to make regular visits to Iran and have been fortunate enough to have remarkable access to every level of that society. Though time does not allow me to share this fascinating and dramatic story, these are also a part of the "they" intended by the apostle.

I find it increasingly difficult to explain the gospel and its implications apart from the need to love individual people and to respond practically and meaningfully to their heartfelt, expressed needs. As we face the enormous task of world evangelization, it is easy to turn to the "responsive," or to stress the priority of salvation-oriented evangelism, and unintentionally end up washing our hands of pressing physical needs and hard, oppressive regimes wherever they may be found. The "they" of our passage are found in such as these.

In another context, I knew of a Christian congregation in the Middle East which was so unwilling to accept a new Muslim convert that when he came forward for communion first in the line, no one else in the church would then touch the cup from which he had drunk. The "they" of our passage includes even such as these.

It embraces the rich and poor on the streets of Bangkok, the free and the oppressed in the countries of Latin America, the illiterate and the well-educated in the continent of Africa, the insensitive affluent and the neglected religious minorities of Australia, and even those who are trapped within the bounds of their own religious prejudices and attitudes.

The "they," therefore, is all-inclusive. It is no surprise to discover this theme throughout the Scriptures (emphasis added):

He is the atoning sacrifice for our sins, and not only for ours but also for the sins of the whole *world* (1 John 2:2).

I am not ashamed of the gospel, because it is the power of God for the salvation of *everyone* who believes; first for the Jew, then for the Gentile (Romans 1:16).

For God so loved the *world* that he gave his one and only Son (John 3:16).

The Recurring Use of the Word *How*

This passage also repeatedly asks the question, "How?":

How, then, can they call on the one they have not believed in? And how can they believe in the one of whom they have not heard? And how can they hear without someone preaching to them? And how can they preach unless they are sent? (Romans 10:14–15).

There are a multitude of possible answers, but we will look at just two:

1. *Through sending.* One of the most remarkable developments in evangelism during the past decade has been the growth of the African, Asian, and Latin American missionary movements. According to one estimate, there have been forty thousand missionaries from five hundred missionary societies sent from these countries over the past twenty-five years.

   In Australia we have a great deal to learn from this. I am convinced the answer to world evangelization lies not in an increased technological or communications efficiency, but in the sacrificial response in word and deed of each local congregation to the needs of those around them and far away.

   I do not believe any local congregation, no matter what its situation, can afford to deprive itself of the encouragement and nourishment that comes by sending missionaries and reading about missionaries beyond their church walls.

2. *Through suffering.* I know of no other pattern for missions (evangelism and service) than that of the Cross. As we partake of the Incarnation, we shall inevitably be drawn into our Lord's lifestyle and share in his sufferings through his people.

On the last evening of our visit to Ethiopia, members of the Christian Relief and Development Association (CRDA) hosted a dinner to say farewell. I sat next to the leader of the Mennonite community. I had read in Michael Bourdeaux's Keston News Service of the suffering of the evangelical churches in Ethiopia. In this special moment, I was able to clarify and fill in the details under the protection of this public place.

During the previous months, two thousand churches had been closed and more than two hundred pastors had been imprisoned or had disappeared without trace. The facts were distressing, but the strength and faith of my new friend provided a lasting memory. Their witness is a shining example to all their people. Their answer to the "how" in our passage is through suffering.

During my time in the Middle East, I visited Saudi Arabia several times. I will never forget the quiet steadfastness of the handful of faithful secret believers who risked their lives to meet with me in clandestine sessions. I have information that they are still holding these meetings.

I am inclined to believe the church which does not know something of the meaning of suffering cannot authenticate its evangelism—either at home or overseas. This is the point where so many of us find the challenge beyond us. We have become comfortable, soft, and utterly ineffectual.

The Emphasis on the *Message*

We are to bring "good news" (v. 15), the Good News that liberates, enlivens, and transforms not only the heart but the circumstances, and brings hope.

Frequently, this message is received through proclamation, as in Cairo, when Pope Shenouda (who is now free after years of confinement) preaches powerfully and effectively to thousands every week. No one should doubt that this message is primarily found in the proclamation of the saving, substitutionary love of Jesus—in his dying for our sins on the cross so we might be set free.

Any dichotomy between proclamation and the activity which godly compassion demands is false and is a denial of the Good News. The message we offer brings the potential for wholeness in every part of life. Christians cannot allow a false division to continue in their proclamation of a message that saves, and a life that transforms.

May the Lord Jesus help us to respond sensitively and humbly to the enormous numbers of people who are without Christ in our world today, by grappling seriously with the "how" (through sending and suffering), and by the sharing of our amazing message of Good News. "How beautiful are the feet of those who preach the Gospel of peace with God and bring glad tidings of good things." In other words, how welcome are those who come [or who go] preaching God's Good News! (Romans 10:15, TLB).

Living Life Fully

David Penman

The Call for Sacrifice: Living Life to Its Fullest (Romans 12:1–2)

The epistle to the Romans does not end at chapter 11, with its ringing "To him [God] be the glory" (v. 35). It takes a crucial new direction—"Therefore, I urge you, . . . "—and issues a call for us to live lives worthy of the one who has called and commissioned us.

As C. K. Barrett wrote:

> [We have] read of the universal sinfulness of mankind and the universal grace of God, of his infinite love in sending his Son to die for our sins, and of the free justification by faith alone which, in his mercy, he offers. We have read of the power of the Spirit of God to bring life out of death; of predestination, and God's eternal purpose for his creation.

There are five chapters remaining in the book of Romans, and a lifetime of faith and hope to be anticipated and applied. In Romans 12:1–2, we find the Pauline application of the principle "faith without deeds is dead" (James 2:26). There is a denial of any division between doctrine and everyday Christian living. In other words, the apostle sees no final distinction between the doctrines of creation, redemption, and sanctification, and the holiness of living that leads to social, economic, and political transformation.

There is vast richness in the teachings of Romans 12 and 13: membership in the body of Christ (12:3–5); differing gifts (12:6–8); the Christian's graces (12:9–13); behavior towards others (12:14–21); and Christian citizenship (13:1–7). But I would like to focus on the theme of the opening verses of chapter 12: the call to sacrifice—or living life to the full.

God has shown us his mercy. This has been made clear in the previous eleven chapters, leading up to the great exultant cry of adoration: "Oh, the depth of the riches of the wisdom and knowledge of God! . . . .To him be the glory forever! Amen." (11:33–36). In response, we are to live as those who have seen with our own eyes, and touched with our hands, the wonders of Jesus, whom we worship. In the Lausanne movement and in the fellowship we represent, we need to rediscover, not only a human and practical application of the doctrines and beliefs imparted to us, but a sense of awe and wonder as we seek to do "his good, pleasing and perfect will" (12:2).

Let's explore briefly the context of these two practical chapters, as we seek to apply the strong theological teaching of the first eleven chapters of the epistle. There are five areas to consider: membership in a body, differing gifts, Christian graces, loving relationships, and Christian citizenship.

1. *Membership in the body of Christ* (12:3–5). These verses remind us of the mutuality in our relationships within the Christian family. We *need* each other and need to depend on each other.

   We used to be a family of six. I have three married children and a nineteen-year-old still at home. One of my daughters brought her boyfriend home often, finally married him, and then they both moved in! They now have a little boy, Hamish, who is fifteen months old. Two of our children have married and moved to their new homes. Today, we are still a family of six with Chris, Hugh, and baby Hamish showing no signs of leaving! Within Aussie culture, this is very unusual and is normally discouraged. Quite frankly, for us it is a joy! We love having them, and we complement and enrich each other's lives. It offers us a glimpse of the mutuality in the family of Jesus, where we are also to complement and enrich one another.

   The metaphor of the body in verse 4 is developed in 1 Corinthians 12, and it appears again in Ephesians 4:16 and Colossians 1:18. The body is healthy when all its parts cooperate, each in its proper sphere. The less visible parts, as medical science demonstrates, are as vital for full health, indeed to life, as the more visible ones. Microscopic malfunctioning can produce tragic diseases. So too with the people of God.

   There are numerous illustrations throughout Christian history of those whose resources seemed small, but who became wonderfully significant. For example, the widow of Zarephath, the child with loaves and fish, Simon of Cyrene, and the woman at the treasury. None of these people realized at the time how important they were to those around them.

2. *Differing gifts* (12:6–8). In verses 6–8, Paul refers to three kinds of gifts. They are important because they sum up the qualities and gifts which the church needs:

   - There are gifts expressed through speech: prophecy, teaching, and exhorting. The church lives by the Word of God, and these gifts (which together we might call preaching) are essential to its life.
   - There are gifts expressed in practical service: serving, contributing, and showing mercy. A church that does not back up its spoken witness with an active witness of love is not the church of Christ.
   - There is the gift of leadership or, as some translations indicate, presiding. We need Christians who are able to guide the community as a whole, and take some responsibility for the welfare of others.

   We expect to see all these gifts exercised in some real measure by ministers of the gospel, but Paul thinks of them as distributed, and exercised, throughout the community.

3. *The Christian's graces* (12:9–13). The passage is dynamic and the action implied is unmistakable. These imperatives imply love, devotion, honor, service, joy, hope, patience, faithfulness, and hospitality. There is a high level of expectation. Who can possibly reflect all these things?

   I have no doubt that Paul is describing the "normal" Christian life: the life that we are to anticipate, the life we are to offer to others, and the life of Jesus, in ours, today.

4. *Behavior towards others* (12:14–21). The remainder of the chapter under-lines the importance of mutual love (vv. 9–10,13,15) and of love even for enemies (vv.14,17,19–21). This is how living sacrifices are to be offered and how our concern for our neighbors is shown.

5. *Christian citizenship* (13:1–7). It is important to keep Christian society in the first century in proper perspective. The Roman Empire—stretching from the Rhine, the Danube, and the Black Sea, bounded to the west by the Atlantic, and to the south and east by the great deserts—had given the Mediterranean world a stable peace. The "Roman peace" was the social and political framework within which the Christian church attained its initial international form. It was also a framework in which relative harmony and peace prevailed throughout the region. The Empire had not yet branded the church as a dissident rebellious group. When Paul was writing, there was still hope of partnership. Chapter 13:1–7 needs to be understood within this context.

It creates real difficulties if we apply them out of their context into the structures of an unequal and unjust society. The temptation to illustrate this issue from a dozen examples of local and national inhumanity is great, but this is not the place or the time to do so.

How can we summarize this call to be living sacrifices? It is expressed clearly in the introduction to the two chapters:

> Therefore, I urge you, brothers, in view of God's mercy, to offer your bodies as living sacrifices, holy and pleasing to God—which is your spiritual act of worship. Do not conform any longer to the pattern of this world, but be transformed by the renewing of your mind. Then you will be able to test and approve what God's will is—his good, pleasing and perfect will" (12:1–2).

What does this mean? This is an important verse with two main points: God has shown us his mercy, and we are to live the Christian life to its fullest.

1. *God has shown us his mercy.* What is this mercy? How shall we see it? Can we experience it today?

A few months ago, my wife and I stood within the ancient walls of Jerusalem on the site believed to be the place of the crucifixion and burial of Jesus. Many arguments exist as to which of several competing locations are genuine, and these discussions will continue for a long time. But one thing is sure, and all the records agree, that Jesus of Nazareth, a carpenter's son who claimed to be the expected Messiah, died in Jerusalem in dramatic circumstances on a Roman cross.

Today, it is often said that history, archaeology, and theology are unimportant, and that what matters is our living and our relationships. This approach is not Christian, and in the end, it is harmful. Many faiths and philosophical systems can offer a similar way to live, but Christianity is rooted in history, and in the gospel—in the Good News. The New Testament constantly affirms this. Otherwise, why bother with Jerusalem, with the Cross, or with the agony of such a terrible death?

For the Christian, the gospel is the fact of Christ crucified—his finished work on the cross. The gospel is not good news of a baby in a manger, a young man at a carpenter's bench, a preacher in the fields of Galilee, or even of an empty tomb. The gospel is that God cared so much about us that he was willing to die on the cross, so we might be set free and be offered a new possibility in life. No other religious system functions like this. "When we were still powerless, Christ died for the ungodly" (Romans 5:6). "But God demonstrates his own love for us in this: While we were still sinners, Christ died for us" (Romans 5:8). "Christ redeemed us from the curse of the law by becoming a curse for us" (Galatians 3:13).

This is the unique nature of our faith. This is the essence of our faith. This is the gospel. *This* is the mercy of God.

2. *We are to live the Christian life to its fullest.* In view of God's mercy, to offer your bodies as living sacrifices, holy and pleasing to God (Romans 12:1). What does this mean? How do we put into practice this gospel life—that which pleases God?

Let me illustrate by telling you what it is not. John Wesley was the son of a clergyman and was a clergyman himself. He was orthodox in belief, religious in practice, upright in conduct, and full of good works. He and his friends visited the inmates of the prisons and workhouses of Oxford. They took pity on the slum children of the city and provided them with food, clothing, and education. They observed Saturday as the Sabbath as well as Sunday. They went to church and to Holy Communion. They gave alms, searched the Scriptures, fasted, and prayed. But they were bound in the limits of their own religion, instead of putting their trust in Jesus as their Lord and Master. A few years later, John Wesley (in his own words) came to "trust in Christ, in Christ only for salvation" and was given an inward assurance that his sins had been taken away. This faith principle, this Jesus-orientation, authenticates works of mercy and a life of service.

During the course of my regular visits to the Middle East, I have met two quite different people who illustrate this truth.

Hassan Dehquani Tafti is the exiled bishop in Iran. He was chairman of a clergy conference I attended in Cyprus several years ago, and has been a part of my life over many years. Before his conversion to Christianity in Iran, he was a devout and devoted Muslim. Eventually, he was ordained and became the first Anglican bishop in that ancient land. During the 1980 uprising, the church was attacked and the bishop's life was threatened. Tragically, the mobs turned on his family and his only son, Bahram, was brutally murdered. The bishop escaped to England, but rather than becoming bitter, he shines as an example of love and forgiveness toward his enemies.

His Holiness, Pope Shenouda III, of Egypt, is leader of the ancient Coptic Orthodox Church and was, during the first few years of the 1980s, confined to his desert monastery in one of the last acts of religious repression by President Anwar Sadat before his assassination.

Until his imprisonment, Pope Shenouda was tremendously effective in the leadership of his six million followers. His weekly Bible studies drew more than six thousand people. Many lives were changed and Shenouda became a target of the conservative Muslim brotherhood. In 1981, they confined him to the monastery.

In 1984, after months of effort, my wife and I were allowed to make the long journey

264/Proclaim Christ Until He Comes

through the desert, past numerous military check-points, to his monastic home. I was one of few overseas church visitors allowed to see him during those years, and my wife certainly was the first woman! We had a marvelous day with that great man and his companions. Their faith was transparent, and even their limited opportunities for service were used to the fullest and rooted in their faith in Jesus. As we prepared to leave later that day, I asked the patriarch if he had a message for the Coptic community in Melbourne. He became quiet and reflected carefully before saying:

> Tell them that God is so good to me. I am well, and they should not worry about me. Remember God is in control, and not this government.

But there is a final story to share. Some years ago, while I was an assistant bishop in Melbourne, I went to St. Aldan's Anglican church in one of our suburbs to announce the decision of their minister to retire due to the rapid advance of cancer. Arthur's honesty and simple trust in Jesus deeply affected many lives. In his last letter to the parish before he died, he wrote:

> Our ways are not God's ways! At times this is very difficult to believe—I freely acknowledge that! But I want to affirm something that I feel deep down in my inner being, that out of every situation God brings good.

This is what it means to live the Christian life to the fullest. The common factor in these lives is not the individual, the life lived, or the interpretation given to varying circumstances. The common factor is: Jesus, who is the Good News of God; Jesus, who infuses our ideas with his purposes; Jesus, who authenticates our behavior and lifestyle; and Jesus, in the words with which we began, who is in himself God's mercy, and who leads us to sacrificial living and shows us how to live life to its fullest.

Love in the End Times

David Penman

The Unifying Power of Love (Romans 13:14)

Over the past few days we have considered God's plan for the Jewish people and the nations, illustrated by a study of the theme of the great missionary passage in Romans 10:14–17: How, and through whom, can they hear the message?

May I say, in passing, to my Jewish friends who are in Christ, and who are such an important part of this Congress, that many of us believe you bring special gifts and insights. We need to hear what you have to say, and we need to accept you in Christ as you are. We love you dearly as brothers and sisters in the Lord, and want to learn from the precious insights you bring to this family. I fear that sometimes we fail to care for you as we ought, and fail to learn from you all we can.

We examined the life and witness of all Christians. We considered that marvelous message in Romans 12–13, with its focus on Christian faith in practice. And we concluded with an exposition of Romans 12:1–2, in which we were exhorted by the apostle to be living sacrifices—living life to the fullest.

I have experienced some difficulty in doing justice to the extensive passages before us each day. I have tried to spend half of the time on general textual comments and the remainder on special focus.

As our Congress draws to a close, in our reading there is a growing emphasis on the approaching end (i.e., the end of all time) and an emphasis on the urgency of love. We will concentrate on the theme: The unifying power of love (Romans 13:8–14).

In Romans 13:12–14 we are reminded that the night is far spent and the day is at hand. The apostle explores the special reasons for ending our old way of life and embarking on a new life in Christ. For this Congress, this chapter is a fresh reminder of the urgency of the times, and of the sacrificial service that is required as the "night is nearly over; the day is almost here" (v. 12). I have no doubt whatsoever of the literal meaning of the passage, nor of its imperative for us as we conclude our considerations in this Congress of World Evangelization.

In terms of earthly time, Paul's new day was not as near as many had thought, but the emphasis is exact. We live in the last chapter of the world's history, however long that chapter may turn out to be. We must live with God's future in mind. It is no wonder verses 13–14 became the "womb" from which Augustine was born in A.D. 386 and became the inspiration of Wesley's comment, "Herein is contained the whole of our salvation."

Let's return to verse 8. In the RSV, this verse is translated, "Owe no one anything," but the New International Version makes it clear that Paul is not forbidding borrowing, but saying, rather, that the believer should not leave debts unpaid. That is, they should be settled promptly. The present imperative has a continuous force: "Don't continue owing. Pay your debts." Not a bad reminder on the last day of Lausanne II in Manila!

Is it too much to apply this more generally to our relationships, as in "let not the sun go down upon your wrath"? How utterly transforming it would be if we were to leave here with all our debts cleared away, all our reconciliations concluded, and our old enmities transformed. It is not too much for God, even if it seems like an unreasonable request to us.

I am aware of the difficulties many people have experienced: the tensions of a missionary past, the memory of paternalistic relationships, the growth of an unhealthy and sometimes ungodly nationalism, and much more. Even in this Congress, there has been much for which we need to ask God for his mercy, and our brothers and sisters for forgiveness.

Paul then applies the same principle to loving. Love is a permanent obligation—a debt impossible to discharge. As Origen put it long ago: "The debt of charity is permanent, we are never quit of it; for we must pay it daily and yet always owe it."

Paul sees this as a simple duty resting on the humblest believer, not just the work of the greatest of saints. Whatever else we do, or do not do, we are to love. Those who love fulfill the commands: do not commit adultery, do not murder, do not steal, do not covet.

Love does no harm to its neighbor, and is in this sense the fulfillment of the law. Paul reminds his listeners they are to live in this way, understanding the present time. The J. B. Phillips paraphrase of 1 Corinthians 13 helps us even more:

This love of which I speak is slow to lose patience—it looks for a way of being constructive. It is not possessive: it is neither anxious to impress nor does it cherish inflated ideas of its own importance.

Love has good manners and does not pursue selfish advantage. It is not touchy. It does not keep account of evil or gloat over the wickedness of other people. On the contrary, it is glad with all good men when Truth prevails.

Love knows no limit to its endurance, no end to its trust, no fading of its hope; it can outlast anything. It is, in fact, the one thing that still stands when all else has fallen (1 Corinthians 13:4–8).

We now come to the famous verse of Augustine's conversion, verse 14. He tells us of it in his *Confessions*. The metaphor is that of being clothed in the moral disposition and character of Christ, taking the garments which are the most visible feature of all. J. B. Phillips expresses it well when he says: "Let us be Christ's men from head to foot, and give no chances to the flesh to have its fling."

My very dear friend, David Bentley-Taylor, writing of Augustine's conversion says:

As he lay there in intense distress he heard what seemed to be a child's voice from one of the other houses, saying, "Take and read," over and over again. He rose and went back to where Alypius was sitting, for he had left the copy of Paul's Epistles there. "I snatched it up, opened it, and in silence read the passage on which my eyes first fell." It was Romans 13:13–14: "Not in orgies and drunkenness, not in sexual immorality and debauchery, not in dissention and jealousy. Rather, clothe yourselves with the Lord Jesus Christ and do not think about how to gratify the desires of the sinful nature." There was not need for him to read on. "In that instant, with the very ending of the sentence it was as though a light of utter confidence shown in my heart and all the darkness of uncertainty vanished." There and then the wayward, proud, immoral Augustine, unhappy and full of doubts, was gone. A new Augustine was born "in that instant" (*Augustine: Wayward Genius* [Grand Rapids, Mich.: Baker, 1981], 39).

In response to this, there are four things I'd like to address. We need to clothe ourselves with the Lord Jesus Christ: in our personal morality, in our worshiping life, in our community concern and involvement, and as we anticipate his coming.

Clothe Ourselves in Personal Morality

Romans 13:13–14 is directed to our individual moral activity: It is a call for purity and godliness. It is suggesting a standard different from the world around us. Today, it is not fashionable to teach or call for such an "apartness" in many of our communities. It wasn't in Paul's day either!

This is not to suggest we won't be tempted, we won't fail, or we won't despair in ourselves. Rather, this tremendous verse seeks to set before us a way of living that: is God's way, is different, protects the family, limits sexual promiscuity, honors personal discipline and restraint, and offers us the unifying power of the Holy Spirit through whom all this is possible

I have a dear friend who lives in Central Asia. He is involved in a tentmaking ministry. For thirty years, he has lived in his adopted land and identified with the language, culture and customs of this strongly Islamic nation. His engineering and construction business has been a blessing to thousands of individual Christians and many national and international mission agencies. In recent years, his determined stand for honesty and truth has been challenged by the authorities. His determination when undertaking any contracts to not offer or accept a bribe (in any form) has meant delayed payments, vilification, and continuous court cases. One case has been proceeding for almost ten years. He is currently before the courts on a new charge and refuses to buy his way out of trouble, but, rather, trusts the Lord for his needs and for his ultimate justification. This is what it means to clothe yourself with personal morality.

Clothe Ourselves in Our Worship Life

The fellowship we are to experience is also included. A detailed description of the partnership of the early church is found in Acts 2:42–47:

> They devoted themselves to the apostles' teaching and to the fellowship, to the breaking of bread and to prayer. Everyone was filled with awe, and many wonders and miraculous signs were done by the apostles. All the believers were together and had everything in common. Selling their possessions and goods, they gave to anyone as he had need. Every day they continued to meet together in the temple courts. They broke bread in their homes and ate together with glad and sincere hearts, praising God and enjoying the favor of all the people. And the Lord added to their number daily those who were being saved.

We need to confess honestly that this fellowship in the Lord Jesus and with each other, has not always been an obvious characteristic in our congregational experience, even though it has been splendidly present at this Congress.

If we do not anticipate a deeper sharing and loving, then we shall be no different from the community of people that surround us, from whom we have been called to become a special people.

The apostle Peter was specific when he said:

But you are a chosen people, a royal priesthood, a holy nation, a people belonging to God, that you may declare the praises of him who called you out of darkness into his wonderful light. (1 Peter 2:9).

From time to time, I share in a worshiping community where such unity and spiritual power is manifestly present. There was a youth convention in Waitarere, New Zealand, about ten years ago, when we prayed and sang and witnessed on an Easter evening until early in the morning. And I remember a mere handful of unlikely believers in Teheran, Iran, in 1986, whose worship was as splendid and awesome as that in any great and magnificent cathedral. Along with three other bishops, I went to consecrate a new bishop. We were the first such official "delegation" in five years. The atmosphere was electric, the welcome overwhelming, and the worship quite indescribable. I returned there again last year and hope to do so again in a few weeks' time. My dear sisters and brothers, please pray for the church, for the people of God in Iran. I shall never forget the vitality and overpowering joy of the worship of the congregation my own mission team visited in Soweto, in South Africa, just twelve months ago.

In the tiny village of Ibillin in Galilee, my Palestinian brother in Christ, Elias Chacour, seeks to apply this same principle in his small Melkite village community. He has told his amazing story in a book titled *Blood Brothers*. In this excerpt, he demonstrates the effect of salvation and repentance in their lives:

The momentum carried us out of the church and into the streets where true Christianity belongs. For the rest of the day and far into the evening, I joined the groups of believers as they went from house to house throughout Ibillin. At every door, someone had to ask forgiveness for a certain wrong. Never was forgiveness withheld. Now I knew that inner peace could be passed from man to man and woman to woman.

As I watched, I recalled, too, an image that had come to me as a young boy in Haifa. Before my eyes, I was seeing a ruined church rebuilt at last, not with mortar and rock, but with living stones.

Clothe Ourselves in Community Concern and Involvement

In 1983, the Australian churches produced a social justice statement entitled, "Changing Australia?" It was issued on behalf of most of the churches and called for a "fair chance" for all Australians, and criticized the inequalities and lack of justice in our society. However we understood the contents of that material (and it was strongly criticized in some sections of our community), the fact that churches together spoke to the society, questioned the direction we were taking, and denied the omnipotence of the politicians, was in itself a marvelous example and achievement.

The Lausanne movement has something to prove, in its spoken and written example, and in its leadership. A dichotomy between gospel and community is a false one. A dichotomy between the sacred and the secular is a travesty of the truth. A dichotomy between salvation and life is a heresy from which the New Testament, when carefully and faithfully read, will rescue us. We need to clothe ourselves with the Lord Jesus Christ in new community concern and involvement.

Clothe Ourselves with the Lord as We Anticipate His Coming

His coming was fulfilled in the Bethlehem event, and is relived again and again in our devotions. His coming is our daily experience, in each of the ways we have been sharing. His coming will be fulfilled again in glory, possibly sooner than we might think or presume.

There is a story that sums up the themes of these studies:

- The urgency of the task (Romans 10:14–17)
- The sacrificial lifestyle required of us (Romans 12:1–2), and
- The unifying power of love-service (Romans 13:13–14).

Several years ago a group of salesmen went to a regional sales convention. They assured their wives that they would be home in plenty of time for dinner. But with one thing and another the meeting ran overtime so the men had to race to the station, tickets in hand. As they charged through the terminal, one man (the one telling this story) inadvertently kicked over a table supporting a basket of apples. Without stopping, they all reached the train and boarded it with a sigh of relief. All but one. He paused, realized what had happened, and experienced a twinge of compunction for the boy whose apple stand had been overturned. He waved good-by to his companions and returned to the terminal. He was glad that he did. The ten-year-old boy was blind. The salesman gathered up the apples, and noticed that several of them were bruised. He reached into his wallet and said to the boy, "Here, please take this ten dollars for the damage we did. I hope it didn't spoil your day." As he started to walk away, the bewildered boy called after him, "Sir, are you Jesus?" The salesman stopped in his tracks. And he wondered! (William J. Bausch, *Storytelling, Imagination and Faith* [Mystic, Conn.: Twenty-Third Pubns., 1986], 177.)

May the Lord in his mercy continue to give us time to be Jesus to one another, and to the millions who do not know him as Savior and Lord. And, may the conclusion of this Congress be the beginning of glory for man.

III. The Whole World

Urban Evangelism

Ray Bakke, with Jember Tafferra, Viju Abraham, David Ngae, and Gary Granada

Today we must confront the awesome impact of global urbanization on world evangelism. World conditions have changed dramatically. It is as though giant magnets pull continents and people together. South is meeting North. East is shifting West. Overall, we're becoming increasingly urbanized.

Our God, the Sovereign Lord of heaven and earth, is not surprised by this. The Holy Spirit is raising up a body of urban witnesses to the gospel on all six continents. The urban church of Jesus Christ has learned many new ways to tell the story of salvation and to live it out in the largest cities of the world. Yes, there is much to lament and an incredible job yet to do, but we are here to testify that there is a gospel as big as the cities.

On Lausanne-sponsored journeys over the past ten years, I have met many of God's choice servants of the gospel serving faithfully in some of the most demanding "frontlines" in world missions today. Many of you in this auditorium fit this description, but we have asked four representatives to come and briefly share what God is teaching them about proclaiming the gospel in their unique context.

First, Jember Tafferra, of Addis Ababa, Ethiopia. Jember, a community health worker, was married to a government official. Following an overthrow of the government, she was imprisoned for five years. Now she and other Christians are ministering to an estimated thirty thousand people even under the constant scrutiny of a hostile Marxist government. Jember, reflect over the past ten years. How did the Lord prepare you for your ministry?

Jember: I have been a Christian from childhood. While growing up, I was exposed to poverty and injustice both at home and at school. Through the years, the Lord gave me an increased sensitivity and compassion for the poor. I first worked among the poor in a large city hospital in Africa. Following that, I worked for humanitarian organizations learning more helping skills and gaining access to valuable resources. My husband was the head of a city organization. Sharing his experiences increased my understanding of social problems within a large city. All of this provided excellent training for helping the poor, but during this time my approach was "top-down" planning and organizing. Something was to happen that would change my viewpoint.

Raymond J. Bakke is Professor of Ministry at Northern Baptist Theological Seminary, Chicago. A Lausanne Senior Associate and an intercity pastor for many years, Dr. Bakke is a citizen of the United States.

For political reasons, I was imprisoned for five years. There I learned what it was really like to be poor. Sharing a mattress and latrine with other prisoners—that was graduate school for me! It was there I learned that effective city ministry—ministry that can change the attitudes of the poor—must begin from the *bottom* up. This ministry begins by establishing caring relationships and really listening to the poor.

Ray: Jember, the principalities and powers of evil seem to rage within some cities. Most often it is women and children who are victims of this evil. Yet, you remain courageous and hopeful. What motivates you to continue your ministry?

Jember: Three elements form the basis of my motivation. First, I have seen that the Lord loves me with unconditional love. He died for me without demanding my automatic loyalty. His is a one-way love—always downward and never dependent upon my response. He loved me first and continues to love me unconditionally. Second, Matthew 25:35–40 tells me that Jesus is with the poor and oppressed in a special way. When I serve them, I serve my Lord Jesus. And third, if Jesus is with the poor and oppressed, they are *special* people—not to be pitied or patronized, but to be loved and served with all the respect I give Jesus.

Ray: One last question. You are a gifted and educated woman with master's studies at the University of Manchester. With your international connections you have generated large sums of money for ministries in the city of Addis. Although this has blessed the ministry, you live under constant, unfriendly scrutiny—even harassment. How do you cope?

Jember: There are difficulties and constraints working in cities where there is oppression and injustice—even those in secular occupations experience difficulties. But for us, the gospel is not a private, personal matter. It must be shared and lived in reality. Therefore, my point of urban entry is holistic and development-oriented. I know God cares about every aspect of our public life together.

The poor are even more suspicious of me than the rich and powerful, for they have been victimized by all. When everyone is suspicious of us it's easy to see why some keep quiet and are reluctant to get involved in social change. Yet I see that even when the rich are suspicious and the poor are fatalistic, my Lord continues to gives me a hopeful vision. He gives us victory over fear, anxiety, and self-pity. He enables us to do above all that we can imagine. He will spread his kingdom through my social-action ministry. That is his promise. That is my testimony.

Ray: Thank you, Jember. And may God go with you to multiply that faithful witness until he comes and calls for you. Let this witness from Addis remind us of those who live faithfully and serve effectively in urban environments. Our witness can—indeed must—contend with principalities and powers, for Christ is Lord of the whole city.

Viju Abraham is from Bombay—the commercial hub of India, a city of more than eleven million persons, it contains the largest slum in Asia. Viju returned to Bombay about five years ago. What did you do when you returned to Bombay? What were your plans?

Viju: My wife and I first moved to Bombay in 1971, feeling a call from God to work with university students. We didn't make much progress, so I decided to pursue theological training. After seminary we returned in 1984 with a renewed call and a four-point agenda committed to the Lord.

My first goal was to start a church that would reach out to nonbelievers from all racial and ethnic groups. With three friends, we began what we called, the Love of Christ Fellowship.

The second goal was to develop a trans-denominational fellowship to support Christian leaders within the city. Four of us began the ministry called Bombay Urban Fellowship after one of your seminars in 1985.

My third goal was to begin a training center that would serve the needs of churches within the city, with the fourth goal to encourage those churches to minister among the poor in Bombay.

Ray: Viju, you planned and prayed. With a vision and some clear goals, you began a small support group, sharing your vision for the evangelization of Bombay. I know you could spend more than all your time pastoring your church. Why are you so concerned about other pastors and other churches? Why is Bombay Urban Fellowship so important?

Viju: We church leaders are often called to organize events like crusades or conventions. While necessary, these events would often leave us drained. Sometimes, we would even feel used by outsiders. We needed to support, encourage, and instruct one another. Four of us began with a vision that God's kingdom was larger than our individual denominations and personal ministries. We belong to each other in the kingdom of God. We meet now as church leaders from a wide spectrum of denominations—historic, evangelical, charismatic, independent, free, and catholic.

We have three primary goals: (1) fellowship in Christ, (2) the pursuit of revival in our personal lives and churches, (3) intercession for ourselves and our city.

Ray: What is unique about urban ministry training for the churches of Bombay?

Viju: Well, first the urban training in our center is done by local people who really understand our unique situation. It's not a program or curriculum package from outside Bombay. Out of the fellowship came a coalition of leaders who in 1986 decided to put a training center together. We've conducted fifteen seminars and workshops on subjects like unreached people groups, management and leadership, family life, early morning prayer, and ministry to the urban poor. All of these training packages focus on Bombay.

We learned that attendees can and will pay to support this program, even in a poor or developing country like India. Paying themselves helps them feel a sense of ownership. Our center has a twofold aim—to stimulate the churches to growth and by this to expand the mission to the city.

Ray: David Ngae comes to us from Hong Kong. He completed theological studies and combined it with a master's degree in social work, specializing in urban studies. Over the past six years, he has planted a church in a high-rise housing estate, established a government-sponsored community social program, lectured in several seminars and served in a host of other ministries besides being senior pastor of a large historic church in Swatow. David, tell us more about the partnership between the government and your new church.

David: The government of Hong Kong had a massive immigration of refugees from the Mainland. They chose to build huge highly populated housing estates. Because of my training I was given a grant to start a social service center in this place. The church started in one corner of the activities center and has grown to a core of one hundred—seventy-five of whom are indigenous to the immediate area which is a low income grass roots community. We have thirteen staff members—the government pays for ten and the church pays for two—to do the work of the center which houses the church.

Ray: Cities are filled with historic churches. Hong Kong is no exception. These churches are often like beached whales, washed in by the tide. They have huge facilities but few people, and most of them are old. In some ways, it's tempting just to ignore these churches and start new ones. One writer described the members as "God's frozen people." David, a few years ago you became senior pastor of a 120-year-old Swatow Chinese Church which had at one time dwindled to just two hundred worshipers. How has that church experienced renewal?

David: I spent the first year trying to enter into the history and memories of my church. I went back to the Swatow region of China. I read and discussed the past. My first task was to explore the roots of our people—my roots—to see how God brought the church into existence. The people learned to love me because I helped them recover their dying past. I reminded them of their once-radical commitment to serve God. My faith in their church enabled them to take my leadership seriously, even though I am young. Now the church is growing again. We're up to six or seven hundred in the services and have many revitalized ministries. Next month we're going to send our first Swatow Chinese missionary to Kenya and at the same time we're starting to plant a new church in a Hong Kong satellite city.

Ray: David, one of the themes of this Congress is "Urgency" and that reminds us of the situation in Hong Kong. The year, 1997 is coming when Hong Kong will become part of China. Since the events of Tiananmen Square in Beijing, there is rising anger, frustration, and even panic in Hong Kong. I know you could tell us many things, but please tell us what all the turmoil in China has done to the church in Hong Kong?

David: Because of 1997, a group of pastors began praying and strategizing several years ago for the renewal of the church in Hong Kong. Hong Kong is facing serious brain and capital drain. Many professional people including church leaders are leaving for North America, but since June 4 surprising things have happened. Almost spontaneously the Christians of Hong Kong have rallied on behalf of democracy on the Mainland. There have been amazing Christian demonstrations where all the churches came together to demonstrate. No one seemed to care what denomination people belonged to. We discovered in the midst of our marches and rallies that we really are Chinese. Many of us never really thought about this before. We grew up in Hong Kong with British passports, and many were educated in Canada and America. We visited the Mainland, but we were tourists. By the grace of God, the church in Hong Kong is learning to embrace being Chinese. The courageous spirits of the Beijing students awakened our moral courage. Our cities are linked together in a world of interconnected cities. We are learning to analyze our situations and take risks. In all this and in many other ways God is preparing the church of Hong Kong for 1997.

Ray: David, article 13 of the Lausanne Covenant commits us to solidarity with Chinese and all other oppressed peoples in the world on behalf of human rights. We thank you and urge everyone to pray anew for Chinese Christians everywhere in the Mainland and scattered throughout the cities of the world.

Now, we introduce Gary Granada from metro Manila, our host city. Gary is a singer-songwriter, evangelist, and community organizer. He used to organize rural areas in Marxist causes, but when he met his wife, Susan, she introduced him to Jesus and her world of ministry. Now they both minister in the slums of metro Manila, especially the garbage city called Smokey Mountain—not too far from this building.

Gary, Jesus Christ radically redirected your life. What we see on you is how the Holy Spirit has produced the fruit of a Christian social conscience. The gospel is shaping your approach to public witness on a host of social and political issues. Can you tell us more about this?

Gary: My wife and I started working with the poor outside the context of the church. We helped farmers and fishermen organize themselves and overcome structures of socio-economic oppression. We have seen incomes and employment rise substantially among rural workers. But we discovered that this increase in material well-being did not necessarily improve their Christianity. On the other hand, I have encountered many Christians who worship Jesus Christ but have nothing to do with social justice. Our work with the poor, therefore, is to witness to the power of Christ and the need to combat social oppression. If the gospel is indeed good news to the poor, then we need to understand poverty—historically, economically, culturally, and spiritually. I believe that our message becomes credible as we live close to the poor and oppressed.

Ray: Gary, you are an artist who lived in slums with the poor. You've written a song about it that won first prize in a national music competition. You're well-known for the song "Bahay" in Tagalog. Tell us about your song, then sing for us please.

Gary: When I sing before our brethren, I look very rich, and yet looking at you today I feel very poor. The Scriptures tell us that in the kingdom of God, those who gathered great material wealth often were spiritually poor. The song that I am going to sing is a simple one to show you contrasts. There are people a couple miles from here who work twelve hours a day picking up garbage for a living. Unless and until we face this dilemma, we should not be surprised if these people think our message is empty—just more trash. My song simply tells you what you already know: They are there and we are here.

One day I visited a house on the garbage dump; squeezed inside was a household of fifteen people, enduring a small makeshift, broken down shanty, while nearby a mansion was almost empty.

Imprisoned inside wooden slabs and corrugated boxes, shaded by rusting zinc sheets and worn out tires, mended together by scraps of trash and held down by stones, I could not understand why such a thing is called a house.

I decided to write a story about what my eyes saw, and even made a song that others may hear and know. I painted what I felt and put on a simple play, and asked knowledgeable people about what they can say.

A famous senator was the first person I came to see, and then an expert professor of a prominent university. And a blessed businessman and the newsmen and the pulpit man, and they all agreed that indeed it was a house.

Day and night they scrape off the mountain of trash, and eat like chickens on the floor as they squat. And force their bodies to sleep on an old torn bed. Far better is the resting place of the dead.

And if one day you'll accidentally pass by that place, and feel and hear and smell and see them face to face, I do not mean to deride, I leave it you to decide. Do you think that in the eyes of the Creator this is a house?

VIDEO PRESENTATION

God Is Building a City

Producers: Peter Blanchard, John Desjarlais

Narrator: "And he [Cain] built a city, and called the name of the city after the name of his son, Enoch" (Genesis 4:17, RSV).

Cities have been in existence from the time people first gathered behind walls after tending their fields. Across the world and through the years, imperial centers of commerce and culture have challenged the imagination. But as we enter the next century, something is happening to the cities for the first time.

In 1800, only 2.5 percent of the world's population lived in sizable cities. By 1900, it was only 9 percent. But by the year 2000, for the first time in history, a majority of the world's population will be living in cities. Of the world's six billion people, over three billion will live in urban centers. And 80 percent of these will live in the exploding metropolises in the developing world of Asia, Africa, and Latin America.

Ray Bakke: Virtually everywhere, cities are increasing in numbers. The percentages are just phenomenal. We're talking about cities like Sao Paulo, Jakarta, Bombay, Calcutta, and Mexico City, which are skyrocketing in sheer numbers.

Narrator: In 1900, there were only twenty cities in the world with a million or more people, and nearly all of the world's largest cities were in the industrialized North. But by 1985, the world had over 270 cities of a million or more. And by the year 2000, there will be over four hundred world-class cities of a million or more people. By then, nine of the world's ten largest cities will be in the developing South.

Two major factors account for the phenomenal growth of Third World cities: high birthrates and massive migrations.

Ray Bakke: The world grows at the rate of more than eight million every month. Half of the children born today will live in cities. Mexico City has a city the size of Seattle born within it every year. Cairo has a new baby born within city limits every twenty seconds. We are talking about massive numbers of new babies.

Craig Ellison: Many people are born in these cities, of course, but the migration into cities amounts to over seventy-five thousand people a day. People living in rural areas by and large are living on a subsistence-level quality of life and are barely surviving. They go to the city hoping to improve their lives.

Narrator: In the nineteenth century, industrialized cities such as London and Chicago grew quickly from the migration of factory workers. However, for the millions pouring into Third World cities today, there are often no jobs or only menial jobs. Entire families of migrant workers, separated from their rural families, move into the overcrowded, disease-ridden squatter settlements, clinging to the hope of a better life.

Ray Bakke: There are massive slums surrounding most of the Third World cities. In Bogota, Colombia—or many of the other cities—shanty towns go high into the mountains, often without running water or sewers. We find enormous problems there. I've read, for example, that 20 percent of the babies born in Third World cities die of water-borne diseases in the first year. Cities like Jakarta have toxic garbage. If they bury it, it poisons the water system; if they burn it, it poisons the air. There are people living on the garbage dumps. And garbage communities are a present reality in every Third World city.

Narrator: In some cities, governments spend more resources on international airports and world-class hotels than on basic services such as power, clean water, and sanitation. The poor are exploited by the unjust structures and systems of the city which favor the rich. Even so, there is hope in the slums of Third World cities, a hope which continues to draw people by the tens of thousands.

Floyd McClung: God is sending the world to us in the city. It is the shifting frontier. Our idea of missions has to realize this. We think the missionary is the man or woman who puts on a pith helmet and takes a butterfly net in one hand and a Bible in the other and goes to the jungles. But the people in the jungles are all moving to the city.

Narrator: Cities are important, but not only for their numbers of people. Cities are strategic centers of communication, commerce, culture, and political power. They are catalysts of social change. Some cities play particular roles: Paris is a cultural city; Delhi is a political city; New York is a commercial city. But most cities of the Third World combine all these roles of influence and are called "primate cities." Many of them once served as colonial capitals and seaports. Today, they are becoming the crossroads of many different cultures.

Some of the fastest growing cities are in areas highly resistant or restricted to Christian work. But global urbanization is making more groups of people accessible to the gospel. Diverse peoples are cross-migrating in large numbers across national boundaries. The world is becoming less a world of independent countries and more a world of interconnected, international cities.

Ray Bakke: I see the whole world is in motion. The Southern Hemisphere is moving north. Asia is moving west. You can see it when you look at London. Paris is becoming Algerian. Amsterdam has large populations of Indonesians, Suranamese, Goan, and Malachan Straits peoples.

Craig Ellison: And in that drawing together into cities, more than ever before, we have an opportunity to reach people with the gospel.

Narrator: Some groups once geographically distant are now near—in the cities. There are large numbers of Turks in Frankfurt; Bengalis in London. And millions of Central American refugees are in Los Angeles, Houston, and Miami.

In addition, a major move can often lead to greater openness to the Good News of Christ and the good works of his church. People in transition are separated from their old traditions and relationships. The urban settler is often more receptive to new ideas.

Despite such possibilities, the vast majority of the global missionary force—nearly 80 percent—remains in rural areas. Rural work should continue, but many people won to Christ by missionaries in rural areas are moving into the cities. There, many are lost from the faith, overwhelmed by the appeal of materialism, and unable to find a supportive Christian community.

Ray Bakke: Imagine cities of eight to ten million people, and far fewer than one hundred churches. The church is just not keeping up with the birthrates and migrations.

Floyd McClung: It's interesting that while the greatest migration in human history is taking place—450 million people in the last twenty-five or thirty years—at the same time, Christians are moving out of the cities. We want to get away from them.

Craig Ellison: As Third World cities progressively become the larger of the cities of our world and are more dominated by non-Christian religions, we are in for a worldwide shift that we have never experienced before. Non-Christian religions will be emanating in their influence from these mega-centers of Third World primate cities.

Narrator: The rapid decline in the number of Christians in major cities is a change from the pattern of the past. Historically, God and his people have had an urban concern.

Ray Bakke: There are far more than one thousand references to cities in Scripture. For example, if you look at the fifty-one references in the Bible to Sodom and Gomorrah, or the literally hundreds of references in the Bible to Nineveh, Babylon, Jerusalem, and Samaria, you are almost overwhelmed by God's concern for these large cities in the Bible.

Narrator: When Abraham prayed for Sodom, God promised to spare the city for the sake of a righteous few. God sent Jonah to Nineveh, a city known for its violence. Jeremiah told the exiles in Babylon to work for the welfare of their oppressor's city. Jesus wept over Jerusalem. The apostle Paul concentrated his missionary strategy in the great commercial centers of his day, and his epistles were letters to urban congregations facing urban pressures. Through the apostle John, Jesus addressed letters to seven city churches in Asia. And the Bible ends with the New Jerusalem of God.

The church has both an urban past and an urban future. The question today's Christians must answer is: *Will we, the church, be compassionate and committed to the urban present?*

George McKinney: A careful survey of biblical history reveals God's unending love affair with the city. Both the New and Old Testaments affirm that God unhesitatingly seeks to redeem the city and its inhabitants.

Those of us involved in the city are here to testify that as everywhere else, where sin abounds, God's grace abounds much more. Christ the wounded healer is present in the concrete jungles, in the overcrowded rat-and roach-infested projects, in the halls of justice, and in the jails of our cities. As our eternal contemporary, Jesus is wherever there is human pain and suffering. God in Christ has never forsaken the city, neither must the church.

Samuel Escobar: As I cross the city of Lima, I feel strengthened by the Lord, who says, "Don't be afraid. There are many troubles, but I have many people in this city."

Narrator: The Lord God says through Isaiah, "If you spend yourselves in behalf of the hungry, and satisfy the needs of the oppressed, you will be called repairer of broken walls, restorer of streets with dwellings." Let us work together in word and deed to proclaim Christ in the urban world until he comes.

Ray Bakke: The Bible may begin in a garden but it ends in a city. What kind of a city is God building? Isaiah gives us a record. It's going to be a city with a housing policy, and a city where children do not die young—that's a public health policy! That's God's agenda, and he's building a city right now. We couldn't honor him more, I suspect, than by loving him and by beginning to love the city. We've got an urban future whether we like it or not.

The Impact of Modernization

Os Guinness

I would like to discuss two theories, and some of their consequences, which are of the utmost gravity to missions.

The first theory is that modernity, or the emerging world civilization which is now being produced by the forces of modernization, represents the single greatest opportunity and the single greatest threat the church of Christ has faced since apostolic times. The second theory is that for most evangelicals worldwide this challenge is unconfronted.

One of my most prized possessions is a little bronze medallion. It was struck in 1900 to celebrate the liberation of Peking by the Boxers. What's fascinating is the symbolism on the medallion. On one side is the Heavenly Gate belching smoke and flames. The Boxers had set the Heavenly Gate on fire as a deliberate political statement. The regime, the Manchu dynasty, had lost the mandate of heaven and they were announcing it to the world. But those who struck the medallion put on the other side other symbols of the same point—the loss of the mandate of heaven. Above was the word, *Ichobod*, "the glory has gone," and underneath the Chaldean words *mene, mene, tekel parsin*, "weighed in the balances and found wanting." That is a rather hypocritical Western observation on the fall of the Manchu regime.

The reason it is so interesting and moving to me is because my grandfather was there and lived through it. It is also interesting the way various commentators have looked at that period and tried to see significance for the world in the twentieth century. At the time, most of them looked at the contrast between modernity and the corrupt ancient regime, the new and the old, the advanced and the backward, and so on. They said the loss of the mandate of heaven showed this would be the American century, or the Christian century.

But at the same time, there were those who looked at the same thing and saw not the contrast between modernity and China, but the similarities. They saw that just as the Chinese regime lost its mandate of heaven under this first impact of modernity, so did Europe and the United States, although they gave it a different name.

Marx looked at modernity and remarked that all that is solid melts into air, all that is holy will one day be profaned. Nietzsche looked across from Germany to England and said that when cultures lose the decisive influence of God, God dies. When God dies for

Os Guinness is Executive Director of the Williamsburg Charter Foundation. An author and scholar, he is a citizen of Great Britain.

a culture, they become weightless; there is a hollowing out. They lose the reality that gives them greatness and staying power, and their energy drains from the inside.

Nietzsche called himself the Anti-Christ. He hated Christ and he hated Christianity. But his understanding was actually profoundly biblical. His word *weightlessness* is precisely the opposite of the biblical word *glory*, and the deepest meaning of *glory* is not "radiance," but "reality." God alone has gravity and reality, and all that's distanced from God slowly loses them both. Idols are nothing—fictions, empty nothings. When cultures fall away from God, they too become weightless.

A hundred and fifty years later we can see Marx was generally wrong, but on that point he was right. A hundred years after Nietzsche, we can see the awful results of what he taught, but on that point he was right. If you look at what modernity has done to religion in general, to the gospel in particular, and to the church in the modernized parts of the world, you perhaps can see it as possibly the greatest threat the church has faced since apostolic times.

Think for a moment of the way modernity encircles individuals. And now it is encircling the globe. First, transcendence is cut off. Second, tradition is closed off. Third, the sense of totality and integration of faith in the whole of life is cramped and confined. And finally, even truth itself is corrupted into shallow sentiment.

We can see this in various situations. Consider any of the religions in the modern world. As yet, no great historic religion has flourished under the conditions of advanced modernity. If we examine the Christian church over 2000 years, we see the challenges of the seduction of gnosticism. Modernity is just as seductive as any gnosticism.

We can see similar challenges in the past in Nero and the Diacletians, and in the Oakland Repression. More people have died in the twentieth century, and more Christians in particular, than in any other century in human history. We can also look at modernity in terms of the Reformation. Protestants have long seen the contrast of the Reformation and what occurred before. But as we meet as Protestant evangelists in the 1980s, let us remember that today the prototypical charlatan in the modern world is no longer the medieval priest. We acknowledge with tears, it is the modern evangelist.

Looking towards the past, at the beginning of the twentieth century didn't they claim the evangelization of the world would be within this generation? A rallying cry, yes; reality, no. The impact of modernity on that movement knocked it off course.

Will we do better? Only if we look at the challenge of modernity straight in the eyes and overcome it by the power of Christ. We are on the threshold of winning the world at a time when the world has called into question what it means to reach anyone. And yet, as evangelicals, we could quite literally win the world and lose our own souls, and in some cases that has already happened.

The Three Revolutions

We need to define *modernization*. Many people incorrectly use it just as a fancy word for change and development. Others improperly use it as a word to describe new philosophical attacks.

Modernity or modernization is the result of three great revolutions in human experience: the oldest goes back to the fifteenth century—the capitalist revolution; the most important goes back to the late eighteenth century in England and France—the industrial, or technological revolution; and the third, and by far the least important, occurred in the late eighteenth and nineteenth centuries—the ideological revolutions.

Another way of saying it is that modernity is the result of a whole constellation of forces working together. The capitalist economy, the modern centralized bureaucratic state, the new industrial technology going everywhere, rapid population growth, the mass media, and globalization. Their tentacles reach to the farthest corners of the world.

Of course, modernity doesn't reach everywhere yet, so much of what I'm saying will not apply to some parts of the world. Different cultures with different values and different value systems refract the growth of modernity and development in different ways. There are great differences between England, the first to be industrialized, and the United States; and between the United States and Japan; and between Japan and a newly industrialized country such as Singapore. There are great differences but also enormous similarities—and tremendous challenges to the gospel.

There are some reminders, or checkpoints, concerning having missions in the modern world without having worldliness in modern missions. Our theme is the whole gospel by the whole church to the whole world. Sounds terrific, doesn't it? And it sounds easier with modernity. After all, with the modern information explosion, with modern technology, with media that are decentralized, that are cheap, that are accessible, more can be known and it can be known better and faster than ever before. That is a very misleading impression. It gives you the impression that the only problem lies between the *knows* and the *know-nots*. But that isn't the problem of modernity; the problem is much deeper. The media themselves have a message and there is a lag between information and comprehension, which is called the "meaning gap."

Unknowing and All Knowing

Modern overload of information leads to a state of unknowing. In many modernized parts of the world, the mentality is, "Happiness is a small circle." We want to know as little as we need, care as little as we can, and get by with it. Advertizing, television, and pop-culture have made a great shift in the way people experience life and understand the world. They shift from words to images, from action to spectacles, from exposition to entertainment, from truth to feeling. They shift from conviction to superficial sentiment. We see it in the church, and even, dare I say, here this week.

People can live in the midst of an explosion of information and know everything about the last twenty-four hours, and next to nothing about the last twenty-four years; all about the immediate, and nothing about the ultimate. Facts without a framework leads to knowledge without obedience, knowledge without wisdom, knowledge without action. At the same time, modernity leads in another direction, towards the state of "all knowing." In other words, the result of the modern explosion, the knowledge explosion, is that we now create a new class of people whose whole life and work is centered around ideas and symbols and information. This in turn has created a new mentality towards information—the ideal of instant total information. As Kant stated, we need to know in order to predict, in order to control. Know everything, predict everything, and control everything.

But if the state of unknowing before the Lord is irresponsible, this illusion of all knowing is a form of idolatry. The idea that we can rely on information to do all these things today has a thousand illusions built into it. It creates a professionalized, specialized class of people in every area: law, academia, missions. And certain common features appear across the world in this class. Expert knowledge begins to be pursued as an end in itself. Experts, understood only by other experts, talk more and more only with other experts. Expertise and professionalism cut experts off from ordinary people and creates a dependency of ordinary people on them—the new paternalism. And finally, it creates experts who live in their own worlds from consultation to congress, and don't touch ordinary reality. That's not an attack on what we're doing, but people fit into it, without thinking, and have fallen for it.

There are two dangers in living with modernity. The old fear was that modernity was against religion altogether. Actually, modernity is hostile only to religions that believe in transcendence and truth; and therefore it is hostile to the gospel.

The modern world creates a great chasm between the private world and the public world. The private world of home and clubs and associations and family and church, and the public world of work and government and Honda and Mitsubishi and the Pentagon and Whitehall, and so on. But religion only flourishes in the private world. Is that the Lordship of Christ?

The founder and first chairman of McDonald's was an evangelical. Before he died, he was interviewed by the *New York Times*. They asked him what he believed in. He said, "I believe in God, the family, and McDonald's. And when I get to the office, I reverse the order." I trust he was joking—the paper didn't say. But every day millions of modern Christians do what he was saying without realizing it. They say Christ is Lord of everything, but they live a part-time, compartmentalized faith.

Another danger is pluralization. Choice and change are the heart of modernity and they profoundly affect faith in many ways—commitment, for example. The increase in choice and change leads to a decrease in commitment, continuity, and conviction. We live in a supermarket—it's pick and choose. And the result in the modern church is a dilettantism and shallowness in terms of old doctrinal commitments. This produces apathy. The gospel flourishes when it's either-or, life or death, darkness or light. But in the modern world the very extension of choice leads to an evasion of choice. There's always another option.

Worst of all, pluralization is touching conversion. As Dr. Packer said last night, conversion is revolutionary because it's total, radical, lasting. But in the modern world, there are people who have been converted fifteen times in the last ten years! They're converted and reconverted and reconverted, or in Christian terms, born again and again and again. But that isn't funny. Even being born again in the conditions of modernized suburbia has become a shallow, sentimental experience that's no longer radical and life changing.

Yet modernity is an ideal reinforcement for two types of religion. First, modernity reinforces a generalized syncretism. Think of the shift back to state Shinto in Japan which replaced post-war democratic values. Think of the way that Europe is not so much post-Christian as pre-Christian. Think of the growth, even in the scientific West, of the New Age movement, or the semi-religious beliefs in environmentalism, feminism, and so on. The modernized world is an ideal breeding ground for syncretism.

And secondly, it is a reinforcement for a generalized secularism—a secular indifference to any religion or faith. It's not so much that religion is untrue, but that religion is utterly irrelevant to modern, secularized people.

All of our contact with any culture is in answer to two questions: How we view that culture and how we view the theology behind our approach. As the church engages extraordinarily powerful cultures, it has been most penetrating when two principles are characterized.

Christ Over All; Christ Against All

The first is the protagonist principle—Christ over all, and the key word is *all*. Modernity shatters that word *all*. We may say it, we may sing it, but we don't live it. The integration of faith needs to be with the whole of life: people witnessing at work, thinking creatively, consistently, coherently about everything they do—not only in the private world but the public world. As the great Dutch leader, Abraham Kuyper, said, there is not an inch of any sphere of life over which Christ the Lord does not say, "Mine." And that is what modernity makes so difficult.

The second principle is the antagonist principle—Christ over all, against all that will not obey him. Here the key word is *tension*. As we follow his Lordship, we are *in*, but we are not *of*. Faithful to him, we're foreign in the world. We are not conformed, we are transformed. The church in the modern world is so accommodating that there is almost no intellectual or social-critical tension left to challenge the cultures profoundly.

In the early seventies at Oxford, one of my professors who was an atheist said that by the end of the seventies in America the worldliest Christians would be the fundamentalists. That was hard to imagine because fundamentalism is world denying by definition. But by the late 1980s, that's the most obvious thing to anyone looking at the scene. Fundamentalism is more worldly in many of its applications, in its use of television, and a hundred other things, than the worldliest liberal you could ever discover.

I'm not against the modern world. I'm very grateful to live in the modern world. But more than that, the modern world represents extraordinary opportunities. What the Greek and the Roman roads were in the first century, what the printing presses and the sailing ships were at the time of the Reformation, modernity represents to us.

Modernity prompts cultural openness. It comes to traditional societies and shatters them and leaves them open. We all know the opportunities for God in societies and classes that have been dislocated from their old ways. When they're dislocated or economically oppressed, they're open. And we know from the early nineteenth century down to the movements of today, what an extraordinary thing it means to see traditional societies which were deeply closed opened up.

Not only that, totalitarianism is challenged to be more open. Totalitarianism, in a way, is the totalitarian enterprise of reconstituting the traditional world in the modern form, with the modern state, with the modern bureaucracy, with the modern technology, all under the party. But even totalitarianism is not immune to the decentralizing forces of modernization. And when we see the struggles in China and the Soviet Union, we realize it's not American ideas, democratic ideas, that have done it. Those who think that flatter themselves. It's modernity.

There are Big Macs in the world of Big Brother. Raisa Gorbachev uses American Express in Red Square. And it's not the writings of Thomas Jefferson. Modernity is the greatest opener of closed societies in history—which also means openness for the gospel.

If we look at Scripture, we see the dynamic of sin is that it always produces ironic results. Sin is never stable. It's the truth held in unrighteousness and it can never be stable. Modernity accelerates this tremendously. The ironies are all around us. For example, modern cities make people closer and lonelier and more alienated all at the same time. Modern lifestyles offer a do-it-yourself freedom that follows fad slavishly and ends in addictions. Modern consumer goods bring happiness closer and take joy further away. Anyone who knows our modern world knows that everywhere it is strewn with ironies, and each one is a "pigsty moment" in which prodigals come to the truth. Modernity destroys its own unbeliefs faster than anything in history.

Overcoming Modernity

There are two points of reliance in overcoming modernity. The first is our part, the second the Lord's. In terms of our part: prayer and fasting. This doesn't come naturally to me—I'd much rather speak on something else. The modern world has reduced fasting to a technique—a form of political or weight control. But we need to see what *Jesus* means by prayer and fasting. When the physical and spiritual are brought together with the purpose of being in touch with spiritual warfare, we see a repudiation of modernity at the heart of its grand lie. Modernity is the greatest example history has ever seen of "by bread alone"—by sex alone, by work alone, by money alone. "By bread alone" is written across modernity. We can see where Adam failed. He did not obey, he broke his fast and he ate. Our Lord sustained both his fast and his obedience, refused to accept the Devil's temptation, and overcame.

The second point of reliance in overcoming modernity is by the Word and the Spirit. Modernity is a world without windows. We live in a world where there's no way to break out because there's nothing left in modern philosophy to break in. The answer is the Word. While traveling around evangelicalism, I hear the cry of the poor, the cry of the dying, the cry of the imprisoned. And I hear the cry of a gasping Word because of evangelicals who say they believe it doesn't belong in preaching. In America, for instance: I know of no country in the world where the churches are so full and the sermons, by and large, are so empty. The loss of transcendence in preaching is horrifying. You can see this shift from Lausanne '74 to Manila '89 in the difference in styles of utterance. That's why Marxism declined. Why is the gospel different from Marxism? Marxism had no transcendental point of critique and could never be renewed. We have, however, the Word which breaks in.

It is my prayer that we will put modernity on our agenda for mission. And that we will analyze its impact at our local levels in our countries, our cities, our audiences, our ministries. And I pray that we will seek to reform the church where the impact of modernity has already been damaging. For example, the loss of truth; sweatless, long-distance evangelism without incarnation; technique without spiritual warfare; a reliance on images until they are coming out of our ears without a trust in the power of words in general, and the Word in particular. I pray we will also abandon our easy excuses.

We need to recover the only reality which will overcome modernity. What's the answer to Nietzsche's philosophy that when God dies for a culture they become weightless? The answer is the glory of God. The answer to Nietzsche is in Moses, in Exodus 33 when he faced the great crisis of his life, with problems all around him. He turned to the Lord and his deepest prayer was, "Lord show me your glory." He wanted all of God that a human being could behold because only that could see him through the problems that he faced.

Do we think we can win the world by A.D. 2000? Or are we overwhelmed by the thought of the task of winning the world at all? We need to face the world and then deliberately turn away and look to the Lord, the source of the only reality stronger than modernity—the only one with power able to overcome the colossus we face. Lord, show us your glory!

Social Concern and Evangelization

Vinay Samuel

Several participants have asked me to explain the difference between the two plenary themes of "Good News to the Poor" and "Social Concern and Evangelization." A clue is found in the table of contents of the electives offered at the Congress. "Good News to the Poor" is placed in the section on "The Whole World," which focuses on the poor as a group to be reached with the gospel. "Social Concern and Evangelization" is included in the section on "The Whole Gospel" and invites us to explore the meaning of the whole gospel.

Their selection reflects the assumptions of the Lausanne Covenant that: (*a*) faithfulness to the gospel includes a call to respond to the needs of the whole person and to all human needs; and (*b*) it is in this context of responding to the whole person that the whole gospel is uncovered and articulated.

Lausanne I affirmed the commitment of evangelicals to the whole gospel. It facilitated a worldwide movement of evangelicals willing to be shaped by the whole gospel, and willing to pay the price of living it out and being eager to share it. Despite some failure, they discovered its effectiveness. Their witness has been shared at this Congress.

We saw the moving and powerful video *The Challenge Before Us*. Luis Bush told the inspiring story of a servant of God who works in the dump city on the edge of Manila. Afterwards, the person sitting next to me remarked, "The problems are so overwhelming. Can we do anything?" Someone else asked, "Does such response to human need really work?"

I would like to present a humble response to such feelings and fears—the response of people who refuse to give up in spite of being overwhelmed by the greatness of the need. They persevered and found Christ empowering them. They looked at the people around them through the eyes of Jesus and sought to respond to their needs in his way. We will hear first from Joni Eareckson Tada, who works with disabled people in the United States:

Vinay Samuel is Coordinator of EFICOR Training Unit, Bangalore, India, and is a citizen of that country.

What Does the Gospel Have to Say to Disabled Persons?

Joni Eareckson Tada

If evangelism is taking the Good News of help to the helpless and hope to the hopeless, shouldn't we be concerned about taking it to the most helpless and hopeless? The gospel of Jesus must be accessible to all—even to a young man with cerebral palsy who cannot speak, who must sit twisted and bent in a wheelchair, and is relegated to a back bedroom.

"But I'm an evangelist," you might say. "I'm called to save people's souls, not to help them find medical care, fix wheelchairs, or build ramps. I'll leave such things to relief agencies who deal with special interest groups like the disabled."

But this is no special interest group. We're talking about the needs of a segment of people which cross all borders, nationalities, ethnic groups, and languages. Experts generally agree that 10 percent of the world population is disabled—over 516 million people. Disabilities do not discriminate—they touch the lives of everyone. For this reason, special attention is required to examine the relationship of our evangelistic efforts to the needs of disabled people in our world. To do so, let's begin with the parable of the banquet in Luke 14:12–14:

> Then Jesus said to his host, "When you give a luncheon or dinner, do not invite your friends, your brothers or relatives, or your rich neighbors; if you do, they may invite you back and so you will be repaid. But when you give a banquet, invite the poor, the crippled, the lame, the blind, and you will be blessed. Although they cannot repay you, you will be repaid at the resurrection of the righteous."

At first glance it might appear the Lord Jesus feels sorry for those "poor crippled folks who don't ever get invited out to fancy banquets. Why, we've got to *do* something to lend a hand to those helpless invalids!" Does this parable intend to foster a "pity-the-poor-unfortunate" attitude toward the helpless?

Who Are the Helpless?

In the Gospels, *all* people are presented as in need of help. In fact, the Pharisees in Luke 14 may not have realized it, but in many ways they were more helpless than the poor and disabled people whom they victimized by prejudice and discrimination.

Yet, there are factors which make physically disabled people "helpless" in a unique

---

Joni Eareckson Tada is founder and President of the Christian Fund for the Disabled, and of Joni and Friends, Inc. An author and painter, she is a citizen of the United States.

way; we cannot evangelize them without first being prepared to address the "helpless-ness" of their physical needs. No evangelistic outreach is possible to disabled people without dealing with their physical impairment in some way, because it is the presence of this impairment which defines "disabled people" as a group—whether it is a birth defect, disease or injury, mental handicaps, blindness, or deafness.

A More Serious Handicapping Condition

However, there are factors other than physical needs which must also be considered. The handicapping conditions of discrimination, fear, and pity imposed by other people must be removed. Disabled people have had to learn to play the part of the cowering and indebted in order to survive in the world of the physically capable. They are often treated as if they are children. These unjust social handicaps keep disabled people locked in dependency and poverty.

This is the real message behind Luke 14:12–14. The parable has less to do with "lending a hand to those helpless invalids," and more to do with landing a knockout blow to the religious and social hierarchy which perpetuated the institutionalized discrimination against disabled people.

How far was the Lord Jesus prepared to take his point? Look at the last verse in Luke 14:12–14. He closed his comments with the reminder that poor people might not be able to repay their hosts, but the hosts would, nevertheless, be repaid at the Resurrection.

Imagine what may have happened next. Jesus probably sat down, put his dinner napkin on his lap, and quietly picked up an *hors d'oeuvre*. Silence, no doubt, hung over the table as the Pharisees exchanged nervous glances. Scripture records what happened next: "When one of those at the table with him heard this, he said to Jesus, 'Blessed is the man who will eat at the feast in the kingdom of God'" (Luke 14:15).

Obviously, the Pharisee was so uncomfortable that he could only relate to a discussion about the Resurrection, certainly not to the topic of entertaining the poor or the disabled. It was as if the Pharisee was saying, "Ah, the Resurrection! I can't say that I follow your odd little ideas about dining with cripples, but I *do* agree with what you say about heaven. It's so comforting to know that everything will work out perfectly in the end." (See R. F. Capon, *The Parables of Grace*, [Grand Rapids, Mich.: Eerdmans, 1988], 13).

But Jesus was not about to let these religious leaders change the spiritual subject. Since they refused to get the point of the first parable, Jesus launched into the next parable of the great banquet in Luke 14:16–24—twice as convicting, three times as forceful. The implication at the close of this parable was that some of these leaders themselves would not even make the guest list: "I tell you, not one of those men who were invited will get a taste of my banquet" (Luke 14:24).

The Lord's message was and is striking, convicting, and foreboding. And the message is for Christian leaders today who might exclude the poor in evangelism, neglect the disabled in Christian service, or systematically avoid persons who are blind, deaf, or mentally or physically handicapped.

What Is Our Message to the Disabled?

We know that our message to people is the Good News that Jesus Christ died for their sins, was raised from the dead, and that as reigning Lord he now offers the forgiveness of sins and the liberating gift of the Spirit to all who repent and believe.

However, in our uneasiness in dealing with the physical needs of disabled people, we may be prone to spiritualize away a person's infirmity. In so doing, we may wrongly focus on the idea that our reigning Lord gives the liberating gift of miraculous healing to *all* those who pray in faith.

As a quadriplegic paralyzed from a diving accident, allow me to share from personal experience the message that truly liberates persons with disabilities. Shortly after I was injured, I read wonderful promises from Scripture such as 1 John 5:14, "This is the confidence we have in approaching God: that if we ask anything according to his will, he hears us."

I prayed in faith that God would hear me and heal me, but my fingers and toes still did not move. I went back to 1 John 5:14 and read it closer; that's when it struck me. It didn't say if we ask we will receive anything we think we might like or anything that would make life easier, but we will receive anything that's actually "according to his will."

But friends said to me, "Why in the world would it be God's will to deny a Christian's request for healing?" That's a good question, but for every verse seeming to guarantee positive answers to our prayers for an easier, happier, more healthy life, there are countless verses about the good things suffering can bring.

My disability helps take my mind off temporary enticements and forces me to think about God (Colossians 3:2). Trials have a way of making us rely on the Lord (2 Corinthians 1:9). Sometimes sickness serves as God's chastiser to wake us from our sin (1 Corinthians 11:29–30). And always God uses suffering to help us relate to others who hurt (2 Corinthians 1:3–4).

This is the message which truly liberates.

But in the meantime, do we abandon disabled Christians to wait for physical liberation in the next life where they will exchange their handicaps for glorified health?

Practical Helps

If we can't assure a disabled person of divine healing in the here and now, we can assure and comfort them with divine help. We need to present the gospel of Christ with one hand and help alleviate the pain with the other.

In your own church, or even when you hold an evangelistic meeting, make the gospel accessible to all. Find out where the disabled people are. Contact the local medical clinic to help locate and invite disabled people. Make certain they can easily gain entrance to your church building or evangelistic meeting. Provide space near the front for people who are hearing impaired, are in wheelchairs, or are on mats or stretchers. When possible, have a Christian interpreter sign your message for those who are deaf.

Greet these people in a friendly, non-condescending manner, and feel free to reach out and touch—your example will speak loudly to those watching. If a person is non-verbal, ask them for their sign for yes and no, then simply ask questions which have yes or no answers. For those who are deaf, communicate with a pencil and pad of paper. If a person is blind, there is no need to shout—they only want to know that you are speaking directly to them, so be sure to look at them when you speak. For mentally handicapped people, don't use "baby talk," but speak simply and clearly.

Enlist church members to help with transportation or even help a disabled person get out of bed and dressed. Encourage church members to help by pushing wheelchairs. Have them hold hymnals and Bibles for those who are paralyzed. This kind of sacrificial service will teach able-bodied Christians what normal Christian living is all about.

Advancing Christ's Gospel to People With Disabilities

The need is overwhelming. Of the more than 516 million people who are disabled in the world, over 42 million are reportedly blind and 294 million are deaf or hearing impaired. There are those disabled by civil strife in countries such as Nicaragua, Lebanon, Sri Lanka, Angola, Ireland, or the West Bank of Israel. World relief agencies remind us of the plight of disabled people further handicapped by famine, drought, or hurricane.

These people need the proclamation and service of the gospel. Other religions may aggravate the desperate circumstances of disabled people, viewing them as victims of fate, but only in Christ can a disabled person be viewed as an individual with worth and dignity. In fact, it is the "least of these brothers" (Matthew 25:40) and "those parts of the body that seem to be weaker " (1 Corinthians 12:22) who are to be given special places of honor.

Christians have the only message which vindicates God's good name as one who is supremely and benevolently sovereign over deformities and disease. Christians have the gospel message which joins the sighted and blind, hearing and deaf, intellectually capable and mentally handicapped. No other ministry better demonstrates Christ's heart of compassion than ministries to persons with disabilities. Helpless people can see themselves in the Man of Sorrows because he became one of them.

What Does the Parable of Luke 14 Say to You?

The Pharisee at the dinner with Jesus could not deal with the cold, hard reality which the Lord presented. He could only retreat into the safety of a spiritualized vision of the future that would demand nothing from him in the here and now.

Our attitudes would be corrected, our motivation focused, and our enthusiasm ignited if we truly understood the advantage of targeting evangelistic efforts toward those who are deemed helpless by the world. "Listen, my dear brothers: Has not God chosen those who are poor in the eyes of the world to be rich in faith and to inherit the kingdom he promised those who love him?" (James 2:5).

If we accept the call to be ministers of his Good News, we agree to be willing to take that message to all people—and that includes those with disabilities.

(VINAY SAMUEL, CONTINUED FROM PAGE 289)

Senator Salongas touched our consciences when he asked, "How can the Philippines have the reputation of being the only 'Christian' country in Asia and also be the most corrupt?"

South Africa represents a similar problem. It is a country with many who dearly love the Lord Jesus Christ, and a country which seeks to apply Christian laws. Yet South Africa is denying basic human rights to a majority of her population.

This is often a stumbling block to faith in Christ. Many Two-Thirds World Christians are convinced that black and white Christians in South Africa are in an ideal position to demonstrate to the whole world the wholeness which the gospel alone can bring. In my own country, I know the harvest will be plentiful once such wholeness is visible. Let's hear from Caesar Molebatsi, who works with young people in South Africa:

Reaching the Oppressed

Caesar Molebatsi

In discussing reaching the oppressed, I will center on those who are outside the church. Therefore, the terms *oppressed* and *suffering* are not referring to the suffering church in areas such as the Eastern bloc countries. Nor is *suffering* used to refer to the alleviation of human suffering as done by social workers. I will focus on those who are oppressed and suffering as a result of injustice perpetrated against them—where people have been rendered powerless by the powerful, poor by the wealthy, and without dignity by those who have not discovered the source of their own humanity.

These situations are generally contexts in which the church already exists. All too frequently, they are contexts in which the church is collaborating with the same powers which are responsible for the oppression.

We will look at what it means for evangelicals to engage in evangelism and mission among the oppressed. In order to do this, we need to define *oppression* and identify some of the major issues at hand. In the light of this, we need to ask the question: *What is the challenge to us as evangelists?*

Oppression and the Gospel

Oppression is the denial of rights, movement, self-expression, and self-fulfillment by those who have the power to do so. Oppression involves subjection and persecution by the unjust, or tyrannical use of force or authority.

From such a description, it is evident that the twentieth century is extremely oppressive! And when oppression has its moorings in religious traditions, evangelism and mission is even more difficult. We have seen this in church histories around the world, and we continue to see it today. South Africa is a case in point. A careful reading of the critiques which have come out of South Africa—such as the "Kairos Document" and the "Evangelical Witness in South Africa" (EWISA) document—clearly demonstrate the church is not only supportive of oppressive systems, but at times is an instigator and perpetrator of such evil. As a result, the credibility of these churches is severely undermined and mission and evangelism becomes impotent—a gospel empty of Good News. The gospel becomes an "oppressed gospel," instead of being a gospel *for* the oppressed.

Oppression is found on all levels: political, economic, and social. It is manifested

---

Caesar Molebatsi is Executive Director of Youth Alive Ministries in South Africa. He has been involved in evangelism, community development, and reconciliation work as a citizen of that country.

in relationships between the establishment and the people; the rich and the poor; the management and the union; the older generation and the youth; between male and female; the disabled and the physically fit; the acceptable and the outcasts; the church leadership and the laity.

There are two familiar faces of oppression. The one is helpless, hopeless, powerless, and shelterless. We see this in the Vietnamese "boat people"and the Mozambican refugees. These people have little strength to champion their cause.

The other face of oppression is militant, angry, and often bitter. These people say, "You have pushed us too far, and you will push us no further!" We see this face among the South African blacks and trade unionists, as well as in the Philippines. They have decided to take their destiny into their own hands.

These people have been sinned against on the basis of factors in which they had no choice (e.g., education, sex, color, ethnic or religious background). They become victims, suffering the consequences of the oppressors' designs.

One of the consequences of oppression is poverty. Though not all poverty is a result of oppression, there is an undeniable link between abject poverty and economic oppression. There is no doubt that the poverty in South Africa is planned poverty—it is no accident. Abject poverty refers to the approximately one billion people who live on less than $100 a year. Evangelicals need to be aware of this startling fact if they are to participate in the bringing of "Good News to the poor." Evangelists, whether they are from the First World or the Two-Thirds World, need to recognize they may well be perceived by the poor as being part of the oppressive and exploitative forces.

Evangelicals and the Gospel

There are two central factors which lie at the heart of the evangelicals' struggle with evangelism and mission among the oppressed:

1. When the evangelical church *supports oppressive structures,* they are seen as ambassadors of the oppressor, rather than as ambassadors of Christ. The evangelist or missionary represents the very problem that the oppressed would like to eradicate. Therefore, the message the evangelist brings cannot be seen as coming out of love.

2. We have not clearly understood that *concern for the oppressed* was always a critical dimension of God's dealing with his creation.

    The biblical concept of *shalom* is "wholeness, which includes the ideas of uninjuredness, totality or completeness, well-being, prosperity, harmony, and having a common will and a mutual responsibility" (Metzler), and "harmony with neighbors, justice, economic equality, and spiritual integrity" (Kraybill). Jesus' understanding of his own mission was, "He has anointed me to preach good news to the poor. He has sent me to proclaim freedom for the prisoners and recovery of sight for the blind, to release the oppressed, to proclaim the year of the Lord's favor" (Luke 4:18–19). The church and its mission needs to be seen clearly as having its source in such a God, as working out the same agenda, and as proclaiming the same message. Then the gospel will truly be seen as Good News for the oppressed.

When we choose to be faithful to such a call, it becomes clear that the focus of the

Lord's concern is *people*. All of our systems and structures should serve God's concern for humankind, not suppress it. It is the job of the evangelist and the missionary to address all forms of oppression—spiritual and structural—which hinder the wholeness which the Lord offers. We cannot be silent about evil structures if our message is Good News to the poor.

A thoroughly contextual gospel will give people a sense of dignity and a hope that their humanity will be redeemed. When context plays a key role in determining the things from which individuals must repent, then the evil in that society—including the oppressive structures or persons—will be identified. Faith in the Lord Jesus then leads to a realization of the ability of the Cross of Christ to bring change and redemption.

This is where hope lies. The Good News touches people in their individual situations of pain, suffering, and oppression. Redemption is transforming, because no area of a person's life is left untouched. When people have this hope, the gospel affirms them and gives them the ability and power to move forward, and the Holy Spirit gives the courage needed to do so.

If the gospel is contextual, it will be transforming; and, if it is transforming, then it will be empowering. It is not possible to impart an empowering gospel which is not contextual. We make transformation a mockery if we think it can occur apart from the context. When people recognize God's concern is holistic and that we are yoke-fellows with Jesus (Matthew 11:29), they are given a reason to believe in the things of the kingdom of God.

The Challenge to the Bearers of Good News

The kingdom of God is *his* kingdom, *his* rule, *his* authority. The kingdom deals with the future in that we will only experience the fullness of the kingdom when the King returns. But the kingdom also has a present dimension which we experience and participate in now. The kingdom's values are consistent with the character of the King, who cries, "For I, the Lord, love justice" (Isaiah 61:8).

"Of prime importance is Jesus' conviction that the kingdom is for the poor, and that the arrival of the kingdom is the beginning of a radical reversal in the world order, a restoration of justice." This does not mean those who are not poor are excluded from the kingdom. Rather, it tells us something of the *nature* of the kingdom. In the same way, the concept of the "preferential option for the poor," which came out of the Catholic Puebla Conference, does not mean there is no hope for the wealthy. On the contrary, it shows that our message in the mission and evangelism of the powerful is *determined by* what the Good News is for the poor.

There are six guiding principles for evangelicals as they take up the challenge of reaching the oppressed:

1. Our message must come out of a heart committed to the one thing most oppressed people desire: Justice.
2. We must never allow strategy to triumph over theology. The concern for growth, numbers, and results often leads to a lack of integrity to the gospel and unfaithfulness to the true biblical mandate.
3. We must never change our message during a crisis because when the crisis is over, we will have no message. One of the Chinese words for *crisis* is a combination of two words meaning "danger" and "opportunity."
4. Our evangelism and mission need to be incarnational if they are to be authentic. If God is on the side of justice, then our message and our lives need to reflect this.

5. We need to do a social analysis. This is essential if we are contextual (transforming and empowering) and it enables us to take a clear biblical stand when challenges arise.
6. It must be clear that we serve only one Master—the Lord. We have primary allegiance to only one King. In mission and evangelism, we proclaim freedom from tyranny and oppression on earth. Our cry is a political cry: the proclamation of a new King!

It is easy to bypass evangelizing the oppressed because of their resistance to the gospel. We need to remember that they are part of the whole world to which the whole gospel must be preached.

(VINAY SAMUEL, CONTINUED FROM PAGE 293)

Join me as we further explore the theme of seeing people through the eyes of Jesus. Our video presentation will share three stories of people who responded to human need around them, and describe what it means in practice to see people through the eyes of Jesus:

VIDEO PRESENTATION

Seeing People Through the Eyes of Jesus

Producers: Mary Fairbrother, Andrew Raynor, Steve Bynon, Mark Townsend and Duncan Murdoch

Vinay Samuel: To see people through the eyes of Jesus is to visualize how Jesus viewed people he ministered to, responding to their physical, social needs, and enabling them to enter into a personal relationship with God.

Jesus went up into the hills and sat down. Great crowds came to him, bringing him the blind, the lame, the crippled, and the dumb. They were laid at his feet and he healed them. The people were amazed, and praised the God of Israel. Seeing the crowd was hungry, Jesus was filled with compassion; and calling his disciples to him, he told them to feed the people.

Bishop Michael Lazario: Jesus' answer to the multitude was quite clear. He told his disciples to feed them. The preaching of the gospel goes hand in hand with the service of our fellow human beings.

Narrator: India! A rich country with many poor people. It has a deep religious awareness, and a great respect for family and community life. It has "Silicon valleys"; a larger film industry than Hollywood; and yet millions live in poverty, bonded labor, and illiteracy.

Colline Samuel is a director at the Divya Shanti Christian Association, based in the heart of the slums of Bangalor. The Association began as a Sunday school, under a tree. Now it is based in a building used as a school and a community center for homeless children, families, drug addicts, alcoholics, battered wives, and the physically disabled. Colline explains that it is only by this privileged involvement with people in the slums that she has gained the right to speak to them about Jesus.

Colline Samuel: The homeless people form a large part of our work. One family we visited had a ten-day-old baby sleeping on the streets, covered in newspaper, so we are struggling now with the government to see that homes are built for people; because we have discovered that, if the government give homes to a woman, they know that the woman is not going to move on. And the woman in our situation, in the lower income group, takes the full burden of the family. We formed this multipurpose women's cooperative, and we find that we are registering two hundred to five hundred of our lower income group so that they will then have a voice. One can thank God for being able to be involved in the life of people. When you pray with someone, you just can't go on praying for them. They have to be also made into the dignified human being that God wanted them to be. Hope gives people something beyond the situation in which they are.

Lazario: Jesus spent most of his ministry among the poor. By effective sign, he showed them where and how the kingdom was coming. And so he healed their diseases, he fed them, he gave them a sense of dignity and worth as children of God.

> True religion is this, to look after orphans and widows in distress, and to keep oneself from being polluted by the world.

Vinay Samuel: To understand an individual is to understand her community: the historical context, the social and economic structures which are a part in which this group exists, and so that the whole of life, not just its behavior, but its political life in relation to other groups, nationally and internationally; all that is taken into consideration, and especially its historical role.

Narrator: Peru! The jewel of the Andes. But beyond its breathtaking landscape is a country gripped by fear, mistrust, and disunity, which began in 1980 with the first public terrorist activities. This violence is met with the government's own violence of repression; armed forces flagrantly transgressing the laws they should defend. Pedro Arana, a pastor working in Peru, finds that a wholistic witness is both effective and essential. Fighting for justice and liberty, Christians like Pedro are admired, and Christ is thus shared with others.

Lazario: There is a kind of preaching that challenges the exploitation of the poor, and the gospel is not wholly preached if these things are not challenged. The most effective preaching is done by those who are serving their fellow human beings.

> The spirit of God is upon me, because he has chosen me to preach good news to the poor; to proclaim freedom to the prisoners, and recovery of sight to the blind. To release the oppressed and to proclaim the coming of the kingdom.

Vinay Samuel: And the whole of the thrust of the Bible in this area is that the kingdom of God is to be proclaimed to the poor, but it is to be proclaimed not only by word of mouth, but by what we do.

Narrator: Kenya is a beautiful country. Home to a mix of city-dwelling sophisticates, urban slum-dwellers, nomads and hard-working farmers, it has one of the largest growing churches in the world. Its enviable political stability is marred by tribal rivalry and economic problems, the cause of much corruption and human rights abuse. Despite victimization, Bishop David Gitari speaks out against this abuse, actively involved in feeding the poor, providing health care, and agricultural development. Hand in hand with this evangelism finds a responsive crowd, as people see Christ's work in action.

Bishop David Gitari: Here in Kenya, we have been able to receive many Ugandan refugees. We try to help and encourage them, and make them feel at home until such time as the situation in their country improves. We have also been very much involved in food distribution during times of famine. We have not wanted to make a commitment to Christianity a condition of receiving food, asserting that anyone, irrespective of their religion, should be fed. As a result, many people came to admire the spirit in which this work was done, and they wanted to know how and why we were spending so much time trying to help them. As a result, we had a great number of people committing their lives to Christ. In Luke 2:52 it says that Christ grew in wisdom, in stature, and in favor with God and humankind. And so he grew in four dimensions: mental, physical, spiritual, and social. And so accordingly, we aim here to look to the whole person. The needs of the whole, both the body and soul, should be met.

Colline Samuel: You just can't go on praying with someone. They have to be also made into the kind of dignified human being that God wanted them to be.

Gitari: Many people came to admire the spirit in which the work was done. They wanted to know how and why we were spending so much time trying to help them. As a result, we had a great number of them committing their lives to Jesus Christ.

Pedro: To see through the eyes of Jesus is to see in every human being a possibility.

Narrator: Seeing people through Jesus' eyes shows us a ministry that is mobile and effective, sensitive to each individual, every situation. A shifting interdependence needs to be respected between evangelism and an immediate, compassionate, sacrificial response to human need.

(VINAY SAMUEL, CONTINUED FROM PAGE 297)

Christian social concern is motivated by seeing people as Jesus saw them. It requires us to experience the life of Jesus in our own lives and to be shaped by his Word, the Bible, until we begin to see people through his eyes. This is also the starting point of Christian social concern—our unconditional commitment to experience the fullness of the life, attitudes, and teachings of the Lord.

It then follows that we will obey the call to share the gospel in Christ's own way.

Like Jesus, we should go to those in need and not expect them to come to us. We can identify with them by sharing our lives with them. This is not just a proposal for a few brave spirits: It is a necessary part of following Christ's own way.

The way of Jesus is the way of the Cross—the way of a suffering servant; of denying our rights (even luxuries); and accepting rebuke, pain, and suffering on behalf of others. How else can the whole gospel be shared with integrity?

Jesus' strategy was not of conquest but of love. He chose to draw people to himself, rather than drag or entice them. To draw them, he had to stand with them; he had to bear the cross and wear the crown of thorns; he had to become poor so that they might become rich. Any authentic strategy to share the whole gospel must reflect love rather than conquest.

The way of Jesus was also to empower the needy. Made whole in body, mind, and spirit, they were enabled and released into the world. This empowerment was first the offer of a new identity as daughters and sons of God. It was given freely by sheer grace. Imagine its powerful impact. They were people who long considered themselves cursed by God. Many poor, oppressed, and disabled people today still feel that way. Some were people who saw themselves as subhuman (the lepers, the outcasts) and were treated as such. It still happens today. All such people heard the offer of a new identity, experienced it, and were released into the world.

This new identity was not merely a label without content. The content was Jesus' power in the Spirit—the power of a new community where people shared what they had; the power of a hope that God is acting to transform the world and will fully restore it when Jesus returns in glory.

The gospel enables God's children not to remain as victims of their circumstances or disabilities, but work in partnership with God, in the power of his Spirit, to address their circumstances and overcome their disabilities. The gospel empowers people to find God's grace not just sufficient to take them to heaven but more than sufficient to address poverty, injustice, oppression, ill health, illiteracy, and physical disability. That is the gospel—the whole gospel which empowers people.

The way of Christ is also the way of the small flock. Jesus called and empowered the little flock—not the wise and powerful. The small flock were to be his ambassadors. It will not be the powerful, the wealthy of the world, however Christian or committed they be, who will be the main players in sharing the whole gospel with the majority of the unreached. They will likely be support staff.

It is the little flock whom Jesus chooses still. It is the foolish and weak, the despised and lowly of the world, whom Jesus calls to be his ambassadors. Jesus' power to transform is revealed and released through them. The roots of the Pentecostal movement at the turn of the century were among such people.

I am of the non-poor. I have a room in the Philippine Plaza Hotel and use a credit card. I try to minister to the poor and live among them. But it is the poor who often teach me what the whole gospel is all about—something which even Cambridge University never taught me.

We have choices before us: Will we commit ourselves to seeing people as Jesus sees them? Will we dare to share the gospel in Christ's way? Practically, it will mean that we need to identify with the needy groups God is calling us to; to begin the process of ministering to them; to learn how to empower them; to release them to change their situations; and by this we will be empowered ourselves. Anything less will not be a witness to the whole gospel.

VIDEO PRESENTATION

The Uniqueness of Christ

Producer: Peter Darg

Narrator: Who was this man who walked among the nation of Israel two thousand years ago? His birth was unique. He was different from every other prophet or teacher. His father was God and his blood was pure enough to atone for the sins of all mankind. Abraham was known as the friend of God; Moses as the servant of God; but at his baptism, this man was declared to be the Son of God.

He is unique in his power to heal. His death was unique. No other man even claimed to lay down his life for all mankind. His resurrection was unique. While the graves of other prophets and religious leaders can still be venerated, his tomb in Jerusalem stands empty as a unique witness to his victory over death and his promise to come again.

But who is Jesus to the billions of frightened, lonely, hungry, indifferent, and confused people living today?

Woman: I don't know.

Punk youth: I don't think he exists.

Man: He was a historical character who lived in Jerusalem.

Hippie: Who is he? He's supposed to be the Son of God.

Young Woman: I'm not very religious.

Man: A lot of people seem to think he's real.

Woman: He was a very good man.

Man: I'm a Christian. He's the Son of God. It's as simple as that.

Narrator: But *is* it as simple as that? The world has many other gods to divert attention from the truth of our Christian witness. Television and sports heroes, gurus and cults, humanism and materialism all compete to lure untold millions away from the one true God we proclaim. In today's world, Christians aren't the only ones offering answers to life's problems. Other voices are making spiritual promises, too.

[*Setting:* Muslim children studying the Koran.]

Chau Wee Hian: This is not a scene from the Middle East. These Moslem youngsters are studying the Koran in a western European mosque. It's not uncommon in cities such as Bradford, England, to find former church buildings now converted into centers for Moslem evangelism. And new mosques are being opened every month.

Narrator: One man who has insight into the serious, contemporary challenges to Christianity in England and around the world is the Reverend John Stott, pastor emeritus of London's famous evangelical church, All Souls.

[Stott comments on his travels in Africa and Asia to discuss the challenge of other faiths to Christianity and how he has seen them grow. He stresses how the message of the church must be clear and uncompromising to proclaim Jesus as Lord.]

Narrator: Vienna, Austria, is a center of inspiring cathedrals and culture. Like most other European cities, its churches have sadly, in many cases, become only museums to a faith that has failed to reach much of today's generation.

[*Setting:* A street in Vienna.]

Woman: Religion doesn't interest me.

Young man: Why not let others believe whatever they want?

Man: Who says Christianity is the only way to salvation?

Young man: I don't care about religion at all.

[*Setting:* Spain]

Narrator: This colorful church pageant in Spain commemorates a time when the witness of Christianity was defended on the battlefield. But the historic event, like the historic faith it symbolizes, has become almost a myth—a distant memory. Our combat in the twentieth century doesn't take place on physical battlefields; so just what shall we do to proclaim the uniqueness of Jesus?

The Uniqueness of Christ

David Wells

Our modern world and modern theology make it hard to believe in the uniqueness of Christ. His uniqueness is subverted by evangelicals and non-evangelicals alike. Why is it that today the church is often in retreat from what Christians believed historically?

From the Nicene Creed in the fourth century, to Chalcedon, to the Reformation and post-Reformation confessions, Christ has been seen as unique. He was the only incarnation of God in human flesh, who died for us on the cross. He did what no one else could do or has done: He bore our sins and rose again for our justification. There was no one else like him in his time, and there is no one else like him in ours. He was and is unique— without rival, peer, equal, or comparison. He is in a category by himself. He is God—the incarnate and sovereign Lord, without whom we would still be hopeless orphans in a cold and indifferent world. Men and women across the ages have worshipped him, served him, suffered for him, and sometimes died for him. He can call forth our highest praise, our deepest commitment, our greatest service because of who he is and what he has done.

Why, then, are so many people today not only embarrassed by this, but think it is wrong. Some even proceed to build their Christian lives without him.

There are cultural factors which, in different parts of the world and in different ways, make belief in Christ's uniqueness difficult. For example:

- In many cultures in the East, the uniqueness of Christ sounds either arrogant or ignorant. They think Christ's uniqueness is a claim made only by the ignorant, who do not know how much of God they could experience outside of Christ; or by the arrogant, who do not realize how much they do not know.
- To some in the Third World, whose memories of colonialism are neither diminished nor happy, the claim of Christ's uniqueness can be misunderstood. It can be heard as a claim for the uniqueness of the West, or it can be misunderstood as a claim for the uniqueness of Western Christian religion. The uniqueness of Christ does not imply the superiority of the West and the inferiority of other cultures, nor is it saying Christian activities are unique. The activities of Christian believing, worshipping, and serving are not unique as activities; the uniqueness lies in *whom* Christians believe, in whose living

David F. Wells is professor of Historical and Systematic Theology at Gordon-Conwell Theological Seminary, South Hamilton, Massachusetts. Born in Zimbabwe, Dr. Wells is a citizen of Great Britain.

presence they gather, whose grace and forgiveness they know, and whose Spirit empowers them. It is Christ who is unique, not the West, or the followers who worship him.

- In the West, Christ's uniqueness often fares no better than in the East, though for different reasons. In the West, secularism robs every religious claim of its finality because secularism is the attitude that God and the supernatural are not meaningful to everyday life. Secularists may say that they believe God exists, but then they look the other way. They are practical atheists. Wherever secularism has triumphed, and it has triumphed over broad areas of Western life, there are truth claims, but no truth; there are beliefs, but nothing to believe in; there are hymns, but no one to sing to. The world has become a stage whose only actors are human and whose Director has vanished.

These and other cultural forces make it difficult to believe in Christ's uniqueness. They make us sound foolish; we may feel embarrassed. But they are not the potent challengers to Christ's uniqueness operating in the theological sphere. There are others far more damaging. The theological challenge is, in fact, many different challenges so we must speak in generalizations.

There has been an accumulation of damage to the credibility of the biblical account, and especially to the Gospels. If it is the case, as it is frequently argued today, that the Gospels tell only of the faith of the early Christians, and has little or nothing of the life, acts, and teaching of Jesus, then with one stroke, his uniqueness has been made inaccessible. He may have been unique, but we have little record of what that uniqueness meant.

This leads to the next step, which is to cut Christ loose from the historical Jesus. Christ takes on an identity which is quite different from what the Gospel record of Jesus is like. A striking example of this is Raimundo Panikkar's argument that Christ is encountered unknown in Hinduism, that his grace is channeled to people through its sacraments.

The results are with us on every side. Norman Pittenger developed a process theology in which Jesus was merely a model of the kind of incarnation that takes place throughout humanity. Liberation theologians, like Juan Segundo, see Christ in today's political struggles, though these events have no cognitive connection with the historical Jesus. Karl Rahner saw Christ so universally present in human life that he spoke of "anonymous Christians," those who were infused by Christ's grace though they knew nothing of him. Wilfred Smith said that there can no longer be any such thing as idolatry since every worshiper, regardless of the object of worship, brings to the act some transcendent sense. Hans Kung declared, "We seem to be witnessing the slow awakening of global ecumenical consciousness." He added that ecumenism "should not be limited to the community of the Christian churches; it must include the community of the great religions."

Common to all these examples is that Jesus can be bypassed because God can be known directly. God can be known directly because he is found beneath the human spirit working within our history, breaking through our consciousness. Jesus, then, is unique only in the sense that we see in him clearly what we sense in ourselves only dimly.

An immediate consequence of this is seen on the liberal Protestant side as well as in Roman Catholicism, where a profound reappraisal of the relationship between

Christian faith and the other religions is underway. It has taken two forms: the Second Vatican Council was tempted by the one form, and the World Council of Churches is now struggling with the other.

One form argues that, though Christian faith is most true, other religions are not untrue and, indeed, they can mediate salvation. The Second Vatican Council allowed that atheists could be saved because Christ's grace infused them even though cognitively they denied his existence (see David F. Wells, *The Search for Salvation* [Downers Grove, Ill.: InterVarsity Press, 1978], 141-162).

Another form, recently advocated by John Hick in his *Myth of Christian Uniqueness,* says all knowledge is relative and all religions are unique to their own context, so no one can say one religion is true and another false.

In either form, the result is the same: Christ is neither central nor necessary to a knowledge of God.

The Reply

The challenge historic Christian faith now faces is not a new temptation. The apostles' world was as filled with gods as ours is with religious claims. We need to reestablish what they had: A deep and unshakable sense that the biblical gospel is true, and that truth matters!

World Spirituality

A common assumption is that there is a world spirituality, regardless of the religious forms it takes on the surface. Beneath all those forms is spirituality, and through this spirituality and within it, is God himself. Jesus Christ is not necessary for us to gain access to it.

Human beings were created as spiritual beings: made for God, made in his image, made to want to know spiritual reality. Human spirituality has remained stubbornly resistant to every assault, whether by the Marxists with their ideological materialism, or by Western secularism with its insatiable appetite for consumption. It cannot be extinguished by dictatorships of the Left or Right who brutalize their captive citizens. The only way human spirituality is destroyed is when the person is killed or, as happens in Western and Marxist countries, its potential is snuffed out when millions of unborn children are discarded each year through abortion. Human beings remain spiritual beings whose hunger for spiritual reality defies all of the misguided attempts either at crushing it or feeding it.

However, human spirituality is not redemptive—even when it takes on religious forms. This is obvious, for example, when we see Paul encountering it in his three missionary sermons (Acts 13:16–41; 14:14–18; 17:22–34). In each case, he recognized that those to whom he spoke, whether Jew or Gentile, were religious. But this spirituality was not recognized as an alternative to Christ!

In the past, God had let the Gentiles go their own way. "In the past God overlooked such ignorance" (Acts 17:30). But through Christ sin has been dealt with decisively, and God now "commands all people everywhere to repent" (Acts 17:30). God "has set a day when he will judge the world with justice by the man he has appointed" (Acts 17:31). That man is Jesus Christ.

Why is human spirituality not redemptive itself? Why is Jesus Christ necessary for redemption? The answer is that human spirituality is inundated with sin. Evil is a reality in this world and it lives through this spirituality, even taking on religious forms, and over it hangs the judgment of God. That is why Jesus died—the just for the unjust.

These truths are an integral part of biblical thought. They have held such a central place in Christian thinking over so many centuries that we have to ask ourselves who has deceived us to think it were otherwise? Is the New Testament vague about this? No, the New Testament is abundantly clear!

Its focus is unremittingly on the Cross and on Christ's work of substitution on the Cross. The New Testament never says he was made hungry for us, or weary for us, or that he thirsted for us, or was made homeless for us, even though this is certainly true. It *does* say repeatedly that he died for us, bore our sin, and he did for us in his death what we could never do in our lives: He bore and satisfied the righteous judgment of God. Why would he have done this if God were already benignly resident in the human race and if through our own spirituality we could bypass Christ in a direct union with God?

Why, then, is the uniqueness of Christ treated so casually in the evangelical world? If Christ is the *only* case of God in human flesh doing for us what he alone could do on the Cross, then why is it we sometimes treat him as a junior partner in the evangelistic enterprise or, worse still, market him in ways that are simply not honest.

The United States is the largest publisher of Christian books. Its products are disseminated throughout the world. In a recent study, it was found that about 80 percent are books catering to the self, to the life of the self, to the needs of the self. In other words, they are like the huge body of secular literature in America. Both secular and Christian literature propose techniques for self-help and tricks for self-conquest. Both markets assume that the fundamental goal in life is to be a whole, happy person.

I am shocked that we have so smoothly, so easily, coupled Christ to this secular interest, and then cast our evangelism in the terms of this new metaphor. If we can do so well with all of the techniques of self-mastery from secular literature, why do we need Christ at all? What we are seeing in the evangelical world is a *subversion* of Christ, one driven not by theology but by popular psychology.

The experience of affluence in the United States puts health care and the good life within reach of many people. When you enjoy these things long enough, you begin to think they are rights—that life would be unthinkable without them. It was not unnatural that some evangelicals, marketing the gospel from America to other parts of the world, would include in the message of salvation through Christ, the promise both of health and wealth.

They have taken this message into some of the poorest countries of the Third World. Countries where disease is rampant and countries whose economies are in shambles. And through Christ, a promise is made that with belief, health and wealth will follow. The disillusionment created among the poor who believe these promises is as devastating as the false theologies I described in the beginning which deny his uniqueness. We are being cruel and heartless to preach this in the shanty towns of the world.

What, then, *does* it mean to believe in Christ's uniqueness in a world that is religiously pluralistic? It means that we have a gospel that cannot be bartered, boiled down, or minimized in order to accommodate those who do not like it. Christ is not up for sale. His gospel is not just one among many items in the market place of religious commerce. It is not a commodity we peddle, nor is it an item we can negotiate about.

He is not one among many possibilities; he is not one among many paths; he is not one among many teachers; and his gospel is not one among many gospels. "Salvation is found in no one else," Peter said. "For there is no other name under heaven given to men by which we must be saved" (Acts 4:12). There is no other name, no other path, no other gospel, no other way of salvation than the salvation which God has wrought through his Son.

What, then, does it mean to affirm the uniqueness, necessity, and centrality of Christ today?

It does *not* mean that men and women of other faiths can be treated insensitively or their beliefs confronted carelessly. Their civil right to disagree with the gospel must be respected. Christ's uniqueness does not give license to use methods of evangelism that are psychologically coercive or manipulative, or which take advantage of the lonely, the poor, the uneducated, and the frightened. If the gospel is about truth, then the reasons for proclaiming it, as well as our methods, *must* have complete integrity.

The Uniqueness of Christ

Ulrich Parzany

It is not enough merely to state and proclaim the uniqueness of Christ: We must be able to give reasons. The more the uniqueness of Christ is being questioned, the more carefully we must explain the reasons.

Reasoning is necessary even within the fellowship of Christians. For only when the uniqueness of Jesus is the center of the church will the task of world evangelization be fulfilled by the church. World evangelization depends on the certainty, "Salvation is found in no one else, for there is no other name under heaven given to men by which we must be saved" (Acts 4:12).

Reasons must be given to those who have not yet accepted Jesus Christ as Lord and Savior. The proclamation of the uniqueness of Christ is the loving invitation which we have to extend in the name of the living God. Yet the question must be asked: *Why do we invite people to follow Jesus?* Adequate reason can only be rooted in the Holy Scriptures which are the document of God's revelation in Jesus Christ.

It is impossible to develop a comprehensive Christology in this short discussion. The uniqueness of Christ proves itself in all aspects of his being and doing. I will just mention one important aspect which has been neglected in Christian teaching and in proclaiming the gospel.

Jesus—the Son of Man

In the four Gospels, Jesus often refers to himself as the "Son of Man." Many Christians mistakenly interpret this title as a description of the humbleness of Christ. But the expression "Son of Man" comes from Daniel 7:13–14:

> In my vision at night I looked, and there before me was one like a son of man, coming with the clouds of heaven. He approached the Ancient of Days and was led into his presence. He was given authority, glory and sovereign power; all peoples, nations and men of every language worshipped him. His dominion is an everlasting dominion that will not pass away, and his kingdom is one that will never be destroyed.

The Son of Man is the Ruler and Judge of the world, as authorized by God. The meaning of the New Testament title "Son of Man" is only properly understood when we add, "Judge and Lord of the world."

Ulrich Parzany is the National General Secretary of the YMCA in the Federal Republic of Germany and a citizen of that country.

Surprisingly, in the New Testament the title "Son of Man" is used in most cases when Jesus speaks about himself. The expression occurs sixty-nine times in the first three Gospels and only when Jesus speaks about himself. It occurs twelve times in the gospel of John. Eleven of these are times when Jesus speaks about himself. Once was when listeners to Jesus quoted him (John 12:34).

Jesus claimed to be the incarnate Judge of the world. He spoke about his coming for the final judgment (Matthew 19:28; 25:31–46; Luke 17:22–30). Already during his lifetime on earth he had the authority to forgive sins—an authority which only God has (Mark 2:10).

It is the uniqueness of Christ that at the same time he is doing the work of the Son of Man (Daniel 7) and the work of the servant of God (Isaiah 53). "For even the Son of Man did not come to be served, but to serve, and to give his life as a ransom for many" (Mark 10:45). In response to Peter's confession, Jesus announces the suffering of the Son of Man (Mark 8:29–31). Although he is Lord of Lords, his basic human need for housing has not been satisfied, "Foxes have holes and birds of the air have nests, but the Son of Man has no place to lay his head" (Luke 9:58).

The uniqueness of Christ is that in him the Lord and Judge of the world has become a human being. The question, "Who is Jesus?" leads to discovering his uniqueness. The uniqueness of what he said, what he did, and what happened to him in suffering, crucifixion, and resurrection is to be derived from the uniqueness of who he is.

Why is the death of Jesus the only way to reconcile men with God? The uniqueness of his death is not in how he died. Thousands were crucified by the Romans with the same brutality and cruelty. The uniqueness of his death is in who he is. The suffering Lord and Judge of the world takes the place of the lost sinner. The Judge himself suffers the consequences of the rebellion and enmity of man against God.

It is impossible for us to claim another person's biography and history. Guilt is not something which we can throw away like a dirty shirt. Rebellion against God is the nature of life. And only the Creator, the Lord and the Judge of the world, is able to break through the barriers of space and time in order to take our sinful lives and crucify them on the Cross, and finish the whole case.

Because of the uniqueness of Christ I can confess, "I have been crucified with Christ and I no longer live, but Christ lives in me. The life I live in the body, I live by faith in the Son of God, who loved me and gave himself for me" (Galatians 2:20).

Criticism

The proclamation of the uniqueness of Christ has been criticized and we need to deal with some aspects of this criticism. Christians who proclaim the uniqueness of Christ have been accused of having a subjective, narrow-minded, and one-sided theological view. Some people feel that in order to improve the greater community of people of different religions, the proclamation of the uniqueness of Christ should be expressed more cautiously. It is more acceptable if the subjective view is kept personal. The uniqueness of Christ is said to be a view of a believer, but not a statement which is obligatory for all people.

Nevertheless, the importance and the meaning of life and death of Jesus Christ does not depend on human judgment, but on God's judgment. By the Resurrection, God has proved, validated, and confirmed that Jesus is the one key figure of the world. Even the disciples thought the death of Jesus disproved his claim. But the risen Lord has overcome the doubts of his disciples and proved himself to be Lord of Lords.

By proclaiming the uniqueness of Christ, we are repeatedly challenged by this truth.

The confession of the first Christians was *Kyrios Jesus,* "Jesus is Lord." It does not only mean, "Jesus is my Lord," Jesus is proclaimed as Lord of Lords. Because Jesus has risen from death, we do not have the right to reduce the uniqueness of Christ merely to a personal, subjective perception.

Intolerance and Fanaticism

Has the proclamation of the uniqueness of Christ led to intolerance and fanaticism against people who believe differently? Has it led even to violence? As Christians, we need to repent of what has happened during the history of the church. The Christian witness of the uniqueness of Christ has been misused and discredited. Christians cannot claim to be the only ones who own the truth. This is an attitude of pride—a superiority complex that is not appropriate for disciples of Jesus.

But Jesus Christ himself *is* the unique way of salvation:

> He is the image of the invisible God, the firstborn over all creation. For by him all things were created: . . . All things were created by him and for him. He is before all things, and in him all things hold together. And he is the head of the body, the church; he is the beginning and the firstborn from among the dead, so that in everything he might have the supremacy (Colossians 1:15–18).

Therefore, only Jesus has been entitled to offer himself as God's absolute truth—for all mankind, but against all who want to compete with him. It is part of his uniqueness that Jesus prayed for his enemies and died on behalf of them. In Jesus, God proves how dearly he loves his enemies.

Those who believe and proclaim the uniqueness of Christ, must realize that to excuse fanaticism or to permit violence in the name of Christianity is to betray Jesus Christ. Proclamation of the uniqueness of Christ must be combined with openness to dialogue and love towards everyone—even if they refuse the gospel of Jesus.

The Joint Action for Justice, Peace, and Integrity of Creation

Facing overwhelming problems of today's world, many people believe that actions for justice, peace, and integrity of creation are of the highest priority. Therefore, it may seem more important to them to cooperate with people of other faiths than to proclaim Jesus Christ as the unique Savior.

When we believe in the uniqueness of Christ, we also realize that God loves and sustains his world and wants to save it through Jesus. The risen Lord Jesus assures us that God will create the new heaven and the new earth. Jesus Christ is God's guarantee of the new world. Therefore, a follower of Jesus should lovingly and carefully work for justice, for peace, and for the integrity of the creation which God has entrusted to us. There are many fields in daily life where Christians can cooperate with people of other faiths without denying Jesus, but cooperation must never lead to compromising the uniqueness of Christ.

Our work in evangelism and in social action for justice, peace, and integrity of creation will not be in vain because Jesus has overcome death (1 Corinthians 15:58). Only Jesus will be able to complete this work. He will create the new world of perfect peace and justice, not us. As we proclaim the uniqueness of Jesus Christ, we need to abandon all utopian concepts of self-redemption. We can no longer believe in the human ability to create a paradise. Due to human selfishness and pride the situation of the world will deteriorate (Matthew 24). Because we trust in the unique Lord Jesus Christ, we will proclaim the gospel of salvation and offer signs of hope because and until Jesus comes.

Trying to Integrate Jesus

In the process of evangelization, we do not just experience either acceptance or refusal of the gospel. There are also many attempts to integrate Jesus into a gallery of religious leaders, prophets, and deities. Jesus then becomes a part of a larger system. He is worshiped along with others. This is also a refusal of the unique and saving offer of Jesus Christ.

In this process, the name of Jesus is being used deceptively. People deny his right to be their Lord by politely putting him alongside other venerable persons or institutions. Such syncretistic integration immunizes people against the true gospel of Jesus Christ as the unique Savior. In Europe today, Jesus appears in a gallery of deities alongside the worshiped god of money, the god of sex, the god of security, the god of health and success.

How far have we accepted the integration of Jesus into the gallery of deities in our own respective cultures? The danger is that we become blind and insensitive to a process of creeping integration. At times we become anesthetized by the approval we receive for proclaiming a type of Jesus who appeases the desires to present Jesus as the God of happiness and success, or as a prophet of the modern, Western "health-and-wealth" cult. These are not only dangers outside the church, but they influence Christians inside the church as well.

Dedicating Ourselves to the Unique Lord Jesus

It is vital to defend the gospel of the unique Christ against all kinds of darkening and misleading interpretations. A deformed gospel no longer has rescuing power.

The biggest temptation comes from within ourselves, not from outside. As long as we worship Jesus in his uniqueness, as long as we surrender our lives to the supreme and loving Lord, we will be faithful messengers of the gospel. Christology must not only shape our thoughts but also our lives. People will easily recognize contradictions between our strong theological statements and our compromising Christian lifestyles.

In February 1988, I met our beloved brother, the late Bishop Festo Kivengere, in a Nairobi hospital. After prayer, I asked him to give me a word which I could take to the young people in my country who had listened to him many times. He bowed his head for a few seconds, then looked up and quoted Paul from his letter to the Philippians, " . . . That now as always Christ will be exalted in my body, whether by life or by death. For to me, to live is Christ and to die is gain" (Philippians 1:20–21).

May our life and death be a credible testimony to the uniqueness of Christ. Let us join the apostle Paul as he puts himself and his ministry of evangelization in the light of the unique Lord Jesus:

> For we must all appear before the judgment seat of Christ, that each one may receive what is due him for the things done while in the body, whether good or bad. Since, then, we know what it is to fear the Lord, we try to persuade men (2 Corinthians 5:10–11).

"UNIQUENESS OF CHRIST" TESTIMONY

Sue Perlman

I was brought up in a traditional Jewish family in Brooklyn, New York. We observed the dietary laws, rested on the Sabbath, and celebrated all Jewish holidays. Most importantly, we held steadfastly to the belief that we were born Jews and we would die Jews. We understood that, at best, we were only tolerated by the non-Jewish world.

I can still remember my first exposure to Christianity. I was told by one of my Christian playmates, "I learned in church that you killed Jesus!" Even though I pleaded with her that I would not kill anybody, let alone this Jesus person, she remained unconvinced. Later, when I experienced Christianity in art, literature, and film, Jesus' appearance seemed unbelievable—looking variously Scandinavian, Asian, or African but seldom like a Middle Eastern Jew!

I agreed with Christians that Jesus was a real person—maybe even a prophet—but not *God!* Jews believe in one, true God. How could Christians say that God is one and at the same time three?

Christians said Jesus is the son of God, sort of a "God, junior" it seemed to me. As a Jew I had been taught that one should not make images of deity and one should not worship anyone other than the almighty. So I saw their worship of Jesus as idolatrous. Certainly, I was *not* going to violate any of the Ten Commandments and consider worshiping this "gentile God!"

Saved? *I* needed to be saved? Saved by who and from what? Jesus could save me? But I was Jewish. Why did I need Jesus? I reasoned that, as Jews, we *were* the chosen people. We were *automatically* related to God! No, being Jewish and believing in Jesus would be like being a carnivorous vegetarian!

Then one day I met a stranger on a street corner in New York City who shattered my misconceptions about the person of Christ. He was the first person to really communicate the gospel to me. He told about a Jesus who was not the king of the Norwegians, but the king of Israel—not Jehovah Junior but very God of very God. He told me that Jesus was not one of *many* paths to God but the *only* way, the *only one* who could forgive my sin—the sin of all mankind!

I reacted in the customary Jewish fashion: "That's a very narrow-minded point of view," I said.

He agreed with me and added, "But it is true!" And something in me knew that I couldn't just dismiss Jesus.

I was invited to attend a church service and I went. Christians began praying for me from that night on, and my defenses started crumbling. I didn't want it to be true that Jesus was the Messiah. I would have been happy to find out that I could find salvation by following the Jewish religion. I would have preferred to believe that my sins were forgiven each year on Yom Kippur, the Day of Atonement. I would *much* rather have believed that my relatives who had died without accepting Christ were in heaven instead of experiencing an eternity apart from God.

But truth isn't always convenient or comfortable. I realized that to deny the truth would be senseless. Jesus *did* die for my sins and he *did* rise from the dead. I, a Jew,

---

Susan Perlman is Assistant Executive Director of Jews for Jesus. She is on the International Steering Committee for Lausanne's Consultation on Jewish Evangelism.

embraced Jesus, the king of the Jews, as my Lord and Savior and, so, became a completed Jew, in the tradition of Peter, Paul, and Priscilla!

Communication and Evangelization

Viggo Sogaard

Communication and Evangelism! Evangelism is communication! It is the communication of the Good News of Jesus Christ to those who do not yet follow him.

Unfortunately, the word *communication* has different connotations. For some, it means fund-raising, for others it is public relations or advertising. For many, communications people are the media people, in particular those working with the mass media. But communication is a subject that is of equal importance for pastors and missionaries, laymen and clergymen, broadcasters and development specialists.

This morning, we will focus on the technology and the use of media in effective evangelism. Some will argue that it is not possible to do so. We would respond: If you are attempting to reach the world, you cannot afford not to seriously consider communication principles and media use. The topic will be presented through videos, a paper by Philemon Choi, some comments and an interview. We will start with the original title of this session, Communication Technology.

Viggo Sogaard is a communications specialist and missionary and a citizen of Denmark. He is a member of both the Communications Working Group and the Strategy Working Group and is the Director of the European Lausanne Committee for World Evangelization.

VIDEO PRESENTATION

Communications Technology and World Evangelization

Producers: Wayne Craig, Cal Bombay
Writers: Tom Houston, Bill Thatcher

Let Us Now Praise Communications Technology

Publishing is being revolutionized by computer technology: from computer graphics to desk top publishing, to simultaneous newspaper production in different locations at once. Add to this, computer assisted translations. Bible agencies lead the way in its application to thousands of languages, and aim to increase their 120 million annual distribution of Bibles and New Testaments.

In the field of sound, radio reception is rapidly increasing, with receivers becoming cheaper and smaller all the time. Cassettes of greater quality and smaller size are being used for every kind of purpose. Cassettes and compact discs are replacing the record for the reproduction of music in a booming industry.

Satellite communications are multiplying. People with relatively simple computers can communicate with their friends half a world away. Personal computers are becoming more and more common with seven hundred million computers in use today. Computers and computer research, which used to require a whole roomful of equipment, can now be done on one's lap.

Films and television multiply space and are extended in their viewing by cable and videos in astonishing numbers. India is now producing more films than Hollywood. Through all of this, information is exploding at the astonishing rate of six hundred million words per hour—beyond the power to keep up.

Let Us Now See the Corruption of Communications Technology

All of this communicating power is in the hands of ordinary sinful mortals who are using it with increasing abandon for their own selfish purposes, and often even for demonic ends.

Much of the output from Hollywood, and its counterparts in other countries, is pouring into the world a portrayal of sexual permissiveness that is undermining the family in every country, regardless of its family tradition. From this field spring the idols, heroes, heroines, and role models of our generation.

Politics is influenced and dominated by what the television can show and say. News reporting is sometimes biased by the sensational and prurient. In many Third World countries, there is some strict censorship and manipulation of the media that distorts truth in ideological directions.

It is tempting to think we are in a losing battle and things can only get worse. No doubt they will get worse for some people, but not necessarily for most if we lay hold of the truth of the gospel and the power of the Spirit. All this tends to deter us from involvement with the media. It seems as though we cannot get near to it without being contaminated by the corrupt use of media by others.

Let Us Now Collect Our Wits About Communications Technology

Let us recognize the media for what they are. They are primarily extension and reinforcement instruments; they can only take and extend what we have and what we are. And they can never be a suitable substitute for the church. With the exception of countries where access to the gospel is denied, our main media thrust has to be linked with our churches where the vertical side of communications is fostered in prayer and fellowship.

The challenge before us is to use these tools to express the life which can be found in God. We must help each other in this by sharing both our successes and failures. We must be willing to ask hard questions, otherwise we will be used by the media rather than using the media.

What are we saying to people through our publishing activities? We publish sixty-five thousand new titles on Christian subjects each year. Why are there so many? And why are there usually such small numbers of each title? Are we writing books which have interest to people outside of our immediate constituency?

What are we saying to people through our radio and TV programs? These tend to be an extension of the letter and the spirit of what we do. If that is vital, then our media will be vital. If it is of poor quality, undisciplined, and unprofessional, that will be extended also.

What are we saying to people through our use of traditional media, such as drama, dance, music, and fine arts? In some cases, our very silence is revealing. The church often swings between the two poles of acceptance and rejection of these media tools. Yet, these traditional media, perhaps more than any other, touch the heart of many cultures.

There is no disputing that today we have unparalleled opportunities through the use of media to touch the lives of many millions of people with the Good News of the gospel. But we must reject the simplistic perspective which views the building of transmitters or the printing of tracts as the magical way to reach the world for Christ.

We do indeed face a challenge today. We must work out our strategy together, not in isolation. Will we choose to mimic the methods and techniques the world offers us in media use? Or will we choose to begin with who we *are* and let that direct the quality of what we *do*.

If in this way, we collect our wits about communication technology, then we will have strong tools for evangelism which will complement, rather than compete, with the local church in its mission.

Communication Technology and Its Impact on the World

Philemon Choi

The communication media are having a tremendous impact on the way people think and live, both for good and for evil. We need to understand this impact so we can fight the negative aspects and utilize the positive ones.

On September 11–15, 1988, a distinguished group of Christian communicators met in Wetzlar, West Germany, to consider the role played by the media in evangelism. They drafted an important "Consultation Statement on Media and Evangelism."

In that Consultation Statement, the centrality of proclamation was stressed, and they emphasized that proclamation needs to be accompanied by presence. The dimension of incarnation was discussed at great length, and they concluded that without incarnation in some form, evangelism is impossible. Evangelism was looked at as a process, and by increasing the sensitivity to an audience, it was less likely that communicators would simply "unload" irrelevant and inappropriate messages or materials upon the audience. Finally, they cautioned that the dimension of worldviews was more than a concern for conflicts at the cognitive level; it involved the clash of competing powers, the conflict of the kingdom of darkness and the kingdom of light.

They went further than merely identifying these four dimensions of evangelism, and attempted to scrutinize them in terms of five key criteria:

- Faithfulness to Scripture
- Contribution to the local church
- Effectiveness—however it could be measured
- Integrity and openness
- Culture and artistic form

As a Christian communicator, I would like to express my gratitude to these fellow warriors for the Lord for laying down some crucial foundations as we study the role of communication technology in the evangelization of a rapidly changing world.

Communication Technology and the Polarization of the World

Futurologists like Alvin Toffler and John Naisbitt vividly portray a world being ushered into the information era by modern technology. Most of these authors look at the world from the perspective of the first world, and they sometimes neglect the further

---

Philemon Choi is General Secretary of Breakthrough Ministries in Hong Kong and is a citizen of Hong Kong.

polarization of the world in terms of economy, values, and lifestyles.

As we attempt to tackle the issue of the Christian response to communication technology and the polarization of the world, we are indebted to the studies of the futurologists and the writings of Christian leaders who have a futuristic outlook.

The Haves and Have-nots

All futurologists are conscious of the "north/south economic inequality." Developments in modern technology make little contribution in terms of economic equality. In reality, there seems to be further polarization of the world into the "haves" and "have-nots." Communication technology, both in terms of hardware and software, is still the monopoly of the first world, that is why the most sophisticated media productions still come from the world economic powers: the United States of America and Japan. Some Asian countries have voiced their resentment towards such modern versions of imperialism in terms of American and Japanese cultures.

Christian organizations who can afford to use modern communication technology still cluster in the first world. As we attempt to proclaim Christ through the modern media (such as communication, satellites, videotapes, or discs), it is crucial that the "haves" involve the "have-nots" in the areas of strategizing, planning, production, and distribution. This would avoid the trap of insensitivity to culture, resulting in poor reception and even rejection.

When modern communication technology has its glamour and power in terms of touching millions at a time, we should not forget that in the Two-Thirds World, many people still consider radios a luxury, and videocassettes and laserdiscs are just myths. We cannot undermine the crucial role of the basic form of communication through the printed page. Yet, in China, two hundred million people are illiterate, so the printed page is meaningless to them. Still, there is no substitute for personal communications when we keep in mind the deprived situations of the "have-nots," which constitute a significant proportion of the unreached peoples in the world.

The Global Village and Segmentalized Cultures

Since the term *global village* was coined, we have been under the impression that the entire world is within our reach. This is true in terms of transportation and communication technology. However, when we think about evangelism, we cannot define people as being reached merely by geographical proximity or accessibility of communication technology. There are other barriers to evangelism that we have to overcome such as racial, ethnic, linguistic, cultural, political, and ethical. We have a paradoxical situation: the people of the world are closer than ever before, yet are more alienated at the same time. We can think in terms of global economics and global politics, but we cannot assume the emergence of a global culture.

With the coming of "the third wave," people's consumer habits tend to be more segmentalized and individualized. Members of the same family view different television programs through cable networks or via satellites. The "pop cultures" of the seventies and eighties are gradually being replaced by the "segmentalized cultures" of the nineties. While mass media still has a role in reaching millions through common denominators, we have to be aware of the trend towards segmentalized media, group media, and even individualized media (each person can read his individualized edition of newspaper each day).

We are deceiving ourselves if we think the task of world evangelization is simplified because of the advancement of communication technology. Statistically, it may be impressive to claim we have proclaimed Christ through the satellite to so many nations and so many millions of people. But are we really communicating, are we being understood correctly? We should not refrain from using communication tools to help us reach millions at a time, but we should also attempt to understand each segmentalized culture carefully in order to bridge the invisible gaps of communication. This cannot be accomplished by a few communication specialists, we need the input of anthropologists, sociologists, theologians, missiologists, and above all, people that live among that particular culture. No wonder Jesus did not communicate the gospel through the trumpets of the angels from the clouds, he chose to live among men in flesh and blood.

As Christian communicators of the gospel, we have to be willing to live among other people. We cannot forget the fact that there are many different peoples in the same global village.

Multiple Option and Real Choice

John Naisbitt identified one of the world trends as the "either/or—multiple option." Modern communication technology has promised the media-consumers a wide range of options. The cable network can easily transmit forty channels of television programs to a household, and the same family can pick up several hundred international television broadcasts via satellites.

However, some TV viewers find there is no real choice among the eye-dazzling parade of options. The television producers only provide them with more of the same. In Hong Kong, for example, the newspaper stands offer the option of over sixty newspapers and over four hundred magazines, radio broadcasters offer their programs through wire channels, and there are four channels for television broadcast. The coming cable network promises to deliver up to forty channels of television programs to the subscribers. In this ocean of mass communication, a Christian presence has been hardly visible until recent years.

The church in Hong Kong has gradually risen to the challenge of communicating the Christian message to the non-Christian world through the mass media. Christian magazines and books are beginning to appear in the newspaper stands and chain stores, and Christian journalists and broadcasters are beginning to make their impact felt through the print media as well as electronic media. The Christian voice is finally being heard outside the four walls of the churches.

Because we are aware of the impact of the media on the way people think and live, we are convinced that the gospel does offer a true alternative, a real choice—the church as a whole cannot afford to give up this strategic battlefront. This implies greater commitment in terms of human and financial resources, training a high caliber of professionals with the ability to master modern communication technology and marketing skills, and production and distribution of good quality media products which can stand the test of the highly competitive secular market.

If we are not willing to pay the price to offer the people a real choice in the midst of multiple options promised by communication technology, then the task of evangelization will be made doubly hard as we present the gospel to them through other means. Evangelism does not take place in a cultural vacuum, the cultural mandate and the evangelistic mandate cannot be dichotomized.

Information and Insight

In the information age, people will be flooded with information, resulting in information overload and indigestion. The picture is not merely one of information explosion, there will be information confusion and pollution.

David McKenna proposed a Christian response, a *megatruth,* which he defines as "the application of the unchanging Word of God to the new and changing information through the work of the discerning Spirit of Truth." People are not satisfied with information alone, they thirst for insight, and megatruth implies that Christians should be able to offer insight by his Spirit.

In the information era, we cannot reduce the task of evangelization to a simple formula, and attempt to present the gospel to everyone in the world in a simplistic form. God's truth has the power to penetrate the barriers of all forms of human knowledge. This is far more complicated than the mastery of communication technology—it involves the integrated efforts of theologians, philosophers, sociologists, psychologists, anthropologists, economists, and lawyers. The day of monopoly of truth by any single discipline is gone. New insights are possible through multi-disciplinary studies, with the Word of God as the basic foundation, and the Holy Spirit as the guiding light.

In the information age, apologetics and evangelism take on new dimensions and reach new heights. With the help of communication technology, the task of proclamation can reach a much wider scope. However, we have to remember that breadth is no substitute for depth.

High Tech and High Touch

Another megatrend identified by John Naisbitt is, "The more high technology around us, the more the need for human touch."

Communication technology is most deceptive in this area. By means of manipulation of the audience's emotions, through the charisma of the performer, and assisted by all kinds of interactive forms, the media can give the consumer a sensation of intimate touch. However, this "pseudotouch" evaporates once the television is turned off, or at the moment you walk out of the cinema hall.

Some Christian communicators are trapped in the game of pseudotouch. The tears of a TV evangelist is no substitute for weeping with the wounded, and the "electronic church" is no substitute for true Christian community life.

Communication through mass media has the strength of offering information and insight to a large audience. It can arouse interest, challenge the mind, and even lead to decision. At the same time, we have to acknowledge the limitations of the communication technology. It cannot offer genuine human touch. Personal communication is more effective in terms of persuasion, decision, and individual problem-solving. There is no real relationship except through real-life interaction.

There is a great need to integrate mass communication and interpersonal communication in the realm of evangelism. High-tech and high-touch should not be mutually exclusive; they complement one another. Christian media organizations need to work closely with the local churches, so each can capitalize on the strength of the other. United in Christ, we can offer a genuine Christian touch to an increasingly technological world.

Eros Defiled and Redeemed Sexuality

John Stott has identified sexuality as an important contemporary issue. John White has defined the problem as "eros defiled." James Dobson has championed the Christian cause in the battle against widespread hard and soft pornography. With the progress in communication technology and the deregulation of media censorship, it is impossible to stop the wildfire of pornography, which has spread worldwide.

Perversion of human sexuality has become a major cause of the disintegration of families, the breakdown of entire cultures, and the corruption of the human soul. Adolescents are deceived by the deceptive sense of intimacy, and adults are addicted to the pursuit of ecstasy.

Christians have been playing the role of police in this whole area of pornography. Efforts in the study of the theology of sexuality are very scarce, and comparatively little is being done in the area of public sex education. As police, Christians play the role of social conscience. If Christians can be more actively involved in sex education, utilizing the modern communication technology, we can offer redemptive measures in the area of human sexuality.

Evangelism involves the redemption of the whole man. There are born-again Christians who need to be redeemed in the area of sexuality. Christian communicators cannot afford to neglect this dimension of the human soul.

Pseudospirituality and True Spirituality

God is Spirit, and man created in his image has an ultimate need which can only be met by a true spiritual encounter with God.

Evangelism is a spiritual battle, which involves encounter with powers and principalities. In recent years, the New Age movement and various religions are using communication technology to promote their cause, and they attempt to offer the audiences all forms of counterfeit spiritual experiences. The pursuit of the occult and all kinds of pseudospirituality has become a worldwide phenomenon.

This is an age that demands spiritual insight and discernment. We need to expose the deceptiveness of the spiritual counterfeits, and we have to avoid falling into the trap of offering pseudospiritual experiences through the mass media. Such experiences may amount to nothing more than manipulation of emotions. In a positive way, the communication technology can be used to point the audience to the only true Way. This requires qualities in the communicator which go beyond techniques. The spirituality of the Christian communicator is far more important that his communication skills. We cannot underestimate the power of communication technology. It changes the patterns of our thinking and living.

When used properly in the hands of truly spiritual Christian communicators, communication technology can be effective tools as we endeavor to fulfill the cultural and evangelistic mandates.

We cannot overemphasize the centrality of incarnation: Christian communicators have to live among the people they attempt to reach, and Christian media productions have to penetrate the secular market in order to offer people a real choice. In our attempt to fulfill the Great Commission, we need to recognize the complementary roles of mass communication and interpersonal communications. There is an urgent need for parachurch media organizations to join hands with the local churches on this strategic battlefront!

VIDEO PRESENTATION

Radio: The Universal Medium

Producer: Christine Rylko
Writer: Phill Butler

Narrator: What medium is powerful enough to penetrate war zones, cross impassable mountain ranges, go through iron and bamboo curtains, speak to hundreds of thousands of people at one time, and yet come to rest intimately in the heart of one individual? Radio.

Since the 1930s, radio has been a major evangelistic tool, used worldwide by God's people to share the Good News. Today there are over nine thousand hours of Christian programming being broadcast internationally each week on radio ELWA, FEBC, Trans World Radio, HCJB, and many others. Many Christian leaders will attest to the fact that radio is unique among mass media.

Keith Fraser-Smith: Radio, for the listener, is cheap, accessible, and private.

Dave Adams: Radio is a surprisingly intimate medium. It can reach people in extremely personal circumstances. It can talk to them when no one else is listening, and they can listen in privacy. They don't even have to admit they are listening to the message of the radio.

Narrator: In India, this young woman lived in a village of high-caste Hindus. They were hostile to Christians, and no one came to tell her about the gospel.

Indian Woman: I began listening to the radio, and in 1983, began corresponding with the people who made the programs. One day, my little brother, Baboo, got lost. We searched and searched but could not find him. I prayed to Jesus and felt that in four days my little brother, Baboo, would return. Lo and behold, on the fourth day, he did come back! My faith in Jesus was greatly strengthened.

Narrator: Despite radio's successful past, its most productive days as a strategic part of world evangelism may still be ahead. Christian leaders around the world are discovering that radio is their most effective evangelistic tool in reaching the two-thirds of our world's unreached people groups that live in countries closed to traditional missionary activity.

Henri Aoun: There are no boundaries for the radio. It flows in freely to homes all over closed nations.

Ab: Where you have thousands and millions of people, radio can find those who are interested in the gospel.

Narrator: The next story from Latin America is true and speaks for itself. A dejected young evangelist was given a radio in 1967. He started listening to Christian broadcasts and was inspired.

Evangelist: I found I could get more radios, and began giving them to people who had placed their faith in Jesus Christ. Many of these people were at a great distance, so I could not get back to each of them to disciple them. That's where listening to the radio programs became so valuable. God began to bless this effort. Around many of these radios, God built little churches. Today there are about eighty-two churches in my area.

Narrator: When broadcasters worked together to beam radio broadcasts into the Soviet Union, the result was scores of radio listening hours for Soviet men and women, and there were life-changing results.

Dr. Robert Bowman: The radio broadcasts came not only from FEBC in the Philippines, Saipan, and Korea, but also from Trans World Radio in Guam. Today, there are areas, European areas like Monte Carlo, Trans World, and HCJB from Quito, Ecuador, broadcasting into the Soviet Union.
Today, there are almost forty thousand isolated "radio churches" scattered across the Soviet Union which have been formed as a result of these radio broadcasts.

Narrator: While radio has been a primary factor in church growth in many countries, it is generally acknowledged that radio is most effective when linked with other evangelism tools such as correspondence, literature, Bible correspondence courses, and personal follow-up contact.

Ab: Radio is a key to open the door for people to hear about the gospel.

David Adams: Yet radio is often weak at the moment of conversion. It's almost like the new birth needs a "midwife," and radio is not a good midwife. It requires that individual to be alongside another individual, as they talk together, and then come to prayer in that moment of conversion.

Narrator: This young believer was living in a Muslim country, when he first heard a Christian radio program and started corresponding.

Amar: But the radio and the correspondence courses weren't enough. I needed to have fellowship with other believers and help to understand Christian doctrine, which I didn't understand as people do when they grow up in a Christian environment.

Narrator: Radio's effective partnering with other forms of evangelistic outreach is being repeated around the world such as in this report from Southern Asia.

Asian Radio Listener: We had never heard about Jesus until one day when we heard a radio broadcast in Manila. We had many questions, so my friend and I walked to an

Anglican mission to try to find someone willing to answer our questions. After four or five visits, we found a lot of people were interested in Jesus. Now, nineteen families have become Christians and about sixty people were baptized.

Narrator: To ensure that radio will achieve its maximum potential as a bearer of the Good News, Christian leaders are calling for new programs and ideas.

Henri Aoun: We produced a special drama that listeners loved. We're getting hundreds of letters from all over the Arab world from people who benefitted and learned a lot from those programs, simply because they were in story and drama form.

Dave Adams: Radio is a flexible medium. It's able to be responsive to the circumstances of a group of people. We've had examples where we've been able to change our message quickly. When there's been a natural disaster in a region, for example, within hours we can be talking about the immediate problems, helping people through those difficulties, and be relating the gospel of Christ to the crisis.

Narrator: But more than anything else, this powerful technology needs native-language speakers from unreached people groups. The power of hearing a radio broadcast in your own language is undeniable. As a convert from a closed country testifies:

Mohand: I speak French, and I understand English. Still, it was something marvelous when God seemed to "lower himself" to speak my language.

Paul Freed: People must speak to their own people. They know their people, they can reach their people. Therefore, nationals are absolutely essential for radio ministry.

Narrator: In addition to the critical need for native speakers from unreached people groups, producing radio programming depends on people of many talents.

Phill Butler: Probably the biggest single problem is finding men and women from the language group who are committed to Christ and who can be trained to do the behind-the-scenes work of producing, airing, writing, and recording radio programs.

Narrator: Radio is a powerful technology. It is even more irresistible when used by the grace of the Holy Spirit, broadcasting in languages that are music to a native listener's ears, and combined with other evangelism tools for a complete presentation of the gospel of Jesus Christ.

Phill Butler: As was said of Esther, she came to the kingdom for such a time as this. It may be that broadcasting, despite the fact that it has been used for five or six decades, possibly has come to the kingdom for such a time as this.

(VIGGO SOGAARD, CONTINUED FROM PAGE 314)

Yes, broadcasting is with us, ready to be used. And so are many other media. We could mention magazines such as *Breakthrough* in Hong Kong and *Step* in Africa.

The question for you and me is not one of saying yes or no to media, but it is one of *how* to use media effectively in the service of evangelization. We must admit that in spite of enormous resources committed to the use of media, we have often seen very few results. Let us not avoid the problems, but let us face the challenges and respond to them.

One of the challenges facing us today is the question of an increasingly non-reading world. The number of illiterates alone is staggering and the number is increasing daily. We are not winning the war against illiteracy. India alone has up to six hundred million non-readers. Bangladesh about one hundred million. Even though we see effective use of printed materials, less than half the world's population can be reached this way. And most of the unevangelized people are among the non-readers.

This is a tremendous challenge to Bible Societies, for example. How do you translate for the non-reader. Maybe we have to learn from the early church that did not have a New Testament, in a time when it has been estimated that only 5 percent of the people were literate. This is also a challenge for the radio people we just met on the video. Most radio organizations use letters as follow-up, but if you cannot write, how do you respond? Radio broadcasters have no choice but to come up with effective follow-up systems that do not require the skills of literacy.

But, let us not just think of the so-called Third World. We want to re-evangelize Europe. In a country like Denmark that claims 100 percent literacy, recent research shows that 22 percent never read or write anything, and you can probably add an equal number who only read headings and pictures. They spend their time in front of videos and television. And most of the programs available on video is at an intelligence level that, to use John Stott's words, "stupidifies" people. We could add, video is probably one of the most destructive elements in our society today. But, if we are to reach these groups, we have to learn how such media can be used effectively in evangelism.

It may be that our main problem as media people has been the exclusion of the local church in strategy development, planning, and programming. But, it is the local church that must give credibility to the message. Let us look at one example of how this can be done. The Cinema Leo ministry in Kenya has movie vans traveling all over the country, showing films. They decided to make their ministry church centered, so when the cinema vans arrive in a community, it is the local church leaders who give the welcome and pray with the seekers.

(A VIDEO PRESENTATION OF THE CINEMA LEO MINISTRY WAS SHOWN AT THIS POINT.)

So the movie vans come as servants of the local churches.

There are four key questions that I often use as my guide in planning effective use of media in evangelism (but they are, of course, of equal importance to the pastor preparing a sermon): The questions are,

1. Who is my listener?
2. Where is my listener?
3. What are the needs of my listener?
4. How can I meet the needs of my listener?

We so often take the audience for granted. We sit in studios and in offices, making programs and sermons for people we do not know. We don't really have the right to produce programs for people whose needs we have not discovered.

When we start with these four questions, we soon realize that they cannot be answered without the help of the local church. I realize the challenge this is to radio and other mass media organizations, but this does not make it less important. I realize that it may seem cheaper and easier to just copy a television program produced in the United States than to produce another one in the Philippines, but we may be seriously mistaken if we are to judge the expense in relation to the number of Filipino viewers and the effectiveness of the program.

If the church is to function as a base for our strategies and communicational activities, ownership, at least felt ownership, must be shared with the church. Often such an approach will turn our attention to the smaller media such as audio cassettes. Of course the use of such media is less prestigious. It sounds much better to be a radio or television producer than a cassette producer, even though cassettes and other smaller media may prove to be of equal or greater value to the church.

One day I was in the village of Sriperampudur in South India with an evaluation team from World Vision. A crowd had gathered around us and a woman came up to us with a young child on her arm. She proudly showed the child to us, telling us how beautiful and healthy he was. "But," she said, "this child has always been sick and weak. Then we heard this tape about water, and it was mentioned that we could pray to Jesus. So we prayed for our child, and see what Jesus has done."

Franklin Joseph works for World Vision India. He has been in charge of the development of this audio cassette project.

Interview: Viggo Sogaard and Franklin Joseph

Viggo Sogaard: Franklin Joseph works for World Vision India. World Vision is a relief and development organization. Franklin has been in charge of the audiocassette project. Why did you start a cassette project?

Franklin: The people we try to help have many problems. Mothers bring their sick children for medical attention; the youth come looking for employment; and others are addicted to alcohol. They come looking for solutions to many problems. We have programs—educational and health-oriented—that attempt to meet their physical needs. But we felt the need to integrate the gospel into our social programs. The people had needs that were social, educational, and spiritual.

Viggo: You have developed quite an extensive strategy. Will you tell us about that?

Franklin: It all started with your visit to us. You asked the simple question, "Who is the audience? Where are they? What are their needs? How best can you meet their needs?" So we began our program by answering these questions.

Viggo: Did you know your audience?

Franklin: To get to know our audience and their needs, I went to live with them. By living closely with them, I sometimes discovered beliefs that were causing some of their medical problems. For example, I found that most of the women think that diarrhea in children is caused by evil spirits. They tie talismans around the child's hand to combat the disease, but they never bother to give the needed medicine.

Viggo: I understand you were a shepherd for a few days?

Franklin: Yes, before producing the cassette, "Good Shepherd," I wanted to spend time with a shepherd to experience some of his feelings and beliefs.

Viggo: Is the local church involved also?

Franklin: Yes. Up in corn hills, a tribal area, the Baptist church is involved in the production, distribution, and follow-up.

Viggo: Could you tell us what's on a program? What does it sound like?

Franklin: Oh, yes, please listen. (An audiocassette is played.)

Viggo: Please describe what's happening?

Franklin: It's about creation of God.

Viggo: What are some of the other programs?

Franklin: We have programs on the evil of drinking, salvation, and eternal life.

Viggo: Would you describe an incident from your ministry?

Franklin: We have many stories to tell, but I'll share a favorite. Up in corn hills, we played the cassette on the evils of drinking. The local village leader came and listened to that cassette. He was so moved that he called all the village people together to listen to the cassette on the evils of drinking. Afterwards, they decided to stop brewing liquor and to heavily fine anyone caught breaking the law. Now almost the whole village is turning to Jesus Christ.

Viggo: What challenge do you have for us?

Franklin: The challenge for us is to unite modern media with personal, caring relationships. That way people are attracted and challenged to Christian action. It is said that anything that holds the attention of the people leads them to act.

(VIGGO SOGAARD, CONTINUED FROM PAGE 326)

Thank you, Franklin. So, how can media be used to reach people with the Good News and to build them in the faith and spiritual maturity? Is it possible to harness the mass media to effective evangelism? It can be done. We certainly do not want to worship technology, nor do we want to reject media because of the corruption and misuse we see.

As we close this session, let me just remind all of us that the master communicator was Jesus himself. He started with the needs and interests of his listeners. From there he led them into a discovery of how those needs could be met and new life in Jesus could be a reality.

In John 3 we have the conversation between Jesus and Nicodemus. The listener—Nicodemus—was a highly educated man, a philosopher, a man with status, someone who would be embarrassed if seen talking alone with Jesus. Jesus showed his acceptance and empathy by sacrificing his sleep to meet with Nicodemus on the roof when nobody would see them. The very language Jesus used shows respect for Nicodemus and an understanding of his needs. Jesus aptly entered into that frame of reference and from there led Nicodemus into new discoveries. Jesus dealt with the questions and assumptions which Nicodemus had.

The language used in the following chapter, John 4, with the Samaritan woman is quite different. The Samaritan woman was an outcast the Jews did not even treat as a human being. But Jesus bowed down and spoke with her, treating her as a person, building up her self-esteem. His language was appropriate, and he quickly led her on to discover the truth.

Let us, like Jesus, be sensitive to the diverse cultural and social backgrounds of the people we are trying to reach. The woman in South India I mentioned earlier had listened to a simple tape, telling about clean water, and relating that to the teachings of Jesus. As a result, dysentery had dropped in the village from 35 to 15 percent, and within a few months, forty to fifty families were attending Bible studies and prayer meetings. Communication principles had been followed carefully, research been done, strategy worked out, holistic tapes produced, and communication technology was used effectively to proclaim the kingdom of God to the poor.

Sacrifice

Eva Burrows

Lausanne II was designed to lead us to a more effective evangelization of the whole world in obedience to Christ's Great Commission. Underlying this program are basic emphases on "urgency, sacrifice, and unity." In the preparatory material, I often noted such phrases as "the costliness of the task," "the demands of love," and "the total mission of sacrificial service."

We are simply and solemnly asking, "If the world is to be evangelized, if men and women of all nations are to be brought into the kingdom of God, what kind of sacrifice will be needed? What is the price to be paid? What will it cost us?"

The Cost of Identifying With Christ

There is no other place to begin our quest than at the cross of Christ, where by his sacrifice he became the Redeemer of the world. Sacrifice was the outstanding principle of Christ's fruitful life. Fruitfulness in evangelism will be ours in proportion to the degree the cross of Christ is operative in us. Christ taught this and lived it.

He taught it as a revolutionary spiritual principle as he spoke to the Greeks in Jerusalem during those final days before Calvary. He said, "Except a corn of wheat fall into the ground and die, it abideth alone: but if it die, it bringeth forth much fruit" (John 12:24, KJV).

The Greek outlook on life was very much that of the world today—seeking self-gratification, self-culture, and self-enjoyment. Jesus proclaimed that only as we die to self, renounce the self-centered life, can we experience the abundant life that produces a harvest for his kingdom. There was no other way for him than the way of the Cross. And we, the followers of a cross-bearing Savior, should not be cross-evading disciples.

The devil has always been aware of this law of spiritual harvest, that is why he often tried to convince Christ to avoid the Cross. That is why Satan tries to draw us back from commitment and sacrifice. But Christ, for the joy that was set before him—the joy of the spiritual harvest in millions of redeemed lives—endured the cross, bearing the shame.

His death, the one grain of wheat that died on Calvary, made possible the harvest of three thousand souls on the day of Pentecost a mere seven weeks later. The sacrifice of those early disciples produced the millions who give allegiance to Jesus Christ throughout the world today.

Sacrifice and commitment were the secret of the effectiveness of the greatest of all

---

Eva E. Burrows is General of the Salvation Army and a former missionary educator. She is a citizen of Australia.

evangelists, the apostle Paul. The New Testament records a catalog of his sufferings for Christ's sake and the gospel's. He was harassed by those who belittled his authority, he worked hard with his own hands to support himself financially, and he bore the defection of fellow workers. Physical persecution was routine for him. He was crucified with Christ, he did not count his life dear to himself, and what things were gain to him those he counted loss for Christ. He not only endured these things but gloried in them, for he said,

> I will boast all the more gladly about my weaknesses, so that Christ's power may rest on me. That is why, for Christ's sake, I delight in weaknesses, in insults, in hardships, in persecutions, in difficulties. For when I am weak, then I am strong (2 Corinthians 12:9–10).

Great revivals and powerful evangelistic endeavors never begin in big ways, but rather by a life given in total dedication on the altar of sacrifice.

How Much Does It Cost You to Be an Evangelist?

Rejection of the principle of sacrifice is deeply rooted in today's world, where modern man's philosophy seems to be concerned with little apart from his own success. The worldly mind clutches at position, power, and wealth as the greatest good. In such a world, we shrink from suffering. Sacrifice does not come easy, but when we center our life on Christ and consecrate ourselves to the religion of the Cross, sacrifice for Christ becomes a privilege, not a penalty.

Norman Grubb said,

> If I am Christ's, then voluntary deaths to the normal advantages of the flesh—comforts, loved ones, material advancement, enlarged income, pleasures, leisure—give me the right to claim and receive the harvest in the Spirit. Instead of regarding such as losses and deprivations to be endured if necessary, but avoided if possible, we deliberately embrace them and glory in them as a way of harvest.

Sacrifice Involves Dying to Self

Samuel Logan Brengle, a Salvation Army leader, has written much about sacrifice as a significant ingredient of the Spirit-filled life. In his book, *The Soul Winner's Secret,* is a chapter entitled, "The Cost of Saving Souls." That language may seem a little old fashioned, but what he says is highly relevant. Isn't that what evangelists are seeking to do—save souls?

There is a price to be paid, says Brengle, in being willing to forgo the world's applause, in letting go of worldly attachments which draw our hearts away from Christ. In a startling phrase, Brengle says, "It is only dead men who are living preachers." That is, death to sin, to self, to personal ambition, and to the praise of men and the hope of earthly rewards.

If God has set us to win souls, the pull of the world must die. We must burn our bridges, have no plans for retreat, and realize the enormity of Paul's words, "Woe unto me if I preach not the gospel." That is the spirit of the true evangelist.

The Cost of Uncompromising Faith

Korea has been a fruitful field for evangelism in the cause of Christ. The cost of discipleship for individual Christians has often been high.

In a cemetery in Korea, boldly inscribed on the tombstone of a servant of Christ, are these words for all the world to see: "If I had a thousand lives, I would give them all for Christ."

The cost of discipleship is often high—as it was for Major Noh Yong Soo, a Korean Salvation Army officer in charge of the corps at Chinju when the town fell to the invading North Korean forces during the Korean civil war.

The victorious North Korean commander brought him in for questioning. In order to make a public example of him, he was marched through the streets with his captors and made to stand in the town square facing the guns of a firing squad. The people were all brought to watch as he was ordered to renounce his faith. When twice he resolutely refused to deny his Lord, the desperate North Korean commander gave him a last chance. Vehemently, he shouted, "Renounce your faith in Jesus Christ!"

But standing calmly, the major raised his Bible in one hand and declared fearlessly, "Whether I live or die matters not. But Christ lives." He fell to his knees, praying for his captors as their rifle shots shattered the silence, and a modern martyr died for his faith. The cruel guards shouldered their rifles and marched away leaving his body where it fell. He was hastily buried by loving hands, but later given a more fitting resting place and a worthy memorial after the North Koreans were driven back. But the greatest memorial to Major Noh Yong Soo is that the gospel of Christ has spread throughout that area. The church, the Salvation Army, has grown. New churches were seeded and the kingdom of Christ has expanded beyond imagination.

The cost of discipleship is seldom low, but its harvest is rich—producing a hundredfold. Few of us may be called upon to face a firing squad, but many will face physical torture, humiliation, and suffering. In hostile environments, antagonistic to the Christian faith because of religious intolerance or political expediency, many of us will be called upon to suffer for Christ's sake and the gospel's.

The Costs of Identification

The need "to spend and be spent" in the service of Christ (2 Corinthians 12:15, KJV) will require identification with the people whom we evangelize and serve. A group of Christian workers were trying to come to grips with the problem of evangelizing the inner cities of Britain—the urban jungles. It was at a time when there were terrible riots, vandalism, and violence in Brixton, an inner London ghetto.

Lord Scarman, the chairman of the commission reviewing these disturbances, was asked to address the Christian group. Someone asked, "Lord Scarman, could you say in a few sentences what you think is the solution to the problems of areas like Brixton?"

He responded by saying, "Yes, I'll tell you. In fact, I'll tell you in one sentence. Go and live there."

It costs something to "go and live there." So often the Christian worker drives home from the ghetto to his comfortable house in some quiet suburban neighborhood, and the effect of his work and witness loses its power. We have to sit where they sit—share their life, identify with them. That was what made the Salvation Army so successful among the working class people in the poverty stricken slums of Britain in the last century. They went and lived there.

Are we prepared to do the same today in the Harlems of this world, in the shanty towns of Africa like "Crossroads," in the overcrowded areas?

In cross-cultural evangelism, costly identification means learning another language and adjusting to new customs and lifestyles. It costs something to step into another person's skin, to feel what that person feels, to discover the pain that person bears, to share that person's poverty. Such self-giving is costly, but fruitfulness in ministry is in direct proportion to our identification with those whom we evangelize and serve.

The Lausanne Covenant reminds us, "Christ's evangelists must humbly seek to empty themselves of all but their personal authenticity in order to become the servants of others."

In the Gospels, Jesus repeatedly condemns the person who refuses to get involved, who refuses to inconvenience himself in order to be of help to others. That is why Jesus told the story of the Good Samaritan. He praised the Samaritan traveler because he became totally involved, and that involved him in personal sacrifice. The Samaritan gave his precious time to the injured traveller, he risked his life on that dangerous lonely road, he overcame racial prejudice, and he used his own money most generously. It is not surprising to hear Jesus say, "Now go and do the same" (Luke 10:37, TLB).

How much does it cost to be an evangelist? Are you willing to pay the price? Our master, Jesus Christ, gives us the perfect example. He identified with us and our humanity. He need not have been born to poverty in a lowly manger; he need not have worked as a common laborer; he need not have endured mockery, persecution, and scorn—but he did. He humbled himself, made himself of no reputation, and became obedient unto death. Let this mind be in you that was also in Christ Jesus.

The Demands of Love

The preeminent place of love in the life of the servant of Christ is a distinctive feature of our Christian faith. Love must be the mainspring of our lives: Love for God, love for the brethren, love for the multitudes who are like sheep without a shepherd.

Love is to be prized before every charismatic gift, above the eloquence of inspired preaching, above intellectual ability, above miracle-working faith, and above sought-after martyrdom (1 Corinthians 13:1–3). Love transcends all and must be the motive and source of all our service. As with Christ, love leads to fruitfulness and victory.

A friend recently told me about the despair of the leaders of the China Inland Mission when they met in Manila during a time of great crisis. It was 1951, and their personnel had been sent out of China. What was to be their next move? One of the missioners described this baffling experience, "There was no awareness of the presence of God. There was no sense of divine direction. We felt completely at a loss as to what to do."

Into this atmosphere of despair came the great woman evangelist, Catherine Booth-Clibbon. As she sat at the table listening to their conversation, she suddenly interrupted, "Gentlemen, what is the meaning of love?" There was an embarrassing silence, as each sought a simple definition. Catherine read their unspoken thoughts and challenged them, "Gentlemen, do you want to know the true meaning of *love?* It is *sacrifice.*"

Into that important conference came the melting and moving power of the Spirit of God. Reborn out of the flame of that moment, the Overseas Missionary Fellowship has accomplished some of the greatest endeavors in missionary history in Southeast Asia.

To love is to give and to give sacrificially. If Mary had been questioned about the sacrifice of her most precious possession, the box of costly perfume to anoint the feet of Jesus prior to his death, she would have replied, "Sacrifice? What sacrifice? It was no sacrifice. You see, I love him." The constraining love of Christ is the very sharing of our actions (2 Corinthians 5:14).

The Price of Wisdom is Sacrifice

In the book of Proverbs is a short but telling sentence, "He who wins souls is wise" (Proverbs 11:30). Soul winners, evangelists, must have the wisdom which enables them to understand and sympathize with those whom they seek to win for Christ. That kind of wisdom cannot be learned at a university; it cannot be bought with silver or gold; it comes only through the experience of knowing Christ. It is gained by entering into all the experiences of the human heart. Whether through personal tragedy or by the path of rejection and self-renunciation, he who wants wisdom must not shrink from sacrifice and suffering.

Oswald Sanders said, "God's method of preparing a preacher is to allow him to bear suffering." A study of the lives of powerful evangelists reveals this—whether it be D. L. Moody, Charles E. Fuller, or William Booth. Are you willing to pay the price for soul-saving wisdom?

The cost is great and it is not paid in one lump sum. It is paid in installments. We are to present ourselves a living sacrifice on his altar (Romans 12:1). A daily giving of ourselves for Christ's sake and the gospel's. Someone has said, "One of the major problems with a living sacrifice is that it keeps crawling off the altar!" Lord, help us to be willing to give whatever it costs.

In his translation of Paul's second letter to the Corinthians, Canon J. B. Phillips entitles chapter 6, "The Hard but Glorious Life of God's Ministers." This statement aptly describes the work of an evangelist. No one expects it to be easy. There will be sacrifices to make and suffering to bear, but it is a glorious life. It is glorious when a lost soul is found, when a man is brought from darkness to light and from the kingdom of Satan to God.

Lord, may we bear any burden, face any demand, be prepared for any sacrifice, and gladly take up our cross and follow you.

Commitment and Sacrifice in World Evangelization

Michael Cassidy

It is a fair assumption that all of us attending this Congress believe in world evangelization. Jesus said we should do it, and we *want* to do it. It is also a fair assumption that many of us are battling with the commitment, cost, and sacrifice involved.

Yet in the same breath, we yearn like Caleb of old, to be undiminished by the chilling winds of discouragement and say, "Let us go . . . at once, and occupy . . . for we are well able to overcome . . . (Numbers 13:30, RSV). Like John Knox, we want to cry for our respective lands, "Give me Scotland, or I die." We want to plead with Caleb, "Give me this mountain" (Joshua 14:12, KJV).

We want to say it—and pray it. And we want deep down to rise to the commitment and sacrifice required by the task. In aiming for this, great encouragement and a vital precedent can be found in the experience, example, and precept of the apostle Paul, particularly in his address to the Ephesian elders (Acts 20:17–35).

This meeting with the Ephesian elders took place during his stop at Miletus in the latter part of Paul's ministry. He was on his way to Jerusalem and the "imprisonment and afflictions" (v. 23, RSV) which awaited him there. The year was A.D. 54. Nero had just begun to rule as emperor and things were getting tense. The challenge of world evangelization was before the apostle. Commitment and sacrifice were going to be vitally important to the Ephesians, and were also marvelously in evidence in the apostle.

Paul speaks volumes in this address, but I want to highlight three things: (*a*) the commitment of Paul's life, (*b*) the sacrifice of Paul's suffering, and (*c*) the secrets of Paul's perseverance.

THE COMMITMENT OF PAUL'S LIFE

A Commitment to Holy Character

The life and character of this messenger of the gospel has been dealt with extensively in this Congress. It is clear that in Paul's commitment to world evangelization his whole life and character were on the line (v. 18).

A Commitment to Servanthood

The apostle had a profound commitment to humble servanthood (v. 19). His entire

---

Michael Cassidy leads the ministry of African Enterprise in South Africa and is a citizen of that country.

evangelistic and missionary commitment flowed from the depths of a servant spirit and was grounded in humility. He was a bondslave to Jesus Christ and his agenda for the world, which made him humble before his Lord and mankind.

A Commitment of Tears

Paul mentions tears twice in Acts 20:19–31. In the first instance, they are related to servanthood and his trials (v. 19) and in the second, to the earnestness of his admonitions to the Ephesian church (v. 31).

These are the only references in Acts which tell us of Paul weeping. Paul is usually seen as a man equal to every situation, crisis, or hardship. Clearly, the apostle knew the anguish of private discouragement, trauma, depression, and hardship, especially from the plots of the Jews (v. 19), and he was often brought to tears.

What brings us to tears? It is important to face these things and seek the Lord's healing and ointment for our wounds. When problems are not dealt with, they impair both our commitment and our capacity to carry out the task of world evangelization.

Many evangelists today, have weepings within. Some of these may be the result of:

1. *Weakness and inadequacies.* Over the years, I have often gone to the Lord to lament my weakness, sinfulness, and inadequacy in trying to evangelize Africa's cities and trying to cope with South Africa's political traumas. I have often cried, "Lord, can't you relieve me of this task and get someone stronger and more capable?" Again and again the Lord has said, "But you're the only kind of material I have ever had to do my work—frail, weak, inadequate, sinful. Besides, you volunteered for the job, so get on with it! And remember, 'My strength is made perfect in weakness'" (2 Corinthians 12:9, KJV).

2. *Strain and tension.* We can't avoid all pressure and tension, even Jesus knew that. Luke 12:50 could be paraphrased, "What tension I suffer until this is all over." But strain is excessive and destructive tension. Stress can bring us not only to tears but to evangelistic paralysis or even nervous exhaustion and emotional breakdown. Yet, it need not happen. Hudson Taylor once wrote, "As to work, mine was never so plentiful, so responsible, or so difficult: but the weight and the strain are all gone."

Sanders describes the way to obtain healing and peace so we that we may continue with the work of the Lord as:

1. *A rediscovery of God.* Nothing less than his will fulfills the deepest need of our complex personality. God himself is the answer and he will grant us a great revelation of himself when we are truly ready for what it involves. To the saints of past ages, he granted a progressive revelation of himself exactly suited to their pressing need. What we need today is a new revelation of him as *El Shaddai,* "God All-sufficient," who is immeasurably greater than our inadequacies.

2. *A recognition of self* as the center and source of strain. Do we feel that more is being asked of us than we are able to bear? God assures us that he "will not suffer you to be tempted above that ye are able" (1 Corinthians 10:13, KJV). He knows our limits. It may also be true that some of our numerous activities are self-imposed rather than divinely ordered, and should be discontinued.

3. *A renewal of mind.* There must be a radical change of attitude, a genuine renewal of mind, if there is to be lasting deliverance. As long as mental attitudes remain unchanged, the tension will continue. Instead of pitying and excusing ourselves because of the pressures under which we labor, we must no longer view them as a burden which crushes us but as a platform for the display of God's glorious sufficiency. We will hear him say, "Now shalt thou see what I will do" (Exodus 6:1, KJV). We need to take our eyes off ourselves and fix them on God. The greater our weakness, the greater his glory will be his as we work in his power.

Tears of Spiritual Concern

As the Lord helps us do these things, our tears over the destructive struggles of our lives will diminish as healing comes. But there are other tears—healthy tears—which flow naturally and freely. These are tears of spiritual concern and passionate intercession for spiritual and other needs of the people in our lives.

Several young Salvation Army officers wrote and asked General Booth, "How can we win the lost?" Booth's return letter simply said: "Try tears."

When I saw the movie *Cry Freedom* about Steve Biko and the South African situation, I went before the Lord for nearly half an hour, weeping in intercession for my country and its needs. When preparing for my address in SACLA in 1979, I had a similar experience which lasted nearly three hours. This can't be artificially induced, and at times we may have to ask the Lord to help us weep even more for our situations and for those within them.

The apostle Paul brought an immense commitment to the task of mission and evangelism. It was a commitment of his entire life and lifestyle—a commitment of utterly self-effacing and humble servanthood. He also demonstrated the commitment of perseverance—sometimes with tears—through trials of ruthless opposition, personal difficulty, and spiritual anguish over those whom he wanted to reach for the Lord. But the apostle's commitment did not end there. It extended into unswerving faithfulness and courage in resolute and actual proclamation of the gospel message in faithfulness to its kerygmatic content. Paul also remained steadfast in setting forth the whole counsel of God with all its implications.

The apostle manifested not just the moral and spiritual courage of "declaring the whole counsel of God" in his evangelism, but also the physical and emotional courage of coping sacrificially with the imminent suffering of "imprisonment and afflictions" in Jerusalem (v. 23). In other words, Paul was ready to face the sacrifice of suffering.

THE SACRIFICE OF PAUL'S SUFFERING

Going to Jerusalem

Paul is "going to Jerusalem, . . . not knowing" what should befall him there except imprisonment and afflictions (Acts 20:22–23, RSV). An effective ministry of evangelism should take evangelists and his colleagues "to Jerusalem" regularly.

In 1980, I went through a "Jerusalem crisis" about returning to South Africa. When my wife Carol and I decided God *was* leading us to return, she said, "We are setting our face to Jerusalem." South Africa is our Jerusalem, not so much in the sense of being our home base, but as our place of pain and affliction.

Jerusalem is inescapably there, wherever we are, if we are committed to fulfill the Great Commission, complete the task of world evangelization, and to honor the Lord's demands of justice for the poor and oppressed. Certainly for Jesus there was no way around it. His face was set throughout his ministry. Nor was there any way around it for James who was stoned, or for Paul and Peter who were imprisoned and martyred, or for John who was exiled to Patmos.

One of the perils of the church in our time is the idea that we can have "all this, and heaven too" (i.e., popularity, prosperity, success, acclaim, the praise of man). Mighty evangelistic achievements for the Lord are desired, and heaven too, but without going through Jerusalem en route! If it has been possible in the past, I seriously doubt it will be possible in the future during what may turn out to be the last days of history.

Matthew 24 describes the last days' events of "wars and rumors of wars" (v. 6), nation rising against nation, famines and earthquakes (v. 7), hatred of believers (v. 9), betrayal within the church (v. 10), false prophets (v. 11), the increase of wickedness, and Christian love growing cold (v. 12). In the midst of that the "gospel of the kingdom will be preached in the whole world as a testimony to all nations" (v. 14).

That is a challenging prospect and we can only cry out, "Lord, who is adequate for these things?" In such a context of social and political upheaval and spiritual hostility, we will not easily minister unscathed.

Going to Prison

For Paul, going to Jerusalem also meant going to prison. Most of us have never faced imprisonment. Perhaps it is time for a new theology of imprisonment. In these last months, this has become quite real to our family. My nephew, an evangelical believer and devout youth of eighteen, was sentenced in South Africa to six years imprisonment. His faith would not allow him to join the South African Defence Force, so he languishes in prison.

Frank Chikane, an evangelical and Pentecostal brother is currently secretary of the South African Council of Churches. He once commented on his prison experiences,

> At times I struggle sitting in a cell, and say "Lord, help me." I want to make sure I am still on the right track, because the theology that is dominant in this country says that you can't go to prison if you are a Christian. But for a person in Soweto who has landed in prison, reading about Peter in prison means something completely different.

In our own African Enterprise ministry in East Africa, our chairman, Janani Luwum, was put in prison by Idi Amin and martyred for his stand in Christ's name.

I am not trying to urge Christians to rush out and try to get thrown in prison. But in the decades ahead, our commitment should include extending our spirit of sacrifice to include the willingness, like Paul's, to face "imprisonment and afflictions."

As for my own nephew, Charles, in his first letter from prison he could say,

> Through it all I know God's unfailing presence.... Be assured I'm well and full of hope. In my weakness and God's strength I persevere. It is imperative that I continue to trust and grow in trusting God, for he alone can keep me and bring me to triumph over this experience and be more than a conqueror. I do feel the pain of separation so much .. . but I rest in the knowledge that the distance between us isn't great enough, nor the walls here thick enough, to keep your love and prayers out, nor mine in!

Those are the words of a young man who knows what commitment and sacrifice in Christian witness are all about.

The irrepressible Paul knew this spirit and wrote from Herod's prison:

I want you to know . . . that what has happened to me has really served to advance the gospel, so that it has become known throughout the whole praetorian guard and to all the rest that my imprisonment is for Christ" (Philippians 1:12–13, RSV).

But what were the inner secrets of Paul's ability to persevere under all these circumstances?

THE SECRETS OF PAUL'S PERSEVERANCE

"Bound in the Spirit"

Paul was under the control of the Holy Spirit—a full captive to the Spirit's work and ways (Acts 20:22, RSV).

Our need has never been greater to know within us the person, work, fruit, gifts, and guidance of the Holy Spirit. We need to be utterly bound to him for whatever he has for us.

"I Do Not Account My Life of Any Value"

In this self-sacrificial posture (Acts 20:24, RSV), the apostle was initiating a tradition of Christian spirit of self-sacrifice and willingness to lose and give all.

In Blantyre, Malawi during a citywide evangelistic campaign, I walked through a graveyard with tombstones of many who had come to preach the gospel in the aftermath of David Livingstone's exploration. Within eighteen months, one by one, they all died. Even as they died, still others came—not counting their lives of any value or as precious to themselves.

"Accomplish My Course"

The apostle was determined and resolved in mind and spirit that there would be no turning back (v. 24, RSV). In 1976, I spoke with Billy Graham in private during the PACLA (Pan-African Christian Leaders' Assembly) Conference in Nairobi about my temptation to leave South Africa for some easier context of ministry. I'll never forget his answer: "Michael, I believe there is a strange blessedness for those who persevere unto the end—even unto death."

That is still true, and is relevant for each one of us.

"Taking Heed to Yourselves"

Paul preached to the Ephesian elders, "Take heed to yourselves" (v. 28, RSV) and to Timothy, "Take heed to yourself" (1 Timothy 4:16, RSV). But he also practiced what he preached and carefully monitored his own spiritual life before the Lord. He knew that if he failed, then both his commitment and his remarkable spirit of sacrifice in the cause of world evangelization would be silently and secretly sabotaged.

"And to All the Flock"

Paul was an overseer to the Ephesian elders as they were to the flock of the church at Ephesus (v. 28, RSV). Sometimes the only thing which holds a man or woman to evangelistic or pastoral service is a sense of deep responsibility for those entrusted to their charge or located in their context of ministry.

How can we leave when there are precious souls who are dependent upon us or in need of our gospel proclamation, pastoral care, and fellowship? If we leave, who will guard or rescue the flock when the "fierce wolves will come in" (v. 29) to devour and devastate?

The Word of His Grace

No other anchor for sacrificial evangelistic commitment can match the inspired Word of God (v. 32). Paul knew this; may we know this as well.

When my nephew was heading into prison, I urged him, "Memorize the Word and hold on to it for dear life!" Thankfully, his last letter from prison said: "I read my Bible a lot and memorize one verse per day." How that warmed my heart! The Word of God will hold us when nothing else can.

Again and again when David Livingstone was tempted to give up, he turned to the Scriptures and was fed and held. It has always been that way for all who have persevered for Christ at their place of divine appointment.

"I Coveted No One's Silver"

One of today's major destroyers of men and women in ministry is money-love or materialism. Unlike Paul, we *do* covet the silver, gold, and apparel of the world around us (v. 32–33, RSV). We let ourselves become rich on the gospel, with all the consequent extravagances this can sometimes breed. Financial and fiscal integrity becomes a major casualty and eventually we are exposed and bring shattering discredit on the gospel. When that happens, commitment and sacrifice in world evangelization is devoted. There is disgrace, shame, Christian embarrassment, the end of otherwise good ministries, and then public glee—which is the most painful of all.

"More Blessed to Give"

Paul was committed to toiling to help the weak. He found tremendous blessing in this because he could help others in greater need than himself. Quoting one of the few authentic sayings of our Lord not recorded in the Gospels, Paul reminds his listeners, "It is more blessed to give than to receive" (v. 35, RSV).

Our Lord has commissioned us to evangelize the world. To do so, we need commitment and sacrifice. Therefore, may we stand by one another in the work of world evangelization with deep commitment of life, with utter faithfulness to the gospel, and with the willingness to suffer if it is necessary. May the Lord bind us as captives to the Holy Spirit. May he give us the determination to finish the task and the humility to continually take stock of our lives. May we be marked by responsibility for the flock and be alert to the dangers of divisive influences, covetousness, and lack of generosity. In all this, may the Lord give us a deep sense of responsibility for the task and privilege that is ours.

There is a story of an imaginary conversation when Jesus returned to heaven after his earthly ministry. Seemingly, the angels gathered around him and said, "But, Lord, you have left your great work of mission on earth with a very weak group of inadequate people. What if they fail? What is your Plan B?"

The Lord replied, "It is true, but I have no Plan B. I am depending on them!"

Closing Addresses

Looking Back—Looking Forward

Floyd McClung

This Congress began with Luis Bush and Leighton Ford presenting a strong challenge to us. The Congress theme is that the whole church is to take the whole gospel to the whole world. The whole world includes Muslims, almost one billion of them. There are less missionaries in the Muslim world than the people who are sitting in this hall tonight. This world includes the Hindu community, almost seven hundred million Hindus in the world, most of whom have never heard the gospel of Jesus Christ.

We think of the urban world. More than half of the people alive today are living in great cities. It's estimated another seven hundred million people will immigrate to the cities in the next eleven years.

This world includes the youth of the world. What some call the "small half" of the world. Forty-five percent of all of the people in Africa, 27 percent of all of the people of Asia, 35 percent of all the people in Latin America are under the age of fifteen. One hundred million children are homeless in our world.

There are the tribal peoples of the world, most of whom still wait to be able to read God's words in the language of their hearts. There's the secularists of the world, in Europe, the United States, and many other nations as well, most of whom sense the gospel is something for the past, who scorn and don't believe and don't take it seriously. There are nominal Christians, 1.3 billion people who profess the name of Jesus Christ— but many of whom do not know what it means to have Jesus Christ as their friend and their Savior.

The Communist world is in turmoil and in ferment. There's a great spirit of change and transition. And yet we remember what has happened in China in the last few weeks.

Many are the poor and the needy of the world.

We're called to this Congress to take seriously the whole world. We're to take the gospel to every person, especially those who have never heard that Jesus loves them. Especially those who are poor and oppressed and have no hope. We were reminded this morning, by Robyn and by Bill, that if we are going to do that, it's going to require a whole new level of cooperation and unity. We can no longer accept the dichotomy, the divisions between male and female, between Western and non-Western, between the young and the old, between the charismatic and the non-charismatic, between those who believe in "incarnational" methods and those who are called to proclamation, between congregational structures and mission structures. It must be the whole church committed in respect and in love to go together to the world.

I believe God is calling us to a new kind of unity in the body of Christ, where we love one another and listen to one another so that in that spirit of unity, we will make a witness of Jesus and his love for the world.

We were also reminded this morning, by Michael Cassidy and Eva Burrows, of the need for sacrifice and commitment.

I wonder how many of us make it a practice to attend conferences around the world. Some of us are required to do that by our responsibility. And yet, it might be time for us to make sure that we are *practicing* all that we hear in these conferences. It's time for many of us who are leaders to begin to lead anew from the front lines, to go where the people are, to sit where the people are. Jesus did not die for the cause of world evangelization. He died for people.

This Congress is first and foremost not about programs and causes and organizations. It's not about all of our various callings and agendas and concerns. It is about people who are lost without Jesus. People who are without hope, who desperately need us to make new levels of commitment and sacrifice, to live amongst them, to listen to them, and to bring grace and truth to them in Jesus' name. So there's a desperate need for us to have a new sense of Godly urgency, a renewed zeal in our hearts, a fire to burn within our spirits to reach people with the gospel of Jesus Christ. We must focus our energies and our efforts, not on maintaining first of all our institutions and our programs, but on people who need Jesus Christ.

Bill O'Brien is going to share with us some developments that have taken place in the last few months that help us to focus our attention on reaching people with the gospel.

The Scope of the Task

Bill O'Brien

In thinking of A.D. 2000 and beyond, we can approach this problem either piece by piece until we come out with a whole, or we can talk about it from the whole back to the particular. I want to focus for just a few moments on the "global scope of the task." Tonight, let us consider that we're gathered here as one body, as Kingdom citizens, pilgrims and aliens in the world, but standing in the middle of hearts as a prayer wish of our Lord, when he said, "O, Father, don't take them out of the world."

About 20 percent of the world's population, or approximately 1.3 billion people, have never heard of Christ. They are doubly lost. Spiritually they are lost to any relationship with Jesus Christ, and physically they are lost to any opportunity to hear the gospel in any form. Fellow pilgrims, the time to change that is now.

When the Great Commission Manifesto was shaped in a global consultation in Singapore last January, two of the four major objectives were to provide every people a valid opportunity to hear the gospel, and to establish a Christian community of worship and evangelism in every human community. Could it be done? Now, let me tell you a scenario. Reach with me across the decades:

Date line—Singapore, January 1, 2001:

A global celebration of Great Commission Christians has just closed in one of the most dramatic moments in Christian history. The celebration was simulcast live via satellite, in fifty languages, directly to the entire world. In addition to home viewers, over seven hundred-thousand Great Commission Christians gathered in major convention centers in seventy-five world-class cities to experience the moment together by big screen. Even a small group of believers working on the L-5 Solar Energy Space Station at the edge of earth's gravity enjoys the celebration by ninety-second-delayed transmission.

The significance of this history-making moment was the spirit of unity reflected throughout. Wherever people viewed the celebration, they thrilled to the music of the thousand-voice choir from Seoul, Korea; the dramatic folk dance interpretation of the Crucifixion and Resurrection of Christ presented by Indonesians; the messages by a Kenyan preacher from Nairobi, and the Brazilian preacher, both originating in Rio's massive Maracanas Stadium. We've heard reports from the representatives of the five intercontinental regional sending agencies that enable six hundred-thousand missionaries to work in cross-cultural, cross-pollinating missions. We've heard testimonies of lay volunteers, of bi-vocational tentmakers, of youth representing over one million short-term youth workers, and from intercessors who have been part of the two hundred million persons praying daily for world evangelization. Four million new churches have been started in the last twelve years. A new church exists now among every people group, and over one billion persons have confessed Christ as Savior and Lord.

Now here we stand at that moment of celebration, but not without pain and not without loss. Our world had been rocked in the past decade with a devastating holy war in one region. A redrawing of national boundaries and new economic coalitions transcended old national boundaries. The synthesis of monetary systems took place as the U.S. dollar fell from universal grace. There was an increasing number of Christian martyrs, and there were rising militant missionary religions penetrating every corner of the earth. The polluted atmosphere began threatening this planet as a habitat for humans. All this and more.

No, we're not talking cheap grace. This celebration bore no marks of triumphalism. It was a pause. A selah. An Ebenezer moment to reflect on how the Lord had brought us hitherto and to once again look to the future. To recollect for the next generation; for obedience is always a present tense verb. It is rooted in revelation, it is related to the will.

Last January 315 leaders met in Singapore to focus on the scope of the task and what we can do as we move toward A.D. 2000 and beyond. Let's watch.

VIDEO PRESENTATION

A.D. 2000 and Beyond

Producer: Van Payne

Thomas Wang: It seems as if God is ringing a bell in heaven and saying, "Hey, ladies and gentlemen, let's get serious. I have been waiting 2000 years for you, the church, to fulfill my command. You have been procrastinating. You have been delaying. Many times you are divided—you are not cooperating."

It is time we get serious. It is time to shift into high gear to fulfill the Great Commission."

Narrator: Thomas Wang's words reflect a growing conviction among missions experts and church leaders around the world. As mankind approaches the dawning of a new century, that conviction, that compelling devotion to Christ's Great Commission, is being translated into action. Christians around the world are dedicating themselves and their resources to the task of world evangelization by the year 2000 and beyond.

Luis Bush: I myself am expectant that Jesus' commission to his disciples will be fulfilled in our time, and perhaps by the year 2000. And I want to give more of my energy, effort, and time to see the task of evangelization completed in our time.

Narrator: The history of the church has seen at least 750 plans for world evangelization. About 250 of these plans are still actively pursued. They represent sincere commitments to evangelism and to the building of God's kingdom, but most have existed in isolation within one part of the body of Christ. These plans were created unrelated to, and usually unaware of, similar efforts elsewhere within the church. As the last century drew to a close, there were high hopes that a new level of cooperation might be achieved, as many organizations stated their desire to reach the world in the nineteenth century's last decade. That plan faltered and eventually failed because there was no mechanism through which the many different groups could cooperate.

Today, however, the era of isolation in the task of world evangelization may be drawing to a close. New openness in planning and coordination among Great Commission Christians; and modern advances in research, communications, and other technologies, are changing the way we approach world evangelization. Mutual respect and cooperation among Christian bodies worldwide have brought the goal of world evangelization within our reach like never before. Earlier this year, for example, more than three hundred world leaders in missions and evangelism representing fifty nations met in Singapore for a global consultation. Their sole agenda: world evangelization by A.D. 2000 and beyond.

John Richard: This consultation is unique because God has been working in the hearts of many people in many parts of the world, laying a burden on their hearts to see that something new happens in the area of evangelization by the turn of the century. And God has used this consultation in order to bring together people with a single, common purpose; and that is to see that this world is evangelized by the year 2000.

David Barrett: We have drawn up five different and distinct scenarios of the future on this subject of world evangelization by A.D. 2000. Each of those scenarios—we call them "alternative futures"—is entirely possible. Each of them is entirely impossible if circumstances develop that we don't know of today. Obviously, the political situation is going to determine to some degree which of those are possible in the next ten years. But from many points of view, the whole thing is not only entirely possible, it would be an outrage if the Christian church did not achieve this particular goal.

Narrator: World evangelization by the year 2000. Can it really be done? Thinking in terms of "alternative futures" reminds us the outcome is ultimately in God's hands. But our responsibility is clear, and as the A.D. 2000 movement gains momentum, our goal is to motivate the church, and to be able to measure our response to the pressing needs of unreached people groups around the world. We can measure our progress in relationship to the dawning of a new century, but no prophetic significance is attached to the year A.D. 2000. Everyone involved realizes that the task of evangelism will enlarge with each new birth in the earth's growing population.

But the leaders who gathered in Singapore, like those here in Manila, represent a growing number of people who believe the Lord is leading them to seek better communication among Christian groups, and to achieve higher levels of cooperation for this specific goal, at this time in history.

Keith Parks: The Lord is saying similar things to so many people of so many denominations in so many countries, that if we don't listen to him now, how in the world is he going to get through to us?

Ralph Winter: This is a place and time where many of us have realized the scope of God's initiative, rather than, the great achievement of some initiative created here.

Narrator: During the course of the consultation, new lines of communication were opened among Christians committed to the Great Commission. People dedicated to world evangelization forged new relationships, making them, in the truest sense, laborers together for God.

David Kitonga: Today, there is a great spirit of understanding. There is a mutual, corporate spirit of understanding about what we want to do, and many people are very enthused.

Elizabeth Javalera: I am going home with higher hopes for a brighter future, as far as the ministry is concerned. I feel there is going to be greater cooperation from here on in.

Simon Havyarimana: It's so good to see people from different organizations together, and thinking together to work together and put all their efforts together, without any strings attached.

John Richard: While we may not see eye to eye, with so many global plans currently in progress because of theological differences, yet there is this fact: We can always learn something from them. We may not be able to cultivate ownership of their plans as such, but there is nothing to prevent us from learning certain good things which can be transferred to our own projects, and see how that can help in the accomplishment of the goals to which we are committed.

Gaetano Sotile: I am excited because, in a couple of years, a consultation like this on a national level is possible in Italy. Evangelicals could come together with the different leaders, so we could share, just as we are doing here, strategies that would allow us to win our country for the Lord.

Narrator: Winning our countries for the Lord. . . .Witnessing to the many unreached people groups within them, and planting a viable church in their midst. . . .Working together as partners in the greatest enterprise of all time. . . .Witnessing God's power, not only in our own lives and in the work of our churches, but witnessing a great movement of his spirit across the face of the earth . . . .

Before us is the twenty-first century. The church, as steward of the gospel, faces a time of momentous decision. We see the Holy Spirit at work all around us: revival in Asia, church growth in Africa, spiritual renewal in South America. But do we dare take up the challenge? Can God expand our vision to see the whole church taking the whole gospel to the whole world? Can we as denominations, as parachurch groups, as churches, and as individuals accept the Great Commission as a task Jesus commanded us to accomplish?

It is not a task for some future generation. It is our task. While many debate whether or not it can be accomplished, the promise of the Scriptures is clear, "At the name of Jesus every knee should bow, in heaven and on earth . . . and every tongue confess that Jesus Christ is Lord" (Philippians 2:10–11).

Why do we wait? Can we not hear the bell ringing in heaven? Can we not hear Jesus' voice in the Scriptures and in our hearts? "Therefore go and make disciples of all nations, baptizing them in the name of the Father and of the Son and of the Holy Spirit, and teaching them to obey everything I have commanded you. And surely, I am with you always, to the very end of the age" (Matthew 28:19–20).

Summary Statement

Luis Bush

At Lausanne I there was a delegation that met every morning to pray before the meeting started. It was the Chinese delegation. And two years later, under the very able leadership of Thomas Wang, there was a movement called the Chinese Coordination Center of World Evangelization (CCCOWE) movement. They have had three major Congresses and in their fourth Congress, which is scheduled for 1991, they will take up the theme "Marching Toward the Year 2000."

Their question is, "What can we do as Chinese Christians around the world to contribute to the fulfillment of the Great Commission by the year 2000 and beyond?" And this is just one of the movements in country after country and region after region that are focusing on a major initiative as the body of Christ to contribute to the mandate that the Lord Jesus has given to us as his disciples, of obeying the Great Commission especially in the light of the year 2000.

And we are starting to see around the world how this movement is almost spontaneously, almost independently one of another beginning to surface. In the countries of Latin America, over the next nine months there will be four major regional consultations. They will be called "Alcanze dos mil," "Reaching to the Year 2000," in Costa Rica for Central America, in Argentina for the six countries of the southern core in November. In January of next year in Colombia for the Andean countries of Latin America. And then further on and a few months later in the Caribbean.

Also in West Asia, Christian leaders have already gathered together in a country to discuss what they can do as Christians in West Asia to assist in the process of evangelization of that part of the world by the year 2000. How they can mobilize their people with their gulf regions, and how they can penetrate those yet unreached peoples of West Asia.

In Europe there are both church-based and mission-based movements. In September of last year in Italy, there was a consultation where some five hundred pastors and Christian leaders came together. And I remember dramatically the evening where they committed unanimously to the task of the evangelization of the country of Italy by the year 2000. In Belgium, next January, there is a consultation planned to challenge the church in Belgium in this respect. There's a mission-base movement just getting started in these days in Europe called "Love Europe," where some seven thousand young people are getting together, and the vision is to see every European have the opportunity to hear the gospel by the year 2000.

We also see in Canada there is a "Vision 2000," which is to multiply churches throughout that country as the decade moves towards the year 2000. In Africa, there is a significant national movement of evangelization taking place right now in Zaire which has the goal of seeing every one of sixty thousand villages with a church in its midst by the year 2000. And in their soon-coming consultation they expect that already seven thousand of these villages will have a church planted in its midst.

In the country of Ghana, fifteen years ago a group made a commitment to see Ghana be discipled as a nation. And over fifteen years of research has been done that has resulted in ten volumes and significant consultation with some six hundred Christian leaders just a few weeks ago, and a mobilization to reach the villages and the cities of Ghana with the gospel of our Lord Jesus Christ. And many other countries are sharing the principles of discipling a whole nation—sometimes referred as the "The DAWN (Discipling a Whole Nation) Principle."

In Africa we see that the vision for Ghana is being taken up also in Nigeria. And there's a consultation coming up on "A.D. 2000 and Beyond" in Nigeria. Next year, Rev. Daidanso Ma Djongwe, General Secretary of the Association of Evangelicals of Africa and Madagascar, was saying to me, a meeting is planned to bring together certain people and city leaders from throughout Africa, so that in each country of Africa, over the next three years, there will be a focus on cross-cultural mission as we look toward the year 2000.

As John Stott said, "Unless the whole church is mobilized, the whole world will not be reached." It is interesting that even in the South Pacific there is a meeting coming up in December and the overall guiding goal of that meeting is to listen to what the Holy Spirit is saying to the churches of the South Pacific about their role in fulfilling the Great Commission by the year 2000.

If the business community can focus on the year 2000, if the political community can focus on the year 2000 and set goals, why can't the Christian community focus on the year 2000 and trust God for the goals? Already twenty-five countries have specific plans focused on that year. And several of the same words are being used to describe these plans. The first word is *mobilization,* the awakening of the church in these countries for this task. The second word is *empowerment*—a recognition that the Lord has provided things like financial and computer resources but, above all, that "It's not by power, it's not by might, but it's by my spirit says the Lord." The third word is *penetration.* It's the focus on the unfinished task, on what is remaining to be done in terms of taking the gospel particularly to those who have not heard. The fourth word is *compassion,* to demonstrate the caring, incarnating love of the Lord Jesus Christ as servants. And the next word is *collaboration.* The need to network and partner together in a new harmonious way.

And then what really distinguishes this particular thrust in different countries is the word *intensification.* It's the intensified process that is already underway, but it's an urgency. It's recognizing that urgent things are things that have to be done now. And in Latin America we love to say *manana.* And we like to postpone things to *manana.* But the vision that is developing is recognizing that we must ask the question: *Why not now? Why postpone until manana, what we can do today?*

As this vision is taking place around the around, the world and national initiatives and global initiatives, the Lord put one light in the heart of Thomas Wang back in February of 1987—the question: *Is God up to something?* You know Thomas sees the many organizational goals being set in the year 2000. Movements, denominations. And these national initiatives. He couldn't sleep one night as he was writing an article for the next edition of the Lausanne magazine. He stayed up until about three in the morning.

And out of that he asked himself the question, *My, what is the Lord doing? So many groups are simultaneously beginning to talk about the year 2000. What is happening? What is God trying to say?* So he wrote the article "By the Year 2000: Is God Trying to Tell Us Something?" And in just a few minutes Thomas will come to help us to understand as God has given him insight into the answer to that question. Let us be praying that God will speak to us clearly.

The Great Commission Decade

Thomas Wang

The book of Isaiah is timeless. It illustrates the relationship between a sovereign God and suffering mankind. The Old Testament prophets did not live in ivory towers—they lived among people. They knew people—their pain and their aspirations.

The book of Isaiah is also the gospel book of the Old Testament. It tells about sin, judgment, redemption, and hope. It not only describes suffering mankind, but also a suffering servant—the Son of God.

The first part of the book warns that the people of Israel will go into captivity because of their sin. And chapter 39 specifically states that they will be taken into Babylon and become slaves. And it happened! Psalm 137 says the Israelites sat down by the rivers of Babylon, and whenever they thought about Zion, they wept. And they said, "O Jerusalem, how can I forget you. If I ever forget Jerusalem, may my right hand forget its skill, and may my tongue cling to the roof of my mouth." In Babylon, they cried out to God from the depth of their sorrow.

The Meaning of the Great Commission

As is always the case, after tears there is joy, and after chastisement there is restoration. And with Isaiah chapter 40, we begin to see a totally different picture. God the loving Father is bringing comfort and joy to his people.

God told them to speak tenderly to Jerusalem. And to tell her that her warfare was accomplished, her sins were pardoned, and that she had received from Jehovah God a double forgiveness. What a wonderful feeling it is: the task is done, sins are forgiven, and we are thoroughly chastened and disciplined. This is the meaning of evangelization: the people of the world hear the Good News, receive Christ, and become his followers. This is the Great Commission.

Agents of the Great Commission

God said, "Comfort ye my people," which means: "*You* comfort my people." He was speaking to the prophets. God did not say, "I will comfort my people," but, "*You, my servants, comfort my people, wipe away their tears, and bring good tidings to them.*"

In New Testament times, God's principle was the same. Before the miracle of five

Thomas Y. H. Wang was International Director of the Lausanne Committee for World Evangelism and Congress Director for Lausanne II in Manila. He is currently Chairman of the A.D. 2000 Movement. He was born in China and is a citizen of United States.

loaves and two fish, he said to the disciples, "You give them things to eat." In John 21, Christ said to Peter three times, "You feed my sheep." We are the agents of evangelization.

Isaiah 40:3 (NKJV) further confirmed this by saying, "The voice of one crying in the wilderness." The Chinese Bible includes an extra word, "A human voice crying in the wilderness." It primarily referred to John the Baptist. In a broader sense, it means God's people. The church is the agent for world evangelization. God uses human instruments to fulfill his Great Commission.

Preparation of the Great Commission

The voice crying in the wilderness said, "Prepare the way for the Lord, make straight a highway for him in the desert." While the wilderness is a place of lawlessness, the desert is an area of lifelessness; an accurate picture of the world today.

It is incorrect to think this passage means literally an engineering operation or a highway construction project. These illustrations have spiritual and moral meanings in our individual and corporate lives.

The voice said to prepare his way in the world. Prepare room for Christ in people's hearts, in our personal life, our family, social, and national life. John the Baptist prepared the way for the Lord's first coming. He called his generation to repent. He stood beside the river Jordan and declared to the world who Jesus was, by saying: "Behold the Lamb of God, which taketh away the sin of the world," (John 1:29, KJV).

Who is responsible today to prepare the way for the Lord's Second Coming? The humanists? The secularists? People of other religions? The politicians? The United Nations? This privilege is the unique and sole responsibility of the church. You and I, *we* are responsible. This is the Great Commission our resurrected Lord gave to his church.

Realization of the Great Commission

A highway for Christ must be built into people's hearts and lives. To achieve this requires spiritual engineering with God as the Chief Engineer.

In Isaiah 40:4, God laid down four spiritual principles to build this spiritual highway. These are the four principles for world evangelization today.

1. "Every valley shall be exalted." *Exaltation.* When a highway comes to a valley, the valley has to be raised up so the highway can be built through. Valleys represent low places in the world, in our lives, in the family, in society, and in the nation.

    Christ came to lift us up physically, socially, and spiritually. When we share the undiluted gospel of Jesus Christ with people, the Holy Spirit will convict them, they will believe, and their lives will be transformed. When individuals are transformed, society is transformed. Christ came to lift us up by his redemption.

2. "Every mountain and hill shall be made low." *Humiliation.* When the highway comes to mountains, hills, and obstacles, they have to be made low, or be removed so the highway can get through.

    The single largest obstacle to world evangelization is not the lack of money; it is not the lack of workers. The biggest hindrance in fulfilling the Great Commission lies in one word, *self.* Self is closely connected with ego and pride. They manifest themselves both within and without the church.

They are like mountains and hills.

For a non-believer to come to God, the first thing he has to overcome is pride: personal pride, intellectual pride, social pride, ethnic pride; the pride of wealth, the pride of position, the pride of age, and the pride of youth, name, authority, and power. When a person says, "I believe in God," he is actually saying, "I recognize there is a higher authority over me," which is something a secularist is not willing to admit. These mountains and hills of pride must be humbled before men are willing to receive Christ.

There are also mountains and hills within the church. One of the serious obstacles in world evangelization is the ever present divisiveness among God's people. The root cause is self and pride. The mountains and hills of self and pride must be made low before world evangelization is possible.

3. "The crooked shall be made straight." *Restoration.* The world is full of crookedness—in society and in people's daily lives. These need to be made straight. In John Wesley's time, one out of every six stores in London was a pub where people went to drink. When revival came to that great city, many pubs closed their doors and went out of business.

About thirty years ago I visited Pastor Petrus of the Philadelphia church in Stockholm, Sweden. I was told that whenever Pastor Petrus walked into a train or bus, people put away their cigarettes.

When the church is truly the light and salt of the world, people will see it, people will be touched and convinced, and they will take the Christian faith seriously.

4. "And the rough places plain . . ." *Levigation.* There are rough places in the church—inconsistencies in Christian lives. Today the eyes of the world are keener than ever before. Sometimes they know us better than we know ourselves. In fact, perhaps they know us too well to take us seriously. We need to ask ourselves the question, *Are we worthy to be taken seriously by the world?*

Men and women of God energized by the Holy Spirit, living a life consistent with their calling, and fully committed to the advancement of the kingdom are indispensable for fulfilling the Great Commission. Technology is important. A database is marvelous. Satellite communication is a scientific wonder. But none of these can replace the centrality of human agency. These are wonderful tools for the ministry and as such should be subservient to the human agency. The tail must not be allowed to wag the dog, although sometimes the tail has a tendency to try to do so.

Rough places in the church and in our lives must be levigated. The uneven surfaces must be made smooth. Our common testimony to the world must be consistent with our words, and then the world will come to Christ.

Vision Regained

The Bible talks about world evangelization as early as Abraham's time, if not earlier. God not only blessed Abraham and his seed, he also promised his blessings to all peoples on earth through Abraham. That includes all peoples, all kindreds, and all races wherever they are.

In New Testament times, Christ gave his church the Great Commission for world evangelization in a more specific manner. The people of God, are to go into all the world and bring the gospel to all peoples and win the world for Christ.

The apostle Paul was forbidden to go into Asia twice, and instead he accepted the Macedonian call and went to Philippi and down to Athens. Thus, the gospel headed West, and the West became the sole custodian of the gospel for almost 1800 years.

From the book of Acts down through the centuries, the church was perpetually baffled by the loss of vision, spirituality, moral integrity, dilution of doctrine, and conflicts within herself. Her presence and influence were largely confined in the areas of Europe and Asia Minor.

Not until more than two hundred years after the Reformation did the church slowly, but finally, begin to wake up to the vision of the Great Commission and her responsibility to fulfill it. And the "Great Century" found its lowly beginning when a Christian cobbler in England began to nag his church board on sending missionaries across the ocean. And in the end he went himself.

William Carey arrived in India in 1793. Following his footsteps, we see the great column of saints marching forth into the world as soldiers of the Cross: Martyn, Duff, Morrison, Judson, Livingstone, Taylor, Mott, the Cambridge Seven, Amy Carmichael, Goforth, Studd, Jones, Schweitzer, Zwemer, Townsend, Gladys Aylward, and the list goes on. Today, we have over eighty thousand missionaries in the Protestant missionary force around the world.

A.D. 2000—The Dawning of a New Era

About one hundred years ago, God's Spirit spoke to a number of his servants in North America, among them D. L. Moody and A. T. Pierson, and then urged them to challenge the churches of their day to evangelize the world by the year 1900. Unfortunately, this heroic effort of world evangelization fell short of its goal. The reasons were many, but clearly the proponents did not receive the responses they sought from the church.

We are coming to the close of the twentieth century, and we are facing a similar movement and calling. While a century ago it was primarily the voice of several individuals, today we are witnessing a worldwide mighty army of church and mission leaders, under the leading of the Holy Spirit , coming forth like a gigantic chorus heralding the evangelization of the world by the year 2000.

God today is doing a new thing. This is a situation we have been praying for. The church has been waiting for twenty centuries for this to happen. According to David Barrett, there are about 250 active global plans today, and half of them make the year 2000 their target year. Among these, eighty-nine of them spend over $10 million a year for their plans. Of them, thirty-three spend over $100 million a year. Between now and the year 2000, a total of $40 billion will be spent for these plans.

Of course, money is not everything, but budgets like these give a projected picture of the enormous amount of work, manpower, prayer, mobilization, and evangelistic effort that will be poured into the task. The task is staggering but possible if God's children in the world today mean business and work together in the next ten years and beyond.

Spiritual Renewal

No matter what we do for God, we can never escape his spiritual principles. No plan or project can expect God's blessings unless it is done in God's way. God is interested in what we do, but he is more interested in what we are. As servants of God, it is important for us to serve, but it is even more important for us to be.

Third-World churchmen are not necessarily impressed with big organizations, big numbers, or technology in church activities. But they are impressed with spiritual discipline, moral integrity, and doctrinal purity.

New Blood

God has raised up new blood and new forces in his church in recent years. They should be recognized as part of the main flow of Christian forces of the world.

1. *Third-World churches and missions.* One of the most encouraging signs today is the emergence and growth of Third-World churches and missions. Dr. David Hesselgrave said the year 1980 was a watershed. In that year, the percentage of all evangelicals in the Third World came to equal the number in the West. Within five years, in 1985, 66 percent of all evangelicals were located in the Third World. The center of gravity in Christianity has shifted from the West to the East and from the northern to the southern hemisphere.

   The West and North should beware—the East and South are coming! They come not to take over, but to work together to fulfill God's command. However, if the West and North continue to decline spiritually and morally, and if they continue to lose grip of their commitments to the kingdom and give themselves to pleasure and ease, then a takeover of leadership is inevitable.

2. *The Holy Spirit movement.* God is turning a new page in history. He is making unprecedented breakthroughs in almost every denomination as well as to independent churches through the movement of his Holy Spirit in the past decades.

   The Pentecostal/charismatic movement brought renewal and growth to churches across the world. They are the fastest growing church, especially in Africa and Latin America. According to David Barrett, its estimated 1988 size is 332 million church members in 240 countries, with a growth rate of 19 million new members renewed in the Spirit every year.

   With their emphasis on evangelism and the working of the Holy Spirit, we have no doubt that this movement will become one of the major thrusts of evangelization in the total task of the Great Commission. However, we should never exalt Pentecost above Calvary because the purpose of the coming of the Holy Spirit was to witness and to glorify Christ. Calvary remains our highest spiritual focus in life and service

Genuine Cooperation

Genuine global cooperation are key words. It is not West versus East, but West *and* East. It was not Jerusalem versus Antioch, but Jerusalem *and* Antioch. These are two arms of world evangelization, and no one can wage a single-armed battle.

To achieve this kind of worldwide cooperation, some mountains and hills need to be made low:

1. *"Elijah syndrome."* Under pressure, Elijah said to the Lord, "I, only I, am left." The Lord had to educate him by letting him know that there were seven thousand just like him who had not bowed down to Baal.

   My dear colleague, Ed Dayton, told me a few months ago that a brother from a remote area of the world wrote to him and said, "You must invite me to the second Lausanne Congress, because world evangelization starts here."

Must we always think that history begins with us? Let us appreciate each other's value and contributions to the kingdom.

2. *"Turfism."* Twenty years ago, I first noticed the word *turf* by reading David Wilkerson's book, *The Cross and the Switchblade*. It described the youth gangs in New York City. Each gang claims a few street blocks as its "turf." They write their names on walls and guard their turf with tenacity and never allow members of the neighboring gangs to intrude. Every turf is a little kingdom.

We have "turfism" in our churches, mission agencies, fellowships, and movements of today. At times I feel we use more time and energy fighting over turf than doing the job.

John Wesley declared, "The world is my parish." Jesus commanded us to go into all the world to preach the gospel. Turfism is unbiblical, self-centered, and deadly to world evangelization.

GREAT COMMISSION COMMITMENT

Begin With Yourself
Commit yourself to be:
(a) a Great Commission Christian; (b) a Great Commission church; (c) a Great Commission mission; (d) a Great Commission seminary; (e) a Great Commission fellowship.

People Groups
Does world evangelization mean that we go to every country, city, town, and village and witness to every person we meet in the street, park, and buildings? Even if we did go out that way, how many people we meet and talk to would receive the gospel?

Since the "people group" idea was popularized in the seventies through McGavran, Winter, and the Lausanne movement, world evangelization suddenly became the "talk of the town" and considered entirely possible. When we talk about world evangelization, we must begin with national evangelization. And when we talk about a nation, we must begin with each people group within that nation. The people group idea breaks down world evangelization into manageable units.

Each nation in the world is made up by mosaic-like people groups. Today there are twelve thousand people groups in the world yet to be reached by the gospel. The idea is to plant vibrant, multiplying churches in each of them so indigenous churches within each people group can evangelize their own people.

Into Each Nation
To plant churches in every people group of a nation, the existing national churches must take the initiative and leadership. They must be thoroughly motivated by the spirit of leadership. They must be thoroughly motivated by the Spirit of God and convinced the task should and can be done. Sometimes God may also use encouragement from churches of other nations to help initiate the spark.

First, a national consultation on evangelization should be held under joint sponsorship of mission groups of that nation. This should be the occasion to inform and to motivate national church leaders, and to relate God's Great Commission to the national level. A national evangelistic task force could be formed during the consultation. And the task force would work out policies, goals, and strategies to mobilize the churches for national evangelization.

Over two hundred plans for world evangelization are going on at this hour. Much like Isaiah's time, God wants his church today to raise up a voice and to comfort his people—to speak tenderly to the peoples in North America, Latin America, Asia, Europe, Africa, Oceania, and to the people groups in Angola, Ethiopia, China, the Soviet Union, North Korea, Cuba, and Eastern Europe. We need to bring true comfort, that is, the gospel of Jesus Christ to all people groups in the world, because Jesus Christ crucified is the only hope of the world. There is no salvation besides him. Rulers come and go, but our Lord Jesus Christ is King of Kings, Lord of Lords, and he shall reign forever.

The churches of the world need to walk together and work together. We need to put away things that divide us and rally upon the one thing that unites us: Christ! Anyone in the world who believes in Christ, who has repented of his sin, and has a born-again experience in Christ, regardless of what church or denomination affiliation, is my brother! There is no biblical ground to exclude believers from fellowship. They have a right in Christ for fellowship and love. Our basis of fellowship is Jesus Christ and him crucified—not labels, not our name or tradition. Because of the grace of the Lamb that was slain, we have fellowship and working relationships with one another.

If you already have a national evangelization movement in your country, please do some praying and planning in two areas:

1. How to make your national evangelization movement more successful, fruitful, and lasting.
2. How to further involve your churches in world evangelization. Are you willing to help other countries, maybe a neighboring country, for their national evangelization? There are some countries which would welcome your help.

If you do not have a national evangelization movement in your country, please pray and think about how to use the next one or two years to prepare and organize a consultation for national evangelization. I am sure God will bless your effort, and that other countries would be more than happy to share their experiences with you to see that you have a successful conference.

Into the Whole World

It is nearly the end of the century. The actual number of years varies depending on how you count it. Whichever method you use, the time is short.

There are more than two hundred nations in the world. Is it possible that within the next few years, by the grace of God and through the cooperative effort of the churches in each country, every nation will have a national evangelistic movement and a task force to serve the churches to achieve the Great Commission?

The readiness of each nation for a national movement is not the same. In some countries national evangelistic movements are already underway such as the Philippines, Guatemala, Ghana, New Zealand, El Salvador, India, and Zaire.

Some are operating in cooperation with international movements, such as the DAWN movement. Some operate independently. And some national movements are in the final phase of preparation and are about to be launched soon. The majority of the rest of the nations will need time for information, motivation, and mobilization efforts.

Can we, by faith, envision a global evangelization movement through each national movement of the world? For instance, today there are twenty nations who already have national movements underway. According to available data, twenty additional nations may have their national movements by 1990. In 1991, fifty more nations may join in the force. That makes a total of ninety.

Through continued efforts of us all, can we believe that God will help make it possible for sixty more in 1992, and still more in 1993, to have their own national evangelization movement underway?

Adopt a People

Data research greatly enhanced modern mission outreach. But the differences of systems and records between leading researchers of today have been a source of frustration to church and mission leaders in the past decades.

In 1988, Dr. David Barrett, author of *The World Christian Encyclopedia,* was commissioned to be coordinator of the LCWE Statistics Task Force for the purpose of working out a unified code and system to enable the researchers to provide the church community with unified data. Marvelous results have been achieved. From now on we will receive unified data.

According to the new statistics, the researchers have generally agreed that there are about twelve thousand unreached people groups in the world today. The immediate goal of national and world evangelization should be to plant vibrant and growing churches in these unreached people groups, and let these indigenous churches evangelize their own people. With the growing number of congregations of the world, and the decreasing number of unreached people groups, today's ratio is over four hundred congregations for every unreached people group. Does this sound simplistic? Maybe so, but it presents a dramatic and reasonable picture of how achievable the task is.

Pray and see if God wants your church or denomination to "adopt" an unreached people group—to get to know the people and be responsible to send and support church planters to go and start the evangelization process. The people group approach has made world evangelization understandable and achievable.

Church history is turning a corner. God has patiently waited for almost twenty centuries for the church to fulfill her responsibility. Today, God is handing us the possibility of evangelizing the world by the year 2000 on a silver platter. Are we willing to accept it?

Acts 12 describes the apostle Peter's release from prison. The church was earnestly praying for his deliverance, but when he was delivered and came to them, they could not believe it and told the messenger that she was mad.

We have been praying for world evangelization, but if God answers our prayers and says to us, "All right, you can evangelize the world in ten years," are we so shocked that we cannot believe it?

God is doing a new thing today. Almost everywhere you go you hear people talk about A.D. 2000. Sometimes it seems God is ringing a bell in heaven, as if he is saying to his church, "Ladies and gentlemen, the hour is late, and the job is not yet done. It is time to get serious. Remember my commission to you. Complete it soon."

Let's work together. Let's open ourselves to each other and to all who take seriously this task of sharing the gospel story. This is our Father's world; it is great and complex. No one can do it alone. Some of us have come into the arena earlier, some later. Let no "early birds" say to the later ones, "Back off, I was here first." Let no "younger birds" say to the early ones, "Time for you to move on. I'm taking over." We need a gigantic global evangelization cooperation across geographical, denominational, ethnic, linguistic, and generation lines.

Perhaps it could be said that today we are writing the next chapter of church history. Just how it shall be written depends on whether we are collectively sensitive and obedient to the leading and prodding of the Spirit of God, who sometimes speaks to us through a still small voice, "This is the way, walk in it."

Reflections

Rolf Scheffbuch

In 1974, when we participated in Lausanne I, some of us Germans were in the midst of preparing our first evangelical rally. It was going to be held some months later in the Stuttgart soccer stadium with an expected participation of about fifty thousand people. After Lausanne, we changed our plans drastically. Instead of just confessing our orthodox viewpoints, we tried to make a joyful, colorful program full of loving invitation to Jesus. The motto of that crowded event became: "Jesus—our refuge and strength!"

In the midst of the preparation, there were two heart-breaking incidents. One of the young volunteers became seriously injured in a tragic traffic accident. And another volunteer was diagnosed with cancer. The Christians in our congregation prayed diligently for both young people. Three weeks later the girl was released from the hospital. The young man died after weeks of suffering. Before he died he said,

> It has been the highlight of my life that I could participate in that Stuttgart meeting. I am knowing and believing that Jesus is and will be my refuge and strength—even in the midst of death!

Wholehearted Thanks

I would like to thank all the Lausanne representatives for the tremendous work they have done to inspire Christians all over the world. In addition, we give thanks to our Lord Jesus Christ. He has blessed and guided the Lausanne movement. Through it he has blessed even us Germans, who so often have behaved as schoolmasters of the world and not as pupils who are anxious to learn their lesson.

Unity

The Lausanne movement has helped Europe to unite our efforts in the field of the new evangelization of Europe. The Lausanne movement made us aware of the common challenge: Get out of the narrow quarters of your churches and denominations; get out of the narrow barriers of your nation! Europe is about to become a "United Europe" as a political unit, as an economical unit, and as a social unit. Shouldn't we also have a unity of mission-minded evangelicals throughout Europe?

Europe is marked by terrible secularization, and also with old mainline churches and

Bishop Rolf Scheffbuch is Dean of the Evangelical Church of Wurttemberg and is a citizen of the Federal Republic of Germany. He is Chairman of the European Lausanne Committee for World Evangelization.

free churches, with the many parachurch agencies, and with all the competition between them. There is the rich European North. But there are also small Christian minorities in Southern Europe, surrounded by much poverty and by the strong Roman Catholic Church. There are also socialistic countries in Eastern Europe with special situations and unique experiences and gifts.

I tried hard to get a European Leaders Conference together. Two years ago, at Calloway Gardens, I understood what the Bible means when it speaks of "brokenhearted people." I was discouraged and exhausted from my efforts, which seemed to be totally in vain. I was discouraged about all European Lausanne work. But the Lord was there. He used brothers and sisters to encourage me. There were Viggo and Patrick, Tormod and Seikku, and others. In spite of their own heavy burdens, they were willing to share the responsibility. They accepted me, a weak, German Lutheran pastor with poor English, just as Christ accepted me.

As a result, we had a wonderful and inspiring European Leaders Conference on World Evangelization. We dedicated ourselves to the Lord Jesus and made a commitment to be obedient in re-evangelizing Europe. More than 140 leaders from all over Europe participated. They came from Iceland and from Greece, from Portugal and from the Scandinavian countries. They even came from the United Kingdom. The Lord gave us a deep understanding of the needs of European people and a vision of the many things which have to be done, and which can only be done with his blessing and presence and with the cooperation of European evangelicals.

Please pray for us as we try to organize a network in Europe between the European Evangelical Alliance and parachurch agencies, and between mainline churches and free churches. In his letter to the Romans, Paul says, "Join me in my struggle by praying to God for me" (Romans 15:30).

Servant Hearts

It is wonderful to have young people with us. I would like to offer a special thank you to those who are younger than forty. Sisters and brothers, you are the ones who will have to carry on the work, to keep the torch burning.

I am also thrilled to have so many sisters among us. It was unfortunate that up until now we had such a poor participation of sisters. Paul expresses my appreciation in his letter to the Romans:

> I commend to you our sister. . . . I ask you to receive her in the Lord in a way worthy of the saints and to give her any help she may need from you, for *she has been a great help to many people,* including me (Romans 16:1–2, emphasis added).

Proclaiming the Gospel

Evangelization and world mission is the central issue of Christ's church. They are not merely tasks "number eleven or twelve" out of a number of other tasks. Evangelization and world mission are the axles for the wheels of all Christian activities; Jesus Christ is the motor. (Please excuse that illustration, but I come from an area in Germany where most people work in Mercedes-Benz plants!) Therefore, like Paul, let us not be ashamed of proclaiming the unique gospel, "because it is the power of God for the salvation of everyone who believes" (Romans 1:16).

The Letter to the Romans

Paul's letter to the Romans is unique. There is still more blessing in that letter than we received during this Congress in the morning Bible studies. The Lord used that letter in the conversions of Augustine, Martin Luther, John Wesley, and many others. He also used that letter to bring real faith to my family.

My great-great-grandmother had heard of a spiritual awakening in the next village. She went there because she was interested in what was going on. Finally, she asked the pastor of that village, "What have I to do in order to get a deeper faith?"

He answered, "Madam, read the New Testament letter to the Romans!"

And she did. However, after she read the first chapters with all those terrible accounts of wickedness, she closed the Bible. She returned and told that pastor, "Maybe you will find all that wickedness in your village; but our situation is different!"

But the pastor didn't give up. He advised, "Just read that letter again!" She was obedient, and the Lord blessed her obedience. She discovered Jesus, the Savior, who gave his life for her—a religious-pagan without Christ, a sinful and lost lady in a desperately poor German village.

The next time she saw the pastor, she confessed, "Pastor, that letter to the Romans has become God's personal message to me!" And so it happened that true Christian faith came to her, to her village, and to our family.

I would also like to urge you, "Read that letter again and again!" We all need to rediscover that the Savior, Jesus, and God, the Father, who justifies the wicked. And the post-Christian, pagan-religious Europe needs to rediscover that faith is more than simply believing in a heavenly being and in some life after death. Faith means that lost people rejoice in God's abundant and full provision of grace.

A major issue of our Congress has been the tension between non-charismatic and charismatic Christians. Just before I came to our Congress, I had finished my fourteenth year of wonderful service as a local pastor. I have witnessed many signs and wonders. Many members of my congregation have said, "It has helped so much when sisters and brothers have prayed with me and for me—that they have laid hands on me!" But my heart is trembling: Have they also accepted the *fullness of grace,* which according to Paul, is the gift of God's righteousness?

It is my conviction that we all need to discover and experience this grace that is the true "full gospel." And we need to see that through this grace, God delivers us from our sin! May the Lord bless us all.

"Fear Not"

Luis Palau

Our brother Ed Dayton asked me to speak on the subject "Fear Not as You Face the Future." But I say to myself, *Who am I to get up here and talk about fear not?* I remember meeting a brother from Nepal who was thrown in jail three times because he's a Christian. He should be here and tell us how to fear not when you're in jail. The closest I've come to suffering for Christ was a bunch of letters telling me I was going to die like a dog in Peru. Though I'm not sure how dogs die, I didn't like the idea. But I'm still alive. Now my brother in Nepal hasn't died like a dog, but he's been penned up like one sometimes, and he should talk. Nevertheless, because the Lord placed me in a position to speak to you on this subject, I will gladly do it.

I'd like to read two passages from the Bible, the first one in the Old Testament, 2 Kings 6:15–17:

> When the servant of the man of God got up and went out early the next morning, an army with horses and chariots had surrounded the city. "Oh, my lord, what shall we do?" the servant asked. "Don't be afraid," the prophet answered. "Those who are with us are more than those who are with them." And Elisha prayed, "O Lord, open his eyes so he may see." Then the Lord opened the servant's eyes, and he looked and saw the hills full of horses and chariots of fire all around Elisha.

What a beautiful passage that is, isn't it?

But now I want to read another passage. John 14 is a favorite. These are beautiful words, and I feel the Lord would have us combine the Old with the New Testament. In John 14:12–14, the Savior is speaking and he says,

> I tell you the truth, anyone who has faith in me will do what I have been doing. He will do even greater things than these, because I am going to the Father. And I will do whatever you ask in my name, so that the Son may bring glory to the Father. You may ask me for anything in my name, and I will do it.

And verse 15, "If you love me, you will obey what I command."

Three of the points I always make in this passage have been hit in this Congress, two of them very much. The first one is obvious: The Lord says to us today, "Fear not, dream

Luis Palau is President of the Luis Palau Evangelistic Association. Born and raised in Argentina, he is now a citizen of the United States.

great dreams and plan great plans, because I am going to the Father." I hardly need to touch on that because we've been overwhelmed by the Word of the Lord from everybody here.

The second word that the Lord seems to say here is, "Fear not. Pray great prayers because I will answer the prayers of my people."

And then the third point is in verse 15, "Fear not as long as you obey my commands." And I feel this morning the Lord would have me emphasize the third one.

When Mary the mother of Jesus went to the marriage in Cana and you remember they ran out of wine, she preached her one and only recorded sermon in the Bible. It's a one-liner, but it's got a lot of power. She said to the servants there, "Do whatever he tells you." And so this morning for this last session, the word that the Lord has laid on my heart is: "Fear not as long as you do it."

We have dreamed great dreams, plans galore, wonderful ideas, and when the year 2000 comes, pray the Lord we'll all be here to see it all happen as was envisioned last night. What a joy it will be on December 31 of the year 2000 to look back and say, "Master, by your grace I was able to do it. The track you put me on I was able to stay on. And by your power we did it. Hallelujah to your name."

Talking about cooperation, the other day I was flying from Budapest to London. Alan Johnson, one of my British team members, and I were chatting about the rally in Budapest where Cliff Richard, a British singer, had sung and I had preached to thousands of Hungarian young people (about twelve hundred came to the Lord). A British lady in front of us was talking to a Hungarian woman, and you could tell she was evangelizing the Hungarian, who turned out to be a young businesswoman going to London to sell plastic cups to the British.

Overhearing us, the English woman turned to me and said, "Excuse me, are you talking about the rally yesterday with Cliff Richard and Luis Palau?" "Yes," I said. "Oh, you know I wasn't able to get in, but I came all the way from western England to pray. I went to Czechoslovakia and Yugoslavia, not as a tourist, just to pray. And then I came to Budapest and for three days I was praying, but I didn't even hear the results. What happened at the rally?"

She didn't know I was Luis Palau, and we told her the blessings and the testimony of Cliff and the power of God, and the tears of the Hungarian brethren. And she said that's wonderful. Then she said, "Do you know where Brother Palau is?"

"Well, that's me," I said.

"Brother, I was praying for you these three days, and I thought you might be on this plane," she said. "I've been talking to this Hungarian lady, and I think she's ready to be converted. Would you talk to her?"

"Why don't you do it?" I said. "I've been listening to what you've been saying. You've done a terrific job."

But she said, "I don't know how to close the deal."

So I agreed, but I thought to myself, *she's got to get this sheep herself.* I stuck my head between the two seats and said to the Hungarian woman, "Did you understand what this lady said to you?"

"Yes," she said.

"Well, look, the final part is this, Revelation 3:20: 'I stand at your door and knock. If you hear my voice and open the door, I'll come in to you.' Are you ready to open the door to Jesus?"

"Oh, yes, I understand," she said.

"Are you willing to open the door?"

"Yes, I'm willing to open the door."

I said to my British sister, "Then lead her in prayer."

She said, "No, no, no. I've never done it."

"Then do it now," I said, and I sat back. I wanted to do it, actually. It would have been a great thing to lead a Hungarian businesswoman to Christ. But the English lady turned to this Hungarian, grabbed her hand, put her arm around her, and led her to Jesus Christ. That is cooperation in evangelism.

We've had a glorious Congress, but I feel on this closing hour I wish I could cheer you up a little bit. I think we've repented a lot. And I think we need to repent. But the Latin Americans said to me, "You better talk about giving glory to God. We've repented enough now; tell about some of the things that have been happening in South America."

The verse that keeps coming to me is this: "Many will come from the east and the west, and will take their places at the feast with Abraham, Isaac, and Jacob in the kingdom of heaven." Since World War II, the Word of the Lord has exploded around the world, and we need to rejoice once in a while. When we glory in the Savior and his power, what a joy that is. When you think that here in Southeast Asia there are now millions upon millions who claim the name of Jesus Christ. We've seen the theologians from Africa and Asia and Latin America, besides those from Europe and America. Most of us didn't have theologians thirty-five to forty years ago. And now we have national leaders. In other words, the Lord has honored the work of the missionaries.

I thank God that the missionaries who came to Latin America had a great vision. I don't think they studied cross-cultural stuff because some of the old British missionaries wore heavy suits in weather like this, and as a little boy I would watch them sweating up a storm as they preached. And I used to think, *Why doesn't he take his coat off?* They made terrible mistakes. Their Spanish was horrid. But they lived among us and our poverty, and we didn't think in terms of whether they adapted or didn't adapt. All we thought was these brothers and their wives and children loved us enough to bring us eternal life, and we just loved them. And I thought the missionaries were saints. It was only when I got older and came to America that I realized they were doing it all wrong. They brought the Word of Life. And they identified with the people, the poor.

We forget that when the gospel came to the Third World, it started with the poor. And most of the gospel even today still goes to the poor. I know that you men and women who are from Europe and America continue to beat your breasts and beat the rich, but in most of the world the gospel is still going to the poor, through the poor, for the poor.

There's a danger that we go from here beating our heads. People might think that since Lausanne we've done nothing but fail, we're nothing but miserable nobodies, the church hasn't grown. Let's first give glory to God.

Some time ago, Os Guinness said, "Our generation is in a shopping mood for answers." Even in Europe, where it may not appear like they are. In America they are searching in Eastern religions. All over the world, they are searching. Summer is here, and so is the harvest. A verse in Proverbs says, "He who gathers crops in summer is a wise son, but he who sleeps during harvest is a disgraceful son."

Four thousand of us have sat for ten days pontificating about evangelism—you have to do it once in a while, but for ten days we probably didn't reach out too much. Now we're going to leave this place and we must go and do it. Mary said to the servants, "Do whatever he tells you." And each one of us, brothers and sisters, has got to find the time now, sifting all that God has said so that we know what the Savior is saying to us. So that we know what we must do, and by the power of the Lord we go with a commitment to do it.

You know, we could continue to multiply congresses and think that we're evangelizing. We could continue to put out volumes and think that we're evangelizing. You and I could be so taken up preparing sermons for conventions that we don't have time to evangelize. But we never outgrow the responsibility. When you get to be middle-aged, there's a great temptation, even for evangelists, to think, *Evangelism is OK for the YWAMers and the OMers and the Youth for Christers and the new generation of Campus Crusaders. But I've got a little dignity now. I've got two free doctorates. I'm president of this university or this organization. And it's a little humiliating to actually go and do it.* There's a great temptation to sit back and say to the young people, "Now you boys and girls go do it. I'll write the books and set up the conventions." But the Lord says to each one of us, "You do it," and stimulate others to do it, too.

If you've read Bready's *England: Before and After Wesley*, you know that England was in as bad a shape as any Third World nation today. Yet Wesley arose, and he and the young people said, "We want to revive the nation, especially the church, and to spread Scriptural holiness across the land." Within fifty years, England began to change, and Wesley, who was kicked out of the churches in his youth, was treated like an honored servant of God.

And though I haven't asked for John Stott's permission to say so, after World War II the Anglican church needed renewal again. And a group of young clergymen, among them our brother, began to dream for another revival. They asked God to raise up a new generation of reborn, Spirit-filled, Bible-centered Anglicans in England, so that England would be awakened again. God has answered the dreams and prayers of our brother John Stott and a group of young evangelicals who now call themselves the senior evangelicals, because forty-five years have gone by. But there's a group of young evangelicals coming up from behind, and when you know the Anglican bishops in the United Kingdom and the key positions that they hold and how alive they are to God, you say, "Lord, how exciting that John Stott, among others, even chose not to get married so that the vision could be fulfilled." What a blessing that has been for the United Kingdom in our day.

And now a new wave has come to the United Kingdom parallel to what's happening among the Anglicans. In the middle seventies some of the young fellows got all worked up about the independent churches and the non-Anglican denominations and they began to dream that God would visit the British Isles again with fire and with blessing. And I tell you, compared to the rest of the continent of Europe, the United Kingdom today is paradise. It's got a ways to go—a few streams to be cleaned and a few trees to be planted—but what fire, what joy, what power, what blessing in the United Kingdom. Politicians are listening to the gospel, and many are being converted to Jesus Christ.

Brothers and sisters, I am committed 100 percent that we must continue to minister among the poor. Most of us were born there, lived there, and ministered there, but praise the Lord for reaffirming it. But there are also one billion rich people whose souls are as valuable to God as the souls of the poor, who need to be converted as much as the poor, although often they are harder to bring to Christ. And yet efforts must be made to reach politicians, to reach wealthy businessmen, to reach university students whom we haven't mentioned enough. Let's not get imbalanced. Yes, compassion. We want the whole world to know that we believers love the poor. I hesitated to make this statement lest it be misunderstood, but let's not lead people to think we're giving up on Europe, that we're giving up on the affluent West. And furthermore, let's not forget that the reason for its wealth isn't just that those nations raped the Third World, but that Reformation principles imbedded in those countries brought so much blessing. And I want Europeans and Americans to know that many people in the Third World dream about winning millions to Christ and, secondly, that this spiritual awakening would reform the nations and in turn bring a better lifestyle. Latin Americans want their children to go to high school, to be able to go to university. They want justice under the law. But we feel this will come by reformation from within by the power of the gospel and the living out of the biblical ethic. And that's what is beginning to happen.

Perhaps in our day, Guatemala will be the first reformed nation in Latin America. Out of seven million people, some three million in Guatemala now claim to have been born again. Already you see the penetration of society. Now you may read in the newspapers about revolution and violence. Of course, there's some of that; there was in Europe during Luther's day and Calvin's day and in England many a time. But as the Christians penetrate economic institutions, the military, education, politics, as they live out the biblical ethic, you can even begin to feel the changes coming along, and we should pray that this would happen. Rather than by violent revolution, by hatred, by bloodshed, why can't we dream that reformation could occur peacefully? Those of us from Latin America want to believe—and we may be naive—but we would love to believe that if enough people who are converted really live out the biblical ethic, the nations could change, bringing blessing to the land. And that's the dream of nation after nation in the Third World.

In honor to everybody here, I want to say that evangelism is the best form of social action. Let's not forget that, because evangelism deals with the root of the problem, not with the symptoms. The root is man's alienation and sinfulness. And although we participate in social action parallel with evangelism—and that's why we love the Lausanne Covenant—nevertheless let's never forget that social action itself is not evangelism. Evangelism is preaching Christ crucified, resurrected with power to change people's lives. Evangelism is John 3:16 and 1 Corinthians 15:1–3 and Romans 1:16. Evangelism is that a person repent and be converted and be born again and begin to live by the power of the Holy Spirit. Evangelism is the presentation of Christ in the power of the Spirit so that lives are changed.

By the year 2000 some of us perhaps will be killed for the gospel. Somehow you sense it. And we will all fear. I don't think any normal person says, "I want to be killed; I'm waiting for the day when some nut comes up and shoots me." But George Whitefield said, "I am immortal till my day is done." None of us will be killed one hour before the Lord says, "OK boy, you've done your duty. Come on home."

Hugh Latimer was sentenced to burn at the stake in 1555, and another bishop, Nicholas Ridley, was tied back to back with him. During those last few moments, Latimer said to his young friend, "Be of good comfort, Master Ridley, and play the man. We shall this day light such a candle by God's grace in England as I trust shall never be put out."

What a way to die. May the Lord give us grace, if some of us should die for the kingdom before we meet in the year 2000, that we would die with that kind of confidence. The Lord says, "Never will I leave you; never will I forsake you." So we say with confidence, "The Lord is my helper; I will not be afraid. What can man do to me?" (Hebrews 13:5–6) And as we get ready to go for it, let's not forget that though we talk big plans, we have massive ideas, bunches of videos, enormous files, documents galore, the Lord is looking at each of us. "Do whatever he tells you." The Lord bless you.

LCWE's Goals for the Future

Tom Houston

I learned an important truth about goals many years ago. My goals are good goals. Your goals are bad goals. If I set goals for myself, I own them, I value them, and they are important to me. If you set goals for me and I have nothing to do with determining what they are or deciding whether I shall adopt them, I have no sense of ownership and my motivation to accomplish them is very low.

I will succeed as International Director of Lausanne if my goals are your goals, but not only for that reason. LCWE is very small. We will have a small staff of eight to ten people with a small budget to match. We can actually do very little. Yet, we are trying to change the whole church and the whole world for Jesus' sake. For that reason, my goals *must* be your goals. You are Lausanne, and the goals that all of you together adopt will determine how effective Lausanne will be. Our job will be to serve you in reaching these goals.

But there is one goal that I believe we all share already. It is that we stay together. We have had tensions in these last ten days but we have survived them: we are surviving them, and we will continue to survive them. This is the nature of the body of Christ.

I learned about creative tension from Stephen Neill in the early sixties. Christians are skillful in polarizing. I don't know why, but we are, and I used to be quite good at it. I was a separatist as a young pastor. Where there were two poles, I wanted to destroy or exclude the other pole. Then I realized God worked with magnetic poles, the North and the South, and they created a field of tension within which things could be done. There is no way you can remove a pole—it is not in the nature of things. So now I am a Baptist—a British Baptist—but I am *glad* the Anglicans are there. I shudder to think what my country or even city would be without them.

David Bosch helped me understand further in South Africa in 1979, with this truth: There are six saving acts of God in Jesus Christ.

The first is the Incarnation. The Word became a human being and lived among us. This is the controlling truth for Anglicans and Roman Catholics. They concentrate on the presence of Christ and emphasize continuity in the life of the people of God.

The second saving act is the Cross, the Atonement. He who knew no sin, God made to be sin that we might be made the righteousness of God in him. The Lutherans and the Evangelicals center on the Atonement. They concentrate on the pardon of Christ and emphasize the discontinuity of conversion.

The third saving act of God is the Resurrection. Christ rose from the dead. This is the paramount truth for the Orthodox churches. I am told their Easter services are deeply moving. Their theology centers on the risen Christ; they emphasize new life in Christ.

The fourth saving act is the Ascension. Christ ascended on high and led captivity captive. Christ is King. This is the great truth for Presbyterians and the Reformed churches, and that is why Presbyterians seem to be permanently dissatisfied with the status quo.

The fifth saving act is Pentecost, the sending of the Spirit. This is the central truth for Pentecostals and charismatics. They emphasize the power of the Holy Spirit.

The sixth saving act is yet to come. It is the Advent, the Second Coming of Christ. This is the theme of the Seventh-day and other Adventists. They present Christ coming again as the hope of glory after this vale of tears. They sometimes spend a great deal of effort in understanding the signs of the times and working out when Christ might come.

All these churches believe in all six saving acts, but they emphasize one and seem to attract people whose need is met by that one. Ideally we should all emphasize all, but no one group is large enough to do that, so it takes all of these to present the whole gospel. And there are tensions between them. Those who emphasize the leadership of the reigning Christ over all things want to see things changed now. The Adventist sees life as a lost and hopeless case that will need to wait for Christ to come to put it right. These views clash regarding social concern.

The Incarnation supporters emphasize the gradual growth of the Christian life beginning in baptism, often in infancy. Those who preach the Cross become impatient with that and pursue the discontinuity of dramatic conversion.

But both views are necessary. God gives us each a torch to carry, but it is one procession. We do not need to apologize for our torch. We need to carry it high, but let us not imagine it is the whole truth. Let us affirm the whole procession and the others in it. Let us maintain our commitment to show to the world the people of God as one— both women and men, poor and rich, young and old, lay and clergy, weak and strong, white and black, yellow and brown, non-reading and reading. Let us be a force for fusion and not send out sparks that ignite inflammatory division. Let us make it our determined goal to stay together under the banner of the Word of God as reflected in the Lausanne Covenant and show the world the fullness of saving acts of God in Christ.

VIDEO PRESENTATION

The Flame Is Now in Us

Producers: Bill Thatcher, Eric Miller

Leighton Ford: On behalf of the Lausanne Committee for World Evangelization, I want to declare the second International Congress on World Evangelization, Lausanne II in Manila, to be officially open.

Thomas Wang: When we say "passing the torch," we do not mean that the older generation pass the torch of the gospel to the younger generation alone. Both generations, and all generations, should uphold and carry on the torch of the gospel of Jesus Christ *together.*

Narrator: In July, 1989, three thousand leaders from nearly two hundred nations and a host of traditions met in Manila for Lausanne II. Since the previous Congress, held in Lausanne, Switzerland, fifteen years before, the world had changed in significant ways: a world more crowded, more urbanized, more mired in poverty. A world less friendly to the Good News of Christ, still unheard by two thousand million people. Building upon a covenant of cooperation and wholistic ministry, the delegates gathered anew to pray, to plan, and to partner together to carry the light of Jesus Christ into a new century.

Leighton Ford: Calling the whole church to take the whole gospel to the whole world. And who is it that calls? Not us. Who is it that calls? Not Lausanne II, but Christ who calls us.

Luis Bush: To work together with new understanding in an increasingly urban world, in an attitude of dependence on the Lord Jesus Christ and his Holy Spirit, to mobilize all the forces within the body of Christ in every country of the world, to fulfill the Great Commission by proclaiming the gospel of our Lord Jesus Christ to every people group, and by obeying the Great Commandment, demonstrating love to the whole person.

Narrator: With a sense of urgency, participants wrestled with the realities of a lost and suffering world, grieved by the pervasiveness of sin, appalled at the inhuman conditions of the poor and oppressed, and newly committed to proclaiming the whole gospel of justification for sinners, and justice in society by word, by deed, and by sign.

Bill Thatcher is an Executive Director of International Christian Media Consortium.
Eric Miller is Director of International 2100, a division of Intervarsity Christian Fellowship, and Media Director of International Fellowship of Evangelical Students.

Senator Salonga: Around 60 to 70 percent of our people live below the poverty level. Eighty-five percent of our schoolchildren suffer from malnutrition. This is the context in which the Good News is being preached today in the Philippines.

Tom Houston: Jesus intended for Good News to be brought to the poor by his followers, giving to the poor as well as telling them about him, and urging them to turn from their sins. This is one part of compassion, the economic part. We may not be required to give up our jobs or sell our property, but we must give up something significant if the compassion of Jesus is to be seen in us.

Gary Granada: Two miles from here there are people working twelve hours a day scraping garbage for a living, perhaps thinking in the back of their minds, "How can the God of these middle-class, privileged, rich, influential Christians really be on the side of the poor?" Unless, and until, we resolve this aberration of our faith, we cannot be surprised if the peoples of the garbage dumps of the cities of the world will think of our message as just another piece of trash.

John Stott: The proper response to the gospel is, indeed, faith and faith alone. But a true and living faith in Jesus includes within itself a measure of *submission,* and it leads *inevitably* into a life of obedience. The presence or absence of saving faith in the heart will be disclosed by the presence or absence of good works of love in our lives.

Interview 1: One of the things that has touched me greatly this morning is the need to embrace my city, to get to love my city.

Interview 2: Most of the Christians, they are trying to do only their evangelism, just their preaching. But it's giving a real challenge, impressing to do, to help the poor people.

Narrator: The call to an authentic witness to a broken world is not without its cost. In a spirit of repentance, participants humbly acknowledged that, in many places, the chief barrier to global evangelization is the church itself—comfortable in its wealth, compromised in its culture, complacent in its lack of integrity and holiness. The Congress appealed to Christians everywhere for moral purity, responsible stewardship, and sacrificial risk, to reflect the character of Christ.

Os Guinness: But in the modern world, there have been people in the last decade who have been converted fifteen times! They're converted, and reconverted, and reconverted; or, in Christian terms, born again, and again, and again. But that isn't valid. Even being born again in the conditions of modernized suburbia has become a shallow and sentimental experience that's no longer radical and life-changing.

Carmelo Teranova: Holiness, holiness, holiness. This is the word for our lives. The world needs to see holy people. Not specialists, not technicians, not executives, not professionals—men and women that look like Jesus.

M.Y. Chan: When I was in prison in the labor camp, the authorities, they thought the best place to remold me, to torture me, was to appoint me to empty the human waste cesspools. Only when I worked in the cesspools, that day, that time, I was alone, so I could pray to our Lord as loudly as I needed and I could also recite the Scriptures—all those psalms of the Bible I still remembered. And no one would come close enough to stop me. That's why I loved to work in the human waste cesspools because I met my Lord's presence in the cesspools.

Ajith Fernando: And if we are to be united with Jesus Christ fully, we must suffer as he suffered. When we suffer for Christ, Christ suffers with us.

Interview 3: I would say that in evangelizing the world, we need to be willing to give ourselves fully to Jesus Christ. Because, when I think about our ministry in Nepal, I would say that many of our people are being imprisoned, but they will say that that is a cost they are willing to pay for because of Christ.

Interview 4: When we become Christians—if we are Hindus or Muslims—if we become Christians, then our families disown us. So the church is the only place where we can find shelter.

Interview 5: And I think the unity of it all has been a challenge to my own heart, that when you get together on an occasion like this you don't worry about who belongs to what, or where you come from, but we're together, united not only in the Lord, but in the challenge of reaching the world for Jesus Christ.

Narrator: In the most representative gathering of Christian leaders ever assembled, Lausanne II embodied the extraordinary diversity and spiritual unity of the international body of Christ. The delegates affirmed a new era of partnership, marked by cooperation and coordination of different gifts. Evangelicals sought to bear witness to the gospel of reconciliation by seeking areas of agreement with the historic Orthodox, Latin, and Coptic traditions, while aware of painful divisions. One agreement recognized the strategic role of the local church, with awakened and equipped laity, as central to advancing the kingdom of God.

Panya Baba: The challenge of the unfinished task of world evangelization in our generation is still too enormous to be left to only a few active Christian workers and missionaries to accomplish. The task calls for the involvement of the whole universal church.

Peter Kuzmic: In the task of world evangelization, it may also, and will also, require less competition and more cooperation; less self-sufficiency and more willingness to serve; less of a drive to dominate others, and more of a desire to develop them.

Juliet Thomas: Help us to see ourselves, not as others see us, not even as we want to see ourselves, but as you see us. For your Word tells us that you have the eyes of blazing fire that look deep within us, into those inmost recesses that no one else sees and no one else knows; those motives that are there, Lord, those attitudes, those relationships, the bitternesses, the unforgiveness, the resentment, the rivalry, the competition, the jealousies. And we know that when our hearts are filled with these, we close ourselves from your presence.

Interview 6: And I tell you, I'll be going back to Fiji a different man, a different minister, a different pastor altogether.

Interview 7: I can take back with me the strength of knowing that I'm part of the body of Christ. And I know that I have a lot of prayer backing from many new people, new friends I've made, and that's a tremendous encouragement.

Narrator: The light of the gospel is in our hands, and the flame of the Spirit is within our hearts, indwelling each believer, called to reach the whole world with the whole gospel of Christ. In the Spirit's power, the whole church is moved by compassion for others, and holy jealousy for God's honor to an incarnational witness in imitation of Jesus Christ.

Jack Hayford: What will result? The result will be fullness in worship, a fullness in the Word, a fullness in integrity and character, a fullness in serving the poor, a fullness in loving one another, a fullness in lay involvement, a fullness in the Spirit with power, gifts, signs, and wonders enhancing a fullness unto evangelism.

Eva Burrows: In cross-cultural evangelism, this costly identification means learning another language, adjusting to their customs and lifestyles. It really does cost us something to step into another person's skin, to feel what that person feels, to discover the hurts that person feels, to share that person's poverty. Such self-giving is costly, but fruitfulness in ministry is in direct proportion to our identification with those whom we seek to evangelize and serve.

Caesar Molebatsi: When we choose to be faithful to such a call, it becomes clear that the focus of the Lord's concern is people. Hence, all systems and structures should serve God's concern for humankind. Our evangelism and mission is to be incarnational if it is to be authentic. If God is on the side of justice, then our message and our lives need to reflect this.

Senator Salonga: (quoting Isaiah):

> The spirit of the Lord is upon me, because he has anointed me to preach the good news to the poor. He has sent me to proclaim freedom for the prisoner, and recovery of sight for the blind, to release the oppressed, to proclaim the year of the Lord's favor.

Luis Palau: The Lord says, "Never will I leave you, never will I forsake you, so that we can confidently say, 'The Lord is my helper, I will not fear. What can man do to me'?" The Lord is looking at each one of us and saying, "Whatever he tells you to do, do it."

"Until He Comes"

Leighton Ford

There is a popular movie in America called *Field of Dreams*. It is about a young farmer and his family who are going through hard times.

One evening as the farmer walks through his cornfield, he hears a voice saying, "If you build it—he will come." He looks around, but no one is there. The voice keeps repeating, "If you build it—he will come," but the farmer has no idea what it means.

The young man's father had died some years before. They had never been close. His father had been bitter and had grown old before his time. He had been a professional baseball player and had become bitter partly because one of his great heroes had been accused of a scandal and had been thrown out of baseball.

The young farmer becomes convinced that the voice is telling him that if he will build a baseball diamond out in his cornfield, then this great athlete and his father might come back to play ball on it. His family and friends think he's crazy, but he goes ahead and builds it. Only his four-year-old daughter believes with him that something will happen.

Then one night, out of the corn walks the figure of the great baseball star from the past. But only the young farmer and his daughter can see him.

On another night, a figure that the farmer recognizes as his father—young and handsome, strong and without bitterness—walks out of the corn. They talk together; they play catch together. At one point, the father looks around and says, "Is this heaven?"

His son replies, "No, this is Iowa. But heaven is the place where dreams become reality."

The story is a wonderful fantasy. But in Christ, heaven is more than a dream; it is reality that is already begun. The young farmer in the story heard a voice that said, "If you build it—he will come." God has given us a similar dream. Will you build? He is coming!

God Has Given a Dream

God calls this dream his kingdom. He put the dream in the hearts of the great prophets. They dreamed of a day when the hearts of the fathers would turn to the children. They dreamed of a day when there would be no war. They dreamed of a day when each family would have their own house and enjoy the fruit of their labors. They dreamed of a day when swords would be turned into plowshares. They dreamed of a day when there would be a new heaven and a new earth, with peace and righteousness. This was the dream God put in their hearts!

Then Jesus came and said; "The kingdom of God is at hand." God's dream is *now*.

He said, "Your kingdom come on earth." God's dream is *here*. The kingdom of heaven—God's dream—was not just in heaven. It was down here. It was an invasion of earth by heaven.

Jesus Christ, the Son of God, came and called his people, died and rose again, sent forth his Spirit and told his people to proclaim this dream until he returned

As Caesar Molebatsi reminded us, we are to pray, "Thy kingdom come—on earth—our proclamation among the oppressed is the proclamation of a new king." And as Ulrich Parzany reminded us, "We must put up signs of hope by working for justice and peace—until Christ comes."

A Crossroad for Christ

In Manila, God has given us a "field of dreams" also. Lausanne II has been a crossroad for Christ. We have seen the King and seen his dream again. As a layman said yesterday:

> The heart of this Congress has not been in the people-to-people meetings. Let's take away, not the differences and not the debates, but what we have seen in Christ and each other. The impact of Lausanne II will be through Christ lifted up in each of us.

A young leader said, "We younger men and women don't have to be convinced about world evangelization. We want to know how to link together and where do we go from here?"

Many have asked: "What is the future? What are the plans for the Lausanne movement? Will there be another Congress? How does the movement go on?"

There will be follow-up plans and ideas. Whether there will be another Congress, we do not know. But as Tom Houston has said, "You and I are Lausanne." If the dream and task of world evangelization is not carried on through you and me, through our churches and ministries, through our national groups, and through the networks formed here, it will not happen.

Lausanne is an enabling and facilitating movement. Lausanne II has been a time to hear God's voice. That young farmer heard a voice say, "If you build it—he will come." God's voice is saying, "Will you build? He is coming!"

Lawrence wrote,

> All men dream, but not equally. Those who dream by night in the dusty recesses of their minds awake to find it was vanity. But the dreamers of the day are dangerous men that they may act their dreams with open eyes to make it possible.

God is calling us to be his "dreamers of the day." He told us that his dream had started, but it would not be fulfilled until he came again. He promised this "gospel of the kingdom" would be proclaimed to all the nations and then the end would come.

What are we, as God's "dreamers," called to be in the light of Christ's return?

God's Dreamers Take Risks

God has given to his people the greatest enterprise in the world and he is asking whether we will have faith that dares to risk in his enterprise. In the parable of the talents, a rich man went away on a long journey and left each of his servants talents to invest. Each talent was probably worth several hundred thousand pesos. One servant got ten talents, another two, and another one.

Two of the servants invested and doubled their money. But the other was afraid—

afraid to risk—and buried his talent. When the owner came back, he asked for an accounting. The two who had risked were rewarded. The one who had buried it, lost everything.

God is like the owner. He has entrusted us to be stewards of the earth itself. God expects us to take care of this beautiful planet, not to waste its natural resources. We are entrusted, and we who follow the King should be concerned about the acid rain which is threatening this magnificent world, killing the great forests.

He has also entrusted to us the great task of world evangelization. He has given each of us a gift to use, and he has gone away and left us. He could have used angels, but he has given us the task because he wants us to grow as we risk.

Like the owner in the parable, Jesus is coming back. And we will have to give an account as to what we have done (2 Corinthians 5:10). *Will you risk? He is coming.*

Which servants do we identify with: the ones who were productive, entrepreneurial, and faithful; or the one who was unproductive, lazy, and fearful? The answer will probably depend on how we see our Lord. Do we see him as someone who has entrusted us? Or do we see him as someone who is hard and that we have to fear?

At a Congress like this, it would be very easy to leave feeling burdened and guilty. There are so many needs. There are so many to reach. It's been a billion minutes since Jesus was born and in the next ten years, a billion and a half babies will be born. All of us may leave here with a sense that we have not done enough, have not given enough, have not sacrificed enough. Michael Cassidy told of the time he was discouraged and ready to give up in South Africa, and the Lord said to him, "Michael, you are the only kind of material I have ever had to work with."

Thank God tonight that he *has* entrusted you and me. "Men ought to regard us as the servants of Christ entrusted," wrote Paul. "We have this treasure in earthen vessels." We are common clay pots, but we have the treasure God has given us. He's entrusted us. He's given us the task. *Will we risk? He's coming back!*

Three words have reverberated throughout this Congress: urgency, sacrifice, and cooperation. Repeatedly, we have heard that world evangelization will not take place without urgency, sacrifice, and cooperation. Each of these demands faith willing to risk.

Urgency—the reaching of the poor, the youth, the cities, the unreached —calls us to say, "My time is not my own. I'm not going to hold back. Where you are calling me to act, I will."

George Otis reminded us of the hidden cost of saying, "No," and that God would judge us, not on the basis of what we have done, but perhaps, on what we could have done.

Sacrifice calls us to say, "My life is not my own. My life is at risk." Someone has said that there are no comfort zones on the cross. And there are few comfort zones in world evangelization.

A Chinese youth stood in front of the tanks on Tiananmen Square in Beijing and dared them to move. As he stood there and put his life on the line, I wondered, "Would I put my life on the line like that for Christ? Would I be like Epaphroditus of whom Paul wrote, 'Welcome Epaphroditus in the Lord with great joy, and honor men like him, because he almost died for the work of Christ, risking his life' (Philippians 2:29–30)?"

Perhaps the risk we need to take is simple—the risk of letting Christ be exposed through his Word and through our lives. It is a risk to stand with Christ in the marketplace of ideas—to let the world see and hear him.

Martin Alphonse told about the Round Tables in India where Muslims, Hindus, and Buddhists were exposed not to Christianity but to Christ. And as Stanley Jones said, when Christianity was defined in terms of the person of Christ, "There was not a single situation where before the close of the conference Christ was not in moral and spiritual command of the situation." We need to take the risk of proclaiming Christ so his uniqueness, his sufficiency, and his attractiveness can be seen as the only hope for all peoples.

Cooperation means that we say, "Lord, our resources are not our own. We are willing to risk sharing those resources—whatever ideas, gifts, finances, and personnel God has given—for the sake of the greater task."

As we go back as leaders from this Congress, the primary job will not be to dispense information. It will be to point people to new frontiers. It will be to make people deal with questions that they won't face if left to themselves. It is the call to turn other followers into leaders who will bring change. If that does not happen, the world will not be evangelized.

Leaders take chances. They take chances on people. Will we take chances on younger leaders, on women, on men, on laypeople? Ford Madison, our lay associate, asked early in the Congress, "Brothers and sisters, will you trust Christ in me as a layman?" Leaders take chances in ideas. Will we be flexible enough to make changes that have to be made?

Jesus ended his story of the talents with a riddle, "He who has, to him it will be given. He who has not, even what he has will be taken away!" That sounds unfair. It sound mysterious. How can you take away something from someone who doesn't have anything? Jesus was revealing a law of spiritual life in a riddle. If we have the opportunity and the faith to act, we will receive more. If we have the opportunity, but not the faith to risk, we will lose that opportunity.

The next ten years may be the greatest opportunity we have ever had for world evangelization. God may open doors that have never been opened—or, if the doors are closed, reveal a window to crawl through.

At the close of Lausanne II, we are poised at a tremendously crucial point. The question is: "Will we as leaders risk taking advantage of it, or will we go back to business as usual and bury our talent in the ground?"

Will you risk? He is coming! Let us proclaim Christ with a faith that risks—until he comes.

God's Dreamers Are Those Who Last

Will you last? He is coming!

One of the great marks of God's "dreamers of the day" is the ability to endure. We have heard tremendous stories of great opportunity, but we have also heard stories of great difficulty. Who can forget Lucien Accad telling of the bombs in Lebanon; or Joseph Bonderanko, the brother from China, of being in prison; or Joni Eareckson Tada of working with the disabled and saying "If all the blind and deaf in the world were in one nation, it would be the largest nation in the world"?

Many of us will go back to places of great difficulty. God's dream calls us to proclaim Christ with a faith that looks forward in hope—like Moses, who endured the wrath of the king because he saw the one who was invisible; like our Lord Jesus, who for the joy that was set before him endured the cross and despised the shame.

Jesus also put the call for enduring hope in the form of another story about his plan to return—the story of the wheat and the weeds (Matthew 13:24–42). God is pictured as a farmer who sows the seed in his field. It reveals God's dream for the salvation of the world.

Jesus is the sower and he calls us to be seed-sowers—the proclaimers of his Word.

He said good seeds are the "sons of the kingdom"—righteous children who belong to the father and will shine like the sun.

God's dream is to produce people like himself. World evangelization is not a program, a plan, or a strategy. It is God the Father reproducing God the Son, through God the Spirit, in his people. As Peter Kuzmic said, "Evangelism is a life before it is a task. It is a call for being before it is an agenda for doing."

But Jesus said there are dreams and there are schemes. The Devil wants to spoil God's dream. He is the Enemy who sows the weeds in the field. He hates what God wants to do with a passion.

As Screwtape, the senior devil, wrote to Wormwood, the junior devil, in C. S. Lewis' *The Screwtape Letters,* "He really does want to fill the universe with a lot of little loathsome replicas of himself." But Satan wants people like himself—people filled with dissension and rivalry, consumed by the lust for money, sex, and power. But Jesus said his angels will "weed out of his kingdom everything that causes sin and all who do evil" (Matthew 13:41).

There is a conflict being played out in this world. God's dream is against Satan's scheme. For every action of God there is a counter-action of Satan. The "lawless one" described in 2 Thessalonians 2 is setting himself up against God's plan.

Jesus taught that God's dream would come in two stages. There would be a time of sowing and growing and a time of conflict. During the growing time he told his servants not to pull up the weeds because they might uproot the wheat. But he also told them that harvest time would come at the end of the world. Then the wheat would be gathered and the weeds destroyed.

We are evangelizing in the "between times." And as his "dreamers of the day," we are called to live by hope. Are we getting discouraged by what we see in the world? In the church? In the struggle between flesh and spirit in our own lives?

The Lord of the harvest says: "I want you to know I am at work. You won't always see it, but I know what I am doing. I sowed the seed. I brought the first fruits. One day the harvest will come swiftly and we will have a harvest home. Until then, I want you to endure with hope and to last."

To endure with hope does not mean to be passive. Augustine said that hope has two daughters: anger that things are as they are and courage to change them. The return of Christ is not an excuse for indifference—whether in evangelism or social justice—it is a spur to obedience.

Sam Escobar taught a class in Peru. He wrote on the blackboard the words of Jesus, "The poor you will always have with you." He asked what the words meant. There was silence. Then an old woman in a black shawl spoke up slowly and firmly, "It means that there will always be inhuman exploiters in this world—until Jesus returns." Hallelujahs and amens greeted her statement.

Many people say, "Because of sin, we can't overcome poverty. The best we can do is evangelize lost souls." But for that old woman in Peru, the return of Christ is a call, not to make a perfect world, but to obey Jesus until he comes.

It is the same way with our evangelistic task. Our hope is not that the whole world will be converted. Our hope is in his coming, and our call is to proclaim Christ and make disciples of all nations until he comes.

"My dear brothers," wrote Paul, "stand firm. Let nothing move you. Always give yourselves fully to the work of the Lord" (1 Corinthians 15:58). That is why he wrote to the Philippians, "We eagerly await a Savior from there [heaven], the Lord Jesus Christ. ...Therefore, my brothers,... that is how you should stand firm in the Lord" (Philippians 3:20–4:1).

John Stott taught about rejoicing in the hope of glory and in our suffering (Romans 5). He said, "Jesus Christ is coming again in the glorious Father and the earth will be suffused with his presence. So we can face evil and suffering even with defiance! His love will never let us go."

God gave Ken Medema a song after our brother from China told of working in the cesspool and of singing:

> Here come the bombs and here come the shells,
> And here come the cesspools, straight out of hell,
> But stand in that garden and don't you dare be moved,
> For we're going to meet this war with love.

Will you last? He is coming! Proclaim Christ until he comes—with enduring hope.

God's Dreamers Are Those Who Burn

Will you burn? He is coming!

Jesus told another story that compared his coming to a wedding. There were ten young women carrying torches which they were supposed to have ready to lead a colorful torch dance and to light the path of the bridal party.

When the bridegroom was delayed, the young women fell asleep. At midnight, the cry rang out, "The bridegroom is coming, come out to meet him!" Only five had enough oil left to keep their lamps burning. The other five had to go to look for oil. When they came back it was too late. "

This is a story of life's greatest opportunity—to come out to meet the Bridegroom. Jesus, the Bridegroom, is coming to fill our lives. One of the loneliest moments in life is when we experience what we think will bring ultimate fulfillment and it lets us down. Even in our modern world, Os Guinness told of the "cultural rebounds," the empty offers of the secular world, and people whom God is preparing to meet Jesus Christ.

Jesus is also coming to fulfill history. History will not end with a capitalist dream. History will not end with a communist utopia. It will not end with a mushroom cloud or the whimper of a dying baby. It will end with the cry, "Here is the bridegroom," for Jesus Christ is the omega of all history. In spite of trouble and war, famine and upheaval, the gospel will be preached in all the world and the end will come. "The Son of Man will come like the lightning which flashes across the whole sky" (Matthew 24:27, TEV).

But this wedding parable is also a story of life's greatest tragedy—an opportunity missed, a door shut, a final word, "I don't know you."

The heart of heaven is "to be with the Lord forever" (1 Thessalonians 4:17). But the hellishness of hell is to be "punished with everlasting destruction and shut out from the presence of the Lord" (2 Thessalonians 1:9). As we proclaim Christ, may we bear in our hearts the glorious hope of heaven, as well as the terrible reality of hell.

This is also the story of life's greatest challenge—to keep the lamp of faith and love burning. God's "dreamers of the day" should wait and watch until the Bridegroom comes, and keep the lamp of faith and love burning through the long night.

Rolf Scheffbuch was visiting missionaries in Nigeria during the civil war. One night they were flying into the city of Kano. Because of the war, the lights on the landing strip could not be left on—they blinked on and off, just enough for the pilot to see the runway. They made what Rolf describes as "My fastest landing ever!"

Rolf told this story to the Lausanne committee and said, "Brothers and sisters, we are in a world at war. We can't always see the full light of the kingdom burning, but there are signals that blink on and off and tell us to hurry down and to be about our task."

Jesus said, "Let your loins be girded and your lamps burning," (Luke 12:35, RSV). Is there fire in our hearts, in our heads, and on our lips? As we return to our homes, our lamps will sometimes burn brightly and sometimes they will burn low. But by God's grace, may our lamps burn on.

The burning lamp is the lamp of love. The greatest motive for evangelism is love for Jesus Christ. "For Christ's love compels us," wrote Paul, "because we are convinced that one died for all, and therefore all died" (2 Corinthians 5:14).

What will keep the lamp of world evangelism burning? Not just the need of the world, or the urgency of the task; at the heart of evangelistic motivation must be a burning jealousy for the name of Christ, and gratitude that springs from the love of Christ.

Lucien Accad testified from the heart of Beirut, "Christianity is not a matter of activities or a set of programs. It is a growing relationship of the believer with his Lord and other believers."

May God help us, and may God keep alive in us our love for the Bridegroom and for his coming! May he help us live in the reality of 1 John 3:1, "How great is the love the Father has lavished on us, that we should be called children of God." And out of that love may there be a passion for holiness to be like Jesus. "We know that when he appears, we shall be like him, for we shall see him as he is. Everyone who has this hope in him purifies himself, just as he is pure" (1 John 3:2–3).

God's dream for world evangelization comes to us as challenges. *Will you risk? He is coming!* Will we proclaim Christ until he comes with faith willing to risk? *Will you last? He is coming!* Will we proclaim Christ with enduring hope until he comes? *Will you burn? He is coming!* Will we keep our lamps burning with love for our Lord and for spreading the gospel?

May God, by his grace and power, enable us to risk, to last, to burn, to proclaim Christ with passion until he comes.

Track Reports

Track 110—A.D. 2000
Coordinators: Bill O'Brien; Luis Bush

Christians and churches worldwide are experiencing and reporting a movement of God. In many places, the harvest is overwhelming. In others, resistance is at an all-time high. In still others, hundreds of millions of people have never heard the gospel.

God's Spirit is prompting the church to bear faithful witness to all peoples in all of the above categories at all costs. It is God's movement.

It is narrow in time frame. The year A.D. 2000 is an arbitrary target date, a point of reference, and serves as a rallying incentive that generates new commitment and intensity.

It is broad in its recognition that all sectors of this body of Christ who relate to Christ personally and are trying to be obedient to his Commission are represented in the movement.

Because it is a movement of the Spirit, it is best served by a cooperative network rather than centralization and control.

Strategic Dimensions of the Movement
1. *Global plans.* Over two thousand plans mirror the diversity of approaches in support of a singular vision.
2. *Great Commission Manifesto.* The Manifesto provides focus for both direction and objectives.
3. *Research.* Macro and micro research is necessary to undergird decisions and strategies at all levels.
4. *National initiatives.* These are essential for local and regional ownership and are key elements in a global movement.
5. *Monitor.* Information sharing in multilevel and multilingual forms is crucial for a forward movement.
6. *Prayer.* A global network of intercession provides the dynamic for energizing the movement.

Track 110 Workshops:
Toward A.D. 2000: Can We Evangelize the World by the Year 2000?
Leaders: Thomas Wang/Luis Bush
Toward A.D. 2000: What Are the Major Hindrances?
Leaders: Bill O'Brien/Luis Bush
Toward A.D. 2000: Three Case Studies
Leaders: Philemon Choi/Ron Cline/Vinson Synan
Toward A.D. 2000: Three Case Studies
Leaders: Paul Eshelman/Gion Henriquez/Bill O'Brien
Toward A.D. 2000 in the Middle East
Toward A.D. 2000 in Asia
Leaders: Petrus Octavianus/B.E. Vijayam/Myung-Hyuk Kim
Toward A.D. 2000 in Latin America (In Spanish)
Leaders: Edison Queiroz/Federico Bertuzzi/Alberto Barrientos

Toward A.D. 2000 in Europe and Africa
Leaders: Floyd McClung/Panya Baby/Modupe T. Pierce
Toward A.D. 2000: Planning for Each Continent in the Workshop
Leaders: Thomas Wang/Luis Bush

Track 120—Research and Evangelism
Coordinator: Samuel Wilson

Summary
1. Participants in the Research Track represented the wide variety of research being done, but highlighted the fact that insufficient resources are committed by church bodies to gather appropriate information to aid the cause of world evangelization.
2. Virtual unanimity was expressed with regard to the fact that research in the context of world evangelization should be:

   a) Applied research: defined and carried out near ministry. Our concerns are ministry concerns.
   b) Researchers ought to be seen as servants to the rest of the church. The researcher has substantive interests and special skills whose use is never independent of the ministries and concerns of some facet of church life from which they draw definition.

3. A profitable session was spent in reviewing the applications of unreached people concepts. Ethno-linguistic research was presented by Barbara Grimes, editor of the *Ethnologue*. The Joshua Model provided a basis for thinking about both methods and concepts relating to people groups in major mission cities. This session included a review of the current status of thinking and research, which defines the remaining needs among ethno-linguistic people groups.
4. Ray Bakke and Kris Gutierrez outlined plans for urban research, based on case studies drawn from eight international regions.
5. Research has a unique purpose to fulfill in providing the basis for developing the vision needed in situations where Christianity has become nominal or notional.
6. Cooperation was described on international and local levels. Strong support existed for the principle of cooperation in the body of Christ to reflect our unity, the profit from the rich variety of gifts, and to responsibly handle steward resources.

Recommendations for Follow-On
1. There is an absolute need for viewing research as a form of ministry.
2. General agreement existed on the need to collect information through the Lausanne network of active researchers regarding the kinds and applica-

Samuel Wilson is Director of Research for the Zwemer Institute of Muslim Studies. He is a former professor and missionary to Peru, and a citizen of the United States.

tions of current research to serve as the basis for researchers themselves to build relationships around common interests. The fine work done by SCEM on the Directory of Evangelical Research Center for the WEF needs to be supplemented and kept up-to-date.

3. The stated hope of the Zeist International Conference of Researchers was affirmed that some popular-level occasional mailing, or other vehicle of information and exchange, was in order to provide:

   a) A channel of identification of and communication with other researchers with similar interests. This should include description of current projects and be continuously updated. Areas of expertise should be described, along with data held and products available. In other words, a sharing of process and product. Current active projects and informational needs should be listed. Capability should be provided to see questionnaire instruments, database structures, and process. In this regard, the "data is the thing" (i.e., broad cataloging should be attempted) but it would be helpful to indicate researchers' and centers' theological stance. Sources should be encouraged to surface the area for which they see themselves responsible.

   b) A vehicle for exchange among those who are charged with development of information to guide strategy and planning for churches and mission agencies.

   c) Basic, popular-level guidance to beginning researchers.

4. The consensus was such a wide variety of research and applications exist that only a loose type of networking was desirable. This probably should occur in conjunction with other conferences and events.

Summary: The means of communication should provide for interaction and mutual learning.

Senior Associate

1. Serve as a catalyst to others in research to promote cooperation in both the actual work of research and to provide needed help. Promote edifying (friendly and constructive) and professional critique.

2. Help establish a possible consortium for publications such as Lausanne occasional papers (LOP).

3. Help in training on a local, national and regional level both to do and use research. Product or Process: Instead of conferences of researchers, a training consortia should be organized in local situations. These would serve to teach and train researchers, not simply communicate instruments of past designs. Tanzania expressed this need, corroborated by others.

4. One goal should be to promote the development of strategic planning at the national level.

5. A listing should be maintained of a pool of potential advisors who could be available to assist and advise in all aspects of research. An annotated bibliography on popular level would be helpful.

Track Publications

The candor in most of the sessions and the particular focus on cases of research signifies the discussions and presentations have a limited market of highly specialized interest, and do not lend themselves in their recorded form for publication. Some of the papers will be reproduced and shared as content for the occasional mailings mentioned above.

An LOP is possible which contains descriptions of the variety of models which were presented in the track. The target audience would be researchers who would learn of the variety of designs now being employed for different ministry circumstances. A similar service could be rendered in describing how research centers have been able to find means of surviving and doing meaningful research.

Track 120 Workshops:

Research and World Evangelization: Where are we?
  Leaders: Robert Oehrig/David Barrett/Gary Packer/James Montgomery
Cooperation in Research for World Evangelization
  Leaders: Patrick Johnstone/Samuel Wilson/David Barrett
People Research for Evangelization and Mission
  Leaders: Patrick Johnstone/Barbara Grimes/Steve Hawthorne
Research, Renewal and Re-Evangelization
  Leader: Peter Brierley
Urban Research
  Leaders: Ray Bakke/Samuel Wilson/Kris Gutierrez
Thinking about Cooperation in National/Regional Research
Thinking about Cooperation in National/Regional Research Cooperation
Track Summary and Future Action
  Leader: Samuel Wilson

Track 130—Cross-Cultural Missions
Coordinators: Theodore Williams; Donald R. Jacobs

This track examined the following question posed by the Lausanne II planners: *How can we communicate the gospel through cultural, linguistic, and ethnic differences?*

Biblical history tells of God's persisting determination to reveal himself to every creature, on the one hand, and on the other, of the human reluctance to join him in that great mission of redemption. God can evangelize only through people, so as he formed a nation of evangelists, the Jews, he made it clear to them that his purpose was to bring the revelation of himself to all people, not only then but through the ages. That the Jews largely failed in understanding God's missionary heart punctuates Old Testament history.

Jesus Christ lived, died, and was resurrected among us; and upon his return to the Father, he urged his believers to fan out across the world, testifying and making disciples

---

Theodore Williams is President of the World Evangelical Fellowship, and is a citizen of India. Donald Jacobs is the Executive Director of the Mennonite Christian Leadership Foundation and a former missionary to Africa. He is a citizen of the United States.

wherever they went. All of Jesus' authority was given to them for this task. Cross-cultural evangelism became absolutely explicit in Jesus' commission. We are the heirs and commissioners of that vision.

If the entire human family is to be introduced to Jesus Christ in our time, the worldwide church must recommit itself to increased efforts in the task of cross-cultural evangelism. Near-neighbor evangelism will not accomplish the task. Over half of the human race will be denied the gospel unless Christians deliberately pay the price to send workers into other cultures. If the whole world is to hear the whole gospel, Christians must enter other "people groups." This is the only method by which the world can be evangelized.

People groups are cultures or sub-cultures which have their own specific identity and which share a common cultural bond. A people group may be a specific ethnic group with its own language, worldview, and value system; or it may be an identifiable group within a larger culture. In any case, to present the gospel to any of these people groups is an exercise in cross-cultural evangelism.

Many of the people groups are rural folk who live scattered or in villages. However, the largest concentration of these people groups is in the great urban centers of the world. And it is in the cities that new people groups are being formed. Therefore, cross-cultural missions will focus more and more on the world's cities.

Almost every urban center in the world is a mission field with a great mosaic of people groups. Cultural pluralism and the growth of cities mark our time. Jesus Christ loves those people and urges his followers to deliberately cross cultural boundaries with the gospel.

This task calls for the creation of hundreds and thousands of sending agencies or groups around the world. It cannot be left to the traditional mission boards of the West which have been pioneers of this work in the past two centuries. Extraordinary initiatives must be taken to quickly multiply the number of cross-cultural workers. The future calls for creative, cooperative efforts which will combine the resources and learning of all of the sending agencies, old and new, in a sacrificial movement to reach all people groups. A comparatively untapped resource lies in local congregations. Most Christian congregations are neighbors to people groups which the believers can, with special effort, reach. Each local church is responsible to take seriously Christ's intention that the gospel be taken to every person on the face of the earth.

Training for cross-cultural evangelism is an essential factor in the endeavor. It is heartening to hear of the multiplication of training institutes and courses for cross-cultural missions. But much more must be done, especially at the congregational and district levels.

Much more study will be required in two areas: How cross-cultural workers are to enter meaningfully into the new culture and how the believers in that new culture are to fully receive the whole gospel. All Christians, including those involved in cross-cultural evangelism, enjoy an understanding of the gospel which is partly influenced by their cultural understandings. The receiving culture will probably have different needs and will therefore seek answers to their particular needs in the gospel.

The receiving culture will wrestle with a great number of issues, because some aspects of their culture are worthy of believers, others are not. The receiving cultures must have freedom under Christ and, in light of the Scriptures, develop a Christian faith which has the same effect on their culture as Jesus Christ had on his.

Every Christian community must be aware of the possibility of slipping into undesirable syncretism as they flesh out the gospel in the particular local context. Yet, unless the churches deliberately contextualize the gospel in their cultures, the church remains a foreign institution and evangelism is throttled.

One of the temptations in cross-cultural evangelism is to lose sight of the reconciling nature of the gospel. While it is understood there will be a high level of homogeneity in the churches, the full impact of the reconciling work of Christ will be exhibited when people of different cultures witness to a common faith, a binding love, and a unified spirit before their communities. Cultural awareness may never be the excuse for ethnocentrism in the fellowship of Christ.

Track 130 Worshops:

Developing Cross-Cultural Strategies
Leaders: Theodore Williams/Don Jacobs
Theologizing in a New Culture
Leaders: Tite Tienou/Don Jacobs
The Gospel in Cultural Context
Leaders: Theodore Williams/Roberta King
Entering Urban "People Groups"; A New Frontier
Leaders: Fletcher Tink/William Pannell/Daniel Serwanga
Unity in Diversity: Maintaining One's Faith in a Culturally Pluralistic Age
Leaders: Edward Muhima/John Tooke
Christology, Anthropology and Christian Faithfulness
Leaders: Bruce Nicholls/Gresford Chitemo
Affinity Group Meeting
Leaders: Theodore Williams/Don Jacobs

Track 140—Two-Thirds World Missions
Coordinator: Panya Baba

The principal concern of Third World missions is found in item 7 of the Lausanne Covenant which declares: "We urge the development of regional and functional cooperation for furtherance of the church's mission, for strategic planning, for mutual encouragement, and for the sharing of resources and experience." The sessions were attended not only by Third World missions leaders, but also Western missions leaders who graciously gave their input.

Overview: The Missions Movement Today in Third World Regions

1. *Africa.* From Nigeria, it was reported that three cross-cultural views are unique in the African situation: the missions movement is vibrant and active because a great number of Christians are young people; the missions movement flows freely as most African countries are already living in a multicultural situation; and the missions movement is experiencing great cooperation through research and training.
2. *Asia.* Asian region was presented through videos showing cooperation of missions agencies of Korea, Japan, and Indonesia. From Indonesia, it was reported that at a consultation on missions held in September 1980, a considerable range of mission agencies was represented with approximately the following division: 50 percent were agencies with foreign roots; about

30 percent represented independent, indigenous churches which have come into being through mission agencies; whereas, 20 percent were new emerging missions agencies.

3. *Latin America.* The missions movement in Latin America started (as reported from Brazil) some fifteen years ago with the main thrust of reaching the Hispanic and Portuguese speaking countries in Latin America and other parts of the world. The small beginning became an explosion in missionary movement with the gathering of thousands of mission leaders during the COMIBAM Congress held in Brazil in 1987.

Interfacing with Western Missions

The concern of developing agencies based in the Third World is their relationship with Western missions and the denominations they have established on the mission field. This was dealt with in two papers (from India and Japan) on, "Interfacing with Western Missions." Possible solutions for the problem of interfacing between the two groups were discussed as suggested in the two papers.

Training and Research

Models of missionary training were presented. The pooling of training personnel and appropriate instructional technology were suggested by some missions agencies who are already doing it. The need for information of mission needs, missionary training, and other mission information was discussed, so that more Third World countries could find out what is available.

Involvement of Third World Professionals in Missions

Dr. P. Octavianus presented his paper, "Cooperation and Partnership in World Mission." His paper was based on two backgrounds: political and missions; theological and biblical. Possibilities for establishing links with mission field and missions agencies for sending Christian professionals must be encouraged.

Mutual Fund for Third World Missions

David Cho presented his paper, "Implementation Plan of Mutual Fund for Third World Mission Advance." The concept of sharing resources in order to best help all Third World agencies was indeed a welcome item. Emphasis was given on accountability and integrity, promoting partnership and not control of any agency or ministry.

Papers Presented

1. "Interfacing with Western Missions"—Philip Abraham, Minoru Okuyama.
2. "The Dramatic Growth of Two-Thirds World Missions"—Larry Pate.
3. "Implementation Plan of Mutual Fund for Third World Missions Advance"—David Cho.
4. "Endangered World and World Missions"—David Cho.
5. "Research in the Total Mission"—Don Smith.
6. "The Status and Future of Two-Thirds World Mission"—Patrick Sookhdeo.

Track 140 Workshops:

Two-Thirds World Missions Today
Leader: David Cho
Panel: Patrick Sookhdeo/Minoru Okuyama/Panya Baba/Petrus Octavianus/ Jonathan Santos

Interfacing with Western Missions
  Leaders: Minoru Okuyama/Petrus Octavianus
Training and Research
  Leaders: Panya Baba/Patrick Sookhdeo
Involvement of Two-Thirds World Professionals in Mission
  Leaders: Panya Baba/Petrus Octavianus
Mutual Funding and Financial Security of Workers
  Leader: Petrus Octavianus
Affinity Group Meeting
  Leader: Panya Baba

Track 150—Mandate of the Laity
Coordinators: Ford Madison; Pete Hammond

In response to Christ's Great Commission, a "sleeping giant" is awakening. Innumerable ranks of ordinary laypeople are taking the gospel to their world (Matthew 13:38). By sharing Christ person to person, and simply living for him in the workplace, in the home, and wherever they go in the world, God has called the inconspicuous 90 percent of the church to a ministry where they spend 97 percent of their time: a ministry found in the world.

As the world becomes increasingly more urbanized, technological, and international in its make-up, and particularly as approximately 80 percent of the world's unreached people live in areas where traditional missionary access is restricted, it is ever more important to recognize, affirm, and equip the laity to serve Christ in full partnership with the clergy.

And what can the spiritual leaders provide to the laity to free them for their task? They can: (1) pray for laborers, (2) encourage the laity, (3) provide role models and mentors who are already laboring, (4) facilitate small accountability groups, (5) promote consistent personal devotional lives, and (6) believe Christ. One key for unleashing the laity is to free them from programs and call them instead to a lifestyle of evangelism. A lifestyle which is not perceived as substandard in spirituality to the clergy, but one which is focused on winning others for Jesus Christ whenever and wherever they are found. In short, the task can be said to be equipping the saints, which is defined as providing whatever it takes for the ordinary person to get the job done.

As over thirteen hundred delegates from more than fifty countries have participated in the various Laity Track workshops, there have been written expressions of interest for a focused conference on mobilizing and equipping the laity. It is a possibility that such a meeting will materialize within the next few years.

We have found nicknames for ourselves at this Congress: The professional Frog, who ministers for Christ by waiting until his prey comes to him; and the layperson Lizard, who slithers into all areas of life to hunt out those who need the gospel of Christ. We now offer a new name for our partnership in world evangelization, a name which expresses what is needed of spiritual leaders: Wisdom. And any wise clergy who help Lizards in the hunt transforms himself into a Wizard—a wise frog who helps lizards—and we are indeed thankful that in the Lausanne movement there are so many Wizards. May God help us all to multiply.

Track 150 Workshops:
>   Equipping and Empowering the Laity
>   *Leader: Kent Humphreys*
>   Theology of the Laity
>   *Leader: Lee Yih*
>   Recovering the Bible of the Laity
>   *Leader: Pete Hammond*
>   What Does Equipping Really Mean?
>   *Leader: Dennis Legaspi*
>   Daily Work Matters to God
>   *Leader: Romy Salvador*
>   Penetrating Urban Industrial Groups for Christ
>   *Leader: D. Arputharaj*
>   Contextualization for Lay People
>   *Leader: Ole Mangus Olafsrud*
>   Liberating the Laity for Ministry
>   *Leader: Ford Madison*
>   A Lay Couple Evangelizing Among Historic Churches
>   *Leaders: Michael and Nancy Timmis*

Track 160—Tentmakers
Coordinators: Ken Touryan; J. Christy Wilson

By January 1987, the Lausanne Committee formed a special focus group, the Tentmaker Task Force, co-chaired by Dr. Ken J. Touryan, adjunct professor at Colorado School of Mines; and Professor J. Christy Wilson of Gordon Conwell Theological Seminary in the United States.

The goal of this task force was to spearhead a worldwide network and dialogue on tentmaking through a series of regional consultations in Europe, Asia, South Africa, North America, the Middle East, and the South Pacific. These regional groups each had opportunity to report on their respective deliberations at the Manila Congress.

Congress Program
Over one hundred participants, including tentmaker advocates, scholars, and practitioners gathered daily to compare notes on past successes and failures, and to plan future cooperative efforts. Workshops offered were: "A Global Report on Tentmaking," "Issues and Case Studies on Tentmaking," "Tools and Resources for Tentmaker Training," and an affinity group meeting to discuss future plans.

The workshops began with discussion of a clearer definition of a tentmaker and culminated with sharper regional focus and plans for future cooperation.

Ken Touryan is Director of Energy Research at the Tetra Corporation and is a citizen of the United States.
J. Christy Wilson is Professor of World Evangelism at Gordon-Conwell Theological Seminary and is a citizen of the United States.

North America

We discussed the need for a database that describes organizations and their work. We decided to conduct ongoing consultations and work with denominational organizations and local churches on awareness seminars for potential tentmakers.

Dr. Howard Foltz presented an integrated plan for training tentmakers within the local church. This plan involves:

1. Basic discipleship
2. The "Perspective on the World Christian Movement" course
3. Training in Power Encounters that would include both theory and experience
4. Practical experience in leading a small group evangelistic Bible study
5. Field work (i.e., ongoing cross-cultural experience within the trainee's own community)
6. An integrative course on tentmaking (three semester hours) touching on ethics, security, accountability, nurture, burnout, cross-cultural work ethics, placement, entrepreneurship, networking, soul winning, government relations, and power encounters

The Middle East and Europe

We discussed a new training center in England and the need for periodic training for tentmakers in their region. We discussed various possibilities for tentmaking ventures and the need for capital investment.

The South Pacific and Asia

We discussed new tentmaker training programs and the need for input from other regions for tentmakers interested in starting business enterprises.

In India, there is a tentmaking training program which uses the following program components:

1. *Land based:* emphasis on agriculture, horticulture, animal husbandry, and water technology
2. *Home based:* emphasis on spinning, weaving, knitting, pickle making, candle making, herbal medicine, bee keeping, toy making, biofertilizers (instead of chemical fertilizers), mushroom growing, basket and mat weaving
3. *Workshop based:* emphasis on agro-mechanics, radio and TV repair, civil construction, electronic parts manufacture
4. *Profession based:* emphasis on medical, legal, and education
5. *Management based:* consulting on business management, secretarial practice, accounting, and auditing

In Singapore, there is a nine-month discipleship/tentmaking training course available for those interested in pursuing tentmaking.

In the South Pacific, an Australian model uses home-study materials, local cross-cultural and mission outreach, discipleship training, and training on world religious and general biblical doctrines. Future courses will include the ethics of tentmaking, time management, power encounter, the singular importance of trusting God, and how people make decisions as a group.

Africa

The Africans felt that the concept of tentmaking was not well understood among churches in their area. To address this problem they decided to identify (or train) and network tentmaker advocates in six regions throughout the continent.

Among the other issues which emerged: The cost of living in the urban areas of developing countries is often high, so tentmaking is a viable (essential) alternative. Urban areas are being neglected due to high cost and the emphasis on (and glamour of) unreached/isolated people groups in the "uttermost parts of the earth." This creates a vacuum in the cities which could otherwise serve as an effective beachhead for penetrating the surrounding countryside (as Paul did at Ephesus).

On the last day of the Manila Congress, the leaders of the Tentmaker Track presented a declarative appeal calling Christian participants to seven courses of action. The following is an abridged version:

1. We encourage Christian laymen and women to seize opportunities for cross-cultural positions as a means of extending God's kingdom. In the first Reformation, the people were given the Word of God. We need a second Reformation where believers are given the work of God (Ephesians 4:12).
2. We call on churches world-wide to recognize the crucial role of tentmaking and the key position congregations can play in mobilizing and equipping the laity for world evangelization.
3. We encourage mission agencies, along with recruiting more missionaries for unreached people groups, to identify and enlist potential Christian tentmakers for cross-cultural witness.
4. We appeal to churches, educational institutions, and mission boards to produce programs and materials to train tentmakers in the Scriptures, linguistics, anthropology, area studies, and church planting.
5. We hope to see a greater involvement by congregations, missions, and coordinating agencies in assisting tentmakers in placement and orientation so they can endure culture shock successfully.
6. We call on organizations and churches to nurture tentmakers through faithful pastoral care. This would include effective prayer backing, careful communications, as well as visits on the field.
7. We urge Christian agencies and congregations to assist tentmakers with reentry into their own culture, to debrief them, and to use them to challenge and recruit others.

Congress Follow-On

In January 1990, the Tentmaker Task Force will be officially disbanded and replaced by a small *ad hoc* group, Tentmaker International Exchange (TIE), with one or two representatives from each of the eight regions. Regional tentmaker meetings and conferences will be encouraged to provide encouragement and accountability for the facilitation and coordination of tentmaking in each region. Dr. Ken Touryan and Dr. Ted Yamamori have agreed to co-chair the ongoing work of TIE.

The Tentmaker Track will produce two Lausanne occasional papers to be completed in mid-1990 on the following subjects: "A Contemporary Mandate for Tentmaking," authored by Dr. Ted Yamamori and Dr. Ken Touryan; and "The Biblical Mandate for Tentmaking," authored by Dr. Christy Wilson.

For further information on Tentmaker Track Follow-On, please write Mrs. Kathy Giske, P.O. Box 6788, Lynwood, Washington 98036, U.S., or telephone (206) 744-0400.

Track 160 Workshops:
Global Report on Tentmaking
  Leaders: Dick Staub/Lynn Buzzard
Issues and Case Studies on Tentmaking
  Leaders: Tetsunao Yamamori/Ken Touryan
Tools and Resources for Tentmaking
  Leaders: Howard Foltz/J. Christy Wilson
Affinity Group Meeting
  Leader: Ken Touryan

Track 170—Women in Evangelism
Coordinator: Robyn Claydon

Over one thousand people—both men and women—have attended the Women's Track workshops and dinner meeting.

We have been greatly encouraged by this support and see it as a clear indication of the fact that the place of women in world evangelization is one of the major concerns of Lausanne II.

We examined the biblical basis for women in ministry and mission looking at Jesus' attitude toward women and the deep involvement of Christian women in all areas of ministry in the early church.

We discussed the roadblocks facing women in world evangelization and identified some of the doors which both culture and the church have closed to women. At the same time, we rejoiced that in many places new doors are opening for women to exercise their gifts. We also rejoiced that wherever Christian women are, whether opportunities abound or are restricted, they are faithfully being used by God. We noted that in the eighteenth and nineteenth centuries, evangelical women were involved in every form of Christian ministry: preaching, teaching, missionary endeavor, and evangelism in the home and in the local church.

We also noted with deep sadness, that some branches of the Christian church began restricting the ministry of women during the twentieth century and some still do. But we rejoiced in the growing awareness of our oneness and our call as women and men of Christ to serve together in full partnership as we take the Good News to the world.

In our track we listened to women from all over the world as they shared something of their ministries and the way the Lord was using them.

- We rejoiced and wept with each other.
- We concluded our track with a recognition of the need to train today's women for tomorrow's task and realized that this will involve churches providing theological and practical training for women, as well as encouraging them in the ministries they already shared.
- We conclude with gratitude to God for this Congress, for the modeling of shared

ministry, for an opportunity to network together, and, in the words of paragraph 14 of the Lausanne Covenant:

We therefore call upon all Christians to pray for such a visitation of the sovereign Spirit of God that all his fruit may appear in all his people and that all his gifts may enrich the body of Christ.

Suggestions for the Future

Lausanne II in Manila, in modeling shared ministry, has been an encouragement and a challenge both to women and to men.

The whole Congress was reminded that the gifts of the Holy Spirit are given to all God's people and that women with their gifts need to be enabled to work alongside men in the task of world evangelization.

In order that this vision of women being fully involved in evangelization across the world be realized, the women's track requests:

1. That a Senior Associate for Women be appointed
2. That we:
   a) Develop a worldwide network of women involved in evangelism and keep them in touch through a newsletter
   b) Endeavor by a variety of means to encourage all women in the work they are doing for the Lord
   c) Set up a resource center to provide women with Bible study materials, articles, journals, magazines, and people to facilitate women in their varied ministries
   d) Consider arranging regional, national, and international conferences for women
   e) Challenge the church to recognize and release the gifts of women in all areas of Christian ministry

We would be very grateful if this request could be considered by the LCWE since Women in World Evangelization has been identified as one of the major challenges of Lausanne.

Track 170 Workshops:

The Biblical Basis for Women in Ministry and Mission
  Leader: Evelyn Jensen
Identifying Road Blocks Facing Women in World Evangelization
  Leader: Kirsti Mosvold
Evangelistic Breakfasts for Women: A European Model
  Leader: Brunhilde Blunck
Esther Across Cultures: Indigenous Leadership Roles for Women
  Leader: Miriam Adeney
Women as Pastors and Evangelists
  Leaders: Midori Okubo/Vincie Thomson
Recognizing and Releasing Ministry Gifts
  Leader: Sakhi Athyal
The Rise and Fall of Evangelical Women in Public Ministry
  Leader: Janette Hassey

Women Ministering in Africa
  Leaders: Sarah Imbuye/Florence Yeboah
Training Today's Women for Tomorrow's Task
  Leader: Neuza Itioka
Special Dinner Meeting: Encouraging the Diversity of Women's Ministries
  Chairperson: Robyn Claydon

Track 180—Communications and Media
Coordinators: Viggo Sogaard; Bill Thatcher

The interrelationship of communication and evangelism was highlighted by the Communication Track. Communication was also seen as more than "media," it concerns all who are dedicated to the proclamation of the Good News. Among the communicators, we need theorists and missiologists, strategists and planners, artists and producers, and evangelists and broadcasters.

In the plenary session, Dr. Philemon Choi focused our attention on the present world of high-tech environment and the need for people to feel warmth in a high-touch situation. The tears of the TV evangelist are no substitute for weeping with the wounded. The communication revolution has brought us technology and multiple choices, but usually just more of the same. Dr. Viggo Sogaard focused on the criteria for effective use of communication technology in evangelism. It is not a question of yes or no, but *how* to use the media. In an increasingly non-reading world, the challenge of finding effective ways of communicating with both the illiterates and "video-viewers" is of utmost importance. To achieve this close cooperation between media organizations and local churches is mandatory.

Twenty workshops were presented, ranging from theory and principles, strategy and research, to specific uses of media. A variety of case studies were presented to show the real possibilities of media use. Case studies from Africa included Cinema Leo in Kenya and comprehensive strategies from Malawi and Uganda; *Step* magazine in East Africa showed how magazines can be used effectively, especially among the younger generation. CBN and 100 Huntley Street presented possibilities for television, and multi-image presentations were provided by different groups. Eagles of Singapore applied it to the city, and World Vision of India showed cassette and traditional media applications in development contexts. A Thai drama and dance team provided both plenary and workshop inputs.

A primary function of a congress is to bring people together, and numerous official and unofficial meetings took place. People met, discussed, prayed, and planned together. Many informal meetings established new friendships and relationships.

As we look to the future for Lausanne, communication needs to receive more attention. We need to study how the various media can be used effectively in evangelism, and we need to develop relationships between church people and media specialists that will help the church to feel joint ownership. Further integration needs to take place, and we could, for example, suggest that the Theology Working Group and Communications develop joint consultations, for example, on the topic of, "The Information Society." We also need to utilize the public media and churches need help in developing approaches to such media.

Track 180 Workshops:
Communication and Evangelism
Leader: Viggo Sogaard
The Role of Media in Evangelism
Leader: Knud Jorgensen
Integration of Radio in Evangelism
Leader: Phill Butler
Cross Barriers by Radio
Leader: Frank Gray
Dance, Drama and Music in Evangelism: A Case Study from CCI in
Thailand
Leader: Pwongduan "Sugar" Yontararak
Press Relations: How to Establish Contacts with Local Media for Evangelistic
Purposes
Leaders: Horst Marquardt/Wolfgang Polzer
Media for the Visual Age: Television in the Service of Evangelism
Leaders: Michael Little/Cal Bombay
Planning the Future Role of Communication in Evangelism
Leader: Viggo Sogaard
The Role of Research in Effective Communication
Leader: Bob Oehrig
Communicating the Gospel God's Way
Leader: Charles Kraft
Urban Evangelism: Message, Methods and Media
Leaders: Peter Chao/John Ng/Mark Chan
The Joys and Sorrows of the Public Media: Not Good, Not Bad, Just
Medium!
Leader: Nick Page
The Power of the Printed Word
Leaders: Richard Crabbe/Connie Kisuke
Audio Cassettes: Integration of Development & Evangelism Through Strategic
Communication
Leaders: Franklin Joseph/Harry Box
Rural Evangelism and Church Integrated Use of Film
Leaders: Peter Margosian/Arnold Mayer
The Why and What and How of Communication Training for Church and
Media Leaders with Case Study from Asia
Leader: Peggy Yeo
The Use of Major Multi-Media Events in Evangelism
Leaders: Wing Tai Leung/Eric Miller
The Preparation and Use of Audiovisuals in Evangelism and Training
Leaders: John Desjarlais/Eric Miller

Track 190—Youth Leadership
Coordinator: Barry St. Clair

Today 1.4 billion people between the ages of thirteen and twenty live in our world. Fifty-five percent of all of the world's population are under twenty years of age. In Latin America, 35 percent of the population is under fifteen years of age. A wide agreement exists that the overwhelming majority of people who become Christians do so in their teenage years.

The Youth Track was the first significant step by the Lausanne movement to focus upon the above need from a global perspective. Two hundred and ninety-three people attended the Youth Track, and unanimously indicated their interest and support for an interdenominational youth representative.

Sixty-seven countries were represented, including North Africa, the Middle East, India, and the Communist bloc countries. While vast differences exist due to culture and sociology, there were many similarities which provided opportunities to become significant resources to each other. Four hundred books and numerous other materials were given as resources. People who didn't know each other before met together from many geographic regions. We spent much time in prayer.

As we met, our vision clarified with many specific examples of God's Spirit moving around the world. For example:

1. *Latvia.* One youth leader expressed, "We have all of this new-found freedom and we are learning to deal with the challenge of how to use that freedom to reach young people for Christ."
2. *Africa.* In one city a school teacher led 138 students to Christ last year.
3. *South Africa.* Youth Harvest, a ministry of Youth for Christ, has inaugurated a specific plan to communicate the gospel to all of South Africa's young people in the next four years. Thirty thousand people received Christ last year alone.
4. *Africa.* Five hundred thousand young people are involved in a Scripture reading program.
5. *United States.* One hundred thirty-five cities have a network of youth ministries, including fifty-five denominations and the major parachurch organizations. Their goal is to establish a ministry to every secondary school by the year 2000.
6. *Philippines.* Young Life is involved in a significant cooperative effort with the Catholic Church in youth evangelism.
7. *Estonia.* A youth association stopped by past Communist pressure has recently been reestablished. Six thousand young people will attend a gospel youth festival in August, 1989.
8. *Germany.* One thousand young people are actively involved in a ministry on military bases.

In Malawi, Zambia, Australia, New Zealand, and many other countries, young people are being reached in significant numbers. In all of this it is obvious that God's Spirit is moving mightily among young people all around the world.

Barry B. St. Clair is Executive Director of Reach Out Ministries and is a citizen of the United States.

But the task is still overwhelming. We have a long way to go to reach half of the world's population by the year 2000:

- Many countries do not have salaried youth workers, or even volunteers, to work with youth. In Greece, there is only one known full-time youth pastor.
- In most areas of the world resources for youth ministry are sparse.
- Very little communication exists between various ministries even within their own countries.
- Often hopelessness and discouragement were reflected as youth workers shared their needs and insights.
- Many expressed a strong need for training and resources.

From these nine sessions came a strong appeal to the LCWE to make known to the church that reaching young people is the greatest challenge, and the greatest human resource available for fulfilling the Great Commission. Young people are both a fruitful mission field, and a powerful mission force.

It must be realized that the resources invested in reaching young people will produce the biggest, quickest, and longest lasting results in the task of world evangelization.

From the Youth Track several recommendations came forth that need to become significant steps of action:

1. We recommend that a Senior Associate of Youth become an integral part of the LCWE.
2. We recommend that Lausanne and the World Evangelical Fellowship plan a consultation for key youth workers worldwide as soon as possible. From that consultation an occasional paper needs to be written to challenge all involved in the Lausanne movement to accept the mandate to reach young people and highlight the priority of youth ministry.
3. We recommend that an international youth workers conference be held that would increase vision, awareness, communication, cooperation, and sharing of resources to reach young people around the world.
4. We recommend that out of that conference, an international network of youth leaders begins.
5. We recommend that an "Adopt a City" proposal be considered to link up existing networks in cities around the world with other cities who desire assistance. Resources would be provided to help raise up youth workers and reach the young people of that city for Christ.
6. We recommend the publication of a regular newsletter to be circulated among youth workers worldwide.
7. We recommend that an international youth conference be considered that would take place in enough regions that young people all over the world could attend at a low cost. Through a satellite hook-up the whole world could link together for inspiration and training to challenge Christian young people around the world to reach their world for Christ.

Obviously, this will never happen through one person or one organization. Nor will it happen by all ministries and all organizations. Only when we fall on our faces before the all powerful God, and call on his power through the Holy Spirit, will we fulfill the Great Commission among the young people of our world.

Track 190 Workshops:

Now and in the Future
God's Spirit Moving: How Is God Working?
Barriers to Reaching Young People: What Barriers Do We Face?
Evangelizing Young People: How Will We Reach Them?
Moving Toward Spiritual Maturity: How Can We Help Them Grow?
Leadership for the Future: How Can They Lead?
A Strategy for Local Ministry: What is my Strategy?
Sending Them To The World: How Do We Mobilize Them?
Networking Around The World: How Do We Link Arms Together?

Track 210—Prayer

Coordinators: Vonette Bright; Glenn Sheppard

Participants from all over the world reported that God is raising up Christians who are committed to prayer. Many reported that God is tearing down strongholds of resistance to the gospel and is opening doors that could not be opened in any other way as they have earnestly and fervently prayed.

They desire to learn how to be more effective in prayer, praise, spiritual warfare, and in learning how to believe God to do great and wonderful things in their lands that will glorify his name.

Over one thousand have already signed up to be a part of the Global Prayer Network. They have indicated they will pray every morning when their eyes first see the light of day for world evangelization, joining the united praying of Christians around the world, using John 17 to inspire their praying for one another and the work of world evangelization. Approximately 130 countries have responded, including restricted areas, saying they will translate the strategy and spread it to the Christians in their lands. Those who cannot worship together can know that they are joining with other Christians in prayer at sunrise. Several organizations have requested to use the Global Prayer Strategy as a prayer teaching tool, and one has indicated it will become their prayer strategy, introducing it at an upcoming conference of approximately fifty thousand people.

Through the Global Prayer Network, we will seek to continue to motivate, train, and unite believers in prayer. We believe the simplicity of the strategy and the emphasis on scriptural praying will be an example of united prayer to prayer leaders in many countries who are seeking a way to unite believers in the work of world evangelization.

Prayer Track leaders, workshop leaders and others have suggested local, national, and regional prayer conferences in the future for the purpose of prayer for world evangelization. Also, they are recommending these prayer movements be united with a Second International Assembly of Prayer, possibly in 1994 or 1995. Those intercessors who met in Room 356, Philippine Plaza, also brought this suggestion to Glenn Sheppard, Senior Associate for Prayer. A recommendation from the intercession working group and prayer track workshop leaders is attached.

Vonette Bright *co-founded Campus Crusade for Christ with her husband, Dr. Bill Bright, and serves as Lausanne's Chairman of the Intercession Advisory Group.*
Glenn Sheppard *is President and co-founder of International Prayer Ministries and is the Lausanne Senior Associate for Prayer.*

In the *Global Prayer Strategy Manual,* John Sung is quoted as saying, "The work of the future is to be the work of prayer." This great Chinese evangelist knew the power of prayer. We join with that statement. We believe that prayer is the power that will break down the walls of resistance and till the soil of the hearts of mankind to receive the precious Seed. Our efforts in evangelism cannot succeed if we fail in prayer.

Recommendations From the Intercession Working Group

As members of the Intercession Working Group of Lausanne II we sense the need for a worldwide prayer movement. The early church was founded in a prayer meeting. The book of Acts is a history of God's answer to the prayers of his people. The prayer commitment of the early church turned the world upside down. The urgency of the hour at the close of the twentieth century demands that we return to united fervent prayer as experienced in the book of Acts.

The Intercessory Prayer Team, along with the Intercession Prayer Track of the Lausanne II Congress in Manila, together have recognized the need to call for a networking of prayer movements worldwide. We, therefore, recommend an International Prayer Assembly in the mid-1990s.

We believe there is a need to network and unify Christians worldwide to pray for spiritual awakening and evangelization so the whole church will take the whole gospel to the whole world. In order to achieve this objective, we recommend the following:

1. *Local.* We believe that the foundation of any worldwide prayer movement must begin with local churches and organizations to develop a prayer strategy for their communities.
2. *National.* As local prayer leadership emerges, we would encourage the networking of leadership into a national prayer movement. We would encourage these national leaders to find God's strategy for reaching their nations through prayer. We also encourage the convening of National Prayer Assemblies to encourage and equip the church for prayer for their nations and communities.
3. *Regional.* We also would suggest that prayer conferences be held in various regions of the world. We recommend that special emphasis be given to prayer for unreached people groups in those regions and the spiritual awakening of the church.
4. *International.* We strongly believe that these prayer movements be united with an International Assembly of Prayer. We would encourage that not only prayer leaders but also local church leaders, missions leaders, evangelism leaders, and parachurch leaders attend the International Assembly. We see the need of a broad spectrum of leaders to participate. We feel the whole church needs to see the necessity of a prayer movement.

Track 210 Workshops:

Prayer and Spiritual Warfare
  Leader: Jack Taylor
Prayer and the Spiritual Leader's Personal Life
  Leader: Dick Eastman
Intercession for Spiritual Leaders
  Leader: C. Peter Wagner
Mobilizing Prayer Groups
  Leader: David Bryant

Prayer and Spiritual Awakening
  Leader: Sammy Tippitt
Prayer and the World Christian
  Leader: John Richard
How to Pray for Leaders of Your Nation
  Leader: Mary Lance Sisk
Praying and Fasting for the Nations
  Leader: Joy Dawson
Praying for the Non-Believer
  Leader: Jim Dawson
Prayer and World Evangelization
  Leader: Crawford Loritts
Prayer and the Family
  Leader: Everett Davis
Prayer Mobilization in the Middle East
  Leader: Iqbal Massey
Prayer Mobilization in Europe, England and USSR
  Leader: Eric Gay
Prayer Mobilization in Africa
  Leader: Dela Adadeyoh
Prayer Mobilization in Asia
  Leader: Joon Gon Kim
Prayer Mobilization in Oceania
  Leader: Brian Caughley
Prayer Mobilization in Latin America
  Leader: Armando Castillo
Prayer Mobilization in North America
  Leader: David Bryant

Track 220—Theology and Evangelization
Coordinator: John R. Reid

Dr. James Packer spoke on "The Kingdom of God and Evangelism," and he propounded the following position: "Evangelism under the kingdom of God must exhibit signs of the kingdom it announces." He asked for a platform for cooperation between Pentecostals/charismatics and evangelicals and suggested the following five points:

1. It is not necessary for anyone to deny the reality of signs and wonders, whatever theology one has had before; but, they should be tested by Scripture to see if spiritual growth accompanied them.
2. It is not necessary to reject either of the two views that are held in the Bible-believing world today. The two hermeneutics being the one stressing that signs authenticating the message do not occur at all times in the church because they are found in the Bible, the other that every phenomenon

---

John Reid is Bishop of Sydney, Australia. He is the head of the Theology Working Group and a member of the Lausanne Executive Committee.

regularly will be found in the church today.

3. It is not necessary to view miraculous signs and wonders as primary sources of the gospel's credibility, the transformed lives of those born again are. It is also not necessary to deny that signs and wonders have some evidential significance.
4. It is not necessary to accept all the claims for all miracles nor full-scale renewal of the sign gifts in order to recognize that what goes on in the Pentecostal/charismatic is a real exhibition of divine power.
5. It is not necessary to affirm the superiority of evangelism with signs and wonders over and against other evangelism. There is no empirical proof that this historically has been more effective.

The Reverend Michael Bourdeaux spoke on, "Suffering and Evangelization" and spoke from the experience of believers in the Soviet Union. He underlined the great need for theological training in the Soviet Union.

Dr. Tormod Engelsviken spoke on,"Scripture and Culture." He showed how the biblical revelation showed the influence of Jewish and Hellenistic culture, and to communicate the gospel, we must be aware of both these cultures. Basic ideas and stories in the cultures need to be understood. While New Testament writers often used Hellenistic concepts, they often poured new meaning into them (e.g., John's use of *logos*). There is a constant need to look at the cultural context of the Bible in the new cultural context where its message is proclaimed.

Dr. Peter Beyerhaus spoke on, "Eschatology and Evangelization." He reviewed the impact the prospect of the Second Coming had until 1910 on evangelism and the reasons why this had declined since that time. Inadequate or wrong views of the kingdom of God had obscured the significance and relevance of the Second Coming. He noted that in this Congress, eschatological aspects of Christ's work had received minimal coverage. He called for a view of the Lord's coming which was relevant to evangelism. This relevance would be seen in:

1. Joyful assurance of Christ's victory
2. Urgency to fulfill the missionary mandate
3. The hope which gives meaning to life
4. The anticipation of the Second Coming to the kingdom by living in the Spirit
5. Patience in the face of false utopian dreams
6. Watchfulness to discern the Antichrist
7. To acknowledge prayer and intercession to be at the heart of the missionary enterprise as we await the kingdom.

Track 220 Workshops:

Eschatology in Evangelism
Leader: Peter Beyerhaus
Kingdom of God in Evangelism
Leader: James Packer
Religious Freedom
Leader: Michael Bourdeaux
Scripture and Culture
Leader: Tormod Engselviken
Theology Working Group Planning Meeting
Leader: John Reid

Track 230—The Holy Spirit in Evangelization
Coordinators: Jack Hayford; Gary Clark

To set the track on ,"The Holy Spirit in World Evangelization" in context, it is important to examine the fifteen-year period between Lausanne I and Lausanne II.

According to some observers, the single most important contribution of Lausanne I to the worldwide task of evangelization was the concept of the "people approach to world evangelization." Speakers such as Ralph D. Winter, Donald A. McGavran and others helped us to understand the magnitude of the challenge of cross-cultural evangelism and began to develop the missiological technology necessary to accomplish the task.

The great, new worldwide fact in the fifteen-year period between the Congresses has been the explosive growth of the Pentecostal and charismatic movements. Many other movements of God have been growing during this period as well. But it was the growth of the Pentecostal and charismatic movements which was highlighted on the first day of the Holy Spirit Track by Vinson Synan and C. Peter Wagner.

Many of the participants in the Holy Spirit Track feel that perhaps the single most important contribution of Lausanne II to the worldwide task of evangelization will prove to be the opening of Lausanne to the Pentecostal and charismatic movements. Whereas little was emphasized in Lausanne I which could be considered as insights gained from Pentecostals and charismatics, much in Lausanne II falls into this category. Not only our track on the Holy Spirit, but also those on prayer, spiritual warfare, and others attest to this fact.

Furthermore, we were encouraged that Jack Hayford, our co-track leader along with Gary Clark, was invited to lead two plenary sessions.

Hayford's address on, "A Passion for Fullness" warmed our hearts. Can we agree with him that whether we desire to be labeled as evangelical or charismatic or whatever, we all want to identify with Jack's new term? That is, "People committed to witness *all* God's word in *all* the Spirit's workings until *all* the world is reached with *all* Christ's fullness."

While we recognize that the Holy Spirit has been powerfully at work in many other Christian traditions throughout history, the current data on the growth of the Pentecostal/charismatic/third wave movements was an eye opener to many:

- In 1945, the number was 16 million
- In 1955, it had grown to 27 million
- In 1965, 50 million
- In 1975, 97 million
- In 1985, 268 million
- And today, 351 million

It was stated that never before in human history has a non-militaristic, non-political

---

Gary Clark is Associate Congress Program Director for the Lausanne Committee for World Evangelization and is a citizen of the United States.

voluntary movement seen such explosive growth. Of the ten largest churches in the world, all ten are Pentecostal/charismatic.

One Pentecostal denomination, the Assemblies of God, has in a relatively short period of time, become the largest or second largest denomination in no fewer than thirty nations of the world. In the city of Sao Paulo, Brazil, alone it counts twenty-four hundred churches.

Here in metro Manila the three largest churches—Jesus is Lord, the Cathedral of Praise, and Word for the World—are Pentecostal/charismatic.

In the Holy Spirit Track, the senior pastors of what some consider to be three of the four largest churches in the world, shared with the group. Paul Yonggi Cho, pastoring the Yoido Full Gospel Church of Seoul, Korea, reported over six hundred thousand active members and related that ministries of divine healing have helped spur this growth.

Omar Cabrera of the ninety thousand member Vision of the Future church in Argentina, gave us a powerful word on how God has used him to identify and break the grip of territorial spirits in his part of the world.

William Kumuyi was privileged to share some of the supernatural dynamics of the evangelistic emphasis of his Deeper Life Bible Church in Lagos, Nigeria, and how they are attempting to crowd over fifty thousand members into a sanctuary accommodating 12,600 in multiple Sunday services.

The three pastors emphasized that only the power of the Holy Spirit, producing supernatural signs and wonders pointing multitudes to salvation through Jesus' work on the cross, could generate such sustained growth.

John Wimber of the Vineyard Christian Fellowship in Anaheim, California, agreed. He instructed us on "power evangelism" which has now become a technical term around the world.

So did Pastor Midori Okubo of the Full Gospel Church of Osaka, Japan. The church she planted two years ago has now grown to 350, a considerable size for Japan. She also told us of a sister church in Tokyo now approaching five thousand members.

The important dynamic of Spirit-directed worship and praise was highlighted by Jack Hayford who has demonstrated its effectiveness not only in our Lausanne II plenary sessions, but also in his ten thousand-member Church on the Way in Van Nuys, California.

We now live in the age of the greatest ingathering of souls into the body of Christ in all of human history. The book of Acts appears to be a mere pilot project in comparison to what God is doing in the world today.

This is a glorious time to be alive and to serve the Lord. Let us raise our voices with the great multitudes around the throne of God—a multitude which no one could number, of all nations, tribes, peoples, and tongues standing before the Throne and before the Lamb, clothed with white robes, crying out with a loud voice saying, "Salvation belongs to our God who sits on the throne and to the Lamb! Hallelujah!"

Track 230 Workshops:

The Worldwide Holy Spirit Renewal
  Leader: Vinson Synan
The Holy Spirit in Church Growth
  Leader: C. Peter Wagner
Holy Spirit's Work in Power Evangelism
  Leader: John Wimber

The Holy Spirit's Presence in Worship Produces Evangelism
Leader: Jack Hayford
The Holy Spirit in Two-Thirds World Mass Evangelism
Leader: William Kumuyi
Open Session for Reports on Power Evangelism
Leader: Gary Clark
Spiritual Conquest Over Evil Spirits
Leaders: Marta and Omar Cabrera
The Spirit's Ministry of Healing and Evangelism
Leader: Paul Yonggi Cho
The Holy Spirit's Penetration of a Secular Oriental Culture
Leader: Midori Okubo

Track 240—The Local Church
Coordinator: James Wong

The local church is God's primary instrument for world evangelization. God's people as the body of Christ are called together as a church to be instructed by the Word of God and empowered by the Holy Spirit to obey the Great Commission of Jesus Christ. The Great Commission calls the local church to teach all members all the things God has commanded, growing strong to reach out for evangelizing their own community, and planting new congregations in their country and the entire world. Only a mature church is able to reach those who need Christ.

The pastor will have a Christlike compassion for the church members and for the lost. Church leaders are servants and equippers of members who will be able to establish a healthy community of believers, praying and working to build each other up in faith by speaking the Word to each other.

God has given his people all the spiritual and material resources required to take the saving gospel of Jesus Christ to all people in the world in our lifetime. We are to use our God-given resources for this task. To accomplish all this the local church will seek to grow in prayer, equipping, worship, fellowship, service and giving, and witnessing:

1. *Prayer.* Together we reach up to the throne of grace, praying for power for victory in spiritual warfare, and for witnessing to Christ (Hebrews 4:16; Acts 1:8; 4:31; Matthew 9:35–39). We believe the total ministry and mission of the local church must be continuously undergirded and accompanied by fervent prayer.

2. *Equipping.* Together we reach in to be educated, nurtured, trained, and strengthened in faith by discipling of leaders and edifying of all members through intensive group and individual Bible study (2 Timothy 2:2; Ephesians 4:7,11–16).

3. *Worship.* Together we reach up in worship, expressing reverence to the triune God in repentance and forgiveness, prayer, praise, thanksgiving (Hebrews 10:24–25; Psalms 150), and we administer baptism and Communion according to Christ's command.

James Wong is Canon in the Anglican Church of Singapore and is a citizen of that country.

4. *Fellowship.* Together we reach around and beyond in fellowship as a healing community, caring for each other and our fellowmen (Acts 2:42; John 13:35; Galatians 6:10; James 1:27), and supporting each according to need.

5. *Service and giving.* Together we reach deeper by God's grace into our God-given resources through faithful stewardship, putting God first in service and giving (2 Corinthians 8:9–15; Matthew 6:33).

6. *Witnessing.* Together we reach out in witnessing and evangelism (Matthew 28:18–20; Mark 16:15; Acts 1:8; 4:33), proclaiming to the lost our Spirit-given faith that Jesus is Savior and Lord.

We believe that it is time for the local church as God's mission to mobilize all our members for the great task of world evangelization, utilizing all of the resources that the Lord has put at our disposal, including those provided by missions and evangelism agencies. We believe that the local church is the God-ordained channel to fulfill the Great Commission.

Recommendations to the Manila Manifesto, Section 8

Every Christian congregation is the local expression of the universal church of Christ, and has the same responsibilities. The body of Christ is both a holy priesthood to offer God the spiritual sacrifices of worship and a "holy nation" to spread abroad his excellence in witness (1 Peter 2:5,9). The church is both a worshipping and witnessing community, gathered and scattered, called and sent. Every Christian must be a responsible member of a local church.

We believe that the local church bears the primary responsibility for the spread of the gospel. Scripture suggests this in the rhythm that "our gospel came to you" and then "rang out from you" (1 Thessalonians 1:5,8). In this way, the gospel creates the church, and the church spreads the gospel, which creates more churches in a continuous chain reaction.

We believe the local church is God's primary instrument for world evangelization. To accomplish this, the local church will seek to grow in prayer, equipping, worship, fellowship, service, giving, and witnessing.

We recommend that every local church should have a vision and goals for growth, and a strategy to accomplish it. There should be continual evaluation of its effectiveness and readjustment of its direction as the Holy Spirit guides through the Word and prayer.

At the same time, the local church must fulfill its global responsibilities. It must be evangelistic in its own locality and have a world vision.

The local church should work with other churches of its own denomination as well as work in creative ways with other churches, avoiding competition and duplication of resources. Church and parachurch organizations should also work together, for the parachurch agency is a servant of the church, while the church can benefit from its specialist expertise.

The church should be a healing community in which righteousness, reconciliation, and peace prevail. As with individuals, so with churches; the gospel has to be embodied if it is to be effectively communicated. It is through our love to one another that the invisible God reveals himself today (1 John 4:12), especially when our fellowship transcends the barriers of race, rank, sex, and age which divide other communities.

God is calling the church away from being inward-looking, organized for maintenance, and holding to institutional forms and traditions rather than being a dynamic mission center. God's purpose is that the whole church (every member of every local church) acknowledge and fulfill the primacy of mission as the priority and task and reason for existence, as individuals, and as churches. To the local church and individual member is given the task of discipling new believers into maturity and fruitfulness (Colossians 1:28; 2 Timothy 2:2). We determine to turn our churches inside out, so they may engage in continuous outreach, until the Lord may again add to them daily those who are being saved (Acts 2:47).

Track 240 Workshops:
The Power of the Local Church
Leader: Robert Schuller
Mobilizing Mission in the Local Church
Leader: Sundo Kim
The Secrets of a Successful Local Church Crusade
Leader: Uma Ukpai
Church Planting by the Local Church
Leader: James Wong
Evangelism in the Local Church
Leader: Paul Cedar
The Importance of Spiritual Formation in the Evangelist
Leader: Roberta Hestenes

Track 250—Social Concern and Evangelism
Coordinator: Vinay Samuel

The Whole Gospel
The Good News is that God has established his kingdom of righteousness and peace through the incarnation, ministry, atoning death, and resurrection of his Son, Jesus Christ. The kingdom fulfills God's purpose in creation by bringing wholeness to humanity and the whole creation. In the kingdom, people receive by grace alone a new status before God and people, a new dignity and worth as his daughters and sons, and empowerment by his Spirit to be stewards of creation and servants of one another in a new community. The kingdom will come in its fullness in a new heaven and a new earth only when Jesus returns.

Those who respond to this Good News who are poor in the material sense or powerless are empowered by the Spirit and served by other members of the kingdom community to experience full humanity as stewards of God's creation. The wealthy who become poor in spirit receive a true dignity replacing false pride in riches and are liberated to be truly human with a passion for justice for the poor. They are to trust in the power of God's Spirit which enables them for who they are rather than for their achievements in material prosperity or status. The task of evangelization among the majority of the unreached who are poor will be carried out primarily by those who are poor, with appropriate support from those economically advantaged who are poor in spirit.

Implications of the Whole Gospel
Since Lausanne I, the social needs of humanity have escalated and the resources to meet them have declined. As we see people through the eyes of Jesus, the proclamation

and demonstration of the whole gospel requires that evangelical Christians make a united and concerted effort to:

- Begin with those aspects of the Good News which relate to people's needs and aspirations
- Build strong families, communities and people's organizations within the will of God implemented in a Christian wholistic way
- Enable the God-given power within people to be released to develop their Christian theology and values within their own culture and context
- Do together what they can do together with other Christians to promote world evangelization and social concern without compromising the invitation to follow Christ
- Engage in prophetic ministry which uses a proper social analysis of the context within which the Good News is to be announced
- Live lifestyles which express holiness and demonstrate kingdom values
- Realize that the source of much Christian money for world evangelization is the excess of first world wealth, much of which is generated from the interest payments of poor nations; make such funds genuinely available to enable the poor to fulfill their legitimate aspirations, and not use them to co-opt, pacify, or frustrate poor people; work for a speedy resolution of the world debt problem which negates much Christian involvement in development
- Encourage economic activities and facilitate access to capital to release poor people from bondage and crippling debt
- Remove discriminatory practices in our church life which prevent people with handicapping conditions from having access to church buildings, programs, and materials used so they can make their needed contributions as church members and/or leaders
- Provide places of safety and trust, and provisions for crisis for the women, children, and young people who are prime victims of urbanization and Third World debt
- Demonstrate God's praise of good government, especially those which receive refugees, and his judgment on those which persistently reward evil, especially those which violently repress the aspirations of people for justice and freedom

We recommend that our Lausanne Committee:
1. Appoint Senior Associates for Evangelism and Social Responsibility
2. Appoint a Strategy Working Group for Evangelism and Social Responsibility
3. Convene a global conference on an evangelical response to contemporary social evils including abortion, abuse of the creation (our environment), drug trafficking, forced displacement of peoples, the international debt crisis, violation of human rights, political oppression, racial injustice, and all forms of unjust discrimination

Notes of Final Session and Recommendations
1. There was complete unanimity among the participants in the final session that there was a need for a continuing structure to further the vision and work of those involved in social concern ministries within the Lausanne movement. It was, however, recognized that there were many other participants

in other tracks who might want to network through such a structure and an additional meeting to bring a wider grouping together was being planned.

2. The need for special interest (disabled, unemployed, voiceless), regional, and other informal networks was identified but would need coordination. It was felt that we should seek to reinforce existing networks, and arrangements to bring them within the gambit of the Lausanne movement, rather than replicate what was already being done, needed to be made.

3. A part of the networking needed was publications, newsletter, or bulletin. It was suggested that *Transformation* or a supplement thereto, might be a suitable vehicle. It was strongly recommended that the Lausanne publication *World Evangelization* should contain a section on social concern ministries in every issue with case studies from around the world and from different fields of work.

4. The final session acknowledged that the Congress had given significant attention to social concern ministries but also agreed that much was still to be done to raise awareness of these issues within the Lausanne movement specifically and among the evangelicals generally. It was agreed that we needed to commission further study into biblical perspective on social analysis in order to develop biblical tools to replace the only other which seems to be available from Marxism.

5. The final session expressed its total solidarity with Joni Eareckson Tada, Peter Sumner, and other participants with disabilities whose special needs appeared to have been totally ignored by the Lausanne Program Planning Committee. It was agreed that all those concerns would be expressed immediately to the committee and would also be collected by Dr. Bryant Myers to ensure that they were made available to the Congress evaluation process.

Recommendations

The Social Concern Track called on the Lausanne movement to take seriously, in action not just words, the Lausanne Covenant's commitment to Christian Social Responsibility (paragraph 5) by:

1. The appointment of a Senior Associate for Social Responsibility ministries
2. The formation of a Lausanne Working Group for Social Responsibilities. The following members of the Social Concern Track and workshop leaders were suggested as candidates for such a working group:

Art Beals (US); Vinay Samuel (India); Chris Sugden (United Kingdom); C. B. Samuel (India); David Adeney (United Kingdom); David Busaau (Australia); Bill Pannel (US); Peter Sumner (Australia); Moss Nithla (South Africa); Michael Eastman (United Kingdom); John Livingstone (Australia); Ann Underland (US); Reg Reimer (Canada); Wanjiku Kirono (Kenya); Evelyn Feliciano (Philippines); Sneel Samonte (Philippines); Pedro Arana (Peru); Sergio Sanchez (Mexico); and others from the "Good News to the Poor," "Urban Evangelism" tracks, and "Healing and Health" workshop.

Track 250 Workshops:
  Reviewing Practices and Identifying Principles
    Leaders: C.B. Samuel/Art Beals
  Discerning Theology
    Leaders: Chris Sugden/Valdir Steurnagel
  Ministry to the Needy
    Leader: Michael Eastman
  Planning for the Future
    Leaders: David Adeney/Bryant Myers/Vinay Samuel

Track 310—Unreached Peoples
Coordinators: Patrick Johnstone; John Robb

Summary Report of the Unreached Peoples (310), Unreached Cities (660), Research and Evangelism (120), Information Sharing (460), and A.D. 2000 (110) Tracks .

We want to share how God has been meeting with us, and giving us an unusual degree of unity of heart and clarity of vision in understanding how the unreached peoples can be reached. We believe that in the power of the Spirit it is an achievable task and that we may be far closer to achieving this goal than we had realized. God's Word also assures us that "This gospel of the kingdom shall be preached in the whole world for a witness to all the nations, and then the end shall come" (Matthew 24:14, NASB). We have the privilege of working together with the Lord for its accomplishment.
    We propose the following global goals as realistic and attainable. We ask each of you to join us in affirming that with God's enabling, we in the Lausanne movement will:

1. Work to see a church planting missionary movement established in every unreached people group by the year 2000. This can best be achieved through a cooperative task force focusing on each group
2. Seek to integrate all supportive ministries such as Bible translation, radio, and literature as fully as possible into these task forces
3. Seek to mobilize a global prayer and information network for each unreached people group and city with major non-Christian populations
4. Give a comprehensive status report to describe the segments of the world's population in understandable terms so everyone can be inspired to reach them
5. Provide a listing of all the known peoples of the world as soon as possible, clearly defining those still unreached. This will initially include two thousand unreached peoples already cataloged. Further research may reveal as many as twelve thousand unreached people groups within the larger groups

---

Patrick Johnstone *is Deputy Director of World Evangelism Crusade and is a citizen of the United Kingdom.*
John Robb *is a former missionary to Malaysia and now Unreached Peoples Program Director for MARC. He is a citizen of the United States.*

6. Provide a listing for the three hundred or more mega-cities of the world with priority given to those with major non-Christian populations
7. Facilitate the establishment of research and information functions in every region and country where possible to serve the body of Christ in conducting national surveys of all areas, peoples and cities. This information can then be used to mobilize the church nationally and worldwide.

We therefore call upon all Christians everywhere to play their part in reaching these unreached peoples as their most urgent priority from now to A.D. 2000 and beyond, so there will be a church for every people and the gospel for every person before he comes!

Affirmations of the Unreached Peoples Track

In Consultation with the Unreached Cities (660), Research (120), Information Sharing (460), and A.D. 2000 (110) Tracks.

We acknowledge the complexity of our world, its peoples and cities. Yet we believe it is our duty to present to the Christian world a clear, unambiguous statement of the extent to which the biblical goals of reaching the nations, peoples, and cities of our world have been achieved. We present our primary goals in simple terms, yet allow for further goals to be set which more clearly define local settings. We desire to provide clear and compelling vision of the means to achieve these goals.

We, therefore, call for the following:

1. A global status report to be presented, including a clear description of the definitions we use to describe the segments of the world population, such that all parts of the body of Christ—whether denominations, local churches, or agencies—be inspired to expedite their evangelization and discipling
2. Interdenominational and interagency task forces with the aim of establishing a church planting movement with a missionary vision within every people group by the year 2000. The gospel should be communicated with relevance in the language of every people on earth
3. Research and publish a locally verified listing of the world's known 11,500 ethno-linguistic peoples and descriptions of the estimated two thousand unreached peoples as soon as possible. Further research of the latter may reveal as many as twelve thousand smaller unreached people groups within these larger groups
4. Adequate research of the more than three hundred megacities of the world, with priority given to those with major non-Christian populations. This should include locally verified lists of ethno-linguistic peoples and sociological subsegments of their populations
5. Mobilization of global prayer and information networks for each of the unreached peoples and cities as soon as possible
6. Coordination of the most effective use of supportive ministries appropriate to expedite these goals—such as Bible translation, literature, audio and video cassettes, radio, TV, and film—as an essential component of these networks and task forces
7. All Christians to embrace the noble enterprise of world evangelization as their primary task and to work together for its accomplishment, that the Lord Jesus Christ may be known and glorified throughout the earth. Further, to

raise vision and hope among all Christians that they may act in full confidence of God's purpose—there *will* be a living testimony of his kingdom among every tribe, language, people, and nation

The Relationship Structures Required and Their Functions

We recommend:

1. The formation of non-hierarchical, global, multilingual, multinational structures which we define as "networks." Such would minimize costs and maximize flexibility and initiative at every level.
2. The setting up of a representative, international committee of reference to endorse and review strategic developments of the global goals. This could be an *ad hoc* group representing all like-minded global movements.
3. The teams now developing global databases to cooperate in:

   a) Facilitating the setting up of regional and national research functions where none exist
   b) Producing a simple yet comprehensive explanation of definitions and numbers relating to all the peoples and people groups of the world
   c) Refining and locally verifying the current list of ethno-linguistic peoples by December 1990
   d) Relating to regional and national research bodies for updating database information
   e) Sharing and disseminating information (within the limits of security considerations) with research bodies and mission agencies
   f) Producing an annual global update on progress
   g) Retaining a regularly updated list of global prayer coordinators for specific peoples, cities, and so on
   h) Presenting research information in a style and form that will give grass roots/frontline workers the means to plan and work strategically

4. That all regions and nations (where possible) set up Research and Mobilization Centers or Functions, or encourage existing research entities to initiate national surveys to discover the present status and give a description of evangelization in all territorial subdivisions, peoples, cities, and communities of the nation or nations by:

   a) Encouraging the involvement of the churches and agencies in the nation
   b) Producing or facilitating the production of:

      i. Single-page profiles for each people and city
      ii. Strategy profiles for each people and community, to motivate and mobilize Christians, churches and agencies nationally and internationally

    c) Maintaining and updating the information for the body of Christ in the region/country, and producing an annual progress report

    d) Maintaining close relationships with the global database teams and prayer coordinators

5. The mobilization of informal global prayer and information networks for each of the unreached peoples and cities with major non-Christian populations which will:

    a) Have one or more global prayer and information coordinators for each people group and city or suitable grouping thereof. The coordinator(s) will relate to the research centers and all agencies, churches, and individual missionaries involved for the compilation of regular prayer and information reports for the national distributors to send out locally.

    b) Be a network of individuals who distribute these prayer reports in the countries and languages required

    c) Feed back new information gained to the local research function

6. The maximum level of interagency/church cooperation in mission task forces with the aims to:

    a) Coordinate all ministries so as to avoid duplication

    b) Employ the best use of supportive ministries appropriate to expedite the goal. These supportive ministries are to be seen as an essential component of these task forces

    c) Enable the production of strategy surveys for reaching the peoples, cities, and so on

    d) Set intermediate goals as appropriate

    e) Ensure the provision of accurate, up-to-date information to both regional/national research bodies and appropriate global prayer coordinators

    f) Carefully define levels of information security needed

7. The establishment of national and international training ministries so Christians worldwide understand the people group approach and the application of research to the task of evangelization. These ministries should seek to awaken and mobilize all churches, denominations, missions agencies, and educational institutions, involving believers at the grass roots level.

Track 310 Workshops:

Unreached Peoples: Global Overview
   Leader: Patrick Johnstone
Biblical Basis and Development of the Unreached Peoples Concept
   Leaders: Ralph Winter/Mary Chung
Researching, Identifying and Targeting Unreaching Peoples: The Macro Level
   Leader: David Barrett
Researching, Identifying and Targeting Unreached Peoples: The Micro Level
   Leaders: Niyi Gbade/Ross Campbell

People Group Strategy and Networking
   Leader: John Robb
Unreached People Group Mission Models
Summation and Planning for the Future
   Leaders: Patrick Johnstone/Luis Bush

Track 320—Urban Evangelism
Coordinator: Ray Bakke

The Urban Track was designed to run major presentations in one room and follow-up discussions in another. We began the track with Eldin Villafane, assisted by Manuel Ortiz, giving a, "Theology of the City." Ray Bakke followed up this paper with a discussion on the scriptural and historical base for a theology of the city.

Day two of the track began a series of presentations by urban ministry practitioners: Viv Grigg, Servants International Resources, "Witness and Ministry Among Third World Squatter Slums"; John Shane, SIM, International, "Ministry with Urban Persons at Risk"; J. Allen Thompson, Worldteam, International, "Urban Church Planting"; Carol Ann McGibbon, Seminary Consortium for Urban Pastoral Education, "Urban Theological Education"; Judy Lingenfelter, Biola University, "Beyond Numbers: Contributions from the Social Sciences"; Robert Linthicum, World Vision, "Uniquely Urban Evangelism: Community Organization."

Follow-up to these presentations gave track participants the opportunity to dialogue further with speakers and with others involved directly in specific urban ministries such as: Elward Ellis, Destiny; Waldinar Carvalho, Brazilian squatter slum church planter, director of Kairos; Bob Moffitt, HARVEST; Myles Lorenzen, Worldteam, International; Ebenezer Bittencourt, Brazilian urban church planter; Viju Abraham, Indian pastor and educator. Special sessions included, "Urban Youth Ministry," Michael Eastman, Frontier Youth Trust, London; and "Strategy Development, Research and Networks," Glenn Smith, Christian Direction, Inc., and Kris Gutierrez, International Urban Associates.

Soon after beginning the Urban Track, workshop leaders came to a decision almost simultaneously: We needed to interact with the unique urban environment surrounding us in Metro Manila and get away from the "programmedness" of the conference. In addition to individually arranged site visits, an urban plunge was arranged for Sunday, July 16. One hundred Urban Track participants left the Holiday Inn in three buses carrying them in three different directions around Metro Manila. Each bus visited a symbol of Filipino wealth and prosperity, and also a church in a local squatter slum.

The three buses returned to the Holiday Inn later that day where people discussed their thoughts and feelings from their site visits. A natural outgrowth of this discussion was a focus on the Manila Manifesto which participants thought did not reflect a true concern for the city or the problems which exist there. This discussion lasted for four hours with the intention of submitting a composite of our discussion for inclusion in the revised Manifesto.

Track 320 Workshops:
Theology of the City Part I
Leader: Luis Cortes
Theology of the City Part II
Leaders: Eldin Villafane/Alvaro Nieves
Witness and Ministry Among Two-Thirds World Squatter Slums
Leader: Viv Grigg
Ministry with Urban Persons at Risk
Leader: Grace Dyrness
Urban Church Planting
Leader: Allen Thompson
Urban Theological Education
Carol Ann McGibbon
Beyond Numbers: Contributions from the Social Sciences
Leader: Judy Lingenfelter
Uniquely Urban Evangelism: Community Organization
Leader: Robert Linthicum
Strategy Development, Research and Networks
Leaders: Kristina Gutierrez/Glenn Smith
Urban Youth Ministries
Leader: Michael Eastman
Theology and the City
Leaders: Manuel Ortiz/Eldin Vallafane/Alvaro Nieves
Witness and Ministry Among Two-Thirds World Squatter Slums
Leaders: Waldinar Carvalho/Bob Moffitt
Urban Persons at Risk
Leader: Grace Dyrness
Urban Church Planting
Leader: Mylan "Myles" Lorenzen
Urban Church Planting
Leader: Ebenezer Bittencourt
Urban Theological Education
Leader: Carol Ann McGibbon

Track 330—Reaching Muslims
Coordinators: Robert Douglas; Dudley Woodberry

Today is the most exciting time in history to be ministering among Muslims, for not only are there now one billion Muslims in the world, but also there are more sizeable movements to Christ in more places than ever before. To meet this challenge, the Muslim exhibit showed examples of evangelistic materials for every part of the Muslim world and counselors advised concerning their use.

We focused on five interrelated issues occasioned or intensified by the new

Robert Douglas is Director of the Zwemer Institute of Muslim Studies, a former missionary and a citizen of the United States. He is a Lausanne Associate for Reaching Muslims.
Dudley Woodberry is Assistant Professor of Islamic Studies at the Fuller School of World Mission and is a citizen of the United States.

responsiveness. First, with unprecedented materials now available from the Muslim world, what can we learn about cooperating with God in the fostering of people movements to Christ? From case studies, we saw the increased results when baptism was only administered if the head of the family was being baptized, when the evangelists were primarily Muslim converts, and when the natural leaders were reached. We saw not only the benefits of wholistic witness through development aid, but also the discord that financial aid can cause.

Second, the increased utilization by converts of forms of worship they also used as Muslims gave us new opportunity to test the advantages and dangers of contextualization. Yet, the very practices which showed the similarities between the converts' old faith and their new allegiance has caused suspicion by existing churches and the banning of the Christian use of words considered "Muslim" in certain Malaysian states. Almost all were seen to have been used first by Jews or Christians.

Third, the major movements to Christ are among folk Muslims, who are initially more concerned with power than sin. This required us to look for practical, biblical guidelines for ministries of power. We saw how Paul at Ephesus dealt with similar power objects, practices, and beings. Case studies show how God often is drawing Muslims to himself by healings, exorcisms, and visions. Some tentmakers even found their prayers for the sick at stated times developed into services of worship and witness.

Fourth, the increased utilization of indigenous art forms is producing promising results among Muslims. *Wayang* is a Hindu shadow puppetry that was used by Muslims to Islamize Java. During the last decade, Christians have adapted the puppets and music to present biblical stories with such success that they were invited to make a presentation on government television with a potential audience of sixty million. Those from other areas of the world discussed how to adapt the form. For example, in orthodox Muslim areas it could be used for the parables about common people but would face opposition if it depicted biblical prophets in historical stories.

Finally, the new movements to Christ are creating new challenges for discipling. Traditionally, apparent converts have drifted back to their former faith communities because they could not find a Christian spouse or because of isolation apart from their families. We dealt with these in a session on reaching Muslim women and families. The newer larger movements toward Christ, however, are raising new challenges of incomplete conversions and the relationship of these converts to the existing churches. The problem of isolation is being dealt with where Christians are consciously providing new extended families for those who have lost theirs. For the problem of incomplete conversions, Bible studies are being prepared. For the problem of relating to existing churches, models were studied from those having separate churches to those that have made transitional gatherings to ease the process of integration.

Our global structure and network has been expanded. Regional conferences are proposed. We are working on a book analyzing conversions from Islam to add to the three books based on our previous gatherings. God is at work, and it was good to have been here.

Track 330 Workshops:

Introduction to Muslim Evangelization
Fostering Contextualized People Movements Amongst Muslims
   Leader: Phil Parshall
Discipling Muslim Converts
Evangelism Among Folk Muslims
   Leader: Dudley Woodberry

Reaching Muslim Women and Families
  Leader: Vivienne Stacey
The Use of Drama in Reaching Muslims
  Leader: Dennis Green
Summation and Planning for the Future

Track 350—The Poor
Coordinators: Betty Sue Brewster; Tom Houston

On the basis of the Lausanne Covenant, section 9 (the reality that 40–50 percent of the urban population of the world are responsive squatter and slum dwellers, and with the understanding that there is a large church growth among the urban poor in Latin American and in English speaking Africa, but that there are not yet significant movements of urban poor in Asia); we propose for consideration in the follow-up of this and the Urban Track that ways be explored of putting the following goals and covenant before churches and other Christian organizations that might contribute to their acceptance.

Goal
The goal we propose would provide: a vital ministering church culturally and geographically accessible to every urban poor person, a movement of churches of the poor in every major city, and transformation of slums and squatter areas. To accomplish this goal we affirm and encourage:

1. An emerging evangelical theology which is wholistic and incarnational and puts more emphasis on Christology—his incarnation, his miracles, his chosen suffering on the cross, his Great Commission, and his kingdom
2. The establishment of churches among the poor that are genuinely churches of and by the people, expressing their leadership patterns and styles of worship, and addressing their needs

   a) Two incarnational workers in every squatter area
   b) A church in every squatter area of the world
   c) A movement among the poor in each mega-city
   d) Transformation of slums and squatter areas
   e) Understanding of leadership emergence patterns and church styles among the poor
   f) Overcoming barriers to redemption and lift
   g) A major thrust from Latin American and Filipino churches of the poor to other Asian squatter areas

3. Churches of the non-poor who are committed to the spread of the gospel among the poor, opening their doors and their hearts to the poor, and

---

Betty Sue Brewster *is Associate Professor for Language and Cultural Learning at Fuller Theological Seminary and is a citizen of the United States.*

accepting them as fully participating members who jointly help shape the style, structure, and future of the church

   a) Christians to work significantly toward transformation of eco-nomic, social, and political structures that are the primary causes of urban poverty
   b) Mission leaders and A.D. 2000 strategies to make the urban poor a priority
   c) Christians to develop an accountable Christian simple lifestyle and share generously
   d) Church of non-poor and church of the poor to learn from one another as equals

Recommendations
   1. Appoint a Strategy Working Group on Evangelizing the Urban Poor
   2. Convene a strategic conference in a Third World city, drawing together leaders with experience in effective church planting among the urban poor, with the aim of learning from one another and engaging in strategic planning
   3. Encourage all A.D. 2000 planners to take seriously the realities of the urban poor and to write their strategies with a primary emphasis on the urban poor

Track 350 Workshops:
The Meaning of Bringing Good News to the Poor
   Leader: Floyd McClung
Where Are the Poor and the Lost Today? A Global Overview
   Leader: Bryant Myers
The Poor in the Bible
   Leader: Duleep Fernando
The Nature of the Good News of Jesus Christ the Poor Need to Hear
   Leader: Agnes Tat Fong Lieu
The Message the Rich Need to Hear in Church/Business/Government
   Leaders: Miriam Adendy/Nico Smith and others
The Church and Leadership Among the Poor
   Leader: Roger Greenway
Lessons from the Poor: Case Studies
   Leader: Viv Grigg
Case Studies/Strategic Planning

Track 410—Countrywide Evangelism
Coordinators: James Montgomery; Wolfgang Fernandez

If the Countrywide Evangelism Track is in any sense a microcosm of the whole Congress—and it could very well be—then we can expect a powerful new thrust in world

James Montgomery is a former missionary to the Philippines. He is head of DAWN (Discipling a Whole Nation) and a citizen of the United States.

evangelization to come out of this incredible gathering in Manila.

In our track, it quickly became obvious that there is considerable interest in developing and extending countrywide evangelism strategies. This was evidenced in several statistical ways:

1. More than three hundred different people attended at least one of the eleven countrywide evangelism workshops.
2. Ninety-five people attended a special luncheon for those now involved in or wanting to develop such projects. These represented twenty-one countries where projects are underway and twenty-seven where there is a desire to start a project.
3. Fifty-three leaders indicated a desire to attend seven-day training sessions for countrywide projects to follow the Congress within eight months. These workshops will be held in five major regions of the world with fifty to seventy leaders expected in each. Over one hundred countries will be represented.

In addition to these expressions of interest were commitments from leaders representing various regional evangelical fellowships, extensive radio ministries, and organizations with worldwide operations. These were considering how they might promote and help develop countrywide evangelism projects in many lands. They included groups with ministries in Eastern Europe and Muslim countries.

Concrete plans for networking with various research entities that can provide the foundation on which national projects can be developed also emerged.

Beyond these statistical and relational evidences of interest, a deep commitment was evidenced to the concept of mobilizing the whole body of Christ in whole countries for a most direct attack on the discipling of those countries and all their people groups.

The concept of working most directly at fulfilling the Great Commission in a country by filling it and its people groups with evangelical congregations incarnating Christ (saturation church planting) seemed to catch fire with workshop participants.

From these sessions we can expect the churches of many nations will set goals for the number of new congregations to be planted in a country. Many denominations will set goals of this nature and develop plans to reach their goals and, in aggregate, the national goals.

Leaders were shown how these goals could lead to the planting of seven million more evangelical churches by A.D. 2000.

Track 410 Workshops:
Discipling a Whole Nation (DAWN) Strategy
  Leaders: Jim Montgomery/Wolfgang Fernandez
Presentation of the DAWN Model in the Philippines
  Leader: Jun Vencer
Discipling a Country through Saturation Church Planting
The Zaire Model of Church Multiplication
  Leader: Willys Braun
Countrywide Projects in Latin America (In Spanish)
  Leader: Wolfgang Fernandez
Doing the Research for a Countrywide Project
  Leader: Wolfgang Fernandez

The Research Model for the Ghana Countrywide Project
  Leader: Ross Campbell
Setting the National Goal and Gaining Goal Ownership
  Leaders: Jim Montgomery/Wolfgang Fernandez
Planning for Each Country in the Workshop

Track 420—Discipling New Believers
Coordinator: John Mallison

Section A: Overview
1. An average of fifty people attended—some sessions exceeded this.
2. The sessions uncovered an obvious and real interest in the task of nurturing new believers. Many are looking for guidance, for resources, and for strategies appropriate to their culture.
3. Concern was expressed that the majority of resources was only in English. Only a minority of participants intimated the capacity to translate existing resources and produce their own.
4. A survey sheet was circulated to ascertain ways in which people are presently involved in nurturing disciples and to discover special needs and interests. This material is to be collated and a report prepared.
5. The survey sheet also identified people with special skills and experience in the nurturing and discipling task. Where these were identified during the session, they were asked to write a brief report and forward it to the track coordinator.
6. The names and addresses of all attendees were recorded.
7. The leadership and content of the track received positive feedback.

Section B: Follow-Through
1. The track designer, Reverend John Mallison, has undertaken to collate all the findings of the track and to compile a master list of the participants.
2. It is hoped that a package will be compiled and sent to all participants in the track by September 1989. The package to include:

   a) The names and addresses of resource people who were identified among the track participants
   b) A complete set of notes used in each session (the notes were deemed very helpful)
   c) Copies of the reports from the above key resource people who have promised to send the same to the track coordinator by the second week in August 1989
   d) A list of readily available resources relating to the total area covered by the track

---

__John Mallison__ is a minister of the United Church in Australia, and is involved in specialist ministries in Australia and overseas.

Section C: Funding
It is anticipated there will be up to five hundred people receiving the follow-up package. The cost of preparing, producing and distributing the package is estimated between $4,000 and $5,000.

Section D: Issues and Concerns Identified in the Track
1. How emphasis upon a covenant relationship in the church, rather than contractual, can provide greater accountability for members
2. The model of Jesus was apprenticing. Disciples are made by other disciples in ongoing ministry. That is, not programmatic but person-centered
3. Evangelism entails dialogue, persuasion and argument (e.g., Paul)
4. Up-to-date methods in evangelism are essential. In the Western world especially we cannot assume any gospel knowledge
5. Evangelism is best done in ongoing relationships, not a "one-off, one-dump" approach
6. Disciplers and disciples require basic knowledge of what Christians need to know to survive and grow in the real world. Tensions include: how to be separate from the world, yet still identified with it; the tension between comfortable and simple lifestyle; and between learning the truth and experiencing it.
7. Nurture groups are not only for new disciples but can be used effectively for any in the community who would respond to an opportunity to hear the basics of the faith. They can be a tool for reaching nominals, especially in churches where simple salvation, teaching, and discipling input is deficient.

Track 420 Workshops:
Catching the Vision
  Leaders: Eddie Gibbs/Michael Bennett
The Importance of an Adequate Understanding of & Response to the
  Gospel
  Leader: Michael Bennett
Bonding/Discipling One on One
  Leader: John Bond
What New Christians Need to Know to Survive and Grow in the Real World
  Leader: Allen Nicholls
The Role of Nurture Groups
  Leaders: John Mallison/Eddie Gibbs
Discipling Different Age Groups
  Leader: Emlyn Williams
Some Models and Resources for Nurturing New Christians
  Leader: Lionel Berthelsen
Small Groups to Keep New Christians Growing
  Leader: John Mallison
Where To From Here?
  Leader: John Mallison

Track 430—Bible Distribution and Translation
Coordinators: Fergus Macdonald; John Bendor-Samuel

The workshop reaffirmed that the whole gospel depends upon God's Word: Without the Word there is no gospel. Scripture is the irreplaceable witness. Christ died and rose again "according to Scripture." Making these Scriptures available in every language and in relevant twenty-first century formats remains the highest priority for the whole church as it seeks to reach the whole world.

The Good News cannot be proclaimed in its wholeness unless the Scriptures are available. The Bible is fundamental for everything we do in evangelism. Men and women of today must be confronted with God's Word. Our gospel is not the word of man nor the result of human reasoning. It is the revelation of God and this revelation is available to us only in the Scriptures.

The gospel needs to be communicated in contemporary language and through contemporary media. The workshop gave a good deal of attention to the issue of illiteracy, recognizing that the whole world contains both hundreds of millions who cannot read and perhaps an equal number who do not read on any regular basis. New ways of using radio, cassettes, and video were presented.

The use of different media inevitably raises a new range of translation problems. What is appropriate for the printed page is inappropriate for the cassette. The spoken word is more demanding on the translator than the written word. For instance, the ambiguities of the written word are no longer possible in the spoken word. Just as the written word has its context, its paragraphs and section headings, so the spoken word has to be placed in a context (e.g., the development of suitable introductory material, the use of appropriate music, the use of discussion questions, and the raising of contemporary issues as a framework for the spoken word).

While the exciting potential for the spoken and visual word clamors for our urgent attention, the vital role of the written word demands continued and creative development. Several case studies were presented which showed how the needs of modern people can be addressed relevantly (e.g., the potential for discipling through Scripture discussion groups as in Project Philip, or local churches cooperating and being trained in Scripture distribution as a means of evangelism as in Project Barnabas). We have never fully exploited the many possibilities for the effective use of God's Word.

In presenting the gospel to those of other faiths, the Scriptures play a key role. Judaism, Islam, and Hinduism all have their holy books. The Holy Scriptures provide a witness that can never be replaced or surpassed. Relevant ways in which God's Word can be used with such readers and audiences were discussed.

To make the nineties the decade of the Word, we must complete the translation task. Scripture needs to be translated in at least another thousand languages, perhaps two thousand. There are still fifty languages with more than a million speakers each that do not have the New Testament.

The workshop participants discussed plans for greater networking and cooperation

---

Fergus Macdonald *is head of the Scottish Bible Society and is a citizen of Scotland. He is a member of the Lausanne Executive Committee.*
John T. Bendor-Samuel *is the Executive Vice President of Wycliffe Bible Translators and is a citizen of Great Britain.*

among those involved in Scripture translation and distribution. As we work together under God's direction, his Word can speak powerfully to all people everywhere.

Track 430 Workshops:

The Bible: An Essential Dynamic in the Process of Evangelization
Leaders: Ramez Atallah/Samuel Escobar
Opening the Bible to the Poor
Leaders: David Cave/Ben Lasigan
Communicating the Bible in an Age of Modernization
Leader: Peter Kaldor
The Bible as a Community-Changer
Leaders: Wayne Dye/Darci Dusilek
The Bible and Other Faiths
Leaders: Colin Chapman/Kenneth Thomas
Bible Translation and Incarnation
Leaders: Wayne Dye/Kenneth Thomas
Letting the Word Speak!
Leaders: Linda Moldez/Roy Pointer
Making the Nineties the "Decade of the Word"
Leaders: John Bendor-Samuel/Richard Worthing-Davies/James Powell
Planning Session: Where Do We Go From Here?
Leaders: John Bendor-Samuel/Fergus Macdonald

Track 440—Cooperative Networks
Coordinator: Michael Cassidy

The following questions were raised as we reviewed the Lausanne movement.

1. What is the relationship between Lausanne as represented by LCWE and WEF? Although different, they have similar goals. Correspondence between them may clarify this. Is it available?
2. Define the evangelical and streams/types within this category of Christians. Are all in Lausanne?
3. Is it clear whom Lausanne/LCWE wants to cooperate with?
4. LCWE is perceived by some as a closed group. How can this be changed? Are people allowed to "gate crash"?
5. The Lausanne Covenant affects cooperation with "non-Protestant evangelicals." Are we saying this supersedes the Creeds as definitive in clarifying who are in Christ? This affects both Roman Catholics and Orthodox.
6. To whom is LCWE (as representing Lausanne) accountable?
7. How can we avoid evangelicals within the Lausanne movement creating closed networks which resist cooperation? This is a real problem in some countries.

Looking at the ecumenical movement and problems of proselytism, a clear need emerged to understand how Lausanne views ecclesiology. Both the Lausanne Covenant and the WCC statements strongly resist proselytizing across the churches based on partisan interests. Proselyte problems can be reduced by entering into dialogue (Roman Catholic/Protestant) so wrong perceptions are avoided.

There are clear advantages in parachurch models. However, we need to encourage all parachurch agencies to maintain constructive links with churches. Often the proliferation seems to create competition which lessens effectiveness in evangelization. In all evangelistic campaigns we saw it as imperative to attract the cooperation of church leaders before the campaign starts. Local parachurch agencies in a given area should be in fellowship, cooperation, and also in servanthood to ecclesiastical groupings.

Dialogue between evangelicals and Roman Catholics was reviewed. Many areas of common concern, including world evangelization, are apparent. Often charismatic renewal spurs cooperation. Lausanne must endorse this obvious movement of the Holy Spirit.

Culture affects cooperation. In the United States and Europe individuals create powerful movements, but in Asia and Africa (most of the world), individuals with no community constituency, or accepted authority, have no credibility.

The most powerful cooperative evangelistic projects seem to come from a serious attempt to combine resources. Roman Catholic/evangelical dialogue in some countries has reduced tension, misunderstandings, and produced a commitment to evangelize and serve the community. Cooperation must include realistic sharing of financial implications. Sharing often breaks down at this point.

We will be networking by correspondence with our core group and the final session working group, and in the next eight months we will produce a Lausanne Occasional Paper of sixty pages.

Track 440 Workshops:
The Lausanne Movement: Unity of Mission, Diversity of Expression
Leader: Gottfried Osei-Mensah
The Ecumenical Movement on Proselytization: An Evangelical Response
*Leader: Samuel Escoba*r
Parachurch Bodies: Common Fronts for Cooperation Together
Leader: Michael Cassidy
Evangelical/Roman Catholic Dialogue on Mission: Its Value and Hindrances
Leader: Martin Goldsmith
Planning Together: The Vehicles of Cooperation
Leader: Michael Cassidy

Track 450—Models of Evangelism
Coordinator: Gary Clark

The first two sessions taught how to evangelize by using the Serendipity methods for small groups, and the Serendipity Bible for lay study and discussion. Ken Anderson and John U'Ren were the speakers. This small group method has been highly developed by Lyman Coleman and used effectively in evangelism around the world.

The third and fourth sessions presented the Evangelism Explosion method of visitation and personal witness evangelism developed by James Kennedy. Buddy Gaines and Bernard Henson led these sessions.

Evangelizing through the method of Christian bookstores was well presented in the model and experience of Dave Adams, who operates his chain of Christian bookstores. He described personal sharing in evangelism and the results achieved.

The sixth and seventh sessions gave means and methods of raising the necessary financial resources for funding evangelism. Waldo Werning's presentation proved to be a helpful session for all participants.

The final two sessions presented the models of Christian camps and conferences as used in evangelism. John Pearson and Oduvaldo Peireira showed how this provides the opportunity for ministering to the whole person—physical, social, mental, and spiritual needs.

The track provided a variety of methods, models, and ideas.

Track 450 Workshops:
Evangelizing Through Serendipity Small Groups Part I
Leaders: Ken Anderson/John U'Ren
Evangelizing Small Groups with the Serendipity Bible Part II
Leader: Ken Anderson
Evangelism Explosion Part I
Leaders: Buddy Gaines/Bernard Henson
Evangelism Explosion Part II
Leaders: Buddy Gaines/Young Man Chan
Evangelizing Through Christian Bookstores
Leader: Dave Adams
How to Get Money for Evangelism Part I
Leader: Waldo J. Werning
How to Get Money for Evangelism Part II
Leader: Waldo J. Werning
Evangelizing Through Camps and Conference Centers Part I
Leader: Oduvaldo Pereira
Evangelizing Through Camps and Conference Centers Part II
Leader: John Pearson

Track 460—Information Sharing
Coordinator: John A. Siewert

Even though information sharing in a general sense was one of the overarching purposes of the Lausanne II meetings, the Information Sharing Track of workshops focused on an emerging major aspect of information sharing—computers. Using portable computers for the storing, processing, and transferring of information on an international scale, yet personal level, has only become feasible in the last few years. At Lausanne I in 1974,

John Siewert is a Senior Researcher for MARC and a citizen of the United States.

no computers were used by participants in the sessions. A large stationary computer had been used prior to the 1974 Congress in processing unreached peoples information which was used in printed form to introduce that concept. The small hand-carried computers used at the July 1989 Congress were more powerful than the room-sized computers of fifteen years ago. It appears as if at least a hundred participants used portable computers at various sessions for such things as word processing, data collection, and the like. On at least one flight from Los Angeles to Manila, there were two Congress participants preparing presentation materials on their battery-powered computers.

But what did this mean to those gathered at Lausanne II? How much help can information sharing with computers be to agencies and individuals engaged in the task of world evangelization? The workshops started with the premise that God works through persons, not computers or any other tools. Computers can make a difference in certain support roles such as research analysis, strategic planning, and by supplying information for decision making, only as God's guidance is sought and received.

In these workshops, it was discovered that Lausanne participants from as many as twenty countries outside of North America and Western Europe have computers and are looking for ways to make them more useful tools in ministry support tasks. There are at least eleven non-Western countries where emerging cooperative computer databases are a part of missions research and information centers.

There were discussions about and demonstrations of computer databases, map-making systems, computer-generated handbooks, electronic mail, and other support applications which are being used by organizations involved in the task of world evangelization. The challenge was heard to make the information in computer databases more accessible for Christian leaders who are occasional, but not technical users of computers. Some think it is feasible to work towards a computer-based network focusing on the transmission of mission-critical information among Christian organizations throughout the world.

In one sense, Lausanne II was like a train station in which Christians from all over the world arrived to fellowship and share. They departed with bundles of new ideas and renewed enthusiasm to proclaim Christ until he comes.

Track 460 Workshops:

An Overview of Computer-Enhanced Information Sharing
   Leader: John Siewert
The Key Role of National Research and Information Activities
   Leader: Bob Waymire
Computer Data-Base and Map-Making Applications
   Leaders: Mike O'Rear/Pete Holzmann
Open Discussions/Demonstrations
Information Sharing Through Computer-Generated Handbooks and Directories
   Leader: Marvin Bowers
Electronic Mail and Information Sharing Across the Globe
   Leader: Phil Sandahl
Future Directions and Areas of Cooperation
   Leaders: Gary Corwin/Mike O'Rear/John Siewert

Track 470—Health and Healing
Coordinators: Eric Ram; Peter A. Boelens

As members of the Health Track, we wish to rescue the concept of health from the narrow perceptions of medical treatment and place it in its rightful context of wholeness, *shalom,* or salvation (i.e., the restoration of harmony within oneself, between person and God, person and person, and person and his community, individual and national environment). It is this wholeness which the Bible proclaims and that our society so desperately needs. Modern lifestyle has increasingly used the results of advanced medical research to devise ways of freeing modern men and women from the normal consequences of a sinful way of life.

Fornication is less likely to result in pregnancy. Pregnancy is easier to terminate by abortion. Venereal diseases that result from promiscuity are mostly controllable by antibiotics. This freedom from consequences has encouraged unfaithfulness in marriage, leading to an epidemic of broken homes and abandoned or battered children.

The AIDS plague is seen as a temporary setback and has not resulted in repentance, but in strident calls for more research for a vaccine.

Most tragic is the failure of the church to provide a strong statement and example of the positive values of continence and the joy of the God-directed lifestyle in marriage, family, and community.

The loose morality of so-called Christian communities, especially in the West, is one of the greatest hindrances to the spread of the gospel. If the church is to be an instrument of evangelism, it needs to begin with a clean-up at home.

In addition to addressing the moral issues in our society, we need to reach the poor in the slums of New York, Calcutta, London, and the Two-Thirds World. To do so, we need more than words. We need an evangelism of compassion patterned after the ministry and strategy of the Great Physician. "Jesus sent them out with these instructions: 'Go and announce to them that the Kingdom of Heaven is near. Heal the sick, raise the dead, cure the lepers, and cast out demons.' . . .As the Father has sent me, even so I am sending you" (Matthew 10:5–8, TLB; John 20:21, TLB).

Those of us called and commissioned by our Savior for this type of ministry have realized through experience its effectiveness in bringing the poor and hurting into the kingdom of God. We have also come to realize that without compassionate evangelism the underprivileged in our societies will never be reached. In the ghettos of Sao Paulo or Manila and the shanty towns of this world, we need more than "street-corner" evangelism. We need an evangelism that brings God's healing to the total person. The words of the gospel needs to be wrapped in the compassionate love of the Savior for the hurting.

Is this compassionate evangelism limited to members of the health profession? The answer is no. Training programs have been developed and models are in existence which equip lay church members, pastors, and evangelists to become health promoters. It has been shown that wherever the wholistic approach has been implemented, the work of pastors and evangelists has been enhanced and churches have grown and multiplied.

Eric Ram is Director of International Health for World Vision International and is a citizen of India.
Peter Boelens is Executive Director of the Luke Society Inc., and is a citizen of the United States.

These are a few of the things we can do now:

- We must promote a God-directed lifestyle and speak out against a loose morality.
- In addition to existing medical ministry, we must promote an evangelism of compassion by the clergy and laity. One way to do this is through training in health promotion and community development.
- We must show the love of Christ through a caring ministry to the victims of AIDS in our communities.

The Lausanne Health and Healing Track wishes to establish contact with the WHO Commission for AIDS in order to provide churches with up-to-date information which will enable them to work together with their respective national and local governments in addressing this devastating disease in a relevant way.

Track 470 Workshops:
Medical Missions Today and Tomorrow
Leaders: Eric R. Ram/Peter A. Boelens
Health, Wholeness and Salvation
Leader: Paul Brand
Congregation as a Healing Community
Leaders: Myung-Soo Lee/Laurence Holst
Congregation-Based Healing Ministry
Leader: E. Anthony Allen
The Church, the Deprived and Health Care
Leaders: Howard Searle/Sonny Olojan
Justice in Health Care
Leaders: Gustavo Parajon/Russel Atonson/Roy Schaefer
Church's Role in AIDS
Leader: Richard Goodgame
Traditional Healing Practices and Evangelization
Leaders: Nyasako-Ni-Nku/Henry Kyeune/Apolos Landa
Planning for the Future
Leaders: Eric R. Ram/Peter A. Boelens

Track 480—Evangelizing College and University Students
Coordinator: Chua Wee Hian

Participants came from all continents and included student workers, students, chaplains, and college professors.

We began by sharing trends in the student world and we attempted to paint a composite word-picture of this student generation. We observe that students today are:

Chua Wee Hian *serves with the International Fellowship of Evangelical Students in England and is a citizen of Singapore.*

- Open but vulnerable to the forces that shape society
- Conformists rather than radical revolutionaries
- More eager to get good grades than to pursue an education
- More job-oriented
- More inclined to feelings than thinking
- Insecure, probably because a good number come from single-parent families
- Anxious regarding their future

Their sense of helplessness leads some to consult the occult or to experiment with Eastern religions or the New Age movement. From various reports, we gain the impression that students today are very receptive to the gospel of Jesus Christ.

Although the gospel is unchanging and focuses on Jesus Christ as Savior and Lord, students must be challenged to commit their lives unreservedly to him. A few participants noted that today's students are not keen to commit themselves fully to any cause. We stressed that we must present him as Lord, and we need to challenge students to wholehearted allegiance to him.

As to the issue of who would be the most effective messengers, we were all agreed that Christian students are the best front-line witnesses. They rub shoulders with their fellow students and through their natural social and academic networks they could spread the Good News. Christian students, however, will need the encouragement and training of experienced older workers who could equip them to serve their student generation.

We explored entry points for the gospel. We realize that there is no universal prepackage that would attract students to Christ. In some situations, we may have to begin by introducing Jesus Christ as the Counselor/Helper. His unconditional love would draw those who feel insecure or who have a low self-esteem. In countries where students feel exploited and oppressed (e.g., black students in South Africa), the presentation of Christ as the Liberator is most meaningful. Students caught in the cross-currents of rapid social and economic changes will find relevance in the unchanging Christ. Entry points, however, must lead students to a personal faith in Christ Jesus as their Savior and Lord.

Participants shared with one another some further means of evangelizing students. At the top of the list was personal evangelism. Students need to be treated and respected as individuals. The witness must listen to their questions and meet their wants and needs. And more important, the witness should introduce the seeker personally to Christ.

In countries where Christians are a minority, evangelistic Bible students have proved productive. As Christian students and their seeking friends study selected passages from the gospels, many have met the living Word through the printed word.

There is still value in the public presentation of the gospel. Campus-wide evangelistic missions with an emphasis on apologetics (to clear the weeds), and proclamation of Christ (to plant the gospel seed) have yielded much fruit.

Other activities included coffee bars, music evangelism (Christian rock bands have scored highly in communication), book tables on campus, and even public debates on the validity and relevance of Christ to today's world.

We also recognized the importance of warm and caring Christian fellowships. These fellowships release concerned messengers of the gospel and new Christians can be nurtured in such loving and accepting communities. To ensure spiritual growth, these believers must be grounded in God's Word and encouraged to pray and participate in the local Christian community.

Track 510—Gospel and Culture
Coordinators: Tite Tienou and Darrell Whiteman

This track made a distinction between the *content* of the gospel and the *context* in which it is communicated in both word and deed.

A theological perspective highlights the importance of God's revelation to human beings in whatever culture they are immersed and his revelation found in Scripture. This is an important starting point because human beings do not invent or create the gospel; its meaning is revealed to them from God.

An anthropological perspective continues from our theological understanding and highlights the importance of the cultural context in which the meaning of the gospel is communicated in both word and deed. Unless we thoroughly understand and appreciate this context, we will communicate the gospel in ways that are not helpful, or are perceived as irrelevant. In other words, if we do not pay attention to the context, the content or meaning of the gospel will be poorly understood or missed altogether by those who receive it.

We recognize two principles in tension in this discussion of gospel and culture. One principle is the indigenizing principle. This idea states that Christians must contextualize the gospel so it is a power and force within their own culture, responding to the felt needs, and answering the urgent questions that people in their culture have. When the indigenizing principle is followed, worshiping communities will be a place to feel at home in because they will be culturally appropriate.

But this indigenizing principle is in tension with the pilgrim principle which reminds us that as children of God our first allegiance is not to our culture. We are only temporarily housed here for we are pilgrims passing through. And so we recognize that this transcendent claim of the gospel will confront our different cultures at different points and in different areas of life.

How do we keep these two principles in dynamic, balanced tension? How do we keep one dimension from overpowering the other? We must avoid the gospel degenerating into an ethnocentric cultural creation, but we must also keep the gospel from becoming so far removed from our culture that it is irrelevant to human concerns. The model of the kingdom of God that is already present and not yet here is one that can encourage us to keep a balance between gospel and culture, between the indigenizing and the pilgrim principles.

Track 510 Workshops:
Gospel and Culture: A Theological Perspective
   Leader: Tite Tienou
Gospel and Culture: An Anthropological Perspective
   Leader: Darrell Whiteman

Tite Tienou *is Associate Professor of Theology and Missiology at Alliance Theological Seminary in Nyack, New York.*
Darrell Whiteman *is Professor of Cultural Anthropology at Asbury Theological Seminary and is a citizen of the United States.*

Track 520—Modernization
Coordinator: Os Guinness

With five major topics and ten lively and well-attended workshops, the broad umbrella topic of modernization received considerable airing at Lausanne II. In addition to the follow-up discussion after the plenary address on the impact of modernization, the following key topics were introduced:

1. "Pop Culture and Evangelization,"by Ken Myer
2. "The New Age Movement and Evangelization," by Dr. Jacob W. Sine
3. "The Recovery of Apologetics and 'Creative Persuasion,'" by Os Guinness
4. "Religious Liberty and Evangelization," by Michael Woodruff

Agenda for the Future
The discussion focused on "coming to grips" with the realities and concepts of modernity as one of the major defining characteristics of the context for modern mission. The following are key topics which were identified as needing ongoing work:

1. Local analysis of modernity. Most evangelicals are unskilled in analyzing modern structures (as opposed to ideas) and need tools and assistance to make such analysis local and practical
2. Critique of the graphics revolution and the triumph of image over word
3. Deeper analysis of the New Age movement as part of modernity's generalized syncretism and the best response to it
4. Strategic planning on how to revive apologetics, take it out of its academic confinement, and release it for the task of winning today's people
5. The internationalizing of the religious liberty issue, including its legal and socio-political implications

Track 520 Workshops:
Modernization
  Leader: Os Guinness
Mission Modernity: Different Models, Strategic Responses
  Leader: John Seel
Modern Spirituality: The New Age Movement
  Leader: James W. Sire
Modernization & the Recovery of the Biblical Style of "Creative Persuasion"
  Leader: Os Guinness
Religious Freedom in the Modern World
  Leader: Michael J. Woodruff
Modernization and the Future
Leader: Os Guinness

Track 530—Spiritual Warfare
Coordinator: Charles H. Kraft

I am pleased to report that the Spiritual Warfare Track was well attended and generated much enthusiasm. Our room held about one hundred people and was full to overflowing for most of the sessions.

The content of the sessions moved from general treatments of the kingdom of God versus the kingdom of Satan, demonization and Brazilian spiritism; through analytical treatments of territorial spirits, and areas of satanic influence; to consideration of strategy in general and with specific reference to Argentina. The final two sessions were devoted to whole panel discussions of the equipment God gives us for battle and the kinds of planning and strategizing we should be involved in over the coming decade.

We are taking steps to set up an international network of people to continue research, writing, ministry, and teaching in this area. We hope to publish the papers presented here. We are encouraging seminars, workshops, and "commando groups" to begin taking offensive action against satanic forces and widescale sharing of information.

We feel that this is an extremely important area for evangelicals to become more involved in. The work of the Enemy seems to be escalating or, at least, becoming more visible. As evangelicals, we dare not continue to live in the widespread ignorance of Satan's devices and powerlessness to oppose him that has characterized evangelicalism for generations. We commend the organizers of Lausanne II for including this track.

Track 530 Workshops:
Two Kingdoms and Their Strategies
  Leader: Charles Kraft
Demonization
  Leader: Edward Murphy
Case Study: Brazilian Spiritism
  Leader: Nueza Itioka
Territorial Spirits
  Leader: C. Peter Wagner
Areas of Satanic Influence
  Leader: Rita Cabezas de Krumm
Taking the Offensive Against Satan
  Leader: Thomas B. White
Case Study: The Argentina Strategy
  Leader: Edgardo Silvoso
Our Strategy: The Weapons at Our Disposal
  Leaders: Charles Kraft and Panel
Our Strategy: Hard, Bold Plans
  Leaders: Charles Kraft and Panel

Charles Kraft *is professor of anthropology at Fuller Theological Seminary. An author and former missionary, he is a citizen of the United States.*

Track 540—Simple Lifestyle
Coordinator: Ronald J. Sider

In section 9 of the Lausanne Covenant, all those who lived in affluent circumstances promised "to develop a simple lifestyle" for both "relief and evangelism."

Probably no part of the Covenant has been more disregarded. With one or two exceptions, participants from many different countries said that since 1974, there has been no progress toward living more simply. The situation in the United States (where the statistics happened to be more readily available) is probably typical. From 1970—1986, the personal income increased by 41 percent (in constant dollars). In the same time period, the giving of the regular church member only increased by 25 percent. Instead of keeping the pledge to live more simply, we moved in the other direction.

Participants in the workshop preferred the phrase, "joyful, sacrificial lifestyle," but felt strongly that this emphasis in the Lausanne Covenant dare not be lost.

Section 9 also spoke of the injustices which cause so much poverty. The workshop explored the biblical concept of social sin, or structural injustice, and urged that this important concept be developed further in evangelical circles. As the 1980 Consultation on Simple Lifestyle, sponsored by the LCWE, said, "Personal commitment to change our lifestyle, without political action to change systems of injustice, lacks effectiveness" (section 7).

The theme of stewardship of the environment from the 1980 consultation was also reaffirmed: "Authentic human fulfillment depends on a right relationship with God, neighbor, and the earth with all its resources" (section 2).

There was also an *extremely strong* feeling that, for future meetings, the LCWE should carefully explore a much less expensive setting (e.g., a university with many dormitories—one model is the IVCF's Urbana in the United States).

Track 540 Workshop:
Living More Simply for Relief and Evangelism: What Progress Since 1974?
Leader: Ronald J. Sider

Track 610—Reaching the Chinese People
Gail Law and James H.Taylor

The Beijing massacre of innocent students and citizens, June 4, 1989, shocked the conscience of the world and stirred Chinese Christians in Hong Kong, Taiwan, and the diaspora to prayer and protest. That moment of China's anger and anguish heightened the awareness of Christians to the urgency of the unfinished task of the evangelization of Chinese people and the Christianization of Chinese culture and society.

Ronald J. Sider is Professor of Theology and Culture at Eastern Baptist College in Pennsylvania.
Gail Law is a professor at the China Graduate School of Theology in Hong Kong and a citizen of Canada.
James H. Taylor is General Director of Overseas Missionary Fellowship.

With the population of 1.1 billion people, China as a nation and the Chinese diaspora present the greatest number of unreached people in the world.

We praise God for the amazing and miraculous growth of the church in China and among some of the Chinese diaspora over the past forty years. However, we recognize that an enormous unfinished task is still before us.

Reaching the Diaspora Chinese

A biblical concept of the diaspora provides the needed basis for the diaspora Chinese church to grapple with her new identity and her mission. Diaspora Chinese need to establish a new identity in their relation to the kingdom of God and to their adopted countries. God's purpose in dispersing the Chinese is redemptive. The evangelistic mission of the diaspora Chinese church should be directed first to their dispersed kinsmen, the displacement of whom has made them a needy and redemptive people group, and second to the peoples of their adopted lands and around the world.

In the task of reaching the diaspora Chinese, six New Testament points were noted: *agape* love, compassion for kinsmen, sacrificial lifestyle, a contextualized gospel, a non-compromising stand with secularism, and planting of small churches which offer ample opportunities in the discovery, use, and development of spiritual gifts.

Seeing the fruits of past labors in the maturing diaspora Chinese church, Western missionaries are encouraged to engage in reaching the Chinese diaspora as partners with Chinese leaders.

Evangelism, Christianization, and the Pro-Democratic Movement

The June 4, 1989, Beijing massacre deepens the conviction among the diaspora Chinese Christians in the dual mandate of evangelization and Christianization. Christianization brings the gospel to bear on the cultural, social, economic, and political realms. Evangelization is basic to Christianization by providing the needed foundation for renewal in the Pro-Democratic Movement. Christianization is conducive to democratic movement on both theological and sociological grounds.

Chinese church history speaks of the failure of the Chinese church to respond to the May 4 movement in 1919. Today, seventy years later, diaspora Chinese churches in Hong Kong, Taiwan, Canada, United States, Australia, and elsewhere are responding in unity of heart and mind to the new May 4 movement (June 4 massacre and Pro-Democratic Movement), through many forms: demonstration, media, declarations, memorial services, prayer meetings, formation of pro-democracy bodies, and writings.

Reaching the Chinese in China: "Three Self" Perspective

It was regrettable that no members of the Three Self Patriotic Movement (TSPM) were able to come as participants to the Lausanne II Congress and also recognized that no one could speak as representative of the TSPM.

The concept of "three self" was defined, the history of the establishment of TSPM in the fifties outlined, and both contributions and errors noted. Since the Cultural Revolution, the TSPM and Chinese Christian Council (CCC) have made significant contributions in opening five thousand churches and more than seventeen thousand Christian meeting points; establishing thirteen seminaries; printing three million Bibles; the amazing growth of the number of Christians in China; and most recently, in voicing support for students in their democratic movement.

From a biblical and missiological standpoint, the TSPM had fundamental problems. It is not a natural expression of the church but a political necessity. A critique of TSPM further highlighted the fact that leaders of the TSPM had a very liberal theological orientation; were early identified with the Communist revolution, and were responsible for the imprisonment, suffering, and even death of many evangelical Christians; opposed house-church Christians, Chinese Christians of the diaspora as well as other non-Chinese Christians in their effort to evangelize the unreached millions of China; and also hindered Christians within TSPM from fulfilling the mandate of the Great Commission.

How to Reach the Chinese in China: House Church Perspective

No brothers and sisters from the house churches in China were able to come to Lausanne II. This was a great disappointment.

The amazing growth of the church in China is directly attributed to God's sovereign work through the house churches. Often deprived of pastors and subjected to severe persecution, the church has contributed to function and growth in new close-knit, low-profile networks.

Every believer is an evangelist and is expected to participate in ministry according to his or her gifts, nevertheless, a Christlike lifestyle and integrity in the marketplace has been the most important factor commending the gospel to non-believers. Miraculous healings and other signs and wonders have also contributed significantly. District leaders meet periodically for prayer, training, and fellowship. Discipline is firm. Bibles and sound Christian literature are in short supply. Gospel broadcasts have been a great help both in evangelism and Christian nurture. Workers come from the prayer meetings.

There are short-term (forty to ninety days) regional training programs for Christian workers. At 4:30 each morning, the day begins with prayer. Teaching focuses on the way of the Cross (even on how to endure beatings), balancing the mastery of Bible knowledge, and the development of Christian life. Trainees are sent out two-by-two for evangelistic service in the field. Workers have been penetrating areas and people groups never before touched by the gospel.

Theological aberrations, extremism, devisiveness, and a lack of forgiveness were noted among some house churches.

How to Reach the Chinese in China: Western Church Perspective

Western missionaries are not welcome in China and any help given must be in a form acceptable to Christians inside China. What is their responsibility and what role can they play?

1. Seek to understand the situation. Since government controlled religious organizations provide neither complete nor entirely reliable information, help must be sought from trustworthy sources in China, Hong Kong, and other places. Invaluable lessons can be learned from the testimonies of Chinese Christians in the independent house churches.
2. Support the church in China in personal prayer and by mobilizing prayer groups for China. In this way, they can participate in the spiritual warfare in which Christians in China are engaged.
3. Reach out to students and scholars studying in the West. Thousands of these students have never been inside a Christian home. Through practical help, hospitality, distribution of Christian literature especially prepared for intellectuals, and small retreats for those deeply interested in the gospel they can share their faith in Christ. This is a time when scholars are especially open to the message of hope and life in Jesus Christ.

4. Encourage and support those engaged in Christian ministries to China such as the production and distribution of greatly needed Bibles and Christian literature and the vitally important radio ministry.
5. Respond to China's welcome to scientists, teachers, and business people in its current Four Modernizations Program. Christians with the right professional qualifications, through their willingness to serve the Chinese people in true Christian character, will be able to share their faith and display the love of Christ. However, during this time of crisis it is important that those who go should be mature and able to deal with difficult situations with wisdom given by the Holy Spirit.
6. Identify with fellow Christians in China and join in protest to the Chinese government when news is received of the violation of human rights and the arrest, imprisonment, and persecution of Christian workers.

How to Reach the Chinese in China: Planning for the Future

We recognize that our Christian brothers and sisters in China will bear primary responsibility for the evangelization of Mainland China. Overseas Chinese and non-Chinese Christians from other parts of the world will serve only in secondary, albeit vital, supportive roles.

Facing the unreached people groups in China's burgeoning urban centers, in the vast rural areas where 75 percent of the population live as well as among the fifty-five minority peoples occupying more than half of China's extensive land area, we view as first priority the nurture and training of gifted spiritual leaders—one hundred for each province and each of the three major municipalities. That would be three thousand mature leaders able to teach others. This would be accomplished through:

- Godly older pastors and spiritual leaders
- Formal and informal Bible and theological training programs
- Radio broadcasts of suitable content and depth
- Preparation (inside and outside China) and distribution of resource materials such as Bible commentaries

Of second priority is the nurture of the millions of new believers—the equipping of the saints (Ephesians 4:11–16). This will be undertaken by the pastors and workers trained by the three thousand gifted spiritual leaders. Radio broadcast and the supply of sound Christian literature, audio tapes, and so on, should complement this urgent task.

Finally, if there are as many as 50 million Christian brothers and sisters in China today, there are 950 million who are still unreached. The task can be accomplished if each Christian in China reaches nineteen others. Then, as brothers and sisters of the Chinese diaspora along with God's people worldwide share in this task through prayer, radio broadcast, Bible and literature support, the service of Christian professionals, and ministry to Chinese students studying abroad, we can hasten the completion of Christ's commission.

Look among the nations! Observe! Be astonished! Wonder! Because I am doing something in your days—You would not believe if you were told (Habakkuk 1:5, NASB).

Track 610 Workshops:
(WEEK ONE: REACHING THE DIASPORA)
Leader: Gail Law
Reaching the Diaspora: A Biblical Perspective
Reaching the Diaspora: Mobilization
Training For Reaching the Diaspora
Outreach Ministry to the Diaspora

(WEEK TWO: REACHING MAINLAND CHINA)
Leader: James Taylor
How to Reach the Chinese in China: Three Self Perspective
How to Reach the Chinese in China: House Church Perspective
How to Reach the Chinese in China: Diaspora Perspective
How to Reach the Chinese in China: A Western Perspective
Planning for the Future

Track 620—Reaching Buddhists
Coordinator: Lakshman Pieris

Much of the world population is Buddhist. *Therevada* is the pure form, and the other type is *Mahayana*.

The monks lecture in pure form, philosophical, but practice is popular form. Let's look at and respect Buddhism for its:

1. *Great teaching.* We must have profound respect, for Buddha was one of the greatest sages. Buddha renounced worldly influence and became a moral giant. One's study of Buddhism increases respect and love of the Lord and conviction of the uniqueness of the gospel of Christ (only it is not logical in modern-day thinking).
2. *Ethics.* Parallel to Christianity, very lofty and great moral teachings, (i.e., ten principles of how to rule a country). Buddhists say their morality is superior to that of Christians (i.e., great respect for all life). They will not even kill ants or bacteria. One out of five precepts prayed each morning is, "I will not destroy life. I will not take intoxicating liquor. I will not tell lies. I will not steal. I will not misbehave sexually." Buddhists have very strict hygiene and personal morality (i.e., eating food so as not to touch palms, only fingers).

Buddhist philosophy has influenced and shaped Asian civilization. Thus, Matthew Arnold wrote the poem, "The Light of Asia" about Buddha. Buddhists respect religious people, even Christian clergy.

Lakshman Pieris *is an Anglican pastor and Missionary Society Chairman in Sri Lanka. He is a citizen of that country.*

1. *Rebirth.* To the Buddhists, killing is a horrible sin, perhaps because they fear that they might be reborn as the life they have destroyed. They also believe that the animal may be one of their ancestors due to their belief in rebirth.
2. *Karma.* Whatever you sow, you will reap, and rebirth are two ingrained doctrines in a Buddhist.

Coveting is to be selfish and the cause of all problems, according to the Buddhists, thus, all desire is to be eradicated. But in Christianity the distinction is made between right desire and wrong.

Buddha manifests great compassion. This attracts the Western mind. Buddha cannot be made angry. He possessed a great equanimity. Thus, we must be careful not to depict Jesus as an angry man, as in cleansing the temple. Despite the great spirit of compassion in Buddhism, Buddhists are often very cruel to animals, only stopping short of killing. All mercy ministry of alleviating suffering and caring for disabled in institutions, such as the lepers, has been started by Christian missionaries. Buddhists' compassion is passive and subjective as opposed to Christian love which is active and objective.

Most Buddhists have never heard of Christ as compassionate. They are amazed to hear that there was another "almost like Buddha." They are very curious to hear of such a person. We must give more information and examples in the New Testament of Christ and his compassion. Then, they will say, "Christ is more compassionate than Buddha." In this process of admiring Jesus, they will come to believe in him.

Likewise, one must be careful not to portray the wrath of God as an emotion. Thus, God's holiness can be illustrated by the brightness of the sun. When man looks on the sun with his naked eye, the sun does not change, but man's weak eyes are hurt. So, when sinning, we cannot face the holiness of God. Our sin has hurt us, not God's having wrath toward us.

The main concept of Buddhists' sin is killing. There is no sense of guilt, which is not surprising as they do not believe in a Supreme Being. Buddhists believe in a pantheon of gods, having been influenced by Hinduism. Thus, when referring to God, they think of him as one of those inferior beings whereas Buddha, to them, is far superior to these gods. We must use the word *Creator* or *Lord* to distinguish God from these gods.

It is difficult for Buddhists to understand how someone else could save them. They believe one must save himself by deeds (i.e., giving alms to the poor). There is a teaching in Buddhism about the transferring of merit which they acquire from their good deeds. Thus, we can show that the Lord Jesus can transfer his merits from his great meritorious act of self sacrifice on the cross, which is large enough to transfer to us and, in fact, cover all our sins.

There is a despair within Buddhism and no room for joy, but Christ is the Good News of the world! We must not be ashamed or afraid to show this by our love.

Spiritual warfare is active. But our enemy is Satan, not Buddhists or even the religion. People must be met at their perceived level of need. Christ can meet every need! Buddhists have a different worldview and are not familiar with Judeo-Greek terminology. Therefore, the need to contextualize our terms and categories is of paramount importance if we are to communicate the glorious gospel of Jesus Christ.

The Christian gospel has not been preached to all sections of Buddhist masses of Asia. In the few areas where it has been done, however, it has not been communicated often in an intelligible manner. This must be the reason for the very small percentage of Christians now in Buddhist nations.

Witnessing to Buddhists is a vital matter with regard to world evangelization. Here is a vast area in the unevangelized world with a huge concentration of people. Christians are challenged to meet this resurgent Asian culture which is making rapid advances into the Western world.

Below are some statistics of the concentration of Buddhist people in Asia:

- Thailand—92 percent of the country
- Kampuchea—85 percent
- Burma—87 percent
- Laos—58 percent
- Japan—60 percent
- Vietnam—54 percent
- North Korea—39 percent
- South Korea—33 percent
- Malaysia—28 percent
- India—5,600,000
- Indonesia—1,120,000
- Bhutan—980,000

Witnessing to Buddhists

Buddhism is an ancient teaching and a very lofty one. The Buddhists are very conscious about this. Therefore, they have a heightened reverence for their religion. This is something that we must take serious note of, and be very careful not to speak with any sense of disrespect of Buddhism. Indeed, Buddhism is a religious teaching of a very high and noble order.

Buddhist ethics are exceedingly high, they are not second to Christian ethics, in fact they are parallel. Therefore, there cannot be and should not be, any sense of superiority on our part. We must admire them and acknowledge their nobleness when they are trying to practice their ethics. We are not trying to teach them better ethics. We are only trying to introduce the Lord Jesus to them so they may find life and life abundant.

The Buddhists have great reverence and devotion to the Buddha. They consider him far superior to the gods, even worthy of their worship, and that the gods are far inferior and far lower in the scale of salvation. Therefore, we should show no disrespect to the greatest son of India, "The light of Asia." We should also take into account their loyalty to the Buddha. Thus, we must present Jesus in all his splendor and perfection so that the Buddhists will begin to admire the Lord Jesus also and then wonder at the great personality and begin to realize that he is comparable to the Buddha. They will begin to respect the Lord Jesus, which is bound to grow to reverence and adoration.

Thus, even the concept and term for God can be misleading to the Buddhists because of their concept of the Buddha and belief in many gods.

The Buddhists of Asia and Far East dislike Western culture, and if Jesus Christ is presented in a Western image or his teaching presented in Western cultural form they would reject him. Therefore, the way we express our message, our worship, and our structure should be carefully thought out so as not to be a stumbling block to them.

The Buddhist worldview is a cyclical one and they have a nontheistic frame of reference, therefore, they have no goal of history or a sense of personal guilt. There are no teachings of origins either. They have an ingrained belief in *karma* and *rebirth* and there is no concept of the spirit or a spirit dimension. Even when they think of gods and heaven and hell, they think in substance or materialistic categories.

Generally speaking, the Buddhists are ignorant of Christian terms and concepts.

Even when they have a cursory acquaintance with those terms they misunderstand them (e.g., God, Son of God, Spirit, Resurrection, guilt, sin, Christ, eternal life, love, heaven).

There is great fear of demons and the demonic among Buddhists. They frequently resort to witch doctors for charms to harm their rivals or to nullify charms done against them or for their own protection and success. These incur great expenses or even debts.

Track 620 Workshops:
The World of the Buddhists
Leader: Lakshman Peiris
Planning for the Future
Leader: Lakshman Peiris

Track 630—Reaching Hindus
Coordinators: Saphir Athyal; Paul Hiebert; Sam Kamaleson

A significant representative body of church leadership and laypeople made the track a useful contribution to the entire Congress. Bearing in mind the complexities of the Hindu religion as well as the diversity of the Hindu people, the following recommendations emerged:

1. The church stands in need of a more positive witness in the Hindu community in order to gain its credibility in the Indian context.
2. There is a need to more fully understand the Hindu mind and *ethos* in order to more effectively communicate the gospel. The methods, language, and so on, need to be properly assessed.
3. India being largely rural, more grass roots level methodologies need to be encouraged. In many such situations, even their knowledge of their religion is superficial and any sincere effort could be successfully employed.
4. Special attention needs to be given to the task of mobilizing Christian women to reach Hindu women. Efforts such as those of Pandita Ramabai have met with national recognition, and Indian Christian women can very effectively reach other women.
5. The Christian community needs to consciously and concretely employ steps to dispel the enthusiasm that we are "Western." This enthusiasm has severely hindered our evangelistic thrust.
6. We must recognize the fact that India is not the only land where Hindus exist. We need to develop careful strategies to reach Hindus. Many are living in

Saphir Athyal *is the former President of Union Biblical Seminary in Poona, India. He is Chairman of the Program Committee for Lausanne II in Manila.*
Paul Hiebert *is Professor of Missions at Fuller School of World Mission, and is a citizen of the United States.*
Sam Kamaleson *is Vice President for Evangelism and Leadership of World Vision International and is a citizen of India.*

the West amid socio-economic and cultural conflicts, and a significant number in Hindu settings such as Nepal.

7. A concentrated penetration into all levels of the Indian life—particularly government service and the revitalizing of our mission in educational and medical institutions—could powerfully utilize our presence for evangelism.

8. In the light of growing concerns of constitutional violations affecting the Christian community, it is imperative for a joint body to be formed to take action at the government level. The Evangelical Fellowship of India could be requested to initiate some such steps in cooperation with the NCCI and other Catholic bodies.

9. Centers for training at all levels of witness to the Hindus need to be established. There are a vast number of institutions and plentiful resources that could be brought together. The Union Biblical Seminary in Puri could be requested to coordinate such an effort. Training was seen to be urgent.

Track 630 Workshops:

Evangelistic Challenges in India Today
  Leaders: Ebenezer Sunder Raj/Sundar Clarke
Reaching Hindus: Rural Setting
  Leader: Atol Agamghar
Reaching Hindus: Urban Settings
  Leaders: George David/Fanai Hrangkhuma
Reaching Hindu Women
  Leaders: Nalina Arles/Sunita Norona
The Indian Christian Missionary Movement
  Leaders: Samuel Devadason/Surendra Parmar
Secularism and Government Attitudes to Evangelism
  Leader: Ken Gnanaken
Hindu Opposition to Christian Evangelism
  Leaders: Johnson Barnabas/C.V. Matthew
Reaching Hindus Outside India
  Leaders: Rabi Maharaj/George Alexander

Track 640—Jewish Evangelism
Coordinator: Moishe Rosen

Provoked to Jealousy? Jewish Evangelism Today

"At Lausanne II, you will hear people discussing 'unreached' peoples and 'hidden' peoples. Well, the Jewish people are not hidden. They are hiding—hiding their hearts," commented Moishe Rosen during the opening session of Lausanne II's Jewish Evangelism Track. Rosen, director of California-based mission, Jews for Jesus, was reflecting on the fact that the Jewish people are among the most gospel-resistant peoples in the

---

Moishe Rosen is head of Jews for Jesus. He is a citizen of the United States.

world today. And not without reason. Folk memories of the horrors of the Middle Ages die hard: to many Jewish people, the name of Christ invokes only the remembrance of state persecution; the cross only the image of the sword; and the very word *mission*, only the experience of coercive proselytization.

Common missiological wisdom advises against concentrating valuable resources on attempting to evangelize resistant peoples, preferring rather to direct effort towards those who are receptive: winning the winnable while they are winnable. And it is of course apparent to anyone engaged in Jewish evangelism that the Jewish community is not easily winnable. So why the effort? Would it not be better to look elsewhere, leaving the Jewish people to "hide" if that is what they wish to do?

In the aftermath of the Holocaust, many Christians have been tempted to do just that. Finding in the two-covenant theory (the notion that Jewish people have their own way to God through the Sinai Covenant and thus do not need redemption through Christ) a panacea for their theological nerves, they have made considerable headway in disestablishing Jewish evangelism as an authentic part of the mission of the whole church to the whole world.

In response, fifteen distinguished theologians, including J. I. Packer, Henri Blocher, and Vernon Grounds, gathered together recently at Willowbank, Bermuda, to prepare a detailed refutation of the two-covenant theory and to reassert the uniqueness of Christ's salvation. "Nevertheless," Moishe Rosen continued in his address at Lausanne II, "there are people at this conference who will question whether or not Jews need Christ, and not many will accept that there is cause to give priority to the consideration of the gospel 'to the Jew first' as a continuing process."

It was in this context that the program for the Jewish Evangelism Track was prepared. Drawing upon the expertise of leading members of the Lausanne Consultation on Jewish Evangelism—a model example of the kind of informal network typical of the Lausanne movement, dating from the Pattaya Consultation of 1980—participants were offered inside glimpses into the progress of those ministering among the Jewish people in North and South America, Europe, Israel, and Australia; into the opposition they face, the charges and countercharges; and into the increasing tendency towards indigenization, particularly in North America and Israel, so that it is Jewish believers evangelizing their fellow Jews. This latter trend has led to dramatic changes in methodology. Increasingly bold approaches have been attempted—most notably the placing of evangelistic advertisements in secular magazines and newspapers in North America, Britain, and Israel. Those who have pioneered these methods presented case studies at the Congress. In addition, David Harley (principal of All Nations Christian College) and Arthur Glasser (dean emeritus of Fuller Seminary's School of World Mission) offered a workshop on educational institutions as vanguards in mission, illustrating from experience the manner in which Bible colleges and seminaries can serve to affirm the legitimacy of missions among the Jewish people in a way which the local church cannot.

Significantly, eight of the thirteen presenters in the Jewish Evangelism Track were Jewish believers in Jesus. A recurrent emphasis of the Congress as a whole was the motif of "passing the torch." It seems that the torch is already being passed in this field, not only from older to younger leaders, but from advocates (outsiders) to innovators (insiders). As the number of Jewish Christians rises—and, despite the odds, it has steadily risen over the fifteen years since Lausanne I, not least in response to the increasing disillusionment among younger Jewish people with the futility of the orthodoxy, empty secularism, and faded Zionism offered as alternatives by their elders—it appears that the day of the old Gentile "missions to Jews" has gone. Those missions which have failed to rethink have found themselves inexorably sinking.

By offering a platform to the leaders of today's Jewish Christian movement in the form of the Jewish Evangelism Track, Lausanne II has taken an important step in affirming their distinctive presence in the church and contribution to its mission. Far from aligning itself with those Christians who inadvertently reinforce the status of the Jewish people as a "hiding" people by offering them shelter from the message of Christ, Lausanne II has given voice to the belief that the whole gospel is for the Jewish people as much as for the rest of the world. True, the Jewish people are not as receptive as many other peoples to the gospel, but, according to this Congress, recourse to a two-covenant theology is not a fitting response to that fact.

Track 640 Workshops:
Evangelizing the Jews: An Overview
  Leader: Moishe Rosen
Networking: The Lausanne Product/A Case Study
  Leaders: C. David Harley/Ole Charles Kvarme
Israel: Today and Tomorrow
  Leader: Baruch Maoz
Provoked to Jealousy: Trends in Jewish Evangelism Around the World
  Leaders: Elizabeth Myers/Betty Baruch/Jhan Moskowitz/Roberto Passo
Getting the Good News in Unexpected Media/Jewish Style
  Leaders: Murdo MacLeod/Susan Perlman
Bible Colleges and Seminaries: Vanguards in Missions
  Leaders: C. David Harley/Arthur Glasser
Proselytizing, Propaganda and Evangelism
  Leader: Arnold Fruchtenbaum
Jewish Evangelism: Future Strategy I and II

Track 650—Nominalism Today
Coordinator: Brian Kingsmore

The workshop on Nominalism Today estimates that 75 to 80 percent of professing Christians are nominal—at least one billion. This makes it the largest religious group in need of evangelization today. The importance of evangelizing nominals cannot be overstated. Not only does obedience to the Great Commission require it, but the fact that their conversion could provide the needed additional manpower for world evangelization makes it most desirable and urgent.

At the outset the workshop asked why a person becomes nominal. Is it a flawed gospel presentation, a flawed messenger or church body? Do our rites of initiation or the way we do or do not exercise discipline promote nominalism? Is it the influence from secularism? Is the demonic involved?

To deal with causes and strategies for a cure, the workshop laid a biblical foundation in a number of directions. It reiterated a biblical view of nominalism as a claim of a

---

Brian Kingsmore is a professor at Columbia Bible School with an interest in evangelism of nominal Christians. He is a citizen of Northern Ireland.

relationship with God which is only superficial and external. It is the unregenerate state of one who claims to identify personally with God but does so in name only. The workshop also wrestled in theological and practical terms with the question: *Should immature Christians also be classified as nominals?*

As the workshop framed the gospel for nominals, it addressed the saving message to four types: the "ethnic/religious identity" nominal, who is literally Christian in name only; the nominal second generation, which does not see the relevance of Christ for them; the ritualistic nominal, whose performance does not flow from a regenerate heart; and the syncretistic nominal, who mixes Christianity with other religious or ideological traditions. This last type also includes the secularized nominal.

Another biblical study considered nominalism as a goal of Satan. A person is persuaded to submit to the world's influence to embrace Christianity simply for its socio-psychological functions: security, power, success, meaning, and values. He is deceived into believing this is synonymous with dynamic Christian commitment.

After a general session on strategy and tactics for reaching nominals as a distinct group with the church, the workshop pursued case studies of work among nominals of a particular tradition: Protestant, Roman Catholic, and Orthodox. These focused on the practical challenges for evangelism as well as successful methods. The workshop found that not all nominals are resistant. Whatever the tradition, effective evangelism is occurring.

The final aspect of the workshop's deliberations was an open discussion in which ideas for strategy and tactics were collected as well as recommendations to the Lausanne movement. The workshop came to consensus on five matters:

1. We are encouraged that the Manila Manifesto draft specifically identifies the nominal as a target group for evangelism. We request that the Lausanne Intercessory Advisory Group make the conversion of nominals an ongoing special focus.
2. In view of the magnitude of the challenge, the keen interest of the participants at this Congress as reflected in the attendance and daily discussion, we urge the LCWE to make nominalism a priority concern.
3. We request that the LCWE Statistics Task Force and other research arms define more clearly the category *Christian* so the nominal ceases to be a "hidden people" and can be specifically identified as a group which may then be targeted for evangelism.
4. We call the church to commit herself to make the gathered church experience a vibrant experience, at once attractive and challenging to nominals.
5. We call all full-time evangelists, tentmakers, and laity to preach the gospel to nominals whether in their own culture or another. What powerful effect, for example, a Ugandan/Anglican evangelist could have in the Church of England, or a tentmaking Korean businessman resident in historic Christian lands, or a Colombian laywoman among her nominal friends. In all these ways, this often overlooked aspect of the whole world will receive the whole gospel through witnesses from the whole church.

Track 650 Workshops:
The Challenge of the Nominal Christian
  Leader: Brian Kingsmore
The Biblical View of Nominalism
  Leader: Paul Ferris
Applying the Gospel Message to the Nominal
  Leader: Bill Larkin
The Nominal Orthodox Christian in Russia
  Leader: Michael Bourdeaux
The Church and Nominals
  Leader: Roy Pointer
The Nominal Christian Among the Orthodox in Kenya
  Leader: Antonious Markos
The Nominal Christian Among Roman Catholics
  Leader: Johanne Lukasse
The Nominal Christian Among Protestants
  Leaders: Roy Pointer/Brian Kingsmore/Bill Larkin/Paul Ferris
Nominal Christians and Spiritual Power
  Leader: Phil Steyne

Track 660—Unreached Cities
Coordinator: Jimmy K. Maroney

Recommendations
Recognizing that cities are the generators of change and new ideas are more acceptable in urban centers, mega-cities (one million or more) represent the key to evangelizing people groups and countries. At least eighty cities ought to be considered as spheres of influence as evangelicals consider a strategy for reaching people living in areas of the world where Christian beliefs and practices are difficult to live out in traditional ways.

What we need is a new way of looking at the unfinished task. One way is to focus our attention on the least evangelized megacities of the world.

1. In-depth research needs to be conducted on these key unreached cities. Demographic, sociological, historical, data are to be gathered along with whatever Christian ministry that may already exist.
2. A "needs survey" should be conducted to assist in determining future strategies.
3. Christian organizations and agencies should dedicate personnel to begin studies and networking activities on these key cities.
4. Preliminary or anticipating strategies need to be developed so as to take advantage of unusual circumstances when Christian ministry is suddenly a possibility.

Jimmy Maroney is a former missionary to Kenya and is Consultant for Evangelism/Church Growth with the Southern Baptist Foreign Mission Board. He is a citizen of the United States.

5. Mini-consultations should be held within the next twelve to eighteen months to discuss:

   a) A list of priority unreached cities
   b) Maps and studies that will provide for more public knowledge of these neglected cities that offer hope and promise to people that have yet to be evangelized
   c) Strategies and models of hope for unreached cities

A Brief Summary of the Track and its Various Workshops and Seminars
A. Introduction to Reaching Unreached Cities

1. *Biblical mandate* (Matthew 28:19–20; Romans 15:18–21)
2. *Global realities.* The present situation is that the vast bulk of Christian community's resources benefit only the Christian world. For example, 85 percent of personnel and money are devoted to Christian countries.
3. *The unreached cities* are located in at least fifteen countries from Northwest Africa, across the northern part of Africa, on through Southwest Asia to the northeast part of China.

B. Southwest Asian Unreached Cities

1. Uniqueness of these cities:

   a) Rapid growth
   b) Massive refugee communities
   c) Poverty
   d) Violent polarizations
   e) Aggressive ethnic minorities
   f) Decline in size and influence of the Christian community

2. Practical strategies:

   a) Security is necessary
   b) Research must be defined
   c) A team ministry is essential
   d) Indigenous Christians are essential if the ministry is to be wholesome and lasting
   e) Effective use of media offers limitless possibilities

C. The Use of Radio in Church Planting in Unreached Cities

1. Radio lends itself naturally to offer support in any overall strategy to evangelize a city.
2. Careful research is needed to determine the audience.
3. The purpose is to increase the audience's appetite for spiritual truth and point them to the Lord. The program should be fifteen minutes daily with a magazine format.
4. A Listeners Rally is an effective way to congregationalize those that respond.

5. The planting of churches/fellowships is the most favorable outcome that such a media approach can hope to achieve.

D. The Nonresidential Missionary as a Strategy to Impact/Evangelize an Unreached City

1. A nonresidential missionary is one who selects an unevangelized segment of the restricted access world as their focus, but does not actually live in the city or country that they are attempting to reach.
2. The nonresidential missionary becomes the chief publicist and advocate for the unevangelized segment.

E. Pioneer Church Planting Efforts in an Urban Context in Restricted Access Countries

1. A team approach (six to ten on a team) has had the most promising results.
2. At times, business and relief projects have proven to be a way to get a hearing.
3. There seems to be, at this particular time, an openness that must be pursued vigorously.

Track 660 Workshops:
Introduction to Reaching Unreached Cities
Leaders: Jim Maroney/David Barrett
Southwest Asian Unreached Cities
Leader: Patrick Johnstone
Radio Broadcasts in Planting Churches in Unreached Cities
Leader: Frank Gay
Non-Residential Missions to Unreached MegaCities
Leader: Bill Smith
Residential Missions in an Unreached City
Leader: Greg Livingston

Track 670—Reaching Children
Coordinator: Ron Buckland

Any society or church that neglects its children sows the seeds of its own destruction. Children make up at least one third of the world's population. In some developing countries, the child population is over 50 percent of the whole.

Children are a significant segment of each missiological focus of this Congress (e.g., urban, restricted access nations, the poor, and handicapped), and are among those most at risk.

Ron Buckland is National Director of Scripture Union of Australia, and is a citizen of that country.

World evangelization strategies must address the specific and special challenges of this large percentage of humanity. Children are not adults, they are not-yet-autonomous people, and have particular needs and limitations. Analysis, theology, and strategies appropriate for adults do not automatically apply to children.

We call on the Lausanne movement to recognize the special nature of evangelization among children, and to establish an international working group to explore all aspects of this challenge. We recommend that consideration be given to the future appointment of a Senior Associate for Children's Evangelism.

We recall that in the official report of Lausanne I (page 734), an insensitivity by the church at large to the need and opportunity of children's evangelism was recorded. In 1974, reasons for this insensitivity included:

- A lack of understanding by church leaders of the nature and psychology of children
- An absence of an evangelical theology of children and children's evangelization
- Inadequate training in children's evangelism in theological education
- Disillusionment with some children's evangelism because of some methods employed

The advances in the fifteen years between Lausanne I and Lausanne II have, on the whole, been insignificant and the situation in 1989 remains much the same as it was in 1974. We submit that the particular challenge and opportunity of children's evangelism remains a blind spot in world evangelization strategies.

This summary report is submitted by the leaders of Track 670 and endorsed by over thirty of the participants.

Track 670 Workshops:
Reaching Children Today: Strategies That Work
  Leader: Ron Buckland
Development and Discipleship (including The Work of the Holy Spirit and the Child)
  Leaders: Virginia Patterson/Donald Miller
Children and Conversion
  Leader: Ron Buckland
Family Evangelism: The Special Challenges of Urban and Rural Children
  Leaders: Cathie Smith/Janet Morgan
Children Under Stress: Children Without Childhood Beyond Lausanne II
  Leader: Ron Buckland

Track 680—Reaching Families
Coordinator: James John Mageria

Declaration of Participants

Whereas:

1. The family is the first institution created by God personally beginning with Adam and Eve. The second institution created by God is the church—The body of Christ.
2. The first institution, the family, sets the model for the second institution, the body or the bride of Christ and Christ's relationship with his bride, the church.
3. Reaching the whole family is the most effective way of reaching the whole world.
4. The crying need from the whole world is the family. The needs families often have present many opportunities for evangelism. As people come to feel their problems, they will be more open to friendship, help, and accepting Christ.
5. Strengthening families results in strengthening local churches and the body of Christ.
6. The subject and teaching on family life is too often overlooked, neglected, or taken lightly.

We, therefore, call for the action of Lausanne Committee in forming a task force or a worldwide Family Life Working Committee that could take a deeper look at these assumptions and develop them further, bringing help to the cry of the world about their hurting and/or lost families. This group should address the following needs:

1. There is a worldwide need for some basic Bible-based family life material that could be used in non-Western countries for their local churches, families, and evangelism.
2. There is a need for more training for laity in marriage counseling in the local churches in many countries of the world.
3. There is a need for a pastors' guide and awareness program on family life, including a section on personal life and family. Pastors' personal lives and families are positive or negative models.
4. There is a need to find more creative ways for family fun and meaningful time together.
5. More prayer time and energy needs to be mobilized worldwide for hurting and/or lost fathers, mothers, families, households, and extended families. It is urgent for the strength and extension of the work of Christ and his church, the bride.

James Mageria is a management consultant and heads the Kenya Family Trust. He is a citizen of Kenya.

Track 680 Workshop:
Reaching Families
Leader: James John Mageria

Track 690—Migrants (Seafarers and Migrant Workers)
Coordinator: John Howell

Seafarers Covenant

An amplification of the Lausanne Covenant of 1974 in relation to the church maritime, as agreed by participants in the elective workshops on "Seafarers' Mission," as well as others attending the Second International Congress on World Evangelization (Lausanne II) in Manila, July 11–20, 1989:

We, as participants in the International Congress on World Evangelization in Manila, on the shores of the South China Sea, are reminded that the first people Christ called to follow him were seafarers—on the shores of the Sea of Galilee. In the Congress workshops on "Seafarers' Mission," we have noted how seafarers were, therefore, the first to whom Christ entrusted the gospel, yet how 1800 years were to roll by before the first organized agencies were established to continue sharing that gospel with seafarers of the world. When it finally happened, it was pioneers of the early world mission movement, like William Carey, Robert Morrison, John Williams, and many more, who helped undergird the efforts of those seafarers' mission agencies, under the banner of the biblically symbolic Bethel Flag.

Today, counting not only merchant seafarers but also fisherfolk, there are well in excess of ten million seafarers worldwide. (That figure needs to be multiplied several times if, as they deserve, their immediate dependents are to be included.) Due to drastic changes in the maritime industry, the majority of today's merchant seafarers are now no longer from a Western world, nominally Christian context, but instead from an Asian, and, therefore, largely non-Christian background. Thus, most of today's merchant seafarers make up a vast, floating global mission field—of Muslims, Hindus, Buddhists, Shintoists, animists, atheists, and others. As one modern day missiologist puts it, major seaports have become urban "gateways" through which fellow humans from all over the world come in by centripetal movement, after which they are "spun back" to all parts of the world again by a contrariwise centrifugal movement.

What a unique, God given opportunity, to share with them the love and life-transforming word of Jesus Christ—where these two movements intersect! Convinced as we are that many churches and agencies committed to the Great Commission have not yet become aware of this great global mission opportunity, we wish to share the following affirmations:

A Doubly Deprived People Group

We affirm that, like most people, we have all too often taken the indispensable

---

John Howell *is an executive assistant for World Vision International. A former missionary to Africa, he is Associate Program Director for Lausanne II and a citizen of Australia.*

services of seafarers for granted, unmindful of how doubly deprived they are as a people group. First, they are socially isolated, for long periods totally removed, by their very vocation, from family and friends, home and country (sociologically speaking, a seagoing total institution). Second, they are spiritually isolated, and most of them have been deprived of any authentic offer of the gospel, much less an accountable relationship within the body of Christ.

Our Double Obligation to Respond

We affirm that commitment to the gospel implies a double duty to respond to the seafarers' social and spiritual isolation. First, in the Great Commandment, Christ calls us to love our neighbors as ourselves. That has to include seafaring strangers at the gates of our port cities. One day he has predicted he will say, "I was a stranger," and relate our final fate to whether we welcomed him or not (Exodus 20:10; Matthew 22:39; 25:31–46).

Second, in the Great Commission, Christ calls us to go make disciples of all people. He made no exceptions for seafarers. On the contrary, he set the example by singling out seafarers as his very first missionaries. He knew that seafarers (as they have always proved wherever they have been given a valid opportunity to accept the gospel) would become the very best missionaries. And there is reason to believe, as doors close to conventional mission around the world, that they may one day prove to be the very last missionaries (Matthew 4:18–22; 28:18–20; John 20:21; Acts 1:8; 18:3; 27:1–44).

The Primacy of Maritime Evangelism

We affirm the biblical primacy of evangelism—in seafarers' mission as in world mission. Through God's general revelation, seafarers in a special sense "see the works of the Lord, his wonderful works in the deep" (Psalm 107:23–24; Acts 17:27; Romans 1:20). However, in the extreme pluralism of the seafaring world, surrounded by a host of other faiths on every side, all more or less pointing out ways to self-salvation, seafarers have an acute need for God's particular revelation of redemption through Christ alone.

To maintain the undiluted uniqueness of salvation through Christ, without making that gospel universally available—by bold but sensitive verbalized witness—would be a betrayal of both Christ's supreme sacrifice and the non-Christian seafarer's chance to benefit by it (Matthew 16:22; John 14:6; Acts 4:12; Romans 10:13–14; Galatians 2:21; 1 Timothy 2:4–5). Meanwhile, to be effective, such witness needs to be responsibly followed up. Furthermore, in order to be credible, it also needs to be wholistically oriented.

Seafarers' Missionary Fellowships

We affirm that Christ calls not only to decision but to discipleship. In the seafarer's context of constant mobility, this calls for an intentional form of follow-up, focusing on both shipboard peer ministry and fellowship. Organized seafarers' missions began with a spontaneous system of Scripture-nurtured, Spirit-bonded lay cell groups, similar to those in the early church (Acts 2:42).

Two reasons make it mandatory to implement the priesthood of all believers and the concept of communion (or *koinonia*) within the maritime context of every age: First, given the limited stay of ships in port, shipboard peer ministry, with seafarers witnessing to fellow seafarers through their daily walk of faith, is the only means by which most of today's non-Christian seafarers can be reached with a genuinely contextualized offer of the gospel; Second, a worshiping, witnessing shipboard fellowship is essential if a newborn Christian is to find strength to be an effective witness—or even survive. Thus, hundreds of so-called "maritime base communities" of (mostly Asian) ministering seafarers have emerged in recent years, and now form a key factor in current-day maritime evangelization.

We thank God for these missionary fellowships, as well as for innovative programs designed to promote them (as currently coordinated by the Tacoma Seamen's Center in the United States Pacific Northwest). They merit encouragement and support by Great Commission Christians everywhere.

Seafarers' Human Rights

We affirm that a faith which does not manifest itself in works of love and compassion is dead (James 2:14–17). In maritime as in world evangelization, though evangelism is primary, social concern is by no means optional but indispensable to a biblically holistic understanding of the faith. No one can claim to be indwelt by the Spirit of Christ, while remaining indifferent to the sufferings of fellow humans—in the body, mind or spirit (Matthew 7:21; 25:31–46; 2 Corinthians 5:14; Galatians 5:6). This applies equally to the prophetic task of confronting the underlying causes of suffering, and seeking to counter them.

With the proliferation of so-called "flags-of-convenience" and mass hiring of Third-World maritime labor, cases of blatant abuse of fundamental human rights have become all too frequent. In advocating for seafarers' God given dignity and humanization of their conditions of life and work, there is a compelling need for specialized resources (as currently provided by the Center for Seafarers' Rights in New York and its associates). However, it must never be forgotten that nothing undermines the human dignity of seafarers (or anyone) more than being deprived of the most basic human right—that of choosing one's own ultimate destiny. Which is precisely what happens when a non-Christian seafarer is not given the means (and therefore freedom) of comparison, through a credible offer of the gospel alternative.

Research and Resources

We affirm the acute need, only increased by recent radical recontextualization of seafarers' mission, for ongoing study and research. These activities should be closely connected with current missiological studies on related themes, such as migration, urban mission, industrial chaplaincy, lay ministry, restricted access ministry, cross-cultural communication, and dialogue and witness. Such study and research must also relate to events, issues, and studies in all aspects of maritime industry which affect the welfare of seafarers.

Since the resources of long established (Caucasian) and emerging (Asian) seafarers' mission agencies are so sorely inadequate in relation to current challenges, there exists a manifest need for resource sharing by world missions agencies, for example, in terms of personnel, media, training, and funding as well as in the crucial areas of awareness raising and intercessory prayer.

Cooperation Without Compromise

We affirm the call of Christ, not to uniformity in specifics, but to unity in the Spirit, in seafarers' mission as in every area of mission. We must not fracture the face of Christ on the waterfront! We deplore the documented failure of many world evangelization plans due to "stand-alone tunnel vision," and where there has been a lack of serious networking among global mission agencies. We see the diversity of agencies and individuals involved in seafarers' mission as a means of achieving together what none could hope to achieve as effectively (if at all) by working in isolation.

We, therefore, pledge ourselves to seek cooperation with both world and seafarers' mission agencies to the extent that we do not in any way compromise our basic commitment to both seafarers and the Great Commission. In so doing, we will seek to promote interagency electronic communication, and gladly share information, plans, and resources.

In light of the above, we appeal to world missions agencies, churches, and committed Christians everywhere to respond to the urgent need and providential opportunity offered by today's maritime migrants, as potential followers of that first great seafaring tentmaker, the apostle Paul. We endorse the words of the Lausanne Covenant of 1974. But we must remind that the whole gospel can never be brought to the whole world, so long as the world of seafarers is not reached.

At Lausanne II in 1989, we have pledged ourselves to "proclaim Christ until he comes." But only by enlisting the unique witness of the church maritime can we expect the glory of the Lord to completely "cover the earth—as the waters cover the sea!"

Track 690 Workshops:
Seafarers' Mission
Leaders: Roald Kverndal/Ray Eckoff/Segundo Big-asan
Migrant Workers
Leader: Nico Smith

Track 810—Athletes/Sports
Coordinators: Eddie Waxer; John K. Cho

The purpose of the sports track was to expose the participants of Lausanne II to the effectiveness and various approaches of sports as an evangelism tool. Therefore, this encompassed sports in the local church, sports as a cross-cultural missions tool, and reaching youth through the use of sports, among other topics.

The response was good as far as the organizers were concerned. Many new relationships were developed and new ministries were exposed to this concept of ministry. Many participants learned that sports and recreation could become a valuable tool within their existing ministry. No matter what ministry one was involved with, it was discovered that sports, recreation, and athletics could be a part of that ministry. For example, church planting groups could use sports to make contacts and develop relationships assisting in their church planting strategy; communication ministries can use testimonies, stories of Christian athletes, and sporting events as part of their strategy to make their medium relevant to their market; urban ministries can include sports

Eddie Waxer is President of World Sports and Vice-chairman of the International Sports Coalition and a citizen of the United States.
John Cho is President of the Seoul Theological Seminary and is a South Korean citizen.

among all classes as sport is a large part of the urban landscape.

There is a great need to continue in the communication and development of sports and recreation type ministries. First, the church (the whole church) is often antagonistic toward sport. This results in isolating many people from the gospel because we put an inaccurate value judgment on those who participate in and are spectators of sport. We also must communicate the methodology and effectiveness of this as an evangelistic tool. Second, it was discovered that we must continue to look for ways to contextualize this ministry in the various countries of the world. It was most encouraging to hear how various countries had taken the basic premise that sports could be used to evangelize and had made it work in their own country. This needs to be encouraged and fostered on a worldwide basis.

The International Sports Coalition will continue to communicate and develop this tool. We look forward to helping the Lausanne movement as a movement for world evangelization.

Track 810 Workshops:

Sports and Recreation—A Tool for Evangelism and Discipleship
 Leaders: Tokunboh/Stuart Briscoe/Loren Cunningham/Klaus Eickoff/Milson Fanini/Carlos Gomez/Ken Tada/Billy Kim/Pracha Thaiwatcharamus
Christian Influence Through Sports in Universities and Colleges
 Leaders: Mike Ryan/Watson Omolukoli/Irfan Jamil
How to Develop an Evangelistic Sports Ministry in the Local Church
 Leaders: Ralph Drollinger/Pracha Thaiwatcharamas/Isam Ghattas
How to Use Sports to Make Contacts and Plant Churches
 Leaders: Tom Randall/Joselito Cabochan/Ric Escobar
Coaches and Athletes as Sports Missionaries
 Leaders: Phill Sunderland/Tim Lewis/Lee Wan Taek
How to Reach and Disciple Athletes
 Leaders: Ralph Drollinger/Pracha Thaiwatcharamas/Isam Ghattas
How to Use a Major Event to Reach Athletes, Visitors and the Host City

Track 820—World Overview Workshop
Coordinator: Frank Kaleb Jansen

The six workshops were rather sparsely attended, but the participants were thrilled and asked, "How can we get this message out to the church?"

To give a satisfactory coverage of the 159 topics and a world overview for the same in forty-five minutes was impossible. I, therefore, concentrated on the two main tracks that will be the "mother of all problems" that the churches have to face in the period 1990 to 2025:

1. Population growth and decline
2. The destruction of our habitat

Frank Kaleb Jansen *is founder and President of Bibles for All and is a native of Norway.*

Population Growth and Decline

The Third World baby boom of the seventies and eighties has taught us to live without noticing 250,000 children under five that die every week, as well as inhumane "birth controls" like ten million abortions in the Soviet Union per year or "one family, one child" in China. As this cohort moves up through the age groups, it will confront the society and the church first with a school problem, and then a pressure on the educational system and budgets.

The next challenge will be to create meaningful work for a working force that will be largely unemployed or underemployed. The average working day in Algeria is for instance today only twelve minutes. Mexico must create fifteen million new jobs in the nineties to keep 1980 level of employment rates.

This generation, the developing countries' baby boomers of the seventies, will in 2020 have increased the elderly population to 300–350 percent over the 1985 elderly population; and the number of workers to support one elderly will have decreased from 9:1 now to 1.5:1 in 2020. The United States, with only an increase of the elderly by 105 percent, will have to increase the expenditure of caring for the elderly from 17 percent in 1970, to 40 percent of the national budget in 2020. An improvement for the elderly over the 1970 level will challenge even the richest country in the world to its economic limits. What a problem that will be for the Third World with a challenge that is three times higher than that of the United States. And what a challenge for the church!

The Destruction of Our Habitat

This generation leaves a legacy that gives little hope for mercy from the children whose assets we have borrowed. Silent springs, dying forests, dead lakes, polluted rivers, depleted ozone shield, hazardous waste, life-threatening air quality, soil erosion, acid rain, and the "greenhouse effect" are just some of the words we taught our grandchildren.

The environment and the structural debt may be the church's greatest problem because we have not yet started a real discussion of whether this relates to us at all.

The biblical mandate of stewardship for God's creation is not touched in the Manila Manifesto. After the young generation has flocked to Greenpeace, WWF, and other environmental and New Age organizations, it will be hard to win them back to a church that has not been concerned with what they consider serious problems.

Track 830—Theological Educators
Coordinators: Carl Lundquist; William Norton

The six sponsors included the International Council of Accrediting Agencies, Fellowship of Evangelical Seminary Presidents, the Overseas Council for Theological Education and Missions, the Lausanne Committee Theological Working Group, and the World

Carl Lundquist is President Emeritus of Bethel College and Seminary, St. Paul, Minnesota, and is a citizen of the United States.
William Norton is Executive Director of the Committee to Assist Ministry Education Overseas; he is a citizen of the United States.

Evangelical Fellowship Theological Commission.

Five one hour sessions were convened, moderated respectively by Peter Kuzmic, Saphir Athyal, Isabelo Magalit, J. E. Modupe Taylor-Pearce and Han Chul-Ha. Five western seminary presidents/principals responded to the reports on area theological education presented by Dieumeme Noelliste, Caribbean; Neil Sneider, Canada; Ray Laird, South Pacific; William Taylor, Latin America; Bruce Stewart, United States; Helmuth Eglekraut, Europe; Bong Rin Ro, East Asia; Ken Gananakan, South Asia; Rene Daidanso, Francophone Africa; Paul Bowers for Cornelius Olowola, Anglophone Africa.

Dr. Yusufu Turaki addressed "Theological Education for World Evangelization" while Robert Ferris spoke to "Renewal in Theological Education for Evangelization."

Discussion sessions were led by Pete Kuzmic, Michael Griffiths, Wilson Chow, Gyoji Nabetani, and Han Chul-Ha.

A follow up session (Wednesday noon) of representatives of the sponsoring groups learned that a panel of four American seminary presidents will report to the January, 1990 meeting. It is expected that representatives of the ICAA and WEFTC will be present to seek proper and adequate means of relating the FESP to ICAA and developing the desired networking.

Proposal for a Global Network of Theological Educators

As a follow up to our conversations about cooperative relationships in theological education in support of world evangelization, it is proposed that:

1. A global network for identification, information and exchange among evangelical theological educators be initiated.
2. The name of the network represent the purpose of the system, such as "Internet" — International Network of Evangelical Theologians.
3. The home base for the network be the WEF through its theological commission.
4. A coordinating committee composed of representatives from the co-sponsors of this meeting be named as the steering committee for initiating the network, consulting on its policy, and supporting its development.
5. The coordinating committee explore links with existing or developing information systems, such as A.D. 2000, to determine the feasibility and economy of system sharing.
6. The initial goal be a computerized directory of theological educators which is expandable, correctable and programmed to permit segmentation by location, institution, academic preparation and specialized area of interest.
7. The coordinating committee prepare a specific statement regarding the role of theological education in world evangelization for inclusion in the Manila Manifesto.
8. This plan, upon approval, be forwarded to the Lausanne II leadership, communicated through the sponsoring agencies and disseminated.

Track 830 Workshops:

Theological Education for Evangelization
   Leader: Peter Kuzmic
Theological Education for Evangelization
   Leader: Saphir Athyal and panel

Theological Education for Evangelization
Leader: Isabelo Magalit
Theological Education for Evangelization
Leader: J.E. Modup Taylor-Pearse
Theological Education for Evangelization
Leader: Han Chul-Ha

Lausanne II in Manila
Congress Schedule

Congress Theme: "Proclaim Christ Until He Comes"

Calling the Whole Church to take the Whole Gospel to the Whole World

Theme bands: **THE WHOLE GOSPEL** · **THE WHOLE WORLD** · **THE WHOLE CHURCH** · (REGISTRATION — July 10 / Day One)

Time	July 1989 Mon/10	Day One Tues/11	Day Two Wed/12	Day Three Thurs/13	Day Four Fri/14	Day Five Sat/15	Day Six Sunday/16	Day Seven Mon/17	Day Eight Tues/18	Day Nine Wed/19	Day Ten Thurs/20
06:45											
07:15				Prayer in Hotels	Prayer in Hotels			Prayer in Hotels	Prayer in Hotels		
08:00				Breakfast (in Hotels)	Breakfast (in Hotels)			Breakfast (in Hotels)	Breakfast (in Hotels)		
08:30				Transport to PICC	Transport to PICC			Transport to PICC	Transport to PICC		
09:30				Eagerness to Preach Gospel — John Stott	Worship and Bible Exposition: The World's Guilt / Amazing Grace — John Stott	Christian and Sin — Ajith Fernando	Worship in Local Churches	Worship and Bible Exposition: Spirit-Filled Life — Ajith Fernando; Living Life Fully — David Penman	Worship and Bible Exposition: Love in End Times — David Penman		
10:30				Coffee Break	Coffee Break	Coffee Break		Coffee Break	Coffee Break		
11:00				The Challenge Before Us — Luis Bush	The Impact of Modernization — Os Guinness; Urban Evangelism — Ray Bakke; Good News for The Poor — Tom Houston, Edna Lee Gutierrez; Sin and Lostness — Stephen Tong	Social Concern — Joni Eareckson-Tada, Vinay Samuel, Caesar Molebatsi; Cross-Cultural Evangelism — Panya Baba		How Can They Hear?; Challenge of Other Religions — Martin Alphonse, Colin Chapman; Uniqueness of Christ — David Wells, Ulrich Parzany; Communication and Evangelism — Viggo Søgaard, Michael Cassidy; Commitment and Sacrifice — Philemon Choi	Gospel and Salvation — Tokunboh Adeyemo, Peter Kuzmic; Cooperation in Evangelism — William O'Brien, Robyn Claydon; Reflections — Rolf Scheffbuch; Preparation for the Future — Luis Palau		
12:00				Transport to Hotels	Transport to Hotels	Transport to Hotels		Transport to Hotels	Transport to Hotels		
12:30				Main meal (in Hotels)	Main meal (in Hotels)	Main meal (in Hotels)		Main meal (in Hotels)	Main meal (in Hotels)		
13:30				FREE	FREE	FREE		FREE	FREE		
14:30			FREE	National Organizing Meetings; Transport to PICC	FREE	FREE	Transport to PICC	National Meetings; Transport to PICC	FREE		
15:00				Electives: Tracks/Workshops	Electives: Tracks/Workshops			Electives: Tracks/Workshops	Electives: Tracks/Workshops		
16:00											
16:30			National Organizing Meetings	Tea Breaks; Electives: Tracks/Workshops	Tea Breaks; Electives: Tracks/Workshops			Tea Breaks; Electives: Tracks/Workshops	National Strategy Meetings; Electives: Tracks/Workshops		
17:30			Light meal (in PICC)	Light meal (in PICC)	Light Meal (in PICC); Transport to PICC		Light Meal (in PICC)	Light meal (in PICC)			
18:00		Opening Ceremony	Congress Introduction			FREE	FREE		FREE		
18:30		"Proclaim Christ" — Leighton Ford	Pre-service Concert: Kerygma Hymn Sing with Ken Medema, The Thai Drama Group	The Local Church — Jong-Yun Lee, Eduardo Maling; Power and Work of the Holy Spirit — J.I. Packer, Jack Hayford	Pre-service Concert; Celebration in Praise and Prayer — Vonette Bright, Jack Hayford			Pre-service: Korean Choir; Celebration in Praise and Prayer			Transport
19:00		Torch Run		Mandate of Laity — Ford Madison, Pete Hammond	Living the Christ-Life — Carmel Terranova, Roberta Hestenes; Communion Celebration — John Reid			Evangelizing in Challenging Settings — Brother Andrew, George Otis, Jr., Lucien Accad			Pre-service Concert: Filipino Choir; Concert; AD 2000 and Beyond — Thomas Wang; "Until He Comes" — Leighton Ford
21:00		Transport to Hotels	Transport to Hotels	Transport to Hotels	Transport to Hotels		Transport to Hotels	Transport to Hotels	Transport to Hotels		Transport to Hotels

Lausanne II Congress Support Personnel

Executive Staff:

Thomas Wang	Congress Director
Paul McKaughan	Congress Coordinator
James Newton	Congress Media Director
Edward R. Dayton	Director of Program
Bradford M. Smith	Director of Participant Selection
Dr. Roger Parrott	Director of U.S. Operations
Brian Allen	Director of Scholarship Development
Ricardo Jumawan	Operations Director

Associate Staff:

Joseph Sindorf	Broadcast Media Director
Carol Kocherhans	Associate Media Director
David Norcross	Director of Finance
Gary K. Clark	Associate Program Director
John R. Howell	Associate Program Director
Bill Thatcher	Associate Program Director
Bob Ainsworth	Exhibits Coordinator
Bill Ditewig	Associate Director of Participant Selection
Gail Branstetter	Associate Director of Scholarship Development
Cathy Green	Associate Director of Scholarship Development
Elmer Wilson	Associate Director of Scholarship Development
Adele Bucy	Accountant
Virgilio G. Enriquez	Associate Operations Director
Richard Ll Lotterhos	Associate Operations Director
Roberto A. Navarro	Associate Operations Director
Bob Klamser	Security

Assisting Staff:

Sharon Chan
Amy Leung
Denise Schubert
Mark Lanford
Julienne Bowman
Charlene Wallace
Rose Gruman
JoAnne Dawson
Tina McKee
Helen Mooradkanian
Tia Marie Tice
Algene Hackett
Sharon Provan
Lisa McKenna

JoAnn Abbas
Sharon Engh
Betty Bradley
Kathy Roth
Peggy Tucker
Judy Harper
Kathy Shay
Irma Roxas
General Honesto Isleta
Brandon E. Elicerio
Noel L. Ticlaw
Mary Grace L. Leones
Rey Halili
Luz T. Handayan
Grace Avante
Joy Magbanua

Program Associates:

Robyn Claydon	Women
Vonette Bright	Prayer
Bob Douglas	Muslims
Ken Touryan and Christy Wilson	Tentmakers
George Otis	Restricted Access Countries
Viggo Soggaard	Communication
Jean Wilson	Bookstore
Barry St. Clair	Youth
John Reid	Theology
Don Jacobs	Cross-Cultural Missions
David Barrett	Statistics
Tom McAlpine	Resource Center
Corean Bakke	Worship
Ray Bakke	Urban
Sam Wilson	Research
Ford Madison	Laity
Vinay Samuel	Social Concern
Jimmy Maroney	Unreached Cities
Bob Ainsworth	Exhibits
Tom Houston/Bett	Poor
Luis Bush/Bill O'Br	A.D. 2000
John Robb	Unreached People
Frank Kaleb Jansen	Statistical Displays
Jack Hayford	Holy Spirit

Video Executive Producers

Michael Little
Kathleen Sindorf
Bill Thatcher